The Future of Business

THIRD CANADIAN EDITION

Norm R. Althouse
University of Calgary

Shirley A. Rose
Mount Royal University

Laura A. Allan
Wilfrid Laurier University

Lawrence J. Gitman
San Diego State University

Carl McDaniel
University of Texas, Arlington

NELSON / EDUCATION

NELSON / EDUCATION

The Future of Business, Third Canadian Edition

by Norm R. Althouse, Shirley A. Rose, Laura A. Allan,
Lawrence J. Gitman, Carl McDaniel

**Vice President,
Editorial Director:**
Evelyn Veitch

**Editor-in-Chief,
Higher Education:**
Anne Williams

Acquisitions Editor:
Jackie Wood/Amie Plourde

Marketing Manager:
Kathaleen McCormick

Developmental Editor:
Karina Hope

Photo Researcher:
Kristiina Paul

Permissions Coordinator:
Kristiina Paul

Content Production Manager:
Christine Gilbert

Production Service:
Elm Street Publishing Services

Copy Editor:
Joan Dooling

Proofreader:
Elm Street Publishing Services

Indexer:
Elm Street Publishing Services

**Manufacturing Manager—Higher
Education:**
Joanne McNeil

Design Director:
Ken Phipps

Managing Designer:
Franca Amore

Interior Design:
Dianna Little

Cover Design:
Greg Devitt

Cover Image:
© artpartner-images/Getty Images

Compositor:
Integra Software Services Pvt. Ltd.

Printer:
RR Donnelly

**Library and Archives Canada
Cataloguing in Publication**

The future of business /
Norm R. Althouse. . . [et al.]. – 3rd
Canadian ed.

Includes bibliographical references
and indexes.
ISBN 978-0-17-650140-2

1. Management—Textbooks.
2. Business—Textbooks. I. Althouse,
Norm

HD70.C3F88 2010
658 C2009-906593-2

ISBN-13: 978-0-17-650140-2
ISBN-10: 0-17-650140-1

BRIEF CONTENTS

CONTENTS

A Unique Integrated Learning System

The Integrated Learning System helps students learn quickly by driving home key chapter concepts and providing a framework for studying. It links all of the instructor and student materials to each chapter's learning outcomes.

Learning outcomes are listed at the beginning of each chapter, and then major headings within the chapter are identified by the relevant chapter learning outcome. Each section of the chapter ends with **Concept Checks** that can be used to self-test understanding of the material.

The chapter **Summary of Learning Outcomes** provides easy review of the chapter's content.

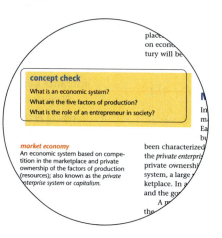

LEARNING OUTCOMES

1 Understand the primary features of th... systems.

2 Explain what economics is and how the economy are linked.

3 Show how economic growth, full employ... stability indicate a nation's economic hea...

4 Define inflation, and discuss how it is m... causes it.

5 Describe how the Bank of Canada use... and how governments use fiscal poli... macroeconomic goals.

6 Discuss the basic microecono... supply, and how they establi...

concept check

What is an economic system?

What are the five factors of production?

What is the role of an entrepreneur in society?

market economy
An economic system based on competition in the marketplace and private ownership of the factors of production (resources); also known as the *private enterprise system* or *capitalism*.

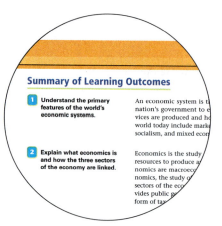

Summary of Learning Outcomes

1 Understand the primary features of the world's economic systems.

An economic system is t... nation's government to e... vices are produced and ho... world today include mark... socialism, and mixed econ...

2 Explain what economics is and how the three sectors of the economy are linked.

Economics is the study... resources to produce a... nomics are macroeco... nomics, the study o... sectors of the ec... vides public g... form of ta...

TEXT ORGANIZATION

The textbook is organized into four parts:

- Trends and the Business Environment
- Canadian Business
- Business Management
- Functional Areas of Business

BRIEF CONTENTS

PROLOGUE

A Quick Guide to Your Future Success in Business The prologue offers practical and inspiring advice for getting the most out of your post-secondary education experience as well as offering suggestions for finding the right career and succeeding in your first job. NEW: New, fun self tests have been added.

CHAPTER ORGANIZATION MATTERS!

Principles of Business The beginning of each chapter gives students a comprehensive overview of current business practices and teaches key principles through real-life examples.

Trends in Business Explores fundamental factors and emerging trends that are reshaping today's business world and altering tomorrow's competitive environment.

Great Ideas to Use Now Brings chapter topics to life with relevant and interesting tips for making the most of a professional career or becoming a smart consumer.

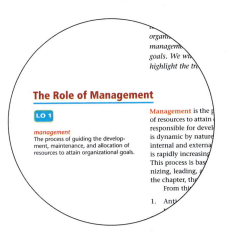

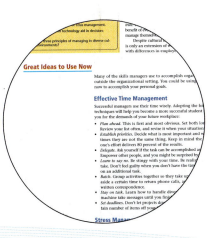

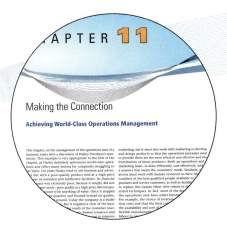

OPENING VIGNETTES THAT CONNECT

Making the Connection **Making the Connection** introduces the chapter's content and is designed to help students connect the chapter concepts to business as a whole.

A Unique Integrated Learning System

FOUR BOXES

NEW Expanding Around the Globe This new boxed feature demonstrates how globalization is important in today's marketplace and its impact on real companies.

Customer Satisfaction and Quality Because customer satisfaction and quality are essential to attracting and keeping customers, the **Customer Satisfaction and Quality** box addresses how these concepts are illustrated and applied in actual companies.

Making Ethical Choices These ethical activities boxes present real-world ethical challenges to stimulate discussion regarding ethical issues faced by organizations.

NEW Sustainable Business, Sustainable World We have added, in selected chapters, "Sustainable Business, Sustainable World" boxes, highlighting the growing importance of sustainability in today's business practices.

Hot Links Provide an opportunity to connect to relevant websites to expand on chapter information.

New Concept in Action Interesting companies and business leaders are profiled in our new "CONCEPT IN ACTION" photo essays. Each "Concept in Action" concludes with a critical thinking question to spark further discussion and study about a business topic.

Key Terms Every business term is carefully defined and is conveniently located in the text margins beside the section where the term is first introduced. A complete glossary of all key terms is included at the end of the text.

END-OF-CHAPTER SKILL-BUILDING ACTIVITIES, EXERCISES, AND RESOURCES

Experiential Exercises This feature allows students to practice and apply the chapter concepts and to expand on the chapter topics. These exercises can be used as assessments, assignments, and to add a real-world application.

Review Questions Review questions confirm student learning and understanding of chapter topics.

Cases These three types of chapter-ending cases encourage the exploration and analysis of business strategies. Many of these cases are new to this edition.

Creative Thinking Cases

Video Cases

E-Commerce Cases

PREFACE

Your Future is Our Business

The Future of Business, Third Canadian Edition, provides a personal roadmap for understanding and navigating the future of business. The third Canadian edition builds on the success of the first and second editions with thorough coverage of business principles and leading-edge practices adopted by business innovators, all illustrated with relevant and interesting business examples. Because the future of business is approaching us at warp speed, the third Canadian edition has been written with the goal of making you the winner in tomorrow's fast-paced marketplace. Each chapter will help you understand what is happening and what will happen in the sometimes chaotic and always exciting world of business.

The Interactive Perspective: Major Business Topics Up Close

Today's most important business topics and trends are thoroughly covered in the third Canadian edition—this means more insight into the key economic and business developments that shape the future. Topics at the forefront of business covered in this edition include:

- integration of business practices,
- customer satisfaction and quality,
- globalization and global management skills,
- sustainable business,
- changing Canadian demographics,
- corporate ethical standards,
- managing multinational cultures in the workplace,
- virtual teams and corporations, and
- nurturing knowledge workers.

Through extensive reviews, we discovered that instructors teaching the introduction to business course place considerable importance on the topics of ethics, customer satisfaction and quality, the role of technology in business, e-commerce, entrepreneurship and small business management, global business opportunities, and careers. Therefore, we gave these topics special emphasis.

The Future of Business is supported by real-world examples to introduce today's students to tomorrow's business careers. The text is written in a friendly and conversational style and helps prepare students of all interests and abilities for future achievements with the information, skills, and techniques they need to get to work and jump on the fast-track to success.

What's New in the Third Canadian Edition

Highlights of new content to the third Canadian edition include the following:

- An updated prologue, **A Quick Guide to Your Future Success in Business,** offers practical and inspiring advice for developing test-taking, interpersonal, time management, and planning skills. The prologue also features suggestions for finding the right career and succeeding in that first professional job. Not only will students find up-to-date guidelines for finding a job using the Internet, they can gain insights into their own readiness for the job market. New, fun Self-Tests explore the following topics:

- Can You Persuade Others?
- Can You Play the Political Game?
- How Well Do You Manage Your Time?
- Are You Good at Managing Money?
- Do You Need to Improve Your Study Habits?
- How Assertive Are You?
- Are You Really a Good Listener?

- In each chapter you will find interesting companies and business leaders profiled in our new "Concept in Action" photo essays. The photos and accompanying essays are fun, contemporary, insightful, and a super learning tool for the visual learner. Each "Concept in Action" concludes with a critical thinking question to spark further discussion and study about a business topic.

Two new boxed features have been added:

Expanding Around The Globe
This new boxed feature demonstrates how globalization is important in today's marketplace and its impact on real companies.

Sustainable Business, Sustainable World
To supplement the "Making Ethical Choices" boxes, we have added, in selected chapters, "Sustainable Business, Sustainable World" boxes highlighting the growing importance of sustainability in today's business practices.

Reorganization

In response to reviewers' suggestions, the following organizational changes were incorporated:

- Reduced the total number of chapters from 18 to 16.
- Moved the discussion of "teams" from Chapter 9 Motivating Employees (previously Chapter 10) to Chapter 8 Designing Organizational Structures.
- Included less theory and more examples in Chapter 9 Motivating Employees.
- Moved *Managing Human Resources and Labour Relations* (previously chapter 9, now chapter 10) to the "Functional Areas of Business" section.
- Consolidated the previous edition's four marketing chapters into two, more manageable chapters—specifically combining the 4P's and presenting them in one chapter, "Creating Marketing Strategies".
- Introduced new International Financial Reporting Standards in the Accounting chapter.
- Reversed the order of the financial chapters to make the content more understandable, interesting, and concise for students.

Great Features Retained from the Previous Editions

Organization matters! Each chapter of *The Future of Business,* Third Canadian Edition has been organized into a unique three-part structure that links principles, trends, and ideas:

Principles of Business
Gives students a comprehensive overview of current business practices, and teaches key principles through real-world examples from the largest global corporate giants to the smallest family start-ups.

Trends in Business

Explores the fundamental factors and emerging trends that are reshaping today's business world and altering tomorrow's competitive environment. This preview of the future gives students a keen advantage when entering the workplace.

Great Ideas to Use Now

Brings chapter topics to life with relevant and interesting tips for making the most of a professional career or becoming a smart consumer. Students develop skills that are applicable immediately.

Customer Satisfaction and Quality boxes

Because customer satisfaction and quality are essential to attracting and keeping customers, the Customer Satisfaction and Quality box addresses how these concepts are illustrated and applied in actual companies.

Making Ethical Choices boxes

These ethical activities boxes present real-world ethical challenges to stimulate discussion regarding ethical issues faced by organizations.

In the **Introduction,** students learn the basic terms that are associated with organizations and business. They are given the foundation of what a business is, how risk can affect the business, revenues, expenses and profits, etc. Here, too, the students are first introduced to the *Integrated Model of a Successful Business.*

Making the Connection introduces each chapter. This section shows how the chapter concepts relate to "The Integrative Model" to help students connect the chapter concepts to business as a whole.

Learning Outcomes are provided at the beginning of each chapter to highlight the learning expectations for students as they read the chapter. These help to guide students' learning by providing key concepts that are presented in the chapter.

Each chapter begins with an **opening vignette** about a prominent, student-friendly company or a business professional that actually previews that chapter's content. We then provide several questions to prompt critical thinking.

Unlike most traditional textbooks that have review or study questions at the end of each chapter only, *The Future of Business* has also included "**Concept Checks**" throughout the chapter. These concept checks are meant to challenge the students' learning as they progress through the chapter. If they are unable to respond to the concept checks, they can simply review the previous few pages instead of trying to search through the entire chapter to locate the information.

Hot Links give the student an opportunity to connect to various websites to expand on the information presented in the chapter. Instructors may also choose to send students to the website links to fulfill assignments.

Key Terms help students to master the business vocabulary. Every key business term is carefully defined within the text. Each term appears in bold type and is defined in the margin where the term is first introduced. A complete glossary of all key terms is also included at the end of the book.

A **Summary of Learning Outcomes** at the end of each chapter helps students to focus on the relevant material in a concise manner. As a supplement to this summary, the Key Terms that were used in the chapter are listed along with their page numbers.

The **Integrated Learning System** anchors chapter concepts, provides a framework for study, and links all of the instructor and student supplements. The Integrated Learning System helps you learn quickly and study efficiently. It also helps ease lecture preparation. Learning outcomes at the beginning of each chapter outline the key concepts in the chapter and provide structure for lesson plans and help exam preparation. Learning outcomes are tied to major headings within the chapter and are supported with concept checks and a chapter summary. Every supplement is also organized by learning outcomes to ensure that each piece of the Integrated Learning System reinforces the other components.

Organization

In Part One of *The Future of Business*, Third Canadian Edition, students learn how the PEST (**p**olitical, **e**conomic, **s**ocial, **t**echnology) model works and its impact on any business. In these first four chapters to either introduce or refresh the students' awareness of certain elementary, but critical components, the book discusses *Understanding Evolving Economic Systems and Competition* (Chapter 1), *The Global Marketplace and Governments' Roles* (Chapter 2), *Social Trends, Social Responsibility, and Making Ethical Decisions in Business* (Chapter 3), and *Using Technology to Manage Information and for Business Success* (Chapter 4) including the role of MIS in the organization.

Part Two introduces the concepts of Canadian business by discussing the *Forms of Business Ownership* (Chapter 5) and *Entrepreneurship and Small Business* (Chapter 6).

Business Management (Part Three) examines *Management and Leadership in Today's Organizations* (Chapter 7), *Designing Organizational Structures* (Chapter 8), and *Motivating Employees* (Chapter 9). This section was revised considerably from the previous editions to reflect the reviewers' thoughts of how the subject matter should be covered and where it should be placed in the book.

The final section, Part Four, gives the students a basic understanding of the functional areas of business. The seven (7) chapters include: *Managing Human Resources and Labour Relations, Achieving World-Class Operations Management, Understanding the Customer, Creating Marketing Strategies, Using Financial Information and Accounting, Understanding Money, Financial Institutions, and the Securities Markets,* and *Managing the Firm's Finances.*

Supplements

Business success is stimulated by access to and mastery of vital resources. The same is true for the classroom. Whether teaching an online course or simply enhancing your course with Web resources, *The Future of Business,* Third Canadian Edition offers a vast, complementary system of teaching and learning resources.

Nelson Education Testing Advantage

NETA Products

Engagement * Assessment * Success

The **Nelson Education Teaching Advantage program** is designed to ensure that instructors and students have access to research-based resources that enable the success of Canadian students and educators.

ENGAGEMENT: NETA GUIDE TO CLASSROOM ENGAGEMENT

The *Guide to Classroom Engagement* for *The Future of Business,* Third Canadian Edition includes a range of activities that give instructors a practical, user-friendly way to incorporate interactive learning activities in both large and small classrooms. The *Guide* is focused on four core principles: student-centred learning, deep learning, active learning, and creating positive classroom environments. All of these principles are based on decades of research into what helps students learn best and are designed to foster classroom engagement.

Each NETA *Guide* includes a section outlining the research underlying these principles, which will help you create engaging classrooms. The *Guide* was written by Dr. Roger Fisher and created in partnership with an interdisciplinary board of scholars of teaching and learning. All NETA *Guide* authors have been trained in the principles underlying the program. *The Future of Business* NETA Guide was authored by textbook author Norm Althouse.

Also included for instructors is a comprehensive Instructor's Manual. Developed in response to numerous suggestions from instructors teaching this course, this resource is designed to provide maximum guidance for delivering the content in an interesting and dynamic manner. Each chapter begins with learning outcomes that anchor the integrated learning system. A lecture outline guides instructors through key terminology and concepts. Each chapter includes lecture support for teaching the cases and guidance for integrating PowerPoint™ slides and other visuals that illustrate and reinforce the lecture and suggested answers to end of chapter material. A comprehensive video guide is included in the Instructor's Manual and includes the running time of each video, concepts illustrated in the video, teaching objectives for the case, and solutions for video case study questions.

EDITORIAL ADVISORY BOARD

NORMAN ALTHOUSE, HASKAYNE SCHOOL OF BUSINESS,
UNIVERSITY OF CALGARY

SCOTT FOLLOWS, MANNING SCHOOL OF BUSINESS ADMINISTRATION,
ACADIA UNIVERSITY

GLEN LOPPNOW, DEPARTMENT OF CHEMISTRY,
UNIVERSITY OF ALBERTA

TANYA NOEL, DEPARTMENT OF BIOLOGY, YORK UNIVERSITY

GARY POOLE, DIRECTOR, CENTRE FOR TEACHING AND
ACADEMIC GROWTH AND SCHOOL OF POPULATION AND
PUBLIC HEALTH, UNIVERSITY OF BRITISH COLUMBIA

DAN PRATT, DEPARTMENT OF EDUCATIONAL STUDIES,
UNIVERSITY OF BRITISH COLUMBIA

BRENDA CHANT-SMITH, DEPARTMENT OF PSYCHOLOGY,
TRENT UNIVERSITY

Assessment: Neta Test Bank In most post-secondary courses, a large percentage of student assessment is based on multiple-choice testing. Many instructors use multiple-choice reluctantly, believing that it is a methodology best used for testing what a student *remembers* rather than what she or he has *learned*. Nelson Education Ltd. understands that a good quality multiple-choice test bank can provide the means to measure **higher-level thinking** skills as well as recall. Recognizing the importance of multiple-choice testing in today's classroom, we have created the Nelson Education Teaching Advantage program (NETA) to ensure the value of our high quality test banks. The testing component of our NETA program was created in partnership with David DiBattista, a 3M National Teaching Fellow, professor of psychology at Brock University, and researcher in the area of multiple-choice testing. NETA for testbanks ensures that subject-matter experts who author test banks have had training in two areas: avoiding common errors in test construction, and developing multiple-choice test questions that "get beyond remembering" to assess higher-level thinking. All NETA test banks include David DiBattista's guide for instructors, "Multiple Choice Tests: Getting Beyond Remembering." This guide has been designed to assist you in using Nelson test banks to achieve your desired outcomes in your course. See the Instructor's Resource CD button "NETA Guidelines" for this valuable resource. The test bank to accompany *The Future of Business,* Third Canadian Edition was authored by textbook author Shirley A. Rose.

Computerized NETA Test Bank in ExamView®

Create, deliver, and customize tests (both print and online) in minutes with this easy-to-use assessment and tutorial system. *ExamView* offers both a *Quick Test Wizard* and an *Online Test Wizard* that guide you step-by-step through the process of creating tests. The test appears on screen exactly as it will print or display online. Using *ExamView's* complete word-processing capabilities, you can enter an unlimited number of new questions or edit existing questions. ExamView is offered in both PC and Mac platforms.

PowerPoint™ Lecture System. The PowerPoint™ Lecture System includes hundreds of slides that illustrate key chapter concepts and actual business examples, many not included in the text. These slides will help improve lecture organization and reduce preparation time. The PowerPoint™ slides were prepared by textbook author Norm Althouse. Both an instructor version and a student version are available.

Instructor's Resource CD (ISBN 0-17-647884-1). For maximum convenience, the NETA *Guide to Classroom Engagement,* the Instructor's Manual, the PowerPoint™ slides, the NETA Test Bank, and the ExamView® Testing System are all available on CD.

JoinIn™ on Turning Point®. Now you can author, deliver, show, assess, and grade all in PowerPoint™ . . . with NO toggling back and forth between screens! JoinIn™ on TurningPoint® is the only classroom response software tool that gives you true PowerPoint™ integration. With JoinIn™ on TurningPoint®, you are no longer tied to your computer . . . you can walk about your classroom as you lecture, showing slides and collecting and displaying responses with ease. There is simply no easier or more effective way to turn your lecture hall into a personal, fully interactive experience for your students. If you can use PowerPoint™, you can use JoinIn™ on TurningPoint®!

DVD to accompany *The Future of Business* 3CE, and DVD Guide (ISBN 0-17-647470-6). Designed to enrich and support chapter concepts, each of the 16 video segments presents real business issues faced by a variety of service and manufacturing organizations. The video cases challenge students to study business issues and develop solutions to business problems. The instructor's DVD guide, included in the instructor's manual, outlines the key teaching objectives of each video case and suggests answers to the critical thinking questions.

***The Future of Business* Website <www.futureofbusiness3e.nelson.com>.** The website for *The Future of Business* provides rich content to maximize student learning and build online skills. Each text chapter is supported by an online Test Yourself quiz that tests student understanding and offers clear, customized feedback for incorrect answers. Also included on the website are Web links, Collaborative Exercises, a business plan template, downloadable supplements, and much more. A unique feature for instructors is Classroom Activities, prepared by textbook author Norm Althouse. Objectives of the Classroom Activities include:

- encouraging students to prepare for class,
- encouraging students to apply materials presented in the chapter,
- learning the chapter material by using an application,
- presenting the material in a format other than lecture style, and
- practicing presentation skills, targeted at students.

Instructors can also use the Classroom Activities for assignment or assessments. Each of the activities can be modified as the instructor sees fit.

CNOW™. This online diagnostic tool, prepared by textbook author Norm Althouse, identifies each student's unique needs with a pre-test that generates a personalized study plan for each chapter, helping students focus on concepts they're having the most difficulty mastering. Students then take a post-test to measure their understanding of the material. An instructor grade book is available to track and monitor student progress. A key component of the study plan is the inclusion of visually and pedagogically rich modules that begin with clearly stated learning objectives followed by knowledge-building animations with audio to present key concepts. Modules also include discovery activities and self-check quizzes that confirm students' understanding of the module material.

InfoTrac College Edition™. Now you can give your students an entire library for the price of one book. With InfoTrac College Edition™, students gain complete, 24-hour-a-day access to full-text articles from hundreds of scholarly journals and popular periodicals such as *Canadian Business, Business Week, Canadian Business Review,* and *HR Professional.* Thousands of full-length, substantive articles spanning the past four years are updated daily, indexed, and linked. And because they're online, the articles are accessible from any computer with Internet access. InfoTrac College Edition™ is perfect for all students, from dorm-dwellers to commuters and distance learners.

Nelson ePacks. Nelson provides cartridge content for this title that's compatible for all versions of BlackBoard (and the former WebCt). Visit the Instructor's Resource area at <www.futureofbusiness3e.nelson.com> for details.

Acknowledgments

We are exceedingly grateful to the many reviewers who offered suggestions and recommendations for enhancing the coverage, pedagogy, and support package of *The Future of Business*. The feedback from these instructors helped guide our efforts and ensures that the textbook surpassed expectations for customer satisfaction and quality. We are deeply appreciative of the insights of the following reviewers:

Ayten Archer, University of Saskatchewan

Barry Boothman, University of New Brunswick

F. Alex Boultbee, Seneca College

Elisabeth Carter, Douglas College

Choon Hian Chan, Kwantlen Polytechnic University

Angela Davis, University of Winnipeg

Johan de Rooy, University of British Columbia

Vic de Witt, Red River College

David Fleming, George Brown College

Jane Forbes, Seneca College

Robert Fournier, Red Deer College

Mary Furey, Memorial University of Newfoundland

Walter Isenor, Acadia University

Sunil Kaplash, University of Victoria

Ed Leach, Dalhousie University

Gordon McFarlane, Langara College

Alan McGee, Acadia University

Dr. C. McLarney, Dalhousie University

Valerie Miceli, Seneca College

Erica Morrill, Fanshawe College

Richard Powers, University of Toronto

John Purcell, Sheridan College

Carson Rappell, Dawson College

Cynthia Riley, Seneca College

Steve Rose, University of Ontario Institute of Technology

Frank Saccucci, Grant MacEwan University

Bob Sproule, University of Waterloo

Patti Stoll, Seneca College

William Thurber, Brock University

Leslie Wilder, Red River College

Terry Wu, University of Ontario Institute of Technology

We would also like to recognize the contribution of Lawrence Gitman and Carl McDaniel, authors of the U.S. edition of *The Future of Business*. Their original work served as the foundation for our writing and set a standard of excellence we conscientiously followed.

We have benefited from the detailed and constructive contributions of many individuals. Specifically, we would like to thank the following people for their insight and contributions to *The Future of Business*:

Cindy Anderson
Bruce Byford
Victoria Calvert
Gordon Campbell
Michael Corbeil
David B. Crawford
Joan Dauter
Doug Dokis
Kathy Drewes
Janice Eliasson
Jeff Everett
Christopher Halpin
Karina Hope
Wayne Irvine
Rafik Kurji
Ryan B. Lee
David Lertzman
Robin Lynas
Robert L. Malach
Sandra E. Malach
Arden Matheson
Leanne McDonald
Doug McDonnell
Fred (Scoop) McKay
Katrina Montgomery
Ron Munaweera
Ron Murch
Albert Nasaar
Gino Panucci
Karen Parsons
Barry Sadrehashemi
Christine Stark
Frank Thirkettle
Elizabeth Watson
Justine Wheeler
Kim Wilson
Claire Wright

And, of course, our talented and patient editorial and production staff at Nelson Education Limited.

Norm R. Althouse
Shirley A. Rose
Laura A. Allan
Lawrence J. Gitman
Carl McDaniel

About the Authors

Norm R. Althouse

Norm Althouse received his Bachelor of Business Administration (Accounting) and worked in the public sector for ten years before returning to continue studies in the Master of Business Program. He has studied in Canada, Australia, Ireland, and Hungary. Currently, Norm teaches at the Haskayne School of Business at the University of Calgary. He has also taught at the University of Lethbridge and Mount Royal College.

After several years of teaching in the Human Resource area at the University of Calgary, Norm transferred to the Strategy and Global Management Area and currently teaches in the Business and Environment Area. Initially, Norm's primary responsibility was to develop a required core-course in business for first- and second-year business students. His commitment to "continuous improvement" has resulted in many new developments, including the integration of materials and changes in the pedagogy of the course.

Norm's research activities include: team building, the changing nature of management and managers and, most currently, studying values and diversity in the workplace. Additionally, Norm has presented at conferences such as the Administrative Sciences Association of Canada (*"The Gendering Component of Diversity: How is it Faring?"*), The Academy of Management (*"Success in the Classroom, Grading Strategies, and Group Work for New Instructors"*) and has been published in a book of readings from the Global Business and Technology Association—Budapest, Hungary (*"Hierarchies in Transition: Hungary and Canada"*).

Shirley A. Rose

Shirley Rose received her Bachelor of Business Administration degree from the University of New Brunswick. She assumed a position with the Alberta Provincial Government in the Department of Advanced Education. Her work history includes banking, oil and gas, land development, electric utility companies, and several entrepreneurial ventures. After some time in industry, Shirley returned to university and completed an MBA at the University of Calgary. Upon completion of the MBA, Shirley taught in a variety of full- and part-time positions at the University of New Brunswick, Athabasca University, Simon Fraser University, University of Calgary, University of Lethbridge, and Thompson River University. She was accepted into the Ph.D. program at the University of Bath in the UK and completed two years of study. Shirley's research and consulting activities are in the fields of health care, oil and gas, union-government relations, unemployment and service learning. She has authored test banks and study guides, as well as served as a contributing author for textbooks in the management and general business areas.

Shirley Rose has been with the Bissett School of Business at Mount Royal University since 1998. During that time she has taught in the areas of management, organizational behaviour, entrepreneurship and general business and served as Program Chair responsible for programs in marketing, human resources, general business, and aviation. In addition to her academic writings, Shirley is also working on a project related to spirituality issues both inside and outside the workplace.

Laura A. Allan

Laura Allan received her Honours Bachelor of Business Administration from Wilfrid Laurier University and, after a brief stint in the private sector working for an advertising agency, she went on to get her Masters of Business Administration in Marketing at York University. Laura went back to her alma mater to teach in 1984, and apart from taking brief time off to have her two children, she has been there ever since. Laura teaches primarily first-year undergraduate classes, but has also taught a second-year decision-making course. She also teaches executive development seminars for the Laurier Institute. Laura has been academic editor on another introductory text, written a study guide, and contributed chapters for two introductory textbooks. She has also co-authored the lab manual for the two first-year courses each semester since 1998, and has developed an online version of both courses for the university's distance education department.

Laura's commitment to the integrative approach to teaching business led to a complete redesign of the first-year courses. Most recently, she helped design the annual New Venture Competition for first-year students. Currently, Laura serves as co-coordinator for the first-year program at Wilfrid Laurier University, and has been recognized as one of the "most popular profs" in *Maclean's* magazine since 2000.

Lawrence J. Gitman

Lawrence J. Gitman is an emeritus professor of finance at San Diego State University. He received his bachelor's degree from Purdue University, his M.B.A. from the University of Dayton, and his Ph.D. from the University of Cincinnati. Professor Gitman is a prolific textbook author and has over 50 articles appearing in *Financial Management, Financial Review, Financial Services Review, Journal of Financial Planning, Journal of Risk and Insurance, Journal of Financial Research, Financial Practice and Education, Journal of Financial Education,* and other publications.

His singly authored major textbooks include: *Principles of Managerial Finance: Brief,* Fourth Edition; *Principles of Managerial Finance,* Eleventh Edition; and *Foundations of Managerial Finance,* Fourth Edition. Other major textbooks include *Personal Financial Planning,* Tenth Edition; and *Fundamentals of Investing,* Ninth Edition; both co-authored with Michael D. Joehnk. Gitman and Joehnk also wrote *Investment Fundamentals: A Guide to Becoming a Knowledgeable Investor,* which was selected as one of 1988's ten best personal finance books by *Money* magazine. In addition, he co-authored *Introduction to Finance* with Jeff Madura and *Corporate Finance,* Second Edition, with Scott B. Smart and William L. Meggison.

An active member of numerous professional organizations, Professor Gitman is past president of the Academy of Financial Services, the San Diego Chapter of the Financial Executives Institute, the Midwest Finance Association, and the FMA National Honor Society. In addition he is a Certified Financial Planner (CFP)® and a Certified Cash Manager (CCM). Gitman served as Vice-President, Financial Education of the Financial Management Association, as a Director of the San Diego MIT Enterprise Form, and on the CFP® Board of Standards. He and his wife have two children and live in La Jolla, California, where he is an avid cyclist.

Carl McDaniel

Carl McDaniel is a professor of marketing at the University of Texas—Arlington, where he is chairman of the marketing department. He has been an instructor for more than 20 years and is the recipient of several awards for outstanding teaching. McDaniel has also been a district sales manager for Southwestern Bell Telephone Company. Currently, he serves as a board member of the North Texas Higher Education Authority, a 1.5 billion member organization that provides immediate financing for student loans across America.

In addition to this text, McDaniel has also co-authored a number of textbooks in marketing. McDaniel's research has appeared in such publications as *Journal of Marketing, Journal of Business Research, Journal of the Academy of Marketing Science,* and *California Management Review.*

McDaniel is a member of the American Marketing Association, Academy of Marketing Science, Society for Marketing Advances, and Southwestern Marketing Association.

PROLOGUE

A Quick Guide to Your Future Success in Business

Your Future in Business: Begin with a Diploma or Degree

What makes someone a winner in life? Winners are people who go through the various stages of life content in knowing that they have done their best: their best at work, at home, and in all pursuits of life. And a big part of having a happy life is pursuing a career that offers job satisfaction and financial rewards. If you are going to "be all that you can be," you need a good education.

A diploma or degree unlocks doors to economic opportunity. Why get a diploma or degree?

- *Get and keep a better job.* Because the world is changing rapidly, and many jobs rely on new technology, more jobs require education beyond high school. With a postsecondary education, you will have more jobs from which to choose.
- *Earn more money.* People who go to postsecondary institutions usually earn more than those who do not. For example, currently a bachelor's degree is worth a minimum of $25,000 a year more than a high school diploma. If your career spans 45 years, you will earn $1,125,000 more than a high school graduate!
- *Get a good start in life.* A postsecondary education helps you acquire a wide range of knowledge in many subjects as well as an advanced understanding of your specialized area of business. Postsecondary institutions also train you to express your thoughts clearly in speech and in writing and to make informed decisions.

Simply stated, a diploma or degree gives you the chance to achieve the quality of life you deserve. The lifestyle, the new friends, the purchasing power of a diploma or degree won't guarantee happiness but will put you well on the road to finding it.

Learning the Basics of Business

You might want to pursue a career as a physician, florist, game warden, systems analyst, or any of a thousand other opportunities. One thing that all careers have in common is that you need to have a basic understanding of business. Your success in whatever you choose will depend partially on your basic business skills. And that is why this course is so important.

Few courses present all the fundamental areas of business and then link them together the way this course does. This is where you get the big picture as well as an introduction to fundamental components of business. Learn it well, because it will be invaluable throughout your life.

Choosing a Career

Because this course gives you a detailed overview of all of the areas of business, it will guide you in selecting a major should you decide to pursue a diploma or degree in business. Choosing a major is one of life's true milestones. Your major essentially determines how you will spend the next four decades of your life! A marketing major will find a career in sales, marketing research, advertising, or other marketing-related field. An accounting major (you guessed it) will become an accountant. Never take selecting a major lightly; working 40 hours a week for the next 45 years (less vacations), you will put in about 90,000 hours on the job. Don't you think that you should choose something that you will enjoy?

Developing Interpersonal Skills is Key to Your Success

A diploma or degree in business is going to offer you many great career opportunities. Once you take your first job, how rapidly you move up the ladder is up to you. People with great interpersonal skills will always do better on and off the job than those who lack them. It has been estimated that up to 95 percent of our workplace success depends on an understanding of other people.[1] Here's how to enhance your interpersonal skills:

1. **Build your people skills.** Learn to build alliances in a group and establish harmony. Make a concerted effort to know what is happening in the lives of those on your team at school and work. About once a month get together with your group and pass out a list of issues, concerns, fears, and potential problems. Then invite everyone to give input to solve little problems before they become big. If something goes wrong, try to find out where things are not running smoothly and improve them. Be sure to compliment someone in your group who is doing an exemplary job.

   Become a good listener. When you listen well, you are in effect telling the other person that he or she is worth listening to. Listening well includes listening to both what is said and not said. Learn to read unspoken gestures and expressions. When giving feedback, plan what you will say in advance. Be positive and be specific. Ask the person receiving the feedback if they would like to discuss your comments further.

2. **Understand how to persuade others.** Remember, we all must sell ourselves and ideas to get ahead in life and business. Influencing others means overcoming objections, igniting passions, or changing minds. The first step is to build esprit de corps, a shared enthusiasm and devotion to the group. Make your vision their vision so that everyone is working toward a common goal. Praise the team as a whole, but recognize the unique contributions different team members have made. The trick is to praise everyone, yet for different reasons. When you and your team successfully solve a problem, change will result.

   Persuasion rests on trust. You can build trust by being honest, fulfilling your commitments, being concerned about others, and minimizing problems and pain for others whenever possible. In short, if you have integrity, building trust becomes a simple task.

   When people raise objections to your plans or ideas, try to fully understand their comments and the motivation for making them. When you feel that you understand the true objection, answer the objection in the form of a benefit: "Yes, you will need to work next Saturday, but then you can have compensatory time off anytime you wish next month." Determine your persuasion skills by taking the quiz in Exhibit P.1.

Rate your level of agreement with the statements below using the following scale:

Strongly Agree	Agree	Neither Agree nor Disagree	Disagree	Strongly Disagree

1. I prefer to work in a team rather than individually.
2. I enjoy motivating others to help accomplish objectives.
3. I avoid working with difficult people or trying to resolve group differences.
4. I can learn more working in a team rather than working by myself.
5. I would prefer to work with individuals I have known previously.
6. I give up if my team members do not agree with me.
7. I may not always convince my team members to agree with my opinions, but I will go ahead and do what I feel is correct.
8. I think people who can persuade others always possess sound judgement.
9. I will do the work myself if others do not agree to do it.
10. To get the work done, I will listen to a person to understand how he/she wants it to be done.
11. I can get people to voluntarily make commitments and get the work done.[2]

See the scoring guidelines at the end of the prologue to obtain your score.

3. **Learn to think on your feet.** Top executives, such as former automobile chairman Lee Iacocca, say that "speaking well on your feet" is the best thing that you can do for your career. If you cannot quickly express yourself with confidence, others will lose confidence in you.

   It will not happen overnight, but you can become an outstanding thinker and speaker. A simple technique is to set a timer for two minutes and ask a friend to begin speaking. When the timer goes off, your friend stops speaking and you begin talking. The challenge is to use the final thought that your friend spoke as the first word of your two-minute talk. Another technique is to have someone supply you with a series of quotes. Then, without hesitation, give your interpretation.

4. **Empower yourself.** No matter who you are, what position you will hold, or where you will work, you probably will have to report to somebody. If you are fortunate enough to work in a culture of empowerment, you are allowed control over your job (not complete control, but enough control to make you feel your opinion matters). When you are not given an opportunity to provide input, you will eventually lose interest in your job. When empowered, you have the confidence to do something to alter your circumstances. On the job, empowerment means that you can make decisions to benefit the organization and its customers.

   If you want to gain empowerment in your life and work, here are a few tips: be assertive, ask for credit for yourself when it is due, propose ideas to your group and your supervisor, initiate projects without being asked, tie your personal goals to those of the organization, develop your leadership skills, plan to learn on a continuous basis, be informed, don't let others intimidate you, and don't complain about a bad situation. Instead, take action to improve it.

5. **Acquire political savvy.** Politics is an inevitable part of every organization in Canada, including your school. Politics has always been a part of the workplace and always will be. The trick is to learn to play the political game to your own advantage and to the advantage of others without causing harm to anyone else. Being political means getting along with others in order to move them toward accomplishing a specific goal. It does not mean manoeuvring for selfish purposes, manipulating in order to deceive, or scheming so others lose while you win.

   Here are some tips and techniques to be an effective player in the political game:

   • *Think about what you say.* Understand the effect your words will have on others before you say or write them.

- *Empathize.* Try to think of a situation from the other person's perspective.
- *Suggest a trial period, if you meet opposition to an idea you're proposing.* If you are as successful as you are confident, you can then ask to have the trial period extended.
- *Learn about the political climate in which you are working.* This means knowing, among other things, what actions have led to failure for others, knowing who is "in" and why, determining who is "out" and why, and learning what behaviours lead to promotion.
- *Volunteer to do the jobs no one else wants to do.* Occasionally pitching in shows your willingness to get the job done. However, do not make this your trademark; you do not want others to think they can take advantage of you.
- *Work hard to meet the needs of those in authority.* Make certain you fully understand management's requirements; then go out of your way to meet them. If in time you do not think you are getting the recognition or respect you deserve, make your own needs known.
- *Give credit.* You never know who may be in a position to hurt or harm you. Consequently, the best policy is to treat everyone with respect and dignity. Show your appreciation to everyone who has helped you. Do not steal credit that belongs to someone else.
- *Learn your supervisor's preferences.* The more you are in sync with your supervisor's style, wishes, and preferences, the better you can do your job. However, do not be a rubber stamp. Rather, work the way your manager works. When necessary, suggest better ways of doing things.
- *Keep secrets—your own and others'.* Resist the temptation to tell all. Not only do you run the risk of being labelled a gossip, but if you share too much about yourself, your words can come back to haunt you. If you are revealing information told to you in confidence, you are bound to lose the trust and respect of those who originally confided in you.

Find out how well you play the political game by taking the quiz in Exhibit P.2.

EXHIBIT P.2 > Fun Self-Test—Can You Play the Political Game?

Rate your level of agreement with the statements below using the following scale:

Strongly Agree	Agree	Neither Agree nor Disagree	Disagree	Strongly Disagree

1. To be successful, you should have a strong relationship with your boss and subordinates.
2. Office politics is not very challenging.
3. Tough people give you a tough time but also teach you tough lessons.
4. Networking and observation plays a major role in being good at office politics.
5. There are no ethics or morals in office politics.
6. Corporate politics is not about the individuals, it is about the survival of the corporation.
7. Office politics is the only way you gain real access to your boss's ear.
8. Those who avoid being political at work may not move forward in their careers, may find themselves resentful and frustrated, and run the risk of being isolated.
9. If you do all of the work on a project, you won't tell the boss because you don't want your coworkers to get in trouble.
10. When faced with gossip and rumours, you prefer to be silent but aware.
11. To master office politics, you should seek a win-lose situation.
12. If a person in authority is out to get rid of you, a good tactic would be to establish allies and position yourself for another job in the company.
13. If you have made any significant contribution to a project, you always make sure that others know about it which, in turn, adds to your reputation.[3]

See the scoring guidelines at the end of the prologue to obtain your score.

EXHIBIT P.3 > Key Questions That Teams Should Answer Before Starting a Project

1. What are the goals?
2. Who provides the mission statement?
3. What are our limits?
4. Where will support come from? Who will be our sponsor?
5. Who will be team leader? How is he or she selected?
6. What are the deadlines we face?
7. What resources are available?
8. What data will we need to collect?
9. For how long will our team exist?
10. Who are the customers for our team results? What do they expect of us?
11. Will our team responsibilities conflict with our regular jobs?
12. What is the reward for success?
13. How will decisions be made?
14. How will our efforts be measured?
15. Will our intended success be replicated? If so, how and by whom?

6. **Become a team builder.** Throughout your college and business career you will participate on teams. Most Canadian organizations employ teamwork. An effective team is one that meets its goals on time and, if a budget is involved, within budget. The first step in creating an effective team is to have goals that are clear, realistic, supported by each team member, and parallels the larger organization goals. Exhibit P.3 lists the questions that teams should answer to ensure their success.

7. **Handle conflict well.** The world is not a perfect place and there are no perfect people inhabiting it. The best we can hope for is people's willingness to improve life's circumstances. If we are truly committed to the idea of reducing school and workplace conflict, there is much we can do to inspire such willingness in others. Bringing conflict into the open has its advantages. Talking about conflict often helps to clear the air, and thinking about the possibility of conflict often helps to avoid it.

When conflicts occur, try the K-I-N-D technique. The letters stand for:

K = Kind
I = Informed
N = New
D = Definite

The technique involves your requesting a meeting with the difficult person, whether he or she is having a conflict with you or with others. Start off with kind words, words that encourage cooperation, words that show your determination to make the conflict situation better. Next, demonstrate that you have taken the time to learn more about the person, what is important to him or her, what he or she prefers in terms of work. Show by your words that you have taken the time to become informed about the individual.

The third step requires you to do something novel, something you have not tried before. Put your creativity to work, and discover a plan to which you can both subscribe (for example, keeping a journal regarding the problem and possible solutions).

Finally, do not permit the exchange to conclude until you have made a definite overture to ensure future success. What can you promise the other person you will do differently? What are you asking him or her to do differently? Set a time to meet again and review your individual attempts to achieve collective improvement.

Make Your Future Happen: Learn to Plan[4]

GEORGE DOYLE/STOCKBYTE/GETTY IMAGES

CONCEPT *in Action* >>>

Life requires planning, and the more important one's goals, the more important planning is to achieve those goals. Whether the objective is to graduate from college, develop a professional career, or build a brighter future for one's family and community, personal success depends on a good plan. How can the six steps of the planning process help individuals achieve their educational, personal, and career dreams?

There is a natural conflict between planning and being impulsive, between pursuing a long-range goal and doing what you feel like doing right now. If you have ever had to study while the rest of the family was in the living room watching television, you know what that conflict feels like. If you have ever been invited to go to the mall to eat pizza and hang out with friends but stayed home to work on a class assignment, you know that sticking to a plan is not easy.

Of course, planning and being impulsive are both good. Each has a place in your life, you need to balance them. Having a plan does not mean that you can't act on the spur of the moment and do something that was not planned. Spontaneous events produce some of the happiest, most meaningful times of your life. Problems arise only when you consistently substitute impulsive actions for goal-oriented planning. Success in life requires a balance between the two.

If you do not engage in long-range planning and lack the discipline for it, you might limit your opportunities to be impulsive. You are not going to take a weekend fun trip just because you need a break, if you haven't saved the money to do it. In the short run, planning involves sacrifice, but in the long run, it gives you more options.

What Is a Plan?

A plan is a method or process worked out in advance that leads to the achievement of some goal. A plan is systematic, which means it relies on using a step-by-step procedure. A plan also needs to be flexible, so that it can be adapted to gradual changes in your goal.

The Planning Process

Whether choosing a postsecondary institution or finding financial aid, you should understand how the planning process helps you accomplish your goals. The following steps outline the planning process.

Step 1: Set a goal. Identify something you want to achieve or obtain: your goal. The goal, which is usually longer term in nature, will require planning, patience, and discipline to achieve. Just living in the present moment is not a goal.

Step 2: Acquire knowledge. Gain an understanding of your goal and what will be required to achieve it. Gather information about your goal through research, conversation, and thought.

Step 3: Compare alternatives. Weigh your options, which are the different paths you might take to achieve your goal. Analyze the pluses and minuses of each—the costs, the demands, and the likelihood of success.

Step 4: Choose a strategy. Select one option as the best plan of action. The choice is based on sound information, the experience of others, and your own interests and abilities.

Step 5: Make a commitment. Resolve to proceed step-by-step toward achieving your goal. Keep your eyes on the prize.

Step 6: Stay flexible. Evaluate your progress and, when necessary, revise your plan to deal with changing circumstances and new opportunities.

An Example of Planning

The following example illustrates the process of buying a new stereo using this planning process.

Step 1: Set a goal. Purchase a wireless media player.

Step 2: Acquire knowledge. Listen to friends' players. Study standards and specifications. Check on dealers, brands, models, and prices. Consult various consumer reports.

Step 3: Compare alternatives.

Alternative 1: Purchase the media player from an online auction such as eBay.
Pro: Affordable high-end equipment. Can buy right now.
Con: Uncertain condition of equipment. Limited warranty.

Alternative 2: Buy a new, lower cost model for $325.
Pro: Can afford now. New equipment with warranty.
Con: Unsuitable for adding extras. Not the best sound quality.

Alternative 3: Buy a high-quality wireless media player for $775.
Pro: Excellent sound. Greatest flexibility. New equipment with warranty.
Con: Costs more than prepared to pay now.

Step 4: Choose a strategy. Decide to buy the high-quality system but, rather than use a credit card and paying interest, delay the purchase for six months to save for it.

Step 5: Make a commitment. Give up going to the movies for the six-month period, packlunches and stop eating out, and place the savings in a stereo fund.

Step 6: Keep flexible. Four months into the plan, a model change sale provides an opportunity to buy comparable equipment for $550. Make the purchase, paying cash.

Planning for Your Life

Using the planning process to make a buying decision is a simple exercise. Making a decision about major parts of your life is far more complex. You will see that no part of life is exempt from the need for planning. It is important to apply thought, creativity, and discipline to all the interrelated phases of our lives. These phases include the following:

Career. Choosing a field of work and developing the knowledge and skills needed to enter and move ahead in that field. We will offer you some tips to get started on a great career later in the Prologue.

Self. Deciding who you are and what kind of person you want to be, working to develop your strengths and overcome your weaknesses, and refining your values.

Lifestyle. Expressing yourself in the nature and quality of your everyday life, your recreation and hobbies, and how you use your time and money.

Relationships. Developing friendships and learning to get along with people in a variety of contexts. Building family and community ties.

Finances. Building the financial resources and the economic security needed to pursue all the other dimensions of your life.

Dreams and Plans

People are natural dreamers. Dreams give us pleasure. They are also part of making a future. If you don't have dreams or think that you are not worthy of dreaming, something very important might be missing from your life. You have a right to your dreams, and you need them—even if there is little possibility that they will ever come true.

Planning is not the same as dreaming, but it uses dreams as raw materials. It translates them into specific goals. It tests them. It lays out a course of action that moves you toward realizing these goals and sets up milestones you need to achieve. Planning brings dreams down to earth and turns them into something real and attainable. For example, assume you have a dream to visit Spain as an exchange student. To translate this dream into a specific goal, you will need to follow the planning process—gather information about the exchange process, discuss the program with parents and teachers, and improve your Spanish-language skills.

Directions for Your Life

One of the best things about pursuing your dreams is that even when you fall short, the effort leads to growth and opens a path to other opportunities. The person who practices the piano every day might not achieve the dream of becoming a concert pianist but might eventually put appreciation of music to work as the director of an arts organization. A hockey player might not make it to a professional team but might enjoy a satisfying career as a coach or a sportswriter. Without a plan, dreams simply dissolve. With a plan, they give shape and direction to our lives.

Planning involves a lot of thinking and finding answers to lots of questions. The answers, and even the plan, will change over time as you gain more knowledge and life experience. Planning is a skill that is useful in every area of your life. It is something you have to pursue consciously and thoughtfully. When you plan, you translate your goals and dreams into step-by-step strategies, specific things you can do to test your goals and bring them to reality. You often have to revise your plans, but even when your plans are not fulfilled, planning will have a positive effect on the course of your life.

Going to a Postsecondary Institution Is an Opportunity of a Lifetime—Grab It, and Don't Let Go[5]

You have already had one of your dreams come true—you are in a postsecondary institution. It is, indeed, a rare privilege, because far less than one percent of traditional postsecondary-age people around the world get to attend a postsecondary institution. You're lucky! So make the best of it by learning the following skills:

Learn to Concentrate

Concentration is the art of being focused, the ability to pay attention. Without concentration, you have no memory of what you hear, see, and read. Concentration is a frame of mind that enables you to stay centred on the activity or work you are doing. You know when you're concentrating, because time seems to go by quickly, distractions that normally take you off task don't bother you, and you have a lot of mental or physical energy for the task.

You are ultimately in charge of how well you concentrate. Here are some ways to make it happen.

- *Choose a workplace.* Avoid the bed—you associate it with relaxing or sleeping. Try a desk or table for studying; you will concentrate better and accomplish more in less time. You will also have a convenient writing space and plenty of space to spread out. Be sure to have good lighting.
- *Feed your body right.* What you eat plays an important role in how well or how poorly you concentrate. Low quality carbohydrates (such as pasta, bread, processed sugars and most junk-foods) make you sleepy.
- *Avoid eating while studying.* Food and serious learning don't mix well. Think about it. When you try to eat and study at the same time, which gets more of your concentration? The food, of course! You will be more effective if you eat first and then study.
- *Listen to your thoughts.* Listening to anything but your own thoughts interferes with good concentration. Eliminating distractions such as music, television, cell phones, e-mail beeps, and other people can greatly increase the amount of studying you can accomplish. Hold all calls, and let e-mail wait.
- *Make a to-do list.* If you are trying to study but get distracted by all of the things you need to do, take time to make a to-do list. Keeping track of your thoughts on paper and referring to the paper from time to time can be very effective for clearing your mind and focusing on your task.
- *Take short, frequent breaks.* Since people concentrate for about 20 minutes or less at a time, it would make sense to capitalize on your natural body rhythms and take a short break every 20 to 30 minutes. If you feel you are fully concentrating and involved in a task, then work until a natural break occurs.

Learn to Manage Your Time

There are two ways to make sure you have more time in a day. *The first and most important way to gain more time is to plan it!* It's like getting in a car and going somewhere. You need to know where you are going and have a plan to get there. Without a plan, you will waste your time and take longer to get to your destination—if you get there at all!

A **weekly project planner** will allow you to keep track of your assignments in more detail. It contains a to-do list specific to one day. It looks like a calendar but is divided into five one-day periods with plenty of space to write. Using a weekly project planner is an effective way of keeping track of assignments and planning study time according to the school calendar.

A second way to gain more time in a day is to do more in less time. This can be as simple as doubling up on activities. For example, if you have three errands, you might try to combine them instead of doing one at a time, making one round-trip instead of three. If you commute on a bus or train, or carpool, you can study during your ride. At lunch, you can review notes. Use your imagination as to how you can get more done in less time.

Here are some ideas to help you master your time.

- *Prepare for the morning the evening before.* Put out your clothes, make lunch, and pack your books.
- *Get up 15 minutes earlier in the morning.* Use the time to plan your day, review your assignments, or catch up on the news.
- *Schedule a realistic day.* Avoid planning for every minute. Leave extra time in your day for getting to appointments and studying.
- *Leave room in your day for the unexpected.* This will allow you to do what you need to do, regardless of what happens. If the unexpected never happens, you will have more time for yourself.
- *Do one thing at a time.* If you try to do two things at once, you become inefficient. Concentrate on the here and now.
- *Learn to say "No."* Say no to social activities or invitations when you don't have the time or energy.

Rate your level of agreement with the following statements using the scale below:

Strongly Agree	Agree	Neither Agree nor Disagree	Disagree	Strongly Disagree

1. I rarely feel driven by the urgencies that come my way.
2. I keep a log of each activity to be performed in a day. I prioritize them accordingly.
3. I prioritize not by the importance of the work but by its nature.
4. I can manage my schedule without preparing a weekly plan that includes specific activities.
5. I always want to do all the work myself, thinking I can do it better than anyone else.
6. I plan my weekends with my family and friends.
7. I can delegate work to people so that the work gets done on time and the people feel they are a part of the team.
8. I allow time for the unexpected things I cannot control.
9. If something doesn't happen as per my schedule, it doesn't get done.
10. To accomplish a set of objectives doesn't mean to avoid other unexpected problems.
11. I seldom work after office hours.
12. I would never work by hand if a machine could do it faster.
13. I feel it is easier and time-saving to try new ways of doing things.
14. I always find time to do what I want to do and what I should do.[6]

See the scoring guidelines at the end of the prologue to obtain your score.

Use Your Money Wisely

You can get postsecondary money from three different sources.

- *Grants and scholarships.* This refers to aid you do not have to repay. Grants are usually based on need, whereas scholarships are frequently based on academic merit and other qualifying factors.
- *Student loans.* The mission of the Canada Student Loans Program (CSLP) is to promote accessibility to postsecondary education for students with a demonstrated financial need by lowering financial barriers through the provision of loans and grants, and to ensure that Canadians have an opportunity to develop the knowledge and skills to participate in the economy and society.
- *Work aid.* This is financial aid you have to work for, frequently 10 or 15 hours a week on campus.

There are many ways to cut the cost of going to a postsecondary institution. Consider:

- going to a community college for the first two years and then transferring to a four-year institution,
- attending a nearby postsecondary institution and living at home,
- enrolling in one of the postsecondary institutions that offer cooperative educational programs that alternate between full-time studies and full-time employment, or
- taking a full-time job at a company that offers free educational opportunities as a fringe benefit.

Check with your postsecondary institution for the various sources of financial aid that are available to you.

Gain some insight into your money management skills by taking the quiz in Exhibit P.5.

Study Smart

The first key to doing well in a subject is completing your assignments on time. Most instructors base their assignments on what they will be discussing in class on a given

Rate your level of agreement with the following statements, using the scale below:

Strongly Agree	Agree	Neither Agree nor Disagree	Disagree	Strongly Disagree

1. I eagerly wait for the day I get my paycheque, because my bank balance is generally below the minimum.
2. I have set my savings and spending priorities and have a budget.
3. When I go shopping, I don't buy anything unless it is on sale or is required.
4. I can easily spend money when I am in school.
5. I can differentiate between what I want and what I truly need.
6. I always max out my credit cards.
7. I don't need to plan for my child's education because there will be plenty of government programs.
8. I don't plan to open or have a savings account.
9. I was raised in a family where I always felt that money was quite tight.
10. Credit cards have been useful to me during times of emergency.
11. It is easy for me to resist buying on credit.[7]

See the scoring guidelines at the end of the prologue to obtain your score.

day. Therefore, if you read the pages you are assigned for the day they are due, you will understand the day's lecture better. If you don't complete an assignment when it is due, not only will you be at a disadvantage in the class, you will also have twice as much work to do for the following class.

Second, know what material to study. This might sound simple, but all too often, students don't ask what material they should study and find out too late that they studied the wrong information. The easiest and most accurate way to learn what will be covered on a test is to ask your instructor or read the syllabus.

Tests measure your working memory and knowledge base. To help yourself remember, you can use several **memory devices** to recall the information you need to study. Here are a few that have been proven to work:

- *Recite information using your own words.* You will learn more when you reinforce your learning in as many ways as possible. You can reinforce your learning through hearing, writing, reading, reviewing, and reciting.
- *Develop acronyms.* **Acronyms** are words or names formed from the first letters or groups of letters in a phrase. Acronyms help you remember, because they organize information according to the way you need or want to learn it. When you study for a test, be creative and make up your own acronyms. For example, COD means "cash on delivery," and GDP refers to "gross domestic product."
- *Try mnemonic sentences, rhymes, or jingles.* **Mnemonic sentences** are similar to acronyms; they help you organize your ideas, but instead of creating a word, you make up a sentence. Creating a rhyme, song, or jingle can make the information even easier to remember. The more creative and silly the sentence, the easier it is to remember. For example, if you are learning to read sheet music, the notes on the lines of the treble clef are EGBDF—you could remember this as Every Good Boy Deserves Fudge.
- *Visualize.* Visualization refers to creating or recalling mental pictures related to what you are learning. Have you ever tried to remember something while taking a test and visualized the page the information was on? This is your visual memory at work. Approximately 90 percent of your memory is stored visually in pictures, so visualizing what you want to remember is a powerful study tool.

Exhibit P.6 helps you evaluate your study skills.

Answer "yes" or "no" to the following questions:

1. Do you usually spend too much time studying for the amount that you are learning?
2. Do you spend hours cramming the night before an exam?
3. Do you find it easy to balance your social life with your study schedule?
4. Do you prefer to study with sound (TV or radio) around you?
5. Can you sit for long periods and study for several hours without getting distracted?
6. Do you always borrow notes/materials from your friends before the exam?
7. Do you review your class notes periodically throughout the semester while preparing for the tests?
8. Is it easy for you to recall what you studied at the beginning of the semester?
9. Do you need to change your reading/learning style in response to the difficulty level of the course?
10. Do you normally write your papers or prepare for your presentations the night before they are due?
11. Do you feel comfortable contacting the instructor and asking questions or for help whenever you need it?
12. Do you prefer to study lying on a bed or couch rather than at a desk or table?[8]

See the scoring guidelines at the end of the prologue to obtain your score.

Become a Master at Taking Tests

Taking a formal test is like playing a game. The object is to get as many points as possible in the time that you are allowed. Tests are evaluations of what you know and what you can do with what you know. Here are the rules of the test-taking game:

Rule 1: Act as if you will succeed. Thought is powerful. When you think negative thoughts, your stress level rises. Your confidence level might drop, which often leads to feelings of failure. When this happens, think about success. Smile and take deep, slow breaths. Close your eyes, and imagine getting the test back with a good grade written at the top.

Rule 2: Arrive ahead of time. Being on time or early for a test sets your mind at ease. You will have a better chance of getting your favourite seat, relaxing, and preparing yourself mentally for the game ahead.

Rule 3: Bring the essential testing tools. Don't forget to bring the necessary testing tools along with you, including extra pens, sharpened pencils, erasers, a calculator, a dictionary, and other items you might need.

Rule 4: Ignore panic pushers. Some people become nervous before a test and hit the panic button, afraid they don't know the material. **Panic pushers** are people who ask you questions about the material they are about to be tested on. If you know the answers, you will feel confident; however, if you don't, you might panic and lose your confidence. Instead of talking with a panic pusher before a test, spend your time concentrating on what you know, not on what you don't know.

Rule 5: Preview the playing field. Here's how to do a preview.

- Listen to instructions, **and** read directions carefully.
- Determine the point spread. Look at the total number of questions and the point value of each. Decide how much time you can spend on each question and still finish the test on time.
- Budget your time. If you budget your time and stick to your time limits, you will always complete the test in the amount of time given.
- Use the test as an information tool. Be on the lookout for clues that answer other questions. Frequently, instructors will test you on a single topic in more than one way.

Rule 6: Write in the margin. Before you begin the test, write key terms, formulas, names, dates, and other information in the margin, so you don't forget them.

Rule 7: Complete the easy questions first. Answering easy questions first helps build your confidence. If you come across a tough question, mark it so you can come back to it later. Avoid spending so much time on a challenging question that you run out of time to answer the questions you do know.

Rule 8: Know if there is a guessing penalty. Chances are your tests will carry no penalty for guessing. If your time is about to run out and there is no penalty, take a wild guess. On the other hand, if your test carries a penalty for guessing, choose your answers wisely, and leave blank the answers you do not know.

Rule 9: Avoid changing your answers. Have you ever chosen an answer, changed it, and learned later that your first choice was correct? Research indicates that three out of four times, your first answer will be correct; therefore, you should avoid changing an answer unless you are absolutely sure the answer is wrong.

Rule 10: Write clearly and neatly. If you are handwriting your test (versus using a computer), imagine your instructor reading your writing. Is it easy to read or difficult? The easier your test is for the instructor to read, the better your chances of getting a higher grade.

Getting Your Career Off on the Right Track

Mark this section of the text with a permanent bookmark, because you are going to want to refer back to it many times during the remainder of your postsecondary institution career. Yes, we are going to give you a roadmap to find, keep, and advance in that job that is perfect for you.

Think Positively

To be successful in life and in a career, you need to be positive. Positive thinking is making a conscious effort to think with an optimistic attitude and to anticipate positive outcomes. *Positive behaviour* means purposely acting with energy and enthusiasm. When you think and behave positively, you guide your mind toward your goals and generate matching mental and physical energy.

Positive thinking and behaviour are often deciding factors in landing top jobs: your first job, a promotion, a change of jobs—whatever career step you are targeting. That's because the subconscious is literal; it accepts what you regard as fact.

Follow these steps to form the habit of positive thinking and to boost your success.

1. *Deliberately motivate yourself every day.* Think of yourself as successful, and expect positive outcomes for everything you attempt.
2. *Project energy and enthusiasm.* Employers hire people who project positive energy and enthusiasm. Develop the habit of speaking, moving, and acting with these qualities.
3. *Practice this positive expectation mind-set until it becomes a habit.* Applicants who project enthusiasm and positive behaviour generate a positive chemistry that rubs off. Hiring decisions are influenced largely by this positive energy. The habit will help you reach your peak potential.
4. *Dwell on past successes.* Focusing on past successes to remind yourself of your abilities helps in attaining goals. For example, no one is born knowing how to ride a bicycle or how to use a computer software program. Through training, practice, and trial and error, you master new abilities. During the trial-and-error phases of development, remind yourself of past successes; look at mistakes as part of the natural learning curve. Continue until you achieve the result you want, and remind yourself that you have succeeded in the past and can do so again. You fail only when you quit trying![9]

Take a Good Look at Yourself

Once you've developed a positive, "can do" attitude, the next step is to understand yourself better. Ask yourself two basic questions: "Who am I?" and "What can I do?"

Who Am I? The first step is to ask "Who am I?" This question is the start of *self-assessment*, examining your likes and dislikes and basic values. You might want to ask yourself the following questions:

- Do I want to help society?
- Do I want to help make the world a better place?
- Do I want to help other people directly?
- Is it important for me to be seen as part of a big corporation?
- Do I prefer working indoors or outdoors?
- Do I like to meet new people, or do I want to work alone?

Are you assertive? Assess your assertiveness by taking the quiz in Exhibit P.7.

What Can I Do? After determining what your values are, take the second step in career planning by asking, "What can I do?" This question is the start of *skill assessment*, evaluating your key abilities and characteristics for dealing successfully with problems, tasks, and interactions with other people. Many skills—for instance, the ability to speak clearly and strongly—are valuable in many occupations.

Be sure to consider the work experience you already have, including part-time jobs while going to school, summer jobs, volunteer jobs, and internships (short-term jobs for students, related to their major field of study). These jobs teach you skills and make you more attractive to potential employers. It's never too early or too late to take a part-time job in your chosen field. For instance, someone with an interest in accounting would do well to try a part-time job with an accounting firm.

In addition to examining your job-related skills, you should also look at your leisure activities. Some possible questions: Am I good at golf? Do I enjoy sailing? Tennis? Racquetball? In some businesses, transactions are made during leisure hours. In that case, being able to play a skillful, or at least adequate, game of golf or tennis might be an asset.

ACESTOCK/GETSTOCK

CONCEPT *in Action* >>>

Part-time jobs can teach you valuable business skills that will make you more attractive to employers. Choose a job, if possible, that gives you experience related to your chosen field. What advantages do you think those with work experience have over those who have no work experience?

EXHIBIT P.7 > Fun Self-Test—How Assertive Are You?

Rate your level of agreement with the following statements using the scale below:

Strongly Agree	Agree	Neither Agree nor Disagree	Disagree	Strongly Disagree

1. I don't easily agree to work for others.
2. There are some people who make jokes about the way I communicate and put me down repeatedly.
3. I speak up without fear of what others will think of me.
4. I rarely have to repeat my thoughts to make people understand.
5. I sound like I am asking a question, when I am making a statement.
6. I'm more reluctant to speak up on the job than in other situations.
7. I can always think of something to say when faced with rude remarks.
8. I tend to suffer in silence when unfairly criticized or insulted.
9. I tend to respond aggressively when criticized unfairly.
10. People don't listen when I am speaking.
11. If I say "no," I feel guilty.
12. When I have a conflict with someone, the results seem to always go their way.
13. When I speak, people listen.[10]

See the scoring guidelines at the end of the prologue to obtain your score.

It's hard to like your job if you don't like the field that you're in. Most career counsellors agree that finding work you're passionate about is one of the critical factors behind career success. That's why so many career counsellors love all those diagnostic tools that measure your personality traits, skill levels, professional interests, and job potential.

Understand What Employers Want[11]

Employers want to hire people who will make their businesses more successful. The most desirable employees have the specific skills, transferable career competencies, work values, and personal qualities necessary to be successful in the employers' organizations. The more clearly you convey your skills as they relate to your job target, the greater your chance of landing your ideal job.

Job-specific skills. Employers seek job-specific skills (skills and technical abilities that relate specifically to a particular job). Two examples of job-specific skills are using specialized tools and equipment and using a custom-designed software program.

Transferable skills and attitudes. Change is a constant in today's business world. Strong transferable career skills are the keys to success in managing your career through change. The most influential skills and attitudes are the abilities to

- work well with people,
- plan and manage multiple tasks,
- maintain a positive attitude, and
- show enthusiasm.

Employers need workers who have transferable career competencies—basic skills and attitudes that are important for all types of work. These skills make you highly marketable, because they're needed for a wide variety of jobs and can be transferred from one task, job, or workplace to another. Examples include

- planning skills,
- research skills,
- communication skills,
- human relations and interpersonal skills,
- critical thinking skills, and
- management skills.

Take, for example, a construction supervisor and an accountant. Both must work well with others, manage time, solve problems, read, and communicate effectively—all transferable competencies. They both must be competent in these areas, even though framing a house and balancing a set of books (the job-specific skill for each field, respectively) are not related. In every occupation, transferable competencies are as important as technical expertise and job-specific skills.

Finding My First Professional Job

The next step is landing the job that fits your skills and desires. You need to consider not only a general type of work but also your lifestyle and leisure goals. If you like to be outdoors most of the time, you might be very unhappy spending eight hours a day in an office. Someone who likes living in small towns might dislike working at the headquarters of a big corporation in Toronto, Calgary, or Vancouver. But make sure that your geographic preferences are realistic. Some parts of the country will experience much greater growth in jobs than others.

You might start answering the question "What will I do" by searching various Internet sites that offer job counselling or job offers.

Using the Internet to Jump-Start Your Job Search

You must start with a great résumé—a written description of your education, work experience, personal data, and interests. Professional Web résumé software (available through <www.webresume.com>) can make the task a lot easier. WebResume software not only helps you format your résumé but also lets you control who sees it. A "confidential" option enables you to create a two-tiered résumé. The first tier offers professional information but doesn't include your name or address. The second contains contact information but is password protected—and you decide who gets the password. WebResume understands what's different about looking for a job online. Its "Search Engine Keywords" function inserts the "tags" that major search engines use to index résumés.

Once you have created a great résumé, the next step is to get it noticed. Here are seven tips for building résumé traffic.

- Post a digital version of your résumé with examples of past work experience on your own home page. Many postsecondary institutions and professional associations offer free or low-cost Web space and resources for posting résumés.
- Place the word *résumé* in the website address to increase your chances of being caught by Internet recruiters.
- Place plenty of links to websites of present and former employers, postsecondary institutions, professional associations, and publications on your digital résumé.
- Create a simpler version of your résumé to send to a recruiter or potential employer, and let them know a longer version is available.
- Read the privacy policies of online job boards to prevent unwanted eyes from viewing your résumé. Some companies have "Web scavengers" who check for their own employees' résumés online. In turn, some job boards let users "block" certain companies from seeing their postings.
- Use niche job boards in your field. Smaller, targeted boards can sometimes be more effective than the big brand-name sites.[12]

There are thousands of places to send your résumé. Don't neglect using the Internet; 83 percent of corporate recruiters use the Internet to advertise their jobs.[13]

Oh My Gosh—I've Got a Job Interview

If some of the companies you contacted want to speak with you, your résumé achieved its goal of getting you a job interview. Look at the interview as a chance to describe your knowledge and skills and interpret them in terms of the employer's specific needs. To make this kind of presentation, you need to do some research on the company. There are many electronic databases and sources that provide company information. Ask your librarians for assistance to access company profiles and information.

EXHIBIT P.8 > Tips for Preparing Your Cyber Résumé

- Use key words to define your skills, experience, education, professional affiliations, and so on.
- Use concrete words rather than vague descriptions to describe your experience. For example, use "managed a team of software engineers" rather than "responsible for managing and training."
- Be concise and truthful.
- Use jargon and acronyms specific to your industry (spell out the acronyms for a human reader).
- Increase your list of key words by including specifics. For example, list the names of software that you use, such as Microsoft Word.
- Use common headings, such as Objective, Experience, Work History, Skills, Education, Professional Affiliations, Licenses, and References.
- Describe your interpersonal traits and attitude. Key words can include *dependable, high energy, leadership, sense of responsibility,* and *good memory.*

SOURCE: "Resume Tool Kit," <www.thespectrum.com> (accessed January 2003).

BARRY ROSENTHAL/THE IMAGE BANK/GETTY IMAGES

CONCEPT *in Action* >>>

For today's wired college grads, preparation for a job interview should include taking time out to Google oneself. The Internet is an easy way for recruiters to learn about prospective employees, and what job candidates post on blogs or on social networking sites could convey an undesirable impression. Do a thorough search on popular search engines to make sure the Web is free of unflattering self-revelations. What can employers learn about you online?

As you do your information search, you should build your knowledge in these three areas.

1. *General information about the industry.* Learn about the current and predicted industry trends, general educational requirements, job descriptions, growth outlook, and salary ranges in the industry.

2. *Information about prospective employers.* Learn whether the organization is publicly or privately owned. Verify company names, addresses, products or services (current and predicted, as well as trends); history; culture; reputation; performance; divisions and subsidiaries; locations (Canada and global); predicted growth indicators; number of employees; company philosophies and procedures; predicted job openings; salary ranges; and listings of managers of your targeted department within the organization. Also learn about competitors and customers.

3. *Information about specific jobs.* Obtain job descriptions; identify the required education and experience; and determine prevalent working conditions, salary, and fringe benefits.[14]

Interview Like a Pro

An interview tends to have three parts: icebreaking (about five minutes), in which the interviewer tries to put the applicant at ease; questioning (directly or indirectly) by the interviewer; and questioning by the applicant. Almost every recruiter you meet will be trying to rate you in 5 to 10 areas. The questions will be designed to assess your skills and personality.

Many firms start with a *screening interview,* a rather short interview (about 30 minutes) to decide whether to invite you back for a second interview. Only about 20 percent of job applicants are invited back. The second interview is a half day or a day of meetings set up by the human resource department with managers in different departments. After the meetings, someone from the human resource department will discuss other application materials with you and tell you when a letter of acceptance or rejection is likely to be sent. (The wait might be weeks or even months.) Many applicants send follow-up letters in the meantime to show they are still interested in the firm.

For the interview you should dress conservatively. Plan to arrive about 10 to 15 minutes ahead of time. Try to relax. Smile and make eye contact with (but do not stare at) the interviewer. Body language is an important communicator. The placement of your hands and feet and your overall posture say a good deal about you. Here are some other tips for interviewing like a pro.

1. *Concentrate on being likable.* As simplistic as it seems, research proves that one of the most essential goals in successful interviewing is to be liked by the interviewer. Interviewers want to hire pleasant people that others will like working with on a daily basis. Pay attention to the following areas to project that you are highly likable.

   - Be friendly, courteous, and enthusiastic.
   - Speak positively.
   - Smile.
   - Use positive body language.
   - Make certain your appearance is appropriate.

2. *Project an air of confidence and pride.* Act as though you want and deserve the job, not as though you are desperate.

3. *Demonstrate enthusiasm.* The applicant's level of enthusiasm often influences employers as much as any other interviewing factor. The applicant who demonstrates little enthusiasm for a job will never be selected for the position.
4. *Demonstrate knowledge of and interest in the employer.* "I really want this job" is not convincing enough. Explain why you want the position and how the position fits your career plans. You can cite opportunities that might be unique to a firm or emphasize your skills and education that are highly relevant to the position.
5. *State your name and the position you're seeking.* When you enter the interviewer's office, begin with a friendly greeting, and state the position you're interviewing for: "Hello, Ms. Levine, I'm Bella Reyna. I'm here to interview for the accounting position." If someone has already introduced you to the interviewer, simply say, "Good morning, Ms. Levine." Identifying the position is important, because interviewers often interview for many different positions.
6. *Focus on how you fit the job.* Near the beginning of your interview, as soon as it seems appropriate, ask a question similar to this: "Could you describe the scope of the job and tell me what capabilities are most important in filling the position?" The interviewer's response will help you focus on emphasizing your qualifications that best match the needs of the employer.
7. *Speak correctly.* Grammatical errors can cost applicants the job. Use correct grammar, word choice, and a businesslike vocabulary, not an informal, chatty one. Avoid slang. When under stress, people often use pet phrases (such as *you know*) too often. This is highly annoying and projects immaturity and insecurity. Don't use *just* or *only*. "I just worked as a waiter." Don't say "I guess." Avoid the word *probably,* because it suggests unnecessary doubt. Ask a friend or family member to help you identify any speech weaknesses you have. Begin eliminating these speech habits now.[15]

In addition, you should avoid these "disqualifiers" at all costs. Any one of these blunders could cost you your dream job:

1. Don't sit down until the interviewer invites you to; waiting is courteous.
2. Don't bring anyone else to the interview; it makes you look immature and insecure.
3. Don't smoke.
4. Don't put anything on or read anything on the interviewer's desk; it's considered an invasion of personal space.
5. Don't chew gum or have anything else in your mouth; this projects immaturity.
6. If you are invited to a business meal, don't order alcohol. When ordering, choose food that's easy to eat while carrying on a conversation.
7. Don't offer a limp handshake; it projects weakness. Use a firm handshake.[16]

Selecting the Right Job for You

Hard work and a little luck can pay off with multiple job offers. Your happy dilemma is deciding which one is best for you. Start by considering the FACTS:

- *Fit.* Does the job and the employer fit your skills, interests, and lifestyle?
- *Advancement and growth.* Will you have the chance to develop your talents and move up within the organization?
- *Compensation.* Is the employer offering a competitive salary and benefits package?
- *Training.* Will the employer provide you with the tools needed to be successful on the job?
- *Site.* Is the job location a good match for your lifestyle and your pocketbook?

A great way to evaluate a new location is through HOMEFAIR <**www.homefair .com**>. This site offers tools to help you calculate the cost of moving, the cost of living, and the quality of life in various places in Canada and the United States. The

Moving Calculator helps you figure out how much it will cost to ship your worldly possessions to a particular city. The **Relocation Crime Lab** compares crime rates in various locations. The **City Snapshots** feature compares demographic, economic, and climate information for two cities of your choosing. The **Salary Calculator** computes cost-of-living differences between hundreds of Canadian and international cities and tells you how much you'd need to make in your new city to maintain your current standard of living.

Starting Your New Job

No time is more crucial, and possibly nerve-racking, than the first few months at a new job. During this breaking-in period, the employer decides whether a new employee is valuable enough to keep and, if so, in what capacity. Sometimes the employee's whole future with the company rides on the efforts of the first few weeks or months.

Most firms offer some sort of formal orientation, but generally speaking, they expect employees to learn quickly—and often on their own. You will be expected to become familiar with the firm's goals; its organization, including your place in the company; and basic personnel policies, such as coffee breaks, overtime, and parking.

Here are a few tips on making your first job rewarding and productive.

Listen and Learn

When you first walk into your new job, let your eyes and ears take everything in. Do people refer to one another by first names, or is the company more formal? How do people dress? Do the people you work with drop into one another's open offices for informal chats about business matters? Or have you entered a "memo mill," where anything of substance is put on e-mail and talks with other employees are scheduled through secretaries? Size up where the power lies. Who seems to assume a leadership role most often? Who is the person others turn to for advice? Why has that person achieved that position? What traits have made this person a "political leader"? Don't be misled by what others say, but also don't dismiss their evaluations. Make your own judgments based on what you see and hear.

Take the quiz in Exhibit P.9 to see if you are a good listener.

EXHIBIT P.9 > Fun Self-Test—Are You a Good Listener?

Rate your level of agreement with the statements below using the following scale:

Strongly Agree	Agree	Neither Agree nor Disagree	Disagree	Strongly Disagree

1. A person who takes time to ask for clarification about something that might be unclear is not a good listener.
2. While listening I am distracted by the sounds around me.
3. I try to understand not only what is being said but also analyze the strength of any ideas that are being presented.
4. I ask questions, make observations, or give opinion when necessary for clarifications.
5. While I am listening, I avoid eye contact but am polite.
6. I am tempted to judge a person whether or not he or she is a good speaker.
7. I feel more comfortable when someone talks to me about a topic that I find interesting.
8. I always jot down key phrases/points that strike me as important points of concern that require a response.
9. My listening style varies from the speaker's style of communication.
10. A good listener requires a good speaker.

See the scoring guidelines at the end of the prologue to obtain your score.

IMAGE SOURCE/GETTY IMAGES

CONCEPT *in Action* >>>

Finding a mentor can be especially helpful when starting a new career. Whether assigned through a corporate mentorship program or sought out on one's own, mentors have inside access to the company and can help protégés learn the ropes. A good mentor is a seasoned veteran who offers insight and advice, boosts morale, and makes networking contacts—while steering mentees away from pitfalls. What lessons can a mentor pass on that aren't necessarily taught in school but are essential to career success?

Do Unto Others

Be nice. Nice people are usually the last to be fired and among the first to be promoted. Don't be pleasant only with those who can help you in the company. Be nice to everyone. You never know who can help you or give you information that will turn out to be useful. Genuinely nice people make routine job assignments, and especially pressure-filled ones, more pleasant. And people who are dealt with pleasantly usually respond in kind.

Don't Start Out as a Maverick

If every new employee tried to change tried-and-true methods to suit his or her whims, the firm would quickly be in chaos. Individual needs must take a back seat to established procedures. Devote yourself to getting things done within the system. Every manager realizes that it takes time for a new person to adjust. But the faster you start accomplishing things, the faster the boss will decide that you were the right person to hire.

Find a Great Mentor

The leading cause of career unhappiness is working for a bad boss. Good jobs can easily be ruined by supervisors who hold you back. In contrast, your career will soar (and you will smile every day) when you have a great mentor helping you along the way. If you find a job with a super mentor, jump at the chance to take it.

Movin' On Up

Once you have been on the job for a while, you will want to get ahead and be promoted. We offer several suggestions for improving your chances of promotion. The first item might seem a bit strange, yet it's there for a practical reason. If you don't really like what you do, you won't be committed enough to compete with those who do. The passionate people are the ones who go the extra mile, do the extra work, and come up with fresh outside-the-box ideas.

So there you have it! In the next chapter we will begin our journey through the world of business, so that you can determine what areas are most interesting to you. Remember, it's never too early to begin planning your career—the future is now.

EXHIBIT P.10 > How to Move Up

- Love what you do, which entails first figuring out who you are.
- Never stop learning about new technologies and new management skills.
- Try to get international experience, even if it is only a short stint overseas.
- Create new business opportunities—they could lead to a promotion.
- Be really outstandingly terrific at what you're doing now, this week, this month.

SCORING GUIDELINES

After you answer the questions in each of the fun self-tests that appear in the "Prologue: A Guide to Your Future Success," determine your score and evaluate your skills using the following scoring guidelines.

Exhibit P.1 Fun Self-Test: Can You Persuade Others?

For questions 1, 2, 4, 8, 10 and 11, use the following to calculate your score:

Strongly Agree	Agree	Neither Agree nor Disagree	Disagree	Strongly Disagree
2 points	1 point	0 points	0 points	0 points

For questions 3, 5, 6, 7, and 9 use the following to calculate your score:

Strongly Agree	Agree	Neither Agree nor Disagree	Disagree	Strongly Disagree
0 points	0 points	0 points	4 points	5 points

If your score is between 40–55 you have an excellent ability to persuade others. A score between 30–39 means you have reasonably good persuasion skills. However, you may need to improve your listening and communicating skills. A score below 30 means that you should consider reading a book or taking a short course on "how to persuade others."

Exhibit P.2 Fun Self-Test: Can You Play the Political Game?

For questions 1, 3, 4, 7, 8, 10, 12 and 13, give yourself 1 point if you said "true." For questions 2, 5, 6, 9 and 11, give yourself 1 point if you said "false." If your score is 9 or below, you may be good at managing your work, but you need to improve your political skills. Being political means getting along with others in order to move them toward accomplishing a specific goal. If your score is low, consider reviewing the tips offered in the Prologue on how to be an effective political player.

Exhibit P.4 Fun Self-Test: How Well Do You Manage Your Time?

For questions 2, 6, 8, 9, 11, 13, 14 and 15, use the following to calculate your score:

Strongly Disagree	Disagree	Neither Agree nor Disagree	Agree	Strongly Agree
0 points	0 points	0 points	4 points	5 points

For questions 1, 3, 4, 5, 7, 10 and 12, use the following to calculate your score:

Strongly Disagree	Disagree	Neither Agree nor Disagree	Agree	Strongly Agree
5 points	4 points	0 points	0 points	0 points

If your score is 60 or above, you have excellent time management skills. Congratulations—you use your time well! If your score is below 60, consider reading a book on time management, taking a course on time management, or investing in time management tools such as a weekly project planner. The Prologue has additional tips that may be useful in improving your time management skills.

Exhibit P.5 Fun Self-Test: Are You Good at Managing Money?

For questions 2, 3, 5, 6, 10 and 11, use the following to calculate your score:

Strongly Disagree	Disagree	Neither Agree nor Disagree	Agree	Strongly Agree
0 points	0 points	0 points	4 points	5 points

For questions 1, 4, 7, 8 and 9, use the following to calculate your score:

Strongly Disagree	Disagree	Neither Agree nor Disagree	Agree	Strongly Agree
5 points	4 points	0 points	0 points	0 points

If your score is 44 or higher, you are able to manage money while balancing your expenses and income. You will be ready to handle financial emergencies without turning to friends or relatives. If your score is 36–43, your savings habits may be inconsistent. To achieve better savings, control your expenses and avoid unnecessary purchases. If your score is 35 or below, you spend too much! Remember it's a lot more painful to earn money than to spend it. You need to gain control of your finances by limiting your spending, paying off credit cards, or investing in a good personal finance book or course. You may also need to meet with a financial advisor to seek direction on your spending and saving habits.

Exhibit P.6 Fun Self-Test: Do You Have Good Study Habits?

If you answered "yes" to questions 3, 5, 7, 8 and 11, give yourself 1 point for each correct answer.

If you answered "no" to questions 1, 2, 4, 6, 9, 10 and 12, give yourself 1 point for each correct answer.

If your score is 10 or above, congratulations! You have good study habits. If your score is below 10, read the tips offered in the Prologue on improving your study skills. You may also meet with someone at your school to help maximize your study time.

Exhibit P.7 Fun Self-Test: How Assertive Are You?

For questions 1, 3, 4, 7, 9 and 13, use the following to calculate your score:

Strongly Agree	Agree	Neither Agree nor Disagree	Disagree	Strongly Disagree
5 points	4 points	0 points	0 points	0 points

For questions 2, 5, 6, 8, 10, 11 and 12, use the following to calculate your score:

Strongly Agree	Agree	Neither Agree nor Disagree	Disagree	Strongly Disagree
0 points	0 points	0 points	4 points	5 points

If your score is 44 or higher, you stand up for your rights while showing respect for others. You quickly respond to unfair criticism. You should be able to fare well in office politics. If your score is 43 or lower, you may want to consider ways to become more comfortable communicating your ideas and opinions and managing your relationships with others.

Exhibit P.9 Fun Self-Test: Are You a Good Listener?

For questions 3, 4, 8 and 9, use the following to calculate your score:

Strongly Agree	Agree	Neither Agree nor Disagree	Disagree	Strongly Disagree
5 points	4 points	0 points	0 points	0 points

For questions 1, 2, 5, 6, 7 and 10, use the following to calculate your score:

Strongly Agree	Agree	Neither Agree nor Disagree	Disagree	Strongly Disagree
0 points	0 points	0 points	4 points	5 points

Listening is an important communication skill that will help you succeed in your career. By becoming an effective listener, you gain respect from your colleagues, pick up insights and ideas on improving your job performance, and develop a skill that is important in managing others. If you have a score of 32 or above, then you are a good listener. If your score falls below 32, you need to improve your listening skills. Search the Web for articles and ideas on becoming a better listener and begin practicing your new skills with your friends and coworkers.

PART 1

TRENDS AND THE BUSINESS ENVIRONMENT

INTRODUCTION

This text on business is important whether you are working in a business today or hope to work in one in the future. Even if your major is in the arts or sciences, you will likely work in an organization that is considered to be a business. Profit or non-profit, the same principles apply.

First let's look at the nature of business.

business
An organization that strives for a profit by providing goods and services desired by its customers.

A **business** is an organization that strives for a profit by providing goods and services desired by its customers. Businesses meet the needs of consumers by providing movies, medical care, autos, and countless other goods and services. **Goods** are tangible items manufactured by businesses, such as laptop computers and BlackBerries. **Services** are intangible offerings of businesses that can't be touched or stored. Accountants, lawyers, restaurants, car washes, and airlines all provide services. Businesses also serve other organizations, such as hospitals, retailers, and governments, by providing machinery, goods for resale, computers, and thousands of other items.

goods
Tangible items manufactured by businesses.

services
Intangible offerings of businesses that can't be touched or stored.

Thus, businesses create the goods and services that are the basis of our standard of living. The **standard of living** of any country is measured by the output of goods and services people can buy with the money they have. This includes not o nly privately purchased goods and services but also collectively consumed goods and services, such as those provided by public utilities and governments.

standard of living
A country's output of goods and services that people can buy with the money they have.

Businesses play a key role in determining our quality of life by providing jobs and goods and services to society. **Quality of life** refers to the general level of human happiness based on such things as life expectancy, educational standards, health, sanitation, and leisure time. Zurich, Switzerland, is ranked as having the world's highest quality of life, followed by Vienna, Austria, and Vancouver, Canada.[1] Building a high quality of life is a combined effort of businesses, government, and not-for-profit organizations.

quality of life
The general level of human happiness based on such things as life expectancy, educational standards, health, sanitation, and leisure time..

risk
The potential for losing time and money or otherwise not being able to accomplish an organization's goals.

Creating a high quality of life is not without risks, however. **Risk** is the potential for losing time and money or otherwise not being able to accomplish an organization's goals. Without enough blood donors, for example, Canadian Blood Services faces the risk of not meeting the demand for blood by victims of disaster. Businesses like Bell Canada Enterprises face the risk of falling short of their revenue goals. **Revenue** is the money a company earns from providing services or selling goods to customers.

revenue
The money a company earns from providing services or selling goods to customers.

costs
Expenses incurred in creating and selling goods and services.

profit
The money left over after all expenses are paid.

not-for-profit organization
An organization that exists to achieve some goal other than the usual business goal of profit.

Costs are expenses for rent, salaries, supplies, transportation, and many other items that a company incurs from creating and selling goods and services. Some of the costs incurred by Research in Motion (featured in our opening) include expenses for research and development, building rental or purchase, advertising, and transportation. **Profit** is the money left over after all expenses are paid.

When a company like Research in Motion uses its resources intelligently, it can often increase sales, hold costs down, and earn a profit. Not all companies earn a profit, but that is the risk of being in business. In Canadian business today, there is generally a direct relationship between risks and profit: the greater the risks, the greater the potential profit (or loss).

Not all organizations strive to make a profit. A **not-for-profit organization** is an organization that exists to achieve some goal other than the usual business goal of profit. The United Way, the Canadian Cancer Society, and Greenpeace are all not-for-profit organizations.

Successful not-for-profit organizations follow sound business principles. These groups have goals they hope to accomplish, but the goals are not focused on profits. For example, a not-for-profit organization's goal might be feeding the poor, stopping destruction of the environment, increasing attendance at the ballet, or preventing drunk driving. Reaching such goals takes good planning, management, and control. Not-for-profit organizations do not compete directly with each other as, for example, Ford and Honda do, but they do compete for people's scarce volunteer time and donations.

If you want to be as successful as you can be, and make your business as successful as it can be, then it is critical that you understand how a successful business works. Most introductory textbooks and courses do a good job of introducing you to the different elements of a business, but often fail to show you how these elements fit together. This objective is achieved mostly in senior business courses. The problem is that by that point, you are so used to studying each piece separately that it's very difficult to see them working together to create the business entity as a whole. And what's important to see is that *"the whole" really is greater than the sum of its parts*. To truly understand what makes a business successful, you must accept it as a fully integrated entity and, as you study each of its parts, study them with the whole in mind.

To this end, we have used an integrative model (shown on page 5) of a successful business as the framework, or basis, of this book. Each chapter will focus on a specific part of this model, and you will be reminded of where and how each piece fits with the other aspects of the model at the beginning of each chapter.

Before we get into the model in detail, take a look at the title—*The Integrative Model of a Successful Business*. Why is this important? What does it tell you?

It Is Integrative.

All the elements of the model work together to create a unified whole. Each piece depends on the others, and they all affect one another. One of the most important lessons to learn about business is that you can't make a decision in one area of a business without considering the impact that it will have on other areas of the business.

For example, according to *Report on Business* magazine's 2008 Top 1000, EnCana Corporation, the largest natural gas producer in North America, was the number one-ranked publicly listed company in Canada on the basis of revenue. Despite the fallout from the global credit crisis and ensuing global recession when Canada's 1,000 largest publicly listed companys' earnings dropped 30% from the year before, EnCana enjoyed a 50% increase. This company has clearly shown that it knows what it takes to be successful in today's environment. Of course given the external environmental context, the top ranks of the Top 1000 were crowded by financial and resource firms, EnCana is not only successful in terms of achieving financial performance, but was also ranked #31 on Corporate Knights "Best 50 Corporate Citizens" for 2009 (**www.corporateknights. ca**), as well as being listed as one of the "Global 100 Most Sustainable Corporations in the World" for 2009 (**www.global100.org**). EnCana certainly appreciates the need to balance all of its *stakeholders*. This is an organization that provides us with an excellent example of the need to act in an integrative fashion to achieve the critical success factors. For example, if the *operations* department of EnCana was able to find a new, less-expensive process to use in its production, could it do so without any impact on other areas of the business? If the process produced a product of lesser quality, or was perceived to be of lesser quality, this would affect the image of the product in the mind of the consumer, making it difficult for the *marketing* department to sell the product. Therefore, the marketing department would be affected in terms of the sales of the product, which, in turn, means that the *finance* department would be affected, as it would affect the expected income for the year, and this might mean that the salaries negotiated in future labour contracts by the *human resources* department might be lower, and so on. All the elements of the business or areas of its *internal environment* (shown by the green circle on the model) affect one another.

By the same token, what if new *technology* was developed that would allow EnCana to produce natural gas by way of machinery exclusively, with absolutely no human input? Then layoffs would likely result and affect the *economy* of the towns where the company was located. This, in turn, would have an impact on the *social* environment of the business with respect to the relationship it has with the residents of the community, and might lead to the government's stepping in to enact a *political* solution for the community.

All the areas of the *external environment* (shown by the pink circle on the model) have an impact on each other as well as on the business as a whole. These four areas of the external environment together can be remembered as the acronym PEST—for political, economic, social, and technological. The external environment can, indeed, be a pest to business! But it can also create enormous opportunities, as you will see.

To make our model more fully integrated, changes in this external environment set off other chain reactions inside the internal environment of the business, just as society's increasing demands for business to be more responsible in the social environment have led to strategic changes within EnCana that have made it into the sustainable business that it is today. The interactions are endless. It's not necessary that you see all these connections. What is necessary is that you understand, as we go through the material section by section, that these sections of material cannot be treated as if they are separate areas of a business that can act on their own. They all work together.

It Is a *Model*

This means several things. A model represents reality—this is how a real business works! A model simplifies reality—you are learning how a successful business works, and that's very complicated. A model summarizes the essential elements in a simple form to give you a base on which to build your knowledge. A model integrates ideas into a whole, as we discussed. And finally, a model provides a framework, so that you can see how the pieces fit together and how you can build on it in later business courses.

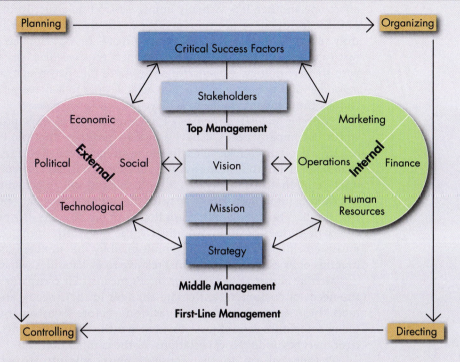

SOURCE: This material was originally published in *Business 111 Lab Manual*, 23rd ed. by Laura Allan and Jim McCutcheon, page xv. Reprinted by permission of Captus Press Inc.

It Is a Model of a *Successful* Business

We're not discussing what all businesses do. We are discussing what successful businesses do that makes them successful over time—not just one year but consistently outperforming year after year. That's how we learn about business—by studying those successful businesses that are leaders in their fields.

What does it mean to be truly successful? Is it simply making money? What does it take to make money? The *critical success factors* for any business, or the factors that indicate success, are:

- achieving financial performance
- meeting and exceeding customer needs
- providing value—quality products at a reasonable price
- encouraging creativity and innovation
- gaining employee commitment[2]

Most businesses exist to make money, but what is often left out of the discussion is how a business becomes successful in the first place. Can a business be truly successful at generating income if it ignores the other four factors? For example, can it make money by selling products that do not satisfy customers' needs, with inferior quality at an unreasonable price, using yesterday's ideas (when the competition is 10 steps ahead), while displaying a negative attitude toward the customer as demonstrated by its employees? Even one of these points would result in lower income and a less successful business. Using EnCana again as an example, according to its website (**www.encana.com**): "At the heart of EnCana's success, are the ingenuity, technical leadership and enthusiasm of (its) over 7,000 staff." Clearly EnCana appreciates the importance of the critical success factors of *gaining employee commitment* in order to *encourage* the *innovation and creativity* so important to its success.

Achieving Success

It's important to remember as well that these factors are also integrative—they all affect one another. It is virtually impossible to find a successful business in which all of these factors have not been achieved. They work together to make the company truly successful. For example, consider Toyota. To *meet customer needs,* Toyota was the first to mass-produce a hybrid vehicle, but it took *creativity and innovation* to come up with the technology, a *committed workforce* to follow through, and a commitment to *providing value through quality at a reasonable price* to achieve success. Because of these factors, the company is able to achieve *financial performance.*

Achieving financial performance is measured in three ways: profit, cash flow, and net worth. A company needs to have a healthy profit, or "bottom line," but it also needs to earn a good profit relative to the money it has invested—the equity of the owners or shareholders. But this means nothing, of course, if it can't pay its bills. It's important to understand that a company that is profitable can still go bankrupt. For instance, while it is waiting for its customers to pay for the products they have purchased, it still has to pay its bills. The timing of the cash flows can put an otherwise profitable business into a very precarious position. And finally, the net worth of the company is important, measured either by its stock price multiplied by the number of shares outstanding, or in terms of its assets (what it owns) relative to its liabilities (what it owes).

Meeting and exceeding customer needs means that companies must be sensitive to the needs of customers, anticipate changes in their needs, and, of course, work to meet these needs in a proactive fashion—before a customer complains. However, today companies cannot just provide what the customer wants. They need to satisfy customers beyond their expectations, or the competition will.

Providing value means that a business must constantly strive to improve the quality of its products and services, and do so at a reasonable cost. Customers demand quality and will stand for nothing less, but they want value for their dollar. They will pay a price that gives them value for their money—the quality that they demand at a price that makes it worthwhile or valuable to them.

Encouraging creativity and innovation involves the process of being creative (or "thinking outside the box"), as well as harnessing that creativity to generate the innovations that keep the company one step ahead of the competition. Danger exists when the company becomes comfortable with its level of success, as it might resist the change needed to stay ahead. But remember, there are only two kinds of businesses—those that constantly innovate and those that go out of business. In today's business world, one of the only constants is change. The status quo doesn't work anymore. Companies need to become "learning organizations," proactively seeking to learn and move ahead every day in everything they do.

And finally, probably the most important success factor is *gaining employee commitment.* Employees need to be empowered to act and motivated to meet the company's objectives in each of the first four factors, or those objectives won't be met. Therefore, every company needs to understand the needs of its employees. Only then can it gain their commitment, for they will be committed to meeting the goals of the company only if their own goals are met at the same time. It is, again, an integrative relationship.

Underneath the critical success factors are the *stakeholders* of the business. These are individuals and groups that have a "stake" in what the business does. They are affected by the decisions that the business makes, and therefore the business has a responsibility to consider them in those decisions.

The three most critical and obvious stakeholder groups are the owners of the business (or shareholders in the case of a corporation), the employees of the business (and their union if represented by one), and the customers. But there is a much wider world out there that must be considered—the government, special interest groups, the community surrounding the business, its suppliers, and so on. All of these groups interact with the business and keep it operating.

The business cannot operate in a vacuum, as if these groups did not exist. They must be considered in every decision the business makes. If we change this material, how will our customers react? Will they keep buying our product? If we move the business, how will it affect the community? How many employees will we lose? If we cut down these trees to build the new plant, how will the environmentalist groups respond? How will the community and the local government respond? If earnings drop in the fourth quarter as expected, will our shareholders sell their shares, making the share price fall even lower? Achieving the critical success factors clearly depends on an intimate knowledge of and relationship with the stakeholders of the business.

It is primarily *top management's* external focus that keeps the business looking at the stakeholders. It is the responsibility of the top management of the company to look outward and chart a course for the company. They examine the external environment of the business and match the threats and opportunities in the external environment with both the expectations of the stakeholders and the strengths and weaknesses of the company, to determine the direction the company should take in the future—their *vision* for the future of the company. This is further refined into a *mission* statement for the company. Next they determine the *strategy* for the company to pursue to achieve this mission—how to go about achieving the company's goals in the future.

For example, perhaps opportunities exist in the external environment to take the company global. Perhaps needs exist within foreign countries for the type of product the company sells, and little competition exists from other firms at the present time. If the company has the internal marketing, operations, human, and financial strength to achieve this objective, then top management might determine that the vision for the future of the company is to make it a strong global competitor. The strategy would then need to take into account such decisions as what countries to enter first, whether to search out foreign firms with which to form a joint venture, and whether to pursue a licensing arrangement with a foreign firm or build its own plants.

It is then *middle management's* job within each of the functional areas of the business to determine and plan out what each area needs to do to help achieve this overall corporate strategy. For example, what type of marketing campaigns will be most successful in these new foreign markets? Do we build new plants or lease/purchase and renovate existing plants? What new skills and attributes are needed to staff our operations in these new foreign markets? Where will the money come from, and how will the budgets be realigned?

First-line management manages the workers who do the actual work in each of the functional areas. It is their job to make sure the higher level plans are implemented—and, most important—by committed workers who are motivated to achieve the goals of the company.

Top managers, middle managers, and first-line managers are responsible for managing the company and its employees to ensure that all five of the critical success factors are achieved. They do this by

- *planning* what the goals are (to achieve the critical success factors) and how to achieve them,
- *organizing* the resources of the company—human, physical, and financial—to achieve the goals,
- *motivating* the workers to gain their commitment to the goals, and then
- *measuring* results and making any changes necessary to continue to steer the company in the direction of the goals, thus maintaining control over the achievement of these five critical success factors.

This is the model we will use in this text to help you integrate the different topics covered into an understanding of how a successful business works as a whole. By studying the topics presented in this textbook, you will gain a solid foundation on which to build your further understanding of successful business practices.

CHAPTER 1

Making the Connection

Understanding Evolving Economic Systems and Competition

In this chapter, you'll learn about different economic systems, basic economic concepts you need to understand how the economy works, and the role of competition in the economic environment. But first, you might be wondering, "Where does all this fit into our understanding of a successful business?"

Take a peek back at the model introduced in the Introduction.

The most obvious relationship between this chapter and the model of a successful business is in the external environment. The PEST model of the external environment is an acronym for the **p**olitical, **e**conomic, **s**ocial, and **t**echnological environments that interact with business.

The *economic* environment is part of our PEST model of the external environment. In this chapter, we will describe the economic system of a country as a combination of policies, laws, and choices made by its government. Remember, this is an integrative model. Here we see a direct link between the *political* and economic environments. But as you'll see throughout the chapter, the economy has an impact on all the other aspects of the external environment, as well as on the internal environment of a business and how it operates.

Take, for example, any of the new hybrid cars, such as the Toyota Prius. You might have seen these sleek, trendy machines racing around your neighbourhood. As a result of pressure from governments and *society* to reduce fuel emissions that cause pollution and increase the threat of global warming—as well as economic pressure from foreign oil companies raising gas prices—Toyota has worked to create the *technology* for hybrid cars that run on gasoline and electricity. This affects the economic environment, because it is an action that other companies need to respond to if they are

going to remain competitive—and many have. Interestingly, the global financial crisis that started in 2008—a change in the economic environment that will continue to show its impact for years to come—pointed out sharply that competing automotive companies hadn't responded sufficiently. The Big Three—General Motors, Ford, and Chrysler—were already in trouble as oil prices skyrocketed leading into the economic crisis because a large part of their market was gas-guzzling SUVs and pick-up trucks. This position put them into even more serious financial trouble when credit tightened up, and had them running to the government for bail-out money. Many groups in society responded negatively, however, as they felt that the Big Three put themselves into that position by not sufficiently responding to the environment by building fuel-efficient cars. There are few examples of the integrative nature of business that create such a large number of complex spinoff effects.

Ideally, the internal environment of the business interacts by creating the product to *meet the needs of the customer*—a critical success factor. *Marketing* works with *operations* to design and build the product through the *human resources* of the company and with the *financial resources* of the company. In Toyota's case, this was a very innovative move on the part of the company that would take several years to create a return on investment. But it is this commitment to *innovation* in response to an environmental threat that has allowed companies like Toyota to remain competitive and turn what would have been a threat into an opportunity for the business. That is what competition and success are all about.

In this chapter, we describe economic systems as differing based on how they manage the factors of production—the

resources needed to produce a company's products. These factors are provided by the **stakeholders** of the business: employees provide human resources, and owners provide financial resources, for example. The economic system that exists in a society depends partly on the relationship between the stakeholders, business, and the government. This stakeholder relationship to the economic environment can also be seen in the discussion of **economics** as a "circular flow": resources are provided by the stakeholders, who then receive something in return from the business. This circular flow also clearly demonstrates the integrative nature of a business, as changes in one flow affect the others.

We have provided numerous examples of the integrative nature of business. One such example is the "crowding out" that occurs when government spending replaces private sector spending. This is an excellent example of how the political and economic environments affect one another as well as affecting the internal environments of companies. When the government spends more on libraries, for example, and individuals spend less on books, how does that affect all the different functional areas of a company? As described in this chapter, this crowding out also occurs when the government raises funds for spending, making corporate financing more expensive and thus crowding out private investment which, in turn, slows economic growth in the private sector.

All the examples in the chapter of news stories that deal with economic matters demonstrate the extent to which the economic environment creeps into the daily workings of a business. Consider the following:

- *"The Bank of Canada lowers interest rates."* This would affect the financial decisions of the company, perhaps making it more feasible financially to expand—affecting the company's overall strategy, as well as its ability to meet the needs of the customer by offering better financing packages.
- *"The Minister of Finance proposes a cut in income taxes."* Lower personal income taxes result in customers' having more disposable income to spend on the company's products. Lower corporate taxes make the economic environment more favourable to business investment domestically

and make it easier for Canadian enterprises to compete with companies from countries with lower taxes.

We will use numerous examples throughout the chapter to demonstrate how factors in the economy affect business decisions: what to produce (marketing and operations), how to price these products (marketing and finance), and how many people to employ and how much to pay them (human resources and finance). The impact of inflation, business cycles, and government policy all provide examples of how economics affects business. But if you look at the factors that cause demand and supply curves to shift, you can also see many other aspects of the environment at play; for example, technology shifts the supply curve, but buyers' preferences (social environment) shift the demand curve.

The economy also affects critical success factors of the business. Many trends in the economic environment relate to these success factors. The chapter describes how "companies are focusing on relationship management, which involves building, maintaining, and enhancing interactions with customers ... so as to develop long-term satisfaction." This comes, in part, as a result of better educated and more demanding customers from the social environment; new technology, which allows customers to find companies that meet their needs and switch to them at the click of a mouse; and the globalization of markets in the economic environment, creating more competition. These environmental factors, combined with an understanding that financially it's better on the bottom line to keep an existing customer than find a new one, results in a trend toward meeting customer needs that takes on more long-term significance. We will describe why "creating and building long-term relationships require a world-class work force." Better training and better technology to improve worker productivity help to build a *workforce committed* to meeting the *quality* needs of the customer and to building long-term relationships with them. And, of course, satisfied long-standing customers and more productive and committed workers result in both higher revenues and cost savings, helping the company achieve better *financial performance*.

CHAPTER 1

Understanding Evolving Economic Systems and Competition

LEARNING OUTCOMES

1 Understand the primary features of the world's economic systems.

2 Explain what economics is and how the three sectors of the economy are linked.

3 Show how economic growth, full employment, and price stability indicate a nation's economic health.

4 Define inflation, and discuss how it is measured and what causes it.

5 Describe how the Bank of Canada uses monetary policy, and how governments use fiscal policy to achieve their macroeconomic goals.

6 Discuss the basic microeconomic concepts of demand and supply, and how they establish prices.

7 Explain the four types of market structure.

8 List some of the trends that are reshaping micro- and macroeconomic environments.

INJECTING CASH INTO A NATIONAL ECONOMY

Imagine you are considering a large purchase—a new car or even your first house—but you do not have the money to pay for it up front. What will you do? Most likely, you will go to the bank to take out a loan. Now, imagine you are the leader of a country. You wish to implement programs to improve the quality of life for your citizens. Where do you turn?

Horst Köhler and the International Monetary Fund (IMF) may provide the answer. The IMF is not a traditional bank as you think of one used for personal banking, but many of its functions are similar to those of personal banks. As Köhler, managing director of the IMF from 2000 until 2005, describes it, "The major goals of the IMF are, first, to provide financial stability in the international financial system and, second, to make a contribution to the international effort to fight poverty, which is far too high."

To achieve that second goal, the IMF established a program to assist developing countries. The program was designed to provide large loans to the developing countries, which they could use to foster growth—similar to the bank that provides you a loan for your car or house purchase. Although the loans were intended to build a country's infrastructure (roads, harbours, airports, utility companies, etc.), the program came under criticism in the 1990s when it was discovered that as little as 30 percent of the money actually was used as intended. The rest was either embezzled or squandered. Borrowing countries were still responsible for the interest and repayment of the loans, so their economic burdens only increased.

Köhler became managing director of the IMF on May 1, 2000, and immediately sought to address these challenges. One of the most respected people in the field, he came to the job with experience as the president of the European Bank for Reconstruction and Development, the president of the German Savings Bank Association, and Germany's deputy minister of finance. Köhler saw an opportunity to correct the problems in the IMF's program to assist developing countries. He instituted a new Poverty Elimination program to concentrate more of the IMF's efforts on humanitarian issues, focusing on the people behind the economy. For this to be successful, though, he knew that the illegal uses of the loan money needed to stop. He insisted on the development of controls to guarantee that the monies were used as intended. In addition, he felt that, along with providing money, the IMF needed to provide training to recipient countries to teach budgeting and fiscal responsibility. In this way, the IMF would be able to greatly influence the economic systems of countries in crisis, creating stability, and, eventually, the potential for growth and entrance into the international economic marketplace.

With the implementation of these policies, Köhler and the IMF have seen great success in developing countries around the world. One such example, Tanzania, set the ambitious goal of cutting the poverty rate from 38 percent to less than 24 percent by 2010. Currently, Tanzania is ahead of schedule and provides the model for other countries looking to plot a course out of poverty.

Critical Thinking Questions

1. **Using the Circular Flow illustration in Exhibit 1.2, examine the impact of a loan by the IMF to Tanzania for infrastructure projects.**

2. **Explain how such a loan would help cut the poverty rate.**

PHOTO SOURCE: From Gitman/McDaniel, *The Future of Business*, 6E. © 2008 South-Western, a part of Cengage Learning Inc. Reproduced by permission. www.cengage.com/permissions

Economics is an analytical science that will help you understand the world around you. As you study this chapter, remember that economics is not something you should learn for an exam and then forget. It can help you be more imaginative and insightful in everyday life. You will understand why prices are going up or down, when interest rates will fall, and when and why the unemployment rate will fall. A knowledge of basic economic concepts can help you decide whether to change jobs (and how much money to ask for) and whether to buy a car now or wait until next year. When you hear that Ford Motor Co. has 115 days of inventory, your understanding of the forces of supply and demand will tell you that now may be the time to buy that new car.

Similarly, economics will help you become a better-informed citizen. Almost every political issue is, in some way, grounded in economic concepts. Economics can also help you understand what is happening in other countries and raise your awareness of opportunities in those countries. Understanding economics and how changes in an economy affect business is important to be successful. Recently we have experienced many changes, from nations changing economic systems to worldwide economic challenges. These have created opportunities for some and threats to others.

Reading this chapter will help you understand how economies provide jobs for workers and also create and deliver products to consumers and businesses. You will also learn how governments attempt to influence economic activity through policies such as lowering or raising taxes. Next, we discuss how supply and demand determine prices for goods and services. We conclude by examining trends in evolving economic systems and competition.

Global Economic Systems

economic system
The combination of policies, laws, and choices made by a nation's government to establish the systems that determine what goods and services are produced and how they are allocated.

A nation's **economic system** is the combination of policies, laws, and choices made by its government to establish the systems that determine what goods and services are produced and how they are allocated. Economic systems found in the world today include market economy (private enterprise or market system), command (planned economies), socialism, and mixed economies.

The major differentiator among economic systems is whether the government or individuals decide how to allocate limited resources—the factors of production—to individuals and organizations to best satisfy unlimited societal needs;

- choose what goods and services to produce, and in what quantities;
- determine how to produce these goods and services and who will produce them; and
- distribute goods and services to consumers.

Companies that do business internationally may discover that they must adapt production and selling methods to accommodate the economic system of another country. Additionally, managers must understand and adapt to the factors of production and the economic system or systems in which they operate to be successful.

Factors of Production: The Building Blocks of Business

factors of production
The resources used to create goods and services, including natural resources, labour, capital, entrepreneurship, and knowledge.

Factors of production are the resources used to create goods and services. By using the **factors of production** efficiently, a company can produce more output with the same resources. Four traditional factors of production are common to all productive activity: natural resources, labour, capital, and entrepreneurship. Many experts now include knowledge as a fifth factor, acknowledging its key role in business success.

natural resources
Commodities that are useful inputs in their natural state.

labour
Economic contributions of people.

capital
The inputs, such as tools, machinery, equipment, and buildings, used to produce goods and services and get them to the customer.

entrepreneurs
People who combine the inputs of natural resources, labour, and capital to produce goods or services with the intention of making a profit or accomplishing a not-for-profit goal.

knowledge
The combined talents and skills of the workforce.

Commodities that are useful inputs in their natural state are known as **natural resources**. They include farmland, forests, mineral and oil deposits, and water. Sometimes natural resources are simply called *land*, although, as you can see, the term means more than just land. Today, urban sprawl, pollution, and limited resources have raised questions about resource use. Conservationists, ecologists, and government bodies are proposing laws to require land use planning and resource conservation.

The economic contributions of people working with their minds and muscles are called **labour**. This input includes the talents of everyone—from a restaurant cook to a nuclear physicist—who performs the many tasks of manufacturing and selling goods and services. The tools, machinery, equipment, and buildings used to produce goods and services and get them to the consumer are known as **capital**. Sometimes the term *capital* is also used to mean the money that buys machinery, factories, and other production and distribution facilities. However, because money itself produces nothing, it is *not* one of the basic inputs. Rather, it is a means of acquiring the inputs. Therefore, in this context, capital does not include money.

Entrepreneurs are people who combine the inputs of natural resources, labour, and capital to produce goods or services with the intention of making a profit. These people make all the decisions that set the course for their firms; they create products and production processes. Because they are not guaranteed a profit in return for their time and effort, they must be risk takers. Of course, if their firms succeed, the rewards can be great.

Today, many Canadians want to start their own businesses. They are attracted by the opportunity to be their own boss and reap the financial rewards of owning a successful firm.

A number of outstanding managers and noted academics are beginning to emphasize a fifth factor of production—knowledge. **Knowledge** is the combined talents and skills of the workforce. As the world becomes ever more uncertain, the very nature of work, organizations, and management is changing. The new competitive environment places a premium on knowledge and learning. Lester Thurow, a leading world expert on economic issues, says, "The dominant competitive weapon of the twenty-first century will be the knowledge of the work force."[1] The companies that will become and remain successful will be the ones that can learn quickly, assimilate this learning, and develop new insights.

---

concept check

What is an economic system?

What are the five factors of production?

What is the role of an entrepreneur in society?

---

market economy
An economic system based on competition in the marketplace and private ownership of the factors of production (resources); also known as the *private enterprise system* or *capitalism*.

Market Economy

In the last decade of the 20th century, many countries shifted toward market economic systems. Sometimes, as in the case of the former East Germany, the transition to a market economy had been painful but fairly quick. In other countries, such as Russia, the movement has been characterized by false starts and backsliding. A **market economy,** also known as the *private enterprise system* or *capitalism,* is based on competition in the marketplace and private ownership of the factors of production (resources). In a competitive economic system, a large number of people and businesses buy and sell products freely in the marketplace. In a pure market economy, all the factors of production are owned privately and the government does not try to set prices or coordinate economic activity.

A market economy guarantees certain economic rights: the right to own property, the right to make a profit, the right to make free choices, and the right to compete. The right to own property is central to a market economy. The main incentive in this system is profit, which encourages entrepreneurship. Profit is also necessary for producing goods and services, building plants, paying dividends and taxes, and creating jobs. The freedom to choose whether to become an entrepreneur or to work for someone else means that people have the right to decide what they want to do on the basis of their own drive, interest, and training. The government does not create job quotas for each industry or give people tests to determine what they will do.

In a market economy, competition is good for both businesses and consumers. It leads to better and more diverse products, keeps prices stable, and increases the

CHAPTER 1 Understanding Evolving Economic Systems and Competition efficiency of producers. Producers try to produce their goods and services at the lowest possible cost and sell them at the highest possible price. But when profits are high, more firms enter the market to seek those profits. The resulting competition among firms tends to lower prices. Producers must then find new ways of operating more efficiently if they are to keep making a profit—and stay in business.

The Command Economy

command economy
An economic system characterized by government ownership of virtually all resources and economic decision making by central-government planning; also known as *planned economy*.

The complete opposite to a market economy is a **command economy**. In a command economy, or planned economy, the government owns virtually all resources and controls all markets. Economic decision making is centralized: the government, rather than the market's competitive force, decides what and how much to produce, where to locate production facilities, where to acquire raw materials and supplies, who will get the output, and what the prices will be. This form of centralized economic system offers little if any choice to a country's citizens.

In the 20th century, countries such as the former Soviet Union and China chose the command economic system, believing that it would raise their standard of living. In practice, however, the tight controls over most aspects of people's lives, such as what careers they can choose, where they can work, and what they can buy, led to lower productivity. Workers had no reasons to work harder or produce quality goods, because there were no rewards for excellence. Errors in planning and resource allocation led to shortages of even basic items.

These factors were among the reasons for the 1991 collapse of the Soviet Union into multiple independent nations. Recent reforms in Russia, China, and most of the Eastern European nations have moved these economies toward more capitalistic, market-oriented systems. North Korea and Cuba are the best remaining examples of command economic systems.

Socialism

socialism
An economic system in which the basic industries are owned either by the government or by the private sector under strong government control.

Socialism is an economic system in which the basic industries are owned by the government or by the private sector under strong government control. A socialist state controls critical large-scale industries such as transportation, communications, and utilities. Smaller businesses may be privately owned. To varying degrees, the state also determines the goals of businesses, the prices and selection of goods, and the rights of workers. Socialist countries typically provide their citizens with a higher level of

CONCEPT *in Action* >>>

Since joining the World Trade Organization in 2001, China has continued to embrace tenets of a market economic system and grow its economy. China is the world's largest producer of mobile phones, PCs, and cameras, and the country's over one billion citizens constitute a gargantuan emerging market. What are some of the benefits that China has experienced by moving toward a market economy?

© FORREST ANDERSON/GETTY IMAGES

services, such as health care and unemployment benefits, than do most capitalist countries. As a result, taxes and unemployment can also be quite high in socialist countries.

Mixed Economic Systems

mixed economies
Economies that combine several economic systems; for example, an economy in which the government owns certain industries but the private sector owns others.

Canada, Great Britain, and Sweden, among others, are also called **mixed economies;** that is, they use more than one economic system. Sometimes, the government is basically socialist and owns basic industries. In Canada, some industries are at least partly owned by the government (e.g., communications, transportation, and utilities industries), but most activities are carried on by private enterprises, as in a market system.

The few factors of production owned by the government include some public lands, Canada Post, and some water resources. But the government is extensively involved in the economic system through taxing, spending, and welfare activities. The economy is also mixed in the sense that the country tries to achieve many social goals—income redistribution (transfer payments) and Canada Pension Plan, for example—that might not be attempted in purely capitalist systems. Exhibit 1.1 summarizes key factors of the world's economic systems.

concept check

What is a market economy, and why is the system becoming more pervasive worldwide?

What is socialism, and why is it still popular?

Why are most economies mixed?

EXHIBIT 1.1 > The Basic Economic Systems of the World

	Market Economy	Command Economy	Socialism	Mixed Economy
Ownership of Business	Businesses are privately owned with minimal government ownership or interference	Governments own all or most enterprises	Basic industries such as railroads and utilities are owned by government; very high taxation as government redistributes income from successful private businesses and entrepreneurs	Private ownership of land and businesses but government control of some enterprises; the private sector is typically large
Control of Markets	Complete freedom of trade; no or little government control	Complete government control of markets	Some markets are controlled and some are free; significant central-government planning; state enterprises are managed by bureaucrats; these enterprises are rarely profitable	Some markets, such as nuclear energy and the post office, are controlled or highly regulated
Worker Incentives	Strong incentive to work and innovate because profits are retained by owners	No incentive to work hard or produce quality products	Private-sector incentives the same as a market and public-sector incentives the same as a planned economy	Private-sector incentives the same as capitalism; limited incentives in the public sector
Management of Enterprises	Each enterprise is managed by owners or professional managers with little government interference	Centralized management by the government bureaucracy; little or no flexibility in decision making at the factory level	Significant government planning and regulation; bureaucrats run government enterprises	Private-sector management similar to capitalism; public sector similar to socialism
Forecast for 2020	Continued steady growth	No growth and perhaps disappearance	Stable with probable slight growth	Continued growth

How Business and Economies Work

economics
The study of how a society uses scarce resources to produce and distribute goods and services.

Economics is the study of how a society uses scarce resources to produce and distribute goods and services. The resources of a person, a firm, or a nation are limited. Hence, economics is the study of choices—what people, firms, or nations choose from among the available resources. Every economy is concerned with what types and amounts of goods and services should be produced, how they should be produced, and for whom. These decisions are made by the marketplace, the government, or both. In Canada, the government and the free-market system together guide the economy.

You probably know more about economics than you realize. Every day, many news stories deal with economic matters: A union wins wage increases at Company X; the Bank of Canada raises/lowers interest rates; Toronto Stock Exchange has a record day; the federal government proposes a cut in income taxes; consumer spending rises as the economy grows; or retail prices are on the rise, to mention just a few examples.

Macroeconomics and Microeconomics

The state of the economy affects both people and businesses. How you spend your money (or save it) is a personal economic decision. Whether you continue in school and whether you work part-time are also economic decisions. Every business also operates within the economy. Based on their owners' and managers' economic expectations, businesses decide what products to produce, how to price them, how many people to employ, how much to pay these employees, how much to expand the business, and so on.

macroeconomics
The sub-area of economics that focuses on the economy as a whole by looking at aggregate data for large groups of people, companies, or products.

microeconomics
The sub-area of economics that focuses on individual parts of the economy, such as households or firms.

Economics has two main sub-areas. **Macroeconomics** is the study of the economy as a whole. It looks at *aggregate* data, data for large groups of people, companies, or products considered as a whole. In contrast, **microeconomics** focuses on individual parts of the economy, such as households or firms.

Both macro- and microeconomics offer valuable outlooks on the economy. For example, Ford might use both to decide whether to introduce a new line of cars. The company would consider such macroeconomic factors as the national level of personal income, the unemployment rate, interest rates, fuel costs, and the national level of sales of new cars. From a microeconomic viewpoint, Ford would judge consumer demand for new cars versus the existing supply, competing models, labour and material costs and availability, and current prices and sales incentives.

CONCEPT *in Action* >>>

The successful introduction of the 787 Dreamliner by aerospace giant Boeing demonstrates that it pays to keep an eye on economic trends. Made from lightweight composites, the jet aircraft's ultra-efficient design reduces fuel consumption by 20 percent per flight. How does the economy affect the types of goods and services that are produced?

© ASSOCIATED PRESS, BOEING CO. AP/WIDE WORLD PHOTOS

Economics as a Circular Flow

circular flow
The movement of inputs and outputs among households, businesses, and governments; a way of showing how the sectors of the economy interact.

Another way to see how the sectors of the economy interact is to examine the **circular flow** of inputs and outputs among households, businesses, and governments, as shown in Exhibit 1.2. Let's review the exchanges by following the purple circle around the inside of the diagram. Households provide inputs (natural resources, labour, capital, entrepreneurship) to businesses, which convert these inputs into outputs (goods and services) for consumers. In return, consumers receive income from rent, wages, interest, and ownership profits (green circle). Businesses receive income from consumer purchases of goods and services.

The other important exchange in Exhibit 1.2 takes place between governments (federal, provincial, and municipal) and both individuals and businesses. Governments supply many types of publicly provided goods and services (highways, schools, police, courts, health services, unemployment insurance, Canada Pension Plan) that benefit individuals and businesses. Government purchases from businesses also contribute to business profits. The contractor who repairs a local stretch of highway, for example, is paid by government for the work. As the diagram shows, government receives taxes from individuals and businesses to complete the flow.

Changes in one flow affect the others. If the government raises taxes, households have less to spend on goods and services. Lower consumer spending causes businesses to reduce production, and economic activity declines; unemployment might rise. In contrast, cutting taxes can stimulate economic activity. Keep the circular flow in mind as we continue our study of economics. The way economic sectors interact will become more evident as we explore macroeconomics and microeconomics.

concept check

What is economics?

What is the difference between macroeconomics and microeconomics?

How do resources flow among the household, business, and government sectors?

EXHIBIT 1.2 > Economics as a Circular Flow

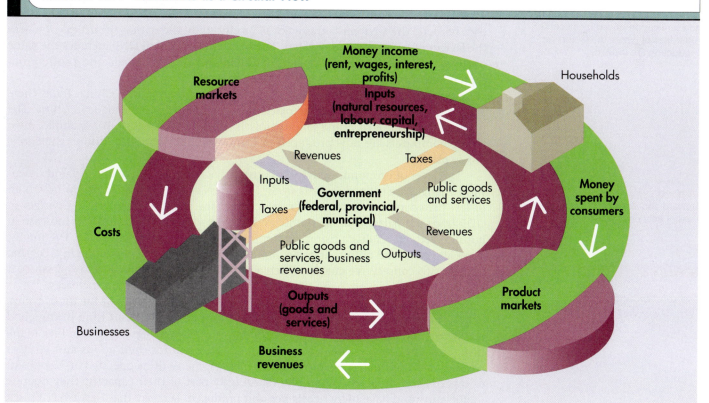

Macroeconomics: The Big Picture

 LO 3

HOT Links

The Canadian Government follows national and regional economic statistics, including the GDP. For the latest economic overview of the Canadian economy, visit (**www.canadianeconomy.gc.ca**).

economic growth
An increase in a nation's output of goods and services.

gross domestic product (GDP)
The total market value of all final goods and services produced within a nation's borders in a year.

gross national product (GNP)
The total market value of all final goods and services produced by a country regardless of where the factors of production are located.

business cycles
Upward and downward changes in the level of economic activity.

recession
A decline in GDP that lasts for at least two consecutive quarters.

Have you ever looked at CBC Newsworld on the Internet (**www.cbc.ca**) or turned on the radio or television and heard something similar to, "Today the government reported that for the second straight month the unemployment rate has risen."? Statements like this are macroeconomic news. Understanding the national economy and how changes in government policies affect households and businesses is a good place to begin our study of economics.

Let's look first at macroeconomic goals and how they can be met. Canada and most other countries have three main macroeconomic goals: economic growth, full employment, and price stability. A nation's economic well-being depends on carefully defining these goals and choosing the best economic policies to reach them.

Striving for Economic Growth

Perhaps the most important way to judge a nation's economic health is to look at its production of goods and services. The more the nation produces, the higher its standard of living. An increase in a nation's output of goods and services is **economic growth**.

Economic growth is usually a good thing, but it also has a bad side. Increased production yields more pollution. Growth can strain public facilities, such as roads, electricity, schools, and hospitals. Thus, the government tries to apply economic policies that will keep growth to a level that does not reduce the quality of life.

The most basic measure of economic growth is the **gross domestic product (GDP)**. GDP is the total market value of all final goods and services produced within a nation's borders each year. It is reported quarterly and is used to compare trends in national output. When GDP rises, the economy is growing.

The *rate* of growth in real GDP (GDP adjusted for inflation) is also important. For example, if the Canadian economy has been growing at about 2 to 3 percent annually, this growth rate has meant a steady increase in output of goods and services. When the growth rate slides toward zero, the economy begins to stagnate and decline.

Another measurement that is often used by economist is the **gross national product (GNP)**. Unlike the GDP, which calculates what is produced within the country's borders, the GNP measures what is produced by the nation regardless of where the factors of production are located. Therefore, the Canadian GNP includes the value of the goods and services produced by Canadian firms in Canada and profits from capital held abroad.

One country that continues to grow more rapidly than most is China. Today there are few things in the global marketplace that are not or cannot be made in China. The primary contributor to China's rapid growth has been technology. For example, most laptop computers are now produced in China, as the Expanding Around the Globe box explains.

The level of economic activity is constantly changing. These upward and downward changes are called **business cycles**. Business cycles vary in length, in how high or low the economy moves, and in how much the economy is affected. Changes in GDP trace the patterns as economic activity expands and contracts. An increase in business activity results in rising output, income, employment, and prices. Eventually, these all peak—and output, income, and employment decline. A decline in GDP that lasts for two consecutive quarters (each a three-month period) is called a **recession**. It is followed by a recovery period, when economic activity once again increases.

Businesses must monitor and react to the changing phases of business cycles. When the economy is growing, companies often have a difficult time hiring good employees and finding scarce supplies and raw materials. When a recession hits, many firms find they have more capacity than the demand for their goods and services requires. During the recession of the early 1990s, many firms operated at 75 percent or less of their capacity. When plants use only part of their capacity, they operate inefficiently and have higher costs per unit produced. Let's say that Nestlé has a plant

Expanding Around The Globe

YOUR LAPTOP: CITIZEN OF THE WORLD

Your new laptop computer has already traveled across the world—before you even open the box! Probably assembled in China by a Taiwanese company, it contains parts from many countries. The power supply may have come from China, the microprocessor from the United States, the hard drive and display from Japan, and the memory chips from South Korea. The graphics processor was probably designed in the United States—but manufactured in Taiwan.

Laptops, the best selling segment of the computer industry, are a good example of how companies and countries cooperate in today's global economic environment. Taiwanese companies manufacture 80 percent of the world's laptops. Dell, Apple, Gateway, and Acer outsource 100 percent of their laptop production (Dell does final assembly in its own offshore factories), and Hewlett-Packard outsources 95 percent. Japanese companies such as NEC, Sony, and Toshiba also outsource, but to a lesser degree—between 35 percent and 60 percent.

Moving laptop production offshore is not a new strategy for computer companies, who needed to reduce costs and find more efficient production methods to stay competitive. Until the 1990s, many laptops were assembled in Japan and Singapore. In the 1990s, Taiwanese firms became the major recipients of the production because of their lower labour costs and high quality.

The rising demand for laptops brought new companies into the market. Although total industry revenues are still rising due to higher demand, profits on laptops have fallen sharply. Low-cost-producers such as Acer and Averatec are willing to accept low profit margins to gain market share. With increased competition came sharply lower prices.

To stay competitive despite continuing cost pressures, most Taiwanese contract manufacturers shifted their production facilities to China after Taiwan's government lifted a ban on manufacturing in China in 2001. Quanta, the world's largest laptop manufacturer, employs 20,000 workers at its factory complex in Shanghai, China.

Today China assembles 68 percent of the world's laptops, followed by Taiwan with 17 percent, and Japan with 8 percent. The Chinese government recognizes the importance of foreign investment to its economic future, especially in technology, and is encouraging companies to locate production facilities there. Producers of hard drives, displays, memory chips, and other components are already setting up shop in China.[2]

Critical Thinking Questions

1. What are the benefits and disadvantages to computer companies of using offshore contract manufacturers to produce their laptops? Are there any risks in this strategy?
2. How would you describe the market structure of the laptop industry (see the section "Competing in a Free Market" later in this chapter), and why?

---

that can produce one million Aero chocolate bars a day, but because of a recession, Nestlé can sell only half a million candy bars a day. Nestlé has a huge plant with large, expensive machines designed to produce a million candy bars a day. Producing Aero chocolate bars at 50 percent capacity does not use Nestlé's investment in the plant and equipment efficiently.

CONCEPT in Action >>>

The housing industry is a leading economic indicator. A rise in new home construction typically translates into a robust economy. What is the current state of Canada's economy?

© KIM STEELE/PHOTODISC/GETTY IMAGES

Keeping People on the Job

full employment
The condition when all people who want to work and can work have jobs.

Another macroeconomic goal is **full employment,** or having jobs for all who want to and can work. Full employment doesn't actually mean 100 percent employment. Some people choose not to work for personal reasons (attending school, raising children) or are temporarily unemployed while they wait to start a new job. Thus, the government defines full employment as the situation when about 94 to 96 percent of those available to work actually have jobs.

Measuring Unemployment

unemployment rate
The percentage of the total labour force that is actively looking for work but is not actually working.

To determine how close we are to full employment, the government measures the **unemployment rate.** This rate indicates the percentage of the total labour force that is not working but is *actively looking for work*. It excludes "discouraged workers," those not seeking jobs because they think no one will hire them. Each month the government releases statistics on employment. These figures help us understand how well the economy is doing.

> **concept check**
>
> What are the three main macroeconomic objectives of Canada?
>
> What is GDP? GNP?
>
> What are business cycles?

Types of Unemployment

Economists classify unemployment into four types: frictional, structural, cyclical, and seasonal. The categories are of small consolation to someone who is unemployed, but they help economists understand the problem of unemployment in our economy.

frictional unemployment
Short-term unemployment that is not related to the business cycle.

Frictional unemployment is short-term unemployment that is not related to the business cycle. It includes people who are unemployed while waiting to start a better job, those who are reentering the job market, and those entering for the first time, such as new college graduates. This type of unemployment is always present and has little impact on the economy.

structural unemployment
Unemployment that is caused by a mismatch between available jobs and the skills of available workers in an industry or region; it is not related to the business cycle.

Structural unemployment is also unrelated to the business cycle but is involuntary. It is caused by a mismatch between available jobs and the skills of available workers in an industry or a region. For example, if the birthrate declines, fewer teachers will be needed. Or the available workers in an area might lack the skills that employers want. Retraining and skill-building programs are often required to reduce structural unemployment.

cyclical unemployment
Unemployment that occurs when a downturn in the business cycle reduces the demand for labour throughout the economy.

Cyclical unemployment, as the name implies, occurs when a downturn in the business cycle reduces the demand for labour throughout the economy. In a long recession, cyclical unemployment is widespread, and even people with good job skills can't find jobs. The government can partly counteract cyclical unemployment with programs that boost the economy.

In the past, cyclical unemployment affected mainly less skilled workers and those in heavy manufacturing. Typically, they would be rehired when economic growth increased. Since the 1990s, however, competition forced many Canadian companies to downsize so they could survive in the global marketplace.

seasonal unemployment
Unemployment that occurs during specific seasons in certain industries.

The last type is **seasonal unemployment,** which occurs during specific seasons in certain industries. Employees subject to seasonal unemployment include retail workers hired for the December buying season, road construction, and restaurant employees in winter ski areas.

Keeping Prices Steady

The third macroeconomic goal is to keep overall prices for goods and services fairly steady. The situation in which the average of all prices of goods and services is rising is called **inflation.** Inflation's higher prices reduce **purchasing power,** the

inflation
The situation in which the average of all prices of goods and services is rising.

purchasing power
The value of what money can buy.

value of what money can buy. If prices go up but income doesn't rise or rises at a slower rate, a given amount of income buys less. For example, if the price of a basket of groceries rises from $30 to $40 but your salary remains the same, you can buy only 75 percent as many groceries ($30 ÷ $40). Your purchasing power declines by 25 percent ($10 ÷ $40).

Inflation affects both personal and business decisions. When prices are rising, people tend to spend more—before their purchasing power declines further. Businesses that expect inflation often increase their supplies, and people often speed up planned purchases of cars and major appliances.

Types of Inflation

demand-pull inflation
Inflation that occurs when the demand for goods and services is greater than the supply.

There are two types of inflation. **Demand-pull inflation** occurs when the demand for goods and services is greater than the supply. In this case, would-be buyers have more money to spend than the amount needed to buy available goods and services. Their demand, which exceeds the supply, tends to pull prices up. This situation is sometimes described as "too much money chasing too few goods." The higher prices lead to greater supply, eventually creating a balance between demand and supply.

cost-push inflation
Inflation that occurs when increases in production costs push up the prices of final goods and services.

Cost-push inflation is triggered by increases in production costs, such as expenses for materials and wages. These increases push up the prices of final goods and services. Wage increases are a major cause of cost-push inflation, creating a "wage-price spiral." For example, assume the Canadian Auto Workers Union negotiates a three-year labour agreement that raises wages 3 percent per year and increases overtime pay. Car makers will then raise car prices to cover their higher labour costs. These higher wages will also give auto workers more money to buy goods and services, and this increased demand might pull up other prices. Workers in other industries will demand higher wages to keep up with the increased prices, and the cycle will push prices even higher.

How Inflation Is Measured

consumer price index (CPI)
An index of the prices of a "shopping basket" of goods and services purchased by consumers.

Economists most commonly measure the rate of inflation by looking at changes in the **consumer price index (CPI)**, an index of the prices of a "shopping basket" of goods and services purchased by consumers. It tracks the retail price of a representative shopping basket of approximately 300 goods and services that an average household would purchase and is published monthly by Statistics Canada. Some of the expenditures include food, housing, transportation, furniture, clothing, and recreation. The index is weighted to reflect typical spending patterns. For instance, greater importance is given to housing than to recreation. Statistics Canada updates the CPI basket to reflect broad changes in consumer spending habits and to acknowledge changes in products and services.

HOT Links

For historical and current information on the CPI, visit Statistics Canada's website at (**www.statcan.ca**).

The CPI sets prices in a base period at 100, currently using the base period of 2002. Current prices are then expressed as a percentage of prices in the base period. A rise in the CPI means prices are increasing. For example, the CPI in January 2008 was measured at 111.8, meaning that the same basket of goods that cost $100.00 in 2002 cost $111.80 in January 2008.

producer price index (PPI)
An index of the prices paid by producers and wholesalers for various commodities such as raw materials, partially finished goods, and finished products.

Changes in wholesale prices are another important indicator of inflation. The **producer price index (PPI)** measures the prices paid by producers and wholesalers for such commodities as raw materials, partially finished goods, and finished products. The PPI is actually a family of indexes for many different product categories. Examples of PPI indexes are raw materials and industrial products. Because the PPI measures prices paid by producers for raw materials, energy, and other commodities, it might foreshadow subsequent price changes for businesses and consumers.

The Impact of Inflation

Inflation has several negative effects on people and businesses. For one thing, it penalizes people who live on fixed incomes. Let's say that a couple receives $1,000 a month retirement income beginning in 2010. If inflation is 10 percent in 2011, then the couple can buy only about 90 percent of what they could purchase in 2010. Similarly, inflation hurts savers. As prices rise, the real value, or purchasing power, of savings deteriorates.

---

concept check

What are the four classifications of unemployment?

Why is full employment usually defined as a target percentage below 100 percent?

What is the difference between demand-pull and cost-push inflation?

How is inflation measured?

Achieving Macroeconomic Goals

HOT Links

For more information on the Bank of Canada and its importance, see (www.bankofcanada.ca).

Bank of Canada
Canada's central bank, which has as its objective to "promote the economic and financial well-being of Canada."

monetary policy
The measures taken by the Bank of Canada to regulate the amount of money in circulation in order to influence the economy.

To reach macroeconomic goals, countries must often choose among conflicting alternatives. Sometimes political needs override economic ones. For example, bringing inflation under control might call for a politically difficult period of high unemployment and low growth. Or, in an election year, politicians might resist raising taxes to curb inflation. Still, the federal government and the **Bank of Canada** must try to guide the economy to a sound balance of growth, employment, and price stability. The two main tools used are the fiscal policy and monetary policy. By having a separation of fiscal and monetary policymakers (i.e., the federal government and the Bank of Canada, respectively), Canada has separated the power to spend money (i.e., fiscal policy) from the power to create money (i.e., monetary policy).

Monetary Policy

Contractionary policy
Expansionary policy

Monetary policy refers to the Bank of Canada's programs for controlling the amount of money circulating in the economy and controlling interest rates. Changes in the money supply affect both the level of economic activity and the rate of inflation. According to the Bank of Canada Act of 1934, the Bank of Canada is the central

contractionary policy
The use of monetary policy by the Bank of Canada to tighten the money supply by selling government securities or raising interest rates.

expansionary policy
The use of monetary policy by the Bank of Canada to increase the growth of the money supply.

fiscal policy
The government's use of taxation and spending to affect the economy.

federal budget deficit
The condition that occurs when the federal government spends more for programs than it collects in taxes.

national debt
The accumulated total of all of the federal government's annual budget deficits.

HOT Links

Want to know the current budget deficit and national debt? Head to (www.fin.gc.ca).

crowding out
The situation that occurs when government spending replaces spending by the private sector.

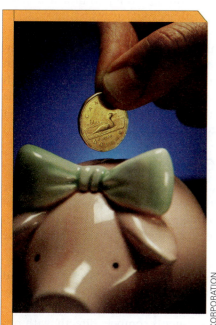

CONCEPT *in Action* >>>

The interest rate set by the Bank of Canada is passed on to consumers and businesses by the banking system. What is the current overnight rate and how has it changed over the last few years?

© 2009 JUPITER IMAGES CORPORATION

banking system that prints money and controls how much of it will be in circulation to "promote the economic and financial well-being of Canada."

As the Bank of Canada increases or decreases the amount of money in circulation, these decisions affect interest rates (the cost of borrowing money and the reward for lending it). The Bank of Canada can change the interest rate on money it lends to banks, signalling to the banking system and financial markets that it has changed its monetary policy. Banks, in turn, may pass along this change to consumers and businesses that receive loans from the banks. If the cost of borrowing increases, the economy slows because interest rates affect consumer and business decisions to spend or invest. The housing industry, business, and investments react the most strongly to changes in interest rates.

As you can see, the Bank of Canada can use monetary policy to contract or expand the economy. With **contractionary policy,** the Bank of Canada restricts, or tightens, the money supply by selling government securities or raising interest rates. The result is slower economic growth and higher unemployment. Thus, contractionary policy reduces spending and, ultimately, lowers inflation. With **expansionary policy,** the Bank of Canada increases, or loosens, growth in the money supply. An expansionary policy stimulates the economy. Interest rates decline, so business and consumer spending go up. Unemployment rates drop as businesses expand. But increasing the money supply also has a negative side: More spending pushes prices up, increasing the inflation rate.

Fiscal Policy *< Spending < Taxation*

The other economic tool used by the government is **fiscal policy,** its program of taxation and spending. By increasing government spending or by cutting taxes, the government can stimulate the economy. Look again at Exhibit 1.2 on page 17. The more government buys from businesses, the greater business revenues and output are. Likewise, if consumers or businesses have to pay less in taxes, they will have more income to spend for goods and services. Tax policies in Canada therefore affect business decisions. High corporate taxes can make it harder for Canadian firms to compete with companies in countries with lower taxes. As a result, companies may choose to locate facilities in other countries to reduce their tax burden.

If the government spends more for programs (social services, education, etc.) than it collects in taxes, the result is a **federal budget deficit**. To balance the budget, the government can cut its spending, increase taxes, or do some combination of the two. When it cannot balance the budget, the government must make up any shortfalls by borrowing (just like any business or household). The accumulated total of all of the federal government's annual budget deficits is known as the **national debt**.

Although fiscal policy has a major impact on businesses and consumers, continual increases in government spending raise another important issue. When government takes more money from businesses and consumers (the private sector) and uses these funds for increased government spending (the public sector), a phenomenon known as **crowding out** occurs. Here are three examples of crowding out:

1. The government spends more on public libraries, and individuals buy fewer books at bookstores.
2. The government spends more on public education, and individuals spend less on private education.
3. The government spends more on public transportation, and individuals spend less on private transportation.

In other words, government spending is crowding out private spending.

bonds
Securities that represent long-term debt obligations (liabilities) issued by corporations and governments

Crowding out Private Investment   Of concern is the effect of the national debt on private investment. If, to sell its **bonds**, the government raises the interest rate on the bonds it offers, it forces private businesses, which must stay competitive as suppliers of bonds in the bond market, to raise the rates they offer on their corporate bonds (long-term debt obligations issued by a company). In other words, financing government spending by government debt makes it more costly for private industry to finance its own investment. As a result, government debt can end up crowding out private investment and slowing economic growth in the private sector.

Another concern is that there is limited supply of investment capital. If the government borrows heavily, there is less for private investment and, therefore, private growth.

Impact of 2008 Economic Crisis

The economic crisis that started in 2008 changed the way that businesses and governments thought about the economy; the first critical recession in Canada since 1990. In many countries the financial institutions were bailed out by governments, taken over by governments, or simply closed their doors. In Canada, we were not immune to the crisis but were less affected than many countries in part due to our strong financial regulations. Yet our governments were forced to respond with sometimes unfavourable decisions. Some of these decisions are discussed below.

Steady Growth   In response to business and consumers opting to reserve spending due to the uncertainty in the economy, the government increased spending for capital infrastructure projects and other initiatives. For example, the government introduced home renovation credits to encourage people to spend money to upgrade or make their homes more energy efficient.

Full Employment   The manufacturing industries, especially those that rely on exports, were greatly affected by the economic crisis, as were commodities and tourism. The government responded by lending money to industries and encouraging upgrades to existing capital assets.

Steady Prices   The Bank of Canada responded to the financial crisis by reducing the overnight rate to record lows. In March 2008 the overnight rate was set at 3.50% and by March 2009, the overnight rate was set at 0.50%. The Bank of Canada used monetary policy with hopes of returning the consumer price index to its 2% target.

Governments' Other Roles in the Economy

We have mentioned that the government uses its fiscal policy to determine public spending and taxation, but it has other roles within our economy. The three levels of governments (federal, provincial, and local) use their many roles to influence businesses and the Canadian economy. Briefly, some of the more important roles are the following:

- *Customer.* Governments purchase thousands of products and services to carry out their functions. Some businesses (e.g., road construction companies) rely on governments for most, if not all, of their revenues.
- *Competitor.* Through Crown corporations, governments compete directly with private companies.
- *Provider of incentives.* Governments use many programs to stimulate economic growth, development, and employment.
- *Provider of essential services.* Governments have traditionally supplied and continue to supply services that private enterprises do not. The armed forces and Statistics Canada are two examples.

- *Regulator.* Governments are responsible for the safety and well-being of the citizens of Canada. This includes the protection of consumers (e.g., consumer rights, as discussed in Chapter 3), protecting businesses and competition (e.g., tariffs and quotas), protection of social goals (e.g., Canadian content laws), environmental protection (e.g., the Fisheries Act and antipollution laws), and so on.
- *Taxation agent.* Taxes are necessary for governments to employ people to provide goods and services. Taxes are the responsibility not only of individuals but also of businesses.

Microeconomics: Zeroing in on Businesses and Consumers

Now let's shift our focus from the whole economy to *microeconomics*, the study of households, businesses, and industries. This field of economics is concerned with how prices and quantities of goods and services behave in a free market. It stands to reason that people, firms, and governments try to get the most from their limited resources. Consumers want to buy the best quality at the lowest price. Businesses want to keep costs down and revenues high to earn larger profits. Governments also want to use their revenues to provide the most effective public goods and services possible. These groups choose among alternatives by focusing on the prices of goods and services.

As consumers in a free market, we influence what is produced. If Vietnamese food is popular, the high demand attracts entrepreneurs who open more Vietnamese restaurants. They want to compete for our dollars by supplying Vietnamese food at a lower price, of better quality, or with different menu choices. This section explains how business and consumer choices influence the price and availability of goods and services.

The Nature of Demand

demand
The quantity of a good or service that people are willing to buy at various prices.

demand curve
A graph showing the quantity of a good or service that people are willing to buy at various prices.

supply
The quantity of a good or service that businesses will make available at various prices.

supply curve
A graph showing the quantity of a good or service that a business will make available at various prices.

Demand is the quantity of a good or service that people are willing to buy at various prices. The higher the price, the lower the quantity demanded, and vice versa. A graph of this relationship is called a **demand curve.**

Let's assume you own a store that sells jackets for snowboarders. From experience, you know how many jackets you can sell at different prices. The demand curve in Exhibit 1.3 depicts this information. The x-axis (horizontal axis) shows the quantity of jackets, and the y-axis (vertical axis) shows the related price of those jackets. For example, at a price of $100, customers will buy (demand) 600 jackets.

In the graph, the demand curve slopes downward and to the right. This means that as the price falls, people will want to buy more jackets. Some people who were not going to buy a jacket will purchase one at the lower price. Also, some snowboarders who already have a jacket will buy a second one. The graph also shows that if you put a large number of jackets on the market, you will have to reduce the price to sell all of them.

Understanding demand is critical to businesses. This is because demand tells you how much you can sell and at what price—in other words, how much money the firm will take in that can be used to cover costs and hopefully earn a profit. Predicting demand is often difficult even for the very largest corporations but is particularly challenging for small firms.

The Nature of Supply

Demand alone is not enough to explain how the market sets prices. We must also look at **supply**, the quantity of a good or service that businesses will make available at various prices. The higher the price, the greater the amount a jacket manufacturer is willing to supply, and vice versa. A graph of the relationship between various prices and the quantities a manufacturer will supply is a **supply curve.**

EXHIBIT 1.3 > Demand Curve for Jackets for Snowboarders

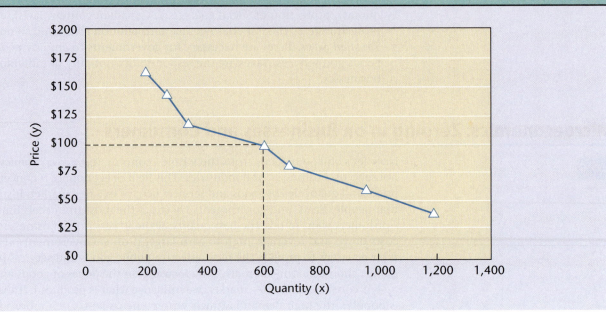

We can again plot the quantity of jackets on the x-axis and the price on the y-axis. As Exhibit 1.4 shows, 800 jackets will be available at a price of $100. Note that the supply curve slopes upward and to the right, the opposite of the demand curve. If snowboarders are willing to pay higher prices, manufacturers of jackets will buy more inputs (Gore-Tex, dye, machinery, labour, etc.) and produce more jackets. The quantity supplied will be greater at higher prices, because producers can earn higher profits.

EXHIBIT 1.4 > Supply Curve for Jackets for Snowboarders

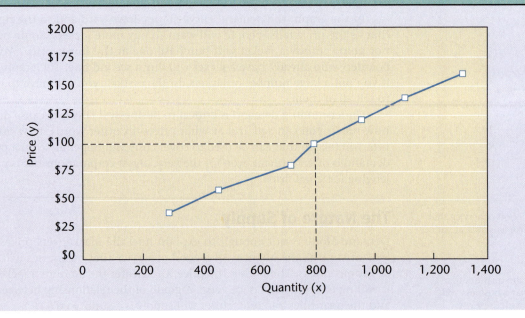

How Demand and Supply Interact to Determine Prices

In a stable economy, the number of jackets that snowboarders demand depends on the jackets' price. Likewise, the number of jackets that suppliers provide depends on price. But at what price will consumer demand for jackets match the quantity suppliers will produce?

To answer this question, we need to look at what happens when demand and supply interact. By plotting both the demand curve and the supply curve on the same graph (Exhibit 1.5), we see that they cross at a certain quantity and price. At that point, labelled E, the quantity demanded equals the quantity supplied. This is the point of **equilibrium**. The equilibrium price is $80; the equilibrium quantity is 700 jackets. At that point there is a balance between the amount consumers will buy and the amount the manufacturers will supply.

Market equilibrium is achieved through a series of quantity and price adjustments that occur automatically. If the price increases to $160, suppliers produce more jackets than consumers are willing to buy, and a surplus results. To sell more jackets, prices will have to fall. Thus, a surplus pushes prices downward until equilibrium is reached. When the price falls to $60, the quantity of jackets demanded rises above the available supply. The resulting shortage forces prices upward until equilibrium is reached at $80.

The number of snowboarder jackets produced and bought at $80 will tend to rest at equilibrium unless there is a shift in either demand or supply. If demand increases, more jackets will be purchased at every price, and the demand curve shifts to the right (as illustrated by line D₂ in Exhibit 1.6). If demand decreases, fewer will be bought at every price, and the demand curve shifts to the left (D₁). If demand decreased, snowboarders bought 500 jackets at $80 instead of 700 jackets. When demand increased, they purchased 800.

equilibrium
The point at which quantity demanded equals quantity supplied.

EXHIBIT 1.5 > Equilibrium Price and Quantity

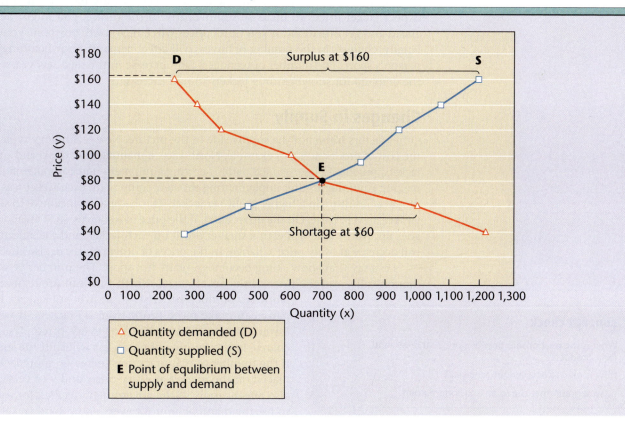

CHAPTER 1 Understanding Evolving Economic Systems and Competition **27**

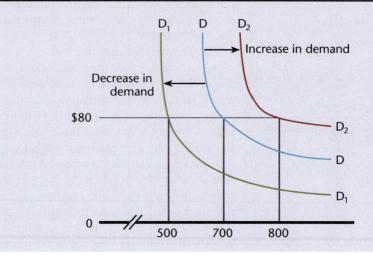

EXHIBIT 1.6 > Shifts in Demand

Changes in Demand

A number of things can increase or decrease demand. For example, if snowboarders' incomes go up, they might decide to buy a second jacket. If incomes fall, a snowboarder who was planning to purchase a jacket might wear an old one instead. Changes in fashion or tastes can also influence demand. If snowboarding were suddenly to go out of fashion, demand for jackets would decrease quickly. A change in the price of related products can also influence demand. For example, if the average price of a snowboard rises to $1,500, some people will quit snowboarding, and jacket demand will fall.

Another factor that can shift demand is expectations about future prices. If you expect jacket prices to increase significantly in the future, you might decide to go ahead and get one today. If you think prices will fall, you will postpone your purchase. Finally, changes in the number of buyers will affect demand. Snowboarding is a young person's sport. The number of teenagers will increase in the next few years. Therefore, the demand for snowboarding jackets should increase.

Changes in Supply

Other factors influence the supply side of the picture. New technology typically lowers the cost of production. For example, North Face, a manufacturer of ski and snowboarder jackets, purchased laser-guided pattern-cutting equipment and computer-aided pattern-making equipment. After implementing the new equipment, each jacket was cheaper to produce, resulting in a higher profit per jacket. This became an incentive to supply more jackets at every price. On the other hand, if the price of resources, such as labour or fabric, goes up, North Face will earn a smaller profit on each jacket, and the amount supplied will decrease at every price. Changes in the prices of other goods can also affect supply.

Let's say that snow skiing becomes a really hot sport. The number of skiers jumps dramatically, and the price of ski jackets soars. North Face can use its machines and fabrics to produce either ski or snowboard jackets. If the company can make more profit from ski jackets, it will produce fewer snowboarding jackets at every price. Also, simply a change in the number of producers will shift the supply curve. If the number of manufacturers increases, more jackets will be placed on the market at every price, and vice versa. Taxes can also affect supply. If the government decides, for some reason, to tax the manufacturer for every snowboard jacket produced,

concept check

What is the relationship between prices and demand for a product?

How is market equilibrium achieved?

Draw a graph that shows an equilibrium point.

EXHIBIT 1.7 > Factors that Cause Demand and Supply Curves to Shift

Shift Demand

Factor	To the Right If:	To the Left If:
Buyers' incomes	increase	decrease
Buyers' preferences/tastes	increase	decrease
Prices of substitute products	increase	decrease
Expectations about future prices	will rise	will fall
Number of buyers	increases	decreases

Shift Supply

Technology	lowers cost	increases cost
Resource prices	fall	increase
Changes in prices of other products that can be produced with the same resources	profit of other product falls	profit of other product increases
Number of suppliers	increases	decreases
Taxes	lowered	increased

then profits will fall and fewer jackets will be offered at every price. Exhibit 1.7 summarizes the factors that can shift demand and supply curves.

Competing in a Free Market

market structure
The number of suppliers in a market.

One of the characteristics of a free-market system is that suppliers have the right to compete with one another. The number of suppliers in a market is called **market structure**. Economists identify four types of market structures: (a) perfect competition, (b) monopolistic competition, (c) oligopoly, and (d) pure monopoly. Exhibit 1.8 illustrates the four types of market structures and Exhibit 1.9 summarizes the primary types of market structures.

Perfect Competition

perfect (pure) competition
A market structure in which a large number of small firms sell similar products, buyers and sellers have good information, and businesses can be easily opened or closed.

Characteristics of **perfect (pure) competition** include:

- a large number of small firms are in the market;
- the firms sell similar products—that is, each firm's product is very much like the products sold by other firms in the market;
- buyers and sellers in the market have good information about prices, sources of supply, and so on; and
- it is easy to open a new business or close an existing one.

In a perfectly competitive market, firms sell their products at prices determined solely by forces beyond their control. Because the products are very similar, and because each firm contributes only a small amount to the total quantity supplied by the industry, price is determined by supply and demand. A firm that raised its price even a little above the going rate would lose customers.

Monopolistic Competition

monopolistic competition
A market structure in which many firms offer products that are close substitutes and in which entry is relatively easy.

Three characteristics define the market structure known as **monopolistic competition**:

- Many firms are in the market
- The firms offer products that are close substitutes but still differ from one another
- It is relatively easy to enter the market

EXHIBIT 1.8 > Types of Market Structures

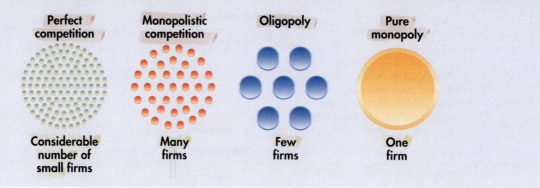

Under monopolistic competition, firms take advantage of product differentiation. Industries in which monopolistic competition occurs include clothing, food, and similar consumer products. Firms under monopolistic competition have more control over pricing than do firms under perfect competition because consumers do not view the products as exactly the same. Nevertheless, firms must demonstrate those product differences to justify their prices to customers. Consequently, companies use advertising to distinguish their products from others. Such distinctions may be significant or superficial. For example, Nike says, "Just Do It", and Tylenol is advertised as being easier on the stomach than aspirin.

Oligopoly

oligopoly
A market structure in which a few firms produce most or all of the output and in which large capital requirements or other factors limit the number of firms.

An **oligopoly** has two characteristics:

- A few firms produce most or all of the output
- Large capital requirements or other factors limit the number of firms

Boeing and Lockheed Martin (aircraft manufacturers), Bombardier Inc. and U.S. Steel Canada (Canada's largest and most diversified Canadian steel producer, previously Stelco Inc.) are major firms in different oligopoly industries.

EXHIBIT 1.9 > Primary Types of Market Structures

Characteristics	Perfect Competition	Pure Monopoly	Monopolistic Competition	Oligopoly
Number of firms in market	Many	One	Many, but fewer than perfect competition	Few
Firm's ability to control price	None	High	Some	Some
Barriers to entry	None	Subject to government regulation	Few	Many
Product differentiation	Very little	No products that compete directly	Emphasis on showing perceived differences in products	Some differences
Examples such as wheat and corn	Farm products gas, water, cable television	Utilities such as clothing stores	Retail specialty automobiles, airlines, aircraft manufacturers	Steel

© PHOTO BY LINDA CRAIG

With so few firms in an oligopoly, what one firm does has an impact on the others. Thus, the firms in an oligopoly watch one another closely for new technologies, product changes and innovations, promotional campaigns, pricing, production, and other developments. Sometimes they go as far as coordinating their pricing and output decisions, which is illegal. Many antitrust cases—legal challenges arising out of laws designed to control anticompetitive behaviour—occur in oligopolies.

Making Ethical Choices

PURCHASING POWER

As a child, you treasured your weekly allowance and delighted in scouting out the best deals. You ended up with more toys than your friends while spending the same amount of money. Your keen sense of the price of goods and ability to buy more quality products for the same money made your college friends envious. Finally, they convinced you to take their money to purchase needed items. You were a natural purchasing agent.

You understood the relationship between supply and demand and the price you were willing to pay for goods. Shortly after graduating, you accepted a position as chief purchasing agent for a public health facility (i.e., hospital).

In the hospital, you became concerned that prices paid for pharmaceutical goods seemed out of alignment with the laws of supply and demand. No more best deals. Perhaps even "a crisis with regard to the cost of prescription drugs." Two pharmaceutical companies seemed to be inflating their drug prices. Your sense about overcharging proved correct. The provincial government filed a lawsuit against the companies, accusing them of offering

drugs to pharmacists at deeply discounted prices as a way of selling more. Part of the issue involved the government's wholesale price system. Could the government be impeding your purchasing power at the hospital? The companies' pricing policies seem to involve inflating the price reported to the government and then offering the pharmacists an opportunity to make money on the difference between the higher reimbursements and promised lower prices from the companies.

All of this is troubling because you haven't been able to identify manufacturers of equivalent drugs at competitive prices.

ETHICAL DILEMMA Would you purchase drugs that were not exactly the same to save the hospital money?

SOURCES: Christopher Bowe, "NY Attorney General Targets Drugmakers", *FT.com*, February 23, 2003, (www.FT.com); and Hollister H. Hovey, "New York State Sues Pharmacia, Glaxo, Alleging Pricing Scheme", *Wall Street Journal*, February 14, 2003. Note: This case has been amended from its earlier publication.

Pure Monopoly

pure monopoly
A market structure in which a single firm accounts for all industry sales and in which there are barriers to entry.

barriers to entry
Factors, such as technological or legal conditions, which prevent new firms from competing equally with a monopoly.

At the other end of the spectrum is **pure monopoly,** the market structure in which a single firm accounts for all industry sales. The firm is the industry. This structure is characterized by **barriers to entry**—factors that prevent new firms from competing equally with the existing firm. Often the barriers are technological or legal conditions. Polaroid, for example, has held major patents on instant photography for years. When Kodak tried to market its own instant camera, Polaroid sued, claiming patent violations. Polaroid collected millions of dollars from Kodak. Another barrier might be one firm's control of a natural resource. De Beers Group, for example, controls most of the world's supply of uncut diamonds.

Public utilities such as natural gas and water are pure monopolies (although many public utilities are being privatized, and competition is being encouraged). Some monopolies have been created by government regulations that prohibit competition. Canada Post Corporation's direct mail service is one such monopoly.

> **concept check**
>
> What is meant by market structure?
>
> Describe the four types of market structure.

Trends in Economics and Competition

LO 8

Trends in business occur at several levels. Never before have the economies of the world been more connected— a "domino effect" is being felt around the world as we experience economic changes. Three of the major trends are meeting competitive challenges, creating a competitive workforce, and increasing entrepreneurship world-wide.

Meeting Competitive Challenges

relationship management
The practice of building, maintaining, and enhancing interactions with customers and other parties to develop long-term satisfaction through mutually beneficial partnerships.

Companies are turning to many different strategies to remain competitive in the global marketplace. One of the most important is **relationship management,** which involves building, maintaining, and enhancing interactions with customers and other parties to develop long-term satisfaction through mutually beneficial partnerships. Relationship management includes both supply chain management, which builds strong bonds with suppliers, and relationship marketing, which focuses on customers. (We'll discuss supply chain management in greater detail in Chapter 11 and return to relationship marketing in Chapter 12.) In general, the longer a customer stays with a company, the more that customer is worth. Long-term customers buy more, take less

CONCEPT in Action >>>
Tim Hortons strives to build strong customer relationships and retain loyal customers with the Quickpay TimCard. How do loyalty cards build customer relations?

Sustainable Business, Sustainable World

The term sustainable development was coined in 1972 at the United Nations Conference on Human Development. It was popularized through *Our Common Future* (1987), the report of the UN *World Commission on Environment and Development*, also known as the Brundtland Commission. One feature of the Brundtland Commission was its challenge that business become part of the solution rather than part of the problem. Since then, sustainable development has been commonly understood as 'development that meets the needs of the present without compromising the ability of future generations to meet their needs.' Linking social and environmental variables within economic agendas is a hallmark of sustainable development. Sustainable development provides a framework to describe the "bigger picture" within which human activities occur, the intention of which is to preserve or enhance the systems—ecological, socioeconomic and cultural—upon which humans and other species depend.[3] This bigger picture is the business environment of the 21st century.

Humans have had an increasing impact on the planet. Along with various forms of pollution and toxic waste, climate change and loss of habitat, humans are responsible for the greatest rate of species extinction the planet has seen since the demise of the dinosaurs in the Mesozoic era 65 million years ago. As a single species, humans have already exceeded the ecological capacity of the biosphere. The wealthiest 20 percent of the world's human population uses 80 percent of the resources. The wealthiest 25 percent of the world gets 75 percent of the income, even after adjustment for the parity of purchasing power.[4] Thus, along with addressing our collective and individual impacts on the biosphere—which has led, amongst other things, to the dwindling of natural resources—sustainable development must also address issues of equity in the sharing of those resources.

The business environment of the 21st century is socially complex, ecologically uncertain and ethically challenging. From a business ethics point of view, sustainable development provides an opportunity to achieve the greatest good or least harm to the Earth's human and non-human inhabitants. Does business have a *moral obligation* to see that its practices are socially just and ecologically sustainable? Markets operate within certain constraints. While business is free to pursue profits, there is a *moral minimum* within which business operates and companies have the *responsibility* to operate within these limits. Traditional models of social responsibility include legal and moral constraints; the sustainable development approach also includes ecological constraints.[5]

Corporate responsibility can be seen to encompass a set of tools for achieving goals and assessing the performance of organizations and individuals within the larger context of the sustainable development business environment. This might include ecological, social, financial, governance, even cross-cultural performance. Corporate leaders in the 21st century innovate strategic capabilities for competitive advantage through sustained, responsible performance in all these areas.

Source: David Lertzman, Ph.D. The University of Calgary, March 2009.

---

of a company's time, are less sensitive to price, and bring in new customers. Best of all, they require no acquisition or start-up costs. Good long-standing customers are worth so much that in some industries, reducing customer defections by as little as five points—from, say, 15 percent to 10 percent per year—can double profits.

Another important way companies stay competitive is through **strategic alliances** (also called strategic partnerships). The trend toward forming these cooperative agreements between business firms is accelerating rapidly, particularly among high-tech firms. These companies have realized that strategic partnerships are more than just important—they are critical. Strategic alliances can take many forms. Some companies enter into strategic alliances with their suppliers, who take over much of their actual production and manufacturing. Nike, the largest producer of athletic footwear in the world, does not manufacture a single shoe. Gallo, the largest wine company on earth, does not grow a single grape.

Others with complementary strengths team up. For example, computer manufacturer Hewlett-Packard (H-P) and retail giant Wal-Mart partnered to improve sales at both. H-P provided Wal-Mart with low-cost electronic products. The two companies worked together to develop special products for Wal-Mart, such as desktop and notebook computers for about $400, digital cameras for $100, and all-in-one printers for $50. H-P was eager to satisfy Wal-Mart, one of its biggest retail partners. For Wal-Mart, H-P's products would lure customers who might otherwise shop for electronics at Best Buy and Circuit City into Wal-Mart where they could spend more of their holiday gift dollars.[6]

Companies in the same industry often form alliances. Smaller companies with unique products or technology may partner with larger companies who can provide wider distribution in exchange for access to the technology. Even rivals find strategic alliances advantageous. South Korean electronics manufacturer Samsung competes with Sony and a few other companies for the top spot in global television sales. Yet since 2003, the two companies have worked together on producing television display panels. Sony, in search of a supplier for its new line of flat-panel televisions, arranged to become a partner in Samsung's new liquid crystal display factory. The result has benefited both companies in many ways. Their engineers now cooperate on panel technologies, leading to speedier improvement cycles. With Samsung's approval,

strategic alliance
A cooperative agreement between business firms; sometimes called a *strategic partnership*.

Sony introduced some of Samsung's LCD technologies before Samsung did—and sold significantly more models equipped with the new technology than Samsung. Why would Samsung want to continue working with Sony? Whereas Samsung had the edge in developing LCD technologies, Sony excelled at applying technology to consumer products, especially televisions. Teaming up with and at the same time competing with Sony has pushed Samsung to new technological breakthroughs and better product design. "If we learn from Sony, it will help us in advancing our technology," says Jang Insik, a Samsung engineer. Other Asian electronics manufacturers are pooling resources to their mutual benefit, despite struggles to overcome concerns about helping rivals and working with companies in other countries.[7]

Creating a Competitive Workforce

Creating and building long-term relationships require a world-class workforce. The goal of leading companies such as McCain Foods Limited and Mark's Work Wearhouse is for all workers to add value to every job they do, every day. Such firms place a strong emphasis on training and the use of technology to improve worker productivity. Mark's Work Wearhouse, for example, values investment in the training of its workers and enjoys significant savings as a result (see Chapter 4).

Entrepreneurship Spreads Worldwide

A key trend in macroeconomics and competition is the rising entrepreneurial spirit in former command economies and other developing nations such as India. As Russia and China have shifted away from centralized economic controls towards greater competitive freedom, many people have embraced the opportunity to start businesses that meet the needs of local consumers.

China itself has been called "the world's largest start-up" as it goes through many of the same eras in the history of business that Canada experienced—but in a greatly compressed time frame. The development of modern business occurred over about 150 years in Canada; China is attempting to accomplish the same thing in about 25 years. A key element in China's economic transformation is setting free the as-yet-untapped entrepreneurial power of its citizens. The Chinese government recognizes the potential of this huge untapped resource and its role in creating new products and a world-class economy that will rival others in the world.[8]

> **concept check**
>
> How do businesses provide customer value?
>
> How does relationship management make a business more competitive?
>
> Explain the entrepreneurial movement in former command economies.

Great Ideas to Use Now

As you study micro- and macroeconomics, remember that economics is not something you should learn for an exam and then forget. Economics is an analytical science that will help you understand the world around you. It can help you be more imaginative and insightful in everyday life. You should now better understand why prices are going up or down, when interest rates will fall, and when and why the unemployment rate will fall.

Understanding these basic economic concepts can help you decide whether to change jobs (and how much money to ask for) and whether to buy a car now or wait until next year. When you hear that an automobile manufacture has 115 days of inventory, understanding supply and demand will tell you that now might be the time to buy that new car.

Similarly, economics will help you become a better informed citizen. Almost every political issue is, in some way, grounded in economic concepts. You should now know what it means to balance the budget and what problems occur with monopoly power. In short, economics can help you make more thoughtful and informed decisions.

Customer Satisfaction and Quality

We spoke earlier in this chapter about China's tremendous growth as a producer of goods and services for the world marketplace. The reason for that growth is that buyers are willingly purchasing the Chinese products because they deliver quality and value.

Customer value is the customer's perception of the ratio of benefits to the sacrifice necessary to obtain those benefits. Customers receive benefits in the form of functionality, performance, durability, design, ease of use, and serviceability. To receive those benefits, they give up money, time, and effort.

Customer value is not simply a matter of high quality. A high-quality product that is available only at a high price will not be perceived as a value. Nor will bare-bones service or low-quality goods selling for a low price. Instead, customers value goods and services of the quality they expect that are sold at prices they are willing to pay. Value marketing can be used to sell a $150,000 Rolls Royce as well as a $5 frozen chicken dinner.

Businesses provide customer value by

- *offering products that perform.* This is the bare minimum. Consumers have lost patience with shoddy merchandise;
- *giving consumers more than they expect.* Soon after Toyota launched Lexus, the company had to order a recall. The weekend before the recall, dealers personally phoned all the Lexus owners in North America and arranged to pick up their cars and provide replacement vehicles;
- *avoiding unrealistic pricing.* Consumers couldn't understand why Kellogg's cereals commanded a premium over other brands, so Kellogg's market share fell 5 percent; and
- *giving the buyer facts.* Today's sophisticated consumer wants informative advertising and knowledgeable salespeople.

Economics not only can help you understand what is happening in other countries but also can help raise your awareness of opportunities in those countries. As more and more countries have moved away from command economies, Canadian and foreign multinational firms are moving in to take advantage of ground-floor opportunities. Consider accepting a foreign assignment. It's a wonderful way to experience other cultures and, at the same time, get ahead in your career. More and more large organizations are requiring that their middle and upper level managers have foreign field experience. When you have an opportunity for a foreign assignment, don't let it slip by.

In today's business world, if a firm doesn't deliver customer value, it doesn't survive. Firms that provide customer value end up with satisfied customers. Some companies that are especially good at satisfying customers are Mercedes-Benz, H. J. Heinz, Lexus, Colgate-Palmolive, Mars, Maytag, Quaker Oats, Hershey Foods, Toyota, and Cadbury Schweppes. All of the companies have won either quality or customer satisfaction awards at one time or another.

Summary of Learning Outcomes

1 Understand the primary features of the world's economic systems.

An economic system is the combination of policies, laws, and choices made by a nation's government to establish the systems that determine what goods and services are produced and how they are allocated. The main economic systems in the world today include market economies (capitalism), command (planned) economies, socialism, and mixed economies.

2 Explain what economics is and how the three sectors of the economy are linked.

Economics is the study of how individuals, businesses, and governments use scarce resources to produce and distribute goods and services. The two major areas in economics are macroeconomics, the study of the economy as a whole, and microeconomics, the study of households and firms. The individual, business, and government sectors of the economy are linked by a series of two-way flows. The government provides public goods and services for the other two sectors and receives income in the form of taxes. Changes in one flow affect the other sectors.

3 **Show how economic growth, full employment, and price stability indicate a nation's economic health.**

A nation's economy is growing when the level of business activity, as measured by gross domestic product, is rising. GDP is the total value of all goods and services produced in a year. The goal of full employment is to have a job for all who can and want to work. How well a nation is meeting its employment goals is measured by the unemployment rate. There are four types of unemployment: frictional, structural, cyclical, and seasonal. With price stability, the overall prices of goods and services are not moving either up or down very much.

4 **Define inflation, and discuss how is it measured and what causes it.**

Inflation is the general upward movement of prices. When prices rise, purchasing power falls. The rate of inflation is measured by changes in the consumer price index (CPI) and the producer price index (PPI). There are two main causes of inflation. If the demand for goods and services exceeds the supply, prices will rise. This is called demand-pull inflation. With cost-push inflation, higher production costs, such as expenses for materials and wages, increase the final prices of goods and services.

5 **Describe how the Bank of Canada uses monetary policy, and how governments use fiscal policy to achieve their macroeconomics goals.**

Monetary policy refers to actions by the Bank of Canada to control the money supply. When the Bank of Canada restricts the money supply, interest rates rise, the inflation rate drops, and economic growth slows. By expanding the money supply, the Bank of Canada stimulates economic growth.

The government uses fiscal policy—changes in levels of taxation and spending—to control the economy. Reducing taxes or increasing spending stimulates the economy; raising taxes or decreasing spending does the opposite. When the government spends more than it receives in tax revenues, it must borrow to finance the deficit. Some economists favour deficit spending as a way of stimulating the economy; others worry about our high level of national debt.

6 **Discuss the basic microeconomic concepts of demand and supply, and how they establish prices.**

Demand is the quantity of a good or service that people will buy at a given price. Supply is the quantity of a good or service that firms will make available at a given price. When the price increases, the quantity demanded falls but the quantity supplied rises. A price decrease leads to increased demand but a lower supply. At the point where the quantity demanded equals the quantity supplied, demand and supply are in balance. This equilibrium point is achieved by market adjustments of quantity and price.

7 **Explain the four types of market structure.**

Market structure is the number of suppliers in a market. Perfect competition is characterized by a large number of buyers and sellers, very similar products, good market information for both buyers and sellers, and ease of entry into and exit from the market. In monopolistic competition, many firms sell close substitutes in a market that is fairly easy to enter. In an oligopoly, a few firms produce most or all of the industry's output. An oligopoly is also difficult to enter, and what one firm does will influence others. In a pure monopoly, there is a single seller in a market.

8 **List some of the trends that are reshaping micro- and macroeconomic environments.**

Three of the major trends are meeting competitive challenges, creating a competitive workforce, and increasing entrepreneurship world-wide. Companies are establishing long-term relationships with both customers and suppliers. To compete in today's environment, companies and industries must build a competitive workforce. At the macro level, budding entrepreneurial spirit is sparking wealth among individual business owners and fuelling the growth of market economies.

Key Terms

Bank of Canada 22
barriers to entry 32
bonds 24
business cycles 18
capital 13
circular flow 17
command economy 14
consumer price index (CPI) 21
contractionary policy 23
cost-push inflation 21
crowding out 23
customer value
cyclical unemployment 20
demand 25
demand curve 25
demand-pull inflation 21
economic growth 18
economic system 12
economics 9
entrepreneurs 13
equilibrium 27
expansionary policy 23
factors of production 12
federal budget deficit 23
fiscal policy 23
frictional unemployment 20
full employment 20
gross domestic product (GDP) 18

gross national product (GNP) 18
inflation 20
knowledge 13
labour 13
macroeconomics 16
market economy 13
market structure 29
microeconomics 16
mixed economies 15
monetary policy 22
monopolistic competition 29
monopoly
national debt 23
natural resources 13
oligopoly 30
perfect (pure) competition 29
producer price index (PPI) 21
purchasing power 21
pure monopoly 32
recession 18
relationship management 32
seasonal unemployment 20
socialism 14
strategic alliance 33
structural unemployment 20
supply 25
supply curve 25
unemployment rate 20

Experiential Exercises

1. Understand your tax commitment. Soon you will enter the permanent job market, if you are not there already. Typically, your earnings will rise over the next 35 years, but as your earnings increase, so will your taxes. The average Canadian works five to six months out of every year just to cover taxes. Are taxes too high in our country? As taxes will be a major part of your financial life for the next 35 to 45 years, you need to be informed. Visit the Web sites of a few organizations that advocate tax reform, such as the Canadian Taxpayers Federation at (**www .taxpayer.com**).

2. Learn a new language. Consider taking a job outside of Canada for a while. If you decide to work overseas, having basic skills in a second language will go a long way toward ensuring that you have a rewarding and pleasant experience. Learning a second language can also bring a lot of self-satisfaction. Go to (**www .learnalanguage.com**) and find out more about learning a foreign language.

3. Use the Internet or go to the library and determine the current trends in GDP growth, unemployment, and inflation. What do these trends tell you about the level of business activity and the business cycle? If you owned a personnel agency, how would this information affect your decision making?

4. As a manufacturer of in-line skates, you are questioning your pricing policies. You note that over the past five years, the CPI increased an average of 2 percent per year, but the price of a pair of skates increased an average of 8 percent per year for the first three years and 2 percent for the next two years. What does this information tell you about demand, supply, and other factors influencing the market for these skates?

5. Write a paper describing an occasion on which you received outstanding customer value and an occasion when you received very poor customer value.

6. Divide the class into four teams. One pair of teams will debate the pros and cons of airline deregulation. The other pair will debate electric-utility deregulation. One team should take the pro and the other the con for each issue. If you have Internet access, use the Dow Jones news service, ABI, or another database to obtain current articles on the subjects.

Review Questions

1. What are the factors of production? How do they work together to produce goods and services?

2. What are the four types of economies? How do they differ regarding the ownership and allocation of the factors of production?

3. Distinguish between macro- and microeconomics. What are the three main macro goals?

4. How do GDP and GNP differ?

5. What are the various types of unemployment?

6. What are monetary policy and fiscal policy? Who is responsible for each?

7. What are contractionary policy and expansionary policy?

8. What is relationship management? How can it be achieved?

9. What is a strategic alliance? What are its benefits to the companies involved?

10. Why is it important for companies to create a competitive workforce?

11. How can understanding economics help you as a consumer? As a business manager or owner?

CREATIVE THINKING CASE >

Inside Intel: It's about Copying—Exactly

Intel Corporation has more than 86,000 employees worldwide, but innovation depends on people like Trish Roughgarden, an Air Force veteran whose job is to copy slavishly. Ms. Roughgarden is known inside Intel as a "seed," an unofficial title for technicians who transfer manufacturing know-how from one Intel chip factory to another. Her job: to help ensure that Intel's latest plant works just like an identical plant in Hillsboro, Oregon. Several hundred other seeds will copy the same techniques to a third plant in Ireland.

It is all part of a major Intel strategy known as "Copy Exactly," which discourages experimentation at individual factories. Instead, engineers and technicians painstakingly clone proven Intel manufacturing techniques from one plant to the next—down to the colour of workers' gloves and wall paint, or other features that would seem to have no bearing on efficiency.

The strategy emerged after Intel's most recent disastrous slump, when maddening variations between factories in the early 1980s hurt productivity and product quality. Japanese competitors nearly drove Intel out of business. Today, Copy Exactly shapes Intel's response to the latest economic downturn, helping accelerate the relentless pace of technology improvements known as Moore's Law, after former Intel chairman Gordon Moore.

Intel's newest plant contains 200,000 square feet of new factory space, linked to an existing 300,000-square-foot facility to create what Intel believes is the world's largest semiconductor "clean room." One corridor stretches 900 feet, an avenue of white, ventilated flooring intersecting side streets called bays and chases. The price: more than $2 billion, roughly the same as the Oregon and Ireland additions.

Although it prohibits willy-nilly changes, the Copy Exactly methodology encourages Intel workers to come up with ideas to boost productivity or make chip features smaller. But the ideas must pass a committee called the Process Change Control Board, which requires workers to come up with tests to prove the value of their suggestions.

Intel's bureaucracy "creates frustration" for some engineers, concedes Youssef Aly El-Mansy, an Intel vice-president in charge of developing manufacturing processes. "We've lost some people from that."[9]

Critical Thinking Questions

- Explain the link between quality and "Copy Exactly."
- How important is technology to a global competitor like Intel? What about product quality?
- Most management consultants claim that employees are happiest when they have freedom to make decisions in the work environment. How does this fit with Copy Exactly? What can be done to let employees exercise their creativity?

SOURCE: Adapted from Don Clark, "In Setting Up Its New Plants, Chip Maker Clones Older Ones Down to the Paint on the Wall", Wall Street Journal (October 28, 2002), pp. B1, B4. Reprinted by permission of the Wall Street Journal, Copyright © 2002 Dow Jones & Company, Inc. All Rights Reserved Worldwide.

VIDEO CASE >

Black Forest Motors: A Triple Whammy that Works

Headquartered in Germany, Mercedes-Benz (**www.mercedes-benz.com**) manufactures luxury automobiles for distribution in Germany, the United States, and elsewhere. To increase sales and perceived customer value in the United States, Mercedes-Benz initiated the "Customer Value Triad," a corporate strategy comprising three key components: quality goods, quality service, and value-based pricing. Although quality goods and value-based pricing are generated by the manufacturer, the 329 independently owned U.S. dealerships and their 16,000 employees are the most important element when it comes to providing customers with quality service.

Black Forest Motors, a Mercedes-Benz dealership in North Acme, Michigan, is a prime example of Mercedes-Benz's corporate strategy in action. Black Forest prides itself on exceeding customers' expectations with fair pricing and quality goods and services. Dedicated employees, who have been with Black Forest Motors since its founding, translate directly into quality customer service, ensuring that the dealership is not only a great place to work but "a great place to buy a car." Enjoying the benefits of the Customer Value Triad initiative, Black Forest's customer base, their "family of owners," continues to grow.

The sales, service, and parts departments all powerfully demonstrate Black Forest's commitment to quality service, quality goods, and value-based pricing. The sales department's sole purpose is to exceed customer expectations, from test drive to vehicle delivery. Customers can schedule their test drive online through Black Forest's website, meet with a sales staff committed to providing the information they need to make an educated buying decision, and drive away in the Mercedes-Benz perfect for them.

The service department is a state-of-the-art facility featuring the latest diagnostic and repair equipment used by highly trained factory technicians. This department operates on the basis that "you and your vehicle deserve only the best of care." Quality goods and quality service are also emphasized in the parts department, which is stocked with a large inventory of the same high-quality parts used in manufacturing Mercedes-Benz vehicles.

Committed to the Customer Value Triad of quality goods, quality service, and value-based pricing, Black Forest Motors asks only one thing of its clients: "If you were treated well, your expectations met, and the service good, please tell your friends."

SOURCE: (**www.mercedes-benz.com**) (accessed December 2008).

Critical Thinking Questions

1. Do you think the Mercedes-Benz Customer Value Triad is an effective corporate strategy?

2. How might a strategy based on the Customer Value Triad help Mercedes-Benz and its dealerships compete effectively in the North American marketplace?

3. Why are product and service quality important elements of operating a successful business? What is the impact on the price of cars?

4. Does Mercedes-Benz operate in an oligopolistic marketplace?

SOURCE: (**www.mercedes-benz.com**) (accessed December 2008).

E-COMMERCE CASE >

Travels with Orbitz

In 2000, five major airlines—American, United, Continental, Delta, and Northwest—announced plans to launch a new online travel site called Orbitz. (**www.orbitz.com**). Like online travel pioneer sites Travelocity and Expedia, Orbitz would let consumers search for the best airfares. Other airlines quickly agreed to post their fares on the Orbitz site, including Air Canada. Each participating airline had to agree to publish its lowest fares on the Orbitz site. The airlines, however, weren't prevented from offering the same low fares elsewhere on the Internet. One airline that decided not to join Orbitz was Southwest. The company explained that it didn't feel comfortable providing information on its fares to a company run by its top competitors, and consequently filed a lawsuit against Orbitz in May, 2001.

Even before Orbitz officially opened, controversy arose. The Interactive Travel Services Association (ITSA), a trade association of online travel sites whose membership includes both Travelocity and Expedia, said the airline industry was jealous of the profits being made by online travel sites and that Orbitz was an organized effort by the airlines to "cash in" on those profits by wiping out competitive travel-booking sites. Orbitz would give airlines an unfair advantage, said the ITSA, by encouraging price fixing between airlines.

After an initial investigation, the U.S. Department of Transportation agreed that Orbitz could provide the potential for unfair competition, but it didn't stop the company's launch. Instead, it agreed to review the case again after Orbitz was in operation for six months. At that point, the Department of Transportation said it hadn't found any unfair trade practices in the Orbitz operation, nor did it see any negative effect on competition or consumer choice. At the ITSA's urging, Orbitz has come under federal scrutiny several times since then, but the government has not found Orbitz in violation of any anticompetition laws.

Antonella Pianalto, ITSA executive director, was unconvinced. "The evidence is clear: Orbitz is harming competition. Prior to Orbitz, both consumers and airlines benefited from independent distributors who fiercely negotiated for the best available fares and placed downward pressure on those fares by forcing the airlines to compete.

Now airlines have little incentive to compete because they don't have to use other online sites."

Nonsense, countered Orbitz former CEO Jeff Katz. "The online travel marketplace was already dominated by a 'Big Two'—Travelocity and Expedia. Their complaints about us are a little like Coke and Pepsi teaming up to run Dr Pepper out of the market."

Although still third in size behind Travelocity and Expedia, Orbitz (now known as Orbitz WorldWide) is currently the fastest-growing online travel site, with revenues topping $1 billion a year. Online air ticket purchases continue to grow. Orbitz brands include: Cheaptickets.com, ebookers.com, hotelClub.com, RatestoGo.com and Away. com. However, the company has not yet turned a profit.

Critical Thinking Questions

1. Do you agree with the ITSA's position or that of Orbitz former CEO Jeff Katz about the effect Orbitz is having on competition and consumer choice? Defend your answer.

CHAPTER 2

Making the Connection

The Global Marketplace and Governments' Roles

In Chapter 1 we looked at economic systems and competition as one factor in the external environment of a business. In this chapter you will learn about global trade and the role of the government in promoting global trade as well as protecting domestic trade. This chapter deals directly with the interrelationship between the *political* environment (the government's role) and the *economic* environment (the global marketplace), two factors in our PEST model. As we saw in Chapter 1, and will see again in this chapter, these two factors are related to each other, and they impact the success of the business.

For example, the external environment presents opportunities and threats for a business. The business considers these opportunities and threats when determining its *strategy* for the future. In this chapter, we discuss Team Canada, a partnership between government and industry to promote global trade. Team Canada is an initiative of the political environment that presents opportunities for Canadian business to gain access to international markets. This opportunity is one that many businesses have capitalized on to develop and expand exposure for their products in global markets. Expanding their businesses globally is one strategy that these companies have chosen to meet their growth objectives. One environmental factor that has affected global trade negatively is the threat of terrorism. As discussed in the chapter, this factor will not stop globalization, but it will

likely slow its growth and make it costlier because of tighter controls.

We will also discuss free trade zones in this chapter. This is another way in which government helps to create opportunities for business to expand. How a business capitalizes on these political initiatives depends on its strategy, and so we will explore different strategies for expanding in the global marketplace: exporting, licensing, joint ventures, and so on.

Other political initiatives result in threats to business. Tariff and non-tariff barriers are obvious examples. In an attempt to protect domestic trade, governments set up obstacles for foreign competition by making foreign goods more expensive through tariffs or by restricting the import of foreign goods through quotas. These barriers are meant to create opportunities for domestic companies to grow within a protected domestic environment; however, they may very well stifle these companies instead, because they don't have to *innovate* (one of the critical success factors) and improve their operations to compete with this foreign competition.

These opportunities and threats exist in the economic environment as well. Companies need to have a global *vision* to recognize and react to international business opportunities, as well as to remain competitive at home. In relation to our model of a successful business, what this means is that the *vision* that is created for the company must take the global economic environment in which it operates into account to

survive and prosper. The environment affects the business. Opportunities exist in the global economic environment—that is certain. But even if a business decides not to pursue a strategy that involves selling in the global marketplace, it cannot ignore the fact that foreign firms can and will still compete in the domestic marketplace. This foreign competition presents a threat to a Canadian enterprise—one that, if ignored, can easily put it out of business.

This chapter also gives several examples of how the other aspects of the external environment affect or are affected by global trade. Technological factors, such as transportation improvements and the Internet, make physical distances less of a barrier to global trade than they used to be. Companies such as Purolator and UPS, for example, can take advantage of both these factors, as transportation improvements have greatly increased the speed and efficiency with which packages are shipped, and advanced computerized tracking software can communicate where packages are at any time. Other barriers still exist, however. Language and cultural differences, and a sense of nationalism, are natural barriers to trade with foreign countries. These differences are part of the *social* environment of these countries that must be considered in terms of the products that are sold and the way business is conducted.

All of these external environmental factors interact when a business enters the global marketplace. They affect the company's vision and its strategy for competing. They also affect the internal environment. The *marketing* department must consider the differing needs of customers in the different countries where the company sells product. The *operations* department must consider the logistics of operating in a global environment depending on the strategic option chosen—exporting to the country or investing in its own facilities in that country, for example. The *human resources* department must consider the skills needed of its employees to do business effectively in foreign countries, language being an obvious example. And the *finance* department must consider differences in exchange rates to maintain the company's profitability.

If a company considers its external environment carefully and develops a global vision for doing business, it can work toward achieving the critical success factors. It can *achieve financial performance* by *meeting the needs* of foreign *customers* with *products of value* to their unique tastes and circumstances. And whether its strategy is to expand into foreign markets or not, it will be forced to innovate to stay ahead of foreign competition. These critical factors of success are, of course, achieved through a *committed workforce*.

CHAPTER 2

The Global Marketplace and Governments' Roles

LEARNING OUTCOMES

1 Show why global trade is important to Canada, and how it is measured.

2 Explain why nations trade.

3 Describe some of the barriers to international trade.

4 Discuss how governments and institutions foster world trade.

5 List some of the international economic communities.

6 Explain how companies can enter the global marketplace.

7 Explain some of the threats and opportunities in the global marketplace.

8 Discuss some of the advantages of multinational corporations.

9 List some of the trends in the global marketplace.

PIZZA GOES GLOBAL

Domino's Pizza has more than 8,700 stores worldwide with stores in every province and territory in Canada as well as countries such as Spain, the Netherlands, Mexico and Australia. As executive vice-president of Domino's International division, Mike Lawton is in charge of every store outside of the United States. In 1983, Domino's opened its first international store in Winnipeg, Manitoba and by the time Lawton joined Domino's in 1999, there were over 1,500 stores beyond the U.S. borders. Today, the International Division oversees more than 3,600 stores in over 60 countries, almost half of all that Domino's operates. Given that Domino's delivers more than 400 million pizzas a year, that's a lot of dough he's responsible for![1]

Such an international scope might seem unusual for someone who has spent much of his life in a single American state: Lawton was born in Michigan, went to school at Michigan State University, and today lives in Ann Arbor, Michigan. However, he was never one to turn down an opportunity. A broad base of accounting and financial skills opened a chance early in his career to work on some international projects, and he took it. "Since the work interested me, I jumped into international business." And from there, he's never looked back. "My career goal has always been to hold interesting and challenging positions. I never focused on attaining a particular level or position in a company, but sought to broaden my experiences so I was prepared when opportunities arose." Along with a strong financial and business background, he has direct international experience in Europe, Latin America, and Asia—experience that he is able to bring to his work heading Domino's International division.

Luckily, too, he doesn't have to do it alone. As he readily admits, "When we look at what has created success in our markets, we have to credit the people who take the responsibility of running our stores with excellence very seriously."

The people Lawton refers to are the master franchisees (see Chapter 5) of Domino's international business. In this case, master franchisees are individuals or entities which, under a specific licensing agreement with Domino's, control all operations within the country. They operate their own stores, set up a distribution infrastructure to transport materials into and throughout the country, and create sub-franchisees. One particular benefit of master franchisees is their local knowledge. As discussed in this chapter, a major challenge when opening a business on foreign soil is negotiating the political, cultural, and economic differences of that country. According to Lawton, master franchisees allow Domino's, and the franchisee, to "take advantage of their local expertise in dealing with marketing, political, and regulatory issues, as well as the local labour markets." It takes local experience to know, for example, that only 30 percent of the people in Poland have phones, so carryout needs to be the focus of the business; or that Turkey has changed their street names three times in the past 30 years so delivery is much more challenging; or even that, in Japanese, there is no word for pepperoni, the most popular topping worldwide. These are just a few of the challenges that Domino's has had to overcome on the road to becoming the worldwide leader in the pizza delivery business. Under the leadership of people like Lawton and with the help of dedicated, local master franchisees, Domino's has been able to not only compete in but lead the global pizza delivery market.

PHOTO SOURCE: From Gitman/McDaniel, *The Future of Buisness*, 6E. © 2008 South-Western, a part of Cengage Learning Inc. Reproduced by permission. www.cengage.com/permissions

Critical Thinking Questions

1. **What are some factors that can make success difficult in the global marketplace?**

2. **What can governments do to protect domestic competitors from firms like Domino's?**

3. **What cultural differences should Domino's consider when entering markets other than those in North America?**

SOURCE: (www.hoovers.com/domino%27s/—ID_40131) accessed June 20, 2009.

---

global vision
The ability to recognize and react to international business opportunities, be aware of threats from foreign competition, and effectively use international distribution networks to obtain raw materials and move finished products to customers.

*Today, global revolutions are under way in many areas of our lives: management, politics, communications, and technology, to name a few. The word global has assumed a new meaning, referring to a boundless mobility and competition in social, business, and intellectual arenas. No longer just an option, having a global vision has become a business imperative. Having a **global vision** means recognizing and reacting to international business opportunities, being aware of threats from foreign competitors in all markets, and effectively using international distribution networks to obtain raw materials and move finished products to the customer.*

Canadian managers must develop a global vision if they are to recognize and react to international business opportunities, as well as remain competitive at home. Often a Canadian firm's toughest domestic competition comes from foreign companies. Moreover, a global vision enables a manager to understand that customer and distribution networks operate worldwide, blurring geographic and political barriers and making them increasingly irrelevant to business decisions. The purpose of this chapter is to explain how global trade is conducted. We also discuss the barriers to international trade and the organizations that foster global trade. We conclude the chapter with a discussion of trends in the global marketplace.

Canada Goes Global

Over the past 25 years, world trade has climbed from $200 billion (USD) a year to more than $8 trillion (USD). Countries and companies that were never considered major players in global markets are now contributing to this growth in world trade. In 2008, Canada exported approximately $500 billion (CAD) and imported approximately $440 billion (CAD) in goods and services.[2]

Go into most Paris McDonald's and you may not recognize where you are. There are no Golden Arches or utilitarian chairs and tables and other plastic features. The restaurants have exposed brick walls, hardwood floors, and armchairs. Some French McDonald's even have faux marble walls. Most restaurants have TVs with continuous music videos. You can even order an espresso, beer, and a chicken on focaccia bread sandwich.[3]

Global business is not a one-way street, where only Canadian companies sell their wares and services throughout the world. Foreign competition in the domestic market used to be relatively rare but now occurs in almost every industry. Nevertheless, the global market has created vast, new business opportunities for many Canadian firms.

The Importance of Global Business to Canada

One reason the United Nations has ranked Canada as one of the best countries in which to live is because of our ability to do business with the "outside world." According to the Department of Foreign Affairs and International Trade, "trade enhances the quality of Canadian life" and helps give Canadians the economic energy we need to create the nation we want.[4]

On the Champs Élysées, this McDonald's is the most frequented restaurant in France. Designed to appeal to local customers, the restaurant offers a cozy Parisian atmosphere. What are some of the considerations for companies expanding internationally?

© AP/WORLD WIDE PHOTOS

HOT Links

For more information about Team Canada Inc see (www.canadabusiness.ca).

Just how important is international trade to Canada? Canada's population, at approximately 33 million, is relatively small versus the 6.5 billion people worldwide. This translates into roughly 200 times more potential customers for Canadian business. Canada exports approximately half of what we manufacture. In terms of a dollar value, we export more than $15,000 in goods and services of what we produce for each Canadian resident. Every $1 billion increase in Canada's exports translates into more than 10,000 jobs, and a fifth of all Canadian jobs are directly related to international trade. We can see that exports are vital to the Canadian economy.[5]

But can we maintain this advantage and keep our economy growing? The simple answer is no—not unless we continue to develop outside markets. Canada has seen international trade increase, helped in part by its proactive partnership between government and industry known as "Team Canada Missions." These missions are led by the prime minister with participation by the provincial premiers, territorial government leaders, and the minister of international trade; their aim is to increase international trade and create or sustain jobs for Canadians. Similar to the Team Canada Missions are the Canada Trade Missions, which are led by the Minister of International Trade with the provincial trade ministers invited to participate.

Successful missions have included Russia, Germany, India, China, Brazil, Mexico, Saudi Arabia, and the United Arab Emirates, to name just a few. The focus of the missions is to emphasize Canadian commercial, political, educational, and cultural links with the countries visited. The presence and support of prominent government leaders facilitates access to crucial economic decision makers for Canadian firms and provides a much greater public profile for the business participants, helping them network with the international business community.[6]

"Team Canada missions send a strong message to prospective partners that Canada is committed to doing business with them. The missions help build prestige and credibility for Canada while helping new exporters, particularly small- and medium-sized firms, to position themselves in markets where competition is fierce. This is important when you consider that smaller businesses create most new jobs in Canada but only about 10 percent of them are currently involved in international markets."[7]

International trade refers to imports as well as exports. If we expect countries to purchase our products, they will need the dollars that are generated by their exports to do so. Imports offer Canadians a wider range and choice of products and services to purchase. Our economy has become more sophisticated in recent decades (see Chapter 1), developing into a knowledge-based economy. Canada's technological potential is ranked first among nations according to the Global *Competitiveness Report*.[8] If Canada is to capitalize on its technical potential, we must convert this potential into global success.

Not only does international trade affect the Canadian economy and provide employment for Canadians, other benefits have been identified. These include

- economies of scale in production and marketing;
- ease of the transfer of experience, technology, and know-how across borders;
- global recognition of products and brand names, allowing for easier introduction of new products and services; and
- the possibility of a uniform global image for the companies.

The Impact of the 2008/2009 Economic Crisis on Global Trade

The economic crisis of 2008/2009 decreased the demand for Canada's exports and had serious implications for employment. Exports in January 2009 decreased by 9% from December 2008 and by approximately 18% compared to January 2008.[9] Governments in Canada provided stimulus packages to keep Canadians working, including financing of public infrastructure projects and loans to some of the automobile manufacturers.

Measuring Trade Between Nations

International trade improves relationships with friends and allies, helps ease tensions among nations, and—economically speaking—bolsters economies, raises people's standard of living, provides jobs, and improves quality of life. The value of international trade is more than $8 trillion (USD) a year and growing. In this section, we take a look at some key measures of international trade: exports and imports, the balance of trade, the balance of payments, and exchange rates.

Exports and Imports

exports
Goods and services produced in one country and sold in other countries.

imports
Goods and services bought from other countries.

The developed nations (those with mature communication, financial, educational, and distribution systems) are the major players in international trade, accounting for about 70 percent of the world's exports and imports. **Exports** are goods and services made in one country and sold to others. **Imports** are goods and services that are bought from other countries. Canada is both an exporter and importer. The main countries (based on dollar amounts) that Canada trades with are listed in Exhibit 2.1.

As Exhibit 2.1 illustrates, approximately 76 percent of Canada's exports are to the United States, and approximately 63 percent of imports come from the United States. This heavy reliance that Canada has on the United States for trade is one rationale for Canada's seeking other international trading partners. Recent studies have shown that Canadian imports are coming less and less from the United States and Japan. In 2008 approximately 37 percent of Canada's imports came from other countries, with China providing much in the consumer and investment goods areas. It should be noted that although these imports are from China, many of these products are assembled in China from parts manufactured elsewhere in Asia.[10]

Balance of Trade

balance of trade
The difference between the value of a country's exports and the value of its imports during a certain time.

The difference between the value of a country's exports and the value of its imports during a certain time is the country's **balance of trade**. A country that exports more

(Balance-of-payments basis)

	2003	2004	2005	2006	2007	2008
	\$ millions					
Exports	399,122.1	429,005.8	450,149.9	453,732.4	463,051.4	489,508.5
United States[1]	328,983.3	350,576.3	368,414.7	361,440.4	356,094.2	369,749.4
Japan	9,799.5	9,846.4	10,168.2	10,279.2	9,989.2	11,855.4
United Kingdom	7,695.3	9,364.0	9,355.4	11,281.2	14,154.8	14,199.9
Other European Economic Community countries	16,423.4	17,533.8	18,630.6	20,900.2	24,187.0	25,372.3
Other OECD[2]	12,754.1	14,189.1	14,528.0	16,773.9	19,690.5	21,046.3
Other countries[3]	23,466.4	27,496.2	29,052.9	33,057.6	38,935.8	47,285.4
Imports	342,709.5	363,157.8	387,804.0	404,252.6	415,005.7	442,794.1
United States[1]	240,356.3	250,038.3	259,348.2	265,023.0	269,752.5	280,684.3
Japan	10,645.5	10,094.5	11,210.8	11,858.3	11,972.3	11,666.8
United Kingdom	9,183.0	9,460.0	9,061.2	9,549.2	9,894.3	11,229.8
Other European Economic Community countries	26,001.0	27,007.0	29,457.0	32,529.8	32,402.9	35,375.5
Other OECD[2]	19,696.9	22,283.6	24,304.5	23,673.3	25,034.2	27,360.7
Other countries[3]	36,826.8	44,274.4	54,422.3	61,618.9	65,949.4	76,477.0
Balance	56,412.6	65,848.0	62,345.9	49,479.8	48,045.7	46,714.4
United States[1]	88,627.0	100,538.0	109,066.5	96,417.4	86,341.7	89,065.1
Japan	−846.0	−248.1	−1,042.6	−1,579.1	−1,983.1	188.6
United Kingdom	−1,487.7	−96.0	294.2	1,732.0	4,260.5	2,970.1
Other European Economic Community countries	−9,577.6	−9,473.2	−10,826.4	−11,629.6	−8,215.9	−10,003.2
Other OECD[2]	−6,942.8	−8,094.5	−9,776.5	−6,899.4	−5,343.7	−6,314.4
Other countries[3]	−13,360.4	−16,778.2	−25,369.4	−28,561.3	−27,013.6	−29,191.6

1. Includes also Puerto Rico and Virgin Islands.
2. Organisation for Economic Co-operation and Development excluding the United States, Japan, United Kingdom and the other European Economic Community.
3. Countries not included in the European Economic Community or the OECD.
SOURCE: Adapted from Statistics Canada Website http://www40.statcan.ge.ca/lol/cstoi/gblec02-eng.htm

trade surplus
A favourable balance of trade that occurs when a country exports more than it imports.

trade deficit
An unfavourable balance of trade that occurs when a country imports more than it exports.

balance of payments
A summary of a country's international financial transactions showing the difference between the country's total payments to and total receipts from other countries.

than it imports is said to have a *favourable* balance of trade, called a **trade surplus**. A country that imports more than it exports is said to have an *unfavourable* balance of trade, or a **trade deficit**. When imports exceed exports, more money from trade flows out of the country than flows into it.

Balance of Payments

Another measure of international trade is called the **balance of payments**, which is a summary of a country's international financial transactions showing the difference between the country's total payments to and total receipts from other countries. The balance of payments includes imports and exports (balance of trade), long-term investments in overseas plants and equipment, government loans to and from other countries, gifts and foreign aid, military expenditures made in other countries, and money transfers into and out of foreign banks.

CONCEPT *in Action* >>>

Many Canadian exports and imports are transported between Canada and the United States by the rail systems. What other transportation methods are used to move products internationally? What are the advantages and disadvantages of each?

COURTESY OF SHIRLEY A. ROSE

HOT Links

Export Development Canada provides Canadian exporters with financing, insurance, and bonding services as well as foreign market expertise. Visit its website at **(www.edc.ca).**

HOT Links

Check out the current Canadian balance of trade with various countries by going to **(ww.statcan.gc.ca)** and then, using the search menu, typing in "balance of trade" for the latest URL.

Although Canada has a favourable balance of trade, it is due to our trade with the United States (i.e., if we exclude our trade with the United States, Canada would have an unfavourable balance of trade). The lower section of Exhibit 2.1 shows that our overall favourable balance of trade is decreasing.

The Changing Value of Currencies

The exchange rate is the price of one country's currency in terms of another country's currency. If a country's currency *appreciates*, less of that country's currency is needed to buy another country's currency. If a country's currency *depreciates*, more of that currency will be needed to buy another country's currency.

How do appreciation and depreciation affect the prices of a country's goods? If, say, the Canadian dollar depreciates relative to the Japanese yen, Canadian residents

Making Ethical Choices

WHAT ARE ACCEPTABLE INTERNATIONAL BUSINESS PRACTICES?

The executives of a clothing manufacturer want to outsource some of their manufacturing to more cost-efficient locations in Indonesia. After visiting several possible sites, they choose one and begin to negotiate with local officials. They discover that it will take about six months to get the necessary permits. One of the local politicians approaches the executives over dinner and hints that he can speed up the process, for an advisory fee of $5,000.

Using a Web search tool, locate articles about this topic and then write responses to the following questions. Be sure to support your arguments and cite your sources.

ETHICAL DILEMMA: Is paying the advisory fee a bribe or an acceptable cost of doing business in that area of the world? If the executives agree to pay the fee, what should they do beforehand?

SOURCES: Jane Easter Bahls, "Illicit Affairs? If You Do Business Overseas, Be Certain Your 'Administrative Fees' Aren't Really Illegal Bribes," *Entrepreneur*, September 2004, p. 80; Paul Burnham Finney, "Shaking Hands, Greasing Palms," *New York Times*, May 17, 2005, p. C10; Phelim Kyne, "Freeport-McMoRan Indonesia Payments Not Graft: Official," *FWN Financial News*, January 18, 2006.

HOT Links

---

concept check

What is the difference between balance of trade and balance of payments?

What impact does international trade have on the Canadian economy?

Explain the impact of a currency devaluation.

---

will have to pay more dollars to buy Japanese goods. To illustrate, presume the dollar price of a yen is $0.012 and a Toyota is priced at 2 million yen. At this exchange rate, a Canadian resident pays $24,000 for a Toyota ($0.012 × 2 million yen = $24,000). If the dollar depreciates to $0.018 to one yen, then the Canadian resident will have to pay $36,000 for a Toyota.

As the dollar depreciates, the price of Japanese goods rises for Canadian residents, so they buy fewer Japanese goods—thus, Canadian imports decline. At the same time as the dollar depreciates relative to the yen, the yen appreciates relative to the dollar. This means prices of Canadian goods fall for the Japanese, so they buy more Canadian goods—and Canadian exports rise.

Currency markets operate under a system called **floating exchange rates**. Prices of currencies "float" up and down based upon the demand for and supply of each currency. Global currency traders create the supply of and demand for a particular currency based on that currency's investment, trade potential, and economic strength. If a country decides that its currency is not properly valued in international currency markets, the government may step in and adjust the currency's value. In a **devaluation**, a nation lowers the value of its currency relative to other currencies. This makes that country's exports cheaper and should, in turn, help the balance of payments.

Why Nations Trade

One might argue that the best way to protect workers and the domestic economy is to stop trade with other nations. Then the whole circular flow of inputs and outputs would stay within our borders. But if we decided to do that, how would we get resources like cotton and coffee beans? Canada simply can't produce some things, and it can't manufacture some products—such as steel and most clothing—at the low costs we're used to. The fact is that nations—like people—are good at producing different things: You might be better at balancing a ledger than repairing a car. In that case, you benefit by "exporting" your bookkeeping services and "importing" the car repairs you need from a good mechanic. Economists refer to specialization like this as *advantage*.

Absolute Advantage

A country has an **absolute advantage** when it can produce and sell a product at a lower cost than any other country or when it is the only country that can provide a product. Canada, for example, has an absolute advantage in softwood and certain technologies.

Assume that Canada has an absolute advantage in air traffic control systems for busy airports and that Brazil has an absolute advantage in coffee. Canada does not have the proper climate for growing coffee, and Brazil lacks the technology to develop air traffic control systems. Both countries would gain by exchanging air traffic control systems for coffee.

Comparative Advantage

Even if Canada had an absolute advantage in both coffee and air traffic control systems, it should still specialize and engage in trade. Why? The reason is the **principle of comparative advantage**, which says that each country should specialize in the products that it can produce most readily and cheaply and trade those products for goods that foreign countries can produce most readily and cheaply. This specialization ensures greater product availability and lower prices.

For example, Mexico and China have a comparative advantage in producing clothing because of low labour costs. Japan has long held a comparative advantage in consumer electronics because of technological expertise. The United States has an advantage in computer software, airplanes, some agricultural products, heavy machinery, and jet engines. Canada's advantages are numerous, including: softwood lumber, oil and gas equipment and services, agricultural products, and technology.

Thus, comparative advantage acts as a stimulus to trade. When nations allow their citizens to trade whatever goods and services they choose without government regulation, free trade exists. **Free trade** is the policy of permitting the people of a country to buy and sell where they please without restrictions. The opposite of free trade is **protectionism**, in which a nation protects its home industries from outside competition by establishing artificial barriers such as tariffs and quotas. In the next section, we'll look at the various barriers, some natural and some created by governments that restrict free trade.

The Fear of Trade and Globalization

The protests in Genoa and Seattle during meetings of the World Trade Organization, and the protests in New York during the convocation of the World Bank and the International Monetary Fund (the three organizations are discussed later in the chapter) showed that many people fear world trade and globalization. What do they fear? The negatives of global trade are as follows:

- Canadians have lost jobs because of imports or production shifts abroad. Most find new jobs, but those jobs often pay less.
- Others fear losing their jobs, especially at those companies operating under competitive pressure.
- Employers often threaten to export jobs if workers do not accept pay cuts.
- Service and white-collar workers are increasingly vulnerable to seeing their operations moving offshore.[11]

Benefits of Globalization

A closer look, however, reveals that globalization has been the engine that creates jobs and wealth. Benefits of global trade include the following:

- Productivity grows more quickly when countries produce goods and services in which they have a comparative advantage. Living standards can go up faster.
- Global competition and cheap imports keep prices down, so inflation is less likely to arrest economic growth.
- An open economy spurs innovation with fresh ideas from abroad.
- Export jobs often pay more than other jobs.[12]

Barriers to Trade

International trade is carried out by both businesses and governments—as long as no one puts up trade barriers. In general, trade barriers keep firms from selling to one another in foreign markets. The major obstacles to international trade are natural barriers, tariff barriers, and non-tariff barriers.

Natural Barriers

Natural barriers to trade can be either physical or cultural. For instance, even though raising beef in the relative warmth of Argentina might cost less than raising beef in the bitter cold of Siberia, the cost of shipping the beef from South America to Siberia might drive the price too high. *Distance* is thus one of the natural barriers to international trade.

---

free trade
The policy of permitting the people of a country to buy and sell where they please without restrictions.

protectionism
The policy of protecting home industries from outside competition by establishing artificial barriers such as tariffs and quotas.

Some other natural barriers include:

- *language differences*—people who can't communicate effectively might not be able to negotiate trade agreements or might ship the wrong goods;
- *cultural differences*—companies that wish to pursue business with countries whose culture is different from theirs must consider these differences and adjust their operations, products, services, and so on, to account for the differences; and
- *legal and regulatory differences*—Canadian companies have to consider not only Canadian laws and regulations but also the laws and regulations of the host country.

Tariff Barriers

tariff
A tax imposed on imported goods.

A **tariff** is a tax imposed by a nation on imported goods. It might be a charge per unit, such as per barrel of oil or per new car; it might be a percentage of the value of the goods, such as 5 percent of a $500,000 shipment of shoes; or it might be a combination. No matter how it is assessed, any tariff makes imported goods more costly, so they are less able to compete with domestic products.

protective tariffs
Tariffs that are imposed to make imports less attractive to buyers than domestic products.

Protective tariffs make imported products less attractive to buyers than domestic products. The United States, for instance, has at times imposed protective tariffs on imported softwood from Canada. On the other side of the world, Japan imposes a tariff on U.S. cigarettes that makes them cost 60 percent more than Japanese brands. U.S. tobacco firms believe they could get as much as a third of the Japanese market if there were no tariffs on cigarettes. With tariffs, they have less than 2 percent of the market.

Arguments for and against Tariffs Tariffs are not a new concept. For centuries industries have tried to protect their products and services and countries have used tariffs to protect employment. The main argument against tariffs is that they discourage free trade, and free trade lets the principle of comparative advantage work most efficiently. The main argument for tariffs is that they protect domestic businesses and workers.

One of the oldest arguments in favour of protectionism is the *infant industry argument.* By protecting new domestic industries from established foreign competitors, so this argument goes, a tariff can give a struggling industry time to become an effective competitor.

A second argument for tariffs is the *job protection argument.* Supporters—especially unions—say we should use tariffs to keep foreign labour from taking away Canadian jobs. Canadian jobs are lost, they say, when low-wage countries sell products at lower prices than those charged in Canada. The higher prices charged by the Canadian firms help pay the higher wages of Canadian workers.

An argument against tariffs is that they cause an increase in prices, thereby decreasing consumers' purchasing power. Over the long run, tariffs can also be too protective if they cause domestic companies to stop innovating and fall behind technologically. An example is the Italian car builder Fiat. Protective tariffs helped keep Fiat's Italian market share very high, but as Europe's trade barriers fell, foreign competitors moved in with cars that Italian drivers preferred. Fiat is now desperately spending billions of dollars to revamp its factories and design new models.

CONCEPT *in Action* >>>

Tariffs on the imported goods arriving on this foreign ship make the products more expensive than those of Canadian competitors. What are some reasons that countries would impose a tariff on an import?

© PHOTODISC COLLECTION/PHOTODISC/GETTY IMAGES

Non-Tariff Barriers

Governments use many tools in addition to tariffs to restrict trade. Among them are import quotas, embargoes, buy-national regulations, customs regulations, and exchange controls.

import quota
A limit on the quantity of a certain good that can be imported; also known as a *quantitative restraint*.

embargo
A total ban on imports or exports of a product.

customs regulations
Regulations on products that are different from generally accepted international standards.

exchange controls
Laws that require a company earning foreign exchange (foreign currency) from its exports to sell the foreign exchange to a control agency, such as a central bank.

Import Quotas   One type of non-tariff barrier is the **import quota**, or limit on the quantity of a certain good that can be imported. The goal of setting quotas is to limit imports to the optimum amount of a given product.

Embargoes   A complete ban against importing or exporting a product is an **embargo**. For instance, Canada does not allow the export of "military goods to countries that threaten Canada's security, are under UN (United Nations) sanction, are threatened by internal or external conflict, and/or abuse the human rights of their citizens."[13]

Customs Regulations   In a more subtle move, a country may make it hard for foreign products to enter its markets by establishing **customs regulations** that are different from generally accepted international standards, such as requiring bottles to be litre size rather than quart size. France seems particularly adept at using this tactic. For example, to reduce imports of foreign VCRs, at one time France ruled that all VCRs had to enter through the customs station at Poitiers. This customs house was located in the middle of the country, was woefully understaffed, and was open only a few days each week. What's more, the few customs agents at Poitiers opened each package separately to inspect the merchandise. Within a few weeks, imports of VCRs in France came to a halt.

Exchange Controls   **Exchange controls** are laws that require a company earning foreign exchange (foreign currency) from its exports to sell the foreign exchange to a control agency, usually a central bank. For example, assume that Rolex, a Swiss company, sells 300 watches to a Canadian retailer for $120,000. If Switzerland had exchange controls, Rolex would have to sell its Canadian dollars to the Swiss central bank and would receive Swiss francs. If Rolex wants to buy goods from abroad, it must go to the central bank and buy foreign exchange (currency). By controlling the amount of foreign exchange sold to companies, the government controls the amount of products that can be imported. Limiting imports and encouraging exports helps a government to create a favourable balance of trade.

> **concept check**
>
> Discuss the concept of natural trade barriers.
>
> Describe several tariff and non-tariff barriers to trade.

Fostering Global Trade

From our discussion so far, it might seem that governments act only to restrain global trade. On the contrary, governments and international financial organizations work hard to increase it, as we explain in this section.

Antidumping Laws

dumping
The practice of charging a lower price for a product in foreign markets than in the firm's home market.

Canadian firms don't always get to compete on an equal basis with foreign firms in international trade. To level the playing field, the federal government has passed antidumping laws. **Dumping** is the practice of charging a lower price for a product (perhaps below cost) in foreign markets than in the firm's home market. The company might be trying to win foreign customers, or it might be seeking to get rid of surplus goods.

When the variation in price can't be explained by differences in the cost of serving the two markets, dumping is suspected. Most industrialized countries have antidumping regulations. They are especially concerned about *predatory dumping*, the attempt to gain control of a foreign market by destroying competitors with impossibly low prices.

The legal test for product dumping is based on two criteria. First, the product must be priced unfairly low—either below its production costs or below the selling price in the home country. Second, the imported product must harm the domestic industry.

The Uruguay Round and the World Trade Organization

Uruguay Round
A 1994 agreement by 117 nations to lower trade barriers worldwide.

The **Uruguay Round** of trade negotiations is an agreement to lower trade barriers dramatically worldwide. Adopted in 1994, the agreement has now been signed by 148 nations. The most ambitious global trade agreement ever negotiated, the Uruguay Round reduced tariffs by one-third worldwide, a move that is expected to increase global income by $235 billion (USD) annually. Perhaps the most notable aspect of the agreement is its recognition of new global realities. For the first time, an agreement covers services, intellectual property rights, and trade-related investment measures, such as exchange controls.

The **World Trade Organization (WTO)** replaced the old General Agreement on Tariffs and Trade (GATT), which was created in 1948. The GATT contained extensive loopholes that enabled countries to evade agreements to reduce trade barriers. Today, all WTO members must comply fully with all agreements under the Uruguay Round. The WTO also has an effective dispute settlement procedure with strict time limits to resolve disputes.

The WTO has emerged as the world's most powerful institution for reducing trade barriers and opening markets. The advantage of WTO membership is that member countries lower trade barriers among themselves. Countries that don't belong must negotiate trade agreements individually with all their trading partners. To date, Russia is the largest country that has not qualified for WTO membership.

The World Bank and International Monetary Fund

Two international financial organizations are instrumental in fostering global trade. The **World Bank** offers low-interest loans to developing nations. Originally, the purpose of the loans was to help these nations build infrastructure such as roads, power plants, schools, drainage projects, and hospitals. Now the World Bank offers loans to help developing nations relieve their debt burdens. To receive the loans, countries must pledge to lower trade barriers and aid private enterprise. In addition to making loans, the World Bank is a major source of advice and information for developing nations.

The **International Monetary Fund (IMF)** was founded in 1945, one year after the creation of the World Bank, to promote trade through financial cooperation and eliminate trade barriers in the process. The IMF makes short-term loans to member nations that are unable to meet their budgetary expenses and operates as a lender of last resort for troubled nations. In exchange for these emergency loans, IMF lenders frequently obtain

---

World Trade Organization (WTO)
An organization established by the Uruguay Round in 1994 to oversee international trade, reduce trade barriers, and resolve disputes among member nations.

HOT *Links*

The World Trade Organization tracks the latest trade developments between countries and regions around the world. For the most recent global trading news, visit the WTO's site (**www.wto.org**).

World Bank
An international bank that offers low-interest loans, as well as advice and information, to developing nations.

International Monetary Fund (IMF)
An international organization, founded in 1945, that promotes trade, makes short-term loans to member nations, and acts as a lender of last resort for troubled nations.

CONCEPT *in Action* >>>

Based in Toulouse, France, Airbus is one of the world's top commercial aircraft manufacturers, operating design and manufacturing facilities in Europe, Japan, China, and the United States. The airliner's current product line-up of 12 jet-aircraft types ranging from 100 seats to 555 seats is heavy competition for Boeing, a top U.S. airline firm with which Airbus has ongoing subsidy-related disputes. What is the World Trade Organization's role in settling disputes between competing multinational corporations?

TIM JESSNER/SHUTTERSTOCK

HOT Links

Gain additional insight into the workings of the International Monetary Fund at (http://imf.org)

significant commitments from the borrowing nations to address the problems that led to the crises. These steps can include curtailing imports or even devaluing the currency.

Some global financial problems do not have a simple solution. One option would be to pump a lot more funds into the IMF, giving it enough resources to bail out troubled countries and put them back on their feet. In effect, the IMF would be turned into a real lender of last resort for the world economy.

The danger of counting on the IMF, though, is the "moral hazard" problem. Investors would come to assume that the IMF would bail them out and might therefore be tempted to take bigger and bigger risks in emerging markets, leading to the possibility of even deeper financial crises in the future.

International Economic Communities

preferential tariff
A tariff that is lower for some nations than for others.

free trade zone
An area where the nations allow free, or almost free, trade among each other while imposing tariffs on goods of nations outside the zone.

Nations that trade with each other frequently might decide to formalize their relationship. In this case, their governments meet and work out agreements for a common economic policy. The result is an economic community or, in other cases, a bilateral trade agreement (an agreement between two countries to lower trade barriers). For example, two nations might agree on a **preferential tariff**, which gives advantages to one nation (or several nations) over others. When members of the British Commonwealth trade with Great Britain, for example, they pay lower tariffs than do other nations. In other cases, nations may form free trade associations. In a **free trade zone**, few duties or rules restrict trade among the partners, but nations outside the zone must pay the tariffs set by the individual members.

North American Free Trade Agreement (NAFTA)

North American Free Trade Agreement (NAFTA)
A 1993 agreement creating a free-trade zone including Canada, Mexico, and the United States.

The **North American Free Trade Agreement (NAFTA)** created one of the world's largest free trade zones. It includes Canada, the United States, and Mexico, with a combined population of more than 449 million and an economy of approximately $16 trillion (USD). Canada and the United States entered a free-trade agreement in 1988. Thus, as NAFTA was established in 1994, most of the new long-run opportunities opened for Canadian business under NAFTA are in Mexico.

The real test of NAFTA will be whether it can continue to deliver rising prosperity to its three members. For Mexicans, NAFTA must provide rising wages, better benefits, and an expanding middle class with enough purchasing power to keep buying goods from Canada and the United States.

HOT Links

Want to learn the latest info about NAFTA? Go to (www.nafta-customs.org).

Mercosur

Mercosur
Trade agreement between Brazil, Argentina, Uruguay, and Paraguay.

The largest new trade agreement is **Mercosur**, which includes Brazil, Argentina, Uruguay, and Paraguay, with Bolivia, Chile, Columbia, Ecuador, and Peru as associate member states. Venezuela is in the process of becoming a member. The elimination of most tariffs among the trading partners has resulted in exports of $119 billion and imports of $135 billion for the year ended 2006. Unfortunately, recent recessions in Mercosur countries have limited economic growth, although trade among Mercosur countries has continued to grow.[14]

HOT Links

See the latest news about Mercosur at (www.mercosur.int).

The European Union

European Union
Trade agreement among 25 European nations.

In 1993, the member countries of the European Community (EC) ratified the Maastricht Treaty, which proposed to take the EC further toward economic, monetary, and political union. Although the heart of the treaty deals with developing a unified European Market, Maastricht was also intended to increase integration among **European Union (EU)** members.

The EU has helped increase this integration by creating a borderless economy for these 27 European nations, shown on the map in Exhibit 2.2. The two newest members, Bulgaria and Romania, were admitted in 2007.

EXHIBIT 2.2 > The European Union Gets Bigger

MEMBER COUNTRIES

CANDIDATE COUNTRIES

ASEAN

The Association of Southeast Asian Nations, which, as of 2006, included 10 member states.

HOT Links

For further in-depth information on ASEAN see (**www.aseansec.org**).

concept check

Explain the pros and cons of NAFTA.

What is Mercosur?

What is the European Union?

One of the principal objectives of the European Union is to promote the economic progress of all member countries. The EU has stimulated economic progress by eliminating trade barriers, differences in tax laws, and differences in product standards, and by establishing a common currency. A new European Community Bank was created along with a common currency called the euro.

ASEAN

The **Association of Southeast Asian Nations** was initially established in 1967, with the original members being Indonesia, Malaysia, the Philippines, Singapore, and Thailand. Today the association has 10 members, the original 5 plus Brunei Darussalam, Vietnam, Laos, Myanmar, and Cambodia. The region has a population of about 560 million, a combined GDP of $1.1 billion (USD), and a total trade of $1.4 billion (USD).[15]

CONCEPT *in Action* >>>
The Eurodollar replaced the individual currencies of many of the European Union nations. The common currency enables the countries to do business as a single trading bloc. What is the advantage of having a single currency?

Participating in the Global Marketplace

LO 6

Companies decide to "go global" for a number of reasons. Perhaps the most urgent is to earn additional profits. If a firm has a unique product or technological advantage not available to other international competitors, this advantage should result in major business successes abroad. In other situations, management might have exclusive market information about foreign customers, marketplaces, or market situations not known to others. In this case, although exclusivity can provide an initial motivation for going global, managers must realize that competitors will eventually

CONCEPT *in Action* >>>
Procter & Gamble introduced Swiffer to a global market, appealing to consumers who share a universal desire for a simple cleaning system. What other consumer products that have an international appeal?

catch up. Finally, saturated domestic markets, excess capacity, and potential for cost savings can also be motivators to expand into international markets. A company can enter global trade in several ways, as we describe in this section.

Exporting

exporting
The practice of selling domestically produced goods to buyers in another country.

When a company decides to enter the global market, usually the least complicated and least risky alternative is **exporting**, or selling domestically produced products to buyers in another country. A company, for example, can sell directly to foreign importers or buyers. Exporting is not limited to huge corporations.

Licensing and Franchising

licensing
The legal process whereby a firm agrees to allow another firm to use a manufacturing process, trademark, patent, trade secret, or other proprietary knowledge in exchange for the payment of a royalty.

One effective way for a firm to move into the global arena with relatively little risk is to sell a licence to manufacture its product to a firm in a foreign country. **Licensing** is the legal process whereby a firm (the *licensor*) agrees to let another firm (the *licensee*) use a manufacturing process, trademark, patent, trade secret, or other proprietary knowledge. The licensee, in turn, agrees to pay the licensor a royalty or fee agreed on by both parties.

Many companies have eagerly embraced the licensing concept. For instance, Philip Morris licensed Labatt Brewing Company to produce Miller High Life in Canada. The Spalding Company receives more than $2 million annually from license agreements on its sporting goods. Fruit-of-the-Loom lends its name through licensing to 45 consumer items in Japan alone, for at least 1 percent of the licensee's gross sales.

The licensor must make sure it can exercise sufficient control over the licensee's activities to ensure proper quality, pricing, distribution, and so on. Licensing might also create a new competitor in the long run, if the licensee decides to void the license agreement. International law is often ineffective in stopping such actions. Two common ways in which a licensor can maintain effective control over its licensees are by shipping one or more critical components from Canada and by registering patents and trademarks locally in its own name.

Franchising, which we will discuss in Chapter 5, is a form of licensing that has grown rapidly in recent years. The Canadian Franchise Association publishes a bimonthly magazine for entrepreneurs wanting to establish a successful franchise and an annual comprehensive directory listing franchises available in Canada.

HOT Links

Find out more about the Canadian Franchise association at **(http://.cfa.ca)**

Contract Manufacturing

contract manufacturing
The practice in which a foreign firm manufactures private label goods under a domestic firm's brand name.

In **contract manufacturing**, a foreign firm manufactures private label goods under a domestic firm's brand. Marketing may be handled by either the domestic company or the foreign manufacturer. Levi Strauss, for instance, entered into an agreement with the French fashion house of Cacharel to produce a new Levi's line called "Something New" for distribution in Germany.

The advantage of contract manufacturing is that it lets a company "test the water" in a foreign country. By allowing the foreign firm (e.g., Cacharel) to produce a certain volume of products to specification and put the domestic firm's brand name on the goods (e.g., Levi's), the domestic firm can broaden its global marketing base without investing in overseas plants and equipment. After establishing a solid base, the domestic firm may switch to a joint venture or direct investment, explained below.

Joint Ventures

joint venture
An agreement in which a domestic firm buys part of a foreign firm or joins with a foreign firm to create a new entity.

Joint ventures are somewhat similar to licensing agreements. In a **joint venture**, the domestic firm buys part of a foreign company or joins with a foreign company to create a new entity. A joint venture is a quick and relatively inexpensive way to enter the global market. It can also be very risky. Many joint ventures fail; others fall victim to takeovers, in which one partner buys out the other.

Sometimes countries have required local partners in order to establish a business in their country. China, for example, had this requirement in a number of industries until recently. Thus, a joint venture was the only way to enter the market. Joint ventures help reduce risks by sharing costs and technology. Often joint ventures will bring different strengths together from each member. In a successful joint venture, both parties gain valuable skills from the alliance.

Foreign Direct Investment

foreign direct investment
Active ownership of a foreign company or of manufacturing or marketing facilities in a foreign country.

Active ownership of a foreign company or of overseas manufacturing or marketing facilities is referred to as **foreign direct investment (also referred to as direct foreign investment)**. Direct investors have either a controlling or a large minority interest in the firm. Thus, they stand to receive the greatest potential reward but also face the greatest potential risks. A firm may make a foreign direct investment by acquiring an interest in an existing company or by building new facilities. It might do so because it has trouble transferring some resources to a foreign operation or obtaining that resource locally. One important resource is personnel, especially managers. If the local labour market is tight, the firm might buy an entire foreign firm and retain all its employees instead of paying higher salaries than competitors.

Sometimes firms make direct investments because they can find no suitable local partners. Direct investments also help businesses avoid the communication problems and conflicts of interest that can arise with joint ventures. IBM, for instance, insists on total ownership of its foreign investments, because it does not want to share control with local partners.

Countertrade

countertrade
A form of international trade in which part or all of the payment for goods or services is in the form of other goods and services.

International trade does not always involve cash. Today, **countertrade** is a fast-growing way to conduct international business. In countertrade, part or all of the payment for goods or services is in the form of other goods or services. Countertrade is a form of barter (swapping goods for goods), an age-old practice whose origins have been traced back to cave dwellers.

Atwood Richards Inc. is the world's largest countertrade organization. Atwood reviews a client's unsold products and issues trade credits in exchange. The credits can be used to obtain other products and services. Atwood has acquired everything from hotel rooms and airline tickets to television advertising time, forklift trucks, carpeting, wood pulp, envelopes, steel castings, or satellite tracking systems.

> **concept check**
>
> Discuss several ways that a company can enter international trade.
>
> Explain the concept of countertrade.

Threats and Opportunities in the Global Marketplace

To be successful in a foreign market, companies must fully understand the foreign environment in which they plan to operate. Politics, cultural differences, and the economic environment can represent both opportunities and pitfalls in the global marketplace.

Political Considerations

We have already discussed how tariffs, exchange controls, and other governmental actions threaten foreign producers. The political structure of a country can also jeopardize a foreign producer's success in international trade.

nationalism
A sense of national consciousness that boosts the culture and interests of one country over those of all other countries.

Intense nationalism, for example, can lead to difficulties. **Nationalism** is the sense of national consciousness that boosts the culture and interests of one country over those of all other countries. Strongly nationalistic countries, such as Iran and New Guinea, often discourage investment by foreign companies. In other, less radical forms of nationalism, the government may take actions to hinder foreign operations. France, for example, requires that pop music stations play at least 40 percent of their songs in French. This law was enacted because the French love American rock and roll. Without airtime, American CD sales suffer. Coca-Cola recently attempted to purchase Orangina, France's only domestically owned and distributed soft drink, but the French government blocked the sale, saying that it would be "anticompetitive." The real reason was nationalism.

In a hostile climate, a government might *expropriate* a foreign company's assets, taking ownership and compensating the former owners. Even worse is *confiscation*, when the owner receives no compensation. This happened during rebellions in several African nations during the 1990s and 2000s.

Cultural Differences

Central to any society is the common set of values shared by its citizens that determine what is socially acceptable. Culture underlies the family, educational system, religion, and social class system. The network of social organizations generates overlapping roles and status positions. These values and roles have a tremendous effect on people's preferences and thus on marketers' options. Inca Kola, a fruity, greenish-yellow carbonated drink, is the largest-selling soft drink in Peru. It was invented in Peru and contains only fruit indigenous to the country. Despite being described as "liquid bubble gum," the drink has become a symbol of national pride and heritage. A local consumer of about a six-pack a day says, "I drink Inca Kola because it makes me feel like a Peruvian." He tells his young daughter, "This is our drink, not something invented overseas. It is named for your ancestors, the great Inca warriors."

Language is another important aspect of culture. Marketers must take care in selecting product names and translating slogans and promotional messages so as not to convey the wrong meaning. For example, Mitsubishi Motors had to rename its Pajero model in Spanish-speaking countries because in Spanish, the term refers to a sexual activity. The MR2 model from Toyota Motors dropped the number 2 in France because the combination sounds like a French swear word. The literal translation of Coca-Cola in Chinese characters means "bite the wax tadpole."

Each country has its own customs and traditions that determine business practices and influence negotiations with foreign customers. In many countries, personal relationships are more important than financial considerations. For instance, skipping social engagements in Mexico might lead to lost sales. Negotiations in Japan often include long evenings of dining, drinking, and entertaining; only after a close personal relationship has been formed do business negotiations begin. See Exhibit 2.3 for some cultural "dos and don'ts."

The Economic Environment

The level of economic development varies considerably worldwide, ranging from countries where everyday survival is a struggle, (such as Sudan and Eritrea), to those that are highly developed, (such as Switzerland and Japan). In general, complex, sophisticated industries are found in developed countries, and more basic industries are found in less developed nations. Average family incomes are higher in the more developed countries than in the least developed markets. Larger incomes mean greater purchasing power and demand not only for consumer goods and services but also for the machinery and workers required to produce consumer goods.

infrastructure
The basic institutions and public facilities on which an economy's development depends.

Business opportunities are usually better in countries that have an economic **infrastructure** in place. Infrastructure is the basic institutions and public facilities on which an economy's development depends. It includes the money and banking system that provides the major investment loans to our nation's businesses; the educational system that turns out the incredible variety of skills; fundamental research on the best production methods and their implementation; the extensive transportation and communications systems—highways, railroads, airports, canals, telephones, Internet sites, postal systems,

concept check

Explain how political factors can affect international trade.

Describe several cultural factors that a company involved in international trade should consider.

How can economic conditions affect trade opportunities?

EXHIBIT 2.3 > Cultural Dos and Don'ts

DO:

- Always present your business card with both hands in Asian countries. It should also be right-side up and print-side showing so that the recipient can read it as it is being presented. If you receive a business card, accept it with gratitude and examine it carefully. Don't quickly put it into your pocket.

- Dress to the culture. If you are in Switzerland, always wear a coat and tie. In other countries, wearing a coat and tie might be viewed as overdressing and make you appear snobbish.

- Use a "soft sell" and subtle approach when promoting a product in Japan. Japanese people do not feel comfortable with North America's traditional hard-selling style.

- Understand the role of religion in business transactions. In Muslim countries, Ramadan is a holy month when most people fast. During this time, everything slows down, including business.

- Have a local person available to interpret culturally and linguistically any advertising that you plan to do. When American Airlines wanted to promote its new first-class seats in the Mexican market, it translated the "Fly in Leather" campaign literally, which meant "Fly Naked" in Spanish.

- In Chile, expect women to greet you with a kiss on the cheek even if you are a stranger. Offer a kiss on both cheeks after you become friends with a French woman (even if you are a woman).

- In Switzerland, offer three kisses.

- Run late for your appointment in some Latin American countries.

- Always be on time for your appointment in Germany.

DON'T:

- Glad-hand, back-slap, or use first names on your first business meeting in Asia. If you do, you will be considered a lightweight.

- Fill a wine glass to the top if dining with a French businessperson. It is considered completely uncouth.

- Begin your first business meeting in Asia by talking business. Be patient. Let your clients get to know you first.

- Kiss someone on the cheek or pat them on the shoulder in Spain before you get to know them.

Expanding Around The Globe

DELL'S SUCCESS IN CHINA TELLS TALE OF A MATURING MARKET

In 2003, Dell Inc. rejected a plan to sell computers online in China. The personal-computer giant worried that most Chinese consumers didn't use credit cards and were too poor to become big Web shoppers.

In 2004, Dell executives in China showed their bosses a startling statistic: More than 90 million people in the country's coastal cities have access to the Internet at home or work. "We're missing a great opportunity," William J. Amelio, Dell's top executive in Asia, recalls thinking.

Today, online sales account for about 6 percent of Dell's orders in China and are becoming a big part of the company's push to shake up the Chinese computer industry the way it did in the United States a decade ago. In China, Dell faced repeated warnings that its strategy—which relies on sophisticated computer buyers willing to purchase a product sight unseen—wouldn't work. But by first going after business customers and then pushing into the consumer market, Dell has become China's third-largest seller of PCs, behind two Chinese rivals, with an 8 percent market share.

Dell has learned some new tricks in China. Rather than create a joint venture with a Chinese firm, it waited to form a wholly owned subsidiary that cultivated close ties with a regional government. And it boosted its reputation in the region by teaching quality-checking and just-in-time manufacturing skills to locals.

Dell stuck to its playbook, concentrating initially on business and institutional buyers who are most familiar with PCs and tend to be the most profitable clients. In China, as in Europe, it started out selling high-margin products, such as server computers, and gradually added less pricey desktop and notebook PCs. Most of its orders are taken by telephone sales representatives who work at a call centre in Xiamen, a city bigger than Dallas, Texas, on China's southeast coast. In nine other Chinese cities, Dell has sales representatives who visit large business and government customers, sending orders back to colleagues in Xiamen.

Critical Thinking Questions

- Do you think that Dell would have been more successful if it had entered into a joint venture with a Chinese company? Why?
- Do you think that Dell should open a sales force to call on businesses in North America?

television stations—that link almost every piece of our geography into one market; the energy system that powers our factories; and, of course, the market system itself, which brings our nation's goods and services into our homes and businesses. When we think about how our own economy works, we tend to take our infrastructure for granted.

The Impact of Multinational Corporations

LO 8

multinational corporations
Corporations that move resources, goods, services, and skills across national boundaries without regard to the country in which their headquarters are located.

Corporations that move resources, goods, services, and skills across national boundaries without regard to the country in which their headquarters are located are **multinational corporations**. Some are so rich and have so many employees that they resemble small countries. The successful ones take political and cultural differences into account. Some examples of successful Canadian multinational companies are Magna International Inc, Cott Corporation, Bombardier Inc, and ScotiaBank.

A multinational company can have several headquarters worldwide, depending on the location of its markets or technologies. Britain's APV, a maker of food-processing equipment, has a different headquarters for each of its worldwide businesses. HP recently moved the headquarters of its personal computer business to Grenoble, France. Siemens A.G., Germany's electronics giant, is relocating its medical electronics division headquarters from Germany to Chicago. Honda has moved the worldwide headquarters for its power products division to Atlanta, Georgia.

The Multinational Advantage

Large multinationals have several advantages over other companies. For instance, multinationals can often overcome trade problems. Taiwan and South Korea have long had an embargo against Japanese cars for political reasons and to help domestic automakers. Yet Honda USA, a Japanese-owned company based in the United States, sends Accords to Taiwan and Korea. In another example, when the environmentally conscious Green movement challenged the biotechnology research conducted by BASF, a major German chemical and drug manufacturer, BASF moved its cancer and immune system research to Cambridge, Massachusetts.

Another advantage for multinationals is their ability to sidestep regulatory constraints. Pharmaceutical company SmithKline and Britain's Beecham decided to merge, in part so that they could avoid licensing and regulatory hassles in their largest markets. The merged company can say it's an insider in both Europe and North America. "When we go to Brussels, we're a member state (of the European Union)," one executive explains. "And when we go to Canada, we're a North American company."

Multinationals can also shift production from one plant to another as market conditions change. When European demand for a certain solvent declined, Dow Chemical instructed its German plant to switch to manufacturing a chemical that had been previously imported from outside the European Union. Computer models help Dow make decisions like these, so it can run its plants efficiently and keep costs down.

Multinationals can also tap new technology from around the world. Xerox has introduced some 80 different office copiers in Canada that were designed and built by Fuji Xerox, its joint venture with a Japanese company. Versions of the super-concentrated detergent that Procter & Gamble first formulated in Japan in response to a rival's product are now being sold under the Ariel brand name in Europe and being tested under the Cheer and Tide labels in Canada. Also, consider Otis Elevator's development of the Elevonic 411, an elevator that is programmed to send more cars to floors where demand is high. It was developed at six research centres in five countries. The Otis group in the United States handled the systems integration, a Japanese group designed the special motor drives that make the elevators ride smoothly, a French group perfected the door systems, a German group handled the electronics, and a Spanish group took care of the small-geared components. Otis says the international effort saved more than $10 million (USD) in design costs and cut the process from four years to two.

Finally, multinationals can often save a lot in labour costs, even in highly union-ized countries. For example, when Xerox started moving copier-rebuilding work to Mexico to take advantage of the lower wages, its union objected because it saw that members' jobs were at risk. Eventually, the union agreed to change work styles and to improve productivity to keep the jobs at home.

The Multinational Challenges

concept check

What is a multinational corporation?

What are the advantages of multinationals?

What are some of the challenges facing multinationals?

The multinationals also face many challenges. These include social and cultural issues (the need to understand diversity and the host country's customs), economic and financial issues (access to finan-cial resources, foreign currency regulations, etc.), legal and regula-tory issues (e.g., government regulations), and environmental issues (e.g., access to raw materials, labour, etc.).

Trends in Global Competition

In this section we will examine several underlying trends that will continue to propel the dramatic growth in world trade. These trends are market expansion, resource acquisition, and the emergence of China and India.

Market Expansion

The need for businesses to expand their markets is perhaps the most fundamental reason for the growth in world trade. The limited size of domestic markets often motivates man-agers to seek markets beyond their national frontiers. The economies of large-scale man-ufacturing demand big markets. Domestic markets, particularly in smaller countries like Denmark and the Netherlands, simply can't generate enough demand. Nestlé was one of the first businesses to "go global," because its home country, Switzerland, is so small. Nestlé was shipping milk to 16 countries as early as 1875. Today, hundreds of thousands of busi-nesses are recognizing the potential rich rewards to be found in international markets.

Resource Acquisition

More and more companies are entering the global marketplace to acquire the resources they need to operate efficiently. These resources may be cheap or skilled labour, scarce raw materials, technology, or capital. Nike, for example, has manufac-turing facilities in many Asian countries in order to use cheap labour. Honda opened a design studio in southern California to put that "California flair" into the design of some of its vehicles. Large multinational banks such as Bank of New York and Citi-group have offices in Geneva, Switzerland. Geneva is the private banking centre of Europe and attracts capital from around the globe.

The Emergence of China and India

China and India—two of the world's hottest economic powerhouses—are impacting businesses around the globe in very different ways. The boom in China's worldwide exports has left few sectors unscathed, be they jeans-makers in Mexico, or plastic-mold manufacturers in South Korea. India's impact has altered how hundreds of service companies from Texas to Ireland compete for billions of dollars in contracts.

The causes and consequences of each nation's growth are somewhat different. China's exports have boomed, largely thanks to foreign investment: lured by low labour costs, big manufacturers have surged into China to expand their production base and push down prices globally. Now manufacturers of all sizes, making everything from windshield wipers to washing machines to clothing, are scrambling either to reduce costs at home or to outsource more of what they make in cheaper locales.[16]

Giant-screen movie exhibitor Imax is taking its trademark big film presentations to an even bigger market: India. The Canadian theatre chain recently expanded into Mumbai and New Delhi where it is dazzling Indian audiences with mega-screen adaptations of today's blockbuster movies. With crystal clear images up to eight stories high and rumbling digital surround sound, the Imax system delivers an unparalleled film experience. What factors make India an attractive market for Imax?

© ARCHIVBERLIN FOTOAGENTUR GMBH/ALAMY

An accelerating trend is that technical and managerial skills in both China and India are becoming more important than cheap assembly labour. China will stay dominant in mass manufacturing and is one of the few nations building multibillion-dollar electronics and heavy industrial plants. India is a rising power in software, design, services, and precision industry.

However, the future for both countries is uncertain. In China, the political system will need to support the country's economic growth in a manner that satisfies other world powers. Issues such as the education and health care systems, the banking system, the land-ownership system, and rural unrest will demand the attention of those in power.[17]

India has been less than enthralled with the multinationals, however, and has chosen to support its own entrepreneurs to foster economic growth, with strength in the information technology (IT) and IT-enabled services fields. With India's strong democracy behind the economic growth, it has the potential to outpace China.[18]

concept check

What trends will foster continued growth in world trade?

Describe some of the ways businesses can take advantage of these trends to "go global."

Great Ideas to Use Now

Continue Your Education

The handwriting is on the wall. Low-skilled jobs are rapidly disappearing in Canada. Canadian businesses know that to compete globally, they must find cheap labour for labour-intensive businesses. This means establishing plants in Mexico, Asia, or other places in the world where labour is inexpensive. It also means that unskilled or low-skilled Canadian workers will find it increasingly difficult to secure permanent jobs. By continuing your education, you can avoid falling into this very undesirable trap.

Study the Role of a Global Manager

Business is becoming more global, so chances are you might become a global manager. Start learning right now what this means and if it's right for you. The life of a global manager can be hectic, as these examples illustrate.

Top overseas performers at Secure Computing, a software developer, are treated to a dinner for two by Christine Hughes, senior vice-president of marketing and business development. Ms. Hughes supervises a 24-person staff in North and South America and Asia. One of her missions on trips is to combat the tendency of foreign-based employees to think the organization is "North American-centric," she says. Because they take much longer flights than the typical corporate road warrior, global managers wind up turning airplanes into offices. When she is overseas, Ms. Hughes has her office ship a package of paperwork overnight to her, so she can work on the flight home.

Indeed, a global manager's workday never really ends. Wherever he or she is, it's still business hours somewhere else. When she's working in Australia, Ms. Hughes usually ends her day in a hotel room, talking with someone at the home office. "I'm on the phone until two in the morning dealing with issues," she says. "You just have to accept that."[19]

Your position might not be as hectic as that of Hughes, but you can easily see the differences between a person who is a global manager and one who is not. Is this the life for you? Would you enjoy living abroad? Can you adapt easily to other cultures?

One way to see if you might be cut out to be a global manager is to spend some time abroad. The ideal situation is to find a job overseas during the summer months. This experience will help you decide if you want to be a global manager. Also, it will look good on your résumé. One source of international jobs information is **(www.internationaljobs.org)**.

If you can't find a job overseas, save your money and travel abroad. Seeing how others live and work will broaden your horizons and give you a more enlightened view of the world. Even international travel can help you decide what you want to do in the global marketplace.

Customer Satisfaction and Quality

Determining *quality* is not always easy in the global marketplace. For example, a manufacturer of garden tools used very high-quality tempered steel to make shovel blades and aged hickory wood for the handles. The shovel is a market leader in Canada but sold poorly in Asia despite a competitive price. The company was puzzled, so it undertook a research project to find out why the shovels weren't selling. The answer proved to be quite simple: People in Asia were of shorter stature than Canadians, making the handles too long to use comfortably! The company shortened the handles and sales skyrocketed.

Quality in developing countries might mean simplifying product features and/or making the parts more durable to withstand a tougher environment. In some cases, a quality sewing machine is one that is foot pedal operated, because buyers don't have access to or can't afford electricity. Yet, companies should not assume that even the poorest people won't pay for quality. Nomads who wander the northern Sahara Desert always buy the highest quality of cloth available to make their clothes. Their garments are all that stand between them and 49°C or hotter in the summer and −20°C in the winter.

So to understand quality in the global marketplace, a business must understand the local culture and listen to the voice of the consumer. A good example is when Universal Studios decided to build a theme park in Japan.

By surveying Japanese visitors at Universal parks in Orlando and Los Angeles, Universal gradually drew a picture of what the Japanese did and didn't like about the parks. For example, cramped in their small homes, they loved the expansive space, but accustomed to modest portions of food, many were turned off by the mountainous servings at restaurants.

A marketing survey in Japan catalogued Japanese expectations for every aspect of Universal Studios Japan, from bathrooms to souvenir sales. One theme was clear, if a bit contradictory: Japanese people wanted an authentic American experience while expecting the park to cater to their cultural preferences.

Searching for the right formula required painstaking attention to detail. Universal set up a test kitchen in Japan, where 10 Japanese and U.S. chefs tested 4,000 recipes to develop U.S.-style dishes with a touch of Japanese flavour. A seafood pizza and gumbo-style soup made the cut. A fried-shrimp concoction with coloured rice crackers didn't. American tasters liked it. Japanese tasters simply found it gross.

In a musical number based on the movie *Beetlejuice*, the main character banters away in Japanese while his sidekicks speak and sing in English. Snippets of Japanese and a Japanese stuntman were injected into a Wild West show to make the gunfight story more understandable to Japanese without ruining the effect of the U.S. performers.

Other features are uniquely Japanese. The nation's penchant for buying edible souvenirs inspired a 6,000-square-foot confection shop packed with Japanese sweets such as dinosaur-shaped bean cakes. Restrooms include Japanese-style squat toilets. Even the park layout caters to the tendency of Japanese crowds to flow clockwise in an orderly manner, contrary to more chaotic U.S. crowds, which steer right.

SOURCE: Adapted from Bill Spindle, "Cowboys and Samurai: The Japanizing of Universal" *Wall Street Journal* (March 22, 2002), pp. B1, B6. Reprinted by permission of the Wall Street Journal, Copyright ©2002 Dow Jones & Company, Inc. All Rights Reserved Worldwide.

Summary of Learning Outcomes

1 **Show why global trade is important to Canada, and how it is measured.**

International trade improves relations with friends and allies, eases tensions among nations, helps bolster economies, raises people's standard of living, and improves the quality of life. With Canada's small population, to meet the economies of scale, we must produce more than we can consume.

Two concepts important to global trade are the balance of trade (the difference in value between a country's exports and its imports over some period) and the balance of payments (the difference between a country's total payments to other countries and its total receipts from other countries). Canada currently has both a positive balance of trade and a positive balance of payments. Another import concept is the exchange rate, which is the price of one country's currency in terms of another country's currency. Currencies float up and down based upon the supply and demand for each currency. Sometimes a government steps in and devalues its currency relative to those of other countries.

2 **Explain why nations trade.**

Nations trade because they gain by doing so. The principle of comparative advantage states that each country should specialize in the goods it can produce most readily and cheaply and trade them for those that other countries can produce most readily and cheaply. The result is more goods at lower prices than if each country produced everything it needed. Free trade allows trade among nations without government restrictions.

3 **Describe some of the barriers to international trade.**

The three major barriers to international trade are natural barriers, such as distance and language; tariff barriers, or taxes on imported goods; and non-tariff barriers. The non-tariff barriers to trade include import quotas, embargoes, buy-national regulations, customs regulations, and exchange controls. The main argument against tariffs is that they discourage free trade and keep the principle of comparative advantage from working efficiently. The main argument for using tariffs is that they help protect domestic companies, industries, and workers.

4 **Discuss how governments and institutions foster world trade.**

The World Trade Organization created by the Uruguay Round has dramatically lowered trade barriers worldwide. For the first time, a trade agreement covers services, intellectual property rights, and exchange controls. The World Bank makes loans to developing nations to help build infrastructures. The International Monetary Fund makes loans to member nations that cannot meet their budgetary expenses. Despite efforts to expand trade, terrorism can have a negative impact on trade growth.

5 **List some of the international economic communities.**

International economic communities reduce trade barriers among themselves while often establishing common tariffs and other trade barriers toward non-member countries. The best-known economic communities are the European Union, NAFTA, and Mercosur.

6 **Explain how companies can enter the global marketplace.**

There are a number of ways to enter the global market. The major ones are exporting, licensing, contract manufacturing, joint ventures, and direct investment.

7 **Explain some of the threats and opportunities in the global marketplace.**

Domestic firms entering the international arena need to consider the politics, economies, and culture of the countries where they plan to do business. For example, government trade policies can be loose or restrictive, countries can be nationalistic, and governments can change. As well, many products fail because companies don't understand the culture of the country where they are trying to sell their products. Some developing countries also lack an economic infrastructure, which can make it very difficult to conduct business.

8 **Discuss some of the advantages of multinational corporations.**

Multinational corporations have several advantages. First, they can frequently side-step restrictive trade and licensing restrictions because they have headquarters in more than one country. Multinationals can also move their operations from one country to the next, depending on which location offers more favourable economic conditions. In addition, multinationals can tap into a vast source of technological expertise by drawing on the knowledge of a global workforce.

9 **List some of the trends in the global marketplace.**

Global business activity will continue to escalate for several reasons. Firms that desire a larger customer base or need additional resources will continue to seek opportunities outside their country's borders. This market expansion requires new sources of resources. China and India, with their emerging middle class, has provided opportunities for many companies to expand their markets.

KEY TERMS

absolute advantage   51
Association of Southeast Asian
 Nations (ASEAN)   57
balance of payments   49
balance of trade   48
contract manufacturing   59
countertrade   60
customs regulations   54
devaluation   51
dumping   54
embargo   54
European Union (EU)   56
exchange controls   54
exporting   59
exports   48
floating exchange rates   51
foreign direct investment   60
free trade   52
free trade zone   56
global vision   46
import quota   54

imports   48
infrastructure   61
International Monetary Fund (IMF)   55
joint venture   59
licensing   59
Mercosur   56
multinational corporations   63
nationalism   60
North American Free Trade Agreement
 (NAFTA)   56
preferential tariff   56
principle of comparative advantage   51
protectionism   52
protective tariffs   53
tariff   53
trade deficit   49
trade surplus   49
Uruguay Round   54
World Bank   55
World Trade Organization (WTO)   55

Experiential Exercises

1. Know the exchange rate between the Canadian dollar and the currencies of the countries you plan to visit before you go. Go to (**www.cnnfn.com/markets/ currencies**) for the latest quotations. Keep up with the changing rates by reading your local paper. Explain the implication in the change of the exchange rate for your next vacation to Mexico.

2. When you travel, avoid changing money at airports, train stations, and hotels. These places usually have the worst rates. Ask local people where they change money. Locals know where the best rates are.

3. Discuss the rise of the Indian and Chinese economies. Investigate what the future might hold for these countries from a political and economic perspective.

4. How can a country's traditions create barriers to trade? Ask foreign students to describe such barriers in their country. Students should give examples of problems that foreign businesspeople might experience with Canadian customs.

5. Should the United Kingdom be admitted to NAFTA? Why might Britain not wish to join?

6. Write a paper on how international economic communities might affect Canadian business.

7. What do you think is the best way for a small company to enter international trade? Why?

8. What impact have foreign multinationals had on the Canadian economy? Give some examples.

9. Identify some Canadian multinational companies that have been successful in world markets. How do you think they have achieved their success?

Review Questions

1. What is a global vision?

2. What is the importance of global business to Canada?

3. What impact has terrorism had on international trade?

4. Define exports and imports.

5. What is the balance of trade? What is the difference between a trade surplus and a trade deficit?

6. What is a country's balance of payments?

7. How does changing values of currencies affect imports and exports?

8. Why do nations trade? What is the principle of comparative advantage?

9. What are some natural barriers to trade?

10. What are tariffs? What are some arguments for and against tariffs?

11. What is the role of the World Bank and the International Monetary Fund?

12. What are some of the main international economic communities?

13. What are some options for Canadian companies that want to participate in the global marketplace?

CREATIVE THINKING CASE >

We Want Our MTV (International)

MTV, a mainstay of American pop culture, is just as popular in Shanghai, China as it is in Sydney, Australia; or in Lagos, Nigeria as it is in Los Angeles, USA. London-based MTV Networks International (MTVNI), the world's largest global network, has taken its winning formula to 167 foreign markets on six continents, including urban and rural areas. It broadcasts in 18 languages to 430 million homes, or about 1.3 billion people, through locally programmed and operated TV channels and websites. While the United States currently generates about 80 percent of MTV's profits, 80 percent of the company's subscriber base lives outside the U.S. "Now a large part of our future will be what happens outside the United States, and that is exciting," says Tom Freston, co-president of parent company Viacom and head of MTV Networks.

The MTV brand has evolved beyond its music television roots into a multimedia lifestyle entertainment and culture brand for all ages. In addition to MTV and MTV2, its channel lineup includes Nickelodeon, VH1, Comedy Central, LOGO, TMF (The Music Factory), Game One, and several European music, comedy, and lifestyle channels. Adding to the complexity is MTV's multimedia and interactive nature, with gaming, texting, and websites as well as television. Another challenge is integrating acquisitions of local companies such as European competitor Viva, which it purchased in 2004.

The company prefers to hire local employees rather than import staff. According to Brent Hansen, president and chief executive of MTV Networks Europe, getting the local perspective is invaluable in helping the network understand its markets, whether in terms of musical tastes or what children like. For example, Alex Okosi, a Nigerian who went to college in the United States, is chief executive for MTV Base, which launched in sub-Saharan Africa in 2005. Okosi recommended that MTV consider each country as an individual market, rather than blending them all together.

One reason for MTVNI's success is "glocalization"—its ability to adapt programs to fit local cultures while still maintaining a consistent, special style. "When we set a channel up, we always provide a set of parameters in terms of standards of things we require," Hansen explains. "Obviously an MTV channel that doesn't look good enough is not going to do the business for us, let alone for the audience. There's a higher expectation." The local unit can tailor content to its market. MTV India conveys a "sense of the colourful street culture," explains Bill Roedy, MTV International's president, while MTV Japan has "a sense of technology edginess; MTV Italy, style and elegance." In Africa, MTV Base will feature videos from top African artists as well as from emerging African music talent. The goal, according to Brent Hansen, is to "provide a unique cultural meeting point for young people in Africa, using the common language of music to connect music fans from different backgrounds and cultures."

Critical Thinking Questions

- Do you agree with Tom Freston that MTV's future lies mostly in its international operations, and why?
- What types of political, economic, and competitive challenges does MTV Networks International face by operating worldwide?
- How has MTVNI overcome cultural differences to create a world brand?

SOURCES: MTV International website, (www.mtv.com/international) (January 18, 2006); "Now, Africa Gets MTV Base", Africa News Service, February 25, 2005, (www.comtexnews.com); Johnnie L. Roberts, "World Tour", *Newsweek*, June 6, 2005, pp. 34–35; and Robin D. Rusch, "MTV Networks Internationally", Brandchannel.com, July 26, 2004, (www.brandchannel.com)

VIDEO CASE >

ESPN Goes Global

If your passion is Indian cricket, Argentinian soccer, or Scottish links golf, tune in to ESPN International for live coverage of your favourite international sports events. The company's initial 1989 foray into international sports broadcasting was in South America, a market that still represents 40 percent of its international business. But ESPN's international programming has since expanded to include 150 to 160 million households worldwide.

"Minimal data was available on basic demographics like household cable penetration, markets, or advertising," said Managing Director of ESPN International Operations, Willy Burkhart. But ESPN followed pioneers CNN and HBO into the international broadcast arena, convinced that sporting events would carry the same global appeal for viewers as news and movies. Their goal was to bring quality programming and journalistic integrity in American sports to a global audience.

Initial distribution partnerships were established with broadcast companies in Europe, Canada, and Asia, followed by penetration into Japan, Australia, New Zealand, the Middle East, Africa, and Antarctica, under ESPN's own banner. Unlike CNN, whose international coverage focuses on bringing news to an American expatriate and tourist audience, ESPN soon realized that sports viewers were mainly interested in local events. As a result, they invested in the "localization" of their coverage, which included being sensitive to different languages and dialects, and hired announcers with accents unlikely to offend or insult any of their viewers.

ESPN's sales pitch to cable operators was the lure of enticing new subscribers to cable and the promise of retaining existing users unwilling to relinquish access to first-rate, up-to-the-minute sports programming. ESPN's two revenue streams are generated from cable operators and the companies that buy ESPN advertising airtime.

Initially ESPN's advertising was designed to encourage viewer tune-in for specific events, with little focus on building the ESPN brand or image. That has changed, however, and the company now features stunts in their own airtime that help build ESPN brand awareness.

As the worldwide leader in sports entertainment, ESPN also recognized the need to identify and even create trends in the world of sports by producing some of its own events. Its phenomenally successful X-Games, staged each year in Thailand, feature edgy "evolving sports" like ramp boarding. Retaining rights to some events is an ongoing challenge for ESPN, but its own production capability provides it with greater control over some of these events.

After 10 years of successfully investing in establishing a worldwide presence, ESPN has now turned its focus to building its brand value and brand name, a name the company hopes worldwide sports viewers will continue to see as synonymous with excellence in sports broadcasting.

Critical Thinking Questions

- Why did ESPN take the risk of moving into the international broadcast arena, even though it did not have solid demographic data available?
- What were some of the main challenges ESPN experienced in this new venture?
- How has ESPN's international presence evolved over the past 10 years? What trends have helped it grow?

SOURCES: Adapted from material contained in the video *ESPN International* and the company website, (www.international.espn.com).

E-COMMERCE CASE >

Auto Manufacturing in China for the Chinese Market or the Global Market?

A May 2006 report on Canada's auto industry suggested that there is a trend emerging to assemble automobiles in the country for which they are ultimately intended. As a result, competition among assemblers of automobiles will be intense. One way to keep costs down is, of course, cheap labour. Assembling the product at its ultimate destination also serves to lower delivery costs. China represents a massive potential market. New car sales in China for the month of February 2009 were up 25% from February 2008 with a total of 827,600 units sold. Production in February was up 12% from the previous year at 807,900 units.

Can Canadian manufacturers take advantage of this? China has many domestic manufacturers who provide low-cost cars of reasonable quality, but the higher end automobiles are generally produced through joint ventures with foreign companies. The Chinese manufacturers might decide to focus on their domestic market, which would create competition for Canadian firms looking to assemble in China to access the huge Chinese market. On the other hand, China might try to move into the export market. Moving into foreign markets will create several problems for Chinese manufacturers. Issues such as environmental and safety concerns will arise, as will the desire to protect domestic manufacturers in Canada, the United States, and Europe. Also, Chinese auto brands are virtually unknown outside China, and service support could be a problem.

The Chinese are moving to introduce battery-powered cars in the near future with a goal of becoming one of the world's largest producers of all-electric cars. The trend toward more environmentally friendly automobiles and away from the gas guzzlers of earlier decades should work in their favour. Outside investment in China's battery manufacturers is coming from, of all places, the United States. Warren Buffett, one of the wealthiest people in the world, has invested heavily in BYD, an important Chinese battery maker. BYD's goal is to become a world leader in batteries *and* cars. An important consideration might be: will the strength of the environmental goals outweigh the safety and service concerns that non-Chinese consumers often associate with Chinese-made automobiles.

Given the advantages of staying domestic, the challenges of exporting globally, and with exports down 33.5% in January 2009 from the previous January, China might choose to focus on the local market. Hence, Canadian manufacturers attempting to assemble in China would be in direct competition with local auto manufacturers.

Critical Thinking Questions

1. How do you see the electric car changing the manufacturing area globally?

2. Do you see a potential for Chinese automakers to export to Canada, the United States and Europe? Google search "Chery," a Chinese automaker, and look at its M14.

3. Check out the video of Warren Buffett with his electric car at (**www.fortune.com/greenbiz**).

SOURCES: Nicholas Van Preet, "Carmakers to Stay Local, TD Says", *National Post,* May 19, 2006. Jim Hemerling, "China's Carmakers at the Crossroads", *Business Week Online,* May 31, 2006, (http://msnbc.msn.com) (accessed June 7, 2006); Associated Press, "*China auto sales jump 25% in February*", business.theglobeandmail.com, March 11, 2009, Alex Taylor, "The Great Electric Car Race", *Fortune ,* Vol. 159, Iss. 8, pg. 38, April 27, 2009.

CHAPTER 3

Making the Connection

Social Trends, Social Responsibility, and Making Ethical Decisions in Business

In this chapter you'll be learning about some very important trends in the social environment. One such trend is the changing demographic composition of the Canadian population, resulting in changing patterns in the workforce and in consumer wants and needs. Another is the trend toward better ethics or, at least, higher expectations with regard to business ethics and increased corporate responsibility.

Just as the other trends in the PEST environment model affect one another, so do social trends. For example, demographic changes in the population—both in age and in multicultural diversity—lead to changing consumer wants and needs (another social trend), and to changes in government/*political* policy. For example, extending the mandatory retirement age to delay the damage to the Canada Pension Plan that will occur as the large bulge of boomers retires. Increasing immigration to offset a shrinking labour force is another good example. Demographic changes also lead to changes in *technology* as businesses look for ways to make up for labour shortages. This has even helped lead to the *economic* trend toward entrepreneurship (which we'll discuss in Chapter 6), as those born at the latter part of the baby boom have difficulty finding jobs at higher levels in companies because the early boomers have taken all of those jobs, and the numbers of visible minorities starting their own businesses increase. This trend toward increased diversity is one that can have a very positive impact on a business if it embraces this diversity in its hiring, making it much more capable of understanding and meeting its increasingly varied customer base.

Business ethics and corporate responsibility also have integrative implications for businesses. Market forces and market failures in the economic environment have motivated greater corporate responsibility for organizations wishing to promote consumer confidence. And of course the political factor is always present; if business does not act ethically and accept its social responsibility voluntarily, governments are likely to step in and enact legislation, as we have seen in response to the Enron and WorldCom scandals in the United States.

On its website, (**www.ic.gc.ca**), Industry Canada presents a "Business Case for CSR" that demonstrates how a company's commitment to corporate social responsibility affects its success by helping it meet the critical success factors in our model. For example, it leads to "operational efficiency gains" that reduce costs to help the company *achieve financial performance*; "improved reputation and branding" that increases sales and customer loyalty (helping to achieve financial success, because the company gains customer trust and better *meets their needs* in the long term); and "enhanced employee relations" that help to gain *employee commitment*.

Recent events would also support the notion that corporate responsibility is necessary to achieving the critical success factors in the long term: a global recession brought on by a focus on short-term wealth, increasing evidence of human-accelerated climate change, and a loss of trust in the private sector brought about by recent scandals. All of these have combined to create a new reality for businesses that, if nothing else, has shed light on the dangers of short-term

thinking. BSR (Business for Social Responsibility—(www. bsr.org)), in its 2008 Report, describes the situation facing business today as one that "future generations are likely to view ... as a pivot point, when old frameworks were discarded and new ones began to emerge ... a "reset," when business as usual was no longer possible, and new ways of thinking and acting were needed."

In fact, acting in an ethical and responsible fashion creates a key opportunity for businesses to be more financially successful; whereas not doing so creates enormous threats to the survival of the business—just look at the famous cases of WorldCom and Enron, as mentioned earlier. Actually all environmental trends create threats that can be turned into opportunities if seen early enough and acted on proactively. For example, the social trend of the growth of dual-income families has resulted in the economic effect of increased purchasing power. As we indicate in this chapter, the "phenomenon of working women has probably had a greater effect on marketing than has any other social change." As women's earnings have grown, so has their impact on purchase decisions, particularly big-ticket items. Working women create opportunities for items such as childcare and eldercare, home-cleaning services, and other convenience items and services. The impact on items such as car sales, however, has created huge market opportunities that many companies have taken advantage of, changing their sales messages to attract female customers.

An interesting and challenging opportunity discussed in this chapter is the trend toward component lifestyles. This makes meeting customer needs very difficult but full of opportunities. Businesses must use technology to track customer needs, and then focus on *innovation* to develop products of *value* to customers while keeping *operations* extremely flexible. Changes can be met as they occur, and the business can adjust to the differing demands of the consumer.

Another major social trend discussed in this chapter is the shift in the demographic composition of the Canadian population created by the baby boom. As this chapter indicates, demographic changes definitely affect the market for products, as well as the size and composition of the workforce, so shifts in demographics have implications for the overall *strategy* of a business as well as its functional areas. Some products will find demand declining, whereas others will experience increased demand as demographics shift—important concerns for *marketing*. The size and composition of the workforce will change, and that's important for *human resources* to understand and plan for. This changing composition of the workforce might necessitate moving operations to other countries in search of labour with the required skills. Clearly, all of these implications have a direct impact on the *finance* area of business, but the demographic shifts we are experiencing in Canada, coupled with a declining birth rate, have also caused the government to respond with changes in economic policy (as discussed earlier) and this inevitably affects finance.

Without a doubt, there is also a connection between functional areas, and ethical and responsible corporate behaviour. According to Canadian Business for Social Responsibility (CBSR (**www.cbsr.ca**)), companies that practice corporate social responsibility develop and practice policies and programs in areas such as employee relations (human resources), international relations (operations), marketplace practices (marketing), and fiscal responsibility and accountability (finance). But if a business is to be truly responsible, commitment must come from the top; it must be part of the *mission* and culture of the company, and therefore part of the decisions made within all functional areas.

Behaving ethically and responsibly involves operating in a manner that recognizes and balances the competing expectations of all the various stakeholders of the business, and building a relationship of trust with them. Furthermore, meeting the company's obligations to its stakeholders helps the company achieve its critical success factors. For example, meeting its responsibility to employees helps gain employee commitment, meeting its responsibility to customers helps meet customer needs, and meeting its responsibility to investors helps achieve financial performance by providing needed capital. In fact, social investing theory would suggest that this is a very big factor. More and more investment funds are moving toward socially responsible companies and, if you follow the Jantzi Social Index or JSI (**www.jantziresearch. com**)—created by Jantzi Research, one of the leading independent, socially responsible investing research firms in the world—you can see they are doing very well.

CHAPTER 3

Social Trends, Social Responsibility, and Making Ethical Decisions in Business

LEARNING OUTCOMES

1. Identify some of the current social factors that have the greatest impact on business.

2. Explain how demographic shifts are creating both challenges and new opportunities for business.

3. Discuss the philosophies and concepts that shape personal ethical standards.

4. Show how organizations can encourage ethical business behaviour.

5. Define social responsibility.

6. Illustrate how businesses meet their social responsibilities to various stakeholders.

7. List some of the global and domestic trends in ethics and social responsibility.

EXPLORING BUSINESS CAREERS

Lord John Browne, BP

Although stories of greedy and unscrupulous business executives have dominated the business news during the last few years, one innovative leader for British Petroleum (BP) has been at the forefront of social responsibility by demonstrating a commitment to preserving the world's fragile environment. Lord John Browne, group chief executive to the world's second largest company, is consistently recognized as one of the 100 most influential British executives, according to the British newspaper *The Times*. But there's a good reason he's so newsworthy: Browne is keenly aware of BP's responsibility to protect and preserve the earth's fragile environment, and he uses his influence and position to make BP more environmentally responsible.

Environmental issues are a growing concern among businesses worldwide. In particular, energy companies face tough scrutiny by their customers and shareholders to make socially and ethically responsible decisions. Recognizing a rapidly increasing demand for energy worldwide, Browne is committed to taking BP "beyond petroleum," although the burden of this increased demand still falls to hydrocarbon-based sources such as oil and natural gas. And although Browne has confidence that the world's oil and natural gas supplies are sufficient, his concerns are clear: "The real challenge is the potential impact of burning ever greater volumes of hydrocarbons on the world's climate."

However, he is not satisfied simply to state the problem and head home. "Business is at heart of the process of taking scientific advances and transforming them into technology ... which can alter the lives of individuals and whole communities, and which can protect the environment." And he is putting his—and BP's—money where his mouth is.

The Kyoto Protocol, a 1997 United Nations treaty on climate change, seeks to reduce the levels of carbon dioxide (CO_2), a harmful byproduct of hydrocarbon use, by 5.2 percent below a 1990 baseline. BP immediately sought to reduce their emissions by twice that amount, a goal they reached by 2002. At the same time, BP increased profitability by almost $650 million, dispelling the belief that environmental concerns cannot coincide with good business sense. They did this by increasing efficiency and eliminating waste in their manufacturing processes.

Additionally, BP has begun several innovative initiatives to help preserve the environment:

- BP built China's first natural gas terminal and pipeline for distribution, which will save approximately 16 million tons of CO2 emissions over coal.

- In Algeria, BP has started to use a process called carbon sequestration in which carbon, produced by natural gas production, is trapped before it can be released into the atmosphere. It is then injected back into reservoirs below the ground where it does not harm the environment. BP estimates this project will prevent the release of 17 million tons of CO_2.

Critical Thinking Questions

As you read this chapter, consider the following questions as they relate to BP:

1. **How have trends affected BP, and what opportunities and threats have these trends offered the company?**

2. **How has BP shown that it is socially responsible, and how does this impact on their profits in the short and long terms?**

3. **Why is ethical behaviour important to companies such as BP?**

PHOTO SOURCE: From Gitman/McDaniel, *The Future of Business*, 6E. © 2008 South-Western, a part of Cengage Learning Inc. Reproduced by permission. www.cengage.com/permissions

No one business is large or powerful enough to create major changes in the external environment. Thus, managers are basically adapters to, rather than agents of, change. Global competition is basically an uncontrollable element in the external environment, as discussed in Chapter 2. In this chapter, we examine the social trends in the business environment that are reshaping today's business landscape. Most important are the trends for companies to consider their social responsibility and the expectation that they will act in an ethical manner.

Every day, managers and business owners make business decisions based on what they believe to be right or wrong. Through their actions, they demonstrate to their employees what is and is not acceptable behaviour and shape the moral standard of the organization. **Ethics** *is a set of moral standards for judging whether something is right or wrong. As you will see in this chapter, personal and professional ethics are important cornerstones of an organization and shape its ultimate contributions to society. Let's consider first the important social trends and then how individual business ethics are formed.*

ethics
A set of moral standards for judging whether something is right or wrong.

Social Trends

Social change is perhaps the most difficult environmental factor for owners and managers to forecast, influence, or integrate into business plans. Social factors include our attitudes, values, and lifestyles. Attitudes include our beliefs about such varied topics as religion, family, and the role of government in providing social services. Whereas some attitudes have an indirect impact on business, others—for example, how we feel about work—directly affect businesses. Examples of values include honesty, job satisfaction, materialism, convenience, and simplicity. Lifestyles are the ways in which consumers and families live, use time, and spend money. Because such social factors are very subjective, they are often difficult to define and measure. They change as we move through different life stages. Recent university and college graduates may value job success most for several years until they establish their careers. Family often becomes their primary concern after they marry.

Social factors influence the products people buy, the prices they pay, the effectiveness of specific promotions, and how, where, and when people expect to purchase products. They are closely tied to and affected by demographics. For example, the living and spending patterns of the young single and empty nester lifestyles relate to those specific age groups. Young singles may spend a higher proportion of their income on entertainment, such as eating out, while empty nesters may travel more.

Companies that track customer attitudes, values, and interests have a competitive advantage. They can use their knowledge of what's in or out to develop goods and services that address changing consumer needs and desires.

Different Lifestyles, Different Choices

The lifestyles we choose have a significant impact on business decisions. If we choose the simple life as a way to reduce stress, we will buy less. If we choose a **component lifestyle**, one made up of a complex set of interests, needs and choices, we become multidimensional rather than following a stereotype. Whereas in the past a person's profession—for instance, banker—defined that person's lifestyle, today a person can be a banker as well as a gourmet, fitness enthusiast, dedicated single parent, and conservationist—all at once. Each of these component lifestyles is associated with different goods and services and represents a unique market, increasing the complexity of consumers' buying habits. For example, this banker may respond to advertisements for cookware, wines, and exotic foods in magazines like Bon Appétit and Gourmet, and for mutual funds in business and

component lifestyle
A lifestyle made up of a complex set of interests, needs and choices.

finance magazines. She may buy Adidas equipment and special jogging outfits to suit her fitness needs and read Runner's World magazine, eat fast-food for lunch but drink French wine for dinner, own sophisticated photographic equipment but listen to a low-priced home stereo, and shop for hosiery at Zellers and suits at Holt Renfrew.

Today's fast paced lifestyles create a "poverty of time." Overworked, tired, and stressed out, we look for ways to gain control of our time. For example, more employees are asking for flex-time and part-time schedules. On-site day care and fitness centres are popular employee benefits. Consumers place a high priority on convenience and healthier lifestyles—and some products meet both needs. Frozen dinners from Healthy Choice, Lean Cuisine, and South Beach Diet make it easy to stay on a low-fat diet. Recently Nabisco introduced 100-calorie "packages of cookies and chips to help calorie-counters limit their portions of snack foods." They were an immediate hit. "We live harried lives," says Stephanie Childs of the Grocery Manufacturers Association. "It's much easier to have somebody else count for you."[1]

Women in the Workforce

A contributing factor to the evolution of component lifestyles is the number of women in the workforce, including those in dual-income families, and the resulting increase in purchasing power. In 2006, approximately 58 percent of all females aged 15 and over had jobs compared to 42 percent in 1976.[2] The phenomenon of working women has probably had a greater effect on marketing than has any other social change. As women's earnings grow, so do their levels of expertise, experience, and authority. Working-age women are not the same group businesses targeted 30 years ago. They expect different things

CONCEPT *in Action* >>>

The tremendous influx of women into the workforce has created a new class of female consumers with enormous purchasing power and unique lifestyle characteristics. Today's working women are busy multitaskers that must balance home, career, and personal needs—they are as preoccupied with home decorating and school supplies as with PDAs and personal fitness. Why do companies that tailor their promotional messages directly to women gain a competitive advantage over those that don't?

© 2009 JUPITER IMAGES CORPORATION

in life—from their jobs, from their spouses, and from the products and services they buy—and they want a say in major economic decisions. Trend expert Faith Popcorn believes that women influence or make 80 percent of all purchasing decisions. "If men and women are different (mentally), why do we market to them in the same way?" she asks. She adds that businesses must target their marketing to women and build relationships, regardless of the type of product they sell.[3]

Demographic Trends

demography
The study of people's vital statistics, such as their age, gender, race and ethnicity, and location.

Demographic factors are another uncontrollable factor in the business environment and extremely important to managers. **Demography** is the study of people's vital statistics, such as their age, gender, race and ethnicity, and location. Demographics help companies define the markets for their products and also determine the size and composition of the workforce. You'll encounter demographics as you continue your study of business. For example, later in this chapter and in chapter 10, we'll examine the challenges of managing a diverse work force. In chapter 12, you'll learn how marketers use demographics to segment markets and select target markets.

The Digital Kids of Generation Y

Those designated by demographers as **Generation Y** were born between about 1977 and 1997 (demographers have reached no consensus as to exact dates, with some starting in 1979 and some ending as late as 2000); also called the Echo Boomers or the Millennium Generation. In Canada there are approximately 33,000,000 people of which about 5.5 million are under the age of 15. See Exhibit 3.1 for the population breakdown by age.

According to Neil Howe and William Strauss, authors of *Millennials Rising: The Next Great Generation*, Generation Y is the most ethnically and socially diverse generation in history.[4]

Generation Y
Canadians born between about 1977 and 1997.

The marketing impact of **Generation Y** has been immense—and they haven't yet reached their peak income and spending years. These technologically sophisticated consumers are the first to grow up with digital technology and the Internet. "They actually go online to be with each other," comments Melissa Payner, chief executive of Bluefly Inc., an online retailer. "It's a different kind of life."[5] Cell phones, iPhones, etc., are loaded with features and come in many colour combinations, allowing Gen Yers to keep up with their peers yet express their individuality through their gadgets.[6] Their spending habits reflect their love of technology, therefore electronic commerce—for example, websites with online ordering capabilities, e-mail newsletters and sale announcements—becomes an important tool to reach them. The best marketing approaches position brands as cutting-edge, fashionable, and popular, but avoid the hard sell.

As the older members of Generation Y enter the work force and approach 30, they are catching the eye of other types of companies. Banks and credit card issuers have already targeted these eager-to-spend consumers. American Express, which for years considered older executives its primary market, is using a very different marketing strategy to court Gen Yers who use debit cards. The result is a new line of no-fee credit cards with award points, including city-specific cards. Its ads tout "the über-glam lifestyle," and the city cards offer points towards discounts at hip restaurants, bars, and other trendy local spots.[7]

Generation X Reaches Middle Age

Generation X
Canadians born between 1964 and about 1977.

Although they are highly educated, **Generation X**—people born between 1964 and 1977—have been overshadowed by the very large baby boomer generation that preceded them (until recently). As the first GenXers turn 40, they are finding their place and entering the mainstream. In the process, they are exhibiting different characteristics than earlier generations.

EXHIBIT 3.1 > Population by Sex and Age Group

Age group	2008					
	Canada	Male	Female	Canada	Male	Female
	Persons (thousands)			% of total of each group		
	Total	Male	Female	Total	Male	Female
Total	33,311.4	16,522.0	16,789.4	100.0	100.0	100.0
0 to 4	1,790.6	920.1	870.6	5.4	5.6	5.2
5 to 9	1,793.3	921.7	871.6	5.4	5.6	5.2
10 to 14	2,013.8	1,031.3	982.5	6.0	6.2	5.9
15 to 19	2,255.7	1,156.3	1,099.4	6.8	7.0	6.5
20 to 24	2,284.3	1,172.6	1,111.7	6.9	7.1	6.6
25 to 29	2,285.2	1,152.7	1,132.5	6.9	7.0	6.7
30 to 34	2,217.0	1,111.9	1,105.1	6.7	6.7	6.6
35 to 39	2,310.0	1,166.8	1,143.2	6.9	7.1	6.8
40 to 44	2,564.1	1,293.5	1,270.7	7.7	7.8	7.6
45 to 49	2,751.8	1,382.1	1,369.8	8.3	8.4	8.2
50 to 54	2,523.4	1,255.0	1,268.4	7.6	7.6	7.6
55 to 59	2,152.4	1,062.5	1,089.9	6.5	6.4	6.5
60 to 64	1,806.6	887.6	919.0	5.4	5.4	5.5
65 to 69	1,346.0	651.1	695.0	4.0	3.9	4.1
70 to 74	1,060.7	497.4	563.2	3.2	3.0	3.4
75 to 79	903.2	404.7	498.5	2.7	2.4	3.0
80 to 84	666.9	268.1	398.8	2.0	1.6	2.4
85 to 89	392.1	134.8	257.3	1.2	0.8	1.5
90 and older	194.2	51.7	142.4	0.6	0.3	0.8

Note: Population as of July 1, 2008.
Source: Adapted from Statistics Canada Website http://www40.statcan.gc.ca/l01/cst01/demo10a-eng.htm

CONCEPT *in Action* >>>

When it launched its red-hot iPod player, Apple Computer revitalized the tech industry and set the standard for digital music. The ultra-hip trademark-white gadgets hold over 15,000 songs and store hundreds of hours of video for display on a stunning 2.5-inch colour screen. Pulsating silhouette ads featuring pop-music icons like U2 and Eminem heighten iPod's mystique and further the player's cultural world-domination. What characteristics of Generation Y made it the ideal target demographic for Apple's ubiquitous iPod?

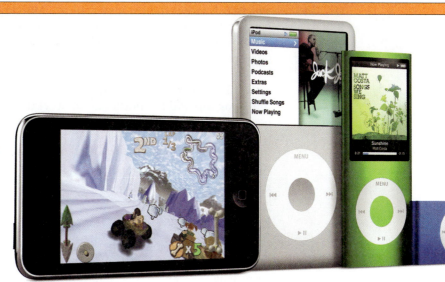

AP/WIDE WORLD PHOTOS

CHAPTER 3 Social Trends, Social Responsibility, and Making Ethical Decisions in Business

It is the first generation of latchkey children—products of dual-career households or, in roughly half of the cases, of divorced or separated parents. This influences their decisions to marry and start families later than their parents. Family and friends, rather than the career success and wealth accumulation that drove their parents, come first. Bombarded by multiple media since their cradle days, Gen Xers are savvy and cynical consumers. "The Xers are the first generation that will not live as well as their parents," says one marketing researcher. They've lived through several rounds of corporate downsizings and spend cautiously, planning for retirement.[8]

Prime Time for Baby Boomers and Beyond

In 2006 the first **baby boomers**, born between 1946 and 1964, turned 60, and in 2008 there were more than half over 50 years of age. This powerful age demographic represents approximately 28 percent of the Canadian population and has significant spending power. Because some boomers are in their peak earning years while others are nearing retirement, it's useful to divide boomers into two subgroups:

- Younger boomers in their 40s and early 50s, whose spending is still directed by their children and have the highest average household incomes and spending of any group.
- Older boomers, ages 55 and above, most of whom are empty nesters.

Shifting Priorities   The two groups exhibit different spending patterns. For younger boomers, home and family are still priorities. Two-thirds of this group own their homes and allocate a larger share of their budgets to home-related expenditures than other ages. Spending on kids and financing their college educations is a high priority for young boomers.

Marketers who chased after the youth market are now catering to the needs of this wealthy and diverse generation of consumers. Research from Home Depot indicates that those over 50 will account for half the growth in home-improvement spending as they remodel their existing homes and buy second homes for investment and retirement purposes. In response, the company introduced in-store kiosks in many of its stores to provide information on making improvements that accommodate the needs of older people. Other industry sectors are courting the older consumer as well. Revlon recently launched a new line of makeup designed for women over 50 called Vital Radiance. L'Oreal followed suit with its own products for older women.[9]

The automotive industry is also taking notice of the over-50 group, which makes more than half of all automobile purchases and will drive auto sales for the next 10 to 15 years. Boomers value quality finishes, safety features and luxury touches, and stylish rather than stodgy vehicles. Muscle cars that were popular with the baby boomer generation have regained their popularity. "They still are caught up in a car-culture mentality where a vehicle is really a primary means of defining who you are," says Art Spinella, president of CNW Marketing Research.[10]

Other industry sectors will be heavily influenced by the extended life spans and active lives of the boomers and their parents. Many are pursuing new passions as they look forward to another 20 to 30 years of life, from hobbies to travel and even new careers. The aging population also places increased demands on health care and related services, and companies are already preparing to meet these needs.

Although many retirees live on fixed incomes, they are still a force in the marketplace. They like convenience and will pay for services, such as home delivery of groceries and prescriptions.

Not Over the Hill Yet

As the huge baby boomer generation ages, so does the workforce.[11] By 2010, 25 percent of all employees will be of retirement age—but the number of people who choose to retire at age 62 or 65 has been declining. Health advances make it possible for them to continue working if they so desire. No longer is retirement an all-or-nothing proposition. Many Canadians expect to work full- or part-time after "retirement," and most would work longer if phased retirement programs were available at their companies.

Financial reasons motivate some of these older workers, who worry that their longer life expectancies will mean outliving their money. Fewer companies offer traditional pension plans, so workers need to supplement social benefits (e.g., Canada Pension Plan payments and Old Age Security payments) and retirement funds. For many, however, the satisfaction of working and feeling productive is more important than money alone. Some stay on with their former companies as consultants or with part-time schedules.

In addition, the number of new entrants to the labour market is not sufficient to replace the retirees, creating resource shortages. Younger workers have different approaches and attitudes to work than their elders.

These converging dynamics create major challenges. Companies must focus not only on recruiting employees to replace retiring workers and track where employees fall in their career lifecycles, but to determine when, whether, and how to replace them. Many companies are developing special programs to retain older workers and benefit from their practical knowledge and problem-solving abilities: employers such as RONA and Home Depot actively seek out older workers because they are disciplined, reliable, and loyal. When older employees do choose to retire, companies discover that they are taking with them vast amounts of knowledge that is difficult—if not impossible—to replace.

Diversity—Canada's Strength

According to the Canadian Policy Research Network, in 2001, 13 percent of the Canadian population identified themselves as belonging to a visible minority group. It is estimated that by 2017, that percentage will rise to approximately 21 percent, excluding First Nations peoples, who are expected to increase their proportion of the Canadian population from 3.4 to 4.1 percent during the same period.[12]

multiculturalism
The fundamental belief that all citizens are equal regardless of their racial or ethnic backgrounds.

Multiculturalism is fundamental to Canada and our belief that all citizens are equal regardless of their racial and ethnic backgrounds. Multiculturalism encourages racial cross-cultural understanding and discourages hatred, discrimination, and violence.[13] Because of the current demographic transition, the trend in Canada is toward greater multiculturalism, although the degree varies in different parts of the country. The majority of the residents of both Toronto and Vancouver might be members of what are now considered visible minorities by 2017.[14]

Changing demographics affect the marketing of goods and services. As Canadians are becoming more health conscious, for instance, companies should promote the "healthiness" of goods and services. As our population ages and becomes more technically sophisticated, organizations need to search for new marketing streams that will encourage the target market to purchase goods and services.

Organizations need to be responsive to customers and, as these buyers change, the organizations need to adjust their marketing efforts. This includes the goods and services they are providing, their price points, their place of availability, and how the organizations promote the goods and services.

If organizations fail to monitor the changing demographics of their customers, they will not be able to respond to these changes and will most likely lose sales.

The Impact of Immigration

Part of the reason for the tremendous shift in Canadian demographics is immigration. Canada's relativity small population simply cannot maintain the current high standard of living. From July 2007 to June 2008, there were approximately 364,000 births in Canada.[15] This rate cannot sustain our economic growth. The federal government—along with the provinces—is trying to determine both the level of need for immigration and various ways to encourage people to move to Canada. For

CONCEPT *in Action* >>>
Employees from different ethnic and racial backgrounds will continue to enrich the workplace with their diverse views and ideas. What can the various governments in Canada do to promote immigration?

© PHOTODISC / GETTY IMAGES

instance, Canada has initiated discussions on the free movement of labour between the NAFTA countries (Canada, United States, and Mexico). Another initiative is the increased use of migrant workers in Canada.

There is no doubt that immigrant entrepreneurs, from the corner grocer to the local builder, are creating jobs for other immigrants and for those born in Canada. Vibrant immigrant communities are revitalizing cities and older suburbs that would otherwise be suffering from a shrinking tax base. And the immigrants' links to their countries of origin are boosting Canadian exports to fast-growing regions such as Asia and Latin America.

Canada is also reaping a bonanza of highly educated foreign-born citizens. High-tech industries, which deal in everything from semiconductors to biotechnology, are depending on immigrant scientists, engineers, and entrepreneurs to remain competitive.

> **concept check**
>
> Explain the impact Generation X, Generation Y, and the baby boomers have on our economy.
>
> How is diversity changing the marketplace?
>
> What has been the impact of immigration in Canada?

Individual Business Ethics

Individual business ethics are shaped by personal choices and the environments in which we live and work. In addition, the laws of our society are guideposts for choosing between right and wrong. In this section, we describe personal philosophies and legal factors that influence the choices people make when confronting ethical dilemmas.

Utilitarianism—Seeking the Best for the Majority

utilitarianism
A philosophy that focuses on the consequences of an action to determine whether it is right or wrong, and holds that an action that affects the majority adversely is morally wrong.

One of the philosophies that might influence choices between right and wrong is **utilitarianism**, which focuses on the consequences of an action taken by a person or organization. The notion that "people should act so as to generate the greatest good for the greatest number" is derived from utilitarianism. When an action affects the majority adversely, it is morally wrong. One problem with this philosophy is that it is nearly impossible to determine accurately how a decision will affect a large number of people.

Another problem is that utilitarianism always involves both winners and losers. If sales are slowing, and a manager decides to release five people rather than putting everyone on a 30-hour workweek, the 20 people who keep their full-time jobs are winners, but the other five are losers.

A final criticism of utilitarianism is that some "costs," although small relative to the potential good, are so negative that some segments of society find them unacceptable. Reportedly, the backs of up to 3,000 animals a year are deliberately broken so that scientists can conduct research that might someday lead to a cure for spinal cord injuries. To a number of people, however, the "costs" are simply too horrible for this type of research to continue.

Individual Rights

HOT Links

For more about the Canadian Charter of Rights and Freedoms and other Canadian legislation, go to (http://laws.justice.gc.ca/en/charter).

In our society, individuals and groups have certain rights that exist under certain conditions regardless of the external circumstances. These rights serve as guides when individuals make ethical decisions. The term *human rights* implies that certain rights are conveyed at birth and cannot be arbitrarily taken away. Denying the rights of an individual or group is considered to be unethical and illegal in most, though not all, parts of the world. Certain rights are guaranteed by the various levels of government and their laws, and these are considered legal rights. The **Canadian Charter of Rights and Freedoms** was enacted in 1982 to guarantee the rights and freedoms of Canadians and is superordinate to any other laws that affect Canadians' rights and freedoms.

Some of the freedoms listed in the Charter include

- freedom of conscience and religion;
- freedom of thought, belief, opinion, and expression (e.g., press and other communications media);
- freedom of peaceful assembly; and
- freedom of association.

Charter rights include

- democratic rights (right to vote at the age of majority);
- mobility rights (the right to enter, remain in, and leave Canada);
- legal rights (the right to life, liberty, and security);
- equality rights (everyone is equal under the law); and
- minority language educational rights (the right to be educated in either English or French).

Justice—The Question of Fairness

justice
What is considered fair according to the prevailing standards of society; in the 21st century, an equitable distribution of the burdens and rewards that society has to offer.

A factor that influences individual business ethics is **justice**, or what is fair according to prevailing standards of society. We all expect life to be reasonably fair. You expect your exams to be fair, the grading to be fair, and your wages to be fair, based on the type of work being done.

In the 21st century, we take justice to mean an equitable distribution of the burdens and rewards that society has to offer. The distributive process varies from society to society. Those in a democratic society believe in the "equal pay for equal work" doctrine, in which individuals are rewarded based on the value that the free market places on their services. Because the market places different values on different occupations, the rewards, such as wages, are not necessarily equal. Nevertheless, many regard the rewards as just. At the other extreme, communist theorists have argued that justice would be served by a society in which burdens and rewards were distributed to individuals according to their abilities and their needs, respectively.

Self-centred stage.

Stages of Ethical Development

We can view an individual's ethical development as having reached one of three levels: preconventional, conventional, or postconventional. The behaviour of a person at the level of **preconventional ethics** is childlike in nature; it is calculating, self-centred, and even selfish, and is based on the possibility of immediate punishment or reward. Thus, a student might not cheat on an exam because he or she is afraid of getting caught and therefore receiving a failing grade for the course. The student's behaviour is based not on a sense of what's right or wrong but, instead, on the threat of punishment.

Conventional ethics moves from an egocentric viewpoint toward the expectations of society. Loyalty and obedience to the organization (or society) become paramount. At the conventional ethics level, a businessperson might say, "I know that our advertising is somewhat misleading, but as long as it will increase sales we should continue the campaign." Right or wrong is not the issue; the only question is whether the campaign will benefit the organization.

Postconventional ethics represents the ethical standards of the mature adult. At the postconventional level, businesspeople are concerned less about how others might see them and more about how they see and judge themselves over the long run. A person who has attained this ethical level might ask, "Even though this action is legal and will increase company profits, is it right in the long run? Might it do more harm than good in the end?" A manager at a fast-food restaurant might refuse to offer Styrofoam cups because they are nonbiodegradable. An advertising agency manager might refuse a tobacco account because of the health hazards of smoking. A lab technician might refuse to recommend a new whitener for a detergent because it could harm the environment. All of these individuals are exhibiting postconventional morality.

Many people believe that the Internet is a vast anonymous place where they can say and do just about anything. When they think that they can't be caught, they sometimes revert to preconventional ethics. Yet e-mail servers owned by businesses and governmental agencies can quickly tell what is being sent and to whom.

Computers and Ethics

The Computer Ethics Institute (CEI) is a research, education, and policy study organization focusing on the interface of information technologies, ethics, and corporate and public policy. Its objective is to undertake research about the actual and potential effects of information technology, and to provide advice to various interested parties (individuals, organizations, communities, etc.) regarding ethical and social responsibilities.

Until recently, there has been a very laissez-faire approach to ethics when it comes to cyberspace, coupled with a great reluctance to restrict information on the Internet, but this is changing in the 21st century. The increased use of the information highway has encouraged more policing. First presented in Dr. Ramon C. Barquin's paper "In Pursuit of a 'Ten Commandments' for Computer Ethics," the CEI has created the "Ten Commandments of Computer Ethics," shown in Exhibit 3.2.

Recognizing Unethical Business Activities

Researchers from Brigham Young University state that all unethical business activities will fall into one of the following categories:

1. *Taking things that don't belong to you.* The unauthorized use of someone else's property or taking property under false pretences is taking something that does not belong to you. Even the smallest offence, such as using the postage meter at your office for mailing personal letters or exaggerating your travel expenses, belongs in this category of ethical violations.

preconventional ethics
A stage in the ethical development of individuals in which people behave in a childlike manner and make ethical decisions in a calculating, self-centred, selfish way, based on the possibility of immediate punishment or reward; also known as self-centred ethics.

conventional ethics
The second stage in the ethical development of individuals in which people move from an egocentric viewpoint to consider the expectations of an organization or society; also known as social ethics.

postconventional ethics
The third stage in the ethical development of individuals in which people adhere to the ethical standards of a mature adult and are less concerned about how others view their behaviour than about how they will judge themselves in the long run; also known as principled ethics.

concept check

Define ethics.

What is utilitarianism?

Discuss the stages of ethical development.

HOT Links

The Canadian Information Processing Society is a professional association providing leadership in information systems and technologies fields. Find out more about their code of ethics at (www.cips.ca).

EXHIBIT 3.2 > Ten Commandments of Computer Ethics

1. Thou shalt not use a computer to harm other people.
2. Thou shalt not interfere with other people's computer work.
3. Thou shalt not snoop around in other people's computer files.
4. Thou shalt not use a computer to steal.
5. Thou shalt not use a computer to bear false witness.
6. Thou shalt not copy or use proprietary software for which you have not paid.
7. Thou shalt not use other people's computer resources without authorization or proper compensation.
8. Thou shalt not appropriate other people's intellectual output.
9. Thou shalt think about the social consequences of the program you are writing or the system you are designing.
10. Thou shalt always use a computer in ways that ensure consideration and respect for your fellow humans.

SOURCE: Computer Ethics Institute, The Brookings Institution, "Ten Commandments of Computer Ethics," (www.brook.edu/its/cei/overview/Ten_Commandments_of_Computer_Ethics.htm) (accessed July 3, 2003; March 2, 2009). Reprinted by permission of The Computer Ethics Institute.

2. *Saying things you know are not true.* When trying for a promotion and advancement, employees might be tempted to discredit their coworkers. Falsely assigning blame or inaccurately reporting conversations is lying. Although "This is the way the game is played around here" is a common justification, saying things that are untrue is an ethical violation.

3. *Giving or allowing false impressions.* The salesperson who permits a potential customer to believe that cardboard boxes will hold tomatoes for long-distance shipping when the salesperson knows the boxes are not strong enough has given a false impression. A car dealer who fails to disclose that a car has been in an accident is misleading potential customers.

4. *Buying influence or engaging in a conflict of interest.* A conflict of interest occurs when the official responsibilities of an employee or government official are influenced by the potential for personal gain. Suppose a company awards a construction contract to a firm owned by the father of a provincial politician while the attorney general's office is investigating that company. If this construction award has the potential to shape the outcome of the investigation, a conflict of interest has occurred.

5. *Hiding or divulging information.* Failing to disclose the results of medical studies that indicate your firm's new drug has significant side effects is the ethical violation of hiding information that the product could be harmful to purchasers. Taking your firm's product development or trade secrets to a new place of employment constitutes the ethical violation of divulging proprietary information.

6. *Taking unfair advantage.* Many current consumer protection laws were passed because so many businesses took unfair advantage of people who were not educated or were unable to discern the nuances of complex contracts. Credit disclosure requirements, truth-in-lending provisions, and new regulations on auto leasing all resulted because businesses misled consumers who could not easily follow the jargon of long, complex agreements.

7. *Committing improper personal behaviour.* Although the ethical aspects of an employee's right to privacy are still debated, it has become increasingly clear that personal conduct outside the job can influence performance and company reputation. Thus, a company driver must abstain from substance abuse because of safety issues. Even the traditional company December party and summer picnic have come under scrutiny because of the possibility that employees at and following these events might harm themselves or others through alcohol-related accidents.

8. *Abusing another person.* Suppose a manager sexually harasses an employee or subjects employees to humiliating corrections in the presence of coworkers or

After the Ford Explorer was linked to rollover accidents and 271 deaths, the Ford Motor Company reached a nationwide settlement that included a national SUV safety campaign that advised consumers on safe SUV driving and loading. At what point should companies ethically inform customers of defects in their products?

JOSE FERNANDEZ WITH HIS FAMILY SHORTLY BEFORE HIS DEATH

© AP / WIDE WORLD PHOTOS

customers. In some cases, laws protect employees. Many situations, however, are simply interpersonal abuse that constitutes an ethical violation.

9. *Permitting organizational abuse.* Many companies with operations outside of their own country have faced issues of organizational abuse. The unfair treatment of workers in international operations appears in the form of child labour, demeaning wages, and excessive work hours. Although a business cannot change the culture of another country, it can perpetuate—or stop—abuse through its operations there.

10. *Violating rules.* Many organizations use rules and processes to maintain internal controls or to respect the authority of managers. Although these rules might seem burdensome to employees trying to serve customers, a violation might be considered an unethical act.

11. *Condoning unethical actions.* What if you witnessed a fellow employee embezzling company funds by forging her signature on a cheque that was to be voided? Would you report the violation? A winking tolerance of others' unethical behaviour is itself unethical.[16]

HOT Links

Visit the Canadian Resources for Business Ethics site at
(www.businessethics.ca).

concept check

How are individual business ethics formed?

How can you recognize unethical activities?

How Organizations Influence Ethical Conduct

LO 4

People choose between right and wrong based on their personal code of ethics. Ethical behaviours (or unethical behaviours) are also influenced by the ethical environment created by their employers. Consider the following newspaper headlines:

- CEO gets paid millions of dollars in salary and bonuses, but when times are tough, it is the middle class tax payers who bail big companies out of their problems.
- "Home Depot Pays $87.5 Million for Not Promoting More Women"[17]

Sustainable Business, Sustainable World

According to Paul Hawken in *The Ecology of Commerce*, "the ultimate purpose of business is not, or should not be, simply to make money. Nor is it merely a system of making and selling things. The promise of business is to increase the general well-being of humankind through service, a creative invention and ethical philosophy."

One of the best ways for a company to demonstrate its corporate responsibility to society is to leave that society better by its actions. And one way a company can do that is by focusing on how "sustainable" it is. For a business to be truly sustainable it has to adapt its practices and be accountable for the environmental impacts of its activities.

Global climate change is perhaps the most important environmental issue of our lifetime. Can we sustain our planet as we've known it, without compromising it for future generations, if we continue to act as we have been toward the environment? One of the major contributors to the problem of global climate change is carbon dioxide (CO_2) emissions, and businesses are a large part of this problem. Most scientists agree that to prevent further changes to the climate, the amount of carbon in the atmosphere must be reduced, and yet the level of carbon emissions continues to grow. In many areas of the country, in regards to CO_2 emissions, businesses are finding that the government is stepping in and mandating them to take some responsibility to reduce the problem.

People often say, "The little bit I could do won't make a difference." But the efforts of each person and each organization acting together, certainly can result in significant positive change. Sustainable Waterloo is one organization that is making a difference. Co-founded by Mike Morrice, a university business and computer electronics graduate, Mike was fueled by a passion to develop a realistic, collaborative, and local solution to the global environmental crisis. The result is Sustainable Waterloo, a not-for-profit organization that facilitates collaboration amongst industry, local government, academia and non-governmental organizations (NGOs) to guide high-tech companies in the Waterloo, Ontario region towards environmental sustainability, initially by developing a voluntary, measurable, and realistic CO_2 reduction target. Its work was inspired by a similar organization in Silicon Valley, California (**www.sustainablesiliconvalley.org**)—that has partnered with 95 high-tech organizations, including Intel, Cisco, and Adobe Systems, to reduce emissions by 20% below 1990 levels by 2010. Sustainable Waterloo offers its "Pledging Partners"—the businesses that are working with it to reduce their CO_2 emissions—(a) a standardized online reporting tool so that companies can measure their carbon footprint and track progress, (b) access to technical information/workshops given by sustainability professionals to help firms reduce their emissions, (c) invitations to ongoing educational forums with experts to share best practices, and (d) public recognition for their accomplishments.

One person, one business, and one community at a time, working together, we can all make a difference.

What changes have occurred in the regulatory environment to deal with greenhouse gas emissions, both federally and provincially? Do you think companies should wait to see what measures are put in place, or act in a proactive fashion? Why? Is this a threat for businesses, or an opportunity? How can you—as a consumer, business student, or young person—be part of the market transition to environmental sustainability?

SOURCE: (www.sustainablewaterloo.org).

As these headlines illustrate, poor business ethics can be very expensive for a company. Organizations can reduce the potential for these types of liability claims by educating their employees about ethical standards through various informal and formal programs. The first step in making a good ethical decision, however, is to recognize unethical business activities when they occur.

Leading by Example

Employees often follow the examples set by their managers. That is, leaders and managers establish patterns of behaviour that determine what's acceptable and what's not within the organization. While Ben Cohen was president of Ben & Jerry's ice cream, he followed a policy that no one could earn a salary more than seven times that of the lowest-paid worker. He wanted all employees to feel that they were equal. At the time he resigned, company sales were $140 million (USD) and the lowest-paid worker earned $19,000 (USD) per year. Ben Cohen's salary was $133,000 (USD) based on the "seven times" rule. A typical top executive of a $140 million (USD) company might have earned 10 times Cohen's salary. Ben Cohen's actions helped shape the ethical values of Ben & Jerry's.

Offering Ethics Training Programs

In addition to providing a system to resolve ethical dilemmas, organizations also provide formal training for employees to help them develop an awareness of questionable business activities and practice appropriate responses. Many Canadian companies have some type of ethics training program. The ones that are most effective begin with techniques for solving ethical dilemmas such as those discussed earlier. Next, employees are presented with a series of situations and are asked to come up with the "best" ethical solution. One of these ethical dilemmas is shown in Exhibit 3.3. Some companies have tried to add a bit of excitement and fun to their ethics training

EXHIBIT 3.3 > An Ethical Dilemma Used for Employee Training

Bill Gannon was a middle manager of a large manufacturer of lighting fixtures in Newark, New Jersey. Bill had moved up the company ladder rather quickly and seemed destined for upper management in a few years. Bill's boss, Dana Johnson, had been pressuring him about the semi-annual reviews concerning Robert Talbot, one of Bill's employees. Dana, it seemed, would not accept any negative comments on Robert's evaluation forms. Bill had found out that a previous manager who had given Robert a bad evaluation was no longer with the company. As Bill reviewed Robert's performance for the forthcoming evaluation period, he found many areas of substandard performance. Moreover, a major client had called recently, complaining that Robert had filled a large order improperly and then had been rude to the client when she called to complain.

Discussion Questions
1. What ethical issues does the situation raise?
2. What courses of action could Bill take? Describe the ethics of each course.
3. Should Bill confront Dana? Dana's boss?
4. What would you do in this situation? What are the ethical implications?

---

programs by presenting them in the form of games. Citigroup, for example, has created The Work Ethic, a board game in which participants strive to answer legal, regulatory, policy-related, and judgment ethics questions correctly.

code of ethics
A set of guidelines prepared by a firm to provide its employees with the knowledge of what the firm expects in terms of their responsibilities and behaviour toward fellow employees, customers, and suppliers.

Establishing a Formal Code of Ethics

Most large companies and thousands of smaller ones have created, printed, and distributed codes of ethics. In general, a **code of ethics** provides employees with the knowledge of what their firm expects in terms of their responsibilities and behaviour toward fellow employees, customers, and suppliers. Some ethical codes offer a lengthy and detailed set of guidelines for employees. Others are not really codes at all but rather summary statements of goals, policies, and priorities. Some companies have their codes framed and hung on office walls or printed on cards to be carried at all times by executives. The code of ethics for the Purchasing Management Association of Canada (PMAC) is shown in Exhibit 3.4.

concept check

What is the role of top management in organizational ethics?

What is a code of ethics?

EXHIBIT 3.4 > Values and Norms of Ethical Behaviour

A. Values

Members will operate and conduct their decisions and actions based on the following values:

Honesty/Integrity

Maintaining an unimpeachable standard of integrity in all their business relationships both inside and outside the organizations in which they are employed;

Professionalism

Fostering the highest standards of professional competence amongst those for whom they are responsible.

Responsible Management

Optimizing the use of resources for which they are responsible so as to provide the maximum benefit to their employers;

Serving the Public Interest

Not using their authority of office for personal benefit, rejecting and denouncing any business practice that is improper;

Conformity to the Laws

In Terms of:

The laws of the country in which they practice;

The Institute's or Corporation's Rules and Regulations;

Contractual obligations

continued

B. Norms of Ethical Behaviour

To consider first, the interest of one's organization in all transactions and to carry out and believe in its established policies.

To be receptive to competent counsel from one's colleagues and be guided by such counsel without impairing the responsibility of one's office.

To buy without prejudice, seeking to obtain the maximum value for each dollar of expenditure.

To strive for increased knowledge of the materials and processes of manufacture, and to establish practical procedures for the performance of one's responsibilities.

To participate in professional development programs so that one's purchasing knowledge and performance are enhanced.

To subscribe to and work for honesty in buying and selling and to denounce all forms of improper business practice.

To accord a prompt and courteous reception to all who call on a legitimate business mission.

To abide by and to encourage others to practice the Professional Code of Ethics of the Purchasing Management Association of Canada and its affiliated Institutes and Corporation.

To counsel and assist fellow purchasers in the performance of their duties.

To cooperate with all organizations and individuals engaged in activities which enhance the development and standing of purchasing and materials management.

RULES OF CONDUCT

In applying these rules of conduct, members should follow guidance set out below:

Declaration of Interest

Any personal interest which may impinge or might reasonably be deemed by others to impinge on a member's impartiality in any matter relevant to his or her duties should be immediately declared to his or her employer.

Confidentiality and Accuracy of Information

The confidentiality of information received in the course of duty must be respected and should not be used for personal gain; information given in the course of duty should be true and fair and not designed to mislead.

Competition

While considering the advantages to the member's employer of maintaining a continuing relationship with a supplier, any arrangement which might prevent the effective operation of fair competition should be avoided.

Business Gifts and Hospitality

To preserve the image and integrity of the member, employer and the profession, business gifts other than items of small intrinsic value should not be accepted. Reasonable hospitality is an accepted courtesy of a business relationship. The frequency and nature of gifts or hospitality accepted should not be allowed whereby the recipient might be or might be deemed by others to have been influenced in making a business decision as a consequence of accepting such hospitality or gifts.

Discrimination and Harassment

No member shall knowingly participate in acts of discrimination or harassment towards any person that he or she has business relations with.

Environmental Issues

Members shall recognize their responsibility to environmental issues consistent with their corporate goals or missions.

Interpretation

When in doubt on the interpretation of these rules of conduct, members should refer to the Ethics Committee of their Institute or Corporation.

ENFORCEMENT PROCEDURES

The following procedures shall apply unless otherwise governed by provincial legislation.

Cases of members reported to have breached the Ethical Code shall be referred to the Institute or Corporation for review by their Ethics Committee.

A. Complaint Process

Allegations of a breach to the Professional Code of Ethics shall be made in writing by the witness to the Institute or Corporation.

Upon receipt of the complaint, the Institute or Corporation will send an acknowledgment of receipt to the witness and will advise the accused in writing that he or she is under investigation, and the nature of the complaint.

B. Investigation

The Ethics Committee will conduct an investigation, which will include the opportunity for the accused to present his or her own version of the facts.

The Ethics Committee will, within a reasonable period of time, present its report to the President of the Institute or Corporation. The report will include the nature of the complaint and the decision as to the dismissal of the complaint, or the sanction to be applied.

The President will then send the decision to the accused, who has thirty days to appeal.

If the accused decides to make a request of appeal, then the request must be in writing to the President.

The President will convene an Appeal Committee meeting with the witnesses, the accused and all other persons who could have new information about the case.

The Appeal Committee will make its decision within 30 days of the receipt of the request of appeal. The decision of the Appeal Committee is final and without appeal.

C. Sanctions

Where a case is proven, a member may, depending on the circumstances and the gravity of the charge, be reprimanded, suspended from membership or expelled and removed from the list of members.

Details of cases in which members are found in breach of the Code may be published in such a manner as the Institute or Corporation shall deem appropriate.

Enforcement shall be in accordance with the requirements of the member's Institute or Corporation.

Do codes of ethics make employees behave in a more ethical manner? Some people believe that they do. Others think that they are little more than public relations gimmicks. If senior management abides by the code of ethics and regularly emphasizes the code to employees, then it will likely have a positive influence on behaviour.

Source: Purchasing Management Association of Canada (PMAC), *PMAC Code of Ethics*, (http://pmac.ca/about/ethics.asp), accessed March 10, 2003. Reprinted by permission.

Managing a Socially Responsible Business

LO 5

social responsibility
The concern of businesses for the welfare of society as a whole; consists of obligations beyond those required by law or contracts.

HOT *Links*

Find out which companies test their products on animals and which don't in the campaign section of the People for the Ethical Treatment of Animals (PETA) website (www.peta.org).

Acting in an ethical manner is one of the four components of the pyramid of corporate social responsibility. **Social responsibility** is the concern of businesses for the welfare of society as a whole. It consists of obligations beyond those required by law or union contract. This definition makes two important points. First, social responsibility is voluntary. Beneficial action required by law, such as cleaning up factories that are polluting air and water, is not voluntary. Second, the obligations of social responsibility are broad. They extend beyond investors in the company to include workers, suppliers, consumers, and communities.

Exhibit 3.5 portrays economic performance as the foundation for the other three responsibilities. At the same time that a business pursues profits (economic responsibility), however, it is expected to obey the law (legal responsibility); to do what is right, just, and fair (ethical responsibility); and to be a good corporate citizen (philanthropic responsibility). These four components are distinct but together constitute the whole.

Understanding Social Responsibility

Peter Drucker, a management expert, says to look first at what an organization does to society and second at what it can do for society. This idea suggests that social responsibility has two basic dimensions: legality and responsibility.

EXHIBIT 3.5 > The Pyramid of Corporate Social Responsibility

Philanthropic Responsibilities
The highest level of the triangle, philanthropic responsibilities can be considered only after economic, legal, and ethical responsibilities.

Legal Responsibilities
Corporations must, of course, follow the law. The second level of the pyramid recognizes that legal considerations are also necessary for a corporation's success.

Ethical Responsibilities
Resting on the foundation set by economic and legal responsibilities are ethical responsibilities. A corporation can turn its attention to ethical matters only after ensuring its economic and legal position.

Economic Responsibilities
Because a corporation must be profitable to survive, its economic responsibilities form the base of the pyramid.

Illegal and Irresponsible Behaviour   The idea of social responsibility is so widespread today that it is hard to conceive of a company continually acting in illegal and irresponsible ways. Nevertheless, such actions do sometimes occur. We have seen acts by those in companies who created   financial ruin for their organizations, extreme financial hardships for many former employees, and general hardships for the communities in which they operated (e.g., Enron and WorldCom). Yet top executives walked away with millions. Some, however, will ultimately pay large fines and be sentenced to jail. Federal, provincial, and local laws determine whether an activity is legal or not.

Irresponsible but Legal Behaviour   Sometimes companies act irresponsibly, yet their actions are legal. The governments are pressuring the advertising industry and the automobile industry for more responsible advertising. The government is concerned about advertisements that place an emphasis on speed and that show vehicles engaging in dangerous driving practices. "It seems that some ads work against road safety rather than for it," according to one spokesperson. Another example is companies that create harm to our environment but are within the acceptable levels of pollutants.

Legal and Responsible Behaviour   The vast majority of business activities fall into the category of behaviour that is both legal and responsible. Most firms act legally, and most try to be socially responsible. Lucent Technologies (formerly Bell Labs) each year has 10,000 employees participate in "Global Days of Caring," assisting community projects worldwide. A recent Global Days of Caring found employees working on specific projects in 20 countries. The projects included engaging in environmental cleanup and fixing up childcare and senior citizens' centres. Ongoing projects include painting maps on elementary school playgrounds to help teach geography and making "smart" teddy bears to ease the trauma of children's hospital stays. Lucent gives employees paid time off for the projects and provides coordination and money. The company also engages in a number of other socially responsible activities including hiring and training the unemployed, giving equipment and grants to schools, and making grants to community agencies where Lucent employees volunteer.

> **concept check**
>
> What are the four components of social responsibility?
>
> Give an example of legal but irresponsible behaviour.

Responsibility to Stakeholders

stakeholders
Individuals or groups to whom a business has a responsibility; employees, customers, the general public, and investors are included.

What makes a company admired or perceived as socially responsible? This type of company meets its obligations to its stakeholders. Stakeholders are the individuals or groups to whom a business has a responsibility. The stakeholders of a business are its employees, its customers, the general public, and its investors.

Responsibility to Employees

An organization's first responsibility is to provide jobs for employees. Keeping people employed and letting them have time to enjoy the fruits of their labours is the finest thing business can do for society. Enron is an example of a company that violated this responsibility. Beyond this fundamental responsibility, employers must provide a clean and safe working environment that is free from all forms of discrimination. Companies should also strive to provide job security whenever possible.

Enlightened firms are also empowering employees to make decisions on their own and suggest solutions to company problems. Empowerment contributes to an employee's self-worth, which, in turn, increases productivity and reduces absenteeism.

Responsibility to Customers

A central theme of this text is that to be successful today, a company must satisfy its customers. A firm must deliver what it promises. It must also be honest and forthright

CONCEPT *in Action* >>>

CIBC's sponsorship of the Run for the Cure represents a legal and socially responsible activity that also enhances the image of the bank in the eyes of many consumers. What other examples can you cite of companies being socially responsible?

CP PHOTO/TORONTO STAR (STUART NIMMO)

social investing
The practice of limiting investments to securities of companies that act in accordance with the investor's beliefs about ethical and social responsibility.

HOT Links

Each year the Financial Post lists the best companies to work for. See the latest at (http://working.canada.com).

HOT Links

Want to see how the global environment is changing and learn the latest about global warming? Check out (www.climatehotmap.org).

with its clients. When the Listeria outbreak occurred at Maple Leaf Foods in 2008, the company took measures to minimize the effect on customers by recalling products and cleaning the machinery. We will discuss this theme in more detail in the, "Customer Satisfaction and Quality" section later in the chapter.

Responsibility to Investors

Companies' relationships with investors also entail social responsibility. Although a company's economic responsibility to make a profit might seem to be its main obligation to its shareholders, many investors increasingly are putting emphasis on other aspects of social responsibility. This includes such actions as the company acting within its legal responsibilities and, at times, doing more than the law mandates.

Some investors are limiting their investments to securities that fit within their beliefs about ethical and social responsibility. This is called **social investing.** For example, a social investment fund might eliminate from consideration the securities of all companies that make tobacco products or liquor, manufacture weapons, or have a history of polluting.

Investors who are dissatisfied with corporate managers tend to be less passive than in the past. They are pressuring corporations with tactics such as exposés on television and in other media, and calling government attention to perceived wrongdoings. Groups of owners are pressuring companies to increase profits, link executive pay to performance, and oust inefficient management. Consequently, executives and managers are giving more weight to the concerns of owner stakeholders in the decision-making process.

Responsibility to Suppliers

Many companies rely on other companies for their survival. Often companies hire other companies to provide products or perform services for them. These suppliers (or business partners) are usually contracted because they can provide the products or perform the services more cheaply. Mark's Work Wearhouse, for example, does not produce its own line of clothing for resale but instead contracts it out to its suppliers. These suppliers are employing people, in turn providing more money to fuel the economy. It is important that businesses support their suppliers (e.g., giving contracts, paying supplier invoices). As we will see in Chapter 4, many companies are tying the e-business technology to their suppliers to realize many efficiencies.

Responsibility to Governments

Governments in Canada rely on tax dollars to operate and provide their services to Canadians. Much of the tax revenue that the governments collect is in the form of corporate taxes. Corporations are responsible for accurately reporting their earnings and fulfilling their tax obligations. Another expectation, for example is that the company operates in a safe and reasonable manner.

Responsibility to Society

A business must also be responsible to society. A business provides a community with jobs, goods, and services. It also pays taxes that go to support schools, hospitals, and better roads. Most companies try to be good citizens in their communities.

Responsibility to society doesn't end at our shores. Global enterprises are attempting to help around the world as explained in the Expanding Around the Globe box.

Expanding Around The Globe

CLEAN WATER, NO PROFIT

Like plenty of multinationals, Procter and Gamble (P&G) rushed to offer aid to tsunami victims in Asia, shipping 15 million packets of water purifier to affected countries and pledging 13 million more if needed. What's less known is that the product P&G airlifted was a commercial bust.

Called Pur, the powder was envisioned as a revolutionary way to clean the world's drinking water. P&G spent four years and $10 million (USD) for research and development before launching Pur in September 2002. But the packets of chlorine salt and iron sulfate are relatively complicated to mix and, at about 10 cents each, expensive for many of the world's poor.

By November of 2003, Pur still hadn't caught on as a profitable venture. In virtually every market where it was available, Pur gained early interest but not broad acceptance. By late 2004, P&G abandoned plans to sell the product for profit in developing countries and dramatically cut back its water-purification ambitions.

P&G wondered how it would unload the millions of packets of Pur sitting in the company's factory in Manila. Then, shortly after the December 26, 2004 tsunami, the phone started ringing with calls from AmeriCares, UNICEF, and the International Federation of the Red Cross with orders for Pur.

The company added a third shift to its factory and had orders to ship 15 million packets of the product to areas hit by the tsunami. Initially, P&G sold the packets to aid organizations at cost—3 1/2 cents, but later decided to donate them because of the enormity of the disaster.

In order to keep the product going, management has examined a list of 40 countries with the highest rates of infant mortality due to unsafe drinking water. P&G has pledged to introduce Pur to two new countries a year. P&G is selling Pur in Haiti and Uganda for 8 or 9 cents a packet and Kenya is the next market to be served.[18]

Critical Thinking Questions

- After the tsunami, should P&G have given Pur away at the beginning?
- Should Pur be given away in Haiti, Uganda, and Kenya? Why?

Source: Sarah Ellison and Eric Bellman, "Clean Water, No Profit," *Wall Street Journal*, February 3, 2005, B1, B2. Reprinted with permission of The Wall Street Journal. Copyright © 2005 Dow Jones & Company, Inc. All Rights Reserved Worldwide.

Environmental Protection   Business is also responsible for protecting and improving the world's fragile environment. The world's forests are rapidly being destroyed. Every second, an area the size of a football field is laid bare. Plant and animal species are becoming extinct at the rate of 17 per hour. A continent-sized hole is opening in the earth's protective ozone shield. Each year we throw out more refuse; as a result, more of our landfills are filled to capacity. To maintain sustainable development, business must be more sensitive to our environment (e.g., recycling, land management, pollution controls).

To slow the erosion of the world's resources, many companies are becoming more environmentally responsible. Canadian Tire, for example, strives to divert as much waste as possible from landfills. Since 1990, it has implemented aggressive pallet reuse and packaging recycling programs.[19]

Corporate Philanthropy   Companies also display their social responsibility through **corporate philanthropy**, which includes cash contributions, donations of equipment and products, and support for the volunteer efforts of company employees. For example, in 2005, Manulife Financial assisted approximately 500 non-profit companies with community building in four main areas: health care, education, community services, and local volunteerism. Its contribution was not only in the form of cash donations and sponsorship but also included more than 44,000 hours of employees' time globally.[20]

corporate philanthropy
The practice of charitable giving by corporations; includes contributing cash, donating equipment and products, and supporting the volunteer efforts of company employees.

> ### concept check
>
> How do businesses carry out their social responsibilities to consumers?
>
> What is corporate philanthropy?
>
> Is a company's only responsibility to its investors to make a profit? Why or why not?

Trends in Ethics and Social Responsibility

LO 7

Four important trends related to ethics and social responsibility are: increased protection for whistle blowers, changes in corporate philanthropy, a new social contract between employers and employees, and the growth of global ethics and social responsibility.

More Protection for Whistle Blowers

whistle blower
An employee, former employee, or any other member of an organization who reports misconduct by others in the organization that have the power to take corrective action.

In the recent past there have been many instances of whistle blowing in Canada. A **whistle blower** is an employee, former employee, or any other stakeholder of an organization who reports misconduct, or harmful or illegal acts by others in the organization.

In Canada, various federal and provincial statutes are designed to protect employees who provide information to law enforcement offices (especially related to health and safety standards). However, little has been done until recently to protect those that have "blown the whistle" on corrupt and/or unethical behaviours of an organization or its employees or directors.

Changes in Corporate Philanthropy

Corporate philanthropy has typically involved seeking out needy groups and then giving them money or company products. Today the focus is shifting to **strategic giving,** which ties philanthropy more closely to the corporate mission or goals and targets donations to regions where a company operates. For example, The Forzani Group supports the Sport Chek Mother's Day Run & Walk each year in Alberta.

Stan Litow, IBM's vice-president of corporate community relations, notes that the company knows it takes more than just money—chequebook philanthropy (the old model)—to have a successful giving program. "With chequebook philanthropy you could contribute a lot of money and accomplish very little," he says. "I think that in the new model, being generous is incredibly important, but the most important aspect of this new model is using our many resources to achieve something of lasting value in the communities where we live, work and do business."[21]

A New Social Contract Trend between Employer and Employee

Another trend in social responsibility is the effort by organizations to redefine their relationship with their employees. Many people have viewed social responsibility as a one-way street that focuses on the obligations of business to society, employees, and others. Now companies are telling employees that they also have a responsibility when it comes to job security. The new contract reads somewhat like this: "There will never be job security. You will be employed by us as long as you add value to the organization, and you are continuously responsible for finding ways to add value. In return, you have the right to demand interesting and important work, the freedom and resources to perform it well, pay that reflects your contribution, and the experience and training needed to be employable here or elsewhere."

Coca-Cola, for example, requires extensive employee retraining each year. The idea, according to a Coke executive, is to become a more valuable employee by adding 25 percent to your existing knowledge every year.

Global Ethics and Social Responsibility

As Canadian businesses expand into global markets, their corporate codes of ethics and policies on social responsibility must travel with them. As a citizen of several countries, a multinational corporation has several responsibilities. These include respecting local practices and customs, ensuring that there is harmony between the organization's staff and the host population, providing management leadership, and developing a cadre of local managers who will be a credit to their community. When a multinational makes an investment in a foreign country, it should commit to a long-term relationship. That means involving all stakeholders in the host country in decision making. Finally, a responsible multinational will implement ethical guidelines within the organization in the host country. By fulfilling these responsibilities, the company will foster respect for both local and international laws.

Multinational corporations often must balance conflicting interests of stakeholders when making decisions regarding social responsibilities, especially in the area of human rights. Questions involving child labour, forced labour, minimum wages, and

strategic giving
The practice of tying philanthropy closely to the corporate mission or goals and targeting donations to regions where a company operates

HOT Links

What does IBM corporation require from its employees in terms of ethical business conduct? It's all presented in the Business Conduct Guidelines, which you will find at (www.ibm.com/us).

HOT Links

How is the International Business Ethics Institute working to promote business ethics worldwide? Find out at (www.business-ethics.org).

HOT Links

The unique corporate culture at Levi Strauss rewards and recognizes employee achievements. To learn about working for a company that values employee efforts, go to the Levi Strauss home page (www.levistrauss.com).

CONCEPT *in Action* >>>

Computer firms that link their product donations with their corporate goals, for example schools, represent the corporate trend of strategic giving. How can other forms of business engage in corporate philanthropy?

LISA F. YOUNG/SHUTTERSTOCK

concept check

Describe strategic giving.

What role do employees have in improving their job security?

How do multinational corporations demonstrate social responsibility in a foreign country?

workplace safety can be particularly difficult. Levi Strauss was strongly praised when it announced it was leaving China because of the country's poor human rights record. However, China is an inexpensive place to manufacture clothing, and the temptation to stay there was simply too great. In fact, Levi Strauss never stopped making clothes in China; its Hong Kong subsidiary continues to manufacture clothes on a contract basis. Levi recently announced that it would begin selling clothes in China. One might argue that Levi Strauss must remain competitive and profitable, or it will not be able to be a leader in the cause of social responsibility. When the announcement came, however, human rights activists quickly set up a picket at Levi's San Francisco headquarters.

Making Ethical Choices

TOO DELICIOUS TO RESIST

We are constantly bombarded with media reports claiming that many people are becoming dangerously overweight. A recent medical study also just classified obesity as a disease in its own right, unconnected to such symptoms as high blood pressure, cholesterol, or heart problems. So perhaps it is not surprising that a recent lawsuit claimed that McDonald's is responsible for the obesity of two teenagers by "getting them hooked" on their burgers and fries.

You are the lawyer approached by the teens' parents to bring suit against McDonald's. You ask yourself some soul-searching questions. Does McDonald's market and sell food in such a manner that it poses a health danger to unsuspecting consumers? And what about personal accountability? Shouldn't the teens and/or their parents be held responsible for their food choices? You wonder whether if this were a local mom and pop restaurant, would the teens' parents be suing? Or are the deep pockets of McDonald's too delicious to resist?

Using a Web search tool, locate articles about this topic and then write responses to the following questions. Be sure to support your arguments and cite your sources.

ETHICAL DILEMMA Do you tell the teens' parents to go home, cook healthy, and put their kids on a diet? Or do you take the case—believing that McDonald's has not acted in a socially responsible way—while recognizing the potential for some serious money?

SOURCES: Dave Carpenter, "DIET: McDonald's to post nutrition facts on packaging next year," The America's Intelligence Wire, October 26, 2005, (http://galenet.thomsonlearning.com); Pallavi Gogoi, "McDonald's New Wrap," Business Week Online, February 17, 2006, (www.businessweek.com); Richard Martin, "Revived McD Obesity Lawsuit Still Suggests Personal-Responsibility Defense—for Now," Nation's Restaurant News, February 14, 2005, (http://galenet.thomsonlearning.com); Wendy Melillo, "Bringing Up Baby: Where's the Line, and Who Should Draw It, In Advertising to Children?" ADWEEK, February 13, 2006, p.14+; Libby Quaid, "House Votes to Block Lawsuits Blaming Food Industry for Obesity," The America's Intelligence Wire, October 19, 2005, (http://galenet.thomsonlearning.com).

In many situations, there are no right or wrong answers. Instead, organizations must provide a process to resolve the dilemma quickly and fairly. Two approaches for resolving ethical problems are the "three-questions test" and the newspaper test.

Resolving Ethical Problems in Business

In evaluating an ethical problem, managers can use the three-questions test to determine the most ethical response: "Is it legal?" "Is it balanced?" and "How does it make me feel?" Many companies such as Texas Instruments, Marriott, and McDonald's rely on this test to guide employee decision-making. If the answer to the first question is "no," then don't do it. Many ethical dilemmas, however, involve situations that aren't illegal. For example, the sale of tobacco is legal in Canada, but given all the research that shows that tobacco use is dangerous to one's health, is it an ethical activity?

The second question, "Is it balanced?" requires you to put yourself in the position of other parties affected by your decision. For example, as an executive, you might not favour a buyout of your company because you will probably lose your job. Shareholders, however, might benefit substantially from the price to be paid for their shares in the buyout. At the same time, the employees of the business and their community might suffer economically if the purchaser decides to close the business or focus its efforts in a different product area. The best situation, of course, is when everybody wins or shares the burden equally.

The final question, "How does it make me feel?" asks you to examine your comfort with a particular decision. Many people find that after reaching a decision on an issue, they still experience discomfort that can manifest itself in a loss of sleep or appetite. Those feelings of conscience can serve as a guide in resolving ethical dilemmas.

Front Page of the Newspaper Test

Many managers use the "front page of the newspaper test" for evaluating ethical dilemmas. The question to be asked is how a critical and objective reporter would report your decision in a front-page story. Some managers rephrase the test for their employees: How will the headline read if I make this decision? This test is helpful in spotting and resolving potential conflicts of interest.

Customer Satisfaction and Quality

Ethics and social responsibility play important roles in customer satisfaction and quality. Acting in an unethical manner, such as overcharging a client or failing to service a product properly after the sale, will normally mean losing that customer for life. Moreover, a dissatisfied customer will often tell other potential customers, resulting in further lost sales. Using cheaper, less reliable parts in the manufacturing process, for example, might save money in the short run but will drive off customers in the long term.

People like to do business with organizations that they feel are good corporate citizens. For example, members of the Retail Council of Canada have a voluntary scanner code, which includes the following policy:

1. THE ITEM FREE SCANNER POLICY. Retailers will implement an Item Free Scanner Policy as follows:

1.1 On a claim being presented by the customer, where the scanned price of a product at checkout is higher than the price displayed in the store or than advertised by the store, the lower price will be honoured; and

(a) if the correct price of the product is $10 or less, the retailer will give the product to the customer free of charge; or

(b) if the correct price of the product is higher than $10, the retailer will give the customer a discount of $10 off the corrected price.

SOURCE: Courtesy the Retail Council of Canada.

Summary of Learning Outcomes

1 **Identify some of the current social factors that have the greatest impact on business.**

The business environment consists of social, demographic, economic, technological, and competitive trends. Managers cannot control environmental trends. Instead, they must understand how the environment is changing and the impact of those changes on the business. Several social trends are currently influencing businesses. First, people choose different lifestyles based on such factors as: economics, interests, resources, etc. Secondly, the phenomenon of working women has probably had a greater effect on marketing than has any other social change. Increasing financial resources have given more opportunities for a component lifestyle.

2 **Explain how demographic shifts are creating both challenges and new opportunities for business.**

Businesses today must deal with the unique shopping preferences of Generations X and Y and the baby boomers. Each must be appealed to in a different way with different goods and services. Generation Y, for example, is the most computer literate and the most interested in computers and accessories. Furthermore, because the population is growing older, businesses are offering more products that appeal to middle-aged and older markets.

3 **Discuss the philosophies and concepts that shape personal ethical standards.**

Ethics is a set of moral standards for judging whether something is right or wrong. A utilitarianism approach to setting personal ethical standards focuses on the consequences of an action taken by a person or organization. According to this approach, people should act so as to generate the greatest good for the greatest number. Every human is entitled to certain rights such as freedom and the pursuit of happiness. Another approach to ethical decision making is justice, or what is fair according to accepted standards.

4 **Show how organizations encourage ethical business behaviour.**

Top management must shape the ethical culture of the organization. They should lead by example, offer ethics training programs, and establish a formal code of ethics.

5 **Define social responsibility.**

Social responsibility is the concern businesses show for the welfare of society as a whole. It consists of obligations beyond just making a profit. Social responsibility also goes beyond what is required by law or union contract. Companies can engage in illegal and irresponsible behaviour, irresponsible but legal behaviour, or legal and responsible behaviour. The vast majority of organizations act legally and try to be socially responsible.

6 **Illustrate how businesses meet their social responsibilities to various stakeholders.**

Stakeholders are individuals or groups to whom business has a responsibility. Businesses are responsible to employees. They should provide a clean and safe working environment. Organizations can build employees' self-worth through empowerment programs. Businesses also have a responsibility to customers to provide good, safe products and services. Organizations are responsible to the general public to be good corporate citizens. Firms must help protect the environment and provide a good place to work. Companies also engage in corporate philanthropy, which includes contributing cash, donating goods and services, and supporting volunteer efforts of employees. Finally, companies are responsible to investors. They should earn a reasonable profit for the owners.

7 **List some of the global and domestic trends in ethics and social responsibility.**

Today, corporate philanthropy is shifting away from simply giving to any needy group and is focusing instead on strategic giving, in which the philanthropy relates more closely to the corporate mission or goals, and targets donations to areas where the firm operates. Corporate philanthropy is coming under increasing attacks from special-interest groups, however.

A second trend is toward a new social contract between employer and employee. Instead of the employer having the sole responsibility for maintaining jobs, now the employee must assume part of the burden and find ways to add value to the organization.

As the world increasingly becomes a global community, multinational corporations are now expected to assume a global set of ethics and responsibility. Global companies must understand local customs. They should also involve local stakeholders in decision making. Multinationals must also make certain that their suppliers are not engaged in human rights violations.

Key Terms

baby boomers 82	justice 85
Canadian Charter of Rights and	multiculturalism 83
Freedoms 85	postconventional ethics 86
code of ethics 90	preconventional ethics 86
component lifestyle 78	social investing 94
conventional ethics 86	social responsibility 92
corporate philanthropy 95	stakeholders 93
demography 80	strategic giving 96
ethics 78	utilitarianism 84
Generation X 80	whistle blower 95
Generation Y 80	

Experiential Exercises

1. **Support a good cause.** You don't have to wait until you graduate to start demonstrating your social responsibility. It will also look good on your résumé when you need to differentiate yourself from all of the other job seekers. Go to (**www.volunteer.ca/index-eng.php**) and find organizations in your area looking for volunteers. Find one that meets your interest and that is related to your career goals, and go to work.

2. **Know your ethical values.** To get a better idea of your own level of ethical development, take an ethics test. Go to (**www.ethicsandbusiness.org/stylequiz.htm**) This test will give you better insight into yourself.

3. If you are thinking about giving money to a charity, check it out first. Find out what charities are registered in Canada at (**www.cra-arc.gc.ca/tax/charities/online_listings/charity_listings-e.html**).

4. **Work for a firm that cares about its social responsibilities.** When you enter the job market, make certain that you are going to work for a socially responsible organization. Ask a prospective employer "how the company gives back to society." If you plan to work for a large company, check out the current list of Canada's most admired corporations in the *Financial Post*.

5. Professor Joseph Badaracco of Harvard Business School believes that "real ethical dilemmas are not choices between right and wrong, but choices between right and right—cases in which both options seem correct for different reasons, yet one must be chosen and one rejected." Here is an example: Many CEOs sold shares of their stock when prices were near their high points. Even though their actions were legal, it soon became apparent that they knew the stock was significantly overpriced. Was the CEO ethically obligated to tell the public that this was the case—even knowing that doing so could cause the stock price to plummet, thereby hurting someone who bought the stock earlier that day?

SOURCE: Geoffrey Colvin, "Between Right and Right," *Fortune,* October 30, 2002, (www.fortune.com).

6. Your company has decided to create a new position for an ethics officer and has asked you to be part of the team that is writing the job description. Using resources such as the website of the Ethics and Compliance Officer Association (ECOA) (**www.theecoa.org**) and other materials, draft a list of job responsibilities for this new role.

7. The Boeing Company makes business ethics a priority, asking employees to take refresher training every year. It encourages employees to take the Ethics Challenge with their work groups and to discuss the issues with their peers. You can take the challenge, too, by going to (**www.boeing.com/companyoffices/aboutus/ethics/education.htm**) Each question presents an ethical dilemma, together with three or four potential answers. Taking the challenge will show you how Boeing approaches workplace ethics. Summarize your findings. Did any answers surprise you?

8. You'll find a comprehensive list of business ethics sites at (**www.web-miner.com/busethics.htm**) Once at the site, go to the section on Corporate Codes of Ethics. Look at three examples of codes in different industries. What elements do they have in common? How are they different? Suggest how one of the codes could be improved.

9. What ethical issues arise as companies add e-business to their operations? Go to the *Information Week* site (**www.informationweek.com**) and perform a search for business ethics. What topics did you find? Identify three areas where the potential for ethical breaches could occur, and briefly discuss each.

10. Visit the Fur Is Dead website from the People for the Ethical Treatment of Animals (PETA), (**http://furisdead.com**) Read about PETA's view of the fur industry. Do you agree with this view? Why or why not? How do you think manufacturers of fur clothing would justify their actions to someone from PETA? Would you work for a store that sold fur-trimmed clothing? Explain your answer.

11. *Green Money Journal,* (**www.greenmoneyjournal.com**) is a bimonthly online journal that promotes social responsibility investing. What are the current topics of concern in this area? Visit the archives to find articles on socially responsible investing and find two areas of corporate social responsibility. Summarize what you have learned.

Review Questions

1. What are some of the social trends affecting Canadian business? Discuss how each of these is affecting business.

2. What are the major demographic groups by age? What are some characteristics of each group?

3. How does diversity and multiculturalism impact Canadian business?

4. What is utilitarianism?

5. What are some of the individual rights we enjoy in Canada?

6. How does the idea of justice affect business?

7. What are some unethical business activities discussed in the chapter?

8. What can organizations do to influence ethical conduct?

9. Define social responsibility.

10. Give examples of legal but irresponsible business behaviours.

11. List the various stakeholders of an organization.

12. What responsibilities does a company have to the various stakeholders?

13. How can being philanthropic help the bottom line of a company?

Timbuk2 Gets the Message

It all started in 1989 with one product: a custom messenger bag designed for bicycle couriers. That unique carrier became popular with not just cyclists, but also students and professionals who loved its stylish yet durable features. Today Timbuk2 manufactures 30 products, including messenger bags, computer cases, totes, duffles, iPod sleeves, and yoga bags that generate more than $10 million in annual revenues. Loyal customers buy Timbuk2 cases at REI, EMS, Apple, and 1,200 independent specialty retail stores. The messenger bags cost from $60 to $90, depending on size; for $10 more customers can select custom colour combinations.

Although other companies have shifted production to low-cost manufacturing centres overseas, Timbuk2 still produces its messenger bags at its original factory. To preserve its local presence and retain jobs while maintaining a financially sound company, Timbuk2 took steps to boost the plant's productivity. Originally Timbuk2 made its bags "on demand" as customer orders came in. Converting to predetermined colour combinations allowed the factory to operate independent of demand and to build inventory, greatly improving productivity. "That change alone saved our factory from going out of business," says Mark Dwight, Timbuk2 president and chief executive officer. "There is value in the made-domestically products, and locally produced bags can be customized to customer requests on a very short lead time. That quick response is a unique advantage."

The company discovered, however, that manufacturing its new lines was more complex than the messenger bags and called for specialized machinery. These factors and the resulting high labour costs led Timbuk2 to explore off-shore manufacturing options. Keeping the headquarters operation and design team in North America but shifting production to a carefully selected factory in China enabled Timbuk2 to continue offering top quality products while keeping prices affordable.

Timbuk2 is proud of its commitment to ethical working conditions and fair wages at all its facilities. Executives visit the China factory every month or two to monitor the work environment and make sure that product quality remains high. The new products have been well-received, increasing Timbuk2's reputation as a lifestyle brand. As a result of its higher sales volume, the company has expanded the domestic factory, doubled its production staff, and added employees in all departments. It continues to roll out new products. "Our goal is to create a solid growth company, to continue delighting our customers with great products, to contribute to our local community, and to make the Timbuk2 swirl as recognizable as the Nike swoosh," says Dwight.[22]

Critical Thinking Questions

- Mark Dwight faced considerable resistance from existing managers when he assumed control of Timbuk2 and wanted to move the production of new products overseas. He has asked for your help in preparing a presentation to win their support. Summarize the arguments in favour of offshore production.
- Now list the arguments against using foreign manufacturers and develop answers to help Dwight counter charges that it is not socially responsible to take jobs offshore.
- How did Dwight's decision to manufacture new products in China support the company's desire to be a good corporate citizen domestically?

SOURCE: Adapted from "In the Bag," *Fast Company*, March 2005, http://www.fastcompany.com; Andrew Tilin, "Bagging the Right Customers," *Business 2.0*, May 2005, pp.56–57; Timbuk2 corporate Web Site, http://www.timbuk2.com (November 13, 2005); David Worrell, "Go for the Gold," *Entrepreneur*, July 2005, http://www.entrepreneur.com; and "It's All in the Bag for Timbuk2," *San Francisco Chronicle*, (May 1, 2006).

Fair Trade Sweetens the Coffee

When you sip your morning coffee, you probably don't wonder who grew the beans. Rink Dickinson did, and when he learned that small coffee growers were at the mercy of agents and middlemen who paid them the lowest possible prices, he decided to do something about it.

Coffee growers, receiving only 40 cents on each $8 to $9 pound of gourmet coffee sold, were fleeing their farms to seek jobs in overcrowded cities. Others were planting illegal crops such as marijuana or coca to generate cash for their next coffee crop. The 20 million coffee farmers who lived in poverty called the middlemen "coyotes," because they preyed on the poor.

Dickinson decided to change these unfair practices and engage in more ethically and socially responsible ways of doing business. In 1986, he cofounded Equal Exchange, a worker-owned cooperative gourmet coffee company. By buying direct and thereby eliminating middlemen, Equal Exchange was able to pay growers 50 cents per pound more than the previous rate.

Coffee is the leading source of foreign currency in Latin America, so this price increase had a significant impact on the economy and lifestyle of the region. Coffee growing provides jobs for people who would otherwise be unemployed. The growers' entire region benefits from projects the farm cooperatives undertake with the additional income, from reforestation programs to building new schools, daycare centres, and carpentry workshops. "We used to live in houses made of corn husks," recalls Don Miguel Sifontes, a farmer in El Salvador. "Now we have better work, better schools, homes of adobe, and a greater brotherhood of decision makers."

Fair trade underscores the idea that businesses are accountable to employees, customers, and the general public. Under exclusive agreements with farming cooperatives, Equal Exchange growers receive better prices, and customers are guaranteed high-quality coffee at fair prices. Receiving a guaranteed minimum price per pound for coffee, even when the market is lower, assures farmers of a living wage during downturns.

Following strict fair-trade guidelines, Equal Exchange enters into long-term relationships with growers, buying directly from cooperatives owned and run by farmers. The farmers govern the even distribution of income and services, such as education and health care. Making credit available to farmers helps them avoid the cycle of debt. "When we sign a contract with growers, we pay up to 50 percent of the contract six months in advance," notes marketing manager Erbin Crowell. "If a hurricane hits, we share the risk." The company pays a premium price for certified organic and shade-grown coffee, and by helping growers use environmentally friendly farming methods, the environment and consumers are protected from toxic chemicals.

When specialty coffee giants Starbucks and Green Mountain announced they were entering into fair-trade agreements with farmers, Equal Exchange congratulated them. "We know these farmers and their struggles. They urgently need more importers to pay a just price, so we encourage our fellow roasters." With this statement, Dickinson raised the bar of ethical standards in the coffee business, knowing that his company can clear it with ease. With $7 million in sales, he is clearly supported by many coffee-loving consumers who do care where their beans come from.

Critical Thinking Questions

- Has Equal Exchange gone beyond other organizations in being socially and ethically responsible? Explain.
- What are the key components of Equal Exchange's fair-trade agreement with coffee growers? How do they support the company's goals and affect coffee growers' regions and lifestyles?
- How might Equal Exchange encourage other companies to adopt fair-trade agreements? Suggest an approach the company could use to launch such a campaign.

SOURCES: Adapted from material in the video case *The Rewards of Paying Fair: Ethics and Social Responsibility at Equal Exchange* and company website, (www.equalexchange.com) (accessed February 8, 2003).

E-COMMERCE CASE >

Geekcorps: Spreading the (IT) Gospel

A Peace Corps for techies? Ethan Zuckerman had a mission: to bring the technology revolution to developing countries such as Rwanda, Mongolia, Lebanon, Bulgaria, and Ghana, via techno-savvy volunteers. Zuckerman, a 1993 graduate of Williams College, became an instant millionaire in 1999 when Lycos bought the online company where he served as vice president of research and development. A self-confessed nethead, he wanted to do something he believed was important.

Geekcorps (**www.geekcorps.com**) was started in February 2000 with $100,000 of Zuckerman's own money. Seven months later, its first team of volunteers was at work in Accra, Ghana, where Zuckerman had spent time on a Fulbright fellowship. Geekcorps now delves into a database of 3,500 volunteers from 11 countries to select teams of seven or eight rigorously screened volunteers; they are given four months to prepare for their stint abroad. Geekcorps pays for travel and provides lodging and a small stipend. On sabbatical from their jobs for periods of one to four months, volunteers are trained to teach their skills to people with different backgrounds.

"We never tell the volunteers to go in and do the project; they teach the in-country staff and company members to do it themselves," says Ana Marie Harkins, Geekcorps director of programs. In return, each business agrees to transfer the skills it acquires to the community, free of charge. "The number one asset for a Geekcorps volunteer is a good sense of humour and the ability to roll with the punches," says Peter Beardsley, 26, who spent six months in Accra. "If you let power outages and leaky roofs get to you, you're going to have a hard time." But it is not all work and no play for the volunteers, who spend their free time exploring the host country and meeting its people.

After the dot-com bubble burst, corporate donations dwindled. The United Nations and other organizations provided some grants to help keep Geekcorps afloat. In 2002, Zuckerman joined forces with the International Executive Service Corps (IESC), an organization with a history of sending business professionals to developing countries. "We both believe that the way to transform an economy is by building small business, by bringing over skilled volunteers," says Zuckerman. Thanks to the IESC partnership and private donations, Geekcorps had enough funding for the next year and a half.

Critical Thinking Questions

1. Ethan Zuckerman still hopes to attract donations from corporate sponsors. If you were Ethan Zuckerman, how would you explain to a high-technology firm why contributing to Geekcorps would be a strategic giving choice?

2. Do you think other consumer goods firms—for instance, a maker of breakfast cereals or a clothing company—would see donating to Geekcorps as an opportunity to meet their social responsibilities to employees, customers, or investors? Explain.

3. Why do you think corporate donations dwindled after the dot-com bubble burst? Do you think companies have a moral obligation to continue corporate sponsorship programs during economic downturns? Defend your answer.

SOURCES: Dawn Calleja, "Heart of Geekness," *Canadian Business Magazine*, April 20, 2002; Laurie O'Connell, "Geekcorps' Savvy Volunteers Bring the Benefits of IT to Developing Countries," *Software Development*, October 2002, (www.sdmagazine.com); material from Geekcorps website, (www.geekcorps.org) (accessed February 25, 2003); and John Yaukey, "Geekcorps Spread Computer Skills Worldwide," *Gannet News Service, HonoluluAdvertiser.com*, March 26, 2002, (www.honoluluadvertiser.com) (accessed February 25, 2003).

CHAPTER 4

Making the Connection

Using Technology to Manage Information and for Business Success

In this chapter, you'll learn about the last piece of our PEST model puzzle—the *technological* environment.

This is a wonderful example of the integrative nature of business, because technology permeates just about every aspect of our model. To begin with, it affects a company's ability to meet its critical success factors. *Financial performance* is affected by technology, because a firm can operate more efficiently and, therefore, increase its bottom line using technology. Technology also allows us to better *meet customer needs* by giving businesses quicker and better access to information on their buyers' needs. Consequently, these needs are better met through the speed of technology, helping us deliver on our promises and provide customer service. In fact, as you'll see in the chapter, a company's technology based information system can "track new orders" to speed order processing; "determine what products are selling best," which can help a company to develop products to meet customer needs; "identify high-volume customers" to focus on enhancing those relationships; "or contact customers about new or related products" to help form relationships. In fact, even greater needs can be met with expanded product offerings, because the Internet does not have the physical limitations of a typical store—any number of items can be sold through a single website. *Quality* is also enhanced through the use of technology. In fact, *innovations* have allowed us

to improve quality and make it a priority at all levels of an organization. The rate of these and other innovations has been boosted to "warp speed" because of technology. Finally, *employees are more committed* to meeting company goals, because companies can make their jobs more interesting; the most repetitive and monotonous jobs can be completed through the use of technology instead of valuable human resources. So technology can definitely help a business be more successful, and since the rapid pace of technological change is a reality for today's business, it is, in fact, a necessity for success.

Technology as an environmental factor affects the other aspects of our PEST model as well. For example, in the *political* environment, the government issues patents on new technology, preventing other firms from copying that technology. This gives a company an advantage over other firms for years to come. From the point of view of *economics*, we saw during the recent "tech bubble" how the rapid growth of technological firms can fuel the stock market to the point of overvalue and then rapid adjustment, to the shock of many investors. Technology also changes the nature of competition. The Internet has removed the geographic and time-related limits to doing business. Customers no longer have to visit a store during business hours—companies don't even need to have a store! And the

traditional relationship between manufacturers, distributors, and retailers has changed because companies can bypass these channels, selling directly over the Internet. From a *social* perspective, it is clear that technology has changed how we, as consumers, see the world—it has given us much more access to information, making us better equipped to make buying decisions and more demanding in our speed of fulfillment expectations. It is also important to understand that, as new technologies are adopted, they promote other waves of technological innovation. In this way, technology enhances our ability to create more technology.

Technology also affects how companies operate. As we emphasize in this chapter, it affects the way businesses communicate and share information in all areas of the company. The company's information system can gather and provide information on what customers want directly to the *marketing* department to enhance its sales efforts. The order information can then be provided directly to *operations* so that managers can obtain the correct inventory needed, when it's needed, and schedule production to meet the customer's needs exactly and on time. Information is also provided to *human resources* to ensure skilled workers are available as the production schedule requires. The final sales information can also be provided directly to *finance* to prepare financial statements. This integration of information brings together the functional areas in an essential way so that they can work together more efficiently to achieve the company's goals and ensure its

success, just like in our opening vignette on Mark's Work Wearhouse.

Technology also affects each specific functional area. For example, on the operational side, it affects how products are built (using computers to help design products and guide manufacturing) as well as what products are built (as technology allows for greater customization to meet customer needs). It affects how products are marketed (such as through the Internet, using e-commerce) and financed. The "bursting of the tech bubble" has had such an impact on capital markets that it's difficult for new technology firms to sell their stock to the public and generate much-needed funds for expansion. Even the human resource function is affected by technology, because computers can take over many tasks done by humans, and companies have the added demand of finding the best people with the necessary skills to use technology, and manage technology workers.

The very nature of business has changed dramatically with technology. E-business has revolutionized the way business is done, affecting the overall *strategies* of many organizations as it has created a new paradigm for business. We have moved beyond the individual enterprise to an interconnected economy through interconnected information systems. As businesses become more interconnected between suppliers, manufacturers, and retailers, they operate more as one company. This allows them to meet the needs of the customer better, providing a seamless integration from the beginning of the business chain to the ultimate consumer.

CHAPTER 4

Using Technology to Manage Information and for Business Success

LEARNING OUTCOMES

1. Explain how information technology has transformed business and managerial decision making.

2. Discuss why computer networks are an important part of today's information technology systems.

3. Give examples of the types of systems that make up a typical company's management information system.

4. Describe how technology management and planning can help companies optimize their information technology systems.

5. Identify some of the best ways to protect computers and the information they contain.

6. List some of the leading trends in information technology.

MARK'S WORK WEARHOUSE: AN E-BUSINESS SUCCESS STORY

According to Robin Lynas, former chief information officer, and now vice-president corporate development and social compliance officer for Mark's Work Wearhouse (MWW), the company's e-business strategy is to "build an integrated multi-channel retailing environment." This strategy is based on the key customer requirements of convenience, access to products, brand loyalty, selection, and information. The main challenges for MWW are the dynamic retail environment and rapidly changing technologies. With more than 370 stores, and sales exceeding $1 billion per year, these challenges require a comprehensive understanding of the organization and its strategies.

MWW is one of Canada's largest retail clothing chains, and its customers include both individuals and corporations. Its target market is built on the philosophy of "Clothes That Work," with the company selling traditional work wear, casual, business casual, and casual outdoor clothing and footwear. The company has been successful, in part, by developing computer applications that put timely customer information in the hands of its sales force. Every MWW store is linked to a database via portal technology that provides information on sales and inventory levels, replenishes inventories at the SKU (stock-keeping unit—the bar code attached to each product) level by store, and reports gross margins as well as expenses by individual stores.

"We have become less 'techie' and much more strategic in our approach to e-business and have become very successful," says Lynas. E-commerce (the actual exchange of transactions using electronic technology, and part of e-business) accounts for less than 10 percent of their e-business. "Our philosophy has been to understand our business, including our customers, and develop an infrastructure that responds to the needs of our stakeholders."

The electronic culture (or e-culture) at MWW incorporates three primary focuses: business to business (B2B), business to consumer (B2C), and business to enterprise (B2E), as shown in Exhibit 4.1.

B2B incorporates both its suppliers and its corporate customers. Each of the stores maintains its minimal level of stock according to product and size. Once the inventory of a particular product reaches its minimal service level in the store, an automatic replenishment system sends an EDI (electronic data interchange) message to the supplier (30 percent of suppliers are domestic and concentrated in the Toronto-Montreal corridor). The supplier completes the order, and all stock for each particular store is then packaged together and transported to the distribution centre where the packages are sorted and sent to the appropriate stores. (MWW picks up the orders from its domestic suppliers two or three times per week and receives about 1500 overseas containers per year from its foreign suppliers.) This procedure ensures that stock levels are maintained (therefore maximizing sales) and markdowns are kept to a minimum.

MWW has been very responsive to its corporate customers. The "Product Knowledge Database" and catalogues specific to a particular corporate purchaser have been very successful. The applications allow the corporations to manage their programs online and track employee purchases with customized purchase vouchers. As each employee of the corporate customer is registered, and purchases are recorded, it is impossible for the employee to purchase more than the authorized amount.

EXHIBIT 4.1 > Mark's Work Wearhouse E-Commerce Focuses

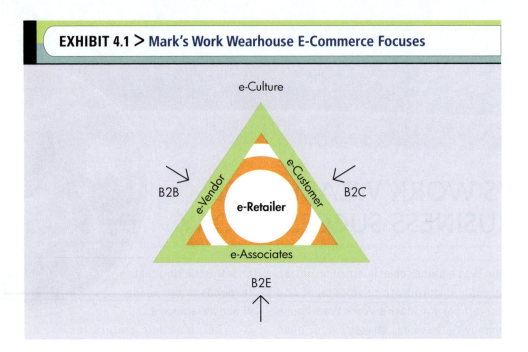

Critical Thinking Questions

As you read this chapter, consider the following questions as they relate to Mark's Work Wearhouse:

1. **What is the difference between e-business and e-commerce? How does MWW use each to satisfy customers' requirements?**

2. **What are the advantages and disadvantages of online retailing to the company and the customer online?**

3. **Identify some of the reasons why MWW has been successful in the retail market.**

4. **Are clothes and footwear well suited for Web sales? Why or why not?**

---

information technology (IT)
The equipment and techniques used to manage and process information.

HOT Links

If you want to know the definition of a computer term or more about a particular topic, Webopedia (**www.webopedia.com**) has the answers.

Harnessing the power of information technology gives a company a significant competitive advantage. ***Information technology (IT)*** *includes the equipment and techniques used to manage and process information.*

Information is at the heart of all organizations. Without information about the processes of and participants in an organization—including orders, products, inventory, scheduling, shipping, customers, suppliers, and employees—a business cannot operate.

Because most jobs today depend on information—obtaining, using, creating, managing, and sharing it—we begin this chapter with the role of information in decision-making and then go on to discuss computer networks and management information systems. The management of information technology—planning and protection—follows. Finally, we'll look at the latest trends in information technology. Throughout the chapter, we will use examples to show how managers and their companies are using computers to make better decisions in a highly competitive world.

Transforming Businesses Through Information

In less than 60 years, we have shifted from an industrial society to a knowledge-based economy driven by information. Businesses depend on information technology for everything from running daily operations to making strategic decisions. Computers are the tools of this information age, performing or helping workers perform extremely complex operations as well as everyday jobs like word processing and creating spreadsheets.

chief information officer (CIO)
An executive responsible for managing all information resources and processes in an organization.

knowledge worker
A worker who develops or uses knowledge, contributing to and benefiting from information used in performing various tasks including planning, acquiring, searching, analyzing, organizing, storing, programming, producing, distributing, marketing, or selling functions.

information system (IS)
The hardware, software, people, data, etc., that provide information about all aspects of a firm's operations.

management information system (MIS)
The methods and equipment that provide information about all aspects of a firm's operations.

database
An electronic filing system that collects and organizes data and information.

© BOB SCHATZ

CONCEPT *in Action* >>>

In today's high-tech world, CIOs must possess not only the technical smarts to implement global IT infrastructures, integrate communications systems with partners, and protect customer data from insidious hackers, but must also have strong business acumen. FedEx's acclaimed tech chief Rob Carter manages the technology necessary to deliver more than 6 million packages daily, with an eye toward greater business efficiency, growth, and profits. Why is it important for CIOs to possess both technological and business expertise?

Change has been rapid since the personal computer became a fixture on most office desks. Individual units became part of small networks, followed by more sophisticated enterprise-wide networks. Now the Internet makes it effortless to connect quickly to almost any place in the world. A manager can share information with hundreds of thousands of people worldwide almost as easily as with a colleague on another floor of the same office building. The Internet and the Web have become indispensable business tools that facilitate communication within companies as well as with customers. The rise of electronic trading hubs, discussed in the Expanding Around the Globe box, is just one example of how technology is facilitating the global economy.

Canadian companies have made considerable contributions to technology use in the world. For example, CGI Group Inc. successfully competes in the competitive IT services industry with over 100 offices in 16 countries. CGI has partnered with many companies across many industries that include banking, distribution, government, healthcare, insurance, retail, oil and gas, etc CGI has been ranked by Mediacorp Canada's "Top 100 Employers" and is among the Corporate Knights' listing of Best 50 Corporate Citizens.[1] Many companies entrust an executive called the **chief information officer (CIO)** with the responsibility of managing all information resources and processes. The importance of this responsibility is immense. As Jerry McElhatton, the retired CIO of MasterCard, points out, "Next to actual cash itself, data is probably the most precious asset a financial institution has. And for good reason." Companies such as MasterCard, banks, and insurance companies don't sell tangible products. "There is nothing to look at in a showroom, nothing to ship, nothing that will make a noise if you drop it. There is simply an agreement that something will happen, such as funds will become available if the customer signs on the dotted line. That's what makes data so precious to us and why we're more protective of it than the average mother lioness is with her cubs," McElhatton explains.[2]

Today most of us are **knowledge workers** who develop or use knowledge. Knowledge workers contribute to and benefit from information they use in performing various tasks including planning, acquiring, searching, analyzing, organizing, storing, programming, producing, distributing, marketing, or selling functions. We must know how to gather and use information from the many resources available to us.

Data and Information Systems

Information systems (IS) are the hardware, software, people, data, etc., that provide information about all aspects of a firm's operations. Information systems and the computers that support them are so much a part of our lives that we almost take them for granted. These **management information systems (MIS)**—methods and equipment that make information available about all aspects of a firm's operations—provide managers with the information they need to make decisions. They help managers properly categorize and identify ideas, which results in substantial operational and cost benefits.

Businesses collect a great deal of *data*—raw, unorganized facts that can be moved and stored—in their daily operations. Only through well-designed IT systems and the power of computers can managers process these data into meaningful and useful *information*, which they can use for specific purposes such as making business decisions. One such form of business information is the **database,** an electronic filing system that collects and organizes data and information. Using software called a *database management system (DBMS)*, you can quickly and easily enter, store, organize, select, and retrieve data in a database. These data are then turned into information to run the business and to perform business analysis.

Databases are at the core of business information systems. For example, a customer database containing name, address, payment method, products ordered, price, order history, and similar data provides information to many departments. Marketing teams can track new orders and determine what products are selling best,

Expanding Around The Globe

ELECTRONIC HUBS INTEGRATE GLOBAL COMMERCE

Thanks to the wonders of technological advancement, global electronic trading now goes far beyond the Internet retailing and trading that we are all familiar with. Special websites known as trading hubs, or eMarketplaces, facilitate electronic commerce between businesses in specific industries such as automotive manufacturing, retailing, telecom provisioning, aerospace, financial products and services, and more.

The trading hub functions as a means of integrating the electronic collaboration of business services. Each hub provides standard formats for the electronic trading of documents used in a particular industry, as well as an array of services to sustain eCommerce between businesses in that industry. Services include demand forecasting, inventory management, partner directories, and transaction settlement services. And the payoff is significant—lowered costs, decreased inventory levels, and shorter time to market—resulting in bigger profits and enhanced competitiveness. For example, large scale manufacturing procurement can amount to billions of dollars. Changing to "just-in-time purchasing" on the hub can save a considerable percentage of these costs.

Electronic trading across a hub can range from the collaborative integration of individual business processes to auctions and exchanges of goods (electronic barter). Global content management is an essential factor in promoting electronic trading agreements on the hub. A globally consistent view of the "content" of the hub must be available to all. Each participating company handles its own content, and applications such as content managers keep a continuously updated master catalogue of the inventories of all members of the hub. The transaction manager application automates trading arrangements between companies, allowing the hub to provide aggregation and settlement services.

Ultimately, trading hubs for numerous industries could be linked together in a global eCommerce Web—an inclusive "hub of all hubs." One creative thinker puts it this way: "The traditional linear, one step at a time, supply chain is dead. It will be replaced by parallel, asynchronous, real-time marketplace decision making. Take manufacturing capacity as an example. Enterprises can bid their excess production capacity on the world eCommerce hub. Offers to buy capacity trigger requests from the seller for parts bids to suppliers who, in turn, put out requests to other suppliers, and this whole process will all converge in a matter of minutes."[3]

Critical Thinking Questions

- How do companies benefit from participating in an electronic trading hub?
- What impact does electronic trading have on the global economy?

SOURCE: "Electronic Trading Hubs," (http://www.com-met2005.org.uk), April 4, 2006; David Luckham, "The Global Information Society and the Need for New Technology," (http://www.informit.com), April 4, 2006; "Trading Hubs," (http://www.investni.com), April 4, 2006; "Trading Hubs in Asia," Oikono, December 6, 2005, (http://www.oikono.com).

---

salespeople can identify high-volume customers or contact customers about new or related products, operations managers need order information to obtain inventory and schedule production of the ordered products, and financial personnel need sales data to prepare financial statements. Later in the chapter, we will see how companies use very large databases called data warehouses and data marts. The data warehouse will help the retailer in many ways, from cutting inventory costs to identifying market trends more quickly.

Companies are discovering that they can't operate well with a series of separate information systems geared to solving specific departmental problems. It takes a team effort to integrate the systems described in Chapter 11 throughout the firm. Company-wide *enterprise resource planning (ERP)* systems that bring together human resources, operations, and technology are becoming an integral part of business strategy. So is managing the collective knowledge contained in an organization using data warehouses and other technology tools. Technology experts are learning more about the way the business operates, and business managers are learning to use information systems technology effectively to create new opportunities and reach their goals.

> **concept check**
>
> What are management information systems? Why are they important to today's business organizations?
>
> Distinguish between data and information. How are they related?
>
> How does systems integration benefit a company?

Linking Up: Computer Networks

computer network
A group of two or more computer systems linked together by communications channels to share data and information.

Today most businesses use networks to deliver information to employees, suppliers, and customers. A **computer network** is a group of two or more computer systems linked together by communications channels to share data and information. Today's networks often link thousands of users and can transmit audio and video as well as data.

Networks include clients and servers. The *client* is the application that runs on a personal computer or workstation. It relies on a *server,* which manages network resources or performs special tasks, such as storing files, managing one or more printers, or processing database queries. Any user on the network can access the server's capabilities.

By making it easy and fast to share information, networks have created new ways to work and increase productivity. They provide more efficient use of resources, permitting communication and collaboration across distance and time. With file sharing, all employees, regardless of location, have access to the same information. Shared databases also eliminate duplication of effort. Employees at different sites can "screen share" computer files, working on data as if they were in the same room. Their computers are connected by phone or cable lines, they all see the same thing on their display, and anyone can make changes, which are seen by the other participants. The employees can also use the networks for videoconferencing.

Networks make it possible for companies to run enterprise software, large programs with integrated modules that manage all of the corporation's internal operations. Enterprise resource planning systems run on networks. Typical subsystems include finance, human resources, engineering, sales and order distribution, and order management and procurement. These modules work independently and then automatically exchange information, creating a company-wide system that includes current delivery dates, inventory status, quality control, and other critical information. Let's now look at the basic types of networks companies use to transmit data—local area networks and wide area networks—and popular networking applications like intranets and extranets.

Connecting Near and Far with Networks

local area network (LAN)
A network that connects computers at one site, enabling the computer users to exchange data and share the use of hardware and software from a variety of computer manufacturers.

Two basic types of networks are distinguished by the area they cover. A **local area network (LAN)** lets people at one site exchange data and share the use of hardware and software from a variety of computer manufacturers. LANs offer companies a more cost-effective way to link computers than linking terminals to a mainframe computer. The most common uses of LANs at small businesses, for example, are office automation, accounting, and information management. LANs can help companies reduce staff, streamline operations, and cut processing costs. LANs can be set up with wired or wireless connections.

wide area network (WAN)
A network that connects computers at different sites via telecommunications media such as phone lines, satellites, and microwaves.

A **wide area network (WAN)** connects computers at different sites via telecommunications media such as phone lines, satellites, and microwaves. A modem connects the computer or a terminal to the telephone line and transmits data almost instantly, in less than a second. The Internet is essentially a worldwide WAN. Long-distance telephone companies operate very large WANs. Companies also connect LANs at various locations into WANs. WANs make it possible for companies to work on critical projects around the clock by using teams in different time zones.

Several forms of WANs—intranets, virtual private networks (VPNs), and extranets—use Internet technology. Here we'll look at intranets (internal corporate networks that are widely available in the corporate world) and VPNs.

Although wireless networks have been around for more than a decade, they are increasing in use because of falling costs, faster and more reliable technology, and improved standards. They are similar to their wired LAN and WAN cousins except that they use radio frequency signals to transmit data. You probably use a wireless WAN (WWAN) regularly when you use your cellular phone.

Wireless LANs (WLANs) that transmit data at one site offer an alternative to traditional wired systems. WLANs' reach is a radius of approximately 150 metres indoors and 300 metres outdoors, which can be extended with antennas, transmitters, and other devices. The wireless devices communicate with a wired access point into the wired network. WLANs are convenient for specialized applications where wires are in the way or when employees are in different locations in a building. Hotels, airports, restaurants, hospitals, retail establishments, universities, and warehouses are among the largest users of WLANs. For example, in recent years hospitals have upgraded their existing WLAN to improve voice quality and reliability. The New WLAN supports many different functions, from better on-site communication among doctors and nurses through both data transmission and voice-over-Internet phone systems to data-centric applications such as Meditech clinical information system and pharmacy mangement.[4]

Making Ethical Choices

ETHICS ACTIVITY

As the owner of a small but growing business, you are concerned about employees misusing company computers for personal matters. Not only does this cost the company in terms of employee productivity, but it also ties up bandwidth that may be required for company operations and exposes the firm's networks to increased risks of attacks from viruses, spyware, and other malicious programs. Installing e-mail monitoring and Web security and filtering software programs would allow you to track e-mail and Internet use, develop use policies, block access to inappropriate sites, and limit the time employees can conduct personal online business. At the same time, the software will protect your IT networks from many types of security concerns, from viruses to Internet fraud. You are concerned, however, that employees will take offense and consider such software an invasion of privacy.

Using a Web search tool, locate articles about this topic and then write responses to the following questions. Be sure to support your arguments and cite your sources.

ETHICAL DILEMMA: Should you purchase employee monitoring software for your company, and on what do you base your decision? If you install the software, do you have an obligation to tell employees about it? Explain your answers and suggest ways to help employees understand your rationale.

SOURCES: Lindsay Gerdes, "You Have 20 Minutes to Surf. Go." *Business Week*, December 26, 2005, p. 16; "Nothing Personal." *Global Cosmetic Industry*, August 2005, p. 19; "Tips on Keeping Workplace Surveillance from Going too Far." *HR Focus*, January 2006, p. 10.

An Inside Job: Intranets

intranet
An internal, corporate-wide area network that uses Internet technology to connect computers and link employees in many locations and with different types of computers.

Like LANs, **intranets** are private corporate networks. Many companies use both types of internal networks. However, because they use Internet technology to connect computers, intranets are WANs that link employees in many locations and with different types of computers. Essentially mini-Internets that serve only the company's employees, intranets operate behind a *firewall*, which prevents unauthorized access. Employees navigate using a standard Web browser, which makes the intranet easy to use. They are also considerably less expensive to install and maintain than other network types and can take advantage of the Internet's interactive features, such as chat rooms and team work spaces. Many software providers now offer off-the-shelf intranet packages, so that companies of all sizes can benefit from the increased access to and distribution of information.

Companies now recognize the power of intranets to connect employers and employees in many ways, promoting teamwork and knowledge sharing. Intranets have many applications, from human resource (HR) administration to logistics. The benefits-administration intranet at a major insurance company quickly became a favourite with employees: instead of having to contact an HR representative to make any changes in personnel records, retirement plan contributions, or submit time sheets, staff members simply log on to the intranet and update the information themselves. The intranet proved to be especially valuable after a merger. With more than 9,000 employees in multiple locations, the insurance company expanded its intranet, which had been used mostly for marketing and client services, to handle more HR functions and improve communications. Managers can now process staffing updates, performance reviews, and incentive payments without filing paperwork with human resources. Employees regularly check an online job board for new positions. Shifting routine administrative tasks to the intranet brought the company additional benefits: it reduced the size of the HR department by 30 percent, and HR staff members can now turn their attention to more substantive projects.[5]

Enterprise Portals Open the Door to Productivity

enterprise portal
A customizable internal website that provides proprietary corporate information to a defined user group, such as employees, supply chain partners, or customers.

Intranets that take a broader view serve as sophisticated knowledge management tools. One such intranet is the **enterprise portal,** an internal website that provides proprietary corporate information to a defined user group. Portals can take one of three forms: business to employee (B2E), business to business (B2B), and business to consumer (B2C). Unlike a standard intranet, enterprise portals allow individuals or user groups to customize the portal home page to gather just the information they need for their particular job situations into one place and deliver it through a single webpage. Because of their complexity, enterprise portals are typically the result of a collaborative project that brings together designs developed and perfected through the joint effort of HR, corporate communications, and information technology departments.

More companies are turning to portal technology to provide

- a consistent, simple user interface across the company;
- integration of disparate systems, and multiple sets of data and information;
- a single source for accurate and timely information that integrates internal and external information;
- a shorter time to perform tasks and processes;
- cost savings through the elimination of "information intermediaries";
- improved communications within the company and with customers, suppliers, dealers, and distributors.

At Intercontinental Hotels Group (IHG), a new enterprise portal will connect staff at the group's 3,500 hotels around the world while supporting marketing, human resources, finance, and IT functions. A major goal is to eliminate duplication of efforts. "All of these departments are tackling similar problems independently," says David House, IHG's senior vice president for global human resources. "For example, you might have marketing efforts going on in one part of the world and someone doing a similar kind of thing in another without knowing it." The portal will facilitate collaboration and teamwork throughout the organization. "We want people to use the intranet to bridge these gaps, to improve availability of information, and to better exploit the intellectual capital in the organization," explains House.[6]

No More Tangles: Wireless Technologies

Wireless technology has become commonplace today. We routinely use such devices as cellular phones, personal digital assistants (PDAs), garage door openers, and television remote controls without thinking of them as examples of wireless technology. Businesses use wireless technologies to improve communications with customers, suppliers, and employees. You might have seen the term Wi-Fi, which refers to wireless fidelity. When products carry the "Wi-Fi Certified" designation, they have been tested and certified to work with each other, regardless of manufacturer.

Companies in the package delivery industry were among the first users of wireless technology. Delivery personnel use handheld computers to send immediate confirmation of package receipt. These companies consider the investment in wireless technology a good one. Not only do customers get better service, the company can also keep expenses down. Without wireless technology, delivery companies would have to hire more call centre and service representatives. You might also have seen meter readers and repair personnel from utility and energy companies sending data from remote locations back to central computers.[7]

Bluetooth short-range wireless technology is a global standard that improves personal connectivity for users of mobile phones, portable computers, stereo headsets, and MP3 players. Bluetooth wirelessly connects keyboards and mice to computers and headsets to phones and music players. A Bluetooth-enabled mobile phone, for example, provides safer hands-free cell phone use while driving. The technology is finding many applications in the auto industry as well. "Bluetooth wireless technology will start to become standard in cars in the near future," predicts David McClure, head of Telematics Research at SBD automotive technology consultants. Many car and cell phone manufacturers—among them Audi, BMW, Honda, Saab, Toyota, Volkswagen, Motorola, and Nokia—already offer Bluetooth hands-free solutions. Other uses include simplifying the connection of portable digital music players to the car's audio system and of transferring music to the system.[8]

Private Lines: Virtual Private Networks

Many companies use **virtual private networks (VPNs)** to connect two or more private networks (such as LANs) over a public network, such as the Internet. VPNs include

virtual private networks (VPNs)
Private corporate networks connected over a public network, such as the Internet. VPNs include strong security measures to allow only authorized users to access the network.

CONCEPT *in Action* >>>

Although designing a true mobile replacement for the desktop PC has proved elusive for computer manufacturers, ultramobile PCs offer wireless functions many professionals want—Web browsing, e-mail, Microsoft Office, and telephony. The Samsung Q1 Ultra Mobile PC runs Microsoft Windows XP and Vista, and with its 17-cm LCD touch screen and stylus, the mini-tablet provides the power of a desktop PC with the freedom of pen and paper. What impact might ultramobile computing have on business?

strong security measures to allow only authorized users to access the network and its sensitive corporate information. Companies with widespread offices might find that a VPN is a more cost-effective option than purchasing equipment and private lines for that purpose alone. A private line network is more limited than a VPN because it doesn't allow users to connect to the corporate network when they are at home or travelling.

As Exhibit 4.2 shows, the VPN uses existing Internet infrastructure and equipment to connect remote users and offices almost anywhere in the world—without long-distance charges. In addition to saving on telecommunications costs, companies using VPNs don't have to buy or maintain special networking equipment and can outsource management of remote access equipment. VPNs are useful for salespeople and telecommuters—they can access the company's network as if they were onsite in the office. On the downside, the VPN's availability and performance, especially when it uses the Internet, depend on factors largely outside of an organization's control.[9]

Software on Demand: Application Service Providers

As software developers release new types of application programs and updated versions of existing ones every year or two, companies have to analyze whether they can

EXHIBIT 4.2 > Virtual Private Networks (VPNs)

VPN Client → Local ISP → Public Network → Internal LAN → VPN Server

application service providers (ASPs)
A service company that buys and maintains software on its servers and distributes it through high-speed networks to subscribers for a set period and price.

HOT Links

For more information about the benefits of ASPs see MarketWeb. **(www.marketweb.ca).**

managed service providers (MSPs)
The next generation of ASPs, offering customization and expanded capabilities such as business processes and complete management of the network servers.

concept check

What is a computer network? What benefits do companies gain by using networks?

How do LANs and WANs differ? Why would a company use a wireless network?

What advantages do VPNs offer a company? ASPs and MSPs?

justify buying or upgrading to the new software in terms of both cost and implementation time. **Application service providers (ASPs)** offer a different approach to this problem. Companies subscribe to an ASP and use the applications much like you'd use telephone voice mail, the technology for which resides at the phone company. Exhibit 4.3 shows how the ASP interfaces with software and hardware vendors and developers, the IT department, and users.

The simplest ASP applications are automated. For example, a user might use one to build a simple e-commerce site. ASPs provide three major categories of applications to users:

- enterprise applications, including customer relationship management, enterprise resource planning (ERP), e-commerce, and data warehousing;
- collaborative applications for internal communications, e-mail, groupware, document creation, and management messaging; and
- applications for personal use e.g., games, entertainment software, and home office applications.

The basic idea behind subscribing to an ASP is compelling. Users can access any of their applications and data from any computer, and IT can avoid purchasing, installing, supporting, and upgrading expensive software applications. ASPs buy and maintain the software on their servers and distribute it through high-speed networks. Subscribers rent the applications they want for a set period and price. The savings in infrastructure, time, and staff could be significant.

Managed service providers (MSPs) represent the next generation of ASPs, offering greater customization and expanded capabilities that include business processes and complete management of the network servers. For example, Bell Canada offered its VoIP Managed Services for large companies such as Cisco and Nortel in 2005. The Global Voice over Internet Protocol can manage customers' voice and data traffic over a single integrated network anywhere in the world.[10]

EXHIBIT 4.3 > Structure of an ASP Relationship

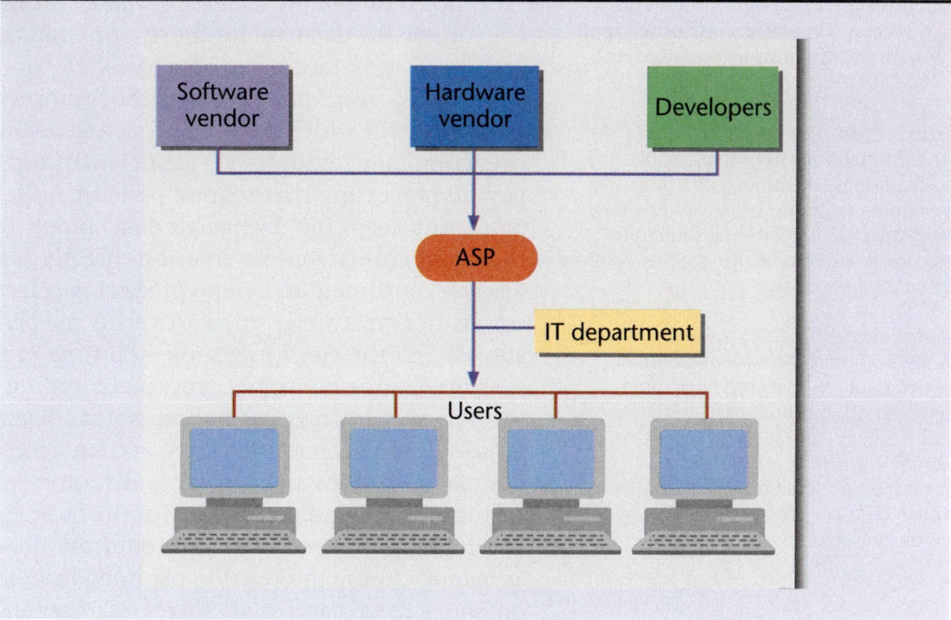

Management Information Systems

© 2009 JUPITER IMAGES CORPORATION

CONCEPT *in Action* >>>

Computer modelling helps Sanofi-Aventis, a major pharmaceutical company, save time and money on later-stage clinical drug trials. When simulation results in one study indicated that a drug's side effects outweighed its benefits, Aventis saved approximately $50 to $100 million by stopping the trial and using that funding for another project with greater potential for success. What are some other applications for computer modelling?

transaction-processing system (TPS)
An information system that handles the daily business operations of a firm. The system receives and organizes raw data from internal and external sources for storage in a database using either batch or online processing.

batch processing
A method of updating a database in which data are collected over some time period, but processed together.

online (real-time) processing
A method of updating a database in which data are processed as they become available.

Whereas individuals use business productivity software such as word-processing, spreadsheet, and graphics programs to accomplish a variety of tasks, the job of managing a company's information needs falls to *management information systems*: users, hardware, and software that support decision making. Information systems collect and store the company's key data and produce the information managers need for analysis, control, and decisions.

Many companies use computer-based information systems to automate production processes and to order and monitor inventory. Most companies use them to process customer orders and handle billing and vendor payments. Banks use a variety of information systems to process transactions such as deposits, ATM withdrawals, and loan payments. Most consumer transactions also involve information systems. When you check out at the supermarket, book a hotel room using a toll-free hotel reservations number, or buy CDs over the Internet, information systems record and track the transaction and transmit the data to the necessary places. Health care providers and insurers use information systems to speed up claims processing.

Companies typically have several types of information systems, starting with systems to process transactions. Management support systems are dynamic systems that allow users to analyze data to make forecasts, identify business trends, and model business strategies. Office automation systems improve the flow of communication throughout the organization. Each type of information system serves a particular level of decision making: operational, tactical, or strategic. Exhibit 4.4 shows the relationship between transaction-processing and management support systems as well as the management levels they serve. Let's now take a more detailed look at how companies and managers use transaction-processing and management support systems to manage information.

Transaction-Processing Systems

A firm's integrated information system starts with its **transaction-processing system (TPS)**. The TPS receives raw data from internal and external sources and prepares these data for storage in a database similar to a microcomputer database but vastly larger. In fact, all the company's key data are stored in a single, huge database which becomes the company's central information resource. As noted earlier, the *database management system* tracks the data and allows users to query the database for the information they need.

The database can be updated in two ways: **batch processing**, whereby data are collected over some time period but processed together, and **online** (or **real-time**), **processing**, in which data are processed as they become available. Batch processing uses computer resources very efficiently and is well suited to applications such as payroll processing that require periodic rather than continuous processing. Online processing keeps the company's data current. When you make an airline reservation, the agent enters your reservation directly into the airline's computer and quickly receives confirmation. Online processing is more expensive than batch processing, so companies must weigh the cost versus the benefit. For example, a factory that operates around the clock might use real-time processing for inventory and other time-sensitive requirements, but process accounting data in batches overnight.

The accounting information system diagrammed in Exhibit 4.5 is a typical TPS. It has subsystems for order entry, accounts receivable (for billing customers), accounts payable (for paying bills), payroll, inventory, and general ledger (for determining the financial status and profitability of the business). The accounting information system provides input to and receives input from the firm's other information systems, such as manufacturing (production planning data, for example) and human resources (data on hours worked and salary increases to generate paycheques).

EXHIBIT 4.4 > A Company's Integrated Information System

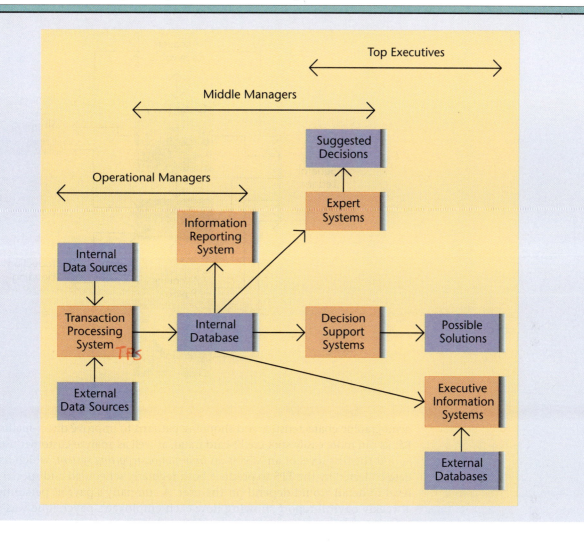

Decisions, Decisions: Management Support Systems

Transaction-processing systems automate routine and tedious back-office processes such as accounting, order processing, and financial reporting. They reduce clerical expenses and provide basic operational information quickly. **Management support systems (MSSs)** use the internal master database to perform the higher-level analyses that help managers make better decisions.

Information technologies such as data warehousing are part of more advanced MSSs. A **data warehouse** combines many databases across the whole company into one central database that supports management decision making. With a data warehouse, managers can easily access and share data across the enterprise, to get a broad overview rather than just isolated segments of information. Data warehouses include software to extract data from operational databases, maintain the data in the warehouse, and provide data to users. They can analyze data much faster than transaction processing systems. Data warehouses may contain many **data marts**, special subsets of a data warehouse that each deal with a single area of data. Data marts are organized for quick analysis.

Companies use data warehouses to gather, secure, and analyze data for many purposes, including customer relationship management systems, fraud detection, product line analysis, and corporate asset management. Retailers might wish to identify customer

management support system (MSS)
An information system that uses the internal master database to perform high-level analyses that help managers make better decisions.

data warehouse
An information technology that combines many databases across a whole company into one central database that supports management decision making.

data mart
Special subset of a data warehouse that deals with a single area of data and is organized for quick analysis.

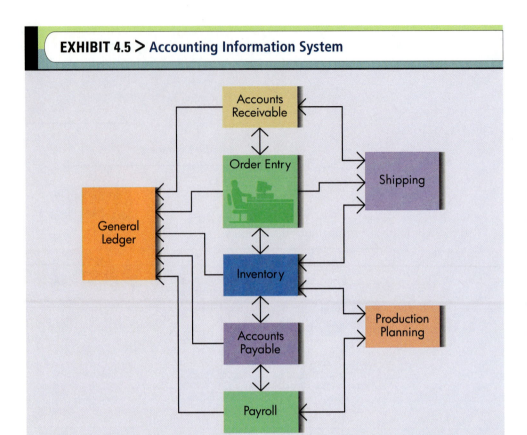

EXHIBIT 4.5 > Accounting Information System

demographic characteristics and shopping patterns to improve direct-mailing responses. Banks can more easily spot credit-card fraud, as well as analyze customer usage patterns.

At the first level of an MSS is an *information-reporting system*, which uses summary data collected by the TPS to produce both regularly scheduled and special reports. The level of detail would depend on the user. A company's payroll personnel might get a weekly payroll report showing how each employee's paycheque was determined. Higher-level managers might receive a payroll summary report that shows total labour cost and overtime by department, and a comparison of current labour costs with those in the prior year. Exception reports show cases that fail to meet some standard. An accounts receivable exception report that lists all customers with overdue accounts would help collection personnel focus their work. Special reports are generated only when a manager requests them; for example, a report showing sales by region and type of customer can highlight reasons for a sales decline.

Decision Support Systems

decision support system (DSS)
A management support system that helps managers make decisions using interactive computer models that describe real-world processes.

.

A **decision support system (DSS)** helps managers make decisions using interactive computer models that describe real-world processes. The DSS also uses data from the internal database but looks for specific data that relate to the problems at hand. It is a tool for answering "what if" questions about what would happen if the manager made certain changes. In simple cases, a manager can create a spreadsheet and try changing some of the numbers. For instance, a manager could create a spreadsheet to show the amount of overtime required if the number of workers increases or decreases. With models, the manager enters into the computer the values that describe a particular situation, and the program computes the results. Marketing executives at a furniture company could run DSS models that use sales data and demographic assumptions to develop forecasts of the types of furniture that would appeal to the fastest-growing population groups.

CONCEPT *in Action* >>>

Medical professionals use expert systems to analyze patients' medications, ensuring that they do not cause allergic reactions or potentially dangerous interactions with the patients' other prescriptions. How can the use of expert systems minimize human error?

Executive Information Systems

executive information system (EIS)
A management support system that is customized for an individual executive; provides specific information for strategic decisions.

Although similar to a DSS, an **executive information system (EIS)** is customized for an individual executive. These systems provide specific information for strategic decisions. For example, a CEO's EIS might include special spreadsheets that present financial data comparing the company to its principal competitors, and graphs showing current economic and industry trends.

Expert Systems

expert system
A management support system that gives managers advice similar to what they would get from a human consultant; it uses artificial intelligence to enable computers to reason and learn to solve problems in much the same way that humans do.

An **expert system** gives managers advice similar to what they would get from a human consultant. Artificial intelligence enables computers to reason and learn to solve problems in much the same way humans do, using what-if reasoning. Although they are expensive and difficult to create, expert systems are finding their way into more companies as more applications are found. Lower-end expert systems can even run on PDAs (personal digital assistants) like the Palm Pilot. Top-of-the-line systems help airlines appropriately deploy aircraft and crews, critical to the carriers' efficient operations. The cost of hiring enough people to do these ongoing analytical tasks would be prohibitively expensive. Expert systems have also been used to help explore for oil, schedule employee work shifts, and diagnose illnesses. Some expert systems take the place of human experts, whereas others assist them.

Office Automation Systems

office automation system
An information system that uses information technology tools such as word-processing systems, e-mail systems, cell phones, personal digital assistants (PDAs), pagers, and facsimile (fax) machines to improve communications throughout an organization.

Today's **office automation systems** make good use of the computer networks in many companies to improve communications. Office automation systems assist all levels of employees and enable managers to handle most of their own communication. Many of the newer devices now combine multiple functions. The key elements, (many of which have been around for years while others are fairly new), include:

- word-processing systems for producing written messages;
- e-mail systems for communicating directly with other employees and customers, and transferring computer files;
- departmental scheduling systems for planning meetings and other activities;

- cell phones for providing telephone service away from the office, with newer models able to receive and send e-mail, text messages, and graphics, and browse the Web;
- PDAs, which replace paper personal planners and address books but can also transfer data to and from the user's PC and run some software;
- wireless e-mail devices, such as the BlackBerry;
- pagers, which notify employees of phone calls and, in the case of alphanumeric models, display more extensive written messages sent from a computer network;
- voice mail systems for recording, storing, and forwarding phone messages;
  - fax systems for delivering messages on paper within minutes; and
  - electronic bulletin boards and computer conferencing systems for discussing issues with others who are not present.

Office automation systems also make telecommuting and home-based businesses possible. Instead of spending time on the road twice a day, telecommuters work at home two or more days a week. This can save time for workers while increasing their flexibility. Companies can save costs by eliminating the need to provide a physical structure for employees.

Technology Management and Planning

With the help of computers, people have produced more data in the past 30 years than in the previous 5,000 years combined. Companies today make sizable investments in information technology to help them manage this overwhelming amount of data, convert the data into knowledge, and deliver it to the people who need it. In many cases, however, the companies do not reap the desired benefits from these expenditures. Among the typical complaints from senior executives are: the company is spending too much and not getting adequate performance and payoff from IT investments, these investments do not relate to business strategy, the firm seems to be buying the latest technology for technology's sake, and communications between IT specialists and IT users are poor.

Optimize IT!

Managing a company's enterprise-wide IT operations, especially when those often stretch across multiple locations, software applications, and systems, is no easy task. Not only must IT managers deal with on-site systems, they must also oversee the networks that connect staff working at locations ranging from the next town to another continent. What makes the IT manager's job even more difficult is providing this technology for remote employees in the face of time constraints and lower budgets, while maintaining a cohesive corporate culture.[11] Add to these concerns the increasing use by employees of handheld devices like PDAs and cell phones that handle e-mail messaging, and you have an overwhelming management task!

Growing companies might find themselves with a decentralized IT structure that includes many separate systems and much duplication of efforts. A company that wants to enter or expand into e-commerce needs systems that are flexible enough to adapt to this changing marketplace. Security for equipment and data, which we will cover later in the chapter, is another critical area.

The goal is to develop an integrated, company-wide technology plan that balances business judgment, technology expertise, and technology investment. IT planning requires a coordinated effort among a firm's top executives, IT managers, and business-unit managers to develop a comprehensive plan. Such plans must take into account the company's strategic objectives and how the right technology will help managers reach those goals.

Technology management and planning are not just about buying new technology. Today companies are cutting IT budgets, so managers are being asked to do more with less. They are implementing projects that leverage their investment in the technology they already have, finding ways to maximize efficiency and optimize utilization.

Managing Knowledge Resources

knowledge management (KM)
The process of researching, gathering, organizing, and sharing an organization's collective knowledge to improve productivity, foster innovation, and gain competitive advantage.

As a result of information proliferation, we are seeing a major shift from information management to a broader view that focuses on finding opportunities in and unlocking the value of intellectual rather than physical assets. Whereas *information management* involves collecting, processing, and condensing information, the more difficult task of **knowledge management (KM)** focuses on researching, gathering, organizing, and sharing an organization's collective knowledge to improve productivity, foster innovation, and gain a competitive advantage. Some companies have even created a new position, *chief knowledge officer,* to head up this effort. The goal of KM is to allow organizations to generate value from their intellectual assets—not just documents but also the knowledge in their employees' heads.[12]

Companies use their IT systems to facilitate the physical sharing of knowledge. But better hardware and software are not the answer to KM. KM is not technology based, but rather a business practice that uses technology. Technology alone does not constitute KM, nor is it the solution to KM. Rather, it facilitates KM. Executives with successful KM initiatives understand that KM is not a matter of buying a major software application that serves as a data depository and coordinates all of a company's intellectual capital.

Effective KM calls for an interdisciplinary approach that coordinates all aspects of an organization's knowledge. It requires a major change in behaviour as well as technology to leverage the power of information systems, especially the Internet, and a company's human capital resources. The first step is creating an information culture, through organizational structure and rewards, which promotes a more flexible, collaborative way of working and communicating. However, moving an organization toward KM is no easy task, but well worth the effort in terms of creating a more collaborative environment, reducing duplication of effort, and increasing shared knowledge. The benefits can be significant in terms of growth, time, and money.

Technology Planning

A good technology plan provides employees with the tools they need to perform their jobs at the highest levels of efficiency. The first step is a general needs assessment, followed by ranking of projects and the specific choices of hardware and software. Exhibit 4.6 poses some basic questions departmental managers and IT specialists should ask when planning technology purchases.

concept check

What are some ways in which a company can manage its technology assets to its advantage?

Differentiate between information management and knowledge management. What steps can companies take to manage knowledge?

List the key questions managers need to ask when planning technology purchases.

Once managers identify the projects that make business sense, they can choose the best products for the company's needs. The final step is to evaluate the potential benefits of the technology in terms of efficiency and effectiveness. For a successful project, you must evaluate and restructure business processes, choose technology, develop and implement the system, and manage the change processes to serve your organizational needs in the best possible way. Installing a new IT system on top of inefficient business processes is a waste of time and money.

EXHIBIT 4.6 > Questions for IT Project Planning

- What are the company's overall objectives?
- What problems does the company want to solve?
- How can technology help meet those goals and solve the problems?
- What are the company's IT priorities, both short- and long-term?
- What type of technology infrastructure (centralized or decentralized) best serves the company's needs?
- Which technologies meet the company's requirements?
- Are additional hardware and software required? If so, will they integrate with the company's existing systems?
- Does the system design and implementation include the people and process changes, in addition to the technological ones?
- Do you have the in-house capabilities to develop and implement the proposed applications, or should you bring in an outside specialist?

Protecting Computers and Information

Have you ever lost a term paper you'd worked on for weeks because your hard drive crashed or you deleted the file by mistake? You were upset, angry, and frustrated. Multiply that paper and your feelings hundreds of times over, and you can understand why companies must protect computers, networks, and the information they store and transmit, from a variety of potential threats. For example, security breaches of corporate information systems—from human hackers or electronic assailants such as viruses and worms—are growing in number at an alarming rate. The ever-increasing dependence on computers requires plans that cover human error, power outages, equipment failure, and as we experienced at the beginning of this century, terrorist attacks. To withstand natural disasters such as major fires, earthquakes, and floods, for example, many companies install specialized fault-tolerant computer systems.

Disasters are not the only threat to data. A great deal of data, much of it confidential, can easily be tapped into or destroyed by anyone who knows about computers. Keeping your networks secure from unauthorized access—from internal as well as external sources—requires formal security policies and enforcement procedures. The increasing popularity of mobile devices—laptops, handheld computers, PDAs, and digital cameras—and wireless networks requires calls for new types of security provisions.

In response to mounting security concerns, companies have increased spending on technology to protect their IT infrastructure and data. Along with specialized hardware and software, companies need to develop specific security strategies that take a proactive approach to prevent security and technical problems before they start.

Data Security Issues

Unauthorized access to a company's computer systems can be expensive, and not just in monetary terms. Computer crooks are becoming more sophisticated all the time, finding new ways to get into ultra-secure sites. "As companies and consumers continue to move towards a networked and information economy, more opportunity exists for cybercriminals to take advantage of vulnerabilities on networks and computers," says Chris Christiansen, program vice president at technology research firm IDC. Whereas early cybercrooks were typically amateur hackers working alone, the new ones are more professional and often work in gangs to commit large-scale Internet crimes for large financial rewards. The Internet, where criminals can hide behind anonymous screen names, has increased the stakes and expanded the realm of opportunities to commit identity theft and similar crimes. Catching such cybercriminals is difficult, and fewer than 5 percent are caught.[13]

Firms are taking steps to prevent these costly computer crimes and problems, which fall into several major categories.

- *Unauthorized access and security breaches.* Whether from internal or external sources, unauthorized access and security breaches are a top concern of IT managers. These can create havoc with a company's systems and damage customer relationships. Unauthorized access also includes employees, who can copy confidential new-product information and provide it to competitors or use company systems for personal business that may interfere with systems operation. Networking links also make it easier for someone outside the organization to gain access to a company's computers.

- One of the latest forms of cybercrime involves secretly installing keylogging software via software downloads, e-mail attachments, or shared files. This software then copies and transmits a user's keystrokes—passwords, PINs, and other personal information—from selected sites, such as banking and credit card sites to thieves.

- *Computer viruses, worms, and Trojan horses.* Computer viruses and related security problems such as worms and Trojan horses are among the top threats to business and personal computer security. A computer program that copies itself into other software and can spread to other computer systems, a **computer virus** can destroy the contents of a computer's hard drive or damage files. Another form is called a worm because it spreads itself automatically from computer to computer. Unlike a virus, a worm doesn't require e-mail to replicate and transmit itself into other systems. It can enter through valid access points.

- *Trojan horses* are programs that appear to be harmless and from legitimate sources but trick the user into installing them. When run, they damage the user's computer. For example, a Trojan horse may claim to get rid of viruses but instead infects the computer. Other forms of Trojan horses provide a "trapdoor" that allows undocumented access to a computer, unbeknownst to the user. Trojan horses do not, however, infect other files or self-replicate.[14]

- Viruses can hide for weeks or months before starting to damage information. A virus that "infects" one computer or network can be spread to another computer by sharing disks or by downloading infected files over the Internet. To protect data from virus damage, virus protection software automatically monitors computers to detect and remove viruses. Program developers make regular updates available to guard against newly created viruses. In addition, experts are becoming more proficient at tracking down virus authors, who are subject to criminal charges.

- *Deliberate damage to equipment or information.* For example, an unhappy employee in the purchasing department could get into the computer system and delete information on past orders and future inventory needs. The sabotage could severely disrupt production and the accounts payable system. Wilful acts to destroy or change the data in computers are hard to prevent. To lessen the damage, companies should back up critical information.

- *Spam.* Although you might think that spam, or unsolicited and unwanted e-mail, is just a nuisance, it also poses a security threat to companies. Viruses spread through e-mail attachments that can accompany spam e-mails. On most days, spam accounts for 70 to 80 percent of all e-mail sent, according to Postini, a message filtering company. In contrast, mail that carries viruses represents just 1.5 percent of all messages on average. The volume of spam has increased five times since just 2003. Spam is now clogging blogs, instant messages, and cell phone text messages

computer virus
A computer program that copies itself into other software and can spread to other computer systems.

as well as e-mail inboxes. Spam presents other threats to a corporation, such as lost productivity and expenses from dealing with spam (like opening the messages), and searching for legitimate messages that special spam filters keep out. Spam filters can greatly reduce the amount of spam that gets through, but spammers continually find new ways to bypass them.[15]

- *Software and media piracy.* The copying of copyrighted software programs, games, and movies by people who haven't paid for them is another form of unauthorized use. Piracy, defined as using software without a licence, takes revenue away from the company that developed the program—usually at great cost. It includes making counterfeit CDs to sell as well as personal copying of software to share with friends.

Preventing Problems

Firms that take a proactive approach can prevent security and technical problems before they start. Creating formal, written security policies—to set standards and provide the basis for enforcement—is the first step in a company's security strategy. Unfortunately, a recent survey of 8,200 IT executives worldwide revealed that only 37 percent have such plans, and just 24 percent of the other companies intend to develop one within a year. Without information security strategies in place, companies spend too much time in a reactive mode—responding to crises—and don't focus enough on prevention.[16]

Security plans should have the support of top management, and then follow with procedures to implement the security policies. Because IT is a dynamic field with ongoing changes to equipment and processes, it's important to review security policies often. Some security policies can be handled automatically, by technical measures, whereas others involve administrative policies that rely on humans to perform them. Examples of administrative policies are: "Users must change their passwords each quarter." and "End users will update their virus signatures at least once a week."[17] Exhibit 4.7 shows the types of security measures companies use to protect data.

Preventing costly problems can be as simple as regularly backing up applications and data. Companies should have systems in place that automatically back up the company's data every day and store copies of the backups off-site. In addition, employees should back up their own work regularly. Another good policy is to maintain a complete and current database of all IT hardware, software, and user details to make it easier to manage software licenses and updates and diagnose problems. In many cases, IT staff can use remote access technology to automatically monitor and fix problems, as well as update applications and services.

Companies should never overlook the human factor in the security equation. One of the most common ways that outsiders get into company systems is by posing as an employee, first getting the staffer's full name and username from an e-mail message, then calling the help desk to ask for a forgotten password. Crooks can also

---

EXHIBIT 4.7 > Methods Companies Use to Protect Data

Method	Percent Using
Anti-virus software	98%
Firewalls	91
Anti-spyware	75
Spam filters	75
VPNs	46
Intrusion prevention or detection systems	23
Smart cards	7
Biometrics	4

get passwords by viewing them on notes attached to a desk or computer monitor, using machines that employees leave logged on when they leave their desks, and accessing laptop computers with sensitive information that have been left unsecured in public places.[18]

Portable devices, from handheld computers and PDAs to tiny plug-and-play flash drives and other storage devices (including MP3 players) pose security risks as well. They are often used to store sensitive data such as passwords, bank details, and calendars. PDAs can spread viruses when users download virus-infected documents to their company computers. Research firm Gartner Inc. reports that only about 10 percent of companies have policies covering security for these portable devices. "It's actually a fairly big problem," says Eric Ouellet, Gartner's vice president of research for security. "You've got so much space on these things now. You can go for an iPod or MP3 player and you've got 60 GB or more on them. You can put a small database on them. It's just a matter of time before we hear about someone losing data because of this."[19]

Imagine the problems that could arise if an employee saw a calendar entry on a PDA like "meeting re: layoffs," an outsider saw "meeting about merger with ABC Company," or an employee lost a flash drive containing files about marketing plans for a new product. Manufacturers are responding to IT managers' concerns about security by adding password protection and encryption to flash drives. Companies can also use flash drive monitoring software that prevents unauthorized access on PCs and laptops.

Companies have many ways to avoid an IT meltdown, as Exhibit 4.8 demonstrates.

Keep IT Confidential: Privacy Concerns

The very existence of huge electronic file cabinets full of personal information presents a threat to our personal privacy. Until recently, our financial, medical, tax, and other records were stored in separate computer systems. Computer networks make it easy to pool these data into data warehouses. Companies also sell the information they collect about you from sources like warranty registration cards, credit card records, registration at websites, personal data forms required for online purchases,

---

EXHIBIT 4.8 > Procedures to Protect IT Assets

- Protect the equipment with stringent physical security measures to the premises.
- Protect data using special *encryption* technology to encode confidential information, so only the recipient can decipher it.
- Stop unwanted access from inside or outside with special authorization systems. These can be as simple as a password or as sophisticated as fingerprint or voice identification.
- Install *firewalls*—hardware or software designed to prevent unauthorized access to or from a private network.
- Monitor network activity with intrusion-detection systems that signal possible unauthorized access and document suspicious events.
- Train employees to troubleshoot problems in advance rather than just react to them.
- Hold frequent staff training sessions to teach correct security procedures, such as logging out of networks when they go to lunch and changing passwords often.
- Make sure employees choose sensible passwords, of at least six and ideally eight characters long or more, containing numbers, letters, and punctuation marks. Avoid dictionary words and personal information.
- Establish a database of useful information and FAQs (frequently asked questions) for employees so they can solve problems themselves.
- Develop a healthy communications atmosphere.

CONCEPT *in Action* >>>

At the heart of the computer-privacy dilemma is the trade-off between confidentiality and convenience. Today's tech-savvy consumers are increasingly willing to give out personal information in exchange for enhanced shopping, more downloads, and user benefits. Entrusting personal data to online merchants eliminates repeat data entry, enables greater personalization of websites, and produces remarkably relevant cross-selling and search results. Can consumers have both convenience and privacy, or will they ultimately have to choose one or the other?

HOT Links

For more information about personal information protection in Canada, see the website of the Office of the Privacy Commissioner of Canada (**www.privcom.gc.ca**).

---

concept check

Describe the various threats to data security.

How can companies protect information from destruction and from unauthorized use?

Why are privacy rights advocates alarmed over the use of techniques such as data warehouses?

---

and grocery store discount club cards. Telemarketers can combine data from different sources to create fairly detailed profiles of consumers. With information about their buying habits, advertisers can target consumers for specific marketing programs.

Increasingly, consumers are fighting to regain control of personal data and how that information is used. Privacy advocates are working to block sales of information collected by governments and corporations. For example, they want to prevent governments from selling driver's license information, and supermarkets from collecting and selling information gathered when shoppers use bar-coded plastic loyalty cards.

The challenge to companies is to find a balance between collecting the information they need and protecting individual consumer rights. Most registration and warranty forms that ask questions about income and interests have a box for consumers to check to prevent the company from selling their names. Many companies now state their privacy policies to ensure consumers that they will not abuse the information they collect.

In Canada the *Personal Information Protection and Electronic Documents Act,* which was enacted in 2000, is intended to support and promote electronic commerce by protecting personal information. In an era of technology that is used to facilitate the exchange of information, the Government of Canada recognized a need for rules that governed the collection, use, and disclosure of personal information in a manner that recognizes the right of privacy of individuals with respect to their personal information.[20]

Trends in Information Technology

LO 6

Information technology is a continually evolving field. The fast pace and amount of change, coupled with IT's broad reach, make it especially challenging to isolate industry trends. From the time we write this chapter to the time you read it—as little as six months—new trends will appear and those that seemed important may fade.

However, some trends that are reshaping today's IT landscape are digital forensics, the shift to a distributed workforce, and the increasing use of grid computing.

Cyber Sleuthing: A New Style of Crime Busting

Digital evidence taken from an individual's computer or corporate network—Web pages, pictures, documents, and e-mails are part of a relatively new science called digital forensics. Digital forensics software safeguards electronic evidence used in investigations by creating a duplicate of a hard drive that an investigator can search by keyword, file type, or access date. Clients can have professional investigators from a firm like Guidance Software access suspect hard drives—Guidance makes EnCase, a forensic software tool used by 17,000 clients including 90 percent of all law-enforcement investigators—or they can buy the software for around $2,400 and do it themselves.[21]

Today digital sleuthing is not limited to the police. Companies like Microsoft have their own secret in-house digital forensics teams. And what if you're in Toronto and need to seize a hard drive in Hong Kong? No problem. Over 75 members of the Fortune 500 now use technology that allows them to search hard drives remotely over their corporate networks.[22] Digital forensics makes it possible to track down those who steal corporate data and intellectual property.

However, there is a downside to having these advanced capabilities. If this kind of software falls into the wrong hands, sophisticated hackers could access corporate networks and individual computers as easily as taking candy from a baby—and the victims would not even know it was happening. In an age of corporate wrongdoing, sexual predators, and computer porn, your hard drive will tell investigators everything they need to know about your behaviour and interests, good and bad. Cyber-sleuthing means we are all potential targets of digital forensics. As evidenced by the huge increase in identity theft, personal privacy—once an unassailable right—is no longer as sacred as it once was.

The Distributed Workforce

When companies shut the doors to some of their operations it may seem that they are in financial trouble. Not necessarily—in fact, far from it. Instead of maintaining expensive offices in multiple locations, many companies are sending employees home to work and adopting a new model for their employees: the distributed workforce. Employees have no permanent office space and work from home or on the road. By shifting to virtual workers, companies save considerable overhead costs and often see more productive employees.

Grid Computing Offers Powerful Solutions

How can smaller companies that occasionally need to perform difficult and large-scale computational tasks find a way to accomplish their projects? They can turn to grid computing, also called utility computing or peer-to-peer computing. Grid technology provides a way to divide the job into many smaller tasks and distribute them to a virtual supercomputer consisting of many small computers linked into a common network. Combining multiple desktop machines results in computing power that exceeds super-computer speeds. A hardware and software infrastructure clusters and integrates computers and applications from multiple sources, harnessing unused power in existing PCs and networks. The grid structure distributes computational resources but maintains central control of the process. A central server acts as a team leader and traffic monitor. The controlling cluster server divides a task into subtasks, assigns the work to computers on the grid with surplus processing power, combines the results, and moves on to the next task until the job is finished. Exhibit 4.9 shows how a typical grid setup works.

With utility computing, any company—large or small—can access the software and computer capacity on an as-needed basis. As John Meyer, vice president of brand strategy at software company Computer Associates, asks, "Why should manufacturers

EXHIBIT 4.9 > How Grid Computing Works

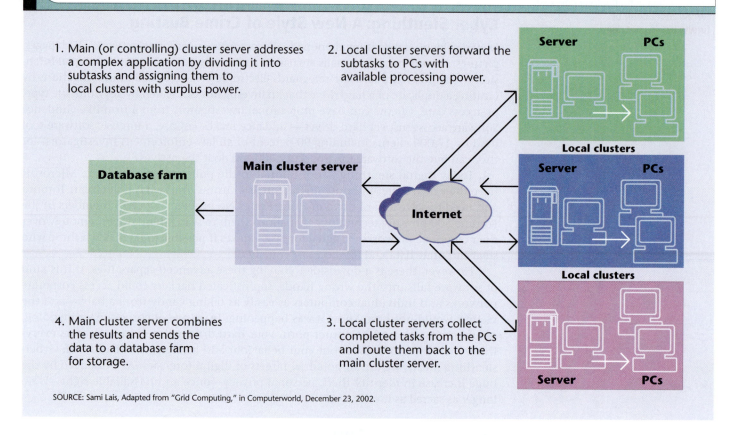

1. Main (or controlling) cluster server addresses a complex application by dividing it into subtasks and assigning them to local clusters with surplus power.

2. Local cluster servers forward the subtasks to PCs with available processing power.

Database farm

Main cluster server

Internet

Server **PCs**

Local clusters

Server **PCs**

Local clusters

Server **PCs**

4. Main cluster server combines the results and sends the data to a database farm for storage.

3. Local cluster servers collect completed tasks from the PCs and route them back to the main cluster server.

SOURCE: Sami Lais, Adapted from "Grid Computing," in Computerworld, December 23, 2002.

pay millions of dollars to run their computer infrastructure, when they can pay on demand for the amount of IT resources they actually consume?"[23]

Oracle Grid Computing, IBM, and Hewlett-Packard are among the companies providing as-needed grid services. Although grid computing appears similar to outsourcing or on-demand software from ASPs, it has two key differences:

- Pricing is set per-use, whereas outsourcing involves fixed-price contracts.
- Grid computing goes beyond hosted software and includes computer and networking equipment as well as services.

Grids provide a very cost-effective way to provide computing power for complex projects in areas such as weather research and financial and biomedical modeling. Because the computing infrastructure already exists—grids tap into computer capacity that is otherwise unused—the cost is quite low. The increased interest in grid technology will contribute to high growth.

concept check

How are companies and other organizations using digital forensics to obtain critical information?

Why do companies find that productivity rises when they offer employees the option of joining the virtual workforce?

What advantages does grid computing offer a company? What are some of the downsides to using this method?

Great Ideas to Use Now

Computer literacy is no longer a luxury. To succeed in business today, almost everyone must develop technological competence. Whether you have a part-time job in a fast-food restaurant that uses computerized ordering systems, or perform financial analyses that guide the future of your company, you will depend on computers. The more you increase your knowledge of technology, the more valuable you will be as an employee in today's information-driven businesses. In addition, the shortage of qualified IT personnel opens up new career avenues to those who enjoy working with technology. You will also have the knowledge required to take steps to protect your privacy.

Preparation Pays Off

Whether you are an employee or a business owner, you need to be aware of how technology affects the way your firm operates. New applications can change fundamental company operations and employees' roles. For example, companies that install ERP systems want individual employees to make more strategic, far-reaching decisions than before. This requires a dramatic shift in employees' roles and the way they should view their jobs. For example, an accountant's responsibilities might now include analyzing budgets, not just auditing expenses. A salesperson's role might expand to include more strategic decision making about customer issues. Your company will see the business benefits sooner if you prepare for these changing roles. A manager should begin teaching employees operational procedures before implementing the new system and help them acquire the necessary analytical skills. As an employee, you can take the initiative to learn as much as possible about the new technology and how it operates.

Protect Your Good Name

HOT Links

For a more complete list of recommendations of the Office of the Privacy Commissioner of Canada, see (**www.privcom.gc.ca**).

Identity theft is on the rise. Recent developments in telecommunications and computer processing make it easier for companies and the public to reach each other; they also cause your personal information to be more widely circulated. If identity theft happens, you could be held responsible for bills and other charges.

Often you have no idea that your identity has been stolen, and you might not be able to prevent it. The Office of the Privacy Commissioner of Canada has compiled the "Top 10 Ways Your Privacy is Threatened":

1. Surveillance cameras, swipe cards, Internet searches—you leave a trail of data as you go about your daily life.
2. Freely sharing your personal information.
3. Personal information being posted on social networking sites.
4. Governments collecting personal data in the name of national security and public safety.
5. Businesses collecting more and more information without having the necessary means to protect it.
6. Data breaches in both the public and private sectors.
7. Fraudsters from all over the globe able to access your personal information through devious, technologically savvy means.
8. Identity theft.
9. Information flows internationally. Not all countries have privacy protection laws and even if they do, the laws are not necessarily created equal.
10. People become complacent about their privacy and share too much too freely.[24]

Customer Satisfaction and Quality

Information technology can be used in many ways to satisfy customers and improve quality. In fact, most IT systems, from customer relationship management systems to enterprise portals, are at the heart of satisfying employees, vendors, and customers. For example, with accurate and timely information, company managers can make decisions that add new products in response to customer requests. Customer databases and order fulfillment systems speed products on their way to customers. Internally, better information allows production managers to forecast inventory accurately, so that it is on-site when needed and the company can avoid paying for rush delivery. Automated systems improve the quality of production, ordering, administration, and finance. Pharmaceutical companies use computer modeling systems to simulate clinical trials, saving time and money when developing new drugs.

Quality, of course, has another side. IT systems must be planned, designed, and implemented to meet the highest quality standards. Many companies have rushed to implement new systems without allowing adequate time to test them before "going live"—with disastrous results.

Summary of Learning Outcomes

1 **Explain how information technology has transformed business and managerial decision-making.**

Businesses depend on information technology for everything from running daily operations to making strategic decisions. Companies must have management information systems that gather, analyze, and distribute information to the appropriate parties, including employees, suppliers, and customers. These systems collect data and process it into usable information for decision-making. Managers tap into databases to access the information they need, whether for placing inventory orders, scheduling production, or preparing long-range forecasts. They can compare information about the company's current status to its goals and standards. Company-wide enterprise resource planning systems that bring together human resources, operations, and technology are becoming an integral part of business strategy.

2 **Discuss why computer networks are an important part of today's information technology systems.**

Computer networks link computers so they can share. Today, companies use networks of computers that share data and expensive hardware to improve operating efficiency. Types of networks include local area networks (LANs), wide area networks (WANs), and wireless local area networks (WLANs). Intranets are private WANs that allow a company's employees to communicate quickly with each other and work on joint projects, regardless of their location. Companies are finding new uses for wireless technologies, such as handheld computers, cell phones, and e-mail devices. Virtual private networks (VPNs) give companies a cost-effective, secure connection between remote locations using public networks such as the Internet.

3 **Give examples of the types of systems that make up a typical company's management information system.**

A management information system consists of a transaction-processing system, management support systems, and an office automation system. The transaction-processing system (TPS) collects and organizes operational data on the firm's activities. Management support systems help managers make better decisions. They include an information-reporting system, which provides information based on the data collected by the TPS to the managers who need it; decision support systems, which use models to assist in answering "what if" types of questions; and expert systems, which give managers advice similar to what they would get from a human consultant. Executive information systems are customized to the needs of top management. All employees benefit from office automation systems, which facilitate communication by using word processing, e-mail, fax machines, and similar technologies

4 **Describe how technology management and planning can help companies optimize their information technology systems.**

To get the most value from information technology (IT), companies must go beyond simply collecting and summarizing information. Technology planning involves evaluating the company's goals and objectives, and using the right technology to reach them. IT managers must also evaluate existing infrastructure to get the best return on the company's investment in IT assets. Knowledge management (KM) focuses on sharing an organization's collective knowledge to improve productivity and foster innovation. Some companies establish the position of chief knowledge officer to head up KM activities.

5 **Identify some of the best ways to protect computers and the information they contain.**

Because companies are more dependent on computers than ever before, they need to protect data and equipment from natural disasters and computer crime. Types of computer crime include unauthorized use and access, software piracy, malicious damage, and computer viruses. To protect IT assets, companies should prepare written security policies. They can use technology, such as virus protection and firewalls, and employee training in proper security procedures. They must also take steps to protect customers' personal privacy rights.

6 **List some of the leading trends in information technology.**

IT is a dynamic industry, and companies must stay current in the latest trends to identify ones that help them maintain their competitive edge, such as digital forensics, the distributed workforce, and grid computing. With digital forensics techniques, corporations, government agencies, lawyers, and lawmakers can obtain evidence from computers and corporate networks—Web pages, pictures, documents, and e-mails. Many knowledge workers now work remotely rather than from an office. Companies adopting the distributed workforce model gain many benefits, such as cost savings, more satisfied and productive employees, and increased employee retention. Grid computing harnesses the idle power of desktop PCs and other computers to create a virtual supercomputer. A company can access the grid on an as-needed basis instead of investing in its own supercomputer equipment. Outsourcing a portion of the company's computing needs provides additional flexibility and cost advantages. Companies can also set up internal grids.

Key Terms

application service providers (ASPs)   117
batch processing   118
chief information officer (CIO)   111
computer network   112
computer virus   125
database   111
data mart   119
data warehouse   119
decision support system (DSS)   120
enterprise portal   114
executive information system (EIS)   121
expert system   121
information technology (IT)   110

intranet   114
knowledge management (KM)   123
knowledge worker   111
local area network (LAN)   113
management information
   system (MIS)   111
management support system (MSS)   119
office automation system   121
online (real-time) processing   118
transaction-processing
   system (TPS)   118
virtual private networks (VPNs)   115
wide area network (WAN)   113

Experiential Exercises

1. **Stay current.** Keeping up with the fast pace of technology change is a real challenge, but it is necessary if you wish to remain up-to-date on the latest IT developments. The Internet has simplified this task, however. Get into the habit of visiting news sites such as ZDNet (**www.zdnet.com**) for current tech news. You can also link to Ziff Davis publications such as *PC Magazine*, read product reviews, find online classes, and even compare prices on technology products. Another excellent site is CNet's News.com (**www.news.com**), which updates the technology news headlines throughout the day. It has sections on enterprise computing, e-business, communications, media, personal technology, and investing, among others.

2. **What jobs are hot?** Managing information is an emerging career area. There are jobs for people to enter the information; for people to "mine" it to find the best markets, as well as to assess the interest and need for new products; and for specialists who understand the complex hardware and software needed to facilitate the loading, maintenance, and use of information. As a result of the increase in outsourcing of some IT functions, and the shift of many IT jobs overseas (where labour costs are lower), companies now are hiring business analysts (BAs), also called subject area experts, or SAEs. BAs serve as business liaisons, interfacing with the company to which the project is outsourced and with offshore personnel. To learn more about these areas and the wide range of other IT positions currently available, read the classified employment ads in your local newspaper and *The Wall Street Journal*. Go online to browse the employment ads from almost any major newspaper and surf through the websites with job listings. Many technology

company websites also post job openings. Make a list of jobs that interest you. In addition, read the general job listings to see how many require computer skills.

3. How has information technology changed your life? Describe at least three areas (both personal and school/work related) where having access to better information has improved your decisions. Are there any negative effects? What steps can you take to manage information more effectively?

4. Should companies outsource IT? According to an interview in the December 9, 2002 San Jose *Mercury News*, Craig Conway, president and chief executive of PeopleSoft, believes that IT is too important to outsource and that application service providers (ASPs) don't have a future. What's your position? Divide the class into groups designated "for" or "against" outsourcing and/or ASPs. Have them research the current status of ASPs using publications like *CIO* and *Computerworld* and websites like ASPnews.com (**www.aspnews.com**).

5. One of the fastest-growing areas of business software is enterprise resource planning (ERP) applications. Visit one of the following company's sites: SAP (**www.sap.com**), PeopleSoft (**www.oracle.com/index.html**), or Baan (**www.ssaglobal.com/solutions/erp/ln.aspx**). Prepare a short presentation for the class about the company's ERP product offerings and capabilities. Include examples of how companies use the ERP software.

6. What can an intranet accomplish for a company? Find out by using such resources as Brint.com's Intranet Portal (**www.brint.com/Intranets.htm**) and *Intranet Journal* (**www.intranetjournal.com**). Look for case studies that show how companies apply this technology. Summarize the features an intranet provides.

7. Learn more about the CERT Coordination Center (CERT/CC), which serves as a centre of Internet security expertise. Explore its website (**www.cert.org**). What are the latest statistics on incidents reported, vulnerabilities, security alerts, security notes, mail messages, and hotline calls? What other useful information does the site provide to help a company protect IT assets?

8. Research the latest developments in computer security at Computerworld's site (**http://computerworld.com/securitytopics/security**). What types of information can you find here? Pick one area, such as security for mobility/wireless devices, and summarize your findings.

Review Questions

1. How has technology been incorporated to help manage business?
2. What is the role of the CIO?
3. What is an MIS, and what are its roles?
4. How do LANs and WANs help in business?
5. How does a transaction-processing system (TPS) help to manage information?
6. Compare data warehouses and data marts.
7. Discuss the role of decision support systems (DSS).
8. How have office automation systems helped businesses?
9. How can we manage knowledge resources?
10. Why is protecting computers and information so important?
11. What are some ways in which computer and information security issues can be breached?
12. How can we prevent security and technical problems?

Canada Takes the Lead

The 2006 Canada Census information formed the basis for the February 2007 release of data by Statistics Canada. The census provided data for such important facts as characteristics of the population, households, dwellings, and families. This information is used to inform planning and decision making in government, and the public and private sector—both profit and not-for-profit.

Canada Post delivered census questionnaires to approximately 70% of households, with the remaining 30% receiving their questionnaires from one of the 20,000 census enumerators. Most households received the short questionnaire, with only about 20% receiving the longer questionnaire.

The census represented a massive project six years in the making; the census website, designed to handle online responses, was more successful than any other in the world. The system had the capacity to handle 15,000 respondents at once and did not go down even during the busiest time of the response activity. Director-general Anil Arora stated that the security was so sophisticated that it exceeded even the level of security on most banking transactions. He also felt that the most important improvement was in the quality of the responses submitted. If respondents were unable to get through because of capacity problems, they were asked to try again later, and they did. About 20 percent of the 13 million households completed the census online, resulting in huge savings in labour, postage, and other costs. For example, having the data already in digital form when submitted eliminates the need for data entry and also eliminates the potential for error. The cost to the government for census administration is about $15 per person, whereas in the United States it is more than $90 per household, six times the Canadian cost. Canadians also had access to a toll-free hotline number that handled one million calls over three days. The total cost for administering the census was approximately $567 million, a saving of over $11 million compared to the 2001 census.

The main cost incurred in collecting the data is the follow-up process for those who do not submit their information. Approximately 30,000 field staff are hired to complete the collection of the data. Even so, Canada has one of the highest response rates in the world, with initial responses of 75 to 80 percent of households.

Critical Thinking Questions

- Given the importance of the data collected by the census, is there any way costs could be lowered further using technology?
- How could the census office encourage more respondents to use the online system?

SOURCES: *The Ottawa Citizen*, "Counter Spin," May 21, 2006, pg. A. 7. Reprinted with permission; David Eadie, *"2007... and still counting,"* Summit, Ottawa: April/May 2007, Vol. 10, Iss. 3, page 7, 2 pages.

Are You Getting Gouged by Geeks?

What do you do if you are having computer problems? Once we have reached the absolute top of our computer diagnostic abilities and desperation sets in, many of us call a computer repair technician. Where do you find these people? The telephone directory offers dozens of options, including everything from small businesses to the more widely recognized names such as Geek Squad, Nerds on Site, Geeks on the Way and Doctor Dave Computer Remedies. Are these techies reliable, responsible, and knowledgeable?

To check this out, Humber College computer experts created a small, relatively common problem—a blown RAM module—in order to assess the service provided by ten computer repair technicians. The solutions offered for the $25 problem ranged from replacing the motherboard or repairing the hard drive, to repairing the CPU. Only three of the ten technicians correctly diagnosed the problem. In a second experiment with the problem of a corrupt system file and an obvious $60 solution, the diagnoses by the computer repair technicians included such disasters as infection by a virus or the need to replace the entire computer.

Why does this happen? Three former technicians from big box stores offer several possible reasons: many of us don't know the basics; tech training is inconsistent and sometimes non-existent; technicians are not well supervised while working, even if they are at the company facilities; there is pressure on the technicians to meet sales targets and bring in the dollars; there is no standard pricing and charges often reflect what the tech thinks the customer is willing to pay. These former techs also confessed to personally taking advantage of consumers' lack of information, and admitted knowledge of technicians copying customer files, stating that there are often no known policies with respect to privacy issues.

How do we protect ourselves, as consumers of these services? Perhaps we need to take the same degree of care as we would if buying a product. Firstly, we need to have a better understanding of our computer and some knowledge about the basics. There are online support sites for many software programs such as Norton or MacAfee and more general support sites for common problems, assuming you can *get* online. We should always have adequate virus protection and firewalls. If we do need help, we should ask around and search out a recommended technician or company doing our research just as we would when buying a product. And of course, back up, back up, back up.

Critical Thinking Questions

- In the video, one of the technicians simply downloaded a client's entire hard drive onto his own computer without permission. How can a large corporation protect its data from unethical and/or unauthorized access by technologically savvy employees?
- Is the issue of corporate espionage still a problem in today's organizations? If so, how can they protect themselves from this practice?
- Check out the Ten Commandments of Computer Ethics at (**www.tekmom.com/ tencommand/index.html**).

SOURCE: CBC Marketplace, "Getting Gouged by Geeks," October 3, 2007.

The Novartis Prescription for Invoice Processing

What do you do when you have more than 600 business units operating through 360 independent affiliates in 140 countries around the world—processing complex invoices in various languages and currencies? You seek out the best technology solution to make the job easier.

At global pharmaceutical giant Novartis, the IT department is a strategic resource, a community of 2,000 people serving 63,000 customers in 200 locations and 25 data centres. Because most of the company's invoices come from international suppliers they have differences in design, language, taxes, and currency. Consequently, many ended up as "query items" requiring manual resolution by Novartis accounting staff—which delayed payments and made those invoices extremely costly to process. In fact, finance personnel spent so much of their time resolving queried invoices that other work suffered. A solution was badly needed.

To maximize its investment, Novartis needed a flexible solution that would meet its current and future needs and function in other business departments in a variety of geographic locations. The solution had to provide fast, accurate document capture, multi-language support, and extend to other types of information—such as faxes and electronic data—in addition to paper documents. Finally, in order to obtain financing for the project, return on investment (ROI) was required within nine months of project implementation.

InputAccel for Invoices from Captiva Software Corporation was the answer. The software extracts data from paper documents, applies intelligent document recognition (IDR) technology to convert them to digital images, and sends relevant data to enterprise resource planning (ERP), accounts payable (A/P), and other back-end management systems. The specialized InputAccel server manages output by recognizing and avoiding holdups in the workflow process. It also ensures if a server goes offline, others will carry on functioning, thus avoiding downtime.

Now Novartis scans incoming invoices at a centrally located site, and the images are transmitted to the InputAccel for Invoices server for image improvement. Invoice data is then extracted and validated against supplier information. Most invoices are transferred directly for payment, with relatively few invoices requiring transfer to one of three accounts payable clerks who deal with queries manually.

Thanks to IT, overall efficiency has increased, processing errors are reduced, and accounting personnel can use their time and expert knowledge for more meaningful tasks than resolving invoice errors. For Novartis it is "mission accomplished."

Critical Thinking Questions

1. What factors contributed to invoice processing at Novartis being so complex?

2. How did IT help the company solve that problem?

3. What other uses and functions does InputAccel serve and how will this be useful to Novartis over the long term? (You may want to visit the Captiva website, (**www.captiva.com**), for more information on InputAccel's capabilities.)

SOURCES: Adapted from Kathryn Balint, "Captiva's Paper Chase Paying Off," *San Diego Union-Tribune*, December 9, 2005, pp. C1, C5. Captiva corporate website, (www.captivasoftware.com), March 22, 2006; "Processing Invoices From Around the World," Captiva Software, (www.captivasoftware.com), February 2, 2006; Novartis corporate website, (www.novartis.com), March 20, 2006)

PART 2

Canadian Business

CHAPTER

Making the Connection

Forms of Business Ownership

In this chapter you'll learn about the different forms of organization taken by business owners. How does an owner set the business up legally, and what does this imply for the business and its owner(s)? This is related directly to our *political* environment in the PEST model, because the government regulates the options for business ownership and the rules to follow. However, you will see that the form of business ownership has implications for all aspects of the integrative business model and thus, ultimately, for the success of the business.

Let's look at the critical success factors. First, the form of business ownership chosen will affect the *financial performance* of the company, because it affects its costs (costs of setting up the organization, for example) and the level of taxes that it must pay. It also affects how much profit is available or distributed to the owner(s). The form of business ownership can also indirectly affect the business' ability to *meet customer needs*, as the degree of flexibility and control for the owner(s) tends to decrease as the business grows larger, which is often when the form of ownership is changed. More directly, the owner is restricted in terms of how to meet the needs of the customer if he or she is under a franchise agreement, for example. This, in turn, will affect the amount of *innovation and creativity* that is possible. Finally, it is perhaps easier to *gain employee commitment* in some forms of business organization, as they offer the possibility of direct ownership beyond purchasing a minority interest in the company's stock.

So the form of business ownership, like all the decisions made in a business, has an integrative impact. It must be chosen with the company's overall goals and *strategy* in mind; for example, it would be difficult for a sole proprietorship to raise sufficient capital to build a chain of hotels worldwide. The form of business ownership also affects how the external environment treats the business and how that business, in turn, affects the environment, in addition to affecting the decisions that are made internally.

Looking back at our PEST model of the external environment, we can examine the effect that the form of business ownership has with regard to those dealing with the business from the outside. For example, within the political environment, the government tends to regulate larger businesses more heavily, especially large public corporations that have a greater impact on society. As well, the amount of legal liability that the owners have for business debts depends on the form of ownership. This might lead to a situation in which a loan is turned down because the lender doubts that the debt can be satisfied out of business assets, and yet the form of ownership chosen (namely, incorporation) does not allow for the debt to be satisfied from the personal assets of the owner(s) unless they are specifically used as collateral.

The form of business ownership chosen affects the amount of taxes paid to the government as well, which, in turn, affects the *economic* environment: paying less tax

allows for greater spending to grow the business. Within the *social* environment, society is becoming ever more demanding of businesses to be socially responsible and act ethically. This extends to all forms of business organization, but perhaps the highest expectations rest on the larger public corporations because of their visibility and resources. The trends in business ownership, as discussed later in this chapter, also have relationships to the social environment. For example, the changing demographics in society—the increasingly prominent role of women in business, the influence women have over purchase decisions, along with political pressure from various groups—have led many franchisors to encourage women to own their own franchises and to facilitate the process for them.

The *technological* environment is perhaps the only area not directly impacted by the form a business takes. Small and large organizations, whether sole proprietorships, partnerships, or corporations, have equal access to technology. This access to technology has allowed different forms of business to compete on more of a level playing field, leading to the creation of many new businesses. These new businesses usually start small, as sole proprietorships, partnerships, or small private corporations—creating a trend that we will discuss in Chapter 6.

When looking at the advantages and disadvantages of each form of ownership, you will see many examples of the integration of the form of ownership and the decisions made within the functional areas. For example, in the *finance* area, the form of ownership directly affects the degree of capital that the business has access to, and the options it has to raise that capital. This, in turn, will affect the size of its *operations*.

In the *human resource* area, taking the large corporation as an example, this form of ownership affects the organization's ability to find and keep quality employees as well as the incentives available to them—the larger the company, the greater the opportunities for employees to advance and the greater the resources to attract and hold onto them.

In a broader sense, the form of ownership affects the ability of the business to make good decisions in all areas. It is very unlikely for a sole proprietor, for example, to be an expert at every function, and thus the business will be weak where he or she is weak unless expert assistance is brought in. This is why businesses often develop partnerships, preferably with people who have complementary skills, and/or create corporations that can, as they grow larger, attract professional talent to round out the company's needs. A good example is Research In Motion (RIM), the maker of the famous BlackBerry Smartphone. The company was built on the strength of its technology, but a major weakness early on was in the area of marketing. Because of the success and visibility of this publicly traded corporation, it was able to attract very strong talent in that area to continue the success of the company. A smaller sole proprietorship would have had much more difficulty.

This issue is the same with respect to the basic tasks of a manager in any of the functional areas or levels of the company. A sole proprietor may be good at *planning*, but bad at executing (*organizing, leading*, and *controlling*), or vice versa. Bringing other people into the company to balance those needs is important to the success of the company, and it is easier as the business grows, which often necessitates a change in the form of ownership.

CHAPTER 5

Forms of Business Ownership

LEARNING OUTCOMES

1 Discuss the advantages and disadvantages of the sole proprietorship form of business organization.

2 Describe the advantages of operating as a partnership, and what downside risks partners should consider.

3 Explain how the corporate structure provides advantages and disadvantages to a company, and identify a special type of corporation.

4 Review some of the other business organization options in addition to sole proprietorships, partnerships, and corporations.

5 Identify when franchising is an appropriate business form, and why it is growing in importance.

6 Understand why mergers and acquisitions can be important to a company's overall growth.

7 List some of the current trends that may affect the business organizations of the future.

THE FREEDOM OF OWNERSHIP

For six years, Christopher Halpin, owner of Manna Catering Services, was frustrated by what he describes as "the lack of respect for employees and lack of choices for the customers." During these six years, Christopher worked for numerous catering companies to supplement his art consulting business. The frustration that Christopher felt convinced him that he could become a successful business owner and demonstrate respect for his employees, all while delivering professional service and products to his customers.

His philosophy is simple: "create the right atmosphere and allow the customers to feel comfortable. The customers must see that the events are flexible, creative, unique, remarkable, and memorable." He says that people in our culture are generally not comfortable with being "served," so this has been his major challenge.

Since Christopher started Manna Catering Services, he has used his prior knowledge of the industry but has also learned some valuable lessons along the way. Because of what he saw while working for other people, he believed that the catering industry was not viewed as being professional or "white-collar." Since opening his business, his approach has been to "treat the industry from a professional aspect and others will see it as being professional."

First he had to design flexible menu choices. "Not all customers want the same experience. By offering a variety of menus and a unique atmosphere around these menus, each event is seen as special and memorable," he says. He was also very aware that it was important to keep his costs to a minimum, without sacrificing quality, so that these savings could be passed on to the customer. With the combination of a variety of experiences and savings to the customers, Christopher ensures that they are receiving the quality and service they want.

Christopher also believes that to be truly customer focused, he must also be considerate of his employees and their needs. "Employees must enjoy their jobs and the customer must be made to realize that it is okay to be served." Christopher continued to share his philosophy about employees:

PHOTO COURTESY OF SHIRLEY A. ROSE

"Typically, employees in the small catering businesses are part time, supplementing their regular income. This often results in employees being very transient. I wanted to have a more secure and stable part-time group. I pay well (about 50 percent more than the standard), I allow the staff to eat the same food as the clients (therefore there is no thieving), they dress professionally (basic black, and of course, the Manna Catering signature natural linen apron, always freshly laundered). I provide training to ensure customers are made to feel comfortable and respected, and to ensure service consistency… Most importantly, I respect my employees."

Because of Christopher's respect for his employees and his fair and equitable treatment of them, the turnover rate of his staff has been very low, and they do not work for other caterers.

Being customer focused has been a very valuable and profitable lesson for Christopher. He warns those who are considering starting their own business not to forget to do their homework. He recommends that after you decide to start a business and determine what the business focus is, you should think about what the legal structure of your enterprise is going to be. "I researched the various types of business ownership and decided to form the simplest, the sole proprietorship, for many reasons," says Christopher.

"I looked into incorporating," he says, "but did not think the added expense and regulations were worth the investment; I could do better things with the money. The limited liability appealed to me, but in this business if you are customer-focused and careful (e.g., handling of food), there is little risk."

The partnership form, on the other hand, held very little interest for him. Christopher sat down and wrote out his qualifications for the catering business. Based on the day-to-day operations, there were no skills that he felt he did not possess or could not learn quickly, so there was no need to have a partner from that perspective. He did acknowledge that he was weak in the accounting and financial management area, but to overcome this situation, he found an accounting firm to help with financial and tax advice. Christopher sums up his sense about the possibility of forming a partnership:

"Besides, I had no interest in sharing the profits with anyone. The sole proprietorship appealed to me the best. I am able to make the decisions by myself and control the growth of the enterprise. I don't ever think that I will take on a partner, but I can see the day that if I want the enterprise to grow to a certain point, I will have to incorporate it."

Today, Christopher enjoys a successful business, the flexibility it offers him, and the respect of both his employees and his customers. He is happy in his venture and suggests that if you want to start a business—"Do your homework."[1]

Critical Thinking Questions

As you read this chapter, consider the following questions as they relate to Christopher Halpin and Manna Catering Services:

1. **What factors did Christopher consider when selecting a form of business organization?**

2. **What are some of the pros and cons of operating the business as a sole proprietorship? If Christopher decided to include a partner, what should that partner bring to the business?**

3. **What would be the benefits of incorporating the business?**

So you've decided to start a business. You have a good idea and some cash in hand, but before you get going, you need to decide what form of business organization will best suit your needs.

So first ask yourself some questions. Would you prefer to go it alone as a sole proprietorship, or do you want others to share the burdens and challenges of a partnership, or do you prefer the limited liability protection of a corporation?

Here are some other questions you need to consider: How easy will it be to find financing? Can you attract employees? How will the business be taxed, and who will be liable for the business' debts? If you choose to share ownership with others, how much operating control will they want, and what costs will be associated with that or other forms of ownership? Most start-up businesses select one of the major ownership categories.

In the following pages, we will discover the advantages and disadvantages of each form of business ownership and the factors that might make it necessary to change from one form of organization to another as the needs of the business change. As your business expands from a small to midsize or larger venture, the form of business structure you selected in the beginning might no longer be appropriate. We will also look at specialized forms of business.

Going It Alone: Sole Proprietorships

Mike Robson was working full time, just finishing a bachelor's degree and starting work on his master's, when having lunch with a fellow student changed everything. His friend mentioned that the company he worked for had trouble obtaining "toppers," metal boxes for ATM (automatic teller machine) modems. Before lunch was over, Robson decided to start a business—building toppers.

sole proprietorship
A business that is established, owned, operated, and often financed by one person.

Eight months after Robson had set up business as a **sole proprietorship,** a business established, owned, operated, and often financed by one person, his $20,000 home equity loan financing was gone without his having sold a single box! Then he made a fateful sales call at a local credit union, where it needed someone to spruce up a dilapidated ATM. Robson drew on his chemical engineering background to clean, polish, and paint the machine until it looked like new, and so his new business restoring and maintaining ATMs was born!

Robson thrived as a sole proprietor. He liked the independence of being his own boss and controlling all business decisions. When he realized that his initial idea was headed nowhere, he was able to change direction quickly when a new opportunity presented itself. Many businesses in your neighbourhood—including florists, dry cleaners, and beauty salons—are sole proprietorships, as are many service providers such as lawyers, accountants, and real estate agents.[2]

Advantages of Sole Proprietorships

Sole proprietorships have several advantages that make them popular:

- *Easy and inexpensive to form.* As Mike Robson discovered, sole proprietorships have few legal requirements and are not expensive to form, making them the business organization of choice for many small companies and start-ups.
- *Profits all go to the owner.* The owner of a sole proprietorship obtains the start-up funds and gets all the profits earned by the business.
- *Direct control of the business.* All business decisions are made by the sole proprietorship owner, without having to consult anyone else. This was beneficial for Mike Robson when he needed to change the direction of his business.
- *Relative freedom from government regulations.* Sole proprietorships have more freedom than other forms of business with respect to government controls.
- *No special taxation.* Sole proprietorships do not pay corporate taxes. Profits are taxed as personal income and are reported on the owner's individual tax return.
- *Ease of dissolution.* With no co-owners or partners, the sole proprietor can sell the business or close the doors at any time, making this form of business organization an ideal way to test new business ideas.

Disadvantages of Sole Proprietorships

Along with the freedom to operate the business as they wish, sole proprietors face several disadvantages:

- *Unlimited liability.* From a legal standpoint, the sole proprietor and the business he or she owns are one and the same, making the business owner personally responsible for all debts the business incurs, even if they exceed the business' value. The owner might need to sell other personal property—his or her car, home, or other investments—to satisfy claims against the business.
- *Difficulty in raising capital.* Business assets are unprotected against claims of personal creditors, and business lenders view sole proprietorships as high risk because of the owner's unlimited liability. Owners often must use personal funds—borrowing on credit cards, securing assets (collateral) for loans or lines of credit, or selling investments—to finance their business, and expansion plans can also be affected by an inability to raise additional funding.
- *Limited managerial expertise.* The success of a sole proprietorship rests solely with the skills and talents of the owner, who must wear many different hats and make all decisions. Owners are often not equally skilled in all areas of running a business. A graphic designer might be a wonderful artist but may not know bookkeeping, how to manage production, or how to market his or her work.
- *Trouble finding qualified employees.* Sole proprietors often cannot offer the same pay, fringe benefits, and opportunities for advancement as larger companies can,

making them less attractive to employees seeking the most favourable employment opportunities.

- *Personal time commitment.* Running a sole proprietorship business requires personal sacrifices and a huge time commitment, often dominating the owner's life with 12-hour workdays and 7-day workweeks.
- *Unstable business life.* The life span of a sole proprietorship can be uncertain. The owner might lose interest, experience ill health, retire, or die. The business will cease to exist unless the owner makes provisions for it to continue operating or puts it up for sale.
- *Losses are the owner's responsibility.* The sole proprietor is responsible for all losses, although tax laws allow these to be deducted from other personal income.

The sole proprietorship might be a suitable choice for a one-person start-up operation with no employees and little risk of liability exposure. For many sole proprietors, however, this is a temporary choice, and as the business grows, the owner might be unable to operate with limited financial and managerial resources. At this point, he or she might decide to take in one or more partners to ensure that the business continues to flourish.

concept check

What is a sole proprietorship?

Why is this a popular form of business organization?

What are the drawbacks to being a sole proprietor?

Partnerships: Sharing the Load

Can partnerships, an association of two or more individuals who agree to operate a business together for profit, be hazardous to a business' health? Let's assume partners Ron and Liz own a stylish and successful beauty salon. After a few years of operating the business they find they have contrasting visions for their company. Liz is happy with the status quo, while Ron wants to expand the business by bringing in investors and opening salons in other locations.

How do they resolve this impasse? By asking themselves some tough questions. Whose view of the future is more realistic? Does the business actually have the expansion potential Ron believes it does? Where will he find investors to make his dream of multiple locations a reality? Is he willing to dissolve the partnership and start over again on his own? And who would have the right to their clients?

Ron realizes that expanding the business in line with his vision would require a large financial risk, and that his partnership with Liz offers many advantages he would miss in a sole proprietorship form of business organization. After much consideration he decides to leave things as they are.

For those individuals who do not like to "go it alone," a **partnership** is simple to set up and offers a shared form of business ownership. It is a popular choice for professional service firms such as lawyers, accountants, architects, and real estate companies.

The parties agree, *either orally or in writing*, to share in the profits and losses of a joint enterprise. A *written partnership agreement*, spelling out the terms and conditions of the partnership, *is recommended* to prevent later conflicts between the partners. These agreements typically include the name of the partnership, its purpose, and the contributions of each partner (financial, asset, skill/talent), as well as outline the responsibilities and duties of each partner and their compensation structure (salary, profit sharing, etc.). It should contain provisions for the addition of new partners, the sale of partnership interests, and the procedures for resolving conflicts, dissolving the business, and distributing the assets.

There are *three basic types of partnerships*: *general, limited, and limited liability partnerships*. In a **general partnership**, all partners share in the management and the profits. They co-own the assets, and each can act on behalf of the firm. Each partner also has unlimited liability for all business obligations of the firm. A **limited partnership** has two types of partners: one or more **general partners**, who have unlimited liability, and one or more **limited partners**, whose liability is limited to the amount of their

partnership
An association of two or more individuals who agree to operate a business together for profit.

general partnership
A partnership in which all partners share in the management and profits. Each partner can act on behalf of the firm and has unlimited liability for all its business obligations.

limited partnership
A partnership with one or more general partners who have unlimited liability, and one or more limited partners whose liability is limited to the amount of their investment.

general partners
Partners who have unlimited liability for all of the firm's business obligations and who control its operations.

limited partners
Partners whose liability for the firm's business obligations is limited to the amount of their investment. They help to finance the business but do not participate in the firm's operations.

investment. In return for limited liability, limited partners agree not to take part in the day-to-day management of the firm. They help to finance the business, but the general partners maintain operational control.

In the **limited liability partnership (LLP),** each individual partner is protected from responsibility for the acts of other partners, and each partner's liability is limited to harm resulting from his or her own actions. Ontario was the first province to allow LLPs in 1998, followed by Alberta in 1999. Today most provinces allow LLPs to operate, and they are common in accounting and legal firms.

Advantages of Partnerships

Some advantages of partnerships come quickly to mind:

- *Ease of formation.* Like sole proprietorships, partnerships are easy to form. For most partnerships, applicable laws are not complex. The partners agree to do business together and draw up a *partnership agreement.*
- *Availability of capital.* Because two or more people contribute financial resources, partnerships can raise funds more easily for operating expenses and business expansion. The partners' combined financial strength also increases the firm's ability to raise funds from outside sources.
- *Diversity of skills and expertise.* Partners share the responsibility of managing and operating the business. Ideal partnerships bring together people with complementary backgrounds rather than those with similar experience, skills, and talents. Combining partner skills to set goals, manage the overall direction of the firm, and problem solve increases the chances of the partnership's success. To find the right partner, however, you must examine your own strengths and weaknesses, and know what you need from a partner. In the Perfect Partners section you'll find some advice on choosing a partner.
- *Flexibility.* General partners are actively involved in managing their firm and can respond quickly to changes in the business environment.
- *No special taxes.* Partnerships pay no income taxes. Each partner's profit or loss is reported on the partner's personal income tax return, with any profits taxed at personal income tax rates.
- *Relative freedom from government control.* Governments exercise little control over partnership activities.

Disadvantages of Partnerships

Business owners must consider the following disadvantages of setting up their venture as a partnership:

- *Unlimited liability.* All general partners have unlimited liability for the debts of the business. In fact, any one partner can be held personally liable for all partnership debts and legal judgments (such as malpractice)—regardless of who caused them. As with sole proprietorships, business failure can lead to a loss of the general partners' personal assets. To overcome this problem, most provinces now allow the formation of limited liability partnerships, which protect each individual partner from responsibility for the acts of other partners, and limit partners' liability to harm resulting from their own actions.
- *Potential for conflicts between partners.* Partners might have different ideas about how to run the business, which employees to hire, how to allocate responsibilities, and when to expand. Differences in personalities and work styles can cause clashes or breakdowns in communication, sometimes requiring outside intervention to save the business.
- *Complexity of profit-sharing.* Dividing the profits is relatively easy if all partners contribute equal amounts of time, expertise, and capital. But if one partner puts in more money and others more time, it might be difficult to arrive at a fair profit-sharing formula.

EXHIBIT 5.1 > Perfect Partners

Picking a partner is both an art and a science. Be prepared to talk about everything. On paper, someone might have all the right credentials, but does that person share your vision and the ideas you have for the business? Is he or she a straight shooter? Honesty, integrity, and ethics are equally important, as you might be liable for what your partner does. Trust your intuition and "your gut feelings—they're probably right," advises Irwin Gray, author of *The Perils of Partners*. So ask yourself the following questions, and then ask a potential partner and see how well your answers match up:

1. Why do you want a partner?
2. What characteristics, talents, and skills does each person bring to the partnership?
3. How will you divide responsibilities? Consider every aspect of the business, from long-range planning to daily operations. Who will handle marketing, sales, accounting, and customer service?
4. What is your long-term vision for the business (size, life span, financial commitment, etc.)?
5. What are your personal reasons for forming this business: Are you looking for a steady paycheque? For independence? To create a small business? Or to build a large one?
6. Are all parties willing to put in the same amount of time and, if not, is there an alternative arrangement that is acceptable to everyone?
7. What are your work ethics and values?
8. What requirements should be in the partnership agreement?

SOURCES: Julie Bawden Davis, "Buddy System," *Business Start Ups*, June 1998, (www.entrepreneurmag.com); Azriela Jaffe, " 'Til Death Us Do Part' Is No Way to Start a Business," *Business Week Online*, October 23, 1998, (www.businessweek.com/smallbiz); Jerry Useem, "Partners on the Edge," *Inc.*, August 1998, 54, 59.

HOT Links

In Canada the provinces have jurisdiction with respect to sole proprietorships and partnerships. To find out more check your provincial government's website.

concept check

How does a partnership differ from a sole proprietorship?

Describe the three main types of partnerships.

Explain the difference between a limited partner and a general partner.

What are the main advantages and disadvantages of a partnership?

- *Difficulty exiting or dissolving a partnership.* As a rule, partnerships are easier to form than to leave. When one partner wants to leave, the value of his or her share must be calculated. To whom will that share be sold, and will that person be acceptable to the other partners? To avoid these problems, most partnership agreements include specific guidelines for transfer of partnership interests and buy-sell agreements that make provision for surviving partners to buy a deceased partner's interest. Partners can purchase special life insurance policies on each partner designed to fund such a purchase.

Business partnerships are often compared to marriages. As with a marriage, choosing the right partner is critical, so if you are considering forming a partnership, allow plenty of time to evaluate your and your potential partner's goals, personality, expertise, and working style. Exhibit 5.1 lists questions that you and a potential business partner can ask each other.

Corporations: Limiting Your Liability

LO 3

corporation
A legal entity with an existence and life separate from its owners, who therefore are not personally liable for the entity's debts. A corporation can own property, enter into contracts, sue and be sued, and engage in business operations.

When people think of corporations, they typically think of major, well-known companies such as Suncor, TD Canada Trust, Bell Canada Enterprises, and the communications corporation Rogers Communications Inc. But corporations range in size from large multinationals, with thousands of employees and billions of dollars in sales, to midsize or even smaller firms, with few employees and little revenue.

A **corporation** is a legal entity with a life separate from its owners, who therefore are not personally liable for its debts. A corporation is subject to the laws of the jurisdiction in which it is incorporated. A corporation can own property, enter into contracts, sue and be sued, and engage in business operations. Unlike sole proprietorships and partnerships, corporations are taxable entities.

In launching his company eEye Digital Security, 21-year-old Marc Maiffret needed the limited liability protection of the corporate business organization model. Maiffret started hacking at age 15, learning how to mangle websites and breach networks.

When the authorities suspected him of breaching a military network, Maiffret and his boss Firas Bushnaq (Maiffret dropped out of school to work for a software firm) decided to capitalize on his expertise. They launched eEye to outsmart the best hackers in the business by designing software to protect corporate network security.

With Maiffret bearing the title "Chief Hacking Officer," the growing company has offices around the world and includes among its 100 employees a team of engineering hackers whose efforts bring eEye an estimated $11 million annually. Its unusual background makes eEye an unconventional corporation.[3] Maiffret has since moved on to become the director of professional services of the Digi Trust Group, a company providing information security consultancy.[4]

Public Versus Private Corporations

public corporation
A corporation whose shares are widely held and available to the general public.

private corporation
A corporation that does not trade publicly; therefore, the shares are not available to the general public.

Corporations can be either public or private. A public corporation's shares are widely held and available to the general public. Once the shares are in the public domain, they are then traded in the secondary markets, either on organized stock markets (e.g., Toronto Stock Exchange) or in the over-the-counter markets (e.g., NASDAQ—see Chapter 15). A private corporation does not trade publicly and is not listed in the markets. The shares are not available to the general public. Most corporations begin as a private corporation but, if they choose, may become public corporations as a means of raising extra money. Just as private corporations can become public corporations, public corporations can become private.

The Incorporation Process

Setting up a corporation is more complex than starting a sole proprietorship or partnership. If the business activity is primarily in only one province, it is necessary to incorporate only as a provincial company under that province's Companies Act (or other similarly named act). A corporation can also be set up under the Canada Business Corporations Act if it is to operate in more than one province or across Canada. Either route of incorporation requires more steps than setting up a sole proprietorship or partnership.

Incorporating a company involves five main steps:

1. Selecting the company's name (including searching existing company names to confirm that you can use the name);
2. writing the articles of incorporation (see below) and filing them with the appropriate government office;
3. paying the required fees and taxes;
4. holding an organizational meeting; and
5. adopting bylaws, electing directors, and passing the first operating resolutions.

The province or federal government issues the corporate charter based on the information in the articles of incorporation. Once the corporation has its charter, it holds an organizational meeting to adopt bylaws, elect directors, and pass initial operating resolutions. Bylaws provide the legal and managerial guidelines for operating the firm.

To distinguish a corporation from other forms of ownership, corporations must use Limited (Ltd./Ltée), Incorporated (Inc.), or Corporation (Corp.) at the end of the company name. This tells the customers, suppliers, and other shareholders that the owners have limited liability for the corporate obligations. See Exhibit 5.2 for a listing of what the Articles of Incorporation include.

The Corporate Structure

shareholders
The owners of a corporation who hold shares of stock that provide certain rights; also known as stockholders.

As Exhibit 5.3 shows, corporations have their own organizational structure, with three important components: shareholders, directors, and officers.

Shareholders, or stockholders, are the owners of a corporation, holding shares of stock that provide them with certain rights. They may receive a portion of the

EXHIBIT 5.2 > Articles of Incorporation

Articles of incorporation are prepared on a form authorized or supplied by the province, or the federal government if the corporation incorporated federally. Although they may vary slightly from province to province, all articles of incorporation include the following key items:

- The name of the corporation;
- The province in which the registered office is to be situated;
- The classes and any maximum number of shares that the corporation is authorized to issue;
- If the issue, transfer, or ownership of shares is to be restricted, a statement that clearly sets out the restrictions;
- The number of directors, or the minimum and maximum number of directors; and
- Any restriction on the business in which the corporation may engage.

board of directors
A group of people elected by the shareholders to handle the overall management of a corporation, such as setting major corporate goals and policies, hiring corporate officers, and overseeing the firm's operations and finances.

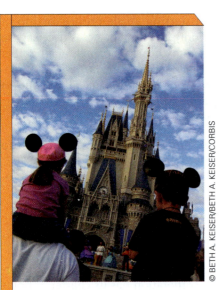

© BETH A. KEISER/BETH A. KEISER/CORBIS

CONCEPT *in Action* **>>>**

When Walt Disney cast his now-famous mouse as Steamboat Willie back in the 1920s, he had little idea that his animation project would turn into one of the largest entertainment companies in the world. The house that Walt built, with its magical theme parks, movie studios, and product lines, is overseen today by visionary directors with accomplished backgrounds in media, technology, and government. What important tasks and responsibilities are entrusted to Disney's board of directors?

corporation's profits in the form of dividends, and they can sell or transfer their ownership—their shares of stock in the corporation—at any time. Shareholders can attend annual meetings, elect the board of directors, and vote on matters that affect the corporation, in accordance with its charter and bylaws. Each share of stock generally carries one vote.

It is possible for one person to own all the shares of a corporation. In some cases, when a private corporations first "goes public," it will issue various classes of stock to be able to retain control (the original owners), on the one hand, and attract capital (new investors), on the other, such as Canadian Tire and Magna International Inc. Also, some corporations issue multiple voting shares (more than one vote per share) to retain control, such as Four Seasons Hotels Inc.

The shareholders elect a **board of directors** to govern and handle the overall management of the corporation. The board of directors is responsible for ensuring that the business is managed with the corporation's best interests in mind. The directors set major corporate goals and policies, hire corporate officers, and oversee the firm's operations and finances.

The boards of large corporations typically include both corporate executives (inside directors) and outside directors (not employed by the organization) chosen for their professional and personal expertise. Outside directors often bring fresh viewpoints to the corporation's activities, because they are independent of the firm. See "Making Ethical Choices" (page 152) for an inside look at some of the decisions corporate boards make.

Hired by the board, the *officers* of a corporation are its top management and include the president and chief executive officer (CEO), vice presidents, the treasurer, and the secretary; they are responsible for achieving corporate goals and policies. Besides the CEO, other common titles of officers of a corporation include chief financial officer (CFO), chief information officer (CIO), and chief operating officer (COO). Officers may also be board members (inside directors) and/or shareholders.

Advantages of Corporations

The corporate structure allows companies to merge financial and human resources into enterprises with great potential for growth and profits:

- *Limited liability.* A key advantage of corporations is that they are separate legal entities that exist apart from their owners. An owner's (shareholder's) liability for the debts of the firm is limited to the amount of the stock he or she owns. If the corporation goes bankrupt, creditors can look only to the assets of the corporation for payment. The main exception is when a shareholder personally

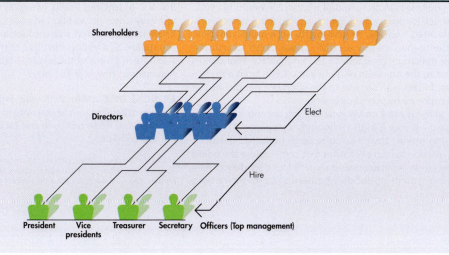

guarantees a business obligation (most common in corporations with one or only a few owners).

- *Ease of transferring ownership.* Shareholders of public corporations can sell their shares at any time without affecting the status of the corporation.
- *Unlimited life.* The life of a corporation is unlimited. Because the corporation is an entity separate from its owners, the death or withdrawal of an owner does not affect its existence, unlike a sole proprietorship or partnership.
- *Ability to attract financing.* Corporations can raise money by selling new shares of stock. Dividing ownership into smaller units makes it affordable to more investors, who can purchase one or several thousand shares. The large size and stability of corporations also helps them get bank financing. All of these financial resources allow corporations to invest in facilities and human resources, and to expand beyond the scope of sole proprietorships and partnerships. It would be impossible for a sole proprietorship or partnership to make automobiles, provide nationwide telecommunications, or build oil or chemical refineries.
- *Ability to attract potential employees.* Corporations often offer better benefit plans and opportunities, which allows them to attract more potential employees. Larger companies also have the advantage of professional management opportunities (e.g., accounting managers).

Disadvantages of Corporations

Although corporations offer companies many benefits, they have some disadvantages:

- *Double taxation of profits.* Corporations must pay federal and provincial income taxes on their profits. The after-tax profit may then be distributed to the shareholders (dividends), and then the shareholders are taxed on the dividends as investment income.
- *Cost and complexity of formation.* As outlined earlier, forming a corporation involves several steps, and costs can run into thousands of dollars, including filing, registration, and licensing fees, as well as the cost of lawyers and accountants.
- *More government restrictions.* Unlike sole proprietorships and partnerships, corporations are subject to many regulations and reporting requirements.
- Business losses cannot be written off against the other income of the owners (shareholders) of the company.

HOT Links

Find out more about corporations and shareholder rights by searching for "corporations Canada" at (http://strategis.gc.ca/engdoc/main.html).

Making Ethical Choices

THE BOARD GAME

After completing your secondary education, you have found your place in the world of business. Everything clicks. You have a knack for seeing the big picture. You excel when working in multifaceted business environments—the more complex, the better. Companies value your fresh approach to structuring businesses for maximum productivity and profitability. Your adeptness has come to the attention of quite a few CEOs from a myriad of companies. In fact, you are one of the youngest people invited to serve on corporate boards of directors.

Wanting to focus most on your career, you accepted a seat on only one board—a young high-technology company, i2T, which has been losing money steadily. You're concerned that decisions about compensation for top executives that come before the board might further erode profitability and shareholder confidence. As a voting member, you must decide whether to approve awarding a severance package, including a $500,000 consulting fee and a BMW Z-8, to Greg Brady, who was removed as CEO after a year of heavy losses. In addition to your concerns about the company's financial picture and shareholder loyalty, you wonder how your reputation as a young member of the board might be affected if you vote in favour of the award. Many fear boards will continue to play games. How will you play?

ETHICAL DILEMMA: With your expertise in structuring for maximum profitability, would you vote in favour of the severance package and the huge bonus in the face of the company's dismal financial condition?

SOURCES: "Corporate Power, Influence, Money and Interlocking Boards of Directors Page," (www.verdant.net/corp.htm) (accessed February 18, 2003); and Arlene Weintraub and Ronald J. Grover, "Look Who's Still at the Trough," *Business Week*, September 9, 2002, 58.

The One-Person Corporation

one-person corporation
A corporation with only one person as the shareholder; common in professional practices (e.g., medical doctors, accountants, or lawyers) and in trades (e.g., plumbers and electricians).

The **one-person corporation** offers certain personal liability protection to owners of a business. This is common in professional practices such as those of doctors, accountants, and lawyers and in the trades such as plumbers and electricians. Usually the personal assets of the shareholder are not at risk, except when the shareholder has personally guaranteed a business debt (this is quite common in small businesses, because the corporation does not have adequate financing or collateral) or there is professional malpractice. It is important that the corporation have adequate business insurance to protect the company from overwhelming legal liabilities.

A one-person corporation might qualify for small-business tax rates, and the owner might be able to secure a dividend tax credit, which can result in lower corporate and personal taxes than in a sole proprietorship or partnership.

Exhibit 5.4 summarizes the advantages and disadvantages of each form of business ownership.

> ### concept check
>
> What is a corporation? Describe how corporations are formed and structured.
>
> Summarize the advantages and disadvantages of corporations. Which features contribute to the dominance of corporations in the business world?

A Special Type of Corporation: The Crown Corporation

Crown corporations
Companies that only the provincial and federal governments can set up.

Corporations that are owned by either a provincial or the federal government are called **Crown corporations.** They are structured similar to private or independent corporations and are established to conduct regulatory, advisory, administrative, financial, or other services or to provide goods and services. Although Crown corporations generally have greater freedom from direct political control than government departments, they are ultimately accountable, through a cabinet minister, to Parliament. Some of the more recognizable Crown corporations are Canada Post Corporation, the Canadian Broadcasting Corporation (CBC), the Bank of Canada, and the National Museum of Science and Technology.

Specialized Forms of Business Organization

In addition to the three main forms, several specialized types of business organization play an important role in our economy. We will look at cooperatives and joint ventures in this section and take a detailed look at franchising in the following section.

EXHIBIT 5.4 > Advantages and Disadvantages of Major Types of Business Organization

SOLE PROPRIETORSHIP	PARTNERSHIP	CORPORATION
ADVANTAGES		
Owner receives all profits	More expertise and managerial skill available	Limited liability protects owners from losing more than they invest
Low organizational costs	Relatively low organizational costs	Can achieve large size due to marketability of stock (ownership)
Income taxed as personal income of proprietor	Income taxed as personal income of partners	Ownership is readily transferable
Independence	Fund-raising ability is enhanced by more owners	Long life of firm (not affected by death of owners)
Secrecy		Can attract employees with specialized skills
Ease of dissolution		Greater access to financial resources allows growth
DISADVANTAGES		
Owner receives all losses	Owners have unlimited liability; may have to cover debts of other, less financially sound partners	Double taxation because both corporate profits and dividends paid to owners are taxed although the dividends are taxed at a reduced rate
Owner has unlimited liability; total wealth can be taken to satisfy business debts	Dissolves or must reorganize when partner dies	More expensive and complex to form
Limited fund-raising ability can inhibit growth	Difficult to liquidate or terminate	Subject to more government regulation
Proprietor may have limited Skills and management expertise	Potential for conflicts between partners	Financial reporting requirements make operations public
Few long-range opportunities and benefits for employees Lacks continuity when owner dies	Difficult to achieve large-scale operations	

Cooperatives

cooperatives
A legal entity typically formed by people with similar interests, such as suppliers or customers, to reduce costs and gain economic power. A cooperative has limited liability, an unlimited life span, an elected board of directors, and an administrative staff; all profits are distributed to the member-owners in proportion to their contributions.

Cooperatives (co-op) in Canada are a vital component in our economy; there are more than 8,000 cooperatives in Canada, four out of every ten Canadians are members of at least one co-op, and they directly employ approximately 150,000 people.[5] Cooperatives are typically formed by people with similar interests, such as customers or suppliers, to reduce costs and gain economic power and are owned by the members who use the services.

Cooperatives differ from other business in three distinct areas:

1. *Purpose.* The primary focus is to meet the common needs of their members, whereas the primary purpose of investor-owned businesses is to maximize the value of the company.
2. *Control structure.* Unlike most businesses, with shares that typically give one vote for each share, cooperatives use the one member—one vote system to ensure that people, not capital, control the organization.
3. *Allocation of profit.* This is based on the extent to which members use the cooperative, not the number of shares held.[6]

A cooperative is a legal entity with several corporate features, such as limited liability for the membership, unlimited life span, an elected board of directors, and an administrative staff. Cooperatives distribute all profits to the members in proportion

HOT Links

For more information about cooperatives in Canada, visit the Canadian Co-operative Association's website (**www.coopscanada.coop**). For an alternative source, see (**www.coopcouncil.mb.ca/links.html**) for the Manitoba Co-operative Association.

- Voluntary and open membership
- Democratic member control
- Member economic participation
- Autonomy and independence
- Education, training, and information
- Cooperation among cooperatives
- Concern for community

SOURCE: "What are Cooperatives," Press Kit, National Cooperative Business Association, (www.ncba.coop).

to their contributions. Cooperatives empower people to improve their quality of life and enhance their economic opportunities through self-help. Throughout the world, cooperatives are providing members with credit and financial services, energy, consumer goods, affordable housing, telecommunications, and other services that would not otherwise be available to them. Exhibit 5.5 outlines the basic principles of operation cooperatives follow.

The Calgary Co-operative Association Limited, Credit Union of Central New Brunswick, Ontario Co-operative Association (OnCoop), and Mountain Equipment Co-op are just a few of the cooperatives in Canada.

concept check

What is a cooperative, and what are the advantages to the membership?

How do cooperatives differ from other forms of ownership?

What are the benefits of joint ventures?

Joint Ventures

joint venture

Two or more companies that form an alliance to pursue a particular project for a specified time period.

In a **joint venture**, two or more companies form an alliance to pursue a particular project, usually for a specified time period. There are many reasons for joint ventures. The project might be too large for one company to handle on its own, and by forming joint ventures, companies can gain access to new markets, products, or technology. Both large and small companies can benefit from this type of endeavour.

For example, Syncrude Canada Ltd. is a joint venture of oil-producing companies, including Nexen Inc., Imperial Oil Resources, and Petro-Canada. By creating the joint venture, infrastructure costs, production costs, and risks were spread

EXHIBIT 5.6 > Ownership of Syncrude Canada Ltd.

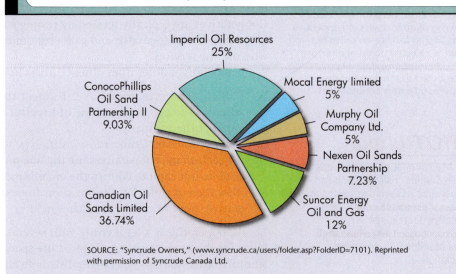

Imperial Oil Resources 25%

Mocal Energy limited 5%

Murphy Oil Company Ltd. 5%

ConocoPhillips Oil Sand Partnership II 9.03%

Nexen Oil Sands Partnership 7.23%

Canadian Oil Sands Limited 36.74%

Suncor Energy Oil and Gas 12%

SOURCE: "Syncrude Owners," (www.syncrude.ca/users/folder.asp?FolderID=7101). Reprinted with permission of Syncrude Canada Ltd.

out among the owners. Syncrude completed phase 3 of the Syncrude 21 expansion program in 2006, bringing its production capacity to 350,000 barrels/day, which represents 13% of Canada's energy needs.[7] Exhibit 5.6 shows the ownership percentages of Syncrude Canada Ltd.

Franchising: A Popular Trend

franchising
A form of business organization based on a business arrangement between a *franchisor*, which supplies the product concept, and the *franchisee*, which sells the goods or services of the franchisor in a certain geographic area.

franchisor
In a franchising arrangement, the company that supplies the product concept to the *franchisee*.

franchisee
In a franchising arrangement, the individual or company that sells the goods or services of the franchisor in a certain geographic area.

Franchises come in all sizes, including McDonald's, the world's largest food service retailer, with 31,000 restaurants in 119 countries (70 percent of which are owned and operated by franchisees) and over 1400 in Canada.[8] Chances are, you deal with one of the more than 2,100 franchise systems in Canada and the United States almost every day. When you have lunch at Tim Horton's or Pizza Pizza, use the services of a UPS store, take your car for servicing at AAMCO, buy candles at Buck or Two, or rent a car from Budget Rent A Car, in each case you are dealing with a franchised business. These and other familiar name brands have come to mean quality, consistency, and value to customers.

Providing a way to own a business without starting it from scratch, franchising is one of the fastest-growing segments of the economy. **Franchising** is a form of business organization that involves a business arrangement between a **franchisor**, the company supplying the product concept, and the **franchisee**, the individual or company selling those goods or services in a certain geographic area. The franchisee buys a package that includes a proven product, proven operating methods, and training in managing the business.

A **franchise agreement** is a contract allowing the franchisee to use the franchisor's business name, trademark, and logo. The agreement also outlines the rules for running the franchise, the services provided by the franchisor, and the financial terms. The franchisee agrees to keep inventory at certain levels, buy a standard equipment package, keep up sales and service levels, follow the franchisor's operating rules, take part in franchisor promotions, and maintain a relationship with the franchisor. In return, the franchisor provides the use of a proven company name and symbols, help finding a site, building plans, guidance and training, management assistance, managerial and accounting procedures, employee training, wholesale prices for supplies, and financial assistance.

Advantages of Franchises

Like other forms of business organization, franchising offers some distinct advantages:

- *Increased ability for the franchisor to expand.* Because franchisees finance their own units, franchisors can grow without making a major investment. Although franchisors give up a share of profits to their franchisees, they receive ongoing revenues in the form of royalty payments.
- *Recognized name, product, and operating concept.* The franchisee gets a widely known and accepted business with a proven track record, as well as operating procedures, standard goods and services, and national advertising. Consumers know they can depend on products from franchises such as Pizza Hut, Hertz, and Holiday Inn. As a result, the franchisee's risk is reduced and the opportunity for success increased.
- *Management training and assistance.* The franchisor provides a structured training program that gives new franchisees a crash course in how to start and operate their business. Ongoing training programs for managers and employees are another plus. In addition, franchisees have a peer group for support and sharing ideas.
- *Financial assistance.* Being linked to a nationally known company can help a franchisee obtain funds from a lender. The franchisor typically also gives the franchisee advice on financial management, referrals to lenders, and help in preparing loan applications. Many franchisors offer payment plans, short-term credit for buying supplies from the franchise company, and loans to purchase real estate and equipment.

Disadvantages of Franchises

Franchising also has some disadvantages:

- *Loss of control.* The franchisor has to give up some control over operations and has less control over its franchisees than over company employees.
- *Cost of franchising.* Franchising can be a costly form of business. Costs will vary depending on the type of business and might include expensive facilities and equipment. The franchisee also pays fees and/or royalties, which are usually tied to a percentage of sales. Fees for national and local advertising and management advice might also add to a franchisee's ongoing costs.
- *Restricted operating freedom.* The franchisee agrees to conform to the franchisor's operating rules and facilities design, as well as inventory and supply standards. Some franchises require franchisees to purchase from only the franchisor or approved suppliers. The franchisor may restrict the franchisee's territory or site, which could limit growth. Failure to conform to franchisor policies could mean the loss of the franchise.

Franchise Growth

Many of today's major names in franchising, such as McDonald's and Kentucky Fried Chicken, started in the 1950s, but franchising grew rapidly through the 1960s and 1970s, with more types of businesses—clothing, convenience stores, business services, and many others—using franchising to distribute their goods and services. Business owners found franchising to be a way to expand operations quickly into new geographic areas with limited capital investment, and many are turning to technology to further expand their businesses.

HOT Links

Considering buying a franchise? Check out the opportunities and costs at (http://canada.franchiseopportunities.com).

Changing demographics drive franchise industry growth, in terms of who, how, and what experiences the most rapid growth. The continuing growth and popularity of technology and personal computing is responsible for the rapidly multiplying number of eBay drop-off stores, and tech consultants like Geeks on Call are in greater demand than ever. Other growth franchise industries are the specialty coffee market, children's enrichment and tutoring programs, senior care, weight control, and fitness franchises.

And the savviest franchisees see multi-unit development as a great way to further expand franchise systems and increase profits. Multi-unit buyers tend to be white-collar workers who have been laid off from middle-management jobs. They are well qualified financially, and bring management skills, financial resources, business acumen, and a lot of drive to their franchise ventures. Exhibit 5.7 shows some of the franchises with a presence in Canada.

The Next Big Thing in Franchising

All around you, people are talking about the next big thing—"always fresh" at Tim Hortons; the half hour workout at Curves, the answer to North America's fitness needs—and you are ready to take the plunge and buy a trendy franchise. But consumers' desires can change with the tide, so how do you plan an entrance—and exit—strategy when purchasing a franchise that's a big hit today but could be old news by tomorrow? Exhibit 5.8 outlines some tips offered by Michael H. Seid, managing director of Michael H. Seid & Associates, a management consulting firm specializing in the franchise industry.

EXHIBIT 5.7 > Examples of Franchises in Canada

MR.SUB	Pizza Hut
Days Inn Canada	Quizno's Canada Corporation
Keg Restaurants Ltd.	Rent-A-Wreck
Kwik Kopy Printing Canada	Royal LePage Real Estate Services
M&M Meat Shops	Second Cup Ltd., The
McDonald's Restaurants Canada Limited	Shoppers Drug Mart
Mr. Lube Canada Inc.	Swiss Chalet Chicken & Ribs
Orange Julius Canada Limited	

EXHIBIT 5.8 > Franchise Purchase Tips

Act fast, yet proceed with caution. Normal trends tend to have a five-year life span, so it's important to get in early. Commit to a shorter term when the investment is not so secure.

Put the franchisor to the test. When you get into a franchise system that needs to be nimble, make certain it can respond quickly to change.

Know what you're getting into. Ask the franchisor what product(s) they plan to add if trends change. If they don't have an answer or aren't talking about research and development, you still might be able to buy into the trend but not with that franchisor.

Don't invest more than you can afford to lose. Bank your money and look at other investments.

Don't fall in love with a trend. Trends are fickle. Adored one day, they can become one-hit wonders the next. Buy on business sense, not on emotions.

SOURCE: Reprinted by permission of Michael H. Seid.

International Franchising

concept check

Describe franchising and the main parties to the transaction.

Summarize the major advantages and disadvantages of franchising.

Why has franchising proved so popular?

Like other forms of business, franchising is part of our global marketplace economy. As international demand for all types of goods and services grows, most franchise systems are already operating internationally or planning to expand overseas. Restaurants, hotels, business services, educational products, car rentals, and non-food retail stores are popular international franchises.

Franchisors in foreign countries face many of the same problems as other firms doing business abroad. In addition to tracking markets and currency changes, franchisors must understand local culture,

Expanding Around The Globe

SETTING UP (SANDWICH) SHOP IN CHINA

Lured by China's fast-food industry—estimated at $15 billion—Jim Bryant, 50, was not the only entrepreneur to discover it is hard to do business in China. In ten years, Bryant has opened 19 Subway stores in Beijing—only half the number he was supposed to have by now—while other companies like Chili's and Dunkin' Donuts have given up their Chinese operations altogether.

Subway, or Sai Bei Wei (Mandarin for "tastes better than others"), is now the third-largest North American fast-food chain in China, right behind McDonald's and KFC, and all its stores are profitable. Although Bryant had never eaten a Subway sandwich before, Jana Brands, the company Bryant worked for in China, sold $20 million in crab to Subway annually, so he knew it was big business. When Subway founder Fred DeLuca visited Beijing in 1994, Bryant took him to a place not on the official tour: McDonald's. It was Sunday night and the place was packed. "We could open 20,000 Subways here and not scratch the surface," Bryant remembers De Luca saying.

Two weeks later Bryant called Subway's headquarters in Milford, Connecticut, and asked to be the company representative in China. He would recruit local entrepreneurs, train them to become franchisees, and act as a liaison between them and the company. He would receive half the initial $10,000 franchise fee and one-third of their 8 percent royalty fees. He could also open his own Subway restaurants. Steve Forman, the founder of Jana Brands, invested $1 million in return for a 75 percent stake.

All foreign businesses in China had to be joint ventures with local partners, so Bryant used the Chinese business practice of relying on local relationships to find a manager for his first restaurant in Beijing. The project ran into problems immediately. Work on the store was delayed and construction costs soared. It didn't take Bryant long to realize that he and Forman had been swindled out of $200,000.

When it finally opened, the restaurant was a hit among Americans in Beijing, but the locals weren't sure what to make of it. They didn't know how to order and didn't like the idea of touching their food, so they held the sandwich vertically, peeled off the paper, and ate it like a banana. Most of all, the Chinese didn't seem to want sandwiches.

But Subway did little to alter its menu—something that still irks some Chinese franchisees. "Subway should have at least one item tailored to Chinese tastes to show they respect local culture," says Luo Bing Ling, a Beijing franchisee. Bryant thinks that with time, sandwiches will catch on in China. Maybe he's right: Tuna salad, which he couldn't give away at first, is now the number one seller.[9]

Critical Thinking Questions
- What are some of the main problems franchisors encounter when attempting to expand their business in a foreign country?
- What steps can franchisors take to ensure a smooth and successful launch of a new franchise business in a foreign country?

language differences, and the political environment. Franchisors in foreign countries also face the challenge of aligning their business operations with the goals of their franchisees, who may be located half a globe away. In the following Expanding Around the Globe box, you will learn about a hugely successful North American company that attempted to replicate its success in the Chinese fast food market, with mixed results.

Mergers and Acquisitions

merger
The combination of two or more firms to form a new company, which often takes on a new corporate identity.

acquisition
The purchase of a corporation by another corporation or by an investor group; the identity of the acquired company might be lost.

friendly takeover
A takeover that is supported by the management and board of directors of the targeted company.

hostile takeover
A takeover that goes against the wishes of the target company's management and board of directors.

horizontal merger
A merger of companies at the same stage in the same industry; done to reduce costs, expand product offerings, or reduce competition.

vertical merger
A merger of companies at different stages in the same industry; done to gain control over supplies of resources or to gain access to different markets.

conglomerate merger
A merger of companies in unrelated businesses; done to reduce risk.

leveraged buyout (LBO)
A corporate takeover financed by large amounts of borrowed money; can be done by outside investors or by a company's own management.

A **merger** occurs when two or more firms combine to form one new company, which often takes on a new corporate identity. In an **acquisition**, a corporation or an investor group buys a corporation, and the identity of the acquired company might be lost. (A company can also acquire divisions or subsidiaries of another firm.) Normally, an acquiring company finds a target company and, after analyzing the target carefully, negotiates with its management or shareholders.

When there is a takeover that is supported by the target company's management and board of directors, it is called a **friendly takeover**. On the other hand, if the takeover goes against the wishes of the target company's management and board of directors, it is called a **hostile takeover**. Hostile takeovers are usually accomplished by the acquiring company buying controlling interest in the targeted company.

The interest of the companies to merge is not the only consideration, however. Some mergers require the approval of the Competition Bureau, which administers and enforces the Competition Act. This is intended to protect not only the general public but also the industry.

Types of Mergers

The three main types of mergers are horizontal, vertical, and conglomerate. In a **horizontal merger**, companies at the same stage in the same industry merge to reduce costs, expand product offerings, or reduce competition. Many of the large mergers in the late 1990s were horizontal mergers to achieve economies of scale.

In a **vertical merger**, a company buys a firm that is in the same industry but is involved in an earlier or later stage of the production or sales process. Buying a supplier, a distribution company, or a customer gives the acquiring firm more control.

A **conglomerate merger** brings together companies in unrelated businesses to reduce risk. Combining with a company whose products have a different seasonal pattern or that responds differently to the business cycle can result in a more stable sales pattern.

A specialized, financially motivated type of merger, the **leveraged buyout (LBO)** became popular in the 1980s but is less common today. LBOs are corporate takeovers financed by large amounts of borrowed money—as much as 90 percent of the purchase price. LBOs can be started by outside investors or the corporation's own management.

Believing that the company is worth more than the value of all the stock, the investors buy the stock and expect to generate cash flow by improving operating efficiency or by selling off some units for cash that can be used to pay the debt. Although some LBOs did improve efficiency, many did not live up to investor expectations or generate enough cash to pay the debt.

Merger Motives

Although the headlines tend to focus on mega-mergers, "merger mania" affects small companies as well. The motives for undertaking mergers and acquisitions are similar regardless of size. Often the goal is strategic: improving the overall performance of the merged firms through cost savings, elimination of overlapping operations, improved purchasing power, increased market share, or reduced competition. Growth, widening of product lines, and the ability to acquire technology or management skill quickly are other motives. Acquiring a company is often faster, less risky, and less costly than developing products internally or expanding internationally.

HOT Links

For more information about the Competition Bureau and the Competition Act, see (**www.competitionbureau.gc.ca**).

Another motive for acquisitions is financial restructuring—cutting costs, selling off units, laying off employees, or refinancing—to increase the value of the company to its shareholders. Financially motivated mergers are based not on the potential to achieve economies of scale but, rather, on the acquirer's belief that the target has hidden value that can be unlocked through restructuring. Most financially motivated mergers involve larger companies.

Trends in Business Ownership

LO 7

As we learned earlier, an awareness of trends in the business environment is critical to business success. Many social, demographic, and technology trends affect how businesses organize. When reviewing options for organizing a business or choosing a career path, consider the following trends.

"Baby Boomers" Drive Franchise Trends

We all hear and read a great deal about the "greying of Canada," which refers to the "baby boomer" generation heading towards retirement age. This unprecedented demographic phenomenon—in 2006 the first members of the Baby Boom generation turned 60—is driving the ongoing battle to stay young, slim, and healthy. Boomers have transformed every life stage they've touched so far, and their demographic weight means that business opportunities are created wherever they go. With their interest in staying fit, boomers are contributing to the growth of fitness and weight-loss franchises.

Another area of boomer-driven franchise growth is elder care. Founded in 1994, Home Instead Senior Care is recognized as one of the world's fastest growing franchise companies in the eldercare market, with a network of over 800 independently owned and operated franchises in 15 countries. And as the world's population continues to age, the need for its unique services will continue to increase.

Home Instead Senior Care provides a meaningful solution for the elderly who prefer to remain at home. Seniors' quality of life is enhanced by Home Instead Senior Care's part-time, full-time, and around-the-clock services, designed for people who are capable of managing their physical needs but require some assistance and supervision. Home Instead Senior Care provides meal preparation, companionship, light housekeeping, medication reminders, incidental transportation, and errands. These services make it possible for the elderly to remain in the familiar comfort of their own homes for a longer period of time.[10]

But the best deal yet may be adult day services, one of the top 10 fastest-growing franchises and "still one of the best-kept secrets around" according to *Entrepreneur* magazine. Based on the concept of day care services for children, Sarah Adult Day Services, Inc. offers a franchising opportunity that meets the two criteria for a successful and socially responsible business: a booming demographic market with great potential for growth, and excellent elder care.[11]

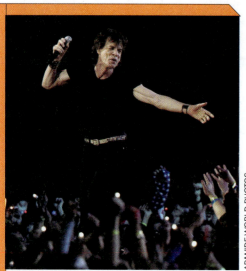

APWIDE WORLD PHOTOS

CONCEPT *in Action* >>>

Baby boomers racing into their 60s and beyond continue to exhibit the free-spirited and independent tendencies that marked their youth. Yet as they age, numerous eldercare services are coming alongside to provide a little extra help as needed. Among the fastest-growing eldercare businesses are those that specialize in non-medical services. Such services can range from illness recovery and emergency monitoring to helping with errands. What other services might have popular appeal with aging baby boomers?

Boomers Rewrite the Rules of Retirement

At age 64, Bob Drucker could be the poster child for retirement except that the concept makes him recoil. Drucker is living his dream. He and his wife have a large house where Drucker kicks back by floating in his pool when he's not spoiling his granddaughters with trips to Disneyland.

"The only way you can get me out of here is to carry me out," Drucker says, referring to the online pharmacy he founded and operates in Port Washington, New York. "I love my work and I cannot imagine sitting home and doing nothing."

Drucker is not alone. Today's boomers are working longer at their jobs and embracing post-retirement second careers, which often means starting their own small businesses.[12] As retirees opt to go into business for themselves, they are choosing different forms of business organizations depending on their needs and goals. Some may start small consulting businesses using the simple sole proprietorship form of business organization, while couples or friends might choose to become partners in a retail or franchise venture.

The more healthy and energetic the baby boomer generation remains, the more interested it is in staying active and engaged—and that may mean postponing retirement or not retiring at all.

Franchise Innovations

As more franchise systems crowd into growing industry categories, established franchises must find ways to differentiate themselves, such as the following:

- *Multiple-concept franchises.* When franchisors can take the competency they have developed and bridge it over to another franchise (i.e., the skills are transferable), these multi-concept franchises improve efficiencies and save money. For example, combination franchise Molly Maid and Mr. Handyman benefit from shared marketing and promotion, hoping to appeal to a similar customer.[13]
- *Expanded product offerings.* When a company can offer its customers multiple products and services, the customers can enjoy reduced costs and one-stop shopping. An example is a business that will deliver and pick up the dry cleaning, go shopping for gifts and essentials, and so on.
- *Cross-branding.* Operating two or more franchises in one location generates more customer traffic and maximizes space, personnel, and management utilization. For instance, gas stations frequently offer fast food outlets.
- *New ideas.* Finding new and innovative products and services that can be offered by a franchise helps to expand its target market and provide better service to its customers. For example, a residential cleaning company might offer house and pet-sitting services to its clients when they travel.

CONCEPT *in Action* >>>

Franchisees enjoy economies of scale and improved efficiency with the multiple-concept franchise by applying expertise learned in one type of franchising to other similar outlets. What other multiple-concept franchises do you think could be successful?

TIM BOYLE/STAFF/GETTY IMAGES NEWS/GETTY IMAGES

It is important to understand the benefits of the different forms of business organization if you start your own company. Even if you decide to work for someone else, this information will help you match a business entity with your goals. Suppose you are considering two job offers for a computer-programming position: a two-year-old consulting firm with 10 employees owned by a sole proprietor, or a publicly traded software developer with sales of $500 million. In addition to comparing the specific job responsibilities, consider the following:

- Which company offers better training? Do you prefer the on-the-job training you'll get at the small company, or do you want formal training programs as well?
- Which position offers the chance to work on a variety of assignments?
- What are the opportunities for advancement? Employee benefits?
- What happens if the owner of the young company gets sick or decides to sell the company?
- Which company offers a better working environment for you?

Answering these and similar questions will help you decide which job meets your particular needs.

Is Franchising in Your Future?

If the franchise route to business ownership interests you, begin educating yourself on the franchise process by investigating various franchise opportunities. You should research a franchise company thoroughly before making any financial commitment. Once you've narrowed your choices, you must research the franchisor, including its

Sustainable Business, Sustainable World

One of the major questions that needs to be answered as a business is created and begins to grow is "who are we?" and "what do we stand for?" Part of the process of creating a business is the development of a mission statement. Every company needs to have a mission, a purpose, a reason for being. Why was the business created in the first place? A company's mission statement puts this into words—the company's purpose, its business, and its values.

Businesses are created for multiple purposes, to achieve many different goals. Numerous businesses in today's environment have decided their purpose is higher than simply profit. Take The Timberland Company, for example. Its mission is "to equip people to make a difference in their world ... by creating outstanding products and by trying to make a difference in the communities where we live and work." Timberland is a sustainable business in the truest sense of the word. Its very reason for being involves sustainability—reducing its carbon footprint and being as environmentally responsible as it can so that the outdoors, the environment in which its products are used, is made better by its actions.

One of the most innovative moves that Timberland has taken in this direction is to create a "nutritional label" for its footwear products entitled "Our Footprint" (www.timberland.com/shop/ad4.jsp). In this way customers know what went into making the shoes they put on their feet and can make responsible choices about the products they buy. It includes the climate impact of the product, which is the percentage of renewable energy used, the chemicals used, and how much PVC plastic alternative was employed ... It also includes resource consumption—what percentage of eco-conscious materials were used and the percentage of recycled content in the shoebox, along with information on the number of trees planted by the company that year.

Timberland's commitment to sustainability is clear right on the home page of its website, where you'll find a link to Earthkeepers. Earthkeepers is an organization that Timberland has created to inspire and engage its customers to protect the earth, by doing small things or big things, but by everyone contributing. As Timberland puts it, it started Earthkeepers "because we love the outdoors. Making outdoor boots, shoes and gear is what we do for a living. No more outdoors means no more living. For us—or anyone else. Of course, we realize that by making our products, we're part of the problem. We believe it's time for companies, like ours, to take a look at how the way they do business affects the environment and do something about it." You can't get much clearer than that.

Does every form of business organization need a mission statement, or just large corporations? In today's business environment can a business be truly successful ignoring sustainability in its mission statement and hence how it operates? Do you think Timberland gains any economic benefit by its actions, or is there a necessary compromise when pursuing sustainability? Most importantly, what would happen if companies like Timberland didn't realize their impact and do something about it?

SOURCE: (www.timberland.com).

EXHIBIT 5.9 > Are You Ready to Be a Franchisee?

What can you to do to prepare when considering the purchase of a franchise? Doing your homework can spell the difference between success and failure, and some early preparation can help lay the groundwork for a successful launch of your franchised business.

Getting to know your banker at an early date should speed the loan process if you plan to finance your purchase with a bank loan. Stop by and introduce yourself. The proper real estate is another critical component for a successful retail/food franchise, so establish a relationship with a commercial real estate broker and begin scouting locations.

Professional guidance while evaluating franchise opportunities can prevent expensive mistakes, so interview advisers to find one that is right for you. Selecting a lawyer with franchise experience will speed the review of your franchise agreement. Most franchise systems use computers, so if you are not computer literate, take a class in the basics.
Then ask yourself some searching questions:

- Are you willing to work hard and put in long hours?
- Do you have the necessary financial resources?
- Are you excited about a specific franchise concept?
- Do you have prior business experience?
- Do your expectations and personal goals match the franchisor's?

SOURCES: Michael H. Seid and Kay Marie Ainsley, "Are You Ready to be a Franchisee?" *FranchiseZone*, December 9, 2002, (www.entrepreneur.com); and Thomas Love, "The Perfect Franchisee," *Nation's Business*, April 1, 1998, (http://ask.elibrary.com).

history, operating style, management, any past or pending litigation, the franchisee's financial obligations, and any restrictions on the sale of units. Interviewing current and past franchisees is another essential step.

Would-be franchisees should check recent issues of small-business magazines such as *Franchise Zone, Entrepreneur, Inc., Business Start Ups,* and *Success,* for industry trends, ideas on promising franchise opportunities, and advice on how to choose and run a franchise. The International Franchise Association website, (**www.franchise.org),** has links to *Franchise World Magazine* and other useful sites.

Is franchising for you? Assertiveness, desire to be your own boss, willingness to make a substantial time commitment, passion about the franchise concept, optimism, patience, and integrity rank high on franchisors' lists. Prior business experience is also a definite plus, and some franchisors prefer or require experience in their field. The information in Are You Ready to Be a Franchisee? can help you make a realistic self-assessment to increase your chances of success.

Customer Satisfaction and Quality

Most companies allocate substantial dollars to winning new business but rarely spend time or money trying to keep the customers they already have. Understanding the importance of satisfying today's demanding consumer can be a matter of business survival. "The fastest, least expensive way to make more money and grow your business is to become a service leader," says John Tschohl, author of *Achieving Excellence through Customer Service.*[14]

An example of this lesson-well-learned is an auto repair franchise called Caliber Collision Centers. Feeling frazzled after a car accident? Let a Caliber Collision Center take care of you—and your vehicle. Offering the vehicle owner unprecedented customer service and a lifetime warranty on all work done, Caliber's innovative approach to automobile collision repair provides state-of-the-art repair work from highly skilled technical staff using sophisticated equipment.

According to Caliber's chairman, Matthew Ohrnstein, "Unparalleled customer service, superior collision repair expertise, and solid relationships with insurers are some of the factors contributing to the company's remarkable growth." All Caliber Centers are affiliated with rental car networks, ensuring that customers have a car to drive while theirs is being repaired, and long-established relationships with insurers avoid the wait for an adjustor to inspect a vehicle before work can begin. An informative "preaccident" checklist of dos and don'ts posted on its website is just another example of how Caliber's management thinks "outside the box," going the extra mile to take care of their customers—one car at a time.

SOURCES: Justin Martin and David Birch, "Slump? What Slump?" *FSB (Fortune Small Business),* December 2002/January 2003, (http://ask.elibrary.com); company website, (www.caliber.com) (accessed December 30, 2002).

Summary of Learning Outcomes

1 **Discuss the advantages and disadvantages of the sole proprietorship form of business organization.**

The advantages of sole proprietorships include ease and low cost of formation, the owner's rights to all profits, the owner's control of the business, relative freedom from government regulation, absence of special taxes, and ease of dissolution. Disadvantages include owner's unlimited liability for debts, difficulty in raising capital, limited managerial expertise, difficulty in finding qualified employees, large personal time commitment, unstable business life, and the owner's personal absorption of all losses.

2 **Describe the advantages of operating as a partnership, and what downside risks partners should consider.**

Partnerships can be formed as either general or limited partnerships. In a general partnership, the partners co-own the assets and share the profits. Each partner is individually liable for all debts and contracts of the partnership. The operations of a limited partnership are controlled by one or more general partners with unlimited liability. Limited partners are financial partners whose liability is limited to their investment; they do not participate in the firm's operations. The advantages of partnerships include ease of formation, availability of capital, diversity of managerial skills and expertise, flexibility to respond to changing business conditions, no special taxes, and relative freedom from government control. Disadvantages include unlimited liability for general partners, potential for conflict between partners, sharing of profits, and difficulty exiting or dissolving the partnership.

3 **Explain how the corporate structure provides advantages and disadvantages to a company, and identify a special type of corporation.**

A corporation is a legal entity chartered by a province. Its organizational structure includes stockholders who own the corporation, a board of directors elected by the stockholders to govern the firm, and officers who carry out the goals and policies set by the board. Stockholders can sell or transfer their shares at any time, and are entitled to receive profits in the form of dividends. Advantages of corporations include limited liability, ease of transferring ownership, and ability to attract financing. Disadvantages include double taxation of profits at a somewhat reduced rate, the cost and complexity of formation, and government restrictions.

A special type of corporation that is owned by either a provincial or the federal government is called a Crown corporation.

4 **Review some of the other business organization options in addition to sole proprietorships, partnerships, and corporations.**

Businesses can also organize as cooperatives, joint ventures, and franchises. Cooperatives are collectively owned by individuals or businesses with similar interests that combine to achieve more economic power. Cooperatives distribute profits to their members. Two types of cooperatives are buyer and seller cooperatives.

A joint venture is an alliance of two or more companies formed to undertake a special project. Joint ventures can be set up in various ways, through partnerships or special-purpose corporations. By sharing management expertise, technology, products, and financial and operational resources, companies can reduce the risk of new enterprises.

A franchise is based on a business arrangement between a *franchisor*, which supplies the product concept, and a *franchisee*, who sells the goods or services of the franchisor in a certain geographic area.

5 **Identify when franchising is an appropriate business form, and why it is growing in importance.**

Franchising is one of the fastest-growing forms of business ownership. It involves an agreement between a franchisor, the supplier of goods or services, and a franchisee, an individual or company that buys the right to sell the franchisor's products in a specific area. With a franchise, the business owner does not have to start from scratch but instead buys a business concept with a proven product and operating methods. The franchisor provides management training and assistance; use of a recognized brand name, product, and operating concept; and financial assistance. Franchises can be costly to start and might restrict operating freedom, because the franchisee must conform to the franchisor's standard procedures. The growth in franchising is attributed to its ability to expand business operations quickly into new geographic areas with limited capital investment.

6 | **Understand why mergers and acquisitions can be important to a company's overall growth.**

In a merger, two companies combine to form one. In an acquisition, one company or investor group buys another. Companies merge for strategic reasons, to improve overall performance of the merged firm through cost savings, elimination of overlapping operations, improved purchasing power, increased market share, or reduced competition. Company growth, broadening product lines, and the ability to quickly acquire new markets, technology, or management skills are other motives. Another motive for merging is financial restructuring—cutting costs, selling off units, laying off employees, and refinancing the company to increase its value to stockholders.

There are three types of mergers. In a horizontal merger, companies at the same stage in the same industry combine to gain economic power, to diversify, or to win a greater market share. A vertical merger involves the acquisition of a firm that serves an earlier or later stage of the production or sales process, such as a supplier or sales outlet. In a conglomerate, unrelated businesses come together to reduce risk through diversification.

7 | **List some of the current trends that may affect the business organizations of the future.**

The baby boomers are demanding more products that enhance their lifestyles. They are living a healthier lifestyle and demanding more independence, which presents opportunities for new and innovative products (both goods and services). Many are delaying retirement, preferring instead to remain employed or self-employed. Many who do retire work as consultants on a part-time basis to supplement the shortage of experienced workers.

Another trend, as the franchise market starts to mature, is many franchise owners expanding their product lines, or cross-branding, to reach more customers with better service.

Key Terms

acquisition   159
board of directors   150
conglomerate merger   159
cooperative   153
corporation   148
Crown corporation   152
franchise agreement   156
franchisee   155
franchising   155
franchisor   155
friendly takeover   159
general partners   146
general partnership   146
horizontal merger   159

hostile takeover   159
joint venture   154
leveraged buyout (LBO)   159
limited liability partnership (LLP)   147
limited partners   146
limited partnership 146
merger   159
one-person corporation   152
partnership   146
private corporation   149
public corporation   149
shareholders or stockholders   149
sole proprietorship   145
vertical merger   159

Experiential Exercises

1. **Learn the laws.** Before starting your own company, you should know the legal requirements in your area. Call the appropriate city or provincial departments, such as licensing, health, and zoning, to find out what licences and permits you need, and any other requirements you must meet. Do the requirements vary depending on the type of company? Are there restrictions on starting a home-based business? Then, check the Web for information on how to incorporate.

2. **Study franchise opportunities.** Franchising offers an alternative to starting your own business from scratch. Do you have what it takes to be successful? Start by making a list of your interests and skills, and do a self-assessment using some of the suggestions in the last section of this chapter. Next, you need to narrow a field of thousands of different franchise systems. At Franchise Handbook Online (**www.franchise1.com**), you'll find articles with checklists to help you thoroughly research a franchise and its industry, as well as a directory of franchise opportunities. Armed with this information, you can develop a questionnaire to evaluate a prospective franchise.

3. Bridget Jones wants to open her own business selling her handmade chocolates over the Internet. Although she has some money saved and could start the business on her own, she is concerned about her lack of bookkeeping and management experience. A friend mentions he knows an experienced businessman seeking involvement with a start-up company. As Bridget's business consultant, prepare recommendations for Bridget regarding an appropriate form of business organization, including outlining the issues she should consider and the risks involved, supported by reasons for your suggestions.

4. You and a partner co-own Swim-Clean, a successful pool supply and cleaning service. Because sales have tapered off, you want to expand your operations to another town 100 kilometres away. Given the high costs of expanding, you decide to sell Swim-Clean franchises. The idea takes off, and soon you have 25 units throughout the region. Your success results in an invitation to speak at a local chamber of commerce luncheon. Prepare a brief presentation describing how you evaluated the benefits and risks of becoming a franchisor, the problems you have encountered, and how you've established good working relationships with your franchisees.

5. Find news of a recent merger using an online search or in a business periodical such as *Canadian Business* or *The Globe & Mail Report on Business*. Research the merger using a variety of sources including the company's website and news articles. Discover the motives behind the merger, the problems facing the new entity, and the company's progress toward achieving its objectives.

Review Questions

1. What are some of the considerations when choosing a form of business ownership to ensure that it suits your needs?

2. Why are proprietorships the most popular form of business ownership?

3. What should a partnership agreement include?

4. Considering some of the disadvantages of corporations, why do so many choose to use the corporation form?

5. When are joint ventures a good idea?

6. Why are franchise operations popular? What opportunities does it offer to the franchisor and franchisee?

7. What are the various types of mergers? Give examples of each.

New Business Takes Shape

Charlie York was trying to read, but the heavy book kept slipping from her lap. She had a vision of a pyramid-shaped book rest and asked her sister, Carolyn Morton, for help in designing it. The result of their collaboration was The Original Peeramid Bookrest, a pyramid-shaped pillow featuring a tasselled cord "bookmark" attached to its peak. York convinced the manager of the bookstore where she worked to display the pillows, and customers bought them and made helpful suggestions for improving the design.

Once the sisters had a final prototype, they needed contract workers to sew them, and months of searching uncovered Hermell Products in Bloomfield, Connecticut, makers of durable medical equipment and pillows for use in homes and hospitals. Hermell agreed to make the pillows, although "it's a very labour-intensive product and the most elaborate pillow we make," says Connie Galli, national sales manager for Hermell.

The company makes two versions of the Peeramid. One features expensive, upscale fabrics provided by Morton and York for sale to their catalogue, bookstore, and gift store customers, with a simpler version made by Hermell for its customers and catalogue, under licence from the sisters, with a royalty paid on every pillow sold.

The sisters incorporated their business, and lawyers helped them obtain a design patent on the Peeramid in 1997. Plans for an inflatable model for poolside use are on the drawing board, as well as a special marketing initiative aimed at the college market—versions of the Peeramid with logos for their bookstores.

Recently obtained permission from the National Institute for Literacy means that each Peeramid's hangtag is printed with the group's hotline number. "One way to sell more bookrests is to encourage more people to read," says York, and the newly established Peeramid Book Club on their website suggests ways to get involved in reading to others.

The sisters' parents, both entrepreneurs themselves, urge their daughters to keep going and growing. "We feel like we are in the infancy stage of the business," says York. They are learning as they go. "An aspect of our company that has been a godsend has been using Ifulfill.com to handle orders," adds Carolyn Morton. "Not having to set up shop for retail sales distribution has been a lifesaver for us!" With time and money invested and their design patent firmly in place, the sisters are pushing forward in the hopes that their pillow will become a "must have" for book lovers everywhere.[15]

Critical Thinking Questions

- Why did Morton and York choose to incorporate instead of organizing as a partnership?
- As the designers of their product, Morton and York also need general business experience to manage a growing company effectively. Should they consider bringing in additional working shareholders?
- What other strategies for growth could they pursue?

SOURCE: Jane Applegate, "Novelty Pillow Catches Manufacturer's Eye," February 2002, http://www.entrepreneur.com ; Carolyn Morton, e-mail correspondence, January 17 and 24, 2003; and Peeramid Web site, http://www.peeramid.com.

Mad Science and Franchising

The Mad Science Group is a successful company operating out of Montreal. The founders, Ariel and Ron Shlien, were interested in science as teenagers, with Ariel purchasing his first laser at the age of 12. By their early teens, Ariel and Ron were doing shows at the local YMCA and at birthday parties for children. From such humble beginnings, a multimillion-dollar enterprise has grown. Today the company has more than 150 franchisees in Canada, the United States, and overseas, and boasts sales in excess of $30 million.

On the franchise side of the business, Mad Science provides support, equipment, and training for their franchisees. In return, the franchisees pay 8 percent of their sales to the company. Franchisees are from a variety of backgrounds, such as air force instructors, clerical workers, and those just wanting a change of pace. The success of the individual franchisees depends on their ability to grow their own business. They must seek out business to become profitable. Birthday parties alone won't do it. The franchise costs approximately $55,000. Performing at two parties every day nets the franchisee only $50,000. Not a great return on your investment. Successful franchisees are the ones who have the drive to excel in a competitive environment. After a three-week training period in Montreal, they are provided with additional support and the necessary equipment to begin their business. The Director of Franchise Support feels that the required support had been lacking in the past and plans to increase the level of support to help franchisees grow their businesses. When the franchises make more money, so does Mad Science. Meanwhile, the head office staff continue to experiment with new and exciting shows and products.

Today, Mad Science has grown beyond all expectations and is found in theme parks in the United States, as well as in all major North American markets.

Critical Thinking Questions

- Franchising has benefits for the franchisee and for the franchisor. What are the benefits for the Mad Science franchisees and for the company?
- Why might someone decide to open his or her own entertainment business rather than buy a franchise?
- What are the advantages and disadvantages of opening your own business instead of buying a franchise?
- What is the status of this company today?

SOURCE: CBC, *Venture*, "Mad Science," July 28, 2002.

E-COMMERCE CASE >

Geeks Rule

"I always wanted to be James Bond," says Robert Stephens, talking about the showmanship that shapes his company's unique corporate culture, and the branding that makes it stand out from its competitors. Stephens originally chose the name Geek Squad to suggest an "army" of employees and disguise the fact that his business originally consisted of just one person—himself.

Who hasn't been in the middle of a project with a looming deadline when the computer crashes and all your files are lost? You would be just one of many individuals happy to see someone from the Geek Squad walk through your door. A quick phone call to 1-800-GEEK-SQUAD answers three important questions—can they fix it, when can they be there, what it will cost—and mobilizes a techie in a distinctively painted black, orange, and white "geekmobile." This uniformed, badge-toting "special agent" visits your home or office site to survey the "crime scene," either fixing the problem on-site, or taking the computer away for repair. Either way, your computer problem is solved. The company prides itself on rapid response times and reasonable rates. Clients are billed on a flat-fee basis rather than an hourly rate and receive a follow-up phone call to make sure everything is working and they are happy.

The company's highly trained techie team makes house calls 365 days a year, providing emergency computer support to panicked cranky clients. These special agents have helped out the likes of rockers U2, Ozzy Osbourne, and the Rolling Stones, even getting to attend their concerts for free.

Started by Stephens in 1994 with $200 and a bicycle, Geek Squad now boasts 5 million customers and 700 locations. Acquired by Best Buy in 2002, Geek Squad now has "precincts" in all Best Buy locations nationwide, in addition to Geek Squad stores in selected cities. The company also operates in Alaska, Hawaii, and Canada.

Even though Stephens set up the business as a corporation, he originally believed it would continue to work best if kept small, and had no interest in franchising the company. "There is always the temptation to expand into other services, through boredom or greed or fear, but I would rather be great at one thing than mediocre at several," he said. Stephens has stayed true to his original vision albeit on a grander scale.[16]

Critical Thinking Questions

Using information from the case and the video, answer the following critical thinking questions:

1. Why did Robert Stephens set up his company as a corporation even though he wanted to keep it small?
2. What was his goal in establishing such a unique identity for his company?
3. What benefits does each party gain from Best Buy's acquisition of Geek Squad? Are there potential disadvantages?

SOURCE: Hilary Potkewitz, "Geek Support: Techies Make House Calls Like Old-Time Docs," Los Angeles Business Journal, June 13, 2005, (http://www.findarticles.com); "Stand Alone Geek Squads Target Small Business," DSN Retailing Today, February 7, 2005, (http://www.findarticles.com); corporate Web sites for Geek Squad, http://www.geeksquad.com, and Best Buy, (http:www.bestbuy.com), (April 27, 2006).

CHAPTER 6

Making the Connection

Entrepreneurship and Small Business

This chapter is an extension of Chapter 5, or put more correctly, this chapter involves the decision that comes before deciding on the form of business ownership—the decision to start the business in the first place. What motivates people to start businesses, and what factors shape the business' success?

Individuals with a desire to start a business, whether they are people who simply want to start a small business of their own or entrepreneurs with a grander vision, need to see the big picture. Every business is affected by its external environment; all those environmental factors have an effect on each other, and they also affect whether the business meets its critical success factors. Also, as discussed in the opening vignette, entrepreneurs and small business owners have a major effect on the economic environment. And the decisions that these individuals make inside their businesses—whether marketing, finance, operations, or human resource decisions—will also affect and be affected by the environment and, in turn, impact the degree to which the business achieves the critical success factors. This is their business—the whole thing, in all its integrative glory! In fact, entrepreneurs and small business owners experience the integrative nature of business more than other business people, because, initially at least, they start off handling all aspects of the business. And because it is so all-consuming to start a new business, these individuals have to ensure that they put balance in their lives—to work hard but to balance

that with taking care of their families and their health. This is a critical lesson for entrepreneurs: the integrative nature of business extends beyond the business to their personal life as well. Since it creeps into life outside of work, the interconnections need to be viewed on a much broader level. You can't get more integrative than that!

This chapter is full of examples of trends in the external environment affecting entrepreneurs and small-business owners. Just look at why people create their own businesses. For example, in the *economic* environment, we see many corporations restructuring and downsizing their staff requirements, and so employees look to creating their own businesses for greater job security. Many of these same corporations have begun to outsource various things they used to do in-house, thus creating an opportunity for small businesses (often the same people that were downsized!) to pick up the slack.

A trend that is both *social* and economic is the fact that there simply aren't as many advancement opportunities for women and minorities as there should be, despite the improvements made in this area, and so many of these people are looking to create their own opportunities in their own businesses. In fact, as you'll read in the chapter, women and minorities are "increasing business ownership at a much faster rate than the national average..." This, in turn, has led to many *innovations* in the workplace, such as more flexible scheduling, family-like environments,

and more socially responsible business practices—changes favoured by women and, therefore, incorporated into their businesses. Furthermore, advancements in the *technological* environment have given small-business people the ability to compete in areas previously inaccessible to them, giving rise to many new small businesses and entrepreneurial ventures. This trend in technology has, in turn, led to a social change in the demographics of small-business owners and entrepreneurs—they are often younger, as most technologically literate people are from the younger generation, which grew up with this technology. Interestingly, as discussed in the chapter, "Web-driven entrepreneurs are 25 percent more likely to be women."

The external environment also presents numerous ideas for new businesses. Often the competition in the economic environment isn't *meeting customer needs* sufficiently, and entrepreneurs see these holes and fill them. There are many examples of this in the chapter. One such example of this is Mike Pratt of OGIO International. Mike was frustrated with "trying to cram his gym bag into a too-small locker" and came up with a solution in The Original Locker Bag. Originally, however, retailers weren't convinced of the products appeal, but because it met the needs of the customer better than other products, the customer ensured its success through demand and forced the retailers' interest. Google is a similar example. The company's founders were not even looking to start a business—they just wanted to find a more efficient way than was currently available to search the infinite amount of information available on the Web.

As we state later in the chapter, "Today's global economy rewards innovative, flexible companies that respond quickly to changes in the business environment." Because our economy today is so global, we have much more competition, and we need to be more concerned with meeting customer needs. Smaller, more entrepreneurial firms tend to be more flexible and innovative (one of our critical success factors, remember); therefore, they can respond more quickly as customer needs change in response to the external environment. But larger businesses can also encourage innovation and creativity by simulating this entrepreneurial environment within the organization through "intrapreneurship."

Thus, *marketing* decisions made by small business owners and entrepreneurs tend to be innovative and responsive to customer needs; *human resource* decisions are also innovative and are often made to rectify problems these business owners saw in their previous jobs (remember Christopher Halpin of Manna Catering Services in Chapter 5). But *financing* can be difficult for new businesses. However, with good ideas and well-thought-out business plans that see the whole business in an integrative way, funds can be generated to cover *operations* and growth—just as Google was able to get their first $100,000 from a Sun Microsystems founder before Google Inc. even existed as a corporation. Perhaps the biggest challenge, though, is for small business owners and entrepreneurs to handle adequately the first of the management functions—*planning*. As discussed in the chapter, economic factors, financial causes, and lack of experience are the most common reasons for business failure. These causes are interrelated and are often directly related to poor management and inadequate planning. It is critical that early on, the new business owner sees the integrative nature of all the parts of the business, and plans accordingly.

CHAPTER 6

Entrepreneurship and Small Business

LEARNING OUTCOMES

1 Explain why people become entrepreneurs, and what the different types of entrepreneurs are.

2 Describe the characteristics that successful entrepreneurs share.

3 Discuss how small businesses contribute to the Canadian economy.

4 Summarize the first steps to take if you are starting your own business.

5 Examine some of the special challenges of a small business owner.

6 Identify the advantages and disadvantages facing owners of small businesses.

7 Describe how the Business Development Bank of Canada helps small businesses?

8 List some of the trends that are shaping entrepreneurship and small-business ownership.

THE EXCITEMENT AND CHALLENGE OF RUNNING YOUR OWN NIGHTCLUB

SHIRLEY A. ROSE

In 1979, Gino Panucci was a student in a public relations program at an Alberta college. Little did he realize how his life would change over the next few years. The college program was going well, but Gino's brother, Dominic, had bought a hotel in a small town in southeastern Alberta and needed help running the business. He invited Gino to join him in the venture. Gino agreed, and thus began his life as an entrepreneur. The hotel had a tavern downstairs, as well as 52 rooms that the brothers had to maintain and rent in order to survive. As Gino says,

"It was a struggle, I was a young guy, we stuck it out through thick and thin. It was a seven-day-a-week job, opening at 11:00 a.m. and closing at 1:00 a.m. or so. Dealing with a combination of the farm community and the oil-patch workers was a challenge, but business was good until the economy took a dive in the mid-eighties."

The brothers were among the casualties of the economic downturn in the 1980s and were unable to continue. Gino moved to Calgary and worked as a construction worker while helping his wife, Shelley, open two successful hairdressing salons. Dominic moved to Kelowna, British Columbia, and worked in a liquor store while scouting out another business opportunity. The desire to own their own business never left the brothers, even though the previous experience had drained them physically, mentally, and financially. They saw the hotel years as a learning experience and were anxious to leave the past in the past. They worked well together. As Gino says, "Dominic is the back end and I am the front end," meaning Gino is the people person and Dominic is the numbers guy. The brothers observed the "scene" in Kelowna and saw an opportunity to take over a nightclub from a previous owner. They invested every penny they could lay their hands on to start the business and have never looked back.

Today, Gotcha is one of the most successful nightclubs in the Okanagan Valley. Dominic has left the partnership, but Gino's brother-in-law, Bob, has joined the business. They have bought two more clubs, are continuing on the road to financial success and are having fun doing it. Gino says,

"I will never forget the lessons we learned in the hotel business. One of the most important was to put some balance in your life … you can't work all the time and ignore your family and your health. It's just not worth it. And then economic conditions can just come along and take you down anyway! You gotta have fun!"[1]

Critical Thinking Questions

As you read this chapter, consider the following questions as they relate to the Panucci brothers:

1. **What type of entrepreneur is Gino? What were his motives in starting the nightclub Gotcha?**

2. **What personal characteristics contributed to Dominic and Gino's success?**

3. **What opportunities and challenges did Dominic and Gino face as small-business owners, and how did they overcome them?**

Typical of many who catch the entrepreneurial bug, Dom and Gino had a vision and pursued it single-mindedly. They are joined by people from all backgrounds and age groups. Teenagers are starting fashion clothing and high-tech companies. Recent college graduates shun the "jacket and tie" corporate world to head out on their own. Downsized employees and mid-career executives form another large group of small-business owners. Retirees who worked for others all their lives might form the company they always wanted to own.

Companies started by entrepreneurs and small-business owners make significant contributions to the Canadian and global economies. Like Gotcha, they are hotbeds of innovation, taking leadership roles in technological change and the development of new goods and services. Small business is hard to define, because different agencies and researchers use different criteria. For our purposes, we define small businesses as being independently owned and operated, and not dominant in their market. Small businesses make a major contribution to our economy. For example, based on Industry Canada's definition of small business having less than 100 employees:

- *Small businesses account for 97.8 percent of all employers;*
- *54.7 percent of Canadian businesses employ one to four (1 to 4) people, 32.5 percent employ five to nineteen (5–19), 7.9 percent employ 20 – 49, and 4.6 percent employ 50 – 500;*
- *Only 0.3 percent of all Canadian businesses have more than 500 employees, and;*
- *Approximately 40 percent of all new jobs in the economy were created by the small-business sector.[2]*

You might be one of the thousands of Canadians who are considering joining the ranks of business owners. As you read this chapter, you'll get the information and tools you need to help you decide whether owning your own company is the right career path for you. You'll discover why entrepreneurship continues to be one of the hottest areas of business activity, as well as the characteristics you need to become a successful entrepreneur. We will offer guidelines for starting, managing, and growing a small business, and discuss their advantages and disadvantages. You will read about the role of the Business Development Bank of Canada. Finally, we will explore the trends that are shaping entrepreneurship and small-business ownership.

Entrepreneurship Today

From experiments with cardboard and tape, 20-something Mike Pratt pieced together a company that today is the top gear bag designer, OGIO. Frustrated with trying to cram his gym bag into a too-small locker, he went home and built a model of his ideal duffle bag. It fit into standard fitness-club lockers and kept all his supplies easily accessible in its rigid-framed interior. Retailers considered The Original Locker Bag too cumbersome. Customers, however, loved the bag that carried like a duffle bag and worked like a locker. In one weekend, they snapped up the 50 bags that Pratt convinced Foot Locker to take on consignment, and soon Pratt's bags were featured at various stores.

Not content to limit OGIO International's fortunes to one bag, Pratt and his employees "geared up" to produce duffles and backpacks with patented design features. His next breakthrough product was the Rig, a protective golf bag designed to go from airport to course that came to market just as golf's popularity began to rise. A complete line of golf bags followed, made in non-traditional colours and fabrics that appealed to younger players. "Today this cutting-edge company has revolutionized bag designs."[3]

Canada is blessed with a rich history of entrepreneurs. And their ranks continue to swell as up-and-coming entrepreneurs aspire to become the next Bill Gates. You may be familiar with some of the following: Grahame Ferguson (IMAX), Tim Horton (Tim Horton's), Christine Magee (Sleep Country Canada), Thomas Ryan (five pin bowling), and Gideon Sundback (Zipper).[4]

Why has entrepreneurship remained a strong part of the foundation of the Canadian business system for so many years? Today's global economy rewards innovative, flexible companies that respond quickly to changes in the business environment. These companies are started by **entrepreneurs**, people with vision, drive, and creativity who are willing to take the risk of starting and managing a business to make a profit.

entrepreneurs
People with vision, drive, and creativity who are willing to take the risk of starting and managing a business to make a profit or greatly changing the scope and direction of an existing firm.

Entrepreneur or Small-Business Owner?

The term entrepreneur is often used in a broad sense to include most small-business owners. The two groups share some of the same characteristics, and we'll see that some of the reasons for becoming an entrepreneur or a small-business owner are very similar. But there is a difference between entrepreneurship and small-business management. Entrepreneurship involves taking a risk, either to create a new business or to greatly change the scope and direction of an existing one. Entrepreneurs typically are innovators who start companies to pursue their ideas for a new product or service. They are visionaries who spot trends.

Although entrepreneurs may be small-business owners, not all small-business owners are entrepreneurs. Small-business owners are managers, or people with technical expertise, who started a business or bought an existing business and made a conscious decision to stay small. For example, the proprietor of your local independent bookstore is a small-business owner. Jeff Bezos, founder of Amazon.com, also sells books. But Bezos is an entrepreneur: He developed a new model—a Web-based book retailer—that revolutionized the bookselling world and then moved on to change retailing in general. Entrepreneurs are less likely to accept the status quo and generally take a longer-term view than the small-business owner.

Types of Entrepreneurs

Entrepreneurs fall into several categories: classic entrepreneurs, multipreneurs, and intrapreneurs.

Classic Entrepreneurs   Classic entrepreneurs are risk takers who start their own companies based on innovative ideas. Some classic entrepreneurs are *micropreneurs*, who start small and plan to stay small. They often start businesses just for personal satisfaction and the lifestyle. Her passion for food led chemistry and psychology major Katrina Markoff to Paris to study at Le Cordon Bleu cooking school. She then took more classes while travelling in Europe, Asia, Australia, and Hawaii, attending cooking schools along the way. Intrigued by the many cultures and tastes she encountered, she returned home and started Vosges Chocolate, a specialty candy company that makes chocolates in unusual flavours, such as curry, spicy wasabi powder from Japan, sweet dulce de leche from Argentina, and a rare white honey from Hawaii. "People are traveling a lot more and wanting more interesting experiences with food," says Markoff. "I want people to take the time to appreciate what's going on in their mouth. What better way to do that than with curry and wasabi?"[5]

In contrast, *growth-oriented entrepreneurs* want their businesses to grow into major corporations. Most high-tech companies are formed by growth-oriented entrepreneurs. Jeff Bezos recognized that with Internet technology, he could compete with large chains of traditional book retailers. Bezos' goal was to build his company into a high-growth enterprise—and he even chose a name that reflected this strategy: Amazon.com. Once his company succeeded in the book sector, Bezos applied his online retailing model to other product lines, from toys and house and garden items to tools, apparel, and services. In partnership with other retailers, Bezos is well on his way to making Amazon's motto—"Earth's Biggest Selection"—a reality.[6]

Multipreneurs   Then there are *multipreneurs*, entrepreneurs who start a series of companies. They thrive on the challenge of building a business and watching it grow. In fact, over half of the chief executives at *Inc. 500* companies say they would start another company if they sold their current one.

Jim Pattison is the Chairman, Chief Executive Officer, and sole owner of The Jim Pattison Group. The Jim Pattison Group started when Mr. Pattison purchased a General Motors automobile dealership. Today the company has more than 30,000 employees with operations in various industries such as food services, packaging, distribution, manufacturing, communications, and entertainment, among others. The Jim Pattison Group, headquartered in Vancouver, BC, is Canada's third largest privately held company.[7]

Intrapreneurs   Some entrepreneurs don't own their own companies but apply their creativity, vision, and risk taking within a large corporation. Called **intrapreneurs**, these employees enjoy the freedom to nurture their ideas and develop new products, while their employers provide regular salaries and financial backing. Intrapreneurs have a high degree of autonomy to run their own mini-companies within the larger enterprise. They share many of the same personality traits as classic entrepreneurs but take less personal risk. According to Gifford Pinchot, who coined the term *intrapreneur* in his book of the same name, large companies, including Intel, IBM, Texas Instruments (a pioneering intrapreneurial company), Eastman Kodak, and Xerox, now provide seed funds that finance in-house entrepreneurial efforts.

Intrapreneurs
Entrepreneurs who apply their creativity, vision, and risk taking within a large corporation rather than starting a company of their own.

Why Become an Entrepreneur?

As the examples in this chapter show, entrepreneurs are found in all industries and have different motives for starting companies. The most common reason cited by CEOs of the *Inc. 500*, the magazine's annual list of fastest-growing private companies,

CONCEPT *in Action* >>>

As a young girl, Helen Greiner loved tech gadgets. But when a spunky droid named R2-D2 helped Luke Skywalker stick it to the Empire in the movie *Star Wars*, Greiner's love became an obsession. Today, Greiner is the cofounder and chairman of iRobot Corporation, a multimillion-dollar robotics firm that creates real-life R2-D2s that do everything from vacuuming household floors to sniffing out terrorist bombs. How might a person's interests and passions lead to a life of successful entrepreneurship?

AP/WIDE WORLD PHOTOS

Expanding Around The Globe

LULULEMON ATHLETIC INC.

Chip Wilson was in the first commercial yoga class offered in Vancouver B.C. and found it very exhilarating. Chip had spent 20 years in the surf, skate and snowboard businesses and liked the post-yoga feeling to these activities. But Chip found the cotton clothing too sweaty and inappropriate for power yoga. With his enthusiasm for technical athletic fabrics and feedback from the yoga instructors wearing his new designs, the lululemon success story was born.

The company was founded in 1998 and its first real store was opened in November of 2000 in Vancouver. The goal was to train his people so that he could have a positive influence on their families, communities, and customers. Initially, the intent was to have one store but soon it was obvious growth was necessary for success.

Today the company's line of apparel includes fitness wear designed for athletic pursuits such as yoga, dance, running, and general fitness.

To complement the apparel line, the company also offers other fitness related products. Manufacturing is contracted to third parties with distribution through its facilities in Vancouver and Washington State.

As of February 2009, lululemon operated 113 corporate-owned and franchise stores in three countries; 43 stores in Canada, 65 in the United States, and 5 Australia. In April 2008 it announced discontinuing its four Japanese stores.

Critical Thinking Questions

- At what point do you think the owners of a company contemplate expanding the company outside of the domestic borders?
- What considerations should a company pondering international expansion think about?

Source: (www.FPInfomart.ca) (2009, May 29, *lululemon athletica inc. corporate survey.* Retrieved from FP Advisor database; (www.lululemon.com).

---

is the challenge of building a business, followed by the desire to control their own destiny. Other reasons include financial independence and frustration working for someone else. Two important motives mentioned in other surveys are a feeling of personal satisfaction with your work, and creating the lifestyle that you want. Do entrepreneurs feel that going into business for themselves was worth it? The answer is a resounding yes. Most say they would do it again. See the "Expanding Around the Globe" box for an example of how one successful Canadian company started.

Characteristics of Successful Entrepreneurs

LO 2

Do you have what it takes to become an entrepreneur? Being an entrepreneur requires special drive, perseverance, passion, and a spirit of adventure in addition to managerial and technical ability. Having a great concept is not enough. An entrepreneur must also be able to develop and manage the company that implements the idea. In addition, entrepreneurs *are* the company; they cannot leave problems at the office at the end of the day. Entrepreneurs tend to work longer hours and take fewer vacations once they have their own companies. They also share other common characteristics, as described in the next section.

The Entrepreneurial Personality

Studies of the entrepreneurial personality generally find that entrepreneurs share certain key traits. Most entrepreneurs are:

- *ambitious*. Entrepreneurs have a high need for achievement and are competitive.
- *independent*. They are self-starters who prefer to lead rather than follow. They are also individualists.
- *self-confident*. They understand the challenges of starting a business but are decisive and have faith in their abilities to resolve problems.
- *risk taking*. Though they are not averse to risk, most successful entrepreneurs prefer situations with a moderate degree of risk, where they have a chance to control the outcome, over highly risky ventures that depend on luck.
- *visionary*. Entrepreneurs' abilities to spot trends and act on them sets entrepreneurs apart from small-business owners and managers.

- *creative.* To compete with larger firms, entrepreneurs need to have creative product designs, marketing strategies, and solutions to managerial problems.
- *energetic.* Starting a business takes long hours. Some entrepreneurs start companies while still employed full-time.
- *passionate.* Entrepreneurs love their work.
- *committed.* They make personal sacrifices to achieve their goals. Because they are so committed to their companies, entrepreneurs are persistent in seeking solutions to problems.

Most entrepreneurs combine many of the above characteristics. Sarah Levy, 23, loved her job as a restaurant pastry chef but not the low pay, high stress, and long hours of a commercial kitchen. So she found a new one—in her parents' home—and launched Sarah's Pastries and Candies. Part-time staffers now help her fill pastry and candy orders to the soothing sounds of music videos playing in the background.

University graduate Conor McDonough started his own Web design firm, OffThe-PathMedia.com, after becoming disillusioned with the rigid structure of his job. "There wasn't enough room for my own expression," he says. "Freelancing keeps me on my toes," says busy graphic artist Ana Sanchez. "It forces me to do my best work because I know my next job depends on my performance."[8]

The "Customer Satisfaction and Quality" box at the end of the chapter describes how Apollonia Poilane made huge sacrifices to maintain her family's business after tragedy struck.

Managerial Ability and Technical Knowledge

A person with all the characteristics of an entrepreneur might still lack the necessary business skills to run a successful company. Entrepreneurs need the technical knowledge to carry out their ideas and the managerial ability to organize a company, develop operating strategies, obtain financing, and supervise day-to-day activities.

Good interpersonal and communication skills are important in dealing with employees, customers, and other business associates such as bankers, accountants, and lawyers. As we will discuss later in the chapter, entrepreneurs believe they can learn these much needed skills.

Mike Becker learned how to manage Funko, Inc. (**www.funko.com**) by trial and error. He started the company to bring back low-tech, nostalgia-based bobble-headed dolls he called Wacky Wobblers. His first character was Bob's Big Boy, the restaurant chain mascot. Putting his licensing background to work, he began producing cartoon, movie, and advertising character Wobblers—Mr. Magoo, Betty Boop, Charlie Tuna, Count Chocula, Pink Panther, and Austin Powers, for example. "(After my first order,) I still didn't understand what the heck I was doing," Becker says. "I didn't have any distribution networks, sales reps, employees, or even a place of business." He quickly had to become competent in every phase of the business, even tasks he hated, like accounting and paperwork.[9]

Entrepreneurs soon learn that they can't do it all themselves. Often they choose to focus on what they do best and hire others to do the rest. Becker learned to delegate many of the operational responsibilities so he could be "Chairman of Fun" and handle product creation and licensing.

concept check

Describe the personality traits and other skills characteristic of successful entrepreneurs.

What does it mean when we say that an entrepreneur should work on the business, not in it?

Small Business: Driving Canada's Growth

Although large corporations dominated the business scene for many decades, in recent years small businesses have once again come to the forefront. Corporate greed and fraud have given large corporations a bad name. Downsizings that accompany economic downturns have caused many people to look toward smaller companies for employment, and they have plenty to choose from.

What Is a Small Business?

How many small businesses are there in the Canada? Using Industry Canada's definition of small business is firms with less than 100 employees. There are approximately 2.3 million business establishments in Canada. About 1.28 million (55 percent) of those 2.3 million businesses represent self-employed individuals. Small businesses account for approximately 48 percent of the total labour force in the private sector. Small businesses that have fewer than 50 employees contribute about 23 percent to Canada's GDP.[10]

So what makes a business "small"? Many different criteria can be used to define a small business. It might be the value of its annual sales or revenues, value of its assets or the number of employees. Industry Canada defines small business generally as having less than 100 employees for goods-producing firms and less than 50 employees for service-producing firms. In addition, a **small business** is

small business
A business that is independently managed, is owned by an individual or a small group of investors, is based locally, and is not a dominant company in its industry.

- independently managed,
- owned by an individual or a small group of investors,
- based locally (although the market it serves might be widespread), and
- not a dominant company (thus, it has little influence in its industry).

Small businesses in Canada can be found in almost every industry group. Services dominate small businesses, accounting for about 75 percent, with the balance of small businesses (25 percent) producing goods.[11] These firms provide everything from health care to computer consulting and food and lodging. Small businesses are found in all of the various sectors, as suggested below.

- *Services.* Service firms are the most popular category of small businesses, because they are easy and inexpensive to start. They are often small; very few service-oriented companies are national in scope. They include repair services, restaurants, specialized software companies, accountants, travel agencies, management consultants, and temporary help agencies.

- *Wholesale and retail trade.* Retailers sell goods or services directly to the end user. Wholesalers link manufacturers and retailers or industrial buyers; they assemble, store, and distribute products ranging from heavy machinery to produce. Most retailers also qualify as small businesses, whether they operate one store or a small chain.
- *Manufacturing.* This category is dominated by large companies, but many small businesses produce goods. Machine shops, printing firms, clothing manufacturers, beverage bottlers, electronic equipment manufacturers, and furniture makers are often small manufacturers. In some industries, small manufacturing businesses have an advantage, because they can focus on customized products that would not be profitable for larger manufacturers.
- *Construction.* Firms employing fewer than 20 people account for many of Canada's construction companies. They include independent builders of industrial and residential properties and thousands of contractors in such trades as plumbing, electrical, roofing, and painting.
- *Agriculture.* Small businesses dominate agriculture-related industry, including forestry and fisheries.

HOT *Links*

See (www.canadaone.ca) for information about starting and growing a business.

Ready, Set, Start Your Own Business

You have decided that you'd like to go into business for yourself. What is the best way to go about it? Start from scratch? Buy an existing business? Or buy a franchise? About 75 percent of business start-ups involve brand-new organizations, with the remaining 25 percent representing purchased companies or franchises. Franchising was discussed in Chapter 5, so we'll cover the other two options in this section.

Getting Started

The first step in starting your own business is a self-assessment to determine whether you have the personal traits you need to succeed and, if so, what type of business would be best for you. (See the exercise "Your Career," featured on pages 198 and 199. It includes a questionnaire and other information to help you make these decisions.) Exhibit 6.1 provides a checklist to consider before starting your business.

Finding the Idea   Entrepreneurs get ideas for their businesses from many sources. It is not surprising that about 80 percent of *Inc. 500* executives got the ideas for their companies while working in the same or a related industry. Starting a firm in a field where you have experience improves your chances of success. Other sources of inspiration are personal experiences as a consumer; hobbies and personal interests; suggestions from customers, family, and friends; and college courses or other education.

EXHIBIT 6.1 > Checklist for Starting a Business

Before you start your own small business, consider the following checklist:

- Identify your reasons
- Self-analysis
- Personal skills and experience
- Finding a niche
- Market analysis
- Planning your start-up
- Finances

Source: "Checklist for Starting a Business," (www.sba.gov/survey/checklist) (March 20, 2006).

COURTESY OF BROTHER INTERNATIONAL CORPORATION

CONCEPT *in Action* >>>

In their start-up stages, small business owners have to be masters of multitasking. Companies like business equipment manufacturer Brother target the high-growth small-business market with multifunction machines that appeal to this group. Can you think of new products or services that you believe would be successful in the marketplace?

business plan
A formal written statement that describes in detail the idea for a new business and how it will be carried out. It includes a general description of the company, the qualifications of the owner(s), a description of the product or service, an analysis of the market, and a financial plan.

An excellent way to keep up with small-business trends is by reading entrepreneurship and small-business magazines and visiting their websites regularly. With articles on everything from idea generation to selling the business, they provide invaluable resources. For example, each year *Entrepreneur* publishes lists of the fastest-growing young, private companies. Reading about companies that are only a few years old but now have more than $1 million in sales will inspire you.

Interesting ideas are all around you. Many successful businesses get started because someone identifies needs and then finds a way to fill them. Do you have a problem that you need to solve or a product that doesn't work as well as you'd like? Maybe one of your coworkers has a complaint. Raising questions about the way things are done is a great way to generate ideas. Many business owners have difficulty filling jobs. On the other hand, many students have problems finding jobs. With websites such as monster.ca and canadajobs.com, employers and students (as well as others) can connect.

Choosing a Form of Business Organization A key decision for a person starting a new business is whether it will be a sole proprietorship, partnership, corporation, or limited liability company. As discussed in Chapter 5, each type of business organization has advantages and disadvantages. The choice depends on the type of business, number of employees, capital requirements, tax considerations, and level of risk involved. Most important, though, is the entrepreneur's tolerance for liability.

Developing the Business Plan Once you have the basic concept for a product or service, you must develop a plan to create the business. This planning process, culminating in a sound **business plan**, is one of the most important steps in starting a business. It can help to attract appropriate loan financing, minimize the risks involved, and be a critical determinant in whether a firm succeeds or fails. Many people do not venture out on their own because they are overwhelmed with doubts and concerns. A comprehensive business plan lets you run various "what if" analyses and "operate" your business as a dry-run, without any financial outlay or risk. You can also develop strategies to overcome problems—well before the business actually opens.

Taking the time to develop a good business plan pays off. A venture that seems sound at the idea stage may not look so good on paper. A well-prepared, comprehensive, written business plan forces entrepreneurs to take an objective and critical look at their business venture and analyze their concept carefully; make decisions about marketing, production, staffing, and financing; and set goals that will help them manage and monitor its growth and performance.

The business plan also serves as the initial operating plan for the business; writing a good business plan can take several months. But many businesspeople neglect this critical planning tool in their eagerness to begin doing business, getting caught up in the day-to-day operations instead.

The key features of a business plan are a general description of the company, the qualifications of the owner(s), a description of the product or service, an analysis of the market (demand, customers, competition), and a financial plan. The sections should work together to demonstrate why the business will be successful, while focusing on the uniqueness of the business and why it will attract customers. Exhibit 6.2 provides an outline of what to include in each section of a business plan.

The most common use of a business plan is to persuade lenders and investors to finance the venture. The detailed information in the plan helps them assess whether to invest. Even though a business plan may take months to write, it must capture

EXHIBIT 6.2 > Outline for a Business Plan

Title page: Provides names, addresses, and phone numbers of the venture and its owners and management personnel; date prepared; copy number; and contact person.

Table of contents: Provides page numbers of the key sections of the business plan.

Executive summary: Provides a one- to three-page overview of the total business plan. Written after the other sections are completed, it highlights their significant points and, ideally, creates enough excitement to motivate the reader to continue reading.

Vision and mission statement: Concisely describes the intended strategy and business philosophy for making the vision happen.

Company overview: Explains the type of company, such as manufacturing, retail, or service; provides background information on the company if it already exists; and describes the proposed form of organization—sole proprietorship, partnership, or corporation. This section should be organized as follows: company name and location, company objectives, nature and primary product or service of the business, current status (start-up, buyout, or expansion) and history (if applicable), and legal form of organization.

Product and/or service plan: Describes the product and/or service and points out any unique features; explains why people will buy the product or service. This section should offer the following descriptions: product and/or service; features of the product or service that provide a competitive advantage; available legal protection—patents, copyrights, and trademarks; and dangers of technical or style obsolescence.

Marketing plan: Shows who the firm's customers will be and what type of competition it will face; outlines the marketing strategy and specifies the firm's competitive edge. This section should offer the following descriptions: analysis of target market and profile of target customer; methods of identifying and attracting customers; selling approach, type of sales force, and distribution channels; types of sales promotions and advertising; and credit and pricing policies.

Management plan: Identifies the key players—active investors, management team, and directors—citing the experience and competence they possess. This section should offer the following descriptions: management team, outside investors and/or directors and their qualifications, outside resource people and their qualifications, and plans for recruiting and training employees.

Operating plan: Explains the type of manufacturing or operating system to be used; and describes the facilities, labour, raw materials, and product-processing requirements. This section should offer the following descriptions: operating or manufacturing methods, operating facilities (location, space, and equipment), quality-control methods, procedures to control inventory and operations, sources of supply, and purchasing procedures.

Financial plan: Specifies financial needs and contemplated sources of financing; presents projections of revenues, costs, and profits. This section should offer the following descriptions: historical financial statements for the last three to five years or as available; pro forma financial statements for three to five years, including income statements, balance sheets, cash flow statements, and cash budgets (monthly for first year and quarterly for second year); breakeven analysis of profits and cash flows; and planned sources of financing.

Appendix of supporting documents: Provides materials supplementary to the plan. This section should offer the following descriptions: management team biographies, any other important data that support the information in the business plan, and the firm's ethics code.

SOURCE: From Longenecker/Moore/Petty. *Small Business Management*, 11E. ©2000 South-Western, a part of Cengage Learning, Inc. Reproduced by permission. (www.cengage.com/permissions).

potential investors' interest within minutes. For that reason, the basic business plan should be written with a particular reader in mind. Then, you can fine-tune and tailor it to fit the investment goals of the investor(s) you plan to approach.

But don't think you can set aside your business plan once you obtain financing and begin operating your company. Entrepreneurs who think their business plans are only for raising money make a big mistake. Business plans should be dynamic documents, reviewed and updated on a regular basis—monthly, quarterly, or annually, depending on how the business progresses and the particular industry changes.

Owners should adjust their sales and profit projections up or down as they analyze their markets and operating results. Reviewing your plan on a constant basis will help

HOT Links

See the RBC Royal Bank website for a business plan template at (**www.royalbank.ca**).

you identify strengths and weaknesses in your marketing and management strategies, and help you evaluate possible opportunities for expansion in light of both your original mission and current market trends.

Financing the Business

Once the business plan is complete, the next step is to obtain financing to set up the company. The funding required depends on the type of business and the entrepreneur's own investment. Businesses started by lifestyle entrepreneurs require less financing than growth-oriented businesses, and manufacturing and high-tech companies generally require a large initial investment.

debt
A form of business financing consisting of borrowed funds that must be repaid with interest over a stated time period.

Who provides start-up funding for small companies? 94 percent of business owners raise start-up funds from personal accounts, family, and friends. Personal assets and money from family and friends are important for new firms, whereas funding from financial institutions may become more important as companies grow. Three-quarters of Inc. 500 companies have been funded on $100,000 or less.[12] The two forms of business financing are **debt**, borrowed funds that must be repaid with interest over a stated time period, and **equity**, funds raised through the sale of stock (i.e., ownership) in the business. Those who provide equity funds get a share of the business' profits. Because lenders usually limit debt financing to no more than a quarter to a third of the firm's total needs, equity financing often amounts to about 65 to 75 percent of total start-up financing.

equity
A form of business financing consisting of funds raised through the sale of stock (i.e., ownership) in a business.

angel investors
Individual investors or groups of experienced investors who provide funding for start-up businesses.

Two sources of equity financing for young companies are angel investors and venture-capital firms. **Angel investors** are individual investors or groups of experienced investors who provide financing for start-up businesses by investing their own funds. This gives them more flexibility on what they can and will invest in, but because it is their own money, angels are careful. Angel investors often invest early in a company's development and they want to see an idea they understand and can have confidence in. Exhibit 6.3 offers some guidelines on how to attract angel financing.

EXHIBIT 6.3 > Making a Heavenly Deal

You need financing for your start-up business. How do you get angels interested in investing in your business venture?

- Show them something they understand, ideally a business from an industry they've been associated with.
- Have respect for your prospective investors. They know things you don't.
- Hone your vision. Be able to describe your business—what it does and who it sells to—in less than a minute.
- Angels can always leave their money in the bank, so an investment must interest them. It should be something they're passionate about. And timing is important—knowing when to reach out to an angel can make a huge difference.
- They need to see management they trust, respect, and like. Present a mature management team with a strong, experienced leader who can withstand the scrutiny of the angel's inquiries.
- Angels prefer something they can bring added value to. Those who invest could be involved with your company for a long time, or perhaps take a seat on your board of directors.
- They are more partial to deals that don't require huge sums of money or additional infusions of angel cash.
- Emphasize the likely exits for investors and have a handle on who the competition is, why your solution is better, and how you are going to gain market share.

SOURCE: Rhonda Abrams, "What Does it Take to Impress an Angel Investor?" Inc.com, (www.inc.com), March 2001. Copyright © 2005 Inc.com, Stacy Zhao, "9 Tips for Winning Over Angels," (www.inc.com), June 2005. Copyright © 2005 Inc.com.

venture capital
Financing obtained from investment firms that specialize in financing small, high-growth companies and receive an ownership interest and a voice in management in return for their money.

Venture capital is financing obtained from venture capitalists—investment firms that specialize in financing small, high-growth companies. Venture capitalists receive an ownership interest and a voice in management in return for their money. They typically invest at a later stage than angel investors.

Buying a Small Business

Another route to small-business ownership is buying an existing business. Although this approach is less risky than starting a business from scratch, it still requires careful and thorough analysis. The potential buyer must answer several important questions: Why is the owner selling? Does he or she want to retire or move on to another challenge, or are there some problems with the business? Is the business operating at a profit? If not, can the problems be corrected? On what basis has the owner valued the company, and is it a fair price? What are the owner's plans after selling the company? Depending on the type of business, customers might be more loyal to the owner than to the product or service. They could leave the firm if the current owner decides to open a similar business. To protect against this situation, many purchasers include a "non-compete clause" in the contract of sale.

Many of the same steps for starting a business from scratch apply to buying an existing company. You should prepare a business plan that thoroughly analyzes all aspects of the business. Get answers to all your questions, and determine, via the business plan, that the business is a good one. Then you must negotiate the purchase price and other terms and get financing. This can be a difficult process, and it might require the use of a consultant or a business broker.

Risky Business

Running your own business might not be as easy as it sounds. Despite the many advantages of being your own boss, the risks are great as well. Businesses close down for many reasons—and not all are failures. Some businesses that close are financially successful and close for nonfinancial reasons. But the causes of business failure can be interrelated. For example, low sales and high expenses are often directly related to poor management. Some common causes of business closure are

- Economic factors—business downturns and high interest rates;
- Financial causes—inadequate capital, low cash balances, and high expenses;
- Lack of experience—inadequate business knowledge, management experience, and technical expertise, and;
- Personal reasons—the owners may decide to sell the business or move on to other opportunities.

Inadequate early planning is often at the core of later business problems. As described earlier, a thorough feasibility analysis, from market assessment to financing, is critical to business success. Yet even with the best plans, business conditions change and unexpected challenges arise. An entrepreneur may start a company based on a terrific new product only to find that a larger firm with more marketing, financing, and distribution clout introduces a similar item.

The stress of managing a business can also take its toll. The business can consume your whole life. Owners may find themselves in over their heads and unable to cope with the pressures of business operations, from the long hours to being the main decision maker. Even successful businesses have to deal with ongoing challenges. Growing too quickly can cause as many problems as sluggish sales. Growth can strain a company's finances when additional capital

HOT Links

Check out the listing of venture capital firms at (**www.cvca.ca**).

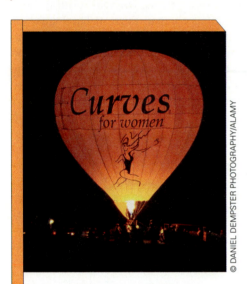

© DANIEL DEMPSTER PHOTOGRAPHY/ALAMY

CONCEPT *in Action* >>>

With over 9,500 locations, Curves International is the fastest growing fitness franchise in the world. The club's all-female clientele and trademark 30-minute workout have generated astounding membership growth in little over a decade. But success didn't come easy for Curves founder Gary Heavin. The pre-med dropout launched a conventional fitness chain during his twenties, became a millionaire by age 30, and soon thereafter declared bankruptcy when his gym business imploded. Undaunted, Heavin went on to launch Curves. Why do small businesses often fail?

concept check

How can potential business owners find new business ideas?

Why is it important to develop a business plan? What should such a plan include?

What financing options do small business owners have?

Summarize the risks of small-business ownership.

is required to fund expanding operations, from hiring additional staff to purchasing more raw materials or equipment. Successful business owners must respond quickly and develop plans to manage its growth.

Managing a Small Business

Managing a small business is quite a challenge. Whether you start a business from scratch or buy an existing one, you must be able to keep it going. The small-business owner must be ready to solve problems as they arise and move quickly if market conditions change.

A sound business plan is key to keeping the small-business owner in touch with all areas of his or her business. Hiring, training, and managing employees is another important responsibility because, over time, the owner's role may change. As the company grows, others will make many of the day-to-day decisions while the owner focuses on managing employees and planning for the firm's long-term success. The owner must constantly evaluate company performance and policies in light of changing market and economic conditions and develop new policies as required. He or she must also nurture a continual flow of ideas to keep the business growing. The types of employees needed may change, too, as the firm grows. For instance, a larger firm may need more managerial talent and technical expertise.

Using Outside Consultants

One way to ease the burden of managing a business is to hire outside consultants. Nearly all small businesses need a good accountant (e.g., CA, CMA, or CGA) who can help with financial record keeping, tax planning, and decision making. An accountant who works closely with the owner to help the business grow is a valuable asset. A lawyer who knows about small-business law can provide legal advice and draw up essential documents. Consultants in other areas, such as marketing, employee benefits, and insurance, can be hired as needed. Outside directors with business experience are another source of advice for small companies. Resources like these free the small-business owner to concentrate on planning and day-to-day operations.

Some aspects of the business can be outsourced, or contracted out to specialists in that area. Among the departments that most commonly use outsourcing are information technology, customer service, order fulfillment, payroll, and human resources. Hiring an outside company—in many cases another small business—can save money, because the purchasing firm buys just the services it needs and has no investment in expensive technology. Management should review any outsourced functions as the business grows. At some point, it might be more cost-effective to bring it in-house.

Hiring and Retaining Employees

A small company might have to be creative to find the right employees and convince applicants to join their firm. Coremetrics, a Web analytics company that tracks habits of site visitors, ran into problems when founder Brett Hurt hired the wrong person to fill a major role. "A big company won't go under because of one bad hire, but a start-up might," Hurt explains. "If you are starting your own business and you hire someone and they're not ethical, or their heart isn't in it, or they're not of the same frame of mind as you, it can crush your business."[13]

Making the decision to hire the first employee is also a major one. Most realize it is time to hire the first employee when the business owner can no longer do it alone. The business might be held back because the owner is working a very long work week and still cannot keep up. In deciding when to hire an employee, it is important to identify all the costs involved in hiring an employee to make sure the business can afford it. Help wanted ads, extra space, employer responsibilities (e.g., CPP and EI), and employee benefits—these will easily add up to substantial costs in addition to the

HOT Links

Want to know more about employment? See (**www.employease.com**).

salary. Having an employee might also mean more work for you at first in terms of training and management. It's a catch-22: To grow you need to hire more people, but making the shift from solo worker to boss can be very stressful.[14]

Attracting good employees can be hard for a small firm, which might not be able to match the higher salaries, better benefits, and advancement potential offered by many larger firms. Once they hire employees, small-business owners must promote employee satisfaction to retain them. Comfortable working conditions, flexible hours, employee benefit programs, opportunities to help make decisions, and a share in profits and ownership are some of the ways to do this.

Going Global with Exporting

More and more small businesses are discovering the benefits of looking beyond Canada for markets. As we learned in Chapter 2, the global marketplace represents a huge opportunity for Canadian businesses, both large and small. Small businesses decide to export because of foreign competition in Canada, new markets in growing economies, economic conditions in Canada, and the need for increased sales and higher profits. When the value of the Canadian dollar declines against other foreign currencies, Canadian goods become less expensive for overseas buyers, and this creates opportunities for Canadian companies to sell globally. Small businesses that choose to do business abroad might also face issues of social responsibility, as "Making Ethical Choices," on page 187, demonstrates.

Like any major business decision, exporting requires careful planning. Many online resources can help you decipher the complexities of preparing to sell in a foreign country and identify potential markets for your goods and services. Export Development Canada (EDC), helps companies grow their export business. Some services that EDC offers are insurance (including political risk insurance) and financing solutions (e.g., foreign customers can access financing through EDC or their partners). EDC recognizes that access to cash is one of the greatest barriers and has developed solutions that can help.

Many small businesses hire international-trade specialists to get started selling overseas. They have the time, knowledge, and resources that most small businesses lack. Export trading companies buy goods at a discount from small businesses and resell them abroad. Export management companies (EMCs) act on a company's behalf. For fees of 5 to 15 percent of gross sales and multi-year contracts, they handle all aspects of exporting, including finding customers, billing, shipping, and helping the company comply with foreign regulations.

HOT Links

"Realize a World of Opportunities" at EDC's website, (**www.keys.edc.ca**).

concept check

How does the small-business owner's role change over time?

What role do technology and the Internet play in creating small businesses and helping them grow?

What are the benefits to small firms of doing business internationally, and what steps can small businesses take to explore their options?

Small Business, Large Impact

An uncertain economy has not stopped people from starting new companies. A poll conducted by Léger Marketing shows that two-thirds of Canadians believe that small business is making a very positive contribution to our economy.[15] This is not surprising when you consider the many reasons why small businesses continue to thrive in Canada:

- *Independence and a better lifestyle.* Large corporations no longer represent job security or offer as many fast-track career opportunities. Mid-career employees leave the corporate world—either voluntarily or as the result of downsizing—in search of new opportunities. Many new college and business school graduates shun the corporate world altogether and start their own companies or look for work in small firms.
- *Personal satisfaction from work.* Many small-business owners cite this as one of the primary reasons for starting their companies. They love what they do.

Making Ethical Choices

MINDING YOUR BUSINESS

As the owner of LT Designs, a small South African company, Lisa Taylor loves her work producing competitively-priced, handcrafted home accessories. She is an advocate for the empowerment of women, recruiting and training workers from nearby towns. These poor rural women are often the sole supporters of their families, and they are grateful for the jobs and eager to learn new skills.

Taylor is thrilled when a Canadian textile wholesaler and distributor, attracted by her unique, well-priced products and socially responsible approach to doing business, starts buying from her. Her business triples, and she hires more workers to handle the extra load. The company is soon Taylor's single largest customer and plans an elaborate and costly marketing campaign to promote her products in Canada. The company assigns you to supervise production and work closely with Taylor on developing appropriate designs for the Canadian market.

At first Taylor welcomes your input, but her receptivity quickly turns into resentment of what she perceives as your company's attempt to "control" her business. Although she has signed an agreement with your company to approve new designs, her new sample ranges reflect none of the agreed-on design elements. After checking with your boss, you tell Taylor that unless she agrees to follow your design standards, you will have no choice but to terminate the relationship. Taylor insists the new designs fall within agreed design specifications and that you are trying to take advantage of the workers' need for jobs to force her to compromise her artistic integrity.

If your company does not buy the products, she will have to lay off the additional workers she hired, and their families will suffer. Everyone will blame the overbearing Canadian company for ruining the local economy. You are in a bind, because the company will lose its investment in the marketing campaign. It could also receive negative publicity, damaging its image as a good corporate citizen.

ETHICAL DILEMMA The Canadian company can afford to buy LT's products and hold them in inventory, waiting for an appropriate marketing opportunity. Should they absorb the cost of doing this to protect workers' jobs?

SOURCE: Case based on experience of Linda Ravden, former owner of Bellissima Designs, as described in a personal interview, February 24, 2003.

COURTESY OF SHIRLEY A. ROSE

CONCEPT in Action >>>

Brent Lane, an entrepreneurship student, is the force behind the growth of Golden Lane Honey, which now offers a wide range of products. Brent is assisted by his twin brother and marketing student, Bryce Lane. What do you think some of Brent's reasons were for starting the company?

HOT Links

Check out the Canadian Federation of Independent Business at (www.cfib.ca).

- *Best route to success.* Small businesses offer their owners the potential for profit. Also, business ownership provides greater advancement opportunities for women and minorities, as we discuss later in this chapter.
- *Rapidly changing technology.* Advances in computer and telecommunications technology, as well as the sharp decrease in the cost of this technology, have given individuals and small companies the power to compete in industries that were formerly closed to them. The arrival of the Internet and World Wide Web is responsible for the formation of many small businesses, as we'll discuss in the trends section later in this chapter.
- *Outsourcing.* As a result of downsizing, corporations often contract with outside firms for services they used to provide in-house. This "outsourcing" creates opportunities for smaller companies, many of which offer specialized goods and services.
- *Major corporate restructurings and downsizings.* These force many employees to look for other jobs or careers. They can also provide the opportunity to buy a business unit that a company no longer wants.

Small businesses are resilient. They are able to respond fairly quickly to changing economic conditions by refocusing their operations.

Why Stay Small?

Owners of small businesses recognize that being small offers special advantages. Greater flexibility and an uncomplicated company structure allow small businesses to react more quickly to changing market forces. Innovative product ideas can be developed and brought to market more quickly, using fewer financial resources and personnel than would be needed in a larger company. And operating more efficiently keeps costs down as well. Small companies can also serve specialized markets that may not be cost effective for large companies. Another feature is the opportunity to provide a higher level of personal service. Such attention brings many customers back to small businesses like gourmet restaurants, health clubs, spas, fashion boutiques, and travel agencies.

Christopher Halpin, the caterer in the opening vignette in Chapter 5, has decided to keep his business small. Christopher believes that to respond to the dynamic tastes of his customers, he can best serve them by not growing too large.

HOT Links

Find out more about small business at (**http://sbinfocanada.about.com**).

---

concept check

Why are small businesses becoming so popular?

Discuss the major advantages and disadvantages of small businesses.

On the other hand, being small is not always an asset. Many small businesses encounter difficulties in obtaining adequate financing. If the founders have limited managerial skills, they might have problems growing the company. As well, complying with regulations is more expensive for small firms. Those with fewer than 20 employees spend about twice as much per employee compared to larger firms. In addition, starting and managing a small business requires a major commitment by the owner. According to Dun & Bradstreet's 21st Annual Small Business Survey, 37 percent of all entrepreneurs work more than 50 hours a week.[16] Long hours, the need for owners to do much of the work themselves, and the stress of being personally responsible for the success of the business can take a toll.

The Business Development Bank of Canada

LO 7

Business Development Bank of Canada (BDC)
Bank that provides small and medium-sized businesses with flexible financing, affordable consulting services, and venture capital.

Many small business owners turn to the **Business Development Bank of Canada (BDC)** for assistance. The BDC is a financial institution that is wholly owned by the Government of Canada. Its mission is to help people start and manage small businesses, help them win federal contracts, and speak on behalf of small business. Through its national network of local offices, the BDC advises and helps small businesses in the areas of finance and management.

Business Service Centres

Business Service Centres (a provincial business service) provide services for start-up and growing small businesses. They typically have both print material and databases that provide not only insight into the industry and the competition but also information on start-up regulations for each city and province. An interactive business planner is also available.

HOT Links

What does it take to start up a business in your province or territory? Go to (**www.canadabusiness.ca/gol/cbec/site.nsf**) then click on the provincial or territorial flag at the bottom of the page.

Trends in Entrepreneurship and Small-Business Ownership

LO 8

Entrepreneurship has changed since the heady days of the late 1990s, when starting a dot-com while still in college or university seemed a quick route to riches and stock options. Much entrepreneurial opportunity comes from major changes in demographics, society, and technology, and at present there is a confluence of all three. A major demographic group is moving into a significantly different stage in life, and minorities are increasing their business ownership in remarkable numbers. We have created a society in which we expect to have our problems taken care of, and the technological revolution stands ready with already-developed solutions. Evolving social and demographic trends, combined with the challenge of operating in a fast-paced technology-dominated business climate, are changing the face of entrepreneurship and small-business ownership.

HOT Links

What services does the Women Business Owners of Canada Inc. provide? Click over to (**www.wboc.ca**).

Doug Dokis, a member of the Ojibwe Nation of Ontario, acts as a liaison between a large college and the Native community in the area. According to Doug, the growth rate in the Native population is the largest of any population segment: "This has tremendous implications for business, and to take advantage of the opportunity, businesses must respond to the demands of this sector." Many Native entrepreneurs are emerging to fill the demand for goods and services, for example, Cree-ative Media (1999) Ltd. of Calgary.

Changing Demographics Create Entrepreneurial Diversity

As we have seen in Chapters 1 and 3, today's baby boomers will indulge in much less knitting and golf. The growing numbers of baby boomer entrepreneurs has prompted some forward-thinking companies to recognize business opportunities in technology. At one time there was a concern that the aging of the population would create a drag on the economy. Conventional wisdom said that the early parenthood years were the big spending years. As we aged, we spent less, and because boomers are such a big demographic group this was going to create a long-term economic decline. Not true, it now appears. The boomer generation has built sizable wealth, and they are not afraid to spend it to make their lives more comfortable.

"In the future, everything from cell phones to computers will be redesigned for users with limited manual dexterity, poor eyesight, and compromised hearing. Intel and other research centres are working on sensor-rich environments that can monitor inhabitants, helping people remember to complete tasks, and watching for sudden behavioural or physical changes," says Jeff Cornwall, who holds the Jack C. Massey Chair in Entrepreneurship at Belmont University in Nashville, Tennessee. "This could be a huge entrepreneurial pot of gold for the next forty years."[17]

Minorities are also adding to the entrepreneurial mix. Minority groups and women are increasing business ownership at a much faster rate than the national average, reflecting their confidence in the Canadian economy.

The Growth of "Web-Driven Entrepreneurs"

Technology, of course, plays a large role in the Canadian economy. According to a survey of 400 small businesses conducted by MasterCard International and Warrillow & Co., a small-business consulting firm, Web-driven entrepreneurs are 25 percent more likely to be women and 25 percent more likely to be university educated.

The study found that Web-savvy companies are also more focused on expansion than their traditional counterparts. "Web-driven entrepreneurs are more growth-focused," said Yoela Harris, director of the Small Business Advisors System at Warrillow & Co. "Internet-based small businesses have a 14 percent growth rate and are 10 years old on average, while traditional small businesses have a 7 percent growth rate and are 14 years old on average."

CONCEPT *in Action* >>>

Doug Dokis, who works extensively with Native students and entrepreneurs, sees the Native population as an increasingly important group offering a wide range of products and services. How does diversity in business ownership benefit customers and employees?

CONCEPT *in Action* >>>

The popularity of eBay and other e-commerce sites has given rise to a new kind of entrepreneur: the "mompreneur." Typically ex-corporate professionals, these Web-driven women launch home businesses specializing in the sale of antiques, jewelry, thrift-store fashions, and other items. Aided by digital photography, wireless technology, and friendly postal workers, these savvy moms are the fastest-growing segment of entrepreneurs building successful businesses on eBay. Why are many professional women leaving the workplace to start entrepreneurial ventures online?

Over the next five years, 54 percent of Web-driven entrepreneurs plan to access new domestic markets, versus 36 percent of traditional small businesses; 52 percent versus 38 percent plan to introduce new products or services, and 18 percent versus 8 percent plan to access international markets. Thanks to these Web-driven entrepreneurs, the technology growth trend doesn't look ready to slow down anytime soon.[18]

Although the desire to strike out on one's own remains widespread, the number of people actually starting businesses or going solo has slowed down a bit in recent years. Reality has set in. Funding is difficult to obtain. No longer do venture capitalists, burned in the dot-com craze, throw money at all sorts of schemes. They want to see a solid idea and a well-developed business plan. People who were eager to join the ranks of the self-employed are thinking twice before giving up the security of a regular paycheque, corporate benefits like paid vacations, subsidized health insurance, retirement plans, and workspace and equipment.

Many would-be entrepreneurs are now choosing to get hands-on experience first at larger companies. They recognize that developing their managerial and technical skills improves their chances of successful business ownership. Their employers benefit as well. Applying their entrepreneurial inclinations within existing companies, these employees open up new opportunities by creating new products and identifying new markets.[19]

That's not to say that entrepreneurship is disappearing, however, but those who do take the entrepreneurial route have reasonable expectations about the time and effort it takes to build a company. They are reverting to basic business management principles, core values, and core competencies. They master their primary vision before diverting money and resources into new areas.

concept check

What significant trends are occurring in small-business management?

How is the Internet affecting small business?

Great Ideas to Use Now

After reading Chapters 5 and 6, you might be ready to go into business. Perhaps you believe you have just the product the world needs. Maybe you want to be your own boss or seek financial rewards. On the other hand, quality-of-life issues might be your primary motive.

Whatever your reasons, you'll have to do a lot of groundwork before taking the plunge. Do you know what you want from life and how the business fits into your overall goals? Do you have what it takes to start a business, from personal characteristics, like energy and persistence, to money to fund the venture? You'll also have to research the market and financial feasibility of your product idea and develop a business plan. No question about it, becoming an entrepreneur or small-business owner is hard work.

Taking the First Steps

Maybe you know that you want to run your own business but don't know what type of business to start. In addition to the advice provided earlier in the chapter, here are some ways to gather possible ideas:

- *Brainstorm with family and friends.* Don't set any limits, and then investigate the best ideas, no matter how impossible they might seem at first.
- *Be observant.* Look for anything that catches your interest wherever you are, in your hometown or when you travel. What's special about it? Is there a niche market you can fill? Look at products that don't meet your needs and find ways to change them. Pay attention to the latest fads and trends. Amy Wolf remembered how thrilled she was to find a music store at London's Heathrow airport. Six years later, she founded AltiTunes Partners LP, a $15 million chain of music stores for

travellers, with outlets in airports and a train station. Wolf knows her idea wasn't new. "I stole the idea, and then did some serious adapting," she says. She saw a need and filled it.[20]

- *Focus on your interests and hobbies.* Opportunities abound, from home-based crafts or consulting businesses to multimillion-dollar companies. Robert Tuchman turned his love of sports into a $10 million company. TSE Sports and Entertainment arranges special travel packages for corporations that want to entertain clients at major sporting and entertainment events.[21]
- *Use your skills in new ways.* Are you computer savvy? You could start a business providing in-home consulting to novices who don't know how to set up or use their computers.

Working at a Small Business

Working for a small company can be a wonderful experience. Many people enjoy the less structured atmosphere and greater flexibility that often characterize the small-business workplace. Several years' experience at a small company can be a good stepping-stone to owning your own company. You'll get a better understanding of the realities of running a small business before striking out on your own. There are other potential benefits as well:

- *More diverse job responsibilities.* Small companies might not have formal job descriptions, giving you a chance to learn a wider variety of skills to use later. In a large company, your job might be strictly defined.
- *Less bureaucracy.* Small companies typically have fewer formal rules and procedures. This creates a more relaxed working atmosphere.
- *Greater sense of your contribution to the business.* Your ideas are more likely to count, and you'll see how your work contributes to the firm's success. You'll have greater access to top management and be able to discuss your ideas.

However, you should also be aware of the disadvantages of being a small-business employee:

- *Lower compensation packages.* Although the gap between large and small businesses is narrowing, salaries are likely to be lower at small businesses. In addition, there might be few, if any, employee benefits, such as health insurance and retirement plans.
- *Less job security.* Small businesses might be affected more profoundly by changing economic and competitive conditions. A change in ownership can put jobs at risk as well. However, small businesses run lean to begin with and, as noted earlier, are at the forefront of job creation.
- *Greater potential for personality clashes.* Conflicts between employees are more apparent in a small company and can affect the rest of the staff. In addition, if your boss owns the company, you don't have anyone to go to if you have a problem with him or her.
- *Fewer opportunities for career advancement.* After a few years, you might outgrow a small firm because there are no chances for promotion. As well, with fewer people within the firm with whom to network, you'll have to join outside organizations for these connections.

Evaluating these factors will help you decide whether working at a small business is the right opportunity for you.

Customer Satisfaction and Quality

How does university student Apollonia Poilane spend her time between classes? Running one of the best French bakeries in the world—in Paris. When people asked her father, baker Lionel Poilane, what his daughter wanted to do when she grew up, Apollonia would announce she planned to take over the bakery. Then when her parents were killed in a 2002 helicopter crash, France lost its most celebrated baker, and Poilane did just that. Because the name Poilane has earned a place with a very small group of prestige bakers, the 18-year-old determined to continue the tradition of customer satisfaction and quality her grandfather established in 1932.

With organization and determination Poilane, who is studying economics, manages the Paris-based business from her apartment in Cambridge, Massachusetts. "I usually wake up an extra two hours before my classes so I can make sure I get all the phone calls done for work. After classes I check on any business regarding the company and then do my homework," she says. "Before I go to bed I call my production manager in Paris to check the quality of the bread." In fact, she receives a shipment of fresh Poilane bread each week as a flavourful and welcome change from cafeteria food.

"Apollonia is definitely passionate about her job," says Juliette Sarrazin, manager of the successful Poilane Bakery in London, the only Poilane shop outside of Paris. "She really believes in the work of her father and the company, and she is looking at the future, which is very good."

Experiments with sourdough distinguished Poilane products from bread produced by Paris' other bakers and it soon evolved into the crusty loaf that has remained the company's signature product. It is baked with a "P" carved into the crust, a throwback to the days when the use of communal ovens forced bakers to identify their loaves. But it was her father, Lionel Poilane, who turned the family's scrumptious bread into a globally recognized brand, shipped daily via FedEx to upscale restaurants and wealthy clients in North America, Japan, and elsewhere.

Poilane has retained control of important decisions, strategy, and business goals, describing herself as the "commander of the ship," determining the company's overall direction. Each day is a juggling act, with Poilane solving problems in Paris while other students sleep. Is it worth it? After surviving numerous changes in consumer tastes over the years, the company is now profiting from a growing interest in healthy eating. "More people understand what makes the quality of the bread, what my father spent years studying, so I am thrilled about that," she says. And this young woman understands the importance of keeping customers happy, albeit from a long way away.[22]

Critical Thinking Questions

- What type of entrepreneur is Apollonia Poilane?
- How does she ensure that customer satisfaction and quality are being maintained after her parents' death?

SOURCE: Gregory Katz, "Her Daily Bread," American Way Magazine, July 15, 2005, p. 34; Poilane Web site (http://www.poilane.com) (October 27, 2005).

Summary of Learning Outcomes

1 Explain why people become entrepreneurs, and what the different types of entrepreneurs are.

Entrepreneurship involves taking the risk of starting and managing a business to make a profit. Entrepreneurs are innovators who start firms either to have a certain lifestyle or to develop a company that will grow into a major corporation. People become entrepreneurs for four main reasons: the opportunity for profit, independence, personal satisfaction, and lifestyle. Classic entrepreneurs may be micropreneurs, who plan to keep their businesses small, or growth-oriented entrepreneurs. Multipreneurs start multiple companies, whereas intrapreneurs work within large corporations.

2 Describe the characteristics that successful entrepreneurs share.

Successful entrepreneurs are ambitious, independent, self-confident, creative, energetic, passionate, and committed. They have a high need for achievement and a willingness to take moderate risks. They have good interpersonal and communication skills. Managerial skills and technical knowledge are also important for entrepreneurial success.

3 Discuss how small businesses contribute to the Canadian economy.

A small business is independently owned and operated, has a local base of operations, and is not dominant in its field. Small businesses play an important role in the economy. More than 95 percent of Canadian businesses have fewer than 50 employees. Small businesses are found in every field, but they dominate the construction, wholesale, and retail categories. Most new private sector jobs created in Canada over the past decade were in small firms. Small businesses also create about twice as many new goods and services as larger firms. Approximately 70 percent of all new jobs in the economy were created by the small-business sector

4 Summarize the first steps to take if you are starting your own business.

After finding an idea that satisfies a market need, the small-business owner should choose a form of business organization. The process of developing a formal business plan helps the business owner to analyze the feasibility of his or her idea. This written plan describes in detail the idea for the business and how it will be implemented. The plan also helps the owner obtain both debt and equity financing for the new business.

5 Examine some of the special challenges of a small business owner.

At first, small-business owners are involved in all aspects of the firm's operations. Wise use of outside consultants can free up the owner's time to focus on planning and strategy in addition to day-to-day operations. Other key management responsibilities are finding and retaining good employees and monitoring market conditions. Expanding into global markets can be a profitable growth strategy for small businesses.

6 Identify the advantages and disadvantages facing owners of small businesses.

Small businesses have flexibility to respond to changing market conditions. Because of their streamlined staffing and structure, they can be operated efficiently. Small firms can serve specialized markets more profitably than large firms and provide a higher level of personal service. Disadvantages include limited managerial skill, difficulty in raising the capital needed for start-up and expansion, the burden of complying with increasing levels of government regulation, and the major personal commitment required on the part of the owner.

7 Describe how the Business Development Bank of Canada helps small businesses.

The BDC is the main federal agency serving small businesses. It provides guarantees of private lender loans for small businesses. The BDC also offers a wide range of management assistance services, including courses, publications, and consulting.

8 List some of the trends that are shaping entrepreneurship and small business ownership.

Opportunities continue to exist for entrepreneurs of all ages and backgrounds. The numbers of women and minority business owners continue to increase. The number of start-ups in the technology sector has declined, but Internet technology is creating numerous opportunities for new types of small businesses and fuelling small-business growth by making it easier to open Web-based businesses.

Key Terms

angel investors   183
Business Development Bank of Canada
  (BDC)   188
business plan   181
debt   183

entrepreneurs   175
equity   183
intrapreneurs   176
small business   179
venture capital   184

Experiential Exercises

1. After working in software development with a major food company for 12 years, you are becoming impatient with corporate "red tape" (regulations and routines). You have an idea for a new snack product for nutrition-conscious consumers and are thinking of starting your own company. What are the entrepreneurial characteristics you will need? What other factors should you consider before quitting your job? Working with a partner, choose one to be the entrepreneurial employee and one to play the role of his or her current boss. Develop notes for a script. The employee will focus on why this is a good idea, reasons he or she will succeed, and so on, whereas the employer will play devil's advocate to convince him or her that staying on at the large company is a better idea. Then switch roles and repeat the discussion.

2. What does it really take to become an entrepreneur? Find out by interviewing a local entrepreneur or researching an entrepreneur you've read about in this chapter or in the business press. Get answers to the following questions, as well as any others you'd like to ask:

   - How did you develop your vision for the company?

   - What are the most important entrepreneurial characteristics that helped you succeed?

   - Where did you learn the business skills you needed to run and grow the company?

   - How did you research the feasibility of your idea?

   - How did you prepare your business plan?

   - What were the biggest challenges you had to overcome?

   - Where did you obtain financing for the company?

   - What are the most important lessons you learned by starting this company?

   - What advice do you have for would-be entrepreneurs?

3. A small catering business in your city is for sale for $150,000. The company specializes in business luncheons and smaller social events. The owner has been running the business for four years from her home but is expecting her first child and wants to sell. You will need outside investors to help you purchase the business. Develop questions to ask the owner about the business and its prospects and a list of documents you'd want to see. What other types of information would you need before making a decision to buy this company? Summarize your findings in a memo to a potential investor that explains the appeal of the business for you and how you plan to investigate the feasibility of the purchase.

4. Does it work? Select a type of business that interests you and go through the checklist presented at (**www.bizmove.com/starting/m1b.htm**), "Starting a Business: Determining the Feasibility of Your Business Idea." Given the results of your feasibility study, should you continue to investigate this opportunity?

5. Do you have what it takes to be an entrepreneur or small-business owner? See (**www.toolkit.cch.com/text/P01_0001.asp**). To evaluate whether you have the character traits of the entrepreneurial personality, take the quiz (**www.2h.com/ entrepreneur-tests.html**). What did your results tell you, and were you surprised by what you learned?

6. Your class decides to participate in a local business plan competition. Divide the class into small groups and choose one of the following ideas:

   - a new computer game based on the stock market,

   - a company with an innovative design for a skateboard, or

   - travel services for college and high school students.

Prepare a detailed outline for the business plan, including the objectives for the business and the types of information you would need to develop product, marketing, and financing strategies. Each group will then present its outline for the class to critique.

7. Home base. Starting a business from your home is one of the easiest ways to become self-employed. Choose an idea that you feel is suited to this type of business. What other issues do you need to investigate before start-up? How feasible is your idea? Use a variety of research resources to answer these questions.

8. Visit Sample Business Plans at (www.bplans.com) to review sample plans for all types of businesses. Select an idea for a company in a field that interests you, and using information from this site, prepare an outline for its business plan.

9. You want to buy a business but don't know much about valuing small companies. Using the "Buy & Sell a Business" column in *Inc.* (also available online at (www.inc.com)) and resources on other small-business sites, including advertisements, develop a checklist of questions to ask when buying a business. Also summarize several ways in which businesses arrive at the sale price ("Business for Sale" includes the price rationale for each profiled business).

Review Questions

1. What is the definition of an entrepreneur? What is the definition of a small business?

2. Why do people become entrepreneurs?

3. What are some of the challenges for entrepreneurs?

4. What impact does small business have on the Canadian economy?

5. Why does small business thrive in Canada?

6. What needs to be included in a business plan? What is the business plan used for?

7. What are some sources of financing for a small business?

8. What role can outside consultants play in a small business?

9. Why does small business have to be creative in hiring and retaining employees?

10. What are some alternatives to starting your own business?

11. Why would a small business decide to remain small?

12. How does Export Development Canada help small businesses?

13. What are some of the trends in entrepreneurship and small business?

CREATIVE THINKING CASE >

180s Gives Old Products New Spin

People laughed when Ron Wilson and Brian Le Gette quit solid investment banking jobs with six-figure salaries to build a better earmuff. The buddies, both engineers, shared a vision based on a simple strategy: to innovate mundane products with redefined style and function.

It all started with the humble earmuff. Walking across campus at his university on a blustery winter day, Ron Wilson mused about keeping his ears warm without looking like a dork, conceptualizing what would later become the company's signature product, the Ear Warmer. Seven years later he and his business school buddy, Brian Le Gette (they both earned MBAs in Entrepreneurial Management), designed and developed prototypes of an expandable, collapsible, fleece-covered ear warmer that wraps around the back of the head.

They charged $7,500 in start-up expenses to credit cards, and the following fall sold their first ear warmers on a university campus—for $20 apiece. Two classmates persuaded Wilson and Le Gette to hawk their product on the home shopping network, and the rest, as they say, is history. Their television debut sold 5,000 Ear Warmers in 8.5 minutes, and three years later home shoppers had bought 600,000 Ear Warmers. Their product was a winner.

Launched by this momentum, their business quickly grew into a booming product design and development company, a creator and marketer of innovative performance wear with 71 employees worldwide. The company's headquarters, known as the 180s Performance Lab, includes an interactive storefront where consumers can test new products. The building's architecture—"floating" conference rooms, a sailcloth roof, four huge windows to the sky—inspires the creative process taking place inside. World-class product design and development teams are constantly working on new innovations, the very core of the 180s culture. And nearly every product has multiple design and utility patents that reflect the unique design solutions the company creates.

Although both founders have now left the company to pursue other interests, it was recently named one of the Most Innovative Companies by *Inc.* magazine, earned Fortune's award for Top Outdoor Products of 2003 for its Exhale gloves, and is number nine on the 2005 *Inc.* 500 list of fastest growing private companies. 180s products posted record sales of over $45 million in 2004, and its products are now available through 18,000 retail stores in more than 40 countries. Wilson and Le Gette are the ones laughing now—all the way to the bank.

Critical Thinking Questions

- What characteristics made Ron Wilson and Brian Le Gette successful entrepreneurs?
- How did their partnership and shared vision serve their business goals?
- Is their departure from the company likely to affect its growth? Why or why not?

SOURCES: Julekha Dash, "180s CEO Le Gette Departs," *Baltimore Business Journal*, July 15, 2005, (www.bizjournals.com); "Winners Announced for Maryland's Business International Leadership Awards," World Trade Center Institute press release, March 9, 2004, "Brian Le Gette, CEO and co-founder, and Tim Hodge, Chief Legal Officer, of 180s, LLC," World Trade Center Institute, (www.wtci.org/events/awards/leadership2004/legette.htm) (November 9, 2005); 180s corporate website (www.180s.com) (March 15, 2006).

VIDEO CASE >

Worm Boy

Tom had his life all laid out for him. He was enrolled in Princeton and with both parents being doctors, there was no problem with tuition and other expenses. So, what did he do? He quit Princeton to start an eco-capitalism company and sell worm droppings. The product involved feeding worms basically garbage so that they would produce twice their body weight daily in fertilizer. With hundreds of thousands of worms doing their thing in the building, it was not an endeavour for everyone. The company, Terra Cycle Inc. used garbage not only to produce the product, but also used garbage, recycled bottles, to package their product.

The composition of the company was rather unusual. Tom was the owner and the boss, his friends were the management team and students from Princeton volunteered as staff. Even with the staff being volunteers, Tom still had monthly expenses of $50,000 and virtually no income. His initial investors contributed $1 million in U.S. dollars. Another $300,000 was needed for factory renovations and more capital was requested to produce enough product to service the big box companies. He was running the business on investors' money and selling potential rather than product.

Many problems occurred for Tom as he tried to develop a viable business. His VP of Sales, Robin, was a good friend but had no experience with the big box companies. While Robin attempted to train the volunteers as sales people, he was missing a very important area of expertise if the company was to crack the big box market. Tom's friend, Alex, who also quit Princeton to be part of the venture, was running the lawn service side of the business. Tom was finding out the difficulties in working with friends. Sometimes Alex's behaviour was inappropriate for a business person representing a company. Tom also had problems with the sloppy work of some of his student volunteers. When people are working for room and board, stock options, and to gain experience, but are not getting paid, it is difficult to motivate them to pay more attention to details.

As Tom continued to invest more time and money into the venture, it became apparent that sales had to be made or they would lose everything.

Critical Thinking Questions

- As an entrepreneur, Tom was under a considerable amount of stress. Is this the sort of situation that would suit any eager 20-something person with a good idea?

- What are the advantages and disadvantages of using friends in your start-up business?

- Check the status of Tom's business today.

SOURCES: CBC, *Venture*, Worm Boy "The Big Adventures of Wormboy Part A and B," February 6, 2005.

E-COMMERCE CASE >

The Ultimate Entrepreneur—K. C. Irving

At the age of 11, Kenneth Colin Irving began a path that would lead him to become one of the richest men in Canada, when he bought a car for eight dollars. His father found out and ordered him to sell it, so K. C. sold the car for $11, a 38 percent profit. The story grows from there. By the age of 25, he opened his first service station in Bouctouche, New Brunswick. The Irving Oil Refinery, built in 1960, is the largest in Canada and produces 300,000 barrels of product per day, an interesting entrepreneurial venture in a province that has no oil wells. The crude oil is brought in and refined into a variety of products, with 175,000 barrels exported daily to the United States. This represents approximately 42 percent of Canadian petroleum exports.

Today Irving Oil serves the Atlantic Provinces, Quebec, and the New England States. In addition to Irving Oil, The Irving Group of companies includes Cavendish Produce, Irving Personal Care, Irving Forest Products, Irving Pulp and Paper, Irving Tissue, Midland Group (transportation services), and ownership of 90 percent of the English language media in New Brunswick. It comprises more than 300 companies worth $4–$5 billion and employs 10 percent of the New Brunswick workforce. The group is managed by K.C.'s three sons, Jack, Arthur, and Jim, and their associates.

K.C.'s early philosophy was to look after customers and they, in turn, would look after you. He believed in hard work and moral behaviour. He worked long hours and expected those around him to do likewise. Today the values of the Irving Group reflect K.C.'s earlier philosophy and include "demonstrating commitment, keeping our word, respecting people as individuals and providing the best for our customers."

K.C. Irving was inducted into the Canadian Business Hall of Fame in 1979, representing one of his few public appearances. The family has always preferred to keep a low profile, and obviously this has done no harm, as the "empire" continues to expand.

Critical Thinking Questions

1. What is the mission and purpose of Irving Oil? (**www.irvingoil.com**) Does it reflect the philosophy of the founder?

2. What is the Irving Group looking for in new employees? Is this somewhere you would want to work? Why or why not? (See (**www.irvingmoncton.com**), (**www.cavendishfarms.com**), or (**www.jdirving.com**).)

SOURCES: (http://collections.ic.gc.ca/heirloom_series/volume4/174-177.htm) (accessed July 12, 2006); and John Demont, *Citizens Irving, K. C. Irving and His Legacy* (Toronto: McClelland and Stewart Inc., 1992).

YOUR CAREER >>

As an Entrepreneur

Do you have what it takes to own your own company? Or are you better suited to working for a corporation? To find out, you need to determine whether you have the personal traits for entrepreneurial success. If the answer is yes, you need to identify the type of business that is best for you.

Know Yourself

Owning a business is challenging and requires a great deal of personal sacrifice. You must take a hard and honest look at yourself before you decide to strike out on your own. The quiz in Exhibit YC.1 can help you evaluate whether you have the personality traits to become a successful entrepreneur. Think about yourself and rate yourself—honestly!—on each of these characteristics.

Which Business Is for You?

If you are well suited to owning your own company, the next question is what type of business to start. You need to consider your expertise, interests, and financial resources. Start with a broad field; then choose a specific good or service. The business can involve a new idea or a refinement of an existing idea. It might also bring an existing idea to a new area.

To narrow the field, ask yourself the following questions:

- What do I like to do?
- What am I good at?
- How much can I personally invest in my business?

- Do I have access to other financial resources?
- What is my past business experience?
- What are my personal interests and hobbies?
- How can I use my experience and interests in my own business?
- Do I want or need partners?

Spending time on these and similar questions will help you identify some possible business opportunities and the resources you will need to develop them.

Prior job experience is the number one source of new business ideas. Starting a firm in a field where you have specialized product or service experience improves your chances for success.

Personal interests and hobbies are another major source of ideas. Gourmet food enthusiasts have started many restaurants and specialty food businesses. For example, Eleni Gianopulos transformed the humble cookie into a specialty item, bringing in more than $1 million in sales each year. Eleni's unique, beautifully decorated cookies come in shapes for every season and occasion, such as several series with Academy Award nominees and movie quotes. Customers, who include corporate and celebrity clients, can also place special orders. One customer ordered a cookie model of Elton John's housel Business at Eleni's NYC is growing; the cookies are now sold online **www.elenis.com** and featured in many specialty catalogues.

Each January, *Entrepreneur* magazines feature lists of top businesses and business trends for the coming year. Check out the current hot lists at **www.entrepreneur. com/hotcenter**.

SOURCE: Eleni's NYC Web site, (http://www.elenis.com); and "Got ID?" *Entrepreneur*, November 2002, downloaded from (http://www.entrepreneur.com).

EXHIBIT YC.1 > How Do You Rate?

The following quiz will help you to assess your personality and determine if you have what it takes to start your own company. Think about yourself and rate yourself—honestly!—on each of these characteristics.

Personality Trait	High	Above Average	Average	Below Average	Low
Ability to handle uncertainty	○	○	○	○	○
Confidence	○	○	○	○	○
Discipline	○	○	○	○	○
Drive/ambition	○	○	○	○	○
Energy	○	○	○	○	○
Flexibility	○	○	○	○	○
Independence	○	○	○	○	○
Ability to seize opportunity	○	○	○	○	○
Persistence	○	○	○	○	○
Problem solving	○	○	○	○	○
TOTAL	_____	_____	_____	_____	_____

Scoring
Give yourself 5 points for every "high," 4 points for every "above average," 3 points for every "average," 2 points for every "below average," and 1 point, for every "low."

Score results
- 46–50: You are already in business for yourself or should be!
- 40–45: Your entrepreneurial aptitude and desires are high.
- 30–39: A paid staff job and owning your own business rate equally.
- 20–29: Entrepreneurial aptitude is apparently not one of your strong suits.
- 10–19: You might find the going tough and the rewards slim if you owned your own business.

SOURCES: "Test Your Aptitude, Attitude to See How You Stack Up," *Los Angeles Times*, September 24, 1997, (http://articles.latimes.com/1997/sep/24/business/fi-35510). Reprinted by permission of The Los Angeles Times.

PART 3

Business Management

CHAPTER 7

Making the Connection

Management and Leadership in Today's Organizations

In this chapter you will be introduced to management and the first function of a manager in the act of managing a business—*planning*. Management is what managers do to ensure that the organization achieves the critical success factors. As we state later in the chapter, "management is the process of guiding the development, maintenance, and allocation of resources to attain organizational goals." That is why the process of management encircles our model of a successful business. It is the process whereby all of the activities of a business toward achieving the factors critical to its success are implemented. It ties everything together and, when done properly, ensures that activities are integrated.

All of the activities within the process of management—planning, organizing, leading, and controlling—are highly integrated. As you'll read in this chapter, they form a tightly integrated cycle of thoughts and actions. They are highly interdependent and are performed in such a way that it is difficult, if not impossible, to separate them. Just watch a manager at work. Let's suppose that she has just made a decision to promote a particular individual and leave that person's previous position permanently vacant. You might say that this was a decision made to reward an individual for a job well done and therefore to *motivate* him to continue to work hard by recognizing his efforts. However, planning would have gone into that decision as well, because managers can't just move people around without looking ahead to the implications of those moves on other employees and

the goals of the firm. One of those implications is that a change would have occurred to the structure of the *organization*, as a position was left vacant, perhaps causing that individual's subordinates to change managers and the number of managers to be reduced at that level. It also would require that the performance of that individual had been monitored to determine that he was worthy of this promotion. This is called *control*—results are measured and compared against objectives, and changes are made to keep everything on track or under control.

But remember that managers don't perform this highly integrative process in a vacuum. They make plans contingent on the opportunities and threats they see in the external environment in relation to the strengths and weaknesses the business has internally. What is done to implement the plan, with respect to organizational structure, motivational tactics, and control mechanisms, also depends on the internal and external environments. For example, a company might choose an open, flexible structure with less bureaucracy to encourage employees to be more creative, and to seek and pursue opportunities that exist in a rapidly changing, highly competitive *economic* environment. This would, in turn, be dependent on the types of employees the company has, whether they would grow and develop in that type of environment, and whether they would need more direction to be motivated to perform. In other words, the strengths and weaknesses of the employees would need to be considered.

The planning process itself is also highly integrative. As mentioned in the chapter, there are different levels of planning—the main ones being strategic, tactical, and operational—but they must all work together. *Strategic* planning is broad based and determines the goals and plans for the entire organization. Then, at the *tactical* level, each functional area determines its own goals and plans, which enable that area to fulfill its role in achieving the overall strategic plan. Finally, at the operational level, each unit within each functional area determines its goals and plans to implement those at the next higher level.

For example, if a company decided strategically to develop a new product line to compete with another company that is threatening to reduce its market share, then, at the tactical level, *marketing* would need to determine how to promote this new product line, and *operations* would need to determine the most efficient and cost-effective way to produce it. At the operational level, sales quotas, territories, and strategies for salespeople would then be set, and production schedules would be established in the plant. The important factor is that all of these plans are related to each other. They are connected as if by a string to the next higher level; each one helps to achieve the objectives of the next level, so ultimately, the company achieves its overall goals and the critical factors of success.

As we indicate in the chapter, there are many trends in the environment that affect management and leadership today. One of these is empowerment. Employees are being given more freedom to make decisions, which, in turn, *increases employee commitment* to the organization and its goals—our most important critical success factor. But this requires really solid communication and integration, so that when employees make decisions, they are in tune with other decisions that are being made, and everyone is moving in the same direction. This is improved by the impact of *technology*, which wires everyone in the organization together with instant, equal access to pertinent information.

This trend toward empowerment is linked to the discussion of leadership. Just as teams need coaches, organizations need leaders to keep everyone moving in the same direction. There are many different leadership styles, but as you'll see in the chapter, the most effective are those that result in individuals working together as a team. These styles result in the greatest commitment which is, of course, our primary objective: that employees take ownership of the results of the company as if it were their own, as mentioned by Max Messmer, Chairman and CEO of Robert Half International. "Most people will work harder … [if] they are trusted to be responsible to make their own decisions. Empowering your employees will likely pay off with … loyalty, and the high level of productivity that comes from effective teamwork." The leader and his or her style are critical to developing a vision for the company and inspiring employees to be committed to that vision, so that all the critical success factors can be achieved.

CHAPTER 7

Management and Leadership in Today's Organizations

LEARNING OUTCOMES

1 Explain the role of management.

2 Discuss the four types of planning.

3 List the primary responsibilities of managers in organizing activities.

4 Describe how leadership styles influence a corporate culture.

5 Examine how organizations control activities.

6 Summarize the roles managers take on in different organizational settings.

7 Identify the set of managerial skills necessary for managerial success.

8 List some of the trends that will affect management in the future.

HAVING FUN AT TIM HORTONS

Working at one of Cindy Anderson's Tim Hortons locations is all about customer service; fresh, high quality products offering value for the dollar; community service, and having fun. Cindy feels that having a cohesive core group of employees has helped her stores become award-winning franchises. How does a manager get and keep these important employees? Cindy believes that a positive work environment is key to keeping your staff and is definitely more important than money. You need keen people who want to be there and who have a strong work ethic. A bad attitude and a bad work ethic can poison the entire team. However, you also have to go with the economic ebb and flow, and understand the needs of your employees. When the economy is booming, and good staff leave for higher paying jobs, "Never close the door," says Cindy, "wish them well and then when the economy slows, they come back."

Tim Hortons was founded in 1964 in Hamilton, Ontario and originally offered only two products, coffee and donuts. The menu expanded as consumer tastes changed but the commitment to quality and service, both customer service and community service, is still much in evidence today. For example, on the annual Camp Day, every Tim Hortons store owner in Canada and the United States donates all proceeds from coffee sales to the Tim Horton Children's Foundation, raising millions to send thousands of children to camp who could not afford to go without the help. Tim Hortons store owners work in conjunction with local non-profit organizations and schools to select children ranging in age from nine to twelve, to attend the camp.

SHIRLEY A. ROSE

Tim Hortons is 95 percent franchise-owned with over 2800 stores operating across Canada and over 400 in the United States. In Cindy's two stores, the commitment to service is operationalized through a focus on goals of cleanliness, time and temperature targets, and food safety. Work-life balance and respect for customers are also a primary goal. These goals are clearly articulated to the staff and are measured whenever possible to identify problem areas. The successes and challenges are communicated to the group and then discussed. This employee buy-in has resulted in award-winning assessments from the Tim Hortons head office. Cindy's approach: "Train your people, set standards, communicate your expectations and follow up on them ... and have fun!"

Critical Thinking Questions

1. **How would you describe Cindy's management style?**

2. **From a customer's point of view, is the atmosphere of the coffee shop created by the staff important to your enjoyment of the coffee experience?**

3. **What can a Tim Hortons manager do to further enhance your experience?**

SOURCE: Personal interview, Cindy Anderson, June 8, 2009 and (www.timhortons.com) accessed June 6, 2009.

Developing consistency in top leadership is critical for the successful future of Canadian organizations. Today's companies rely on managers to guide the daily process using human, technological, financial, and other resources to create a competitive advantage. For many beginning business students, being in "management" is an attractive, but somewhat vague, future goal. This vagueness is due in part to an incomplete understanding of what managers do and how they contribute to organizational success or failure. In this chapter, we introduce the basic functions of management and the skills required by managers to drive an organization toward its goals. We will also discuss how leadership styles influence a corporate culture and highlight the trends that are shaping the future role of managers.

The Role of Management

management
The process of guiding the development, maintenance, and allocation of resources to attain organizational goals.

Management is the process of guiding the development, maintenance, and allocation of resources to attain organizational goals. Managers are the people in the organization responsible for developing and carrying out this management process. Management is dynamic by nature and evolves to meet needs and constraints in the organization's internal and external environments. In a global marketplace where the rate of change is rapidly increasing, flexibility and adaptability are crucial to the managerial process. This process is based in four key functional areas of the organization: planning, organizing, leading, and controlling. Although these activities are discussed separately in the chapter, they actually form a tightly integrated cycle of thoughts and actions.

From this perspective, the managerial process can be described as:

1. Anticipating potential problems or opportunities and designing plans to deal with them.
2. Coordinating and allocating the resources needed to implement plans.
3. Guiding personnel through the implementation process.
4. Reviewing results and making any necessary changes.

efficiency
Using the least amount of resources to accomplish the organization's goals (doing things right).

effectiveness
The ability to produce the desired results or goods (doing the right thing).

This last stage provides information to be used in ongoing planning efforts, and thus the cycle starts over again.

The four management functions can help managers increase organizational **efficiency** and **effectiveness**. Efficiency is using the least possible amount of resources to get work done, whereas effectiveness is the ability to produce a desired result. Managers need to be both efficient and effective in order to achieve organizational goals.

As shown in Exhibit 7.1, managerial work can be divided into four activities: planning, organizing, leading, and controlling. The four functions are highly interdependent, with managers often performing more than one of them at a time and each of them many times over the course of a normal workday. As you will learn in the following sections, all of the functions require sound decision-making and communication skills.

concept check

Define the term management.

What are the four key functions of managers?

What is the difference between efficiency and effectiveness?

Planning

planning
The process of deciding what needs to be done to achieve organizational objectives, identifying when and how it will be done, and determining by whom it should be done.

Planning begins with the anticipation of potential problems or opportunities that the organization might encounter. Managers then design strategies to solve current problems, prevent future problems, or take advantage of opportunities. These strategies serve as the foundation for goals, objectives, policies, and procedures. Put simply, planning is deciding what needs to be done to achieve organizational objectives, identifying when and how it will be done, and determining by whom it should be done. Effective planning requires extensive information about the

EXHIBIT 7.1 > What Managers Do and Why

Good management consists of these four activities:		Which results in	And leads to
Planning • Set objectives and state mission • Examine alternatives • Determine needed resources • Create strategies to reach objectives	**Leading** • Lead and motivate employees to accomplish organizational goals • Communicate with employees • Resolve conflicts • Manage change	Organizational efficiency and effectiveness	Achievement of organizational mission and objectives
Organizing • Design jobs and specify tasks • Create organizational structure • Staff positions • Coordinate work activities • Set policies and procedures • Allocate resources	**Controlling** • Measure performance • Compare performance to standards • Take necessary action to improve performance		

external business environment in which the firm competes, as well as its internal environment.

There are four basic types of planning: strategic, tactical, operational, and contingency. Most of us use these different types of planning in our own lives. Some plans are very broad and long term (more strategic in nature), such as planning to attend graduate school after earning a bachelor's degree. Some plans are much more specific and short term (more operational in nature), such as planning to spend a few hours in the library this weekend. Your short-term plans support your long-term plans. If you study now, you have a better chance of achieving some future goal, such as getting a

CONCEPT *in Action* >>>

After the Disney Magic cruise ship had a second outbreak of flu-like symptoms among passengers, 1,000 workers began cleaning and disinfecting the ship for a second time within a month. Disney Cruise Line offered free cruises to sick passengers and to travellers who stayed in the same room as sick people. This contingency plan, in the face of an unexpected crisis, helped Disney rebound and regain customer confidence. What is the importance of contingency plans?

CHRIS LIVINGSTON/STRINGER/GETTY IMAGES NEWS/GETTY IMAGES

strategic planning
The process of creating long-range (one to five years), broad goals for the organization and determining what resources will be needed to accomplish those goals.

mission 佳命
An organization's purpose and reason for existing; its long-term goals.

mission statement 任务宣言,任命证明书
A formal document that states an organization's purpose and reason for existing, and describes its basic philosophy.

tactical planning
The process of beginning to implement a strategic plan by addressing issues of coordination and allocation of resources to different parts of the organization; has a shorter time frame (less than one year) and more specific objectives than strategic planning.

HOT Links

How does a company translate its mission statement into company action? Find out at Ben & Jerry's home page, (www.benjerry.com).

job interview or attending graduate school. Like you, organizations tailor their plans to meet the requirements of future situations or events. A summary of the four types of planning appears in Exhibit 7.2.

Strategic planning involves creating long-range (one to five years), broad goals for the organization and determining what resources will be needed to accomplish those goals. An evaluation of external environmental factors, such as economic, technological, and social issues, is critical to successful strategic planning. Strategic goals, such as the organization's long-term mission, are formulated by top-level managers and put into action at lower levels in the organization. For example, Carly Fiorina, when she was CEO of Hewlett-Packard, engineered the merger with Compaq to create a vast organization that could effectively compete with Dell Computer and IBM. She believed that the merger gave her a technology company with enough products and services to satisfy all customers. "We are betting on heterogeneity," she says. "We'll be the only systems provider to support everything."[1]

An organization's **mission** is formalized in its **mission statement**, a document that states the purpose of the organization and its reason for existing. For example, Ben & Jerry's mission statement addresses three fundamental issues and states the basic philosophy of the company (see Exhibit 7-3).

In all organizations, plans and goals at the tactical and operational levels should clearly support the organization's mission statement.

Tactical planning begins the implementation of strategic plans. Tactical plans have a shorter (less than one year) time frame than strategic plans and more specific objectives designed to support the broader strategic goals. Tactical plans begin to address issues of coordination and allocation of resources to different parts of the organization.

For an example of how planning affects an organization, look at Procter & Gamble—makers of such products as Mr. Clean, Tide detergent, Zest, and Pringles.[2] Prior to the tenure of the current CEO, A. G. Lafley, P&G had lost $70 billion in market value in just 6 months. Following a strategy of aggressive new-product introduction and brand-name changes that contributed to the loss of market value, Mr. Lafley's mission was simple: turn around the current situation and grow the $40 billion company.

EXHIBIT 7.2 > Types of Planning

Type of Planning	Time Frame	Level of Management	Extent of Coverage	Purpose and Goal	Breadth of Content	Accuracy/ Predictability
Strategic 战略计划	1–5 years	Top management (CEO, vice-presidents, directors, division heads)	External environment and entire organization	Establish mission and long-term goals	Broad and general	High degree of uncertainty
Tactical 战术性计划	Less than 1 year	Middle management	Strategic business units	Establish mid-range goals for implementation	More specific	Moderate degree of certainty
Operational 作业性计划	Current	Supervisory management	Geographic and functional divisions	Implement and activate specific objectives	Specific and concrete	Reasonable degree of certainty
Contingency 应急计划	When an event occurs or a situation demands	Top and middle management	External environment and entire organization	Meet unforeseen challenges and opportunities	Both broad and detailed	Reasonable degree of certainty once situation occurs

EXHIBIT 7-3 > Ben & Jerry's Mission Statement

Ben & Jerry's is founded on and dedicated to a sustainable corporate concept of linked prosperity. Our mission consists of three interrelated parts:

Product Mission

To make, distribute and sell the finest quality all natural ice cream & euphoric concoctions with a continued commitment to incorporating wholesome, natural ingredients and promoting business practices that respect the Earth and the Environment.

Economic Mission

To operate the Company on a sustainable financial basis of profitable growth, increasing value for our stakeholders and expanding opportunities for development and career growth for our employees.

Social Mission

To operate the Company in a way that actively recognizes the central role that business plays in society by initiating innovative ways to improve the quality of life locally, nationally and internationally.

Central to the mission of Ben & Jerry's is the belief that all three parts must thrive equally in a manner that commands deep respect for individuals in and outside the Company and supports the communities of which they are a part.

SOURCE: (www.benjerry.com/our_company/our_mission). Reprinted with permission of Ben & Jerry's Homemade, Inc.

Unlike his predecessor, Mr. Lafley's strategy was straightforward and direct: refocus on the top brands. On a tactical level, he chose the top 10 brands and made them the highest priority. These products got most of the company's human resources and financial backing. The goal was to sell more of what were already winners instead of trying to invest in a new blockbuster product. Additionally, to reduce expenses, Mr. Lafley eliminated 9,600 jobs, shut down weak product lines, and sold product lines that were not a good strategic fit. Even in day-to-day operations, Lafley is a very hands-on CEO. He frequently visits retail stores to talk directly to both employees and customers to find out exactly what they think about his company's products. He also likes to make suggestions to store owners on where Procter & Gamble's products will sell best.

operational planning
The process of creating specific standards, methods, policies, and procedures that are used in specific functional areas of the organization; helps guide and control the implementation of tactical plans.

Operational planning creates specific standards, methods, policies, and procedures that are used in specific functional areas of the organization. Operational objectives are current, narrow, and resource focused. They are designed to help guide and control the implementation of tactical plans.

In an industry where new versions of software have widely varying development cycles, Autodesk, maker of software tools for designers and engineers, has implemented new operational plans that are dramatically increasing profits. CEO Carol Bartz shifted the company away from the erratic release schedule it had been keeping to regular, annual software releases. By releasing upgrades on a defined and predictable schedule, the company is able to use annual-subscription pricing, which is more affordable for small and mid-size companies. The new schedule keeps Autodesk customers on the most recent versions of popular software and has resulted in an overall increase in profitability.[2]

contingency plans
Plans that identify alternative courses of action for very unusual or crisis situations; typically stipulate the chain of command, standard operating procedures, and communication channels the organization will use during an emergency.

The key to effective planning is anticipating future situations and events. Yet even the best-prepared organization must sometimes cope with unforeseen circumstances, such as a natural disaster, an act of terrorism, or a radical new technology. Therefore, many companies have developed **contingency plans** that identify alternative courses of action for very unusual or crisis situations. The contingency plan typically stipulates the chain of command, standard operating procedures, and communication channels the organization will use during an emergency. An effective contingency plan can make or break a company.

concept check

What is the purpose of planning, and what is needed to do it effectively?

Identify the unique characteristics of each type of planning.

Organizing

organizing
The process of coordinating and allocating a firm's resources to carry out its plans.

A second key function of managers is **organizing,** which is the process of coordinating and allocating a firm's resources to carry out its plans. Organizing includes developing a structure for the people, positions, departments, and activities within the firm. Managers can arrange the structural elements of the firm to maximize the flow of information and the efficiency of work processes. They accomplish this by

- dividing up tasks (*division of labour*),
- grouping jobs and employees (*departmentalization*), and
- assigning authority and responsibilities (*delegation*).

These and other elements of organizational structure are discussed in detail in Chapter 8. In this chapter, however, you should understand the three levels of a managerial hierarchy. This hierarchy is often depicted as a pyramid, as in Exhibit 7.4. The fewest managers are found at the highest level of the pyramid. Called **top management,** they are the small group of people at the head of the organization (such as the CEO, president, and vice-president). Top-level managers develop *strategic plans* and address long-range issues, such as which industries to compete in, how to capture market share, and what to do with profits. These managers design and approve the firm's basic policies and represent the firm to other organizations. They also define the company's values and ethics and thus set the tone for employee standards of behaviour. For example, Jack Welch, the former CEO of General Electric, was a role model for his managers and executives. Admirers say that he had an extraordinary capacity to inspire hundreds of thousands of people in many countries and that he could change the direction of a huge organization like General Electric as if it were a small firm. Following his leadership, General Electric executives turned in impressive results. During his tenure, the average annual shareholder return with General Electric was 25 percent.[3]

top management
The highest level of managers, including CEOs, presidents, and vice-presidents; they develop strategic plans and address long-range issues.

middle management
Managers who design and carry out tactical plans in specific areas of the company.

supervisory management
Managers who design and carry out operational plans for the ongoing daily activities of the firm.

The second and third tiers of the hierarchy are called **middle management** and **supervisory management,** respectively. Middle managers (such as division heads, departmental managers, and regional sales managers) are responsible for beginning the implementation of strategic plans. They design and carry out *tactical plans* in specific areas of the company. They begin the process of allocating resources to meet organizational goals, and they oversee supervisory managers throughout the firm. Supervisors, the most

---

EXHIBIT 7.4 > The Managerial Pyramid

Top management
CEO, CFO, COO, CIO, President, etc.

Chief Executive Officer

Middle management
Regional manager, Division head, Director, Plant manager, Sales manager, etc.

Supervisory management
(first-line management)
Supervisor, Team leader, Foremen, etc.

---

numerous of the managers, are at the bottom of the managerial pyramid. These managers design and carry out *operational plans* for the ongoing daily activities of the firm. They spend a great deal of their time guiding and motivating the employees who actually produce the goods and services.

Leading, Guiding, and Motivating Others

LO 4

leadership
The process of guiding and motivating others toward the achievement of organizational goals.

power
The ability to influence others to behave in a particular way.

legitimate power
Power that is derived from an individual's position in an organization.

reward power
Power that is derived from an individual's control over rewards.

coercive power
Power that is derived from an individual's ability to threaten negative outcomes.

expert power
Power that is derived from an individual's extensive knowledge in one or more areas.

referent power
Power that is derived from an individual's personal charisma and the respect and/or admiration the individual inspires.

leadership style
The relatively consistent way in which individuals in leadership positions attempt to influence the behaviour of others.

autocratic leaders
Directive leaders who prefer to make decisions and solve problems on their own with little input from subordinates.

HOT Links

Search (**www.canadianbusiness .com**) for recent articles relating to business leaders who interest you.

Leadership, the third key management function, is the process of guiding and motivating others toward the achievement of organizational goals. Managers are responsible for directing employees on a daily basis as the employees carry out the plans and work within the structure created by management. Organizations need strong, effective leadership at all levels to meet goals and remain competitive.

To be effective leaders, managers must be able to influence others' behaviour. This ability to influence others to behave in a particular way is called **power**. Researchers have identified five primary sources, or bases, of power:

- **legitimate power,** which is derived from an individual's position in an organization;
- **reward power,** which is derived from an individual's control over rewards;
- **coercive power,** which is derived from an individual's ability to threaten negative outcomes;
- **expert power,** which is derived from an individual's extensive knowledge in one or more areas; and
- **referent power,** which is derived from an individual's personal charisma and the respect and/or admiration the individual inspires.

Many leaders use a combination of all of these sources of power to influence individuals toward goal achievement. A. G. Lafley gets his legitimate power from his position as CEO of Procter & Gamble. His reward power comes from reviving the company and making the stock more valuable. Also, raises and bonuses for managers who meet their goals is another form of reward power. Lafley is also not hesitant to use his coercive power. He has eliminated thousands of jobs, sold underperforming brands, and killed weak product lines. With nearly 30 years of service to the company, Lafley has a unique authority when it comes to P&G's products, markets, innovations, and customers. He has captained the purchase of Clairol, Wella AG, IAMS, as well as the multi-billion dollar merger with Gillette. As a result, Lafley has a substantial amount of referent power. Lafley is also widely respected, not only by people at P&G, but by the general business community as well.

Leadership Styles

Individuals in leadership positions tend to be relatively consistent in how they attempt to influence the behaviour of others, meaning that each individual has a tendency to react to people and situations in a particular way. This pattern of behaviour is referred to as **leadership style**. As Exhibit 7.5 shows, leadership styles can be placed on a continuum that encompasses three distinct styles: autocratic, participative, and free rein.

Autocratic leaders are directive leaders, allowing for very little input from subordinates. These leaders prefer to make decisions and solve problems on their own and expect subordinates to implement solutions according to very specific and detailed instructions. In this leadership style, information typically flows in one direction, from manager to subordinate. The military, by necessity, is generally autocratic. When autocratic leaders treat employees with fairness and respect, they may be considered knowledgeable and decisive. But often autocrats are perceived as narrow-minded

EXHIBIT 7.5 > Leadership Styles of Managers

Amount of authority held by the leader

Autocratic Style	Participative Style (democratic, consensual, consultative)	Free-Rein (laissez-faire) Style
• Manager makes most decisions and acts in authoritative manner.	• Manager shares decision making with group members and encourages teamwork.	• Manager turns over virtually all authority and control to group.
• Manager is usually unconcerned about subordinates' attitudes toward decisions.	• Manager encourages discussion of issues and alternatives.	• Members of a group are presented with task and given freedom to accomplish it.
• Emphasis is on getting task accomplished.	• Manager is concerned about subordinates' ideas and attitudes.	• Approach works well with highly motivated, experienced, educated personnel.
• Approach is used mostly by military officers and some production line supervisors.	• Manager coaches subordinates and helps coordinate efforts.	• Approach is found in high-tech firms, labs, and colleges.
	• Approach is found in many successful organizations.	

Amount of authority held by group members

participative leaders ← democratic consensual consultative
Leaders that share decision making with group members and encourage discussion of issues and alternatives; includes democratic, consensual, and consultative styles.

and heavy-handed in their unwillingness to share power, information, and decision making in the organization. The trend in organizations today is away from the directive, controlling style of the autocratic leader.

Instead, Canadian businesses are looking more and more for **participative leaders,** meaning leaders who share decision making with group members and encourage discussion of issues and alternatives. For example, they might enlist frontline workers to

CONCEPT *in Action* >>>

Many successful organizations use participative leadership styles that involve group members in discussing issues and making decisions. How can participative leadership enhance decision-making?

© EYEWIRE / GETTY IMAGES

Sustainable Business, Sustainable World

Leadership is about being at the front of a movement—not following, not being reactive—but instead being proactive. Sustainability is a movement. It is a movement that is gathering momentum every day. Some companies are leaders; others are followers. Coca-Cola is one company that has taken a leadership role. In fact, it was named to the 2008 list of the Global 100 Most Sustainable Corporations in the World (www.global100.org/2008/index.asp); one of only 17 US and 20 North American companies, and the only US company in the Consumer Staples industry category. Other North American firms included as leaders in sustainability, with names you'd recognize, were the Royal Bank of Canada, Eastman Kodak, General Electric, Hewlett-Packard, Nike, and Walt Disney.

Go to Coca-Cola's website and you'll see "Sustainability" as a prominent page link second only to "Our Company." Under "Our Company" you'll find a page link to "Leadership," and the title on that page encapsulates Coca-Cola's role in sustainability leadership: "Leading the Industry and Refreshing the World Responsibly." At the top of Coca-Cola's written values is "Leadership: the courage to shape a better future." Coca-Cola is a company that sees its leadership role as one that is focused on its commitment to its consumers and the communities in which it operates. Coca-Cola's strategic vision with respect to sustainability recognizes that the "health of (the) business is directly linked to the health of the communities (it) serves" and, as a result, sustainability is now one of the key criteria by which the company evaluates its business plans and performance. That's what leaders do—they hold themselves accountable for their actions. In fact, Coca-Cola proudly provides a prominent link to its "Sustainability Review" on its website (www.thecoca-colacompany.com/citizenship/index.html).

The areas in which Coca-Cola is focusing its sustainability efforts include respecting people, protecting the environment, supporting communities, and offering safe, quality products in the marketplace. Respecting people involves efforts such as improving global workplace rights, eliminating child labour, increasing diversity, and creating programs to prevent and treat HIV/AIDS in Africa. Protecting the environment involves efforts in the areas of water stewardship, sustainable packaging, energy management and climate protection, as well as partnering with the World Wildlife Federation for global conservation. The company's efforts to support communities includes the Coca-Cola Foundation—supporting projects most relevant to community needs, improving access to safe drinking water, providing access to higher education, and supporting employee volunteerism. And finally, offering safe, quality products through efforts to identify and implement solutions to prevent obesity and encourage active, healthy lifestyles, and innovative nutritional labelling projects like its recent Guideline Daily Amount labelling.

The list is enormous, but the commitment more so. That's what leadership is about—committing to a goal, creating the culture to support that goal, and providing the resources to implement it. That's what Coca-Cola has done.

Is Coca-Cola a company that instantly comes to mind when you think of sustainability? Did you expect Nike to be in the Global 100 list? Check out the websites of companies you wouldn't instantly think of—you might change your perception. If you don't see a commitment to sustainability, what actions do you feel they could be taking? Is the company you work for making efforts to be sustainable. How do you feel about that?

SOURCES: (www.thecoca-colacompany.com) and (www.global100.org)

---

democratic leaders
Leaders who solicit input from all members of the group and then allow the members to make the final decision through a vote.

consensual leaders
Leaders who encourage discussion about issues and then require that all parties involved agree to the final decision.

consultative leaders
Leaders who confer with subordinates before making a decision but who retain the final decision-making authority.

free-rein (laissez-faire) leadership
A leadership style in which the leader turns over all authority and control to subordinates.

concept check

What are the five power bases mentioned? What is the source of each base?

What are the three types of leadership styles mentioned? When is each appropriate?

Explain each: democratic leaders, consensual leaders, and consultative leaders.

help design the assembly lines, or involve employees in programs to improve safety, quality, and process efficiency. The goal is to create a business where workers are passionately involved in their work. Participative leaders can be classified as either democratic, consensual, or consultative.

Democratic leaders solicit input from all members of the group and then allow the group members to make the final decision through a voting process. This approach works well with highly trained professionals. **Consensual leaders** encourage discussion about issues and then require that all parties involved agree to the final decision. This style is often used when consensus is necessary. **Consultative leaders** confer with subordinates before making a decision but retain the final decision-making authority. This technique has been used in some situations to increase productivity dramatically.

The third leadership style, at the opposite end of the continuum from the autocratic style, is **free-rein**, or **laissez-faire** (French for "leave it alone") **leadership**. Managers who use this style turn over all authority and control to subordinates. Employees are assigned a task and then given free rein to determine the best way to accomplish it. The manager doesn't get involved unless asked and then usually acts only as a facilitator. Under this approach, subordinates have unlimited freedom as long as they do not violate existing company policies. This approach is sometimes used with highly trained professionals, as in a research laboratory.

Although one might at first assume that subordinates would prefer the free-rein style, this approach can have several drawbacks. If free-rein leadership is accompanied by unclear expectations and lack of feedback from the manager, the experience can be frustrating for an employee. Employees might perceive the manager as being uninvolved and indifferent to what is happening or as unwilling or unable to provide the necessary structure, information, and expertise.

There is no one best leadership style. The most effective style for a given situation depends on elements such as the characteristics of the subordinates, the complexity of the task, the source of the leader's power, and the stability of the environment.

Employee Empowerment

empowerment
The process of giving employees increased autonomy and discretion to make decisions, as well as control over the resources needed to implement those decisions.

Participative and free-rein leaders use a technique called empowerment to share decision-making authority with subordinates. **Empowerment** means giving employees increased autonomy and discretion to make their own decisions, as well as control over the resources needed to implement those decisions. When decision-making power is shared at all levels of the organization, employees feel a greater sense of ownership in, and responsibility for, organizational outcomes.

Max Messmer, Chairman and CEO of Robert Half International, says, "Most people will work harder and do a better job if they feel their opinions are respected and that they are trusted to be responsible to make their own decisions. Empowering your employees will likely pay off with respect, loyalty, and the high level of productivity that comes from effective teamwork."[4]

See the Expanding Around the Globe box for a discussion of some of the challenges Canadian companies encounter when they decide to go global.

Corporate Culture

corporate culture
The set of attitudes, values, and standards of behaviour that distinguishes one organization from another

The leadership style of managers in an organization is usually indicative of the underlying philosophy, or values, of the organization. The set of *attitudes, values,* and *standards of behaviour* that distinguishes one organization from another is called **corporate culture.** A corporate culture evolves over time and is based on the accumulated history of the organization, including the vision of the founders. It is also influenced by the dominant leadership style within the organization. Evidence of a company's culture is seen in its heroes (e.g., Andy Grove of Intel), myths (stories about the company that are passed from employee to employee), symbols (e.g., the Nike swoosh), and ceremonies.

Although culture is intangible and its rules are often unspoken, it can have a strong impact on a company's success. Therefore, managers must try to influence the corporate culture so that it will contribute to the success of the company. Companies can most often match the competition on the spreadsheet, but they can create a competitive advantage with the corporate culture.

HOT Links

See Waterstone's complete list of Canada's 10 Most Admired Corporate Cultures™ list at (http://canadasmostadmired.com).

CONCEPT in Action >>>
Each employee on the Toyota assembly line has been empowered to act as a quality control inspector, stopping the line if necessary to correct a problem. How can empowerment increase productivity and a company's profitability?

© MICHAEL S. YAMASHITA / CORBIS

Expanding Around The Globe

LEADERSHIP IN FOREIGN SUBSIDIARIES

Canadian companies are often seeking new opportunities and many of these are presented outside of our borders. These opportunities provide new markets to service and the potential of increased profits. But associated with these benefits are challenges, especially from a leadership perspective.

Many of these challenges result from cultural differences. For example, some cultures are more comfortable with autocratic leadership styles than participative or free rein styles. This can present problems for Canadian managers working internationally, especially when they are accustomed to allowing more autonomy for the employees. Suddenly they may have to use more "hands-on" management techniques that may seem insulting to employees in Canada.

When a Canadian company purchases an existing foreign company, another challenge may be adapting the Canadian corporate culture to those of the host country's company. Corporate culture evolves over time and based on the history of the organization, it will be most likely resistant to sudden changes in the new attitudes and standards of behaviours. Canadian managers assigned to foreign subsidiaries must understand the current corporate culture and modify their leadership styles accordingly.

Some other issues that may create challenges for Canadian managers in foreign subsidiaries include the decision-making process, timing of decisions, how to disseminate the decisions, etc.

Critical Thinking Questions

- Is it possible to change the attitudes of workers regarding the appropriateness of the leadership style? If so how?
- How can managers assigned to foreign subsidiaries learn the corporate culture?

Since 2005, Waterstone Human Capital has interviewed hundreds of senior Canadian executives in a wide range of industries for their annual Canadian Corporate Culture Study™. For a third consecutive year, WestJest Airlines Ltd has been named number one in the "Canada's 10 Most Admired Corporate Cultures" in 2007. Some of the other interesting findings in the 2007 study were

concept check

How do leaders influence other people's behaviour?

How can managers empower employees?

What is corporate culture?

- 93 percent of the executives see a correlation between their corporate culture and corporate performance;
- 37 percent say that company leadership creates the corporate culture; and
- 86 percent say that cultural fit is more important than skills in finding executive-level candidates.[5]

CONCEPT *in Action* >>>

Innovative organizations empower their employees to present and implement new ideas. The WestJet Airline scorporate culture, for example, encourages employees to solve problems and keep customers happy. What correlations do you see between corporate culture and corporate success?

COURTESY OF WESTJET

Making Ethical Choices

WAITING AND WAITING AND WAITING

You've always been in a hurry, whether it's to get to a party or to find a job. You were in a hurry to land a supervisory position immediately on college graduation and looked for an organization that satisfied your goals of providing community service and moving up quickly. As an adept organizer with an innate sense of the right number of people and amount of money necessary to complete a task, you wanted your ability to plan and stay focused on goals to be recognized.

Your search led you to the police department of a major metropolitan city, as the supervisor of 911—the perfect job for someone in a hurry. On taking over, you analyzed the department's requirements and determined you needed more operators to service the growing call volume. You shared your findings with the chief of police, who had to approve all staffing allocations, and he agreed with your evaluation. Human resources, however, repeatedly denied your requests for more operators, even though your department received numerous complaints from callers who were left waiting and waiting. Even more serious, you knew people were dying because of missed calls and delayed responses.

Investigating further, you discovered that although he told you otherwise, the chief of police never, in fact, approved your proposal, which would have permitted human resources to hire the additional staff. When the mayor called to discuss complaints his office had received about poor 911 service, the chief told the mayor the call centre was fully staffed and placed the blame on your department's inefficiency. Based on current call volume, your department is short approximately 25 percent of the operators needed to service the 911 calls it receives efficiently.

ETHICAL DILEMMA: Once you realize your staffing proposal has been ignored and take into account the serious ramifications that result from this, do you report this to the mayor and the city's board of elected officials?

SOURCES: Mike Fitzgerald, "911 Problem Began Months Ago," *Belleville News-Democrat*, October 13, 2002, (www.belleville.com); and Phil Mendelson, "Want an Explanation of D.C.'s 911 Deficiencies? Hold, Please," *The Washington Post*, March 9, 2003, B8.

Controlling

LO 5

controlling
The process of assessing the organization's progress toward accomplishing its goals; includes monitoring the implementation of a plan and correcting deviations from it.

The fourth key function that managers perform is **controlling**. Controlling is the process of assessing the organization's progress toward accomplishing its goals. It includes monitoring the implementation of a plan and correcting deviations from that plan. As Exhibit 7.6 shows, controlling can be visualized as a cyclical process made up of five stages:

1. Setting performance standards (goals).
2. Measuring performance.
3. Comparing actual performance to established performance standards.
4. Taking corrective action (if necessary).
5. Using information gained from the process to set future performance standards.

Performance standards are the levels of performance the company wants to attain. These goals are based on its strategic, tactical, and operational plans. The most effective performance standards state a measurable behavioural objective that can be achieved in a specified time frame. For example, the performance objective for the sales division of a company could be stated as "$100,000 in gross sales for the month of January." Each individual employee in that division would also have a specified performance goal. Actual firm, division, or individual performance can be measured against desired performance standards to see if a gap exists between the desired level of performance and the actual level of performance. If a performance gap does exist, the reason for it must be determined and corrective action taken.

Feedback is essential to the process of control. Most companies have a reporting system that identifies areas where performance standards are not being met. A feedback system helps managers detect problems before they get out of hand. If a problem exists, the managers take corrective action. Toyota uses a simple but effective control system on its automobile assembly lines. Each worker serves as the "customer" for the assembly process and is empowered to act as a quality control inspector. If a part is defective or not installed properly, the next worker won't accept it. Any worker can alert the supervisor to a problem by tugging on a rope that turns on a warning light (i.e., feedback). If the problem isn't corrected, the worker can stop the entire assembly line.

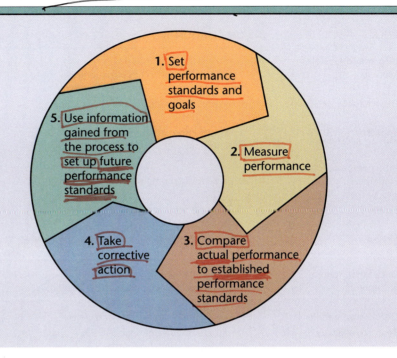

EXHIBIT 7.6 > The Control Process

1. Set performance standards and goals
2. Measure performance
3. Compare actual performance to established performance standards
4. Take corrective action
5. Use information gained from the process to set up future performance standards

concept check

Describe the control process.

Why is the control process important to the success of the organization?

Why is controlling such an important part of a manager's job? First, it helps managers to determine the success of the other three functions: planning, organizing, and leading. Second, control systems direct employee behaviour toward achieving organizational goals. Third, control systems provide a means of coordinating employee activities and integrating resources throughout the organization.

Managerial Roles

LO 6

informational roles
A manager's activities as an information gatherer, information disseminator, or spokesperson for the company.

interpersonal roles
A manager's activities as a figurehead, company leader, or liaison.

decisional roles
A manager's activities as an entrepreneur, resource allocator, conflict resolver, or negotiator.

In carrying out the responsibilities of planning, organizing, leading, and controlling, managers take on many roles. A role is a set of behavioural expectations, or a set of activities that a person is expected to perform. Managers' roles fall into three basic categories: *informational roles, interpersonal roles,* and *decisional roles.* These roles are summarized in Exhibit 7.7. In an **informational role,** the manager may act as an information gatherer, information distributor, or spokesperson for the company. A manager's **interpersonal roles** are based on various interactions with other people. Depending on the situation, a manager might need to act as a figurehead, company leader, or liaison. When acting in a **decisional role,** a manager might have to think like an entrepreneur, make decisions about resource allocation, help resolve conflicts, or negotiate compromises.

Managerial Decision Making

In every function performed, role taken on, and set of skills applied, a manager is a decision maker. Decision making means choosing among alternatives. Decision making occurs in response to the identification of a problem or an opportunity. Managers make decisions in two basic categories: programmed and non-programmed.

EXHIBIT 7.7 > The Many Roles that Managers Play in an Organization

ROLE	DESCRIPTION	EXAMPLE
Informational Roles		
Monitor	Seeks out and gathers information relevant to the organization.	Finding out about legal restrictions on new product technology.
Disseminator 信播者	Provides information where it is needed in the organization.	Providing current production figures to workers on the assembly line.
Spokesperson	Transmits information to people outside the organization.	Representing the company at a shareholders' meeting.
Interpersonal Roles		
Figurehead	Represents the company in a symbolic way.	Cutting the ribbon at ceremony for the opening of a new building.
Leader	Guides and motivates employees to achieve organizational goals.	Helping subordinates to set monthly performance goals.
Liaison	Acts as a go-between among individuals inside and outside the organization.	Representing the retail sales division of the company at a regional sales meeting.
Decisional Roles		
Entrepreneur	Searches out new opportunities and initiates change.	Implementing a new production process using new technology.
Disturbance handler	Handles unexpected events and crises.	Handling a crisis situation such as a fire.
Resource allocator	Designates the use of financial, human, and other organizational resources.	Approving the funds necessary to purchase computer equipment and hire personnel.
Negotiator	Represents the company at negotiating processes.	Participating in salary negotiations with union representatives.

programmed decisions
Decisions made in response to frequently occurring routine situations.

Programmed decisions are made in response to routine situations that occur frequently in a variety of settings throughout an organization. For example, the need to hire new personnel is a common situation for most organizations. Therefore, standard procedures for recruitment and selection are developed and followed in most companies.

Infrequent, unforeseen, or very unusual problems and opportunities require **non-programmed decisions** by managers. Because these situations are unique and complex, the manager rarely has a precedent to follow. For example, after Hurricane Katrina in New Orleans, many non-programmed decisions were needed. The overwhelming magnitude of the disaster was unforeseen, and rescue and emergency workers responded to the disaster to the best of their abilities but were unable to keep up with the needs. Had this situation been anticipated, more and better planning would have resulted.

non-programmed decisions
Responses to infrequent, unforeseen, or very unusual problems and opportunities where the manager does not have a precedent to follow in decision making.

Managers typically follow five steps in the decision-making process, as illustrated in Exhibit 7.8:

1. Recognize or define the problem or opportunity. Although it is more common to focus on problems because of their obvious negative effects, managers who do not take advantage of new opportunities might lose the company's competitive advantage over other firms.
2. Gather information so as to identify alternative solutions or actions.
3. Select one or more alternatives after evaluating the strengths and weaknesses of each possibility. This must be based not only on the ability to solve the problem or take advantage of the opportunity but also on the available resources.
4. Put the chosen alternative into action.
5. Gather information to obtain feedback on the effectiveness of the chosen plan.

concept check

What are the three types of managerial roles?

Give examples of things managers might do when acting in each of the different types of roles.

List the five steps in the decision-making process.

EXHIBIT 7.8 > The Decision-Making Process

5. Check plan effectiveness

4. Put the plan into action

3. Select one or more alternatives

2. Identify possible solutions/actions

1. Define the problem/ recognize the opportunity

Managerial Skills

LO 7

To be successful in planning, organizing, leading, and controlling, managers must use a wide variety of skills. A *skill* is the ability to do something proficiently. Managerial skills fall into three basic categories: conceptual, human relations, and technical skills. The degree to which each type of skill is used depends on the level of the manager's position, as seen in Exhibit 7.9. Additionally, in an increasingly global marketplace, it pays for managers to develop a special set of skills to deal with global management issues.

Technical Skills

technical skills
A manager's specialized areas of knowledge and expertise, as well as the ability to apply that knowledge.

Specialized areas of knowledge and expertise and the ability to apply that knowledge make up a manager's **technical skills**. Preparing a financial statement, programming a computer, designing an office building, and analyzing market research are all examples of technical skills. These types of skills are especially important for supervisory managers, because they work closely with employees who are producing the goods and/or services of the firm.

Human Relations Skills

human relations skills
A manager's interpersonal skills that are used to accomplish goals through the use of human resources.

Human relations skills are the interpersonal skills managers use to accomplish goals through the use of human resources. This set of skills includes the ability to understand human behaviour, to communicate effectively with others, and to motivate individuals to accomplish their objectives. Giving positive feedback to employees, being sensitive to their individual needs, and showing a willingness to empower subordinates are all examples of good human relations skills. Identifying and promoting managers with human relations skills is important for companies. A manager with little or no people skills can end up using an authoritarian leadership style and alienating employees.

	Conceptual Skills	Human Skills	Technical Skills
Top Management			
Middle Management			
Supervisory Management			

Very important   Not as important

At many service companies, one of the keys to success is genuinely friendly service. Achieving their service standards requires genuinely enthusiastic staff. The capacity for such enthusiasm must be determined before the employee is hired. Prospective employees might be asked to take a written test that measures skills and gives personality insights. Once an applicant is hired, the coaching process should begin almost immediately.

Conceptual Skills

conceptual skills
A manager's ability to view the organization as a whole, understand how the various parts are interdependent, and assess how the organization relates to its external environment.

Conceptual skills include the ability to view the organization as a whole, understand how the various parts are interdependent, and assess how the organization relates to its external environment. These skills allow managers to evaluate situations and develop alternative courses of action. Good conceptual skills are especially necessary for managers at the top of the management pyramid, where strategic planning takes place.

Global Management Skills

global management skills
A manager's ability to operate in diverse cultural environments.

Increasingly, Canadian companies are participating in the international marketplace, as discussed in Chapter 2; this has created a need for managers who have global management skills, that is, the ability to operate in diverse cultural environments. With more and more companies choosing to do business in multiple locations around the world, employees are often required to learn the geography, language, and social customs of other cultures. It is expensive to train employees for foreign assignments and pay their relocation costs; therefore, choosing the right person for the job is especially important. Individuals who are open-minded, flexible, willing to try new things, and comfortable in a multicultural setting are good candidates for international management positions.

CONCEPT *in Action* >>>

For many managers, accepting an international position might mean helping their spouses and children adapt to the new environment. What special skills do you think Canadian managers need to be successful in international assignments?

---

concept check

Define the basic managerial skills.

How important is each of these skill sets at the different levels of the management pyramid?

What new challenges do managers face due to increasing globalization?

Although a single manager might possess some or most of the skills described above, rarely does one person excel in all types of managerial skills. Every business needs a leader, but in today's marketplace things move too quickly, the need for specialization is too great, and competition is too fierce for a one-person show to survive.

Trends in Management and Leadership

Three important trends in management today are: crisis management, the growing use of information technology, and the increasing need for global management skills.

Crisis Management

Crises can occur in even the best-managed organizations. For example, the economic crisis of 2008 and beyond was, for the most part, unexpected in the business environment. Another example is power grid meltdowns, where the supply of electricity was suspended because of a system overload. No manager or executive can be completely prepared for these types of unexpected crises. However, how a manager handles the situation could mean the difference between disaster, survival, or even financial gain.

No matter what the crisis, there are some basic guidelines that managers should follow to minimize negative outcomes. Managers should not become immobilized by a problem, nor should they ignore it. Managers should face the problem head on. They should always tell the truth about the situation and then put the best people on the job to correct the problem. They should ask for help if they need it, and, finally, managers must learn from the experience to avoid the same problem in the future.[6]

Managers and Information Technology

The second trend having a major impact on managers is the proliferation of information technology. An increasing number of organizations are selling technology, and an increasing number are looking for cutting-edge technology to make and market the products and services they sell. One particularly useful type of technology is dashboard software. Much like the dashboard in a car, dashboard software gives managers a quick look into the relevant information they need to manage their companies. Most large companies are organized in divisions (which you'll learn about in more detail in Chapter 8), and often each division relies on a particular type of application or database software. Dashboard software allows employees to access information from software they don't routinely use, for example, from an application used by a different division from their own. More important, however, is the ability of a dashboard to show up-to-the-minute information and to allow employees to see all the information they need—like financial and performance data—on a single screen. Such integrated functionality is making dashboards extremely popular.

Managing in Diverse Cultural Environments

The increasing globalization of the world market, as discussed in Chapter 2, has created a need for managers who have global management skills, that is, the ability to operate in diverse cultural environments. As companies expand around the globe, managers will face the challenges of directing the behaviour of employees around the world. They must recognize that because of cultural differences, people respond to similar situations in very different ways. The burden, therefore, falls on the manager to produce results while adapting to the differences among the employees he or she manages. How a manager gets results, wins respect, and leads employees varies greatly among countries, cultures, and individuals.

The best way to meet this challenge of managing international employees is to develop an individual-level program that is based on values and principles. Managers should apply three specific principles to this process: example, involvement, and trust. *Example* means that managers should set and live out the standard for others to follow. They must act as role models for all employees of the organization. Leaders must also create personal *involvement*

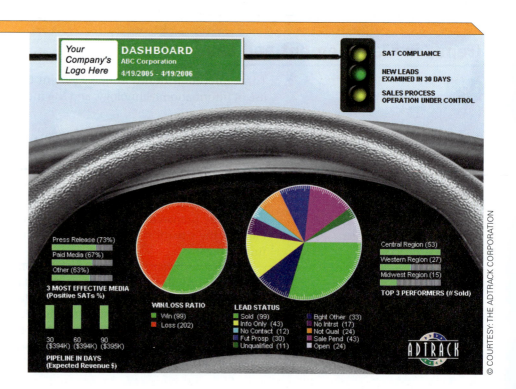

CONCEPT *in Action* >>>

Marketing and sales professionals are increasingly turning to advanced software programs called "dashboards" to monitor business and evaluate performance. These computer tools help managers identify valuable customers, track sales, and align plans with company objectives—all in real time. A typical dashboard might include sales and bookings forecasts, monthly close data, customer satisfaction data, and employee training schedules. How does information technology affect managerial decision making?

concept check

Describe several guidelines for crisis management.

How can information technology aid in decision-making?

What are three principles of managing in diverse cultural environments?

in the organization for all members. Involvement brings the whole person into the company's operations. People are treated like valuable partners, not just as an expense to the company. Leaders must develop a culture of *trust*. This is essential to getting people to invest themselves for the mutual benefit of everyone. When these principles are applied, people are able to manage themselves, and they can release incredible talent and energy.[7]

Despite cultural differences, managing within a different culture is only an extension of what managers do every day. That is, working with differences in employees, processes and projects.

Great Ideas to Use Now

Many of the skills managers use to accomplish organizational goals can be applied outside the organizational setting. You could be using these skills in your life right now to accomplish your personal goals.

Effective Time Management

Successful managers use their time wisely. Adopting the following time management techniques will help you become a more successful student now and will help prepare you for the demands of your future workplace:

- *Plan ahead.* This is first and most obvious. Set both long- and short-term goals. Review your list often, and revise it when your situation changes.
- *Establish priorities.* Decide what is most important and what is most urgent. Sometimes they are not the same thing. Keep in mind the 80–20 rule: 20 percent of one's effort delivers 80 percent of the results.
- *Delegate.* Ask yourself if the task can be accomplished as effectively by someone else. Empower other people, and you might be surprised by the quality of the outcome.
- *Learn to say no.* Be stingy with your time. Be realistic about how long tasks will take. Don't feel guilty when you don't have the time, ability, or inclination to take on an additional task.
- *Batch.* Group activities together so they take up less of your day. For example, set aside a certain time to return phone calls, answer e-mail, and do any necessary written correspondence.
- *Stay on task.* Learn how to handle diversions. For example, let your answering machine take messages until you finish a particular task.
- *Set deadlines.* Don't let projects drag on. Reward yourself each time you cross a certain number of items off your "to do" list.

Stress Management

One of the things that can stop any career in its tracks is burnout. One way to prevent burnout is to examine how well you are dealing with the current stress you are experiencing and learn how to develop coping mechanisms. To start this process, look to see if you are exhibiting any of the warning signs of being overstressed. Students under stress can have a wide range of symptoms, including headaches, asthma attacks, nail biting, and sleep problems.[8] More serious symptoms can include stomach problems and even depression.

If you feel that you are not coping with the stress in your life, now is the time to learn some stress management skills. Here are some helpful ideas:

- Make sure to include physical exercise in your schedule. Try some mind/body work, such as yoga or stretching.
- Find someone you trust and can confide in. Talking out your problems can help a lot.
- If there is no one you feel comfortable talking to, try keeping a diary to work out your stressful situations.
- For more information, visit the Canadian Institute of Stress website: (**www.stresscanada.org**).

Customer Satisfaction and Quality

Dieter Zetsche, CEO of Daimler Chrysler, is known for his participative leadership style, the hallmark of which is listening to the company's employees. But Zetsche also pays very close attention to what the customer is saying. When he became CEO of Chrysler shortly after the company merged with Daimler Benz, Zetsche was charged with turning around the faltering Detroit automaker. During crisis years, the company had historically turned to design as a way to emerge from the brink of disaster. Zetsche, however, knew that design was only part of the solution. He wanted the company to apply its crisis-driven intensity to quality.

Zetsche began by importing the quality-control measures used at Mercedes. If Chrysler's designs and prototypes did not meet quality standards and pass quality checks, the car would not be allowed to move to the next stage of development. Zetsche showed up at test drives for the Chrysler 300, recommended changes and improvements, solicited feedback, and then returned to the test-track to see the results of the changes. He praised the improvements and the engineers' motivation to create the best-quality car the company had ever made. Chrysler sold 120,857 300s in 2004 and received a slew of awards, not to mention rave reviews.

Zetsche paired his focus on quality with a renewed focus on customers—not competitors. Although Chrysler was the originator of the minivan in 1979, the company let its competitive advantage slip away. Twenty years after the first minivans were introduced to the market, Chrysler faced dozens of competitors, including the tremendously successful Honda Odyssey and Toyota Sienna. Management took its eyes off what consumers wanted and spent billions of dollars to keep up with innovations by its Japanese rivals. Chrysler's dominance in the minivan market eroded.

Recognizing a misplaced focus, Zetsche pointed his designers back toward the customer. What did minivan drivers want out of their vans? Engineers identified a common problem: Drivers wanted to be able to reconfigure their vans for more parcels or people on a moment's notice. Other companies were working on this problem as well, but their solutions were difficult to use and their seats were heavy, some weighing over 50 pounds. Chrysler's solution was "Stow and Go" seating that allowed the driver to transform a minivan with seating for eight to a vehicle that could carry two passengers up front and a full-size motorcycle in the back—in less than one minute! As a result, sales of Chrysler minivans began booming, up 20 percent for its flagship Dodge Caravan and Chrysler Town & Country models.[9]

Critical Thinking Questions

- Do you think Chrysler could have achieved its innovation breakthroughs if Dieter Zetsche had been an autocratic leader? Why or why not?
- What kind of participative leader does Zetsche seem to be? Explain your choice.

SOURCE: Fara Warner, "Keeping the Crisis in Chrysler," *Fast Company,* September, 2005, pp. 69–73.

Summary of Learning Outcomes

1 Explain the role of management.

Management is the process of guiding the development, maintenance, and allocation of resources to attain organizational goals. Managers are the people in the organization responsible for developing and carrying out this management process. The four primary functions of managers are planning, organizing, leading, and controlling.

2 Discuss the four types of planning.

Planning is deciding what needs to be done, identifying when and how it will be done, and determining by whom it should be done. Managers use four types of planning: strategic, tactical, operational, and contingency planning. Strategic planning involves creating long-range (one to five years), broad goals and determining the necessary resources to accomplish those goals. Tactical planning has a shorter time frame (less than one year) and more specific objectives that support the broader strategic goals. Operational planning creates specific standards, methods, policies, and procedures that are used in specific functional areas of the organization. Contingency plans identify alternative courses of action for very unusual or crisis situations.

3 List the primary responsibilities of managers in organizing activities.

Organizing involves coordinating and allocating a firm's resources to carry out its plans. It includes developing a structure for the people, positions, departments, and activities within the firm. This is accomplished by dividing up tasks (division of labour), grouping jobs and employees (departmentalization), and assigning authority and responsibilities (delegation).

4 **Describe how leadership styles influence a corporate culture?**

Leading is the process of guiding and motivating others toward the achievement of organizational goals. Managers have unique leadership styles that range from autocratic to free rein. The set of attitudes, values, and standards of behaviour that distinguishes one organization from another is called corporate culture. A corporate culture evolves over time and is based on the accumulated history of the organization, including the vision of the founders.

5 **Examine how organizations control activities.**

Controlling is the process of assessing the organization's progress toward accomplishing its goals. The control process is as follows: set performance standards (goals), measure performance, compare actual performance to established performance standards, take corrective action (if necessary), and use information gained from the process to set future performance standards.

6 **Summarize the roles managers take on in different organizational settings.**

In an informational role, the manager may act as an information gatherer, an information distributor, or a spokesperson for the company. A manager's interpersonal roles are based on various interactions with other people. Depending on the situation, a manager might need to act as a figurehead, company leader, or liaison.

7 **Identify the set of managerial skills necessary for managerial success.**

Managerial skills fall into three basic categories: technical, human relations, and conceptual skills. Specialized areas of knowledge and expertise, and the ability to apply that knowledge, make up a manager's technical skills. Human relations skills include the ability to understand human behaviour, to communicate effectively with others, and to motivate individuals to accomplish their objectives. Conceptual skills include the ability to view the organization as a whole, understand how the various parts are interdependent, and assess how the organization relates to its external environment.

8 **List some of the trends that will affect management in the future.**

Three important trends in management today are: crisis management, the increasing use of information technology, and the need for global management skills. Crisis management requires quick action, telling the truth about the situation, and putting the best people on the task to correct the situation. Management must learn from the crisis to prevent it from happening again. Using the latest information technology, managers can make quicker, better informed decisions. As more companies "go global," the need for multinational cultural management skills is growing. Managers must set a good example, create personal involvement for all employees, and develop a culture of trust.

Key Terms

autocratic leaders   211
coercive power   211
conceptual skills   220
consensual leaders   213
consultative leaders   213
contingency plans   209
controlling   216
corporate culture   214
decisional roles   217
democratic leaders   213
effectiveness   206
efficiency   206
empowerment   214

expert power   211
free-rein (laissez-faire) leadership   213
global management skills   220
human relations skills   219
informational roles   217
interpersonal roles   217
leadership   211
leadership style   211
legitimate power   211
management   206
middle management   210
mission   208
mission statement   208

Experiential Exercises

1. **Would you be a good manager?** Do a self-assessment that includes your current technical, human relations, and conceptual skills. What skills do you already possess, and which do you need to add? Where do your strengths lie? Based on this exercise, develop a description of an effective manager.

2. You are planning to start one of the following companies. Develop a mission statement that defines its vision and give examples of how you would apply each of the four types of planning (strategic, tactical, operational, and contingency) in building the business.

   • Ethnic restaurant near your campus
   • Custom skateboard manufacturer
   • Computer training firm
   • Boutique specializing in Latin American clothing and jewellery

3. Focusing on either your educational institution or a place where you have worked, prepare a brief report on its unique culture. How would you describe it? What has shaped it? What changes do you see occurring over time?

4. Strategic Advantage, (**www.strategy4u.com**), offers many reasons why companies should develop strategic plans, as well as a strategy tip of the month, assessment tools, planning exercises, and resource links. Explore the site to learn the effect of strategic planning on financial performance, and present your evidence to the class. Then select a planning exercise and, with a group of classmates, perform it as it applies to your school.

5. Are you leadership material? Go to the Leadership section at About.com, (**http://management.about/cs/leadership**). Read several articles that interest you to develop a list of characteristics of effective leaders. How do you measure up?

6. How do entrepreneurs develop corporate culture in their companies? Do a search on the term "corporate culture" in *Inc.* (**www.inc.com**), *Entrepreneur* (**www.entrepreneur.com**), or *Fast Company* (**www.fastcompany.com**). Prepare a short presentation for your class that explains the importance of corporate culture and how it's developed in young firms.

Review Questions

1. Briefly describe the four primary management functions.

2. How does proper planning help the organization to achieve its mission statement?

3. What are the impacts on a company that does not allocate its resources properly? (Relate this to their stakeholders.)

4. What are the various power bases? What determines the power in each of these?

5. How do the various leadership styles impact a corporate culture?

6. In what situation would each of the three leadership styles be appropriate?

7. Why is it important for leaders to set performance standards? After the performance standards have been set, what actions should follow?

8. As a manager what are the roles you have to play?

9. What skills are necessary to be an effective manager? How does the focus change between the various levels of management?

10. What are the trends that are becoming more important in leadership?

CREATIVE THINKING CASE >

Managing an Extreme Makeover

During a tour of a Toyota Corolla assembly plant located near their headquarters in Bangalore, India, executives of Wipro Ltd. hit on a revolutionary idea—why not apply Toyota's successful manufacturing techniques to managing their software development and clients' back-office operations business.

"Toyota preaches continuous improvement, respect for employees, learning, and embracing change," says T. K. Kurien, President of Wipro Consulting Services, Global Programs & Strategic Initiatives, Communication & Media. "What we do is apply people, technology, and processes to solve a business problem."

Among the problems spotted early on by Kurien? Cubicles. They're normal for programmers but interrupt the flow for business-process employees. Deciding to position people side by side at long tables assembly-line style "was a roaring disaster," admits Kurien. "The factory idea concerned people." So based on feedback from his middle managers, Kurien arranged classes to explain his concepts and how they would ultimately make life easier for employees.

Wipro also adopted Toyota's kaizen system of soliciting employee suggestions. Priya, who had worked for Wipro for several years, submitted several kaizen and was delighted when her bosses responded promptly to her suggestions. "Even though it's something small, it feels good. You're being considered," she says. Empowerment in the workplace washed over into her private life. As the first woman in her family to attend college, she told her parents they may arrange her marriage only to a man who will not interfere with her career.

Kurien and his managers work hard at boosting employee morale, offering rewards—pens, caps, or shirts—to employees who submit suggestions to kaizen boxes. And each week a top-performing employee receives a cake. Murthy, formerly an accountant and now Senior Vice-president, Retail, Consumer Goods, Transportation & Services, spearheaded an effort to cut government import approval times from 30 to 15 days. He got a cake with his name written on it in honey. "I was surprised management knew what I was doing," he says. "Now I want to do more projects."

With over 900 clients, 95,000+ employees, and 54 development centres across the globe, Wipro is a star of India's burgeoning information technology industry. Today, the company's paperwork processing operations in Pune, Bangalore, and Chennai bear a clear resemblance to a Toyota plant. Two shifts of young men and women line long rows of tables. At the start of each shift team leaders discuss the day's goals and divide up tasks. And just like in a Toyota factory, electronic displays mounted on the walls shift from green to red if things get bogged down.

This obsession with management efficiency has helped India become the back office operation for hundreds of Western companies, resulting in the transfer of many thousands of jobs offshore. "If the Indians get this right, in addition to their low labour rates, they can become deadly competition," says Jeffrey K. Liker, a business professor at the University of Michigan and author of The Toyota Way, a book about Toyota's lean manufacturing techniques. If Kurien's management initiatives succeed, experts may soon be extolling the Wipro way.

Critical Thinking Questions

- What type of manager is T. K. Kurien? How would you characterize his leadership style?
- What managerial role does T. K. Kurien assume in his approach to attaining his division's goal of improved customer service?
- What management skill sets does he exhibit?

SOURCES: Steve Hamm, "Taking a Page from Toyota's Playbook," BusinessWeek Online (www.businessweek.com) August 22, 2005; Theodore Forbath, "Developing an Effective Global Sourcing Strategy," CIO Update, July 22, 2005, (www.cioupdate.com); Toyota company website (www.toyota.com) December 29, 2005; Wipro company website (www.wipro.com) , accessed June 8, 2009.

VIDEO CASE >

SAS Knows How to Keep Employees. . .

Insanity Inc.? "It's been called worse," says James H. Goodnight, CEO, of the company he helped co-found, SAS Institute, Inc. "If you treat people right they will make a difference. What we do here makes good business sense." The millions SAS saves annually, thanks to an employee defection rate of less than 4 percent, proves him right. And what does SAS do with the dollars its saves? It rewards its employees by creating a work environment that no one wants to leave. For the 12th consecutive year SAS has made the FORTUNE magazine " 100 Best Companies to work for" list, ranking number 20, with points awarded for such items as healthcare, childcare and work-life balance.

What would keep you happy on the job? A 35-hour workweek? A health-and-recreational centre with Olympic-sized pool, gym, and basketball court? How about an on-site massage therapist and free daily laundering of your workout clothes? Or unlimited sick days, with free comprehensive health insurance and access to on-site health care at a company-run clinic? And of course there are the usual financial rewards: a competitive salary, bonuses, and a profit-sharing plan.

Impossible you say? Welcome to SAS (**www.sas.com**), the world's largest privately held software company and leader in e-business solutions, where every day is a dress-down day for the over 4,000 people working at the company's 200-acre campus in North Carolina. This group represents a fraction of the 11,000 SAS employees working in more than 50 countries and 400 SAS offices.

Goodnight's free-rein leadership and belief in employee empowerment reflects a corporate culture that supports employees' independent working styles. SAS "hires hard and manages easy." It makes sure employees have the technical and intellectual skills for the job, then lets them get on with it. "We are not into 'face time' here," says Goodnight. "If you need to leave at 4 p.m. on a Wednesday to go watch your child's soccer game, we trust that you will get your work done."

SAS also offers employees unlimited opportunity for growth. Many staffers come as students and stay because they are able to leapfrog around the organization, learning new skills and tackling fresh challenges. Says Goodnight, "SAS is in the intellectual-property business and our employees work on cutting-edge products. Developing employees' intellectual prowess makes them increasingly valuable to the company. It is not a disgrace to fail, as long as they learn something from it and share the information so we can all learn. Our people are our assets and we believe in taking good care of our assets."

Critical Thinking Questions

- Describe the corporate culture at SAS.
- How does Goodnight's leadership support this culture?
- Given your personal experiences in the workplace, compare the SAS environment with what you have experienced.

SOURCE: Adapted from material in the video "Work Hard, Play Hard, and Have a Nice Lunch: Corporate Culture at SAS"; SAS website, (www.sas.com) (accessed March 16, 2003), (www.sas.com/presscenter/bgndr_statistics.html) (accessed May 28, 2009), (www.sas.com/awards/index.html) (accessed May 28, 2009).

Stapling Together an E-Commerce Strategy

Wander into one of more than 300 Staples stores, and you will soon reach an Access Point. These online kiosks link you to Staples.ca or Staples.com, where you can order products, build PCs to order, and tap into an online library with product and service information.

Why have online kiosks in the regular stores? "We're letting customers do business the way they want to do business, not the way we want them to," says Paul Gaffney, executive vice-president and chief information officer (CIO) of the Framingham, Massachusetts-based office supplies superstore chain. The Access Point system increases the available products from about 7,500 stocked in the typical store to 45,000 products and dozens of business services. The build-to-order PC feature is so popular that about 35 percent of Staples stores no longer carry computers on-site.

Access Point is just one of many Staples e-commerce initiatives. The Staples.com website focuses on small-business users, whereas 20,000 medium- to large-size companies use StaplesLink.com, their own specialized business-to-business (B2B) e-commerce site. About 70 percent of Staples Contract Division customers place orders through StaplesLink, where users can pull up real-time inventory availability, company-specific contract pricing, and order status. Corporate purchasing managers like the site, which lets them decentralize office supply purchasing while centralizing and controlling costs.

E-commerce is an integral part of the Staples long-term strategy to redefine the customer experience. The company's slogan—"Staples: That was easy"—is now guiding its business decisions. Making sure the firm's customer-focused, e-commerce technology does, indeed, simplify purchasing for customers falls to CIO Gaffney. The behind-the-scenes integration work that facilitates shoppers buying online or in-store calls for a big-picture, comprehensive strategy. "To best serve our customers, we follow a disciplined approach to our technology and process integration initiatives," he explains. "That approach aligns our portfolio of projects to our overall business goals."

Gaffney has appointed several groups to help him implement his strategies. An e-commerce steering committee composed of both IT and business managers from these areas has become a primary forum for sharing technology across units and creating a common technology infrastructure. As a result, Staples.com and StaplesLink.com now share applications like order processing. Another team with people from all business areas is examining business processes at Staples and looking at how people, process, and technology relate. The goal is to identify projects that will have the greatest impact.

Critical Thinking Questions

1. What special challenges does the CIO face in developing and implementing a firm's e-commerce strategy? Discuss and evaluate Gaffney's approach at Staples.

2. What managerial roles does Gaffney take? How would you describe his leadership style and the corporate culture he is promoting?

3. According to a recent article in CIO magazine, the CIO's role in e-commerce has passed through three stages. In the early years of e-commerce (1996–2000), the CIO took a back seat to the dedicated e-commerce business unit managers. From 2000 to 2002, as the dot-com bubble burst, the CIO moved into a major role in overall e-commerce management, focusing on execution, cost control, and consolidation. Now that e-commerce is considered an essential part of corporate strategy, many industry experts expect business unit leaders to want more control. How should the CIO's role shift to accommodate the maturing of e-commerce? What has Gaffney done to adapt his management approach to this third stage?

SOURCES: Todd Datz, "Strategic Alignment," *CIO*, August 15, 2002, (www.cio.com); "Staples Inc. Corporate Overview," Staples corporate website, (www.staples.com) (accessed April 20, 2003); "Staples Launches National Advertising Campaign to Introduce New Brand Promise," *Business Wire*, February 27, 2003, (www.staples.com); "Staples Launches New Version of StaplesLink.com B-to-B Procurement website," *Business Wire*, February 18, 2003, (www.staples.com); "Staples Inc. Receives CIO Magazine's CIO-100 Award for Technology and Process Integration," *Business Wire*, August 15, 2002, (www.staples.com); Elana Varon, "The New Lords of E-Biz," *CIO*, March 15, 2003, (www.cio.com); (www.staples.ca/ENG/images/pdf/042209.pdf), accessed May 25, 2009.

CHAPTER 8

Making the Connection

Designing Organizational Structures

We saw in the previous chapter how all of the functions of a manager are highly integrated. They are done almost simultaneously, and they affect and are affected by one another. They are the glue that binds the organization together, because it is the process of management that guides the internal organization to achieve its critical success factors, within the external environment that it is faced with, and to the satisfaction of its stakeholders. Sounds complicated, doesn't it? Well, management isn't easy. The rewards of a successful business don't come without effort, but they are definitely worth it. To make it easier, we will examine each of the functions of a manager separately. Just remember that they are connected.

In this chapter, we will examine the design of organizational structures suitable for achieving the goals of the company. Take the example of Navistar, discussed in this chapter. This multi-billion dollar company manufactures, distributes and provides financing for diesel vehicles and engines. It has developed a structure that allows each of its units—trucks, engines, and financing—to operate as independent businesses so each can be flexible enough to deal with its own unique market. However, it still keeps decision-making relatively centralized in order to keep the company working in the most integrative and efficient fashion, and moving in the direction best for the corporation as a whole while maintaining a unified "strategic story." Companies design their structures to suit their own environmental circumstances. Another example is Procter & Gamble (P&G) (discussed in Chapter 7). It made changes to its organizational structure in 2005 to better reach its goal of faster product *innovation*, and increased flexibility and response time. This goal came in reaction to today's rapidly changing business environment, which demands that businesses act more quickly to meet both competitive threats and changing customer needs. Innovation, we know, is a critical success factor, and P&G needed to be a step ahead of the competition. To achieve this goal, it shifted from a geographically-based structure to a structure based on products. It also introduced a new compensation system to encourage innovation. Like Navistar, this is a very integrative example. We can see that the strategic plan fits with the environment, that the organizational structure fits with the strategic plan, and that the tactical plan, in the case of P&G for compensation, was changed to fit with the strategic plan as well.

In fact, you'll see that when organizations change their structures, they are attempting to increase their ability to *satisfy the customer*, the central ingredient to organizational success—whether through centralizing some operations to improve customer service, reduce costs, and ultimately reduce price; decentralizing to be more responsive to customer needs; or using information technology to get closer to the customer.

One of the structural building blocks of the organization is the managerial hierarchy. The traditional configuration is a pyramid structure with employees at the bottom and top management at the top. However, some companies alter this to *improve employee commitment*. One such company is Halsall Associates. As discussed in the chapter, it is one of Canada's leading engineering firms and is considered one of the best places to work in Canada. Halsall has followed the trend that some companies have followed—inverting the pyramid and putting employees at the top.

This demonstrates graphically that "employees are the priority within the company," in the same way that we understand how important a factor employee commitment is to a company's success.

As discussed in the chapter, the organizing or structuring process is accomplished by dividing the work to be done, grouping the parts together, and assigning authority and responsibility. A formal organizational structure is the result of this design process. In this chapter, we describe this formal organization as "human, material, financial, and information resources deliberately connected to form the business organization." In other words, the resources of each functional area are structured in such a way that even though they are in separate areas—human resources, operations, finance, and marketing—they are linked together so that the organization can achieve its goals. If the organization is not structured in this way, with all the parts working together in an integrative way, success is not possible. We know from our discussion in the introduction to the model that all of the critical success factors are connected. They are also connected to each of the functional areas. The most obvious connections are

- achieving financial performance (*finance*);
- meeting and exceeding customer needs (*marketing*);
- providing value—quality products at reasonable prices (*operations* and *marketing*);
- encouraging creativity and innovation (all areas); and
- gaining employee commitment (*human resources*).

However, the parts of the business can't work independently and achieve these success factors. It all starts, as we've said, with the customer. As you'll see in the chapter, every organization is structured with the customer as the central thread. With this in mind, operations and marketing must work together. Marketing determines customer needs and works with operations to design a product to meet those needs. Operations provides the product in a quality manner, and marketing prices it to reflect the level of quality, providing something of value to the customer. They can't do this without people committed to making it work, and they can't keep doing it without fresh ideas that keep the organization providing something that distinguishes it from the competition. All of these areas provide the income for the business, but that money must flow back to each of the areas as needed to fuel the plans. It is therefore necessary that whatever structure is designed should take into consideration the inseparable connections among the different areas of the business.

Certain structures specifically integrate the different functional areas intentionally, so that they are working together on specific projects. A matrix structure is one such example. All areas are represented so that conflicting objectives can be balanced and overall goals, rather than individual ones, become the priority. This structure also allows for other factors that contribute to success—different minds working together increases creativity and innovation, for example.

In a matrix structure, individuals work together on teams. As discussed in the chapter, team-based structures are becoming increasingly used in organizations today. They help the organization in many ways; in particular they help to integrate the different areas of the business as well as to gain employee commitment to the organization's goals. This integration is crucial, as we'll see in our discussion of the functional areas, and is achieved when the teams are cross-functional—made up of employees from different functional areas working together on a common task. Without this integration, and commitment of the employees toward this integration, the areas can't work together to achieve the overall company goals. We've also seen this through our discussion of planning. Different departments or areas within the organization have different roles to play in the overall plan, but they must work together in an integrative fashion to achieve these overall goals.

Another type of structure takes the topic of integration beyond the borders of the business, as is the case with most successful businesses today. As we describe in the chapter, the virtual corporation is a "network of independent companies linked by information technology," which allows them to take advantage of opportunities they couldn't act on alone and share each other's key competencies to become a truly integrative organization. Cisco is one such company at the forefront of this new type of structure. Cisco CEO John Chambers' beliefs reflect the essence of this integrative structure—organizations should be built on change, organized as networks, and based on interdependencies.

CHAPTER 8

Designing Organizational Structures

LEARNING OUTCOMES

1 Identify the five structural building blocks that managers use to design organizations.

2 Examine the tools companies use to establish relationships within their organizations.

3 Show how the degree of centralization/decentralization can be altered to make an organization more successful.

4 Describe the differences between a mechanistic and organic organization.

5 Discuss the contemporary organizational structures companies are using.

6 Summarize why companies are using team-based organizational structures.

7 Explain how the informal organization affects the performance of the company.

8 List some of the trends that are influencing the way businesses organize.

NAVISTAR INTERNATIONAL CORPORATION

As director of corporate communications for Navistar International Corporation, Karen Denning's role in the structuring of the organization might not be apparent initially. After all, you might ask, doesn't communication typically involve marketing? And what does that have to do with organizational structure? As it turns out, quite a bit.

Named to the Fortune 500 Hall of Fame, Navistar history extends back over 175 years when Cyrus Hall McCormick invented the mechanical reaper in 1831 and decided he needed a way to advertise his new invention. Today, it is a $12 billion corporation whose principal activities are divided into three separate industry segments: truck, engine, and financial services. Accounting for almost 70 percent of the corporation's revenues, the truck segment manufactures and distributes a full line of diesel-powered trucks and school buses. The engine segment, which earns Navistar approximately 25 percent of its revenue, designs and manufactures diesel engines for use in selected vehicles produced by the truck industry segment. It also sells engines for industrial, agricultural, and marine applications. The financial services segment, which accounts for the remaining 5 percent of revenue, provides retail, wholesale, and lease financing of products sold by the truck segment and its dealers within the United States and Mexico. Each segment operates as a separate business and is structured to reflect that independence, with its own marketing, manufacturing, engineering, and finance departments. This separation enables each segment to specialize in its own market and to be able to focus on that market's unique challenges and opportunities.

Denning's role, in large part, is to bring these three segments together in a unified "strategic story" and single corporate culture. Despite the separation between its three segments, Navistar maintains a relatively centralized decision-making process. In part, this is due to the nature of manufacturing, an industry with high capital investments and long product development timetables. Decisions made today have the potential to significantly affect outcomes several months or years down the line, and how issues are handled in one segment can easily impact the entire organization. Even management issues that seem simple, such as those involving hourly workers, are sensitive—in this case, due to the workers' union representation by the United Auto Workers. Thus, each decision needs the careful attention of the management that oversees the whole corporation, and these decisions need to be communicated to the rest of the corporation in a way that ensures the successful execution of a unified vision. "As director of corporate communication, I work with the CEO and executive council to craft the strategic story and communicate where they want to take the company, both to those internally and externally. Additionally, I help them communicate with the board of directors and shareholders who are influential in approving and directing where the company is going strategically. In this way, I facilitate the smooth use of the organizational structure by ensuring communication between all levels of Navistar."

This chapter focuses on the different types of organizational structure, the reasons an organization might prefer one structure over another, and how the choice of an organizational structure ultimately can impact that organization's success.

Critical Thinking Questions

1. **What organizational structure does Navistar International seem to reflect?**

2. **What are the advantages and disadvantages of this structure?**

SOURCE: From Gitman/McDaniel, *The Future of Business*, 6E. © 2008 South-Western, a part of Cengage Learning Inc. Reproduced by permission. www.cengage.com/permissions

In today's dynamic business environment, organizational structures need to be designed so that the organization can respond quickly to new competitive threats and changing customer needs. Future success for companies will depend on the company's ability to be flexible and respond to the needs of customers. In this chapter, we'll look first at how companies build organizational structures. Then, we'll explore how managers establish the relationships within the structures they have designed, including determining lines of communication, authority, and power. We will examine some contemporary structures and the use of teams in organizations. Finally, we'll examine the new trends that are changing the choices companies make about organizational design.

Building Organizational Structures

As you learned in Chapter 7, the key functions that managers perform include planning, organizing, leading, and controlling. This chapter focuses specifically on the organizing function. Organizing involves coordinating and allocating a firm's resources so that the firm can carry out its plans and achieve its goals. This organizing, or structuring, process is accomplished by

- determining work activities and dividing up tasks (division of labour),
- grouping jobs and employees (departmentalization), and
- assigning authority and responsibilities (delegation).

formal organization
The order and design of relationships within a firm; consists of two or more people working together with a common objective and clarity of purpose.

The result of the organizing process is a formal organizational structure. A **formal organization** is the order and design of relationships within the firm. It consists of two or more people working together with a common objective and clarity of purpose. Formal organizations also have well-defined lines of authority, channels for information flow, and means of control. Human, material, financial, and information resources are deliberately connected to form the business organization. Some connections are long lasting, such as the links among people in the finance or marketing department. Others can be changed at almost any time, as when a committee is formed to study a problem.

Every organization has some kind of underlying structure. Traditional structures are more rigid and group employees by function, products, processes, customers, or regions, as described in the next section. Contemporary and team-based structures

CONCEPT *in Action* >>>
Founded in 1943, IKEA has grown from a small mail-order operation into an international home-furnishings retailer with over 230 stores in 33 countries throughout Europe, North America, and Asia. Best known for its intriguing modern furniture designs, highly trafficked store openings, and quirky advertising, the IKEA Group consists of multiple corporate divisions corresponding to the company's retail, purchasing, sales, and design and manufacturing functions. What factors likely influenced the development of IKEA's organizational structure as the company changed over the years?

©PAT GOH SENG/BLOOMBERG NEWS/LANDOV

are more flexible and assemble employees to respond quickly to dynamic business environments. Regardless of the structural skeleton a company chooses to implement, all managers must first consider what kind of work needs to be done within the firm.

Division of Labour

division of labour
The process of dividing work into separate jobs and assigning tasks to workers.

specialization
The degree to which tasks are subdivided into smaller jobs.

The process of dividing work into separate jobs and assigning tasks to workers is called **division of labour**. In a fast-food restaurant, for example, some employees take or fill orders, others prepare food, a few clean and maintain equipment, and at least one supervises all the others. In an auto assembly plant, some workers install rear-view mirrors, whereas others mount bumpers on bumper brackets. The degree to which the tasks are subdivided into smaller jobs is called **specialization**. Employees who work at highly specialized jobs, such as assembly-line workers, perform a limited number and variety of tasks. Employees, who become specialists at one task, or a small number of tasks, develop greater skill in doing that particular job. This can lead to greater efficiency and consistency in production and other work activities. However, a high degree of specialization can also result in employees who are disinterested or bored due to the lack of variety and challenge. In Chapter 9, we will discuss ways managers can mitigate the disadvantages of a highly specialized workforce.

Departmentalization

departmentalization
The process of grouping jobs together so that similar or associated tasks and activities can be coordinated.

functional departmentalization
Departmentalization that is based on the primary functions performed within an organizational unit.

product departmentalization
Departmentalization that is based on the goods or services produced or sold by the organizational unit.

process departmentalization
Departmentalization that is based on the production process used by the organizational unit.

customer departmentalization
Departmentalization that is based on the primary type of customer served by the organizational unit.

geographic departmentalization
Departmentalization that is based on the geographic segmentation of the organizational units.

organizational chart
A visual representation of the structured relationships among tasks and the people given the authority to do those tasks.

After a company divides into jobs the work it needs to do, managers then group the jobs together so that similar or associated tasks and activities can be coordinated. This grouping of people, tasks, and resources into organizational units is called **departmentalization** and facilitates the planning, leading, and control processes. As Exhibit 8.1 shows, five basic types of departmentalization are commonly used in organizations:

1. *Functional departmentalization*, which is based on the primary functions performed within an organizational unit (marketing, finance, production, sales, and so on).
2. *Product departmentalization*, which is based on the goods or services produced or sold by the organizational unit (such as outpatient/emergency services, pediatrics, cardiology, and orthopedics).
3. *Process departmentalization*, which is based on the production process used by the organizational unit (such as lumber cutting and treatment, furniture finishing, shipping).
4. *Customer departmentalization*, which is based on the primary type of customer served by the organizational unit (such as wholesale or retail purchasers).
5. *Geographic departmentalization*, which is based on the geographic segmentation of organizational units (such as Canadian and U.S. marketing, European marketing, South American marketing).

Once companies choose a method of departmentalization, they must then establish the relationships within that structure. In other words, the company must decide how many layers of management it needs and who will report to whom. The company must also decide how much control to invest in each of its managers and where in the organization decisions will be made and implemented.

Organizational Chart for a Typical Retailer

An **organization chart** is a visual representation of the structured relationships among tasks, responsibilities, and the people given the authority to do those tasks. In the organization chart in Exhibit 8.2, each figure represents a job, and each job includes several tasks.

EXHIBIT 8.1 > Five Traditional Ways to Organize

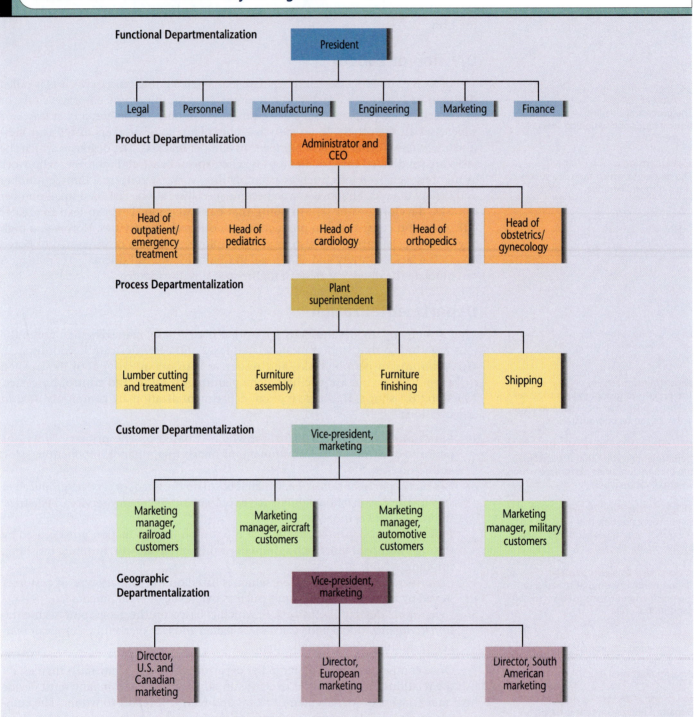

Functional Departmentalization

President

Legal | Personnel | Manufacturing | Engineering | Marketing | Finance

Product Departmentalization

Administrator and CEO

Head of outpatient/ emergency treatment | Head of pediatrics | Head of cardiology | Head of orthopedics | Head of obstetrics/ gynecology

Process Departmentalization

Plant superintendent

Lumber cutting and treatment | Furniture assembly | Furniture finishing | Shipping

Customer Departmentalization

Vice-president, marketing

Marketing manager, railroad customers | Marketing manager, aircraft customers | Marketing manager, automotive customers | Marketing manager, military customers

Geographic Departmentalization

Vice-president, marketing

Director, U.S. and Canadian marketing | Director, European marketing | Director, South American marketing

As an example, Exhibit 8.2 shows the executive as departmentalized by function. Reporting to the Chief Operating Officer are the District Managers (geographical) who are then responsible for the Sales Managers (by customer/consumer). The Sales Managers oversee the Sales Associates (by product).

People are assigned to a particular organizational unit because they perform similar or related tasks, or because they are jointly responsible for a product, client, or market. Decisions about how to departmentalize affect the way in which management assigns

EXHIBIT 8.2 > Organizational Chart for a Typical Retailer

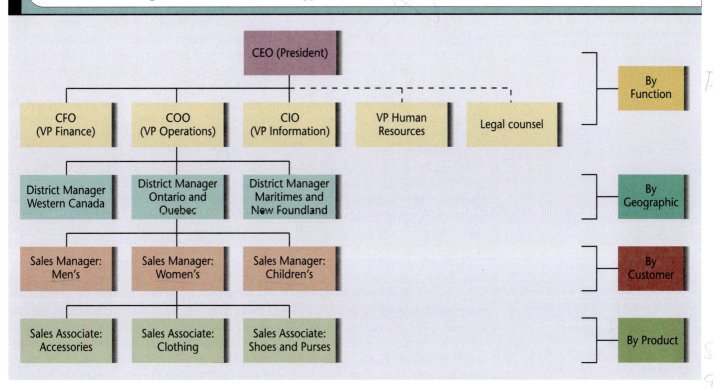

authority, distributes resources, rewards performance, and sets up lines of communication. Many large organizations use several types of departmentalization. For example, a global company might be departmentalized first geographically (North American, European, and Asian units), then by product line (foods/beverages and health care), and finally by functional area (marketing, operations, finance, and so on).

Managerial Hierarchy

managerial hierarchy
The levels of management within an organization; typically includes top, middle, and supervisory management.

Managerial hierarchy (also called the *management pyramid*), is defined by the levels of management within an organization. Generally, the management structure has three levels: top, middle, and supervisory management. These three levels were introduced in Chapter 7.

In a managerial hierarchy, each organizational unit is controlled and supervised by a manager in a higher unit. The person with the most formal authority is at the top of the hierarchy. The higher a manager, the more power he or she has. Thus, the amount of power decreases as you move down the management pyramid. At the same time, the number of employees increases as you move down the hierarchy.

Not all companies today are using this traditional configuration. An interesting trend in designing a company's management structure is the inverted pyramid. For instance, Toronto-based Halsall Associates Ltd., an engineering firm, describes itself just that way.[1] When the president of the company, Peter Halsall, discusses his management structure, he draws an upside-down pyramid. At the bottom of the pyramid, he puts himself. Above him, he lists the layers of management and, finally, the front-line employees. The reason he does this is to show graphically that the employees are the priority within the company. He explains, "Decisions are made so these people maximize their opportunities." This unusual view must pay off: Halsall Associates is one of Canada's leading engineering firms and is considered one of the best places to work.

An organization with a well-defined hierarchy has a clear **chain of command,** which is the line of authority that extends from one level of the organization to the next, from top to bottom, and makes clear who reports to whom. The chain of command is shown in the organization chart and can be traced from the CEO all the way down to the employees producing goods and services. Under the *unity of command* principle, everyone reports to and gets instructions from only one boss. Unity of command guarantees that everyone will have a direct supervisor and will not be taking orders from a number of supervisors. Unity of command and chain of command give everyone in the organization clear directions and help coordinate people doing different jobs.

The growth of the global marketplace has led some companies to examine the traditional principle of unity of command with a single person at the top of the organization. These organizations are finding the need for quick decision making and flexibility in every worldwide location too difficult for any one individual to handle. Many companies are moving to alternative management models, including co-CEOs or even a committee model of leadership.

Individuals who are part of the chain of command have authority over other persons in the organization. **Authority** is legitimate power, granted by the organization and acknowledged by employees, that allows an individual to request action and expect compliance. Exercising authority means making decisions and seeing that they are carried out. Most managers delegate, or assign, some degree of authority and responsibility to others below them in the chain of command. The **delegation of authority** makes the employees accountable to their supervisor. *Accountability* means responsibility for outcomes. Typically, authority and responsibility move downward through the organization as managers assign activities to, and share decision making with, their subordinates. Accountability moves upward in the organization as managers in each successively higher level are held accountable for the actions of their subordinates.

Span of Control

The fourth structural building block is the managerial span of control. Each firm must decide how many managers are needed at each level of the management hierarchy to effectively supervise the work performed within organizational units. A manager's **span of control** (sometimes called *span of management*) is the number of employees

chain of command
The line of authority that extends from one level of an organization's hierarchy to the next, from top to bottom, and makes clear who reports to whom.

authority
Legitimate power, granted by the organization and acknowledged by employees, that allows an individual to request action and expect compliance.

delegation of authority
The assignment of some degree of authority and responsibility to persons lower in the chain of command.

span of control
The number of employees a manager directly supervises; also called span of management.

CONCEPT *in Action* >>>

The span of control is wide for employees who have highly special ized and similar skills like these memory chip technicians. A wide span of control means that managers can supervise more employees. Discuss what criteria determines how many subordinates a manager can manage.

© CHARLES O'REAR/CORBIS

EXHIBIT 8.3 > Narrow and Wide Spans of Control

	Advantages	Disadvantages
Narrow span of control	• High degree of control. • Fewer subordinates may mean manager is more familiar with each individual. • Close supervision can provide immediate feedback.	• More levels of management, therefore more expensive • Slower decision making due to vertical layers. • Isolation of top management. • Discourages employee autonomy. • Less control.
Wide span of control	• Fewer levels of management means increased efficiency and reduced costs. • Increased subordinate autonomy leads to quicker decision making. • Greater organizational flexibility. • Higher levels of job satisfaction due to employee empowerment.	• Possible lack of familiarity due to large number of subordinates. • Managers spread so thinly that they can't provide necessary leadership or support. • Lack of coordination or synchronization.

the manager directly supervises. It can be as narrow as 2 or 3 employees or as wide as 50 or more. In general, the larger the span of control, the more efficient the organization is. As Exhibit 8.3 shows, however, both narrow and wide spans of control have benefits and drawbacks.

If hundreds of employees perform the same job, one supervisor might be able to manage a very large number of employees. Such might be the case at a clothing plant, where hundreds of sewing machine operators work from identical patterns. But if employees perform complex and dissimilar tasks, a manager can effectively supervise only a much smaller number. For instance, a supervisor in the research and development area of a pharmaceutical company might oversee just a few research chemists because of the highly complex nature of their jobs.

The optimal span of control is determined by the following five factors:

1. *Nature of the task.* The more complex the task, the narrower the span of control.
2. *Location of the workers.* The more locations, the narrower the span of control.
3. *Ability of the manager to delegate responsibility.* The greater the ability to delegate, the wider the span of control.
4. *Amount of interaction and feedback between the workers and the manager.* The more feedback and interaction required, the narrower the span of control.
5. *Level of skill and motivation of the workers.* The higher the skill level and motivation, the wider the span of control.

Degree Of Centralization

centralization
The degree to which formal authority is concentrated in one area or level of an organization.

decentralization
The process of pushing decision-making authority down the organizational hierarchy.

The final component in building an effective organizational structure is deciding at what level in the organizational decisions should be made. **Centralization** is the degree to which formal authority is concentrated in one area or level of the organization. In a highly centralized structure, top management makes most of the key decisions in the organization, with very little input from lower-level employees. Centralization lets top managers develop a broad view of operations and exercise tight financial controls. It can also help to reduce costs by eliminating redundancy in the organization. But centralization can also mean that lower-level personnel don't get a chance to develop their decision making and leadership skills, and that the organization is less able to respond quickly to customer demands.

Decentralization is the process of pushing decision-making authority down the organizational hierarchy, giving lower-level personnel more responsibility and power to make and implement decisions. Benefits of decentralization can include quicker decision making, increased levels of innovation and creativity, greater organizational flexibility, faster development of lower-level managers, and increased levels of job satisfaction and employee commitment. But decentralization can also be risky. If lower-level personnel don't have the necessary skills and training to perform effectively, they might make costly mistakes. Additionally, decentralization can increase the likelihood of inefficient lines of communication, incongruent or competing objectives, and duplication of effort.

Several factors must be considered when deciding how much decision-making authority to delegate throughout the organization. These factors include the size of the organization, the speed of change in its environment, managers' willingness to give up authority, employees' willingness to accept more authority, and the organization's geographic dispersion.

Decentralization is usually desirable when the following conditions are met:

- The organization is very large, such as Magna, Petro-Canada, or Ford.
- The firm is in a dynamic environment where quick, local decisions must be made, as in many high-tech industries.
- Managers are willing to share power with their subordinates.
- Employees are willing and able to take more responsibility.
- The company is spread out geographically, such as The Bay, Parmalat Canada, and Prudential Financial.

As organizations grow and change, they continually re-evaluate their structure to determine whether it is helping the company achieve its goals.

concept check

What factors determine the optimal span of control?

What are the primary characteristics of a decentralized organization?

What factors should be considered when choosing the degree of centralization?

Organizational Design Considerations

You are now familiar with the different ways to structure an organization, but as a manager, how do you decide which design will work the best for your business? What works for one company may not work for another. In this section, we'll look at two generic models of organizational design and briefly examine a set of contingency factors that favour each.

Mechanistic Versus Organic Structures

mechanistic organization
An organizational structure that is characterized by a relatively high degree of job specialization, rigid departmentalization, many layers of management, narrow spans of control, centralized decision making, and a long chain of command.

organic organization
An organizational structure that is characterized by a relatively low degree of job specialization, loose departmentalization, few levels of management, wide spans of control, decentralized decision making, and a short chain of command.

Structural design generally follows one of the two basic models described in Exhibit 8.4: mechanistic or organic. A **mechanistic organization** is characterized by a relatively high degree of job specialization, rigid departmentalization, many layers of management (particularly middle management), narrow spans of control, centralized decision making, and a long chain of command. This combination of elements results in what is called a tall organizational structure. The Canadian Armed Forces and the United Nations are typical mechanistic organizations.

In contrast, an **organic organization** is characterized by a relatively low degree of job specialization, loose departmentalization, few levels of management, wide spans of control, decentralized decision making, and a short chain of command. This combination of elements results in what is called a flat organizational structure. Colleges and universities tend to have flat organizational structures, with only two or three levels of administration between the faculty and the president. Exhibit 8.5 shows examples of flat and tall organizational structures.

Factors Influencing the Choice Between Mechanistic Versus Organic Structures

Although few organizations are purely mechanistic or purely organic, most tend more toward one type or the other. The decision to create a more mechanistic or a more

EXHIBIT 8.4 > Mechanistic Versus Organic

Structural Characteristic	Mechanistic	Organic
Job specialization	High	Low
Departmentalization	Rigid	Loose
Management hierarchy (levels of management)	Tall (many levels)	Flat (few levels)
Span of control	Narrow	Wide
Decision-making authority	Centralized	Decentralized
Chain of command	Long	Short

organic structural design is based on factors such as the firm's overall strategy, the size of the organization, the types of technologies used in the organization, and the stability of its external environment, among others.

A company's organizational structure should enable it to achieve its goals, and because setting corporate goals is part of a firm's overall strategy-making process, it follows that a company's structure depends on its strategy. Recall the example of how Hewlett-Packard's CEO, Mark Hurd, is working to untangle the unwieldy organizational structure put in place by his predecessor. Hurd has flattened H-P's 14 layers of

EXHIBIT 8.5 > Flat Versus Tall Organizational Structures

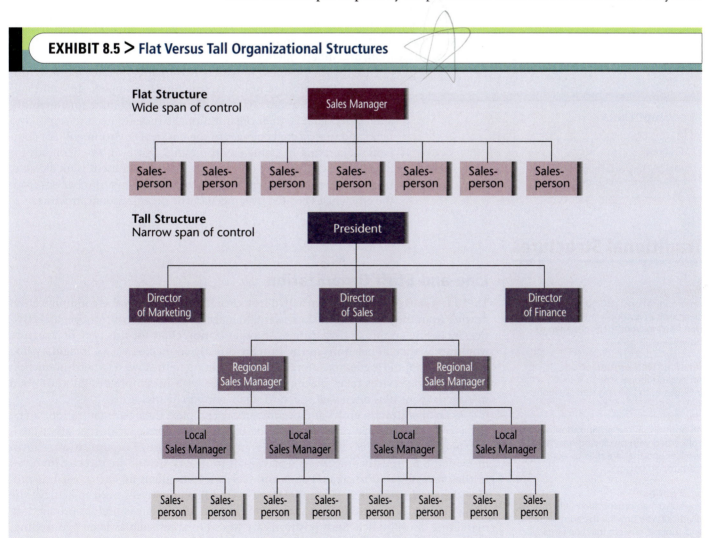

management to have more executive vice-presidents reporting directly to the CEO. Business units will have more autonomy to execute their plans combined with increased accountability for their results. H-P has simply aligned its structure with its strategy.[2]

That alignment can be challenging for struggling companies trying to accomplish multiple goals. For example, a company with an innovation strategy will need the flexibility and fluid movement of information that an organic organization provides. But a company using a cost-control strategy will require the efficiency and tight control of a mechanistic organization. Often, struggling companies try to simultaneously increase innovation and reduce costs, which can be organizational challenges for managers. Such is the case at Sony, whose CEO, Howard Stringer, cut 10,000 jobs, closed factories, and shuffled management in an attempt to control costs and improve efficiency. At the same time, he is also trying to encourage cross-divisional communication (like between the music and electronics divisions) and increase the pace of innovation. Stringer will need to balance these two strategies regardless of which organizational model he relies on most.[3]

Another factor that affects how mechanistic or organic a company's organizational structure is, is its size. Much research has been conducted that shows a company's size has a significant impact on its organizational structure.[4] Smaller companies tend to follow the more organic model, in part because they can. It is much easier to be successful with decentralized decision making, for example, if you have only 50 employees. A company with that few employees is also more likely, by virtue of its size, to have a lesser degree of employee specialization. That's because when there are fewer people to do the work, those people tend to know more about the entire process. As a company grows, it becomes more mechanistic, as systems are put in place to manage the greater number of employees. Procedures, rules, and regulations replace flexibility, innovation, and independence.

Lastly, the business in which a company operates has a significant impact on its organizational structure. In complex, dynamic, and unstable environments, companies need to organize for flexibility and agility. That is, their organizational structures need to respond to rapid and unexpected changes in the business environment. For companies operating in stable environments, however, the demands for flexibility and agility are not so great. The environment is predictable. In a simple, stable environment, therefore, companies benefit from the efficiencies created by a mechanistic organizational structure.

concept check

Compare and contrast mechanistic and organic organizations.

What factors determine whether an organization should be mechanistic or organic?

Traditional Structures

line organization
An organizational structure with direct, clear lines of authority and communication flowing from the top managers downward.

line-and-staff organization
An organizational structure that includes both line and staff positions.

line positions
All positions in the organization directly concerned with producing goods and services and that are directly connected from top to bottom.

staff positions
Positions in an organization held by individuals who provide the administrative and support services that line employees need to achieve the firm's goals.

Line-and-Staff Organization

The **line organization** is designed with direct, clear lines of authority and communication flowing from the top managers downward. Managers have direct control over all activities, including administrative duties. An organization chart for this type of structure would show that all positions in the firm are directly connected via an imaginary line extending from the highest position in the organization to the lowest (where production of goods and services takes place). This structure with its simple design and broad managerial control is often well suited to small, entrepreneurial firms.

As an organization grows and becomes more complex, the line organization can be enhanced by adding staff positions to the design. Staff positions provide specialized advisory and support services to line managers in the **line-and-staff organization,** shown in Exhibit 8.6. In daily operations, individuals in **line positions** are directly involved in the processes used to create goods and services. Individuals in **staff positions** provide the administrative and support services that line employees need to achieve the firm's goals. Line positions in organizations are typically in areas such as production, marketing, and finance. Staff positions are found in areas such as legal counselling, managerial consulting, public relations, and human resource management.

EXHIBIT 8.6 > Line-and-Staff Organization

Line functions
Staff functions

President

Corporate attorney — Assistant to president

Vice-president of marketing | Vice-president of manufacturing | Vice-president of finance

Marketing research specialist — Advertising specialist | Quality-control engineer | Internal auditor

Sales manager | Sales manager | Sales manager | Supervisor | Supervisor | Supervisor | Supervisor | Cost accountant | Credit analyst

Contemporary Structures

LO 5

Although traditional forms of departmentalization still represent how many companies organize their work, newer, more flexible organizational structures are in use at many firms. Let's look at matrix and committee structures, and how those two types of organizations are helping companies better leverage the diverse skills of their employees.

Matrix Structure

matrix structure (project management)
An organizational structure that combines functional and product departmentalization by bringing together people from different functional areas of the organization to work on a special project.

The **matrix structure** (also called the *project management* approach) is sometimes used in conjunction with the traditional line-and-staff structure in an organization. Essentially, this structure combines two different forms of departmentalization, functional and product, that have complementary strengths and weaknesses. The matrix structure brings together people from different functional areas of the organization (such as manufacturing, finance, and marketing) to work on a special project. Each employee has two direct supervisors: the line manager from her or his specific functional area and the project manager. Exhibit 8.7 shows a matrix organization with four special project groups (A, B, C, D), each with its own project manager. Because of the dual chain of command, the matrix structure presents some unique challenges for both managers and subordinates.

Advantages of the matrix structure include the following:

- *Teamwork.* By pooling the skills and abilities of various specialists, the company can increase creativity and innovation and tackle more complex tasks.
- *Efficient use of resources.* Project managers use only the specialized staff they need to get the job done instead of building large groups of underused personnel.
- *Flexibility.* The project structure is flexible and can adapt quickly to changes in the environment; the group can be disbanded quickly when it is no longer needed.
- *Ability to balance conflicting objectives.* The customer wants a quality product and predictable costs. The organization wants high profits and the development of technical capability for the future. These competing goals serve as a focal point for directing activities and overcoming conflict. The marketing representative can

CONCEPT *in Action* >>>

Like the futuristic characters trapped in a dizzying web of confusion in the movie The Matrix Revolutions, some managers experience chaos within a contemporary organizational structure known as the matrix. Advocates of matrix structures claim that combining the functional and product forms of departmentalization leads to greater innovation and responsiveness to markets, but others say having multiple supervisors and hierarchies invariably leads to power struggles and confusion among team members. Are workers capable of serving two masters?

EXHIBIT 8.7 > Matrix Organization

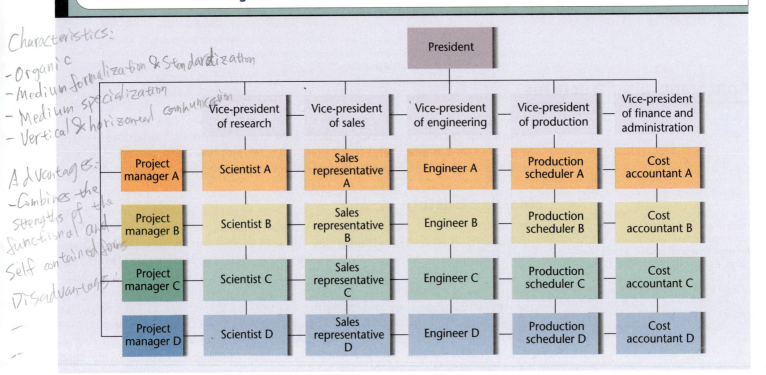

Handwritten margin notes:

Characteristics:
- Organic
- Medium formalization & Standardization
- Medium specialization
- Vertical & horizontal communication

Advantages:
- Combines the strengths of the functional and self contained form

Disadvantages:
-
--

Unitee of Comand

represent the customer, the finance representative can advocate high profits, and the engineers can push for technical capabilities.

- *Higher performance.* Employees working on special project teams may experience increased feelings of ownership, commitment, and motivation.
- *Opportunities for personal and professional development.* The project structure gives individuals the opportunity to develop and strengthen technical and interpersonal skills.

Disadvantages of the matrix structure include the following:

- *Power struggles.* Functional and product managers might have differing goals and management styles.

- *Confusion among team members.* Reporting relationships and job responsibilities might be unclear.
- *Lack of cohesiveness.* Team members from different functional areas might have difficulty communicating effectively and working together as a team.

Although project-based matrix organizations can improve a company's flexibility and teamwork, some companies are trying to unravel complex matrix structures that create limited accountability. For example, during the first year as CEO of Hewlett-Packard, Mark Hurd worked diligently to untangle the complex matrix structure implemented by his predecessor, Carly Fiorina. The reason Hurd gave for tossing out Fiorina's matrix management structure, which muddied responsibilities, was to give business heads more control of their units. "The more accountable I can make you, the easier it is for you to show you're a great performer," says Hurd. "The more I use a matrix, the easier I make it to blame someone else."[5]

Committee Structure

committee structure
An organizational structure in which authority and responsibility are held by a group rather than an individual.

In **committee structure,** authority and responsibility are held by a group rather than an individual. Committees are typically part of a larger line-and-staff organization. Often the committee's role is only advisory, but in some situations the committee has the power to make and implement decisions. Committees can make the coordination of tasks in the organization much easier. For example, Novartis, the huge Swiss pharmaceutical company, revamped the structure of its committees, which report to its board of directors. The company reflects best practices in global corporate governance. Novartis has four permanent committees reporting to the board: the chairman's committee, the compensation committee, the audit and compliance committee, and the corporate governance committee. The chairman's committee deals with business matters arising between board meetings and is responsible for high-level appointments and acquisitions. The compensation committee looks at the remuneration of board members, whereas the audit and compliance committee oversees accounting and financial reporting practices. The corporate governance committee's duties include focusing on board nominations, board performance evaluations, and possible conflicts of interest.[6]

Committees bring diverse viewpoints to a problem and expand the range of possible solutions, but there are some drawbacks. Committees can be slow to reach a decision and are sometimes dominated by a single individual. It is also more difficult to hold any one individual accountable for a decision made by a group. Committee meetings can sometimes go on for long periods of time with little seemingly being accomplished.

Using Teams to Enhance Motivation and Performance

One of the most apparent trends in business today is the use of teams to accomplish organizational goals. Using a team-based structure can increase individual and group motivation and performance. This section gives a brief overview of group behaviour, defines work teams as specific types of groups, and provides suggestions for creating high-performing teams.

Understanding Group Behaviour

Teams are a specific type of organizational group. Every organization contains groups, social units of two or more people who share the same goals and cooperate to achieve those goals. Understanding some fundamental concepts related to group behaviour and group processes provides a good foundation for understanding concepts about work teams. Groups can be formal or informal in nature. Formal groups are designated and sanctioned by the organization; their behaviour is directed toward accomplishing organizational goals. Informal groups are based on social relationships and are not determined or sanctioned by the organization.

Formal organizational groups, like the sales department at Dell Computers, must operate within the larger Dell organizational system. To some degree, elements of the larger Dell system, such as organizational strategy, company policies and procedures, available resources, and the highly motivated employee corporate culture, determine the behaviour of smaller groups, like the sales department, within Dell. Other factors that affect the behaviour of organizational groups are individual member characteristics (e.g., ability, training, personality), the roles and norms of group members, and the size and cohesiveness of the group. Norms are the implicit behavioural guidelines of the group, or the standards for acceptable and non-acceptable behaviour. For example, a Dell sales manager may be expected to work at least two Saturdays per month without extra pay. Although this isn't written anywhere, it is the expected norm.

group cohesiveness
The degree to which group members want to stay in the group and tend to resist outside influences.

Group cohesiveness refers to the degree to which group members want to stay in the group and tend to resist outside influences (such as a change in company policies). When group performance norms are high, group cohesiveness will have a positive impact on productivity. Cohesiveness tends to increase when the size of the group is small, individual and group goals are similar, the group has high status in the organization, rewards are group based rather than individual based, and the group competes with other groups within the organization. Work group cohesiveness can benefit the organization in several ways including increased productivity, enhanced worker self-image because of group success, increased company loyalty, reduced employee turnover, and reduced absenteeism. Southwest Airlines is known for its work group cohesiveness. On the other hand, cohesiveness can also lead to restricted output, resistance to change, and conflict with other work groups in the organization.

The opportunity to turn the decision-making process over to a group with diverse skills and abilities is one of the arguments for using work groups (and teams) in organizational settings. For group decision making to be most effective, however, both managers and group members must understand its strengths and weaknesses (see Exhibit 8.8).

Work Groups Versus Work Teams

work groups
The groups that share resources and coordinate efforts to help members better perform their individual jobs.

We have already noted that teams are a special type of organizational group, but we also need to differentiate between work groups and work teams. **Work groups** share

---

EXHIBIT 8.8 > Strengths and Weaknesses of Group Decision Making

Strengths	Weaknesses
• Groups bring more information and knowledge to the decision process.	• Groups typically take a longer time to reach a solution than an individual takes.
• Groups offer a diversity of perspectives and, therefore, generate a greater number of alternatives.	• Group members may pressure others to conform, reducing the likelihood of disagreement.
• Group decision making results in a higher-quality decision than does individual decision making.	• The process may be dominated by one or a small number of participants.
• Participation of group members increases the likelihood that a decision will be accepted.	• Groups lack accountability, because it is difficult to assign responsibility for outcomes to any one individual.

work teams
Like a work group, but also requires the pooling of knowledge, skills, abilities, and resources to achieve a common goal.

resources and coordinate efforts to help members better perform their individual duties and responsibilities. The performance of the group can be evaluated by adding up the contributions of the individual group members. Work teams require not only coordination but also collaboration, the pooling of knowledge, skills, abilities, and resources in a collective effort to attain a common goal. A work team creates synergy, causing the performance of the team as a whole to be greater than the sum of team members' individual contributions. Simply assigning employees to groups and labelling them a team does not guarantee a positive outcome. Managers and team members must be committed to creating, developing, and maintaining high-performance work teams. Factors that contribute to their success are discussed later in this section.

Types of Teams

problem-solving teams
Usually members of the same department who meet regularly to suggest ways to improve operations and solve specific problems.

The evolution of the team concept in organizations can be seen in three basic types of work teams: problem solving, self-managed, and cross-functional. Problem-solving teams are typically made up of employees from the same department or area of expertise and from the same level of the organizational hierarchy. They meet on a regular basis to share information and discuss ways to improve processes and procedures in specific functional areas. Problem-solving teams generate ideas and alternatives and may recommend a specific course of action, but they typically do not make final decisions, allocate resources, or implement change.

self-managed work teams
Teams without formal supervision that plan, select alternatives, and evaluate their own performance.

Many organizations that experienced success using problem-solving teams were willing to expand the team concept to allow team members greater responsibility in making decisions, implementing solutions, and monitoring outcomes. These highly autonomous groups are called self-managed work teams. They manage themselves without any formal supervision, taking responsibility for setting goals, planning and scheduling work activities, selecting team members, and evaluating team performance.

Making Ethical Choices

TEAM SPIRIT—OH, REALLY?

You work in the HR department of a corporation that focuses on training and organizational development. Over the next year, you will be creating a division devoted to managing virtual teams that are responsible for developing new training materials or updating existing ones. The job is organized so that you are spending your first year being mentored by your boss, the vice-president of HR.

With full understanding of the benefits technology brings to virtual teams, you are also aware of the need for trust among members of virtual teams. The first project you are following is a virtual team tasked with updating one of the corporation's most sought-after guides. The HR vice-president appointed all team members and assigned one person as the team leader. None of the team members knows the others, and the team leader is the only team member who has direct contact with your boss. In following the team's work, you realize that no one knows exactly what each member has contributed, because members are not in contact with each other. Their only contact is with the team leader.

Your sense is that the team leader is taking full credit for all the work. Not only is she the only one with direct contact to your boss, she lives in the same area as the corporation's headquarters. The other team members are located across the country. Your sense is confirmed when only the team leader is invited to the annual awards dinner and at the dinner receives singular acknowledgment for her work on updating the guide.

ETHICAL DILEMMA How can the vice-president of HR, and eventually you, determine whether each team member pulled his or her weight or the team lead had to step in to complete or redo the guide?

SOURCES: Sirkka L. Jarvenpaa and Dorothy E. Leidner, "Communication and Trust in Global Virtual Teams," *Journal of Computer-Mediated Communication*, June 1998, (www.ascusc.org); Carla Joinson, "Managing Virtual Teams: Keeping Members on the Same Page without Being in the Same Place Poses Challenges for Managers," *HR Magazine*, June 2002, (www.findarticles.com); and Charlene Marmer Solomon, "Managing Virtual Teams," *Workforce*, June 1, 2001, (www.findarticles.com).

In 2006, over 70 percent of production workers were members of an empowered or self-directed work team.[7] One example is at Chrysler's pickup truck assembly plant in Saltillo, Mexico, where self-directed work teams comprised of 10 to 12 employees take on a set of tasks and tools, including specified maintenance, quality control, and productivity and safety jobs. Team members rotate among different tasks every few hours and are encouraged to find ways to cut time and wasted effort. Those whose jobs become redundant as a result are reassigned. Production has increased to about 38 vehicles an hour from 30, all without additional hiring or overtime.[8] A more extreme version of self-managing teams can be found at W. L. Gore, the company that invented Gore-Tex fabric and Glide dental floss. The three employees who invented Elixir guitar strings contributed their spare time to the effort and persuaded a handful of colleagues to help them improve the design. After working three years entirely on their own—without asking for any supervisory or top management permission or being subjected to any kind of oversight—the team finally sought the support of the larger company, which they needed to take the strings to market. Today, W. L. Gore's Elixir has a 35 percent market share in acoustic guitar strings.[9]

cross-functional team
Members from the same organizational level but from different functional areas.

An adaptation of the team concept is called a **cross-functional team**. These teams are made up of employees from about the same hierarchical level, but different functional areas of the organization. Many task forces, organizational committees, and project teams are cross-functional. Often the team members work together only until they solve a given problem or complete a specific project. Cross-functional teams allow people with various levels and areas of expertise to pool their resources, develop new ideas, solve problems,

> **concept check**
>
> What is the difference between a work team and a work group?
>
> Identify and describe three types of work teams.
>
> What are some ways to build a high-performance team?

Expanding Around The Globe

HARNESSING TALENT TO HARNESS THE WIND

Many companies boast a global workforce, but few are as skilled at mobilizing experts from diverse disciplines and locales in pursuit of a common goal. At General Electric, executives are encouraged to think beyond the boundaries of their particular business. They come together frequently for training or joint projects. Executives are apt to move among units several times in their careers, letting them build up a rich network of internal contacts. There's also a tradition of plucking people from their day jobs for other projects. At any given time, thousands of GE employees are on so-called bubble assignments—lending their skills to another function or business that pays their salaries for the duration of the project.

James Lyons, a chief engineer at the GE Global Research Center, is the fulcrum for GE's Wind Energy project. The 30-year veteran has brought in engineers from other units and navigated cultural hurdles worldwide. He has recruited materials experts from down the hall who developed the composites for the fan blades of the GE90 aircraft engine; design teams in South Carolina and Salzbergen, Germany; engineers from Ontario, who are tackling the generators; Bangalore researchers who are drafting analytical models and turbine system design tools; and Shanghai engineers who conduct high-end simulations. Chinese researchers design the microprocessors that control the pitch of the blade. And technicians in Munich have created a smart turbine that can calculate wind speeds and signal other turbines to pitch their blades for maximum electricity production. Lyons keeps his global team focused with e-mails, teleconferences, and clear deadlines.

One way he builds team spirit is to foster familiarity. In addition to regular teleconferences, engineers take stints working in other parts of the operation. That has meant trading engineers from Bangalore and Salzbergen, for example, for a week or two at a time. Along with learning about the core design tools being created in Bangalore or the actual products being made in Salzbergen, they establish better lines of communication. With its $2 billion in annual revenues, the far-flung Wind Energy team is getting results. Among the innovations so far is a new generation of land-based wind turbines with new blade and advanced control technologies for customers who want to generate energy on sites where space is limited. One unit designed for offshore locations sits 30 storeys above the ocean, has turbine blades each longer than a football field, and can power 1,400 average American homes a year. Current projects range from a wind farm in Inner Mongolia to working on smaller turbines that could help provide clean water to villages in developing countries.[10]

Critical Thinking Questions

1. What challenges do you think face James Lyons in managing his global Wind Energy team?
2. Would you be interested in participating in such a geographically widespread team? Why or why not?

SOURCE: Diane Brady, "Reaping the Wind: GE's Energy Initiative Is a Case Study in Innovation - without Borders," *Business Week*, October 11, 2004, p. 201; Patricia Sellers, "Blowing in the Wind: To Build a Better Wind Turbine, General Electric Built a Global Team of - Researchers in Germany, China, India, and the U.S.," *Fortune*, July 25, 2005, p. 130.

and coordinate complex projects. Both problem-solving teams and self-managed teams may also be cross-functional teams. Read the Expanding around the Globe box for an example of how General Electric is implementing—and succeeding with—global cross-functional teams.

Building High-Performance Teams

A great team must possess certain characteristics, so selecting the appropriate employees for the team is vital. Employees who are more willing to work together to accomplish a common goal should be selected, rather than employees who are more interested in their own personal achievement. Team members should also possess a variety of skills. Diverse skills strengthen the overall effectiveness of the team, so teams should consciously recruit members to fill gaps in the collective skill set. To be effective, teams must also have clearly defined goals. Vague or unclear goals will not provide the necessary direction or allow employees to measure their performance against expectations. Next, high-performing teams need to practice good communication. Team members need to communicate messages and give appropriate feedback that seeks to correct any misunderstandings. Feedback should also be detached, that is team members should be careful to critique ideas rather than criticize the person who suggests them. Nothing can degrade the effectiveness of a team like personal attacks. Lastly, great teams have great leaders. Skilled team leaders divide work up so that tasks are not repeated, help members set and track goals, monitor their team's performance, communicate openly, and remain flexible to adapt to changing goals or management demands.

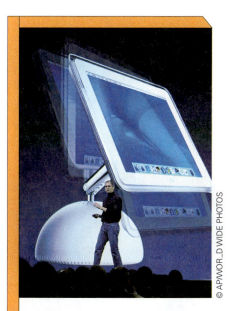

© AP/WORLD WIDE PHOTOS

CONCEPT *in Action* >>>

Apple Computer's CEO Steve Jobs uses an organic structure to develop new products like the iMac computer. Organic structures allow firms like Apple to succeed in rapidly changing environments. Why else do you think that Apple has chosen a organic structure?

The Informal Organization

informal organization
The network of connections and channels of communication based on the informal relationships of individuals inside an organization.

Up to this point in the chapter, we have focused on formal organizational structures that can be seen in the boxes and lines of the organization chart. Yet many important relationships within an organization do not show up on an organization chart. Nevertheless, these relationships can affect the decisions and performance of employees at all levels of the organization.

The network of connections and channels of communication based on the informal relationships of individuals inside the organization is known as the **informal organization.** Informal relationships can be between people at the same hierarchical level or between people at different levels and in different departments. Some connections are work related, such as those formed among people who car-pool or ride the same train to work. Others are based on non-work commonalties, such as belonging to the same religious group or health club, or having children who attend the same school.

Functions of the Informal Organization

The informal organization has several important functions. First, it provides a source of friendships and social contact for organization members. Second, the interpersonal relationships and informal groups help employees feel better informed about and connected with what is going on in their firm, thus giving them some sense of control over their work environment. Third, the informal organization can provide status and recognition that the formal organization cannot or will not provide employees. Fourth, the network of relationships can aid the socialization of new employees by informally passing along rules, responsibilities, basic objectives, and job expectations. Finally, the organizational grapevine helps employees to be more aware of what is happening in their workplace by transmitting information quickly and conveying it to places that the formal system does not reach.

CONCEPT *in Action* >>>

Smart managers understand that not all of a company's influential relationships appear on the organization chart. Off the chart there exists a web of informal personal connections between workers, across which vital information and knowledge pass constantly. Using social network analysis software and communication-tracking tools, managers are able to map and quantify the normally invisible relationships that form between employees. How might identifying a firm's informal organization aid managers in fostering teamwork, motivating employees, and boosting productivity?

Informal Communication Channels

The informal channels of communication used by the informal organization are often referred to as the grapevine, the rumour mill, or the intelligence network. Managers need to pay attention to the grapevines in their organization, because their employees increasingly put a great deal of stock in the information that travels along it. A recent survey found that many business leaders have their work cut out for them in the speeches and presentations they give employees. Survey participants were asked if they would believe a message delivered in a speech by a company leader or one that they heard over the grapevine. Forty-seven percent of those responding said they would put more credibility in the grapevine. Only 42 percent said they would believe senior leadership, and another 11 percent indicated they would believe a blend of elements from both messages.[11] Perhaps even more interesting is how accurate employees perceive their company grapevine to be: Fifty-seven percent gave it favourable ratings. "The grapevine may not be wholly accurate, but it is a very reliable indicator that something is going on," said one survey respondent.[12]

With this in mind, managers need to learn to use the existing informal organization as a tool that can potentially benefit the formal organization. An excellent way of putting the informal organization to work for the good of the company is to bring informal leaders into the decision-making process. That way, at least the people who use and nurture the grapevine will have more accurate information to send it.

> **concept check**
>
> What is the informal organization?
>
> How can informal channels of communication be used to improve operational efficiency?

Trends in Organizational Structures

To improve organizational performance and achieve long-term objectives, some organizations seek to re-engineer their business processes or adopt new technologies that open up a variety of organizational design options, such as virtual corporations and virtual teams. Other trends that have strong footholds in today's organizations include outsourcing and managing global businesses.

Re-engineering Organizational Structure

re-engineering
The complete redesign of business structures and processes to improve operations.

Periodically, all businesses must re-evaluate the way they do business. This includes assessing the effectiveness of the organizational structure. To meet the formidable challenges of the future, companies are increasingly turning to **re-engineering**—the complete redesign of business structures and processes to improve operations. An even simpler definition of re-engineering is "starting over." In effect, top management asks, "If we were a new company, how would we run this place?" The purpose of re-engineering is to identify and abandon the outdated rules and fundamental assumptions that guide current business operations. Every company has many formal and informal rules based on assumptions about technology, people, and organizational goals that no longer hold. Thus, the goal of re-engineering is to redesign business processes to achieve improvements in cost control, product quality, customer service, and speed. The re-engineering process should result in a more efficient and effective organizational structure that is better suited to the current (and future) competitive climate of the industry.

concept check

What is meant by re-engineering?

What is the purpose of re-engineering?

The Virtual Corporation

virtual corporation
A network of independent companies linked by information technology to share skills, costs, and access to one another's markets; allows the companies to come together quickly to exploit rapidly changing opportunities.

One of the greatest challenges for companies today is adapting to the technological changes that are affecting all industries. Organizations are struggling to find new organizational structures that will help them transform information technology into a competitive advantage. One alternative that is becoming increasingly prevalent is the **virtual corporation,** which is a network of independent companies (suppliers, customers, even competitors) linked by information technology to share skills, costs, and access to one another's markets. This network structure allows companies to come together quickly to exploit rapidly changing opportunities. These are the key attributes of a virtual corporation:

- *Technology.* Information technology helps geographically distant companies form alliances and work together.
- *Opportunism.* Alliances are less permanent, less formal, and more opportunistic than in traditional partnerships.
- *Excellence.* Each partner brings its core competencies to the alliance, so it is possible to create an organization with higher quality in every functional area and to increase competitive advantage.
- *Trust.* The network structure makes companies more reliant on one another and forces them to strengthen relationships with partners.
- *No borders.* This structure expands the traditional boundaries of an organization.

In the concept's purest form, each company that links with others to create a virtual corporation is stripped to its essence. Ideally, the virtual corporation has neither a central office nor an organization chart, no hierarchy, and no vertical integration. It contributes to an alliance only its core competencies, or key capabilities. It mixes and matches what it does best with the core competencies of other companies and entrepreneurs. For example, a manufacturer would only manufacture, while relying on a product design firm to decide what to make and a marketing company to sell the end result.

Although firms that are purely virtual organizations are still relatively scarce, many companies are embracing several of the characteristics of the virtual structure. One great example is Cisco Systems. Cisco has 34 plants that produce its products, but the company only owns two of them. Human hands touch only 10 percent of customer orders. Less than half of all orders are processed by Cisco employees. To the average customer, the interdependency of Cisco's suppliers and inventory systems makes it look like one huge, seamless company.

HOT Links

Go to (www.google.ca) and, using the search words "virtual corporation concepts," read about new approaches by Canadian companies.

Virtual Teams

Technology is also enabling corporations to create virtual work teams. Geography is no longer a limitation when employees are considered for a work team. Virtual teams mean reduced travel time and costs, reduced relocation expenses, and utilization of specialized talent regardless of employee location.

When managers need to staff a project, all they need to do is make a list of required skills and a general list of employees who possess those skills. When the pool of employees is known, the manager simply chooses the best mix of people and creates the virtual team. Special challenges of virtual teams include keeping team members focused, motivated, and communicating positively despite their location. If feasible, at least one face-to-face meeting during the early stages of team formation will help with these potential problems.

Outsourcing

Another organizational trend that continues to influence today's managers is outsourcing. For decades, companies have outsourced various functions. For example, payroll functions such as recording hours, benefits, wage rates, and issuing pay deposits have been handled for years by third-party providers. Today, however, outsourcing includes a much wider array of business functions: customer service, production, engineering, information technology, sales and marketing, janitorial services, maintenance, and more. Outsourcing is evolving from a trend to a way of doing business.

Companies outsource for two main reasons: cost reduction and labour needs. Often, to satisfy both requirements, companies will outsource work to firms in foreign countries. It seems that nearly every day an article in the business press mentions global outsourcing. That is because more and more companies are integrating global outsourcing into their business strategy.

Structuring for Global Mergers

Recent mergers creating mega firms raise some important questions regarding corporate structure. How can managers hope to organize the global pieces of these huge,

CONCEPT *in Action* >>>

In today's high-tech world, teams can exist anyplace where there is access to a wireless network. With globalization and outsourcing on the rise, organizations are increasingly utilizing virtual teams to coordinate people and projects—often from halfway around the world. Unlike coworkers in traditional teams, members of virtual teams rarely meet in person, working from different locations and even from different continents. What practical benefits do virtual teams offer to businesses and employees?

©2009 JUPITER IMAGES CORPORATION

complex new firms into a cohesive, successful whole? Should decision making be centralized or decentralized? Should the firm be organized around geographic markets or product lines? And how can managers consolidate distinctly different corporate cultures? These issues and many more must be resolved if mergers of global companies are to succeed.

Beyond designing a new organizational structure, one of the most difficult challenges when merging two large companies is uniting the cultures and creating a single business. Failure to effectively merge cultures can have serious effects on organizational efficiency.

concept check

How does technology enable firms to organize as virtual corporations?

What are some organizational issues that must be addressed when two large firms merge?

Great Ideas to Use Now

How is organizational structure relevant to you? A common thread linking all of the companies profiled in this chapter is you, the consumer. Companies structure their organizations to facilitate achieving their overall organizational goals. To be profitable, companies must have a competitive advantage, and competition is based on meeting customer expectations. The company that best satisfies customer wants and demands is the company that will lead the competition.

When companies make changes to their organizational structures, they are attempting to increase in some way their ability to satisfy the customer. For example, several of the companies profiled in this chapter were consolidating or centralizing parts of their operation. Why? Those companies hope to become more efficient and reduce costs, which should translate into better customer service and more reasonable prices. Some companies are decentralizing operations, giving departments or divisions more autonomy to respond quickly to changes in the market or to be more flexible in their response to customer demands. Many companies are embracing new information technology because it brings them closer to their customers faster than was previously possible. Internet commerce is benefiting consumers in a number of ways. When you buy books at (**www.amazon.ca**) or use (**www.ebay.ca**) to sell a used bicycle, you are sending the message that the virtual company is a structure you will patronize and support. Increasing globalization and use of information technology will continue to alter the competitive landscape, and the big winner should be the consumer, in terms of increased choice, increased access, and reduced price!

Customer Satisfaction and Quality

There was a time when large organizations needed only open their doors and customers were waiting to do business. They didn't need to worry about being responsible to customers or having a structure flexible enough to respond to customer needs. Today, no company can afford to take its customers for granted. To keep a strong and loyal customer base, an organization structure must be created to constantly monitor the level of satisfaction the customer is experiencing and then be able to address any problems. One recent example of just how far a company is willing to go to keep its customers happy is Enterprise Rent-A-Car.

After the attacks of September 11, 2001, Enterprise found itself faced with many stranded customers. With all airports shut down, stranded travellers found themselves with no way to get home other than by car. In an unprecedented move, Andy Taylor, Chairman and CEO, told the 4,300 U.S. neighbourhood locations to permit out-of-state one-way rentals for stranded travellers and waive or reimburse drop-off fees. In an e-mail message to the employees, Taylor said, "Right now, we're just concerned about taking care of our customers."[8] As a result of this decision, thousands of Enterprise cars were displaced in other cities without any means of return. Some cars were sold, employees retrieved others, and still others were shipped back on flatbed trucks. By putting customers' needs first during this national emergency, Enterprise incurred significant costs but maintained its firm policy on customer satisfaction.

Summary of Learning Outcomes

1 **Identify the five structural building blocks that managers use to design organizations.**

To build an organizational structure, companies first must divide the work into separate jobs and tasks (division of labour). Managers then group related jobs and tasks together into departments (departmentalization). Five basic types of departmentalization (see Exhibit 8.1) are commonly used in organizations:

- *Functional*. Based on the primary functions performed within an organizational unit.
- *Product*. Based on the goods or services produced or sold by the organizational unit.
- *Process*. Based on the production process used by the organizational unit.
- *Customer*. Based on the primary type of customer served by the organizational unit.
- *Geographic*. Based on the geographic segmentation of organizational units.

The relationships within the organization must be established by determining how many layers of management there will be and who will report to whom (managerial hierarchy and span of control). Finally it must be decided at what level the organizational decisions should be made (centralization/decentralization).

2 **Examine the tools companies use to establish relationships within their organizations.**

The managerial hierarchy (or the management pyramid) comprises the levels of management within the organization, and the managerial span of control is the number of employees the manager directly supervises. In daily operations, individuals in line positions are directly involved in the processes used to create goods and services. Individuals in staff positions provide the administrative and support services that line employees need to achieve the firm's goals. Line positions in organizations are typically in areas such as production, marketing, and finance. Staff positions are found in areas such as legal counselling, managerial consulting, public relations, and human resource management.

3 **Show how the degree of centralization/decentralization can be altered to make an organization more successful.**

In a highly centralized structure, top management makes most of the key decisions in the organization with very little input from lower-level employees. Centralization lets top managers develop a broad view of operations and exercise tight financial controls. In a highly decentralized organization, decision-making authority is pushed down the organizational hierarchy, giving lower-level personnel more responsibility and power to make and implement decisions. Decentralization can result in faster decision making and increased innovation and responsiveness to customer preferences.

4 **Describe the differences between a mechanistic and organic organization.**

A mechanistic organization is characterized by a relatively high degree of work specialization, rigid departmentalization, many layers of management (particularly middle management), narrow spans of control, centralized decision making, and a long chain of command. This combination of elements results in a tall organizational structure. In contrast, an organic organization is characterized by a relatively low degree of work specialization, loose departmentalization, few levels of management, wide spans of control, decentralized decision making, and a short chain of command. This combination of elements results in a flat organizational structure.

5 **Discuss the contemporary organizational structures companies are using.**

In recent decades, companies have begun to expand beyond traditional departmentalization methods and use matrix, committee, and team-based structures. Matrix structures combine two types of traditional organizational structures (for example, geographic and functional). Matrix structures bring together people from different functional areas of the organization to work on a special project. As such, matrix organizations are more flexible, but because employees report to two direct supervisors, managing matrix structures can be extremely challenging. Committee structures give authority and responsibility to a group rather than to an individual. Committees are part of a line-and-staff organization and often fulfill only an advisory role. Team-based structures also involve assigning authority and responsibility to groups rather than individuals, but different from committees, team-based structures give these groups autonomy to carry out their work.

6 **Summarize why companies are using team-based organizational structures.**	Work groups share resources and coordinate efforts to help members better perform their individual duties and responsibilities. The performance of the group can be evaluated by adding up the contributions of the individual group members. Work teams require not only coordination but also collaboration, the pooling of knowledge, skills, abilities, and resources in a collective effort to attain a common goal. Four types of work teams are used: problem solving, self-managed, cross-functional, and virtual teams. Companies are using teams to improve individual and group motivation and performance.
7 **Explain how the informal organization affects the performance of the company.**	The informal organization is the network of connections and channels of communication based on the informal relationships of individuals inside the organization. Informal relationships can be between people at the same hierarchical level or between people at different levels and in different departments. Informal organizations give employees more control over their work environment by delivering a continuous stream of company information throughout the organization, thereby helping employees stay informed.
8 **List some of the trends that are influencing the way businesses organize.**	Reengineering is a complete redesign of business structures and processes in order to improve operations in the areas of cost control, product quality, customer service, and speed.

The virtual corporation is a network of independent companies (suppliers, customers, even competitors) linked by information technology to share skills, costs, and access to one another's markets. This network structure allows companies to come together quickly to exploit rapidly changing opportunities.

Many companies are now using technology to create virtual teams. Team members may be down the hall or across the ocean. Virtual teams mean that travel time and expenses are eliminated and the best people can be placed on the team regardless of where they live. Sometimes, however, it may be difficult to keep virtual team members focused and motivated.

Outsourcing business functions—both globally and domestically—is evolving from trend to regular business practice. Companies choose to outsource either as a cost-saving measure or as a way to gain access to needed human resource talent. To be successful, outsourcing must solve a clearly articulated business problem, and managers must closely match third-party providers with their company's actual needs. |

Key Terms

authority 238
centralization 239
chain of command 238
committee structure 245
cross-functional team 248
customer departmentalization 235
decentralization 239
delegation of authority 238
departmentalization 235
division of labour 235
formal organization 234
functional departmentalization 235
geographic departmentalization 235
group cohesiveness 246
informal organization 249
line organization 242
line positions 242
line-and-staff organization 242

managerial hierarchy 237
matrix structure (project management) 243
mechanistic organization 240
organic organization 240
organization chart 235
problem-solving teams 247
process departmentalization 235
product departmentalization 235
re-engineering 251
self-managed work teams 247
span of control 238
specialization 235
staff positions 242
virtual corporation 251
work groups 246
work teams 247

Experiential Exercises

1. Evaluate your leadership skills. If you want to evaluate your own leadership skills, go to (www.humanlinks.com/skilhome.htm) and scroll down to "Managerial Skills." By taking the self-assessment quizzes offered here, you will gain insight into your ability to manage virtual teams, test your ability to think logically and analogically, and even your perceptions about management. Companies are seeking managerial leaders who have leadership traits that will guide employees through the competitive business landscape.

2. Draw an organization chart of the firm you work for, your college, or a campus student organization. Show the lines of authority and formal communication. Describe the informal relationships that you think are important for the success of the organization.

3. How would you restructure a large mechanistic organization to be more customer-friendly and to increase customer satisfaction? Choose a specific organization and give a detailed plan to accomplish your organizational goals.

4. Using a search engine such as Google or Yahoo! to search for the term "company organizational charts," find at least three examples of organizational charts for corporations, nonprofits, or government agencies. Analyze each entity's organizational structure. Is it organized by function, product/service, process, customer type, or geographic location?

5. At either the *Business Week* (www.businessweek.com), *Fortune* (www.fortune.com), or *Forbes* (www.forbes.com) website, search the archives for stories about companies that have re-engineered. Find an example of a re-engineering effort that succeeded and one that failed and discuss why. Also visit the BPR Online Learning Center at (www.prosci.com) to answer the following questions: What is benchmarking and how can it help companies with business process re-engineering (BPR)? What were the key findings of the best-practices surveys for change management and benchmarking?

6. Visit the *Inc.* magazine website (www.inc.com) and use the search engine to find articles about virtual corporation. Using a search engine, find the website of at least one virtual corporation and look for information about how the company uses span of control, informal organization, and other concepts from this chapter.

7. Managing change in an organization is no easy task, as you've discovered in your new job with a consulting firm that specializes in change management. To get up to speed, go to Bpubs.com, the Business Publications Search Engine, (www.bpubs.com), and navigate to the Change Management section of the Management Science category. Select three articles that discuss how companies approached the change process and summarize their experiences.

8. After managing your first project team, you think you might enjoy a career in project management. The Project Management Institute is a professional organization for project managers. Its website, (www.pmi.org), has many resources about this field. Start at the Professional Practices section to learn what project management is; then go to the professional Development and Careers pages. What are the requirements to earn the Project Management Professional designation? Explore other free areas of the site to learn more about the job of project manager. Prepare a brief report on the career and its opportunities. Does what you've learned make you want to follow this career path?

Review Questions

1. What is division of labour? Specialization?

2. What does the organizational chart show?

3. What are the five basic types of departmentalization that are commonly found in organizations?

4. What is managerial hierarchy? Span of control (span of management)?

5. What is the difference between a centralized and decentralized organization?

6. What are a line organization, line-and-staff organization, committee structure, and matrix structure?

7. What is the informal organization? What are its functions?

8. What is a virtual corporation? What are virtual teams?

CREATIVE THINKING CASE >

Meet the Gore Family

Imagine an organization with more than 7,000 employees working at 45 facilities around the world—with no hierarchy structure. W. L. Gore & Associates, headquartered in Newark, Delaware, is a model of unusual business practices. Wilbert Gore, who left Dupont to explore new uses for Teflon, started the company in 1958. Best known for its breathable, weatherproof Gore-Tex fabric, Glide dental floss, and Elixir guitar strings, the company has no bosses, no titles, no departments, and no formal job descriptions. There is no managerial hierarchy at Gore, and top management treats employees, called associates, as peers.

In April 2005, the company named 22-year associate Terri Kelly its new chief executive officer. Unlike large public corporations, Gore's announcement was made without much fanfare. "It's never about the CEO," she says. "You're an associate, and you just happen to be the CEO. We don't like anyone to be the center of attention." She considers the idea that the CEO of W. L. Gore manages the company a misperception. "My goal is to provide the overall direction. I spend a lot of time making sure we have the right people in the right roles. . . . We empower divisions and push out responsibility. We're so diversified that it's impossible for a CEO to have that depth of knowledge—and not even practical."

The company focuses on its products and company values rather than individuals. Committees, comprised of employees, make major decisions such as hiring, firing, and compensation. They even set top executives' compensation. Employees work on teams, which are switched around every few years. In fact, all employees are expected to make minor decisions instead of relying on the "boss" to make them. "We're committed to how we get things done," Kelly says. "That puts a tremendous burden on leaders because it's easier to say, 'Just do it' than to explain the rationale. But in the long run, you'll get much better results because people are making a commitment."

The company tries to maintain a family-like atmosphere by dispersing its employees into 60 buildings, with no more than 200 employees in any one place. Because no formal lines of authority exist, employees can speak to anyone in the company at any time. This arrangement also forces employees to spend considerable time developing relationships. As one employee described it, instead of trying to please just one "boss," you have to please everyone.

The informal organizational structure is working well. With revenues of almost $2 billion, the company produces thousands of advanced technology products for the electronics, industrial, fabrics, and medical markets. Its corporate structure fosters innovation and has been a significant contributor to associate satisfaction. Employee turnover is a low 5 percent a year, and the company can choose new associates from the 38,000 job applications it receives annually. For the ninth consecutive year, W. L. Gore was near the top of the list of Fortune's "100 Best Companies to Work For."

Critical Thinking Questions

- Given the lack of formal structure, how important do you think the informal structure becomes? Does Gore's reliance on committee work slow processes down?

- Is W. L. Gore a mechanistic or an organic organization? Support your answer with examples from the case.
- How do you think Gore's organizational structure affects the division of labour?

SOURCES: Alan Deutschman, "What I Know Now: Terri Kelly, CEO, W. L. Gore & Associates," Fast Company, September 2005, p. 96; "Gore Marks 9th Year as One of Nation's Best, Company Earns #5 Position on FORTUNE Magazine '100 Best Companies to Work For' List," W. L. Gore & Associates, press release, January 9, 2006, (www.gore.com); Robert Levering and Milton Moskowitz, "And the Winners Are …," Fortune, January 23, 2006, p. 89; Sara J. Welch, "GORE The Fabric of Success," Successful Meetings, May 2005, p. 49–51; and W. L. Gore & Associates website, (www.gore.com) (February 10, 2006).

VIDEO CASE >

Lonely Planet Travels the Globe

With offices on three continents and a distribution centre in a fourth, Lonely Planet is as global as its travel books. A leading publisher of guides for free-spirited, independent travelers, the company started in the early 1970s, when founders Tony and Maureen Wheeler wrote the first guidebook, Across Asia, at their kitchen table. Today Lonely Planet publishes more than 650 books in multiple languages that cover every area of the world, from Antarctica to Greenland and the Arctic, Belize to Sri Lanka—and all points in between. Travelers turn to its guidebooks, website, and the Lonely Planet Six Degrees television series on the Discovery Channel for high quality, accurate, and insightful travel information. "We tell it like it is, we try to raise a smile, and we never take ourselves too seriously," says Lonely Planet Travel Information Manager, Tom Hall. "Our pioneering spirit keeps us searching for new experiences to offer our readers and it's obviously paying off."

Headquartered in Melbourne, Australia, the company also has offices in Oakland, California; London; and Paris. The editors who commission guides are responsible for a specific region and based in the appropriate office. This allows them to acquire in-depth expertise on their areas and follow the latest local trends. Production is centralized at the Melbourne headquarters, and its centralized distribution centre is located in Singapore, near its printers. This provides greater control, reduces redundancy on a worldwide basis, and saves money. In addition to its 400 regular employees, Lonely Planet contracts with about 250 professional authors worldwide who provide an insider's perspective on their countries.

This global workforce presents challenges in structuring the company. "Lonely Planet is a very flat organization . . . a very lean organization," says Vice President Robin Goldberg, who heads up marketing and business development. "When you're lean, you need to allow everyone to grow to their greatest potential, to make decisions, to make them fast. If we had too much hierarchy, it would slow us down dramatically." Lonely Planet is structured as a global company and consolidates publishing, information technology, and distribution functions across locations to avoid duplication of efforts. At the same time, Lonely Planet acknowledges the need to customize its products to meet the needs of regional markets, of which many have different retailers, languages, and images to appeal to local audiences.

Although its multinational nature makes operations more complex—from time zone changes to cultural differences—it also brings advantages. Authors can get answers from staff members during their work day, regardless of where they happen to be traveling. With information technology personnel based on three continents, the company can offer 24-hour global technical support. Teams can collaborate on projects, handing off their work when they go home for the day to colleagues in another time zone, shortening time to completion. Working with people in other countries provides fresh ideas and different perspectives.

Critical Thinking Questions
- Describe the Lonely Planet organizational structure. Does it support the company's goals?
- How does Lonely Planet incorporate teams into its organizational structure? Suggest other areas where the company could use teamwork effectively.

- Is Lonely Planet a mechanistic or an organic organization? Support your answer with examples from the case and video.

SOURCES: Adapted from Daft Video Series, Chapter 10, "Lonely Planet: Designing Adaptive Organizations," Lonely Planet corporate website, (www.lonelyplanet.com) (February 11, 2006); "Lonely Planet Publications," Hoover's Inc., (www.hoovers.com) (February 1, 2006); "Lonely Planet voted best guidebook series," Lonely Planet press release, February 10, 2006, (www.lonelyplanet.com); and "Tony and Maureen Wheeler Honored with Lifetime Achievement Award," Lonely Planet press release, September 20, 2005, (www.lonelyplanet.com).

E-COMMERCE CASE >

In Charge at Oracle

Oracle is one of the world's largest software firms, second only to Microsoft in size. Selling $22.4 billion of business software a year, Oracle has more than 84,000 employees and operates around the world. The Internet has long been an integral part of founder and CEO Larry Ellison's vision for the company. Oracle introduced a line of e-business software applications several years ago that allow businesses to manage all of their computers and databases through the Internet. Since then, Ellison has constantly pushed the benefits of using the Web as a business tool. He claims Oracle saved $1 billion in operating costs in the first year after the firm began using its own Web-based software.

Before 2000, Ellison shared leadership of Oracle with company president Ray Lane and chief financial officer Jeff Henley. Each ran their own area—technology, sales, and finances, respectively—relatively independently. Lane was credited with helping to streamline Oracle's bloated organizational structure, opening the door for the company to compete more effectively in the e-commerce marketplace.

In 2000, however, after a power struggle with Ellison, Ray Lane abruptly resigned. Since then, Ellison has refused to name a new president. "The problem I found is that it's hard to have two leaders," Ellison says. "What happened with Oracle was we had two separate visions of where the company should go. The company was divided into two factions. It's not a healthy thing."

Many analysts, however, think Ellison needs a counterbalance, especially since Oracle's sales started to slip after Lane's departure. "When Ray Lane was there, he was a good complement to Larry," explains one analyst. "When he left, some of the things weren't managed quite as effectively. You don't need to have Ray Lane, but you do need that skill set." However, today Oracle has three senior VP's and six executive VP's as well as Jeff Henley as Chairman of the Board.

Oracle's most pressing problem is that many customers complain that the firm's sales force has been overly aggressive and made false claims about the performance of the company's e-commerce software products. Several customers—including the state of California—have actually filed lawsuits against Oracle because of its sales practices.

Ellison says a recent company restructuring will solve the problem. Before, each salesperson was responsible for selling all of Oracle's products to customers. Now, salespeople will specialize in selling just a few particular products. Ellison says this new structure will allow salespeople to understand and serve customer needs better. "We can't possibly have salespeople who are experts in everything," Ellison says. "That's simply impossible."

Critical Thinking Questions

1. Do you agree or disagree with Ellison's decision not to name a new company president? Discuss the benefits and disadvantages of centralizing company control in Ellison's hands.

2. How effective do you think Ellison's new sales force structure will be? How can the Internet help implement and support Ellison's plan?

3. What organizational structure do you think is most appropriate for Oracle? Why?

SOURCES: David Futrelle, "Jumping Ship at Oracle and Sun," Fortune, May 2, 2002, (www.business2.com); Eric Hellweg, "Oracle's Larry Ellison, a Solitary Man," Business 2.0, July 15, 2002, (www.business2.com) (accessed date); G. Christian Hill, "Updates: Trouble with Larry," eCompany, May 2001, (www.ecompany.com); Ian Mount, "Out of Control," Business 2.0, August 2002, (www.business2.com); (www.oracle.com/corporate/information-powers-profitability.pdf), accessed December 9th, 2008.

CHAPTER 9

Making the Connection

Motivating Employees

In this chapter we'll look at the third step in the process of management—*motivating* employees toward the accomplishment of organizational goals. As we saw in Chapter 8, organizational structures are designed to support the accomplishment of the overall plans of the company. But these plans cannot be accomplished, appropriate structure or not, if the individuals responsible for their implementation are not committed to the outcome. As we've said numerous times, without the final critical success factor—*gaining employee commitment*—none of the critical success factors can be accomplished. This is, therefore, perhaps our most important management function but, unfortunately, also one of the most difficult. We're dealing with human beings, not push-button machines, and, therefore, it is extremely important that managers understand what makes people tick.

For example, have you ever walked into a restaurant, gone up to a service counter in a store, or called a company's customer service department on the phone and been served by an employee that didn't appear to be overjoyed to answer your questions? Most of us have. The important question here is—did you just assume that the employee was having a bad day and not let it affect your perception of the company, or did it enter your mental database and register as a less-than-pleasurable experience with that company as a whole? Probably the latter. We all see our contact with employees in different companies as a contact with the

company, and one employee's attitude as the company's attitude—consciously or not. As customers we see it in a very integrative way—we see it as the whole company. As managers in that company, we need to recognize that and focus on understanding our employees' needs to gain their commitment. Recent research, discussed in this chapter, demonstrates that employee turnover has a significant impact on customer satisfaction. Employee turnover results when employee commitment is low; therefore, the higher the commitment, the greater the likelihood that customer needs will be met.

In this chapter we discuss different motivation theories that will help you understand what motivates individuals to work harder to please the customer. But everyone is different. Therefore, a manager must play a truly integrative role here. He or she must see each employee as an individual but also in the context of how that person fits into the larger organization. Managers must integrate the different theories to find a style that works both for them and for their employees. Just as Jennifer Shroeger, a district manager for UPS, does in the opening vignette. Faced with a 50 percent turnover rate for part-time employees, one of things she did was identify different groups of employees and tailor her communication to each group to address the areas of concerns that affected each employee. It is essential that managers understand how to gain the commitment of all of the different individuals that make up their team, as many

different personalities are needed to make a successful business work, but people with different skills and motivations must work together as one.

You'll learn that when a company shows commitment to its employees it gets commitment in return—something discovered initially through the Hawthorne experiments, when researchers saw that employees performed better when they felt that management was concerned for their welfare. A commitment to education and training—one of the trends in employee motivation discussed in the chapter—goes a long way toward showing employees that they are valued and that the organization is a place where they can grow to their full potential. The trends of employee ownership and work-life benefits are other examples.

Remember as you learn the different theories of motivation to keep in mind that the manager's job here is to gain employee commitment to achieve the other factors critical to a successful business. Each of the success factors is achieved through people, and thus the people at all levels in the organization must be motivated to achieve these success factors. They must be committed to the organization's success for it to happen.

One factor not discussed so far, but integral to achieving this success, is the external environment. The external environment can and does have concrete implications on the work environment, as well as affecting the mindset that people bring to work every day, thereby affecting their levels of motivation. Managers must therefore take into consideration the elements in the external environment that might affect employee motivation. Examples are the political environment and its effect on legislation pertaining to employment standards, the economy and its effect on job security and levels of pay, the *social* environment and the resulting expectations that people have regarding the work environment, and the *technological* environment and how it changes the demands of different jobs. One obvious instance of the effect of the environment that is discussed in the chapter is the effect of culture on motivation. The *societal* culture of different countries makes certain motivation theories inapplicable. As a company hires a more diverse workforce, it gains the benefit of a better understanding of its diverse customers—especially if it competes in the global marketplace—but it also becomes even more necessary to understand workers' individualities to gain their commitment to work toward the goals of the organization.

CHAPTER 9

Motivating Employees

LEARNING OUTCOMES

1 Explain the basic principles of Frederick Taylor's concept of scientific management.

2 Summarize what Elton Mayo's Hawthorne studies revealed about worker motivation.

3 Discuss Maslow's hierarchy of needs, and how these needs relate to employee motivation.

4 Identify how McGregor's Theories X and Y, and Ouchi's Theory Z are used to explain worker motivation.

5 Explain the basic components of Herzberg's motivator-hygiene theory.

6 Describe how three contemporary theories of employee motivation offer insights into improving employee performance.

7 Discuss how managers can redesign existing jobs to increase employee motivation and performance.

8 List some of the initiatives organizations are using today to motivate and retain employees.

GETTING THE LEAD OUT AT UPS

© WALTER HODGES / STONE / GETTY IMAGES

United Parcel Service (UPS), (**www.ups.com**), has more than 400,000 employees worldwide, and provides service to every address in Canada, the United States, and more than 200 countries and territories. Suppose your job at UPS consisted of unloading packages from a truck and placing them on a conveyor belt. After unloading the first package, you unload another and then another. You unload one box every three seconds, 1,200 every hour. This might not sound like a very exciting job, but it is a job that is essential to UPS which hires thousands of part-time workers to move millions of packages daily. However, keeping a well-trained workforce motivated was a major problem for UPS.

In an article in "Fast Forward," Keith Hammond described the efforts of Jennifer Shroeger when she became a district manager for UPS. Her region was experiencing a 50 percent turnover rate among its part-time employees. This was both costly and disruptive, as part-time employees made up half of the workforce. Shroeger made attracting, retaining, and motivating a part-time workforce her immediate priority. She addressed the problem by focusing on better hiring and more effective communication and by giving frontline supervisors more responsibility for keeping employees motivated.

Specifically, Shroeger changed the "first applicant through the door" hiring practice to targeting people whose need for a part-time job matched the company's need. Then she identified different groups of employees by age and career stage. By tailoring her communication to each group, she was able to address those areas of concern that really affected each employee. Another initiative was to provide a positive work environment by upgrading the facilities. Employee retention committees were installed to mentor new employees through their initial hiring phase, when fears and frustration were at their highest levels. Finally, to increase effectiveness, frontline supervisors were given additional training on how to communicate, listen, and solve problems facing the large and diverse workforce.[1]

Critical Thinking Questions

1. **Do the new initiatives at UPS help employees feel more empowered?**

2. **How do you think these efforts will affect turnover?**

3. **Do you think that matching the needs of the employees with the company's needs will increase an employee's motivation?**

motivation
Something that prompts a person to release his or her energy in a certain direction.

need
The gap between what is and what is required.

want
The gap between what is and what is desired.

People can be a firm's most important resource. They can also be the most challenging resource to manage well. Employees who are motivated and work hard to achieve personal and organizational goals can become a crucial competitive advantage for a firm. The key then is to understand the process of motivation, what motivates individuals, and how an organization can create a workplace that allows people to perform to the best of their abilities. **Motivation** is the set of forces that prompt a person to release energy in a certain direction. As such, motivation is essentially a need- and want-satisfying process. A **need** is best defined as the gap between what is and what is required. Similarly, a **want** is the gap between what is and what is desired. Unsatisfied needs and wants create a state of tension that pushes (motivates) individuals to practice behaviour that will result in the need being met or the want being fulfilled. That is, motivation is what pushes us to move from where we are to where we want to be because expending that effort will result in some kind of reward.

Rewards can be divided into two basic categories: intrinsic and extrinsic. Intrinsic rewards come from within the individual; things like satisfaction, contentment, sense of accomplishment, confidence, and pride. By contrast, extrinsic rewards come from outside the individual and include things like pay raises, promotions, bonuses, prestigious assignments, and so forth. Exhibit 9.1 illustrates the motivation process.

Successful managers are able to marshal the forces to motivate employees to achieve organizational goals. And just as there are many types of gaps between where organizations are and where they want to be, there are many motivational theories from which managers can draw to inspire employees to bridge those gaps.

EXHIBIT 9.1 > Model of Motivation

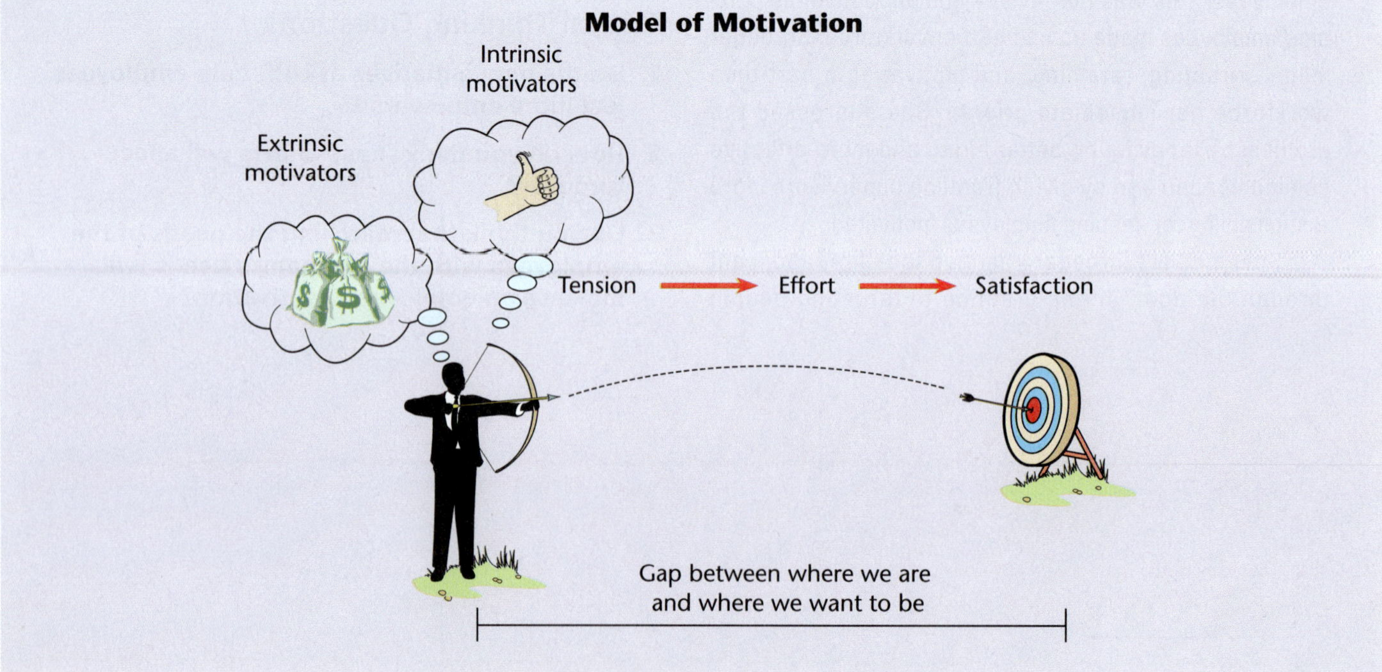

Model of Motivation

Intrinsic motivators

Extrinsic motivators

Tension ⟶ Effort ⟶ Satisfaction

Gap between where we are and where we want to be

In this chapter, we will first examine motivational theories that grew out of the industrial revolution and early ideas of organizational psychology. Then we will examine needs-based theories and more contemporary ideas about employee motivation like equity, expectancy, goals, and reinforcement theories. Finally, we will show you how managers are applying these theories in real-world situations.

Early Theories of Motivation

How can managers and organizations promote enthusiastic job performance, high productivity, and job satisfaction? Many studies of human behaviour in organizations have contributed to our current understanding of these issues. A look at the evolution of management theory and research shows how managers have arrived at the practices used today to manage human behaviour in the workplace. We will discuss a sampling of the most influential of these theorists and research studies in this section.

LO 1

Frederick Taylor's Scientific Management

scientific management
A system of management developed by Frederick W. Taylor and based on four principles: developing a scientific approach for each element of a job, scientifically selecting and training workers, encouraging cooperation between workers and managers, and dividing work and responsibility between management and workers according to who can better perform a particular task.

One of the most influential figures of the classical era of management, which lasted from about 1900 to the mid-1930s, was Frederick W. Taylor, a mechanical engineer sometimes called the "father of **scientific management**." Taylor's approach to improved performance was based on economic incentives and the premise that there is "one best way" to perform any job. As a manager at the Midvale and Bethlehem Steel companies in Philadelphia in the early 1900s, Taylor was frustrated at the inefficiency of the labourers working in the mills.

Convinced that productivity could be improved, Taylor studied the individual jobs in the mill and redesigned the equipment and the methods used by workers. Taylor timed each job with a stopwatch and broke down every task into separate movements. He then prepared an instruction sheet telling exactly how each job should be done, how much time it should take, and what motions and tools should be used. Taylor's ideas led to dramatic increases in productivity in the steel mills and resulted in the development of four basic principles of scientific management:

1. Develop a scientific approach for each element of a person's job.
2. Scientifically select, train, teach, and develop workers.
3. Encourage cooperation between workers and managers, so that each job can be accomplished in a standard, scientifically determined way.
4. Divide work and responsibility between management and workers according to who is better suited to each task.

Taylor published his ideas in *The Principles of Scientific Management*. His pioneering work vastly increased production efficiency and contributed to the specialization of labour and the assembly line method of production. Taylor's approach is still being used nearly a century later in companies such as United Parcel Service (UPS), where industrial engineers maximize efficiency by carefully studying every step of the delivery process, looking for the quickest possible way to deliver packages to customers. Though Taylor's work was a giant step forward in the evolution of management, it had a fundamental flaw in that it assumed that all people are motivated primarily by economic factors. Taylor's successors in the study of management found that motivation is much more complex than he envisioned.

LO 2

The Hawthorne Studies

The classical era of management was followed by the *human relations era*, which began in the 1930s and focused primarily on how human behaviour and relations affect organizational performance. The new era was ushered in by the Hawthorne studies, which changed the way many managers thought about motivation, job productivity, and

Employers of factory workers in the early 1900s applied scientific methods to improve productivity. During this classical era of management, employers believed performance was motivated only by economic incentives. How did his work affect today's organizations?

© MINNESOTA HISTORICAL SOCIETY/CORBIS

Hawthorne effect
The phenomenon that employees perform better when they feel singled out for attention or feel that management is concerned about their welfare.

employee satisfaction. The studies began when engineers at the Hawthorne Western Electric plant decided to examine the effects of varying levels of light on worker productivity—an experiment that might have interested Frederick Taylor. The engineers expected brighter light to lead to increased productivity, but the results showed that varying the level of light in either direction (brighter or dimmer) led to increased output from the experimental group. In 1927, the Hawthorne engineers asked Harvard professor Elton Mayo and a team of researchers to join them in their investigation.

From 1927 to 1932, Mayo and his colleagues conducted experiments on job redesign, length of workday and workweek, length of break times, and incentive plans. The results of the studies indicated that improvements in performance were tied to a complex set of employee attitudes. Mayo claimed that both experimental and control groups from the plant had developed a sense of group pride because they had been selected to participate in the studies. The pride that came from this special attention motivated the workers to increase their productivity. Supervisors who allowed the employees to have some control over their situation appeared to increase the workers' motivation further. These findings gave rise to what is now known as the **Hawthorne effect**, which suggests that employees will perform better when they feel singled out for special attention or feel that management is concerned about employee welfare. The studies also provided evidence that informal work groups (the social relationships of employees) and the resulting group pressures have positive effects on group productivity. The results of the Hawthorne studies enhanced our understanding of what motivates individuals in the workplace. They indicate that in addition to the personal economic needs emphasized in the classical era, social needs play an important role in influencing work-related attitudes and behaviours.

LO 3

Maslow's Hierarchy of Needs

Another well-known theorist from the behavioural era of management history, psychologist Abraham Maslow, proposed a theory of motivation based on universal human needs. Maslow believed that each individual has a hierarchy of needs, consisting of physiological, safety, social, esteem, and self-actualization needs, as shown in Exhibit 9.2.

EXHIBIT 9.2 > Maslow's Hierarchy of Needs

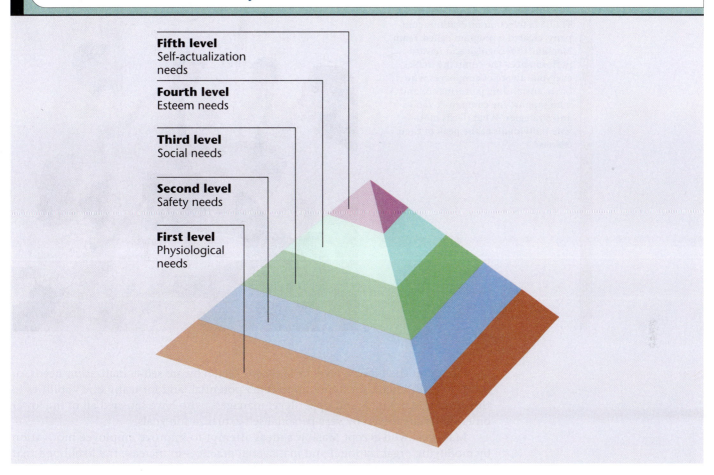

Fifth level
Self-actualization
needs

Fourth level
Esteem needs

Third level
Social needs

Second level
Safety needs

First level
Physiological
needs

Maslow's hierarchy of needs
A theory of motivation developed by
Abraham Maslow; holds that humans
have five levels of needs and act to
satisfy their unmet needs. At the base
of the hierarchy are fundamental
physiological needs, followed in order
by safety, social, esteem, and self-
actualization needs.

Maslow's theory of motivation contends that people act to satisfy their unmet needs. When you're hungry, for instance, you look for and eat food, thus satisfying a basic physiological need. Once a need is satisfied, its importance to the individual diminishes, and a higher level need is more likely to motivate the person.

According to **Maslow's hierarchy of needs**, the most basic human needs are physiological needs, that is, the needs for food, shelter, and clothing. In large part, it is the physiological needs that motivate a person to find a job. People need to earn money to provide food, shelter, and clothing for themselves and their families. Once people have met these basic needs, they reach the second level in Maslow's hierarchy, which is safety needs. People need to feel secure, to be protected from physical harm, and to avoid the unexpected. In work terms, they need job security and protection from work hazards. Many companies provide their permanent employees with the job security they need by having no-layoff policies.[2] When times are good, these companies are careful about bloating the workforce; and when times are bad, they use creative ways to keep the staff working until business improves.

Physiological needs and safety are physical needs. Once these are satisfied, individuals focus on needs that involve relationships with other people. At Maslow's third level are social needs, or needs for belonging (acceptance by others) and for giving and receiving friendship and love. Informal social groups on and off the job help people satisfy these needs. At the fourth level in Maslow's hierarchy are esteem needs, which are needs for the respect of others and for a sense of accomplishment and achievement. Satisfaction of these needs is reflected in feelings of self-worth. Praise and recognition from managers and others in the firm contribute to the sense of self-worth.

CONCEPT *in Action* >>>

TELUS, a telecommunications company, created a program called Team Machine to recognize and reward performance. The company makes everyone aware of employees who have outstanding performance and who support the company's values and strategies. What needs motivate individuals at the peak of their careers?

Finally, at the highest level in Maslow's hierarchy are self-actualization needs, or needs for fulfillment, for living up to one's potential, and for using one's abilities to the utmost. Many mid- and upper-level managers, who have satisfied all of the lower order needs, are driven by very personal self-actualization goals.

Managers who accept Maslow's ideas attempt to improve employee motivation by modifying organizational and managerial practices to increase the likelihood that employees will meet all levels of needs. Maslow's theory has also helped managers understand that it is hard to motivate people by appealing to already satisfied needs. For instance, overtime pay might not motivate employees who earn a high wage and value their leisure time.

Maslow's theory is not without criticism, however. Maslow claimed that a higher level need was not activated until a lower level need was met. He also claimed that a satisfied need is not a motivator. A farmer who has plenty to eat is not motivated by more food (the physiological hunger need). Research has not verified these principles in any strict sense. The theory also concentrates on moving up the hierarchy without fully addressing moving back down it. Despite these limitations, Maslow's ideas are very helpful for understanding the needs of people at work and for determining what can be done to satisfy them.

McGregor's Theories X and Y

Douglas McGregor, one of Maslow's students, influenced the study of motivation with his formulation of two contrasting sets of assumptions about human nature—Theory X and Theory Y.

The **Theory X** management style is based on a pessimistic view of human nature and assumes the following:

- The average person dislikes work and will avoid it if possible.
- Because people don't like to work, they must be controlled, directed, or threatened with punishment to get them to make an effort.
- The average person prefers to be directed, avoids responsibility, is relatively lacking in ambition and wants security above all else.

HOT Links

How do you keep employees satisfied? The Business Research Lab has a series of articles on this topic at (**www.busreslab.com/tips/tipses.htm**).

Theory X
A management style formulated by Douglas McGregor that is based on a pessimistic view of human nature and assumes that the average person dislikes work, will avoid it if possible, prefers to be directed, avoids responsibility, and wants security above all.

This view of people suggests that managers must constantly prod workers to perform and must closely control their on-the-job behaviour. Theory X managers tell people what to do, are very directive, like to be in control, and show little confidence in employees. They often foster dependent, passive, and resentful subordinates.

In contrast, a **Theory Y** management style is based on a more optimistic view of human nature and assumes the following:

- Work is as natural as play or rest. People want to and can be self-directed and self-controlled and will try to achieve organizational goals they believe in.
- Workers can be motivated using positive incentives and will try hard to accomplish organizational goals if they believe they will be rewarded for doing so.
- Under proper conditions, the average person not only accepts responsibility but seeks it out. Most workers have a relatively high degree of imagination and creativity and are willing to help solve problems.

Managers who operate on Theory Y assumptions recognize individual differences and encourage workers to learn and develop their skills. An administrative assistant might be given the responsibility for generating a monthly report. The reward for doing so might be recognition at a meeting, a special training class to enhance computer skills, or a pay increase. In short, the Theory Y approach builds on the idea that worker and organizational interests are the same. The SAS Institute, a leader in business intelligence and analytics, has successfully created a corporate culture based on Theory Y assumptions. With a four percent turnover rate and a recruitment ratio of 200 applicants for each open position, the success of this culture is evident. VP Human Resources Jeff Chambers claims that employee retention has more to do with the company's environment than any other factor:

> "The two key concepts are flexibility and trust. We have a flat organizational structure so usually an employee is no more than four to five levels away from the CEO. And we treat people like adults and allow them to do their jobs. We hire hard and then manage easy. Just leave them alone and trust them to do the right thing for the company."[3]

Theory Z

William Ouchi (pronounced O Chee), a management scholar at the University of California, Los Angeles, has proposed a theory that combines North American and Japanese business practices. He calls it **Theory Z**. Exhibit 9.3 compares the traditional North American and Japanese management styles with the Theory Z approach. Theory Z emphasizes long-term employment, slow career development, moderate specialization, group decision making, individual responsibility, relatively informal control over the employee, and concern for workers. Theory Z has many Japanese elements but reflects North American cultural values.

In the past decade, admiration for Japanese management philosophy, which centres on creating long-term relationships, has declined. The cultural beliefs of groupthink, of not taking risks, and of employees not thinking for themselves are passé. Such conformity has limited Japanese competitiveness in the global marketplace. Today there is a realization that Japanese firms need to be more proactive and nimble to prosper.

The average profitability of a Japanese company on the Tokyo Stock Exchange declined from about 9 to 1 percent in the past decade. This is often attributed partially to Japanese management philosophy. Sony, Hitachi, and other big companies are moving away from lifetime employment and now emphasize information disclosure, profitability, and management accountability.

Herzberg's Motivator-Hygiene Theory

Another important contribution to our understanding of individual motivation came from Frederick Herzberg's studies, which addressed the question "What do people really

Theory Y
A management style formulated by Douglas McGregor that is based on a relatively optimistic view of human nature; assumes that the average person wants to work, accepts responsibility, is willing to help solve problems, and can be self-directed and self-controlled.

Theory Z
A theory developed by William Ouchi that combines U.S. and Japanese business practices by emphasizing long-term employment, slow career development, moderate specialization, group decision making, individual responsibility, relatively informal control over the employee, and concern for workers.

LO 5

EXHIBIT 9.3 > Differences in Management Approaches

Factor	Traditional North American Management	Japanese Management	Theory Z (Combination of North American and Japanese Management)
Length of employment	Relatively short term; worker subject to layoffs if business is bad	Lifetime; layoffs never used to reduce costs	Long term but not necessarily lifetime; layoffs "inappropriate"; stable, loyal workforce; improved business conditions don't require new hiring and training
Rate of evaluation and promotion	Relatively rapid	Relatively slow	Slow by design; manager thoroughly trained and evaluated
Specialization in a functional area	Considerable; worker acquires expertise in single functional area	Minimal; worker acquires expertise in organization instead of functional areas	Moderate; all experience various functions of the organization and have a sense of what's good for the firm rather than for a single area
Decision making	On individual basis	Input from all concerned parties	Group decision making for better decisions and easier implementation
Responsibility for success or failure	Assigned to individual	Shared by group	Assigned to individual
Control by manager	Very explicit and formal	More implicit and informal	Relatively informal but with explicit performance measures
Concern for workers	Focuses on work-related aspects of worker's life	Extends to whole life of worker	Is relatively concerned with worker's whole life, including the family

SOURCE: Based on information from Jerry D. Johnson, Austin College. Dr. Johnson was a research assistant for William Ouchi.

want from their work experience?" In the late 1950s, Herzberg surveyed numerous employees to find out what particular work elements made them feel exceptionally good or bad about their jobs. The results indicated that certain job factors are consistently related to employee job satisfaction, whereas others can create job dissatisfaction. According to Herzberg, **motivating factors** (also called *job satisfiers*) are primarily intrinsic job elements that lead to satisfaction. **Hygiene factors** (also called *job dissatisfiers*) are extrinsic elements of the work environment. A summary of motivating and hygiene factors appears in Exhibit 9.4.

One of the most interesting results of Herzberg's studies was the implication that the opposite of satisfaction is not dissatisfaction. Herzberg believed that proper management of hygiene factors could prevent employee dissatisfaction but that these factors could not serve as a source of satisfaction or motivation. Good working conditions, for instance, will keep employees at a job but won't make them work harder. Poor working conditions, which are job dissatisfiers, on the other hand, might make

motivating factors
Intrinsic job elements that lead to worker satisfaction.

hygiene factors
Extrinsic elements of the work environment that do not serve as a source of employee satisfaction or motivation.

EXHIBIT 9.4 > Herzberg's Motivating and Hygiene Factors

Motivating Factors	Hygiene Factors
Achievement	Company policy
Recognition	Supervision
Work itself	Working conditions
Responsibility	Interpersonal relationships at work
Advancement	Salary and benefits
Growth	Job security

AP/WIDE WORLD PHOTOS

HOT *Links*

What are ways to motivate your employees without raising their pay? Visit (**www.biztrain.com/motivation/stories/20ways.htm**).

concept check

What did Elton Mayo's studies reveal about employee productivity?

How can a manager use an understanding of Maslow's hierarchy to motivate employees?

How do the Theory X, Theory Y, and Theory Z management styles differ?

What is the difference between Herzberg's hygiene factors and motivating factors?

employees quit. According to Herzberg, a manager who wants to increase employee satisfaction needs to focus on the motivating factors, or satisfiers. A job with many satisfiers will usually motivate workers, provide job satisfaction, and prompt effective performance, but a lack of job satisfiers doesn't always lead to dissatisfaction and poor performance. Instead, a lack of job satisfiers might merely lead to workers doing an adequate job rather than their best.

Although Herzberg's ideas have been widely read and his recommendations implemented at numerous companies over the years, there are some very legitimate concerns about his work. Although his findings have been used to explain employee motivation, his studies actually focused on job satisfaction, a different concept from motivation, though related to it. Other criticisms focus on the unreliability of Herzberg's method, the fact that the theory ignores the impact of situational variables, and the assumed relationship between satisfaction and productivity. Nevertheless, the questions raised by Herzberg about the nature of job satisfaction and the effects of intrinsic and extrinsic factors on employee behaviour have proved a valuable contribution to the evolution of theories of motivation and job satisfaction.

Contemporary Views on Motivation

The early management scholars laid a foundation that enabled managers to understand their workers better and how best to motivate them. Since then, new theories have given us an even deeper understanding of worker motivation. Three of these theories are explained in this section: the expectancy theory, the equity theory, and the goal-setting theory.

Expectancy Theory

expectancy theory
A theory of motivation that holds that the probability of an individual's acting in a particular way depends on how strongly that person believes the act will have a particular outcome, and on whether they value that outcome.

One of the best-supported and most widely accepted theories of motivation is expectancy theory, which focuses on the link between motivation and behaviour. According to **expectancy theory**, the probability that an individual will act in a particular way depends on how strongly that person believes the act will have a particular outcome, and on whether they value that outcome. The degree to which an employee is motivated depends on three important relationships, shown in Exhibit 9.5:

EXHIBIT 9.5 > How Expectations Can Lead to Motivation

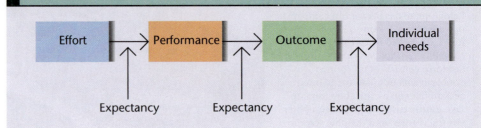

1. The link between *effort and performance*, or the strength of the individual's expectation that a certain amount of effort will lead to a certain level of performance.
2. The link between *performance and outcome*, or the strength of the expectation that a certain level of performance will lead to a particular outcome.
3. The link between *outcomes and individual needs*, or the degree to which the individual expects the anticipated outcome to satisfy personal needs. Some outcomes have more valence, or value, for individuals than others do.

Based on the expectancy theory, managers should do the following to motivate employees:

- determine the rewards valued by each employee,
- determine the desired performance level and then communicate it clearly to employees,
- make the performance level attainable,
- link rewards to performance,
- determine what factors might counteract the effectiveness of an award, and
- make sure the reward is adequate for the level of performance.

Equity Theory

Another contemporary explanation of motivation, **equity theory** is based on individuals' perceptions about how fairly they are treated compared to their coworkers. Equity means justice or fairness, and in the workplace it refers to employees' perceived fairness of the way they are treated and the rewards they earn. Employees evaluate their own *outcomes* (e.g., salary, benefits) in relation to their *inputs* (e.g., number of hours worked, education, and training) and then compare the outcomes-to-inputs ratio to one of the following:

1. Their past experience in a different position in the current organization.
2. Their past experience in a different organization.
3. Another employee's experience inside the current organization.
4. Another employee's experience outside the organization.

According to equity theory, if employees perceive that an inequity exists, they will make one of the following choices:

- *change their work habits* (exert less effort on the job),
- *change their job benefits and income* (ask for a raise, steal from the employer),
- *distort their perception of themselves* ("I always thought I was smart, but now I realize I'm a lot smarter than my coworkers"),
- *distort their perceptions of others* ("Joe's position is really much less flexible than mine"),
- *look at the situation from a different perspective* ("I don't make as much as the other department heads, but I make a lot more than most graphic artists"), or
- *leave the situation* (quit the job).

Margin

equity theory
A theory of motivation that holds that worker satisfaction is influenced by employees' perceptions about how fairly they are treated compared to their coworkers.

COURTESY OF BEN & JERRY'S HOMEMADE, INC.

CONCEPT *in Action* >>>

Ben & Jerry's founders Ben Cohen and Jerry Greenfield firmly believe the maxim that companies "do well by doing good." This idealism led the founders to once famously swear that no Ben & Jerry's executive would ever make more than seven times the lowliest worker's wage. But when growth required attracting exceptional top-level management, the company eventually abandoned its self-imposed ratio between its lowest and highest compensation rates. How might perceived inequities in pay affect worker satisfaction and motivation?

Managers can use equity theory to improve worker satisfaction. Knowing that every employee seeks equitable and fair treatment, managers can make an effort to understand an employee's perceptions of fairness and take steps to reduce concerns about inequity.

Goal-Setting Theory

goal-setting theory
A theory of motivation based on the premise that an individual's intention to work toward a goal is a primary source of motivation.

Goal-setting theory is based on the premise that an individual's intention to work toward a goal is a primary source of motivation. Once set, the goal clarifies for the employee what needs to be accomplished and how much effort will be required for completion. The theory has three main components:

1. Specific goals lead to a higher level of performance than do more generalized goals ("do your best").
2. More difficult goals lead to better performance than do easy goals (provided the individual accepts the goal).
3. Feedback on progress toward the goal enhances performance.

Feedback is particularly important, because it helps the individual identify the gap between the *real* (the actual performance) and the *ideal* (the desired outcome defined by the goal). Given the trend toward employee empowerment in the workplace, more and more employees are participating in the goal-setting process.

> **concept check**
>
> Discuss the three relationships central to expectancy theory.
>
> *Explain the comparison process that is a part of equity theory.*
>
> *How does goal-setting theory contribute to our understanding of motivation?*

Expanding Around The Globe

MOTIVATION IS CULTURE BOUND

Most motivation theories in use today were developed in the United States.[4] Of those that were not, many have been strongly influenced by the U.S. theories. In Canada, although to a lesser extent than in the United States, there is a relatively strong emphasis on individualism. This has led to expectancy and equity theories of motivation: theories that emphasize rational, individual thought as the primary basis of human behaviour. The emphasis placed on achievement is not surprising, given a willingness to accept risk and high concern for performance, but several motivation theories do not apply to all cultures.

Maslow's theory does not often hold outside of Canada and the United States. For instance, in countries whose citizens on average rate higher on uncertainty avoidance (such as Greece and Japan) as compared to those lower on uncertainty avoidance (such as Canada), security motivates employees more strongly than does self-actualization. Employees in high uncertainty-avoidance countries often consider job security and lifetime employment more important than holding a more interesting or challenging job. Also contrasting with the U.S. and, to a lesser extent, the Canadian pattern, social needs often dominate the motivation of workers in countries such as Denmark, Norway, and Sweden, whose residents stress the quality of life over materialism and productivity.

When researchers tested Herzberg's theory outside the United States, they encountered varied results. In New Zealand, for example, supervision and interpersonal relationships appear to contribute significantly to satisfaction and not merely to reducing dissatisfaction. Similarly, researchers found that citizens of Canada, Asia, Europe, Latin America, the Republic of Panama, and the West Indies cited certain extrinsic factors as satisfiers more frequently than did their American counterparts. The factors that motivate employees might not spark the same motivation in employees in other cultures.

Even the expectancy theory, considered a well-accepted contemporary motivation theory, does not always hold up in other cultures. Some of the major differences among the cultural groups include the following:

1. Citizens of English-speaking countries rank higher than average on individual achievement and lower on the desire for security.
2. Citizens of French-speaking countries, although similar to those of English-speaking countries, give greater importance to security and somewhat less to challenging work.
3. Northern Europeans have less interest in "getting ahead" and work recognition goals, instead placing more emphasis on job accomplishment. In addition, they have more concern for people and less for the organization as a whole (it is important that their jobs not interfere with their personal lives).
4. Latin Americans and southern Europeans find individual achievement somewhat less important; southern Europeans place the highest emphasis on job security, whereas citizens of both groups of countries emphasize fringe benefits.
5. Germans rank high on security and fringe benefits, and among the highest on "getting ahead."
6. The Japanese, although placing a low priority on advancement, also rank second highest on challenge and lowest on autonomy, with a strong emphasis on good working conditions and a friendly working environment.

Expectancy theories are universal to the extent that they do not specify the types of reward that motivate a given group of workers. Managers themselves must determine the level and type of reward most sought after by a particular group.[5]

From Motivation Theory to Application

LO 7

The material presented thus far in this chapter demonstrates the wide variety of theorists and research studies that have contributed to our current understanding of employee motivation. Now we turn our attention to more practical matters: to ways in which these concepts can be applied in the workplace to meet organizational goals and improve individual performance.

Reinforcing Behaviour

Reinforcement is described as the application of consequences in response to behaviour. According to B. F. Skinner's operant learning theory, the premise behind reinforcement is that consequences *influence* behaviour. The rules of consequences describe the outcomes that typically occur.

1. Introducing a positive consequence increases or maintains desired behaviours.
2. Removing a negative consequence increases or maintains desired behaviours.
3. Introducing a negative consequence (punishment) decreases behaviours.
4. Activities that do not give positive or negative consequences decrease behaviours.

Say, for example, that you have an employee who is consistently meeting or exceeding his or her sales targets. You might consider giving that person a bonus (positive reinforcement), but when this person no longer meets the targets, you remove the bonus (extinction). On the other hand you might have other employees who are not meeting their sales targets, and so you give them warnings whenever they don't meet their targets (punishment). When the employees meet the targets, you no longer give the warnings (negative reinforcement).

Several factors are important with respect to using reinforcement strategies. Positive reinforcement must be clearly contingent on specific behaviour, diversity must be considered with respect to the choice of reinforcer, and other sources of reinforcement within the workforce must be taken into consideration (e.g., peer pressure).

Handwritten margin notes:

Reinforcing Behaviour (Skinner)

	Introduce Consequence	Remove Consequence
Increase or maintain behaviour	Positive reinforcement (Add reward)	Negative reinforcement (Remove punishment)
Decrease or eliminate behaviour	Punishment	Extinction

CONCEPT *in Action* >>>

With employees clocking longer hours at work, office romances have become more frequent and less taboo than in the past. Regular collaboration between dedicated colleagues can very easily spill over into lunch breaks, happy hour, or even after-hours work assignments. While such tight teamwork raises fewer eyebrows today, companies concerned about workplace distractions and dramatic breakups often frown upon inter-office dating. How might managers utilize reinforcement theory to discourage employees from pursuing office trysts?

ANTONIO MO/PHOTODISC/GETTY IMAGES

Motivational Job Design

How might managers redesign or modify existing jobs to increase employee motivation and performance? The following three options have been used extensively in the workplace:

- *Job enlargement.* The horizontal expansion of a job, through an increase in the number and variety of tasks that a person performs, is called **job enlargement**. Increasing task diversity can enhance job satisfaction, particularly when the job is mundane and repetitive in nature. A potential drawback to job enlargement is that employees might perceive that they are being asked to work harder and do more with no change in their level of responsibility or compensation. This can cause resentment and lead to dissatisfaction.
- *Job enrichment.* **Job enrichment** is the vertical expansion of an employee's job. Whereas job enlargement addresses the breadth or scope of a job, enrichment is an attempt to increase job depth by providing the employee with more autonomy, responsibility, and decision-making authority. In an enriched job, the employee can use a variety of talents and skills and has more control over the planning, execution, and evaluation of the required tasks. In general, job enrichment has been found to increase job satisfaction and reduce absenteeism and turnover.
- *Job rotation.* Also called *cross-training*, **job rotation** is the shifting of workers from one job to another. This might be done to broaden an employee's skill base or because an employee has ceased to be interested in or challenged by a particular job. The organization might benefit from job rotation, because it increases flexibility in scheduling and production; employees can be shifted to cover for absent workers or changes in production or operations. It is also a valuable tool for training lower level managers in a variety of functional areas. Drawbacks of job rotation include an increase in training costs and decreased productivity while employees are getting "up to speed" in new task areas.

Work-Scheduling Options

As companies try to meet the needs of a diverse workforce and retain quality employees, while remaining competitive and financially prosperous, managers are challenged to find new ways of keeping workers motivated and satisfied. Increasingly popular are alternatives to the traditional work schedule, such as the compressed workweek, flextime, job sharing, and telecommuting.

One option for employees who want to maximize their leisure hours, indulge in three-day weekends, and avoid commuting during morning and evening rush hours is the *compressed* workweek. Employees work the traditional 40 hours but fit those hours into a shorter workweek. Most common is the 4-40 schedule, whereby employees work four 10-hour days a week. Organizations that offer this option claim benefits ranging from increased motivation and productivity to reduced absenteeism and turnover.

Another scheduling option, called *flextime*, allows employees to decide what their work hours will be. Employees are generally expected to work a certain number of hours per week but have some discretion as to when they arrive at work and when they leave for the day.

Job sharing is a scheduling option that allows two individuals to split the tasks, responsibilities, and work hours of one 40-hour-per-week job. Though used less frequently than flextime and the compressed workweek, this option can also provide employees with job flexibility. The primary benefit to the company is that it gets "two for the price of one"—the company can draw on two sets of skills and abilities to accomplish one set of job objectives.

Telecommuting is a work-scheduling option that allows employees to work from home via a computer that is linked with their office, headquarters, or colleagues. It is the fastest growing of the four scheduling options.

Options for Increasing Motivation (OSS)

① job enlargement (variety)
The horizontal expansion of a job based on an increase in the number and variety of tasks that a person performs.

② job enrichment (depth)
The vertical expansion of a job based on an increase in the employee's autonomy, responsibility, and decision-making authority.

③ job rotation (breadth)
The shifting of workers from one job to another; also called cross-training.

job sharing
A scheduling option that allows two individuals to split the tasks, responsibilities, and work hours of one 40-hour-per-week job.

Telecommuting
An arrangement in which employees work at home and are linked to the office by phone, fax, and computer.

HSBC, like many Canadian companies, recognized that its policies and practices around work-life balance were important in the competition for talent. They now offer flextime and job sharing to assist employees in meeting both their professional and their personal responsibilities.

Many companies have found themselves in a similar position to that of HSBC: recognizing that their policies and practices around work-life balance—important for an employer competing for talent in a small pool—could be enhanced and improved. And although some employers might not have accepted this challenge, HSBC took it as an opportunity to improve its policies related to work-life and change its culture to be more supportive and flexible.

Although each of these work scheduling options might have some drawbacks for the sponsoring organizations, the benefits far outweigh the problems. For this reason, not only is the number of companies offering compressed work increasing, so is the number of companies offering other options.

Recognition, Empowerment, and Economic Incentives

All employees have unique needs that they seek to fulfill through their jobs. Organizations must devise a wide array of incentives to ensure that a broad spectrum of employee needs can be addressed in the work environment, thus increasing the likelihood of motivated employees. A sampling of these motivational tools is discussed here.

Formal recognition of superior effort by individuals or groups in the workplace is one way of enhancing employee motivation. Recognition serves as positive feedback and reinforcement, letting employees know what they have done well and that their contribution is valued by the organization. Recognition can take many forms, both formal and informal. Some companies use formal awards ceremonies to acknowledge and celebrate their employees' accomplishments. Others take advantage of informal interactions to congratulate employees on a job well done and offer encouragement for the future. Recognition can take the form of an employee-of-the-month plaque, a monetary reward, a day off, a congratulatory e-mail, or a verbal "pat on the back."

As described in Chapter 7, employee empowerment, sometimes called employee involvement or participative leadership, involves delegating decision-making authority to employees at all levels of the organization. Employees are given greater responsibility for planning, implementing, and evaluating the results of decisions. Empowerment is based on the premise that human resources, especially at lower levels in the firm, are an underutilized asset. Employees are capable of contributing much more of their skills and abilities to organizational success if they are allowed to participate in the decision-making process and are given access to the resources needed to implement their decisions.

Any discussion of motivation has to include the use of monetary incentives to enhance performance. Currently, companies are using a variety of variable-pay programs, such as piece-rate plans, profit sharing, gain sharing, and bonuses, to encourage employees to be more productive. Unlike the standard salary or hourly wage, variable pay means that a portion of an employee's pay is linked directly to an individual or organizational performance measure. In *piece-rate pay plans*, for example, employees are paid a given amount for each unit they produce, directly linking the amount they earn to their productivity. *Profit-sharing plans* are based on overall company profitability. Using an established formula, management distributes some portion of company profits to all employees. *Gain-sharing* plans are incentive programs based on group productivity. Employees share in the financial gains attributed to the increased productivity of their group. This encourages them to increase productivity within their specific work area regardless of the overall profit picture for the organization as a whole. A *bonus* is simply a one-time lump-sum monetary reward.

<aside>
concept check

Explain the difference between job enlargement and job enrichment.

What are the four work scheduling options that can enhance employee performance?

Are all employees motivated by the same economic incentives? Explain.
</aside>

Making Ethical Choices

VOLUNTEERISM—OR SELF BENEFIT

You join a large financial institution that encourages and promotes employee volunteerism, allowing employees one day a month, or up to 12 days a year, to volunteer for a cause of their choosing. Shortly after you start working there as a junior teller, your boss' wife is diagnosed with a particularly aggressive form of breast cancer which carries a very poor prognosis. Realizing it will win you kudos with your boss, you choose the local chapter of a foundation—a breast cancer charity that sponsors an annual Race for the Cure—for your company-sponsored volunteer work.

In addition to working at the foundation's office one day a month, you spend your own time actively soliciting other staffers at your firm to sign up for the charity walk in a few months' time. Impressed with your qualities of tireless dedication, your boss puts your name forward for promotion to junior bank officer, well before the customary two years of service normally required for being considered for promotion.

Using a Web search tool, locate articles about this topic and then write responses to the following questions. Be sure to support your arguments and cite your sources.

ETHICAL DILEMMA: Your company is generous in its approach to employee volunteerism. It gives you paid time off and you acquire enhanced job skills through your volunteer activities. Have you just been smart in recognizing the value of volunteering for a charity that you know will earn your boss' personal appreciation? Or are you taking unfair advantage of your boss' vulnerability and manipulating the situation?

SOURCES: Margarita Bauza, "Companies Find Volunteering Makes Good Business Sense," Detroit Free Press, November 20, 2005, (http://galenet.thomsonlearning.com); "Deloitte Volunteer IMPACT Survey Reveals Link Between Volunteering and Professional Success," Internet Wire, June 3, 2005, (http://galenet.thomsonlearning.com); Charley Hannagan, "Can Work Help?" Post-Standard (Syracuse, NY), September 30, 2005, p. C1

Trends in Employee Motivation

LO 8

This chapter has focused on understanding what motivates people and how employee motivation and satisfaction affect productivity and organizational performance. Organizations can improve performance by investing in people. In reviewing the ways in which companies are currently choosing to invest in their human resources, we can spot four trends:

1. Education and training.
2. Employee ownership.
3. Work-life benefits.
4. Nurturing knowledge workers.

All of the companies making the *Canada's top 100 Employers* list know the importance of treating employees properly. They all have programs that allow them to invest in their employees through programs such as these and many more. Today's businesses also face the challenge of increased costs of absenteeism. In the next section, we discuss each of these trends in motivating employees.

Education and Training

Companies that provide educational and training opportunities for their employees reap the benefits of a more motivated, as well as a more skilled, workforce. Employees who are properly trained in new technologies are more productive and less resistant to job change. Education and training provide additional benefits by increasing employees' feelings of competence and self-worth. When companies spend money to upgrade employee knowledge and skills, they convey the message "we value you and are committed to your growth and development as an employee."

Employee Ownership

A recent trend that seems to have levelled off is employee ownership, most commonly implemented as employee stock ownership plans, or ESOPs. ESOPs are not the same as stock options, however. In an ESOP, employees receive compensation in the form of company stock. Recall that stock options give employees the opportunity to purchase company stock at a set price, even if the market price of the stock increases above that point. Because employees are compensated with stock, over time they can become the owners of the company. Behind employee ownership programs is the belief that employees who think like owners are more motivated to take care of customers' needs, reduce unnecessary expenses, make operations smoother, and stay with the company longer.

Work-Life Benefits

Another growing trend in the workplace involves companies helping their employees to manage the numerous and sometimes competing demands in their lives. Organizations are taking a more active role in helping employees achieve a balance between their work responsibilities and their personal obligations. The desired result is employees who are less stressed, better able to focus on their jobs, and therefore, more productive. Many companies provide work-life benefits for employees. For example, some companies offer telecommuting, part-time positions, job sharing, subsidized childcare, eldercare referral, and on-site fitness centres.

Nurturing Knowledge Workers

Most organizations have specialized workers, and managing them all effectively is a big challenge. In many companies, knowledge workers (now two-fifths of the workforce) might have a supervisor, but they are not "subordinates." They are "associates." Within their area of knowledge, they are supposed to do the telling. As knowledge is effective only if specialized, knowledge workers are not homogeneous, particularly the fast-growing group of knowledge technologists, such as computer systems specialists, lawyers, programmers, and others. And because knowledge work is specialized, it is deeply splintered.

A knowledge-based workforce is qualitatively different from a less skilled workforce. True, knowledge workers are still a minority, but they are fast becoming the largest single group. And they have already become the major creator of wealth. Increasingly the success, indeed the survival, of every business will depend on the performance of its knowledge workforce. The challenging part of managing knowledge workers is finding ways to motivate proud, skilled professionals to share expertise and cooperate in such a way as to advance the frontiers of their knowledge for the benefit of the shareholders and society in general. To achieve that auspicious goal, several companies have created what they call "communities of practice." Schlumberger Limited, an oilfield services company, uses this innovative tool to motivate its highly technical knowledge workers.

Coping with the Rising Costs of Absenteeism

The rate of employee absenteeism is relatively consistent from year to year, but the costs continue to rise very rapidly. Short-term absence costs have doubled in the past decade. Much of this is due to the cost of health-related absences.

As Canadian workers age, they will experience more responsibilities for caring for elderly parents. An older workforce also means more health-related time off. Experts speak about the "entitlement mentality" of many workers; that is, "I am entitled to take time off when I want or need to." Stress-related absenteeism is also on the rise.

Companies are trying to lower absenteeism in the following ways:

- allowing employees who arrive late or miss a day to do "make-up time," usually the same day or within the same week;
- establishing a grace period of a certain number of minutes for late arrivals that won't count as tardiness;
- eliminating advance-notice requirements for tardiness, which lets employees call at the last minute and be excused for a late arrival if operations won't be disrupted;

ANDRESR/SHUTTERSTOCK

CONCEPT in Action >>>

Companies sometimes create unusual perks to help attract and retain talented workers. Timberland employees receive a $3,000 subsidy to buy a hybrid automobile. Worthington Industries offers workers onsite haircuts for just $4. And at SC Johnson, retirees receive a lifetime membership to the company fitness center. What trends are emerging in the ways companies seek to motivate workers and keep them happy on the job?

concept check

What benefits can an organization derive from training and educational opportunities, stock ownership programs, and work-life benefits?

How are knowledge workers different from traditional employees?

Why is the cost of absenteeism rising, and what can be done about it?

- if mandatory overtime is permitted, allowing employees to refuse mandatory overtime occasionally—for example, for 25 percent of the time;
- eliminating formal attendance policies altogether. Instead, they treat poor attendance as they do performance problems. Employees who slip receive feedback and counselling, followed by a performance or development plan. The employee is discharged if the behaviour doesn't improve;[6]
- providing on-site day care for employees' children; and/or
- contracting with a firm specializing in eldercare to make in-home visits to employees' older relatives.

Great Ideas To Use Now

We've come a long way from the days of Taylor's scientific management. Organizations now offer a wide variety of incentives to attract and retain high-quality employees. A knowledgeable, creative, committed, and highly skilled workforce provides a company with a source of sustainable advantage in an increasingly competitive business environment. What does that mean to you? It means that companies are working harder than ever to meet employee needs. It means that when you graduate from college or university, you may choose a prospective employer on the basis of its daycare facilities and fitness programs as well as its salaries. It means that you need to think about what motivates you. Would you forgo a big salary to work for a smaller company that gives you lots of freedom to be creative and make your own decisions? Would you trade extensive health coverage for a share of ownership in the company? Most organizations try to offer a broad spectrum of incentives to meet a variety of needs, but each company makes trade-offs, and so will you in choosing an employer. Do a little research on a company you are interested in working for (paying particular attention to its corporate culture); then use the first exercise in the "Experiential Exercises" to help you determine how well your values fit with the company's values.

Customer Satisfaction and Quality

So often we think of employee motivation as a purely internal process. However, recent research shows that happy, satisfied employees who stay in jobs can affect an organization's level of customer satisfaction. Unifi, a division of PricewaterhouseCoopers, and Roper Starch Worldwide, recently conducted a survey of customers of businesses in six industries. Across all six, the survey results showed that employee turnover has a significant impact on customer satisfaction. Customers felt that employee retention affected the quality of the service they received from the organization.

Gary Wallace, the CEO of a credit union, recognized this connection between motivated employees and happy customers some time back. With customer satisfaction as his primary goal,

Wallace first went about implementing programs to find new and better ways to serve his employees. The credit union redecorated the employee lounge in the colours of the local football teams and offered employees an enjoyable place to relax. It also installed multimedia stations at each branch to offer motivational messages and information about employee benefits and upcoming company and community events. The company also built larger employee cubicles and constructed an outdoor patio with umbrella tables.[7]

How has all of this worked? Quite well for Mr. Wallace and the credit union. The company has expanded its market share, and its assets have passed the $500 million mark. Service has improved, employee turnover is down, and customer satisfaction has never been higher.

Summary of Learning Outcomes

1 **Explain the basic principles of Frederick Taylor's concept of scientific management.**

Scientific management is based on the belief that employees are motivated by economic incentives and that there is "one best way" to perform any job. The four basic principles of scientific management developed by Taylor are as follows:

1. Develop a scientific approach for each element of a person's job.

2. Scientifically select, train, teach, and develop workers.

3. Encourage cooperation between workers and managers, so that each job can be accomplished in a standard, scientifically determined way.

4. Divide work and responsibility between management and workers according to who is better suited to each task.

2 **Summarize what Elton Mayo's Hawthorne studies revealed about worker motivation.**

The pride that comes from special attention motivates workers to increase their productivity. Supervisors who allow employees to have some control over their situation appeared to increase the workers' motivation further. The Hawthorne effect suggests that employees will perform better when they feel singled out for special attention or feel that management is concerned about their welfare.

3 **Discuss Maslow's hierarchy of needs, and how these needs relate to employee motivation.**

Maslow believed that each individual has a hierarchy of needs, consisting of physiological, safety, social, esteem, and self-actualization needs. Managers who accept Maslow's ideas attempt to increase employee motivation by modifying organizational and managerial practices to increase the likelihood that employees will meet all levels of needs. Maslow's theory has also helped managers understand that it is hard to motivate people by appealing to already satisfied needs.

4 **Identify how McGregor's Theories X and Y and Ouchi's Theory Z are used to explain worker motivation.**

Douglas McGregor influenced the study of motivation with his formulation of two contrasting sets of assumptions about human nature—designated Theory X and Theory Y. Theory X says people don't like to work and will avoid it if they can. Because people don't like to work, they must be controlled, directed, or threatened to get them to make an effort. Theory Y says that people want to be self-directed and will try to accomplish goals that they believe in. Workers can be motivated with positive incentives. McGregor personally believed that Theory Y assumptions describe most employees and that managers seeking to motivate subordinates should develop management practices based on those assumptions.

William Ouchi's Theory Z combines North American and Japanese business practices. Theory Z emphasizes long-term employment, slow career development, and group decision making. The recent decline of the Japanese economy has resulted in most North American firms moving away from Japanese management practices.

5 **Explain the basic components of Herzberg's motivator-hygiene theory.**

Frederick Herzberg's studies indicated that certain job factors are consistently related to employee job satisfaction, whereas others can create job dissatisfaction. According to Herzberg, motivating factors (also called satisfiers) are primarily intrinsic job elements that lead to satisfaction, such as achievement, recognition, the (nature of) work itself, responsibility, advancement, and growth. What Herzberg termed hygiene factors (also called dissatisfiers) are extrinsic elements of the work environment, such as company policy, relationships with supervisors, working conditions, relationships with peers and subordinates, salary and benefits, and job security. These are factors that can result in job dissatisfaction if not managed well. One of the most interesting findings of Herzberg's studies was the implication that the opposite of satisfaction is not dissatisfaction. Herzberg believed that proper management of hygiene factors could prevent employee dissatisfaction but that these factors could not serve as a source of satisfaction or motivation.

6 **Describe how three contemporary theories of employee motivation offer insights into improving employee performance.**

According to expectancy theory, the probability that an individual will act in a particular way depends on: how strongly that person believes the act will lead to a certain level of performance; whether that performance will have a particular outcome; and whether they value that outcome. Equity theory is based on individuals' perceptions about how fairly they are treated compared to their coworkers. Goal-setting theory states that employees are highly motivated to perform when specific goals are established and feedback on progress is offered.

7 **Discuss how managers can redesign existing jobs to increase employee motivation and performance.**

The horizontal expansion of a job by increasing the number and variety of tasks that a person performs is called job enlargement. Increasing task diversity can enhance job satisfaction, particularly when the job is mundane and repetitive in nature. Job enrichment is the vertical expansion of an employee's job to provide the employee with more autonomy, responsibility, and decision-making authority. Other popular motivational tools include work-scheduling options, employee recognition programs, empowerment, and variable-pay programs.

8 **List some of the initiatives organizations are using today to motivate and retain employees.**

Today, firms are using several key tactics to motivate and retain workers. First, companies are investing more in employee education and training, which make workers more productive and less resistant to job change. Second, managers are offering employees a chance for ownership in the company. This can strongly increase employee commitment. Enlightened employers are providing work-life benefits to help employees achieve a better balance between work and personal responsibilities. Businesses are also recognizing the importance of managing knowledge workers and reducing the growing cost of employee absenteeism.

Key Terms

expectancy theory   271
goal-setting theory   273
Hawthorne effect   266
hygiene factors   270
job enlargement   275
job enrichment   275
job rotation   275
job sharing   275

Maslow's hierarchy of needs   267
motivating factors   270
scientific management   265
telecommuting   275
Theory X   268
Theory Y   269
Theory Z   269

Experiential Exercises

1. The accompanying table lists 17 personal characteristics and 13 institutional values you might encounter at a company. Select and rank-order the 10 personal characteristics that best describe you; do the same for the 10 institutional values that would be most evident in your ideal workplace. Test your fit at a firm by seeing whether the characteristics of the company's environment match your top 10 personal characteristics.

The Choice Menu

Rank Order (1–17) You Are	Rank Order (1–13) Your Ideal Company Offers
_____ 1. Flexible	_____ 1. Stability
_____ 2. Innovative	_____ 2. High expectations of performance
_____ 3. Willing to experiment	_____ 3. Opportunities for professional growth
_____ 4. Risk taking	_____ 4. High pay for good performance
_____ 5. Careful	_____ 5. Job security
_____ 6. Autonomy seeking	_____ 6. A clear guiding philosophy
_____ 7. Comfortable with rules	_____ 7. A low level of conflict
_____ 8. Analytical	_____ 8. Respect for the individual's rights
_____ 9. Team oriented	_____ 9. Informality
_____ 10. Easygoing	_____ 10. Fairness
_____ 11. Supportive	_____ 11. Long hours
_____ 12. Aggressive	_____ 12. Relative freedom from rules
_____ 13. Decisive	_____ 13. The opportunity to be distinctive, or different from others
_____ 14. Achievement oriented	
_____ 15. Comfortable with individual responsibility	
_____ 16. Competitive	
_____ 17. Interested in making friends at work	

2. How are job satisfaction and employee morale linked to job performance? Do you work harder when you are satisfied with your job? Explain your answer.

3. Review the assumptions of Theories X, Y, and Z. Under which set of assumptions would you prefer to work? Is your current or former supervisor a Theory X, Theory Y, or Theory Z manager? Explain by describing the person's behaviour.

4. Think about several of your friends who seem to be highly self-motivated. Talk with each of them and ask them what factors contribute the most to their motivation. Make a list of their responses and compare them to the factors that motivate you.

5. Both individual motivation and group participation are needed to accomplish certain goals. Describe a situation you're familiar with in which cooperation achieved a goal that individual action could not. Describe one in which group action slowed progress and individual action would have been better.

6. Using expectancy theory, analyze how you have made and will make personal choices, such as a major area of study, a career to pursue, or job interviews to seek.

7. If you're looking for 1,001 ways to motivate or reward employees, Bob Nelson can help. Visit the "Recognition" resources section of his Nelson Motivation site at (**www.nelson-motivation.com**) to get some ideas you can put to use to help you do a better job, either as an employee or as a manager.

8. More companies are offering their employees stock ownership plans. To learn the differences between an employee stock ownership plan (ESOP) and stock options, visit the National Center for Employee Ownership (NCEO), at (**www.nceo.org**), and the Foundation for Enterprise Development (FED), at (**www.fed.org**). Which stock plan would you rather have? Why? Also visit the "Ownership Culture" area of the NCEO site. What does research on employee ownership indicate? Cite specific examples.

9. Open-book management is one of the better known ways to create a participatory work environment. More than 2,000 companies have adopted this practice, which involves sharing financial information with non-management employees and training them to understand financial information. Does it really motivate employees and improve productivity? Do a search for this topic at the NCEO site, (**www.nceo.org**). You'll find survey results, case studies, related activities, and links that will help you answer this question.

10. Use a search engine to find companies that offer "work-life benefits." Link to several companies and review their employee programs in this area. How do they compare? Which benefits would be most important to you if you were job hunting, and why?

Review Questions

1. Summarize the following:

   - Frederick Taylor's scientific management,
   - Hawthorne studies,
   - Maslow's hierarchy of needs,
   - McGregor's Theories X and Y,
   - Ouchi's Theory Z, and
   - Herzberg's motivator-hygiene theory.

2. Explain E > P > O of expectancy theory. How does this explain employee behaviour?

3. What are the choices available when an employee feels that there is unfairness on the job?

4. How can the use of goal-setting theory lead to motivation?

5. Explain

   - job enlargement, job enrichment, and job rotation;
   - work-scheduling options and how they can be a motivator; and
   - how motivation is affected by recognition, empowerment, and economic incentives.

6. Explain how the following affect employee motivation:

   - education and training opportunities,
   - employee ownership,
   - work-life benefits, and
   - the nurturing of knowledge workers.

CREATIVE THINKING CASE >

De-Motivating Your Top Producer

The Max Call Centre had been home to Sandy Rolf for many years. She had a good salary, excellent bonus system (cash and other incentives), and a reasonable benefits package and pension plan. Sandy's job was outbound cold calls to bring customers back to the company. Many of us would cringe at the thought of spending eight hours a day doing this. Sandy loved it, as she said, "my two favourite things, talking on the phone and making money." As a top producer in the area, she received gift certificates in the hundreds of dollars for various local merchants, as well as her base salary and commissions. She was celebrated at company functions by upper management, received congratulatory e-mails and plaques, and was honoured at departmental meetings. Her managers could not say enough positive things about her.

So what did the company ultimately do to reward this loyal and valued employee? They outsourced her job. As a result of an executive decision, the department no longer existed. Sandy was told not to worry, she still had a job. The job turned out to be fielding inbound calls, most of which were complaints against the company for perceived wrongs against the customer.

Sandy's health began to deteriorate because of extreme stress, and the once happy, outgoing, fun-loving woman now spent most of her leisure time sleeping, watching TV, and avoiding her friends and family.

Research suggests that small pleasures (e.g., a job you enjoy) are more likely to yield long-term joy than high-profile positive events. "It's the frequency and not the intensity of the positive events in your life that leads to happiness, like comfortable shoes or a single malt scotch," according to Daniel Gilbert, a Harvard University psychology professor. By going to a job she loved, Sandy experienced happiness and job satisfaction on a daily basis. Now that this situation had changed, her happiness and motivation levels dropped, leaving Sandy in a depressed state, struggling for the energy and interest even to access the online job search sites.

Critical Thinking Questions

- Using the motivation theories in the chapter, explain why Sandy was so motivated in a job such as cold calling.
- Given that she still had a salary, benefits, and a pension plan, why did she become so extremely unmotivated after the change?

SOURCE: Judy Stoffman, "You're Happy. Imagine That!: Why People Are So Bad at Predicting What Will Make Them Feel Good," *Toronto Star*, May 21, 2006, D4.

SOURCE: Judy Stoffman, "You're Happy. Imagine That!: Why People Are So Bad at Predicting What Will Make Them Feel Good," *Toronto Star*, May 21, 2006, D4.

VIDEO CASE >

One Red Paperclip: Motivated to Follow Your Dream

On July 12, 2005, Kyle MacDonald, a 26 year old unemployed geography major living in Montreal, set a goal to trade one red paperclip for a house by the end of one year. He succeeded and became an international celebrity. How did he do this? And *why* did he do this? What would possibly motivate someone to embark on such an outrageous undertaking?

Probably the 'how' is the easier question to answer. Kyle began by setting up a website called, of course, "oneredpaperclip.com". As Kyle was unemployed, he paid his bills by selling advertisements on his website. He announced his plan on Craigslist and the trading began. The paperclip was traded for a fish pen, which was then traded for a door knob, which was traded for a Coleman camp stove and on it went. Kyle's story was featured on CNN, CBC, ABC, BBC, a Japanese TV station and an Israeli station, all of these representing free advertising for his project. All of the trades were posted online, each trade represented another story, and Kyle invited everyone to participate in his adventure. He traded an afternoon with Alice Cooper for a motorized KISS snow globe which he then traded to producer Corbin Bersen for a role in the movie *Donna on Demand*.

The movie role was traded for a two storey farmhouse in Kipling, Saskatchewan within the one year timeframe that Kyle had hoped for . The final trade was carefully contemplated by the town before the offer was extended. Proposed by Bert, the town's head of development, the deal had to be sold to the voting members of the town council and the mayor. Fortunately this group of individuals had the vision to predict what the whole story could do for the town in the form of publicity and jobs. The deal was signed and in September 2006, a huge house-warming was held in Kipling with 12 of the 14 traders in attendance as well as the media and many hundreds of guests.

Kyle's insight and drive lead him to succeed in this undertaking. As he suggested, the value of the house was irrelevant, the value was in the story. Little did he know at the time that he was predicting the future. He now has a book, in English and in

French, and a major movie company has the rights to his story. Never one to sit quietly and enjoy what is, Kyle and his fiancée, Dom, are trading the house. As Kyle says," With who? For what? Well that's where things get interesting: We have no idea yet."

Critical thinking questions

- Using material from the chapter, discuss what might motivate someone to do something like this.
- What motivates others to participate?
- Check out Kyle's website and see where he is now in his trading story. Did he trade the house? To whom and for what? Is there a movie? If so, how does the movie address the issue of motivation?

SOURCE: CBC, *Venture*, Y8V-06-06 (From CBC learning website).

E-COMMERCE CASE >

Motivating Employees: A Monster of a Problem

As mentioned in earlier chapters, businesses will face a decrease in the available workforce due in part to a smaller generation of talented workers replacing retiring baby boomers. "Our study reveals that recruiters and hiring managers are not only cognizant of the issue but are concerned about its current and future impact on organizational growth," said Dr. Jesse Harriott, vice-president of research at Monster Worldwide (www.monster.com), the leading global online career and recruitment resource. "Businesses of all sizes and across all industries must develop and implement creative programs and strategies to attract and hire top candidates while retaining and motivating current employees. As the talent pool shrinks, it is imperative that immediate action is taken to ensure businesses are properly prepared and staffed for the future."

In a sampling of over 600 human resource managers, Monster's survey showed that over 75 percent believe compensation is one of the top three motivators that prevent employees from leaving their jobs. The fact that money motivates top-performing employees is supported by almost half the human resources professionals surveyed for the 2005 Rewards Program and Incentive Compensation Survey released by the Society of Human Resource Management. The survey also found that neither monetary nor non-monetary rewards were effective motivators for underperformers.

While compensation is clearly a significant issue, not all companies can offer this advantage. Other strategies that motivate employee loyalty and commitment are necessary. Some of these include: making supervisors more accountable for worker retention; promoting work/life balance for employees; fostering a workplace where employee expectations are clearly articulated; learning and development programs that groom employees for future management roles; performance-based systems that identify and proactively manage top employees and, when possible, to promote from within; mentoring programs that match new employees with seasoned veterans; monitoring sentiment throughout the employee lifecycle; creating an employment brand "experience" that not only motivates and energizes employees, but can be used to attract new talent.

Diana Pohly, president and owner of The Pohly Company, keeps vigilant watch over the morale of the office, ensuring that employees are satisfied. "Business owners of growing companies must possess strong leadership and management skills in order to solidify the foundation of their business," said Pohly. "Effective team leadership is imperative to sustain efficient team workflows and contribute to employee morale."

"Employees are the lifeblood of any organization. Building a positive work environment is an important strategy in attracting, retaining and motivating a team," says Michelle Swanda, corporate marketing manager of The Principal. Improving employee morale with creative and effective management tactics ultimately boosts employee productivity, and that goes straight to the bottom line.

Critical Thinking Questions

1 How are social and economic factors influencing companies' approaches to hiring, motivating, and retaining employees?

2 What are some of the non-monetary strategies companies must develop to attract, reward, and keep employees motivated?

3 What "reward factors" would be important to you when working for a company? List at least five in order of importance and your reasons for each.

SOURCES: "70 Percent of HR Managers Concerned about Workforce Retention, According to Monster Study," Business Wire, Jan 9, 2006, (www.findarticles.com); "Poll Says Top-Performing Workers Motivated By Money," Nation's Restaurant News, April 25, 2005, (www.findarticles.com). "Team Motivation: Women Business Owners Increase Productivity Through Effective Leadership," Business Wire, Oct 27, 2005, (www.findarticles.com).

PART 4

Functional Areas of Business

CHAPTER 10

Making the Connection

Managing Human Resources and Labour Relations

In this section of the text we will take a look at the internal environment of a business or, more simply, the functional areas of a business. These areas are what most people think of when they think of a business or a career in business—human resources, operations, marketing, accounting, and finance.

Before we take a look inside each of the functional areas in detail, in separate chapters, one very important message must be communicated clearly at the outset. Even though each of these areas is discussed separately in different chapters of introductory textbooks, and later in separate courses in business schools, they cannot act separately if the business is to be successful. They are all part of the integrated business model that has been the central theme of this text. Each of these areas must work together to make the business successful overall. For example, a company cannot design and market a product for which it does not have the human, operational, and financial resources. Just imagine The Bay attempting to produce a new all-terrain vehicle and introduce it to the market. It could perhaps alter its store setup to sell the vehicle, but does it have the facilities and people skills to produce it? Would it even have the financial resources to put toward this type of endeavour, considering the tight budgets most businesses are working with today to keep their core business alive?

It was clear from Chapter 7, which deals with management and planning, that all decisions made at the tactical level in the functional areas come from decisions made at a higher *strategic* level that affect the whole company. Top management first scans the external environment (PEST model) to look for opportunities and threats and matches those with the strengths and weaknesses of the company in the different functional areas to decide the direction for the company. It is therefore unlikely that a decision like this one would ever be made by The Bay. Even if there were opportunities in the market for ATVs, it would not match with the strengths of the company. Financial resources would therefore not be released for this type of project to begin with.

In this chapter we'll take a look at our first functional area. The old adage "last but not least" certainly applies here. As we discussed earlier, *gaining the commitment of employees* is the most critical factor, because all of the other four critical success factors are achieved through the people in the company. Without a strong human resource area and the strong commitment of the employees toward organizational goals, the company simply cannot be successful in any functional area or overall.

The business environment today provides many challenges for the human resource manager. In the *political* environment, regulations govern many aspects of the human resource function, such as how workers can be selected (e.g., drug testing, human rights legislations governing the application and interview process). The mix of people hired is also regulated for some companies through employment equity legislation. Issues relating to diversity are critically important, because without a diverse workforce, companies will have a difficult time both understanding the global marketplace and, subsequently, designing products and marketing plans to appeal to this multifaceted society. Therefore, companies must consider this trend toward greater diversity in the make-up of society very seriously, taking proactive steps rather than just reacting to government legislation. The importance of diversity to a company's success can be seen in the example of PepsiCo in the opening vignette to this chapter. PepsiCo has

a long-standing commitment to diversity within its marketing and human resources that has made it both more responsive to the marketplace and a better place to work, giving it a competitive advantage. In the *economic* environment, organizations are competing not only for customers but also for a shrinking pool of qualified job applicants, and they must also pay attention to the salaries of the competition to remain competitive. In the *social* environment, workers are seeking to better balance their home and work lives, making it more critical and more difficult to gain commitment in the traditional ways;the aging workforce is also creating difficulties. The *technological* environment is reshaping how work is done, offering options to human labour and changing the nature of many jobs and the skills required to do them. Technology also affects how the human resource department does its job. You'll find many examples both in the chapter and in trying to find a job yourself, such as using the Internet to recruit workers and using specially designed software to pick out key phrases from résumés to sort through them more quickly.

An environmental factor that has a dramatic impact on how a company operates is the presence of unions. This is a very integrative factor as it has implications for all the environmental factors and all the areas of the business. It is *political*, because legislation governs how unions become involved with a group of workers and how the union-management relationship works; it is social, because the culture and attitude of the workers affect how they view unions and whether they would want to work in a unionized environment; it is technological, because the union contract could impact the rights of management to use technology if it replaces workers; and it is economic, because a unionized workplace often has less flexibility and higher compensation costs than a non-unionized environment, and that can impact a company's competitiveness. Unions can therefore affect the financial success of the company, and they can definitely signal an issue with respect to worker commitment when the workers feel compelled to have a third party represent them with management. This point stresses the importance of management operating with the commitment of the workers foremost in its mind if it wishes to operate without a union. It is management's job to create a work environment that gains commitment and loyalty, where the human resource policies are so worker focused that unions are the last thought on the workers' minds.

As with the other functional areas, the main basis for all decisions in the human resource area is the company's goals and *strategy*. The role of the human resource area is to provide the right numbers of the right kinds of people in the right places at the right times to assist the other functional areas to help the organization achieve its objectives. To do this, the human resource area must work very closely with *marketing, operations,* and *finance* to understand their objectives and thus their human resource requirements. It must also understand the jobs that need to be done to determine the skills that it must recruit and train for.

One area in which human resources must work especially closely with finance is in the area of employee compensation and benefits. Because of the relative size of this expense, it has a tremendous impact on the bottom line on the one hand, but on the other it also affects the level of commitment from employees. Therefore, an integrative approach must be taken in determining compensation. This matter is becoming more important as workers are changing jobs more often.

Compensation is just one decision area in which the human resource manager must develop and implement policies in an integrative way to create a more committed workforce. For example, one common approach in recruitment and selection is to promote first from within. This practice shows employees that the organization is committed to them, which is an essential ingredient in gaining commitment from employees. Another particularly integrative way to increase commitment is by offering telecommuting. The technological environment has made telecommuting possible, thus improving the productivity of workers and saving companies money. This, in turn, has helped firms retain key people who would otherwise have to leave. In training and development as well, the organization can show its commitment to the employees by helping them to achieve their potential. Again, employees will be more committed to an organization that shows commitment to them in its human resource policies. This effort to train and develop employees makes them both better at their jobs and more loyal, which translates into being more *innovative,* providing greater *quality,* and working harder to meet and exceed *customer needs,* thereby allowing the organization to *achieve financial performance* both through lower turnover and through greater customer satisfaction.

CHAPTER **10**

Managing Human Resources and Labour Relations

LEARNING OUTCOMES

1 Discuss the human resource management process, and how human resource needs are determined.

2 Explain how firms recruit applicants.

3 Summarize how firms select qualified applicants.

4 List some of the types of training and development programs organizations offer their employees.

5 Show how performance appraisals are used to evaluate employee performance.

6 Analyze the various methods for compensating employees.

7 Explain how labour–management relations are different in a unionized environment.

8 Describe some of the key laws and federal agencies affecting human resource management and labour relations.

9 List some of the trends and issues affecting human resource management and labour relations.

PEPSICO IS COMMITTED TO DIVERSITY

PepsiCo (**www.pepsico.com**) is the parent company of some of Canada's best-known brands, including Pepsi, Frito-Lay, Tropicana, and Quaker Oats. With more than 185,000 employees around the world, PepsiCo employees share a common set of values and goals. Top executives and human resource managers know that success takes the work of talented and dedicated people who are committed to making an impact every day. Their ability to grow year after year is driven by their ability to attract, develop, and retain world-class people who will thrive in a dynamic environment. To achieve this, PepsiCo recognizes that they need employees who are anxious to be part of a dynamic, results-oriented company, with powerful brands and top-notch people.

Early in the firm's history—as far back as the 1940s—Pepsi-Cola acknowledged the importance of diversity within its workplaces and in the marketplace. Recognizing the importance of tailoring its marketing to minority groups, Pepsi pioneered advertising specifically to minority groups. These ads featured minority actors and actresses and focused on minority lifestyles. The company also developed education and sports programs spotlighting minorities, and sponsored major musical tours by entertainers such as Michael Jackson and Tina Turner. The firm also spends millions of dollars advertising in minority media such as *Ebony* and *Black Enterprise*.

PepsiCo has been nationally recognized as one of the top places for women and minorities to work. The firm has been hiring minorities in professional positions for more than 65 years. Pepsi was the first Fortune 500 Company to have an African American vice-president. PepsiCo has developed a number of diversity initiatives to ensure that the firm's core value of diversity is a competitive advantage. These initiatives include the following:

© DIGITAL VISION / GETTY IMAGES

- Within Pepsi-Cola, Frito-Lay, and Tropicana operating divisions, executives are completely dedicated to managing diversity in the workplace.

- Multiyear strategic plans for diversity are developed with the same vigour and goal-setting process as other business issues. Goals include turnover reduction, increased diversity hiring, and creation of an "inclusion" culture.

- An External Diversity Advisory Board consisting of educators, politicians, practitioners, and customers advises PepsiCo senior management on how to leverage diversity in the marketplace.

- Annual employee reviews incorporate the need to "Act with Integrity," "Create a Positive Work Environment," and "Align and Motivate Teams."

- A mandatory annual Affirmative Action Planning process is in place.

- An annual organizational health survey incorporates diversity questions and requires analysis of the minority and female employees. Senior management is held accountable for results.

- A corporate program is dedicated to training employees on how to work and manage in an inclusive environment.

- Employee networks mentor and support minority and female employees.

Human resource management and labour relations involve acquisition, development, use, and maintenance of a human resource mix (people and positions) to achieve strategic organizational goals and objectives. Successful human resource management is based on a company's ability to attract and hire the best employees, equip them with the knowledge and skills they need to excel, compensate them fairly, and motivate them to reach their full potential and perform at high levels. Today's business environment presents numerous challenges to effectively managing employees:

- *Technology continues to advance, which places great importance on knowledge workers, especially when demand outstrips the supply of high talent individuals.*
  - *Global business operations involve rapid data transfer and necessitate accelerated decision making by executive and technical employees.*
  - *The workforce is increasingly more diversified and multicultural, which places increased emphasis on communication and cultural understanding.*
  - *Work life and family priorities are more difficult to balance as dual worker families populate the labour force.*
  - *Employment and labour laws continue to greatly influence employee recruitment and hiring, compensation decisions, and employee retention and turnover in both union and non-union organizations.*

Each day, human resource experts and front-line supervisors deal with these challenges while sharing responsibility for attracting and retaining skilled, motivated employees. Whether faced with a large or small human resource problem, supervisors need some understanding of difficult employee relations issues, especially if there are legal implications.

In this chapter, you will learn about the elements of the human resource management process, including human resource planning and job analysis and design, employee recruitment and selection, training and development of employees, performance planning and evaluation, and compensation of the workforce. The chapter also describes labour unions and their representation of millions of Canadian workers in construction, manufacturing, transportation, and service-based industries.

© PHOTODISC RED/GETTY IMAGES

CONCEPT *in Action* >>>

As business expands around the globe, human resource managers need to develop communication systems and training strategies that build teamwork among diverse employees who may be located around the world. What human resource challenges are caused by increasing globalization of Canadian companies?

Achieving High Performance Through Human Resource Management

LO 1

human resource management
The process of hiring, developing, motivating, and evaluating employees to achieve organizational goals.

Human resource (HR) management is the process of hiring, developing, motivating, and evaluating employees to achieve organizational goals. The goals and strategies of the firm's business model form the basis for making human resource management decisions. HR practices and systems comprise the firm's human resource decision support system that is intended to make employees a key element for gaining competitive advantage. To this end, the HR management process contains the following sequenced activities:

EXHIBIT 10.1 > Human Resource Management Process

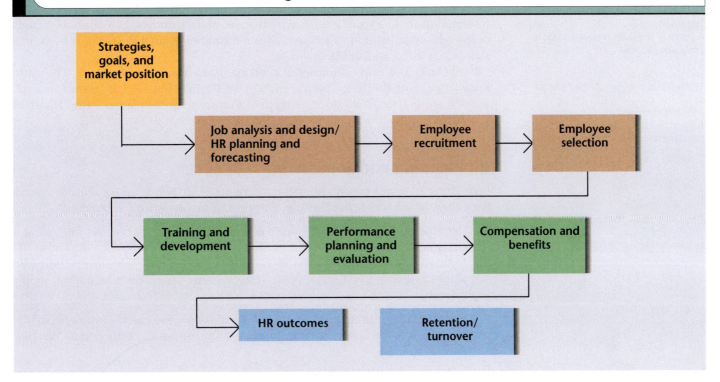

- job analysis and design,
- human resource planning and forecasting,
- employee recruitment,
- employee selection,
- training and development,
- performance planning and evaluation, and
- compensation and benefits.

The human resource management process shown in Exhibit 10.1 encourages the development of high performance employees. The process is sequential because employees can't be trained and paid until selected and placed in jobs, which follows recruitment, which is preceded by human resource planning and job analysis and design. Good HR practices used along this sequence foster performance improvement, knowledge and skill development, and loyal employees who desire to remain with the organization.

HR Planning and Job Analysis and Design

Two important, and somewhat parallel, aspects of the human resource management process are determining the employee needs of the firm and the jobs to be filled. Firms need to have the right number of people, with the right training, in the right jobs, to do the organization's work when it needs to be done. Human resource specialists are the ones who must determine future human resource needs and assess the skills of the firm's existing employees to see if new people must be hired or existing ones retrained.

human resource (HR) planning
Creating a strategy for meeting future human resource needs.

Creating a strategy for meeting future human resource needs is called **human resource (HR) planning**. Two important aspects of HR planning are job analysis and forecasting the firm's people needs. The HR planning process begins with a review of corporate strategy and policy. By understanding the mission of the organization, planners can understand its human resource needs.

Human resource planners must know what skills different jobs require. Information about a specific job is typically assembled through a **job analysis**, a study of the tasks required to do a job well. This information is used to specify the essential skills, knowledge, and abilities.

The tasks and responsibilities of a job are listed in a **job description**. The skills, knowledge, and abilities a person must have to fill a job are spelled out in a **job specification**. These two documents help human resource planners find the right people for specific jobs. A sample job description is shown in Exhibit 10.2.

job analysis
A study of the tasks required to do a particular job well.

job description
The tasks and responsibilities of a job.

job specification
A list of the skills, knowledge, and abilities a person must have to fill a job.

HR Planning and Forecasting

Forecasting an organization's human resource needs, known as an HR *demand forecast*, is an essential aspect of HR planning. This process involves two forecasts:

1. Determining the number of people needed by some future time (in one year, for example).
2. Estimating the number of people currently employed by the organization who will be available to fill various jobs at some future time. This is an *internal* supply forecast.

By comparing human resource demand and supply forecasts, a future personnel surplus or shortage can be determined and appropriate action taken. WestJet,

---

EXHIBIT 10.2 > Job Description

Position:	College Recruiter	**Location:**	Corporate Offices
Reports to:	Vice President of Human Resources	**Classification:**	Salaried/Exempt

Job Summary: Member of HR corporate team. Interacts with managers and department heads to determine hiring needs for college graduates. Visits 20 to 30 college and university campuses each year to conduct preliminary interviews of graduating students in all academic disciplines. Following initial interviews, works with corporate staffing specialists to determine persons who will be interviewed a second time. Makes recommendations to hiring managers concerning best-qualified applicants.

Job Duties and Responsibilities:

Estimated time spent and importance

15 percent	Working with managers and department heads, determines college recruiting needs.
10 percent	Determines colleges and universities with degree programs appropriate to hiring needs to be visited.
15 percent	Performs college relations activities with numerous colleges and universities.
25 percent	Visits campuses to conduct interviews of graduating seniors.
15 percent	Develops applicant files and performs initial applicant evaluations.
10 percent	Assists staffing specialists and line managers in determining who to schedule for second interviews.
5 percent	Prepares annual college recruiting report containing information and data about campuses, number interviewed, number hired, and related information.
5 percent	Participates in tracking college graduates who are hired to aid in determining campuses that provide the most outstanding employees.

Job Specification (Qualifications):

Bachelor's degree in human resource management or a related field. Minimum of two years of work experience with the firm in HR or department that annually hires college graduates. Ability to perform in a team environment, especially with line managers and department heads. Very effective oral and written communication skills. Reasonably proficient in Excel, Word, and Windows computer environment and familiar with PeopleSoft.

---

a low-cost airline, has continuously added planes and routes that require adding personnel. In contrast, some other airlines have reduced flights and decreased employee head count. In both cases, the firms had to forecast the number of employees needed, given their respective competitive positions with the industry. Exhibit 10.3 summarizes the process of planning and forecasting an organization's people needs.

Many firms with employee shortages are hiring **contingent workers**, or persons who prefer temporary employment, either part- or full-time. Postsecondary students and retired persons make up a large portion of Canada's contingent workforce. Other people who want to work but don't want to be permanent employees can join a temporary employment agency. A temporary employment agency performs staffing, training, and compensation functions by contracting with a business to provide employees for a specified period. A firm with a shortage of accountants can rent or lease an accountant from the temporary employment agency for the expected duration of the shortage.

contingent workers
Persons who prefer temporary employment, either part- or full-time.

concept check

Distinguish between job analysis, job description, and job specification.

Describe the job analysis and design process.

What is the process for human resource forecasting?

EXHIBIT 10.3 > Human Resource Planning Process

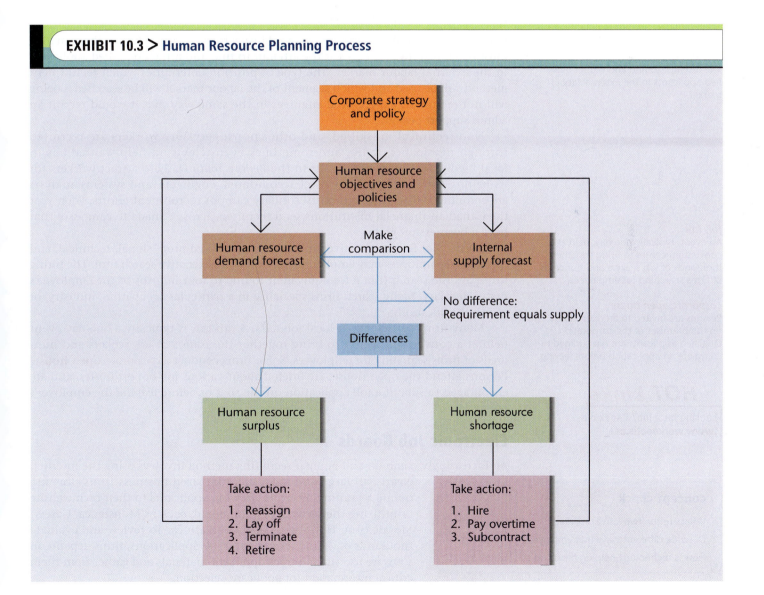

Employee Recruitment

When a firm creates a new position or an existing one becomes vacant, it starts looking for people with qualifications that meet the requirements of the job. Two sources of job applicants are the internal and external labour markets. The internal labour market consists of employees currently employed by the firm; the external labour market is the pool of potential applicants outside the firm.

Internal Labour Market

Internal recruitment can be greatly facilitated by using a human resource information system containing a skills inventory, or computerized employee database of information about an employee's previous work experience, education and certifications, job and career preferences, performance, and attendance. Promotions and job transfers are the most common results of internal recruiting. Most companies, including UPS, WestJet Airlines, and Wal-Mart, follow a policy of promotion from within and try to fill positions with their existing employees. The internal search for job applicants usually means that a person must change his or her job. People are typically either promoted or transferred.

External Labour Market

If qualified job candidates cannot be found inside the firm, the external labour market must be tapped. **Recruitment** is the attempt to find and attract qualified applicants in the external labour market. The type of position determines which recruitment method will be used and which segment of the labour market will be searched. Boeing will not recruit an experienced engineer in the same way that it would recruit an admin support person.

Non-technical, unskilled, and other nonsupervisory workers are recruited through newspaper, radio, and sometimes even television help-wanted ads in local media. Starbucks placed ads in the *Beijing Youth Daily* to attract workers for its Beijing coffee shops. Entry-level accountants, engineers, and systems analysts are commonly hired through postsecondary campus recruitment efforts. Each year the Canadian financial institutions send recruiters across Canada to campuses that have a business program.

A firm that needs executives and other experienced professional, technical, and managerial employees may employ the services of an executive search firm. The hiring firm pays the search firm a fee equivalent to one to four months of the employee's first-year salary. Many search firms specialize in a particular occupation, industry, or geographic location.

Many firms participate in local job fairs. A **job fair** is typically a one-day event held at a convention center to bring together thousands of job seekers and hundreds of firms searching for employees. Some firms conduct a **corporate open house**. Persons attend the open house, are briefed about various job opportunities, and are encouraged to submit a job application on the spot or before leaving the employer's premises.

Electronic Job Boards

An increasingly common and popular recruiting method involves using the Internet. Nearly all large and most medium-sized business firms now use online recruiting by either drawing applicants to their own website or utilizing the services of a job board, such as Monster.ca, Career-Mosaic.com, Hotjobs.ca, or CareerPath.ca. To review and evaluate thousands of online résumés and job applications, firms depend on software to scan and track applicant materials and gather from them critical information for applicant selection.

---

recruitment
The attempt to find and attract qualified applicants in the external labour market.

job fair
An event, typically one day, held at a convention centre to bring together thousands of job seekers and hundreds of firms searching for employees.

corporate open house
Persons are invited to an open house on the premises of the corporation. Qualified applicants are encouraged to complete an application before leaving.

HOT Links

Looking for a job? Check out (www.workopolis.ca).

---

concept check

What are the two labour markets?

Describe different ways that employees are recruited.

How is technology helping firms find the right recruits?

Job fairs bring together hundreds of employers and thousands of job seekers. Job fairs are one of the ways human resource managers identify employees from the external job market. What are some of the benefits of job fairs to employers and potential employees?

Employee Selection

selection
The process of determining which persons in the applicant pool possess the qualifications necessary to be successful on the job.

After a firm has attracted enough job applicants, employment specialists begin the selection process. **Selection** is the process of determining which persons in the applicant pool possess the qualifications necessary to be successful on the job. The steps in the employee selection process are shown in Exhibit 10.4. An applicant who can jump over each step, or hurdle, will very likely receive a job offer; thus, this is known as the successive hurdles approach to applicant screening. Alternatively, an applicant can be rejected at any step or hurdle. Selection steps or hurdles are described below:

1. *Initial screening.* During the initial screening, an applicant usually completes an application form and has a brief interview of 30 minutes or less. The application

EXHIBIT 10.4 > Steps of the Employee Selection Process

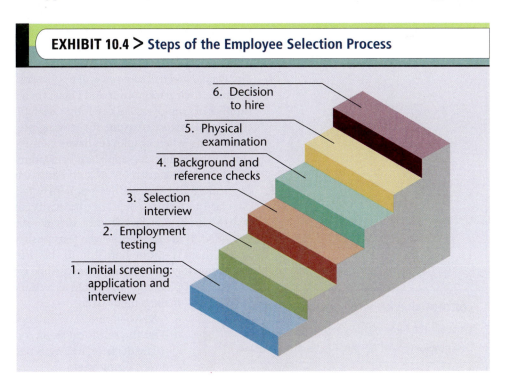

6. Decision to hire
5. Physical examination
4. Background and reference checks
3. Selection interview
2. Employment testing
1. Initial screening: application and interview

form includes questions about education, work experience, and previous job duties. A personal résumé may be substituted for the application form. If the potential employer believes that the potential employee is suitable, then the next step is the interview. The interview is normally structured, consisting of a short list of specific questions. For example: Are you familiar with any accounting software packages? Did you supervise anyone in your last job? Did you use a company car when making sales calls?

2. *Employment testing.* Following the initial screening, an applicant may be asked to take one or more employment tests, such as the Wonderlic Personnel Test, a mental-ability test. Some tests are designed to measure special job skills, others measure aptitudes, and some are intended to capture characteristics of one's personality. The Myers-Briggs Type Indicator is a personality and motivational instrument widely used on college campuses as an aid in providing job and career counselling as well as assisting a student in selecting his or her major. In recent years some firms have begun to use a test that assesses one's emotional intelligence. Frequently called the e-quotient, the emotional intelligence quotient reveals how well a person understands his or her own emotions and the emotions of others, and how he or she behaves based on this understanding.

3. *Selection interview.* The tool most widely used in making hiring decisions by Intel, Merck, and other firms is the **selection interview**, an in-depth discussion of an applicant's work experience, skills and abilities, education, and career interests. For managerial and professional positions, an applicant may be interviewed by several persons, including the line manager for the position to be filled. This interview is designed to determine an applicant's communication ability and motivation. It is also a means for gathering additional factual information from the applicant such as college major, years of part-time work experience, computer equipment used, and reason for leaving the last job. The applicant may be asked to explain how to solve a particular management problem or how she or he provided leadership to a group in a previous work situation when an important problem had to be solved quickly. United Airlines asks prospective flight attendants how they handled a conflict with a customer or coworker in a previous job.

Carolyn Murray, a recruiter for W. C. Gore and Associates, makers of Gore-Tex, says she pays little attention to a candidate's carefully scripted responses to her admittedly easy questions. Instead, she listens for a casual remark that reveals the reality behind an otherwise thought-out reply. Using a baseball analogy, Carolyn's examples of how three job candidates struck out are presented in Exhibit 10.5.[1]

4. *Background and reference check.* If applicants pass the selection interview, most firms examine their background and check their references. In recent years an increasing number of employers are carefully researching applicants' backgrounds, particularly their legal history, reasons for leaving previous jobs, and even creditworthiness. Retail firms, where employees have extensive contact with customers, tend to be very careful about checking applicant backgrounds. It is important to note that reference checks must be carried out in accordance with current regulations and legislations.

5. *Physical exams.* Companies frequently require job candidates to have a medical checkup to ensure they are physically able to perform a job. In Canada, drug testing can be conducted only after a conditional offer of employment has been extended. If the new employee tests positive, he or she will probably still be hired unless there is undue hardship to the firm as a result. If the condition turns out to be an addiction, the employee will be treated under the new employer's benefit plan, and any issues as a result of the addiction become performance management issues.[2]

6. *Decision to hire.* If an applicant progresses satisfactorily through all the selection steps, a decision to hire the individual is made. The decision to hire is nearly always made by the manager of the new employee.

---

selection interview
An in-depth discussion of an applicant's work experience, skills and abilities, education, and career interests.

---

concept check

What are the steps in the employee selection process?

Describe some ways in which applicants are tested.

EXHIBIT 10.5 > Striking Out with Gore-Tex

The Pitch (Question to Applicant)	The Swing (Applicant's Response)	The Miss (Interviewer's Reaction to Response)
"Give me an example of a time when you had a conflict with a team member."	"Our leader asked me to handle all of the FedExing for our team. I did it, but I thought that FedExing was a waste of my time."	"At Gore, we work from a team concept. Her answer shows that she won't exactly jump when one of her teammates needs help."
"Tell me how you solved a problem that was impeding your project."	"One of the engineers on my team wasn't pulling his weight, and we were closing in on a deadline. So I took on some of his work."	"The candidate may have resolved the issue for this particular deadline, but he did nothing to prevent the problem from happening again."
"What's the one thing that you would change about your current position?"	"My job as a salesman has become boring. Now I want the responsibility of managing people."	"He's probably not maximizing his current territory, and he is complaining. Will he find his next role 'boring' and complain about that role, too?"

Employee Training and Development

 LO 4

training and development
Activities that provide learning situations in which an employee acquires additional knowledge or skills to increase job performance.

orientation
Training that prepares a new employee to perform on the job; includes information about job assignments, work rules, equipment, and performance expectations, as well as about company policies, salary and benefits, and parking.

To ensure that both new and experienced employees have the knowledge and skills to perform their jobs successfully, organizations invest in **training and development** activities. Training and development involves learning situations in which the employee acquires additional knowledge or skills to increase job performance. Training objectives specify performance improvements, reductions in errors, job knowledge to be gained, and/or other positive organizational results. Training is done either on or off the job. The process of creating and implementing training and development activities is shown in Exhibit 10.6.

New employee training is essential and usually begins with **orientation**, which entails getting the new employee ready to perform on the job. Formal orientation (often a half-day classroom program) provides information about company policies, salary and benefits, and parking. Although this information is very helpful, the more important orientation is about job assignments, work rules, equipment, and performance expectations provided by the new employee's supervisor and coworkers. This second briefing tends to be more informal and can last for several days or even weeks.

EXHIBIT 10.6 > Employee Training and Development Process

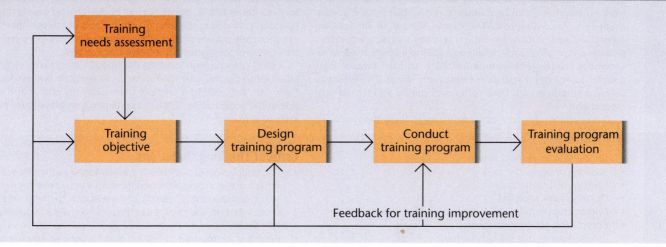

For the latest news in the human resources field, visit the website of the Society for Human Resource Management at (www.shrm.org).

on-the-job training
Training in which the employee learns the job by doing it with guidance from a supervisor or experienced coworker.

job rotation
Reassignment of workers to several different jobs over time so that they can learn the basics of each job.

apprenticeship
A form of on-the-job training that combines specific job instruction with classroom instruction.

mentoring
A form of on-the-job training in which a senior manager or other experienced employee provides job- and career-related information to a protégé.

On-the-Job Training

Continuous training for both new and experienced employees is important to keep job skills fresh. Job-specific training, designed to enhance a new employee's ability to perform a job, includes **on-the-job training**, during which the employee learns the job by doing it with guidance from a supervisor or experienced coworker.

On-the-job training takes place at the job site or workstation and tends to be directly related to the job. This training involves specific job instructions, coaching (guidance given to new employees by experienced ones), special project assignments, or job rotation. **Job rotation** is the reassignment of workers to several different jobs over time. It is not uncommon for management trainees to work sequentially in two or three departments, such as customer service, credit, and human resources, during their first year on the job.

An **apprenticeship** usually combines specific on-the-job instruction with classroom training. It might last as long as four years and can be found in the skilled trades of carpentry, plumbing, and electrical work.

With **mentoring**, another form of on-the-job training, a senior manager or other experienced employee provides job- and career-related information to a protégé. Inexpensive and providing instantaneous feedback, mentoring is becoming increasingly popular with many firms. For an example of mentoring for cultural orientation, explore Expanding Around the Globe.

Expanding Around The Globe

EMPLOYEES ON THE (INTERNATIONAL) MOVE

Is an international job assignment a step up the ladder to a more rewarding career path or a potential mine-field of professional and family risk? The answer depends as much on an employee's family situation as their ambition, according to a new survey that explores worldwide employee-relocation trends. And it also depends on how well their company supports and handles a transfer to an international location.

Working abroad at one of the Canadian or foreign multinational firms can be exciting and look good on your résumé. Increasing numbers of recent college graduates and experienced professionals are offered opportunities for overseas work assignments ranging from a few days to 24 months, or longer. But acclimating to a new country and culture, as well as a new work environment, can be daunting and involves some unique challenges. According to GMAC Global Relocation Services, an assignment and mobility consulting service that helps employees settle in a foreign country, retaining expatriate talent remains an enormous challenge for companies. With attrition rates at least double that of non-expatriate employees, about 21 percent of overseas employees left their companies during an international assignment.

Other challenges face expatriates aside from the demands of work:

- Choosing schools for children
- Securing housing
- Finding medical facilities
- Opening bank accounts
- Finding transportation and obtaining a driver's license
- Completing government forms
- Locating stores that sell familiar foods
- Learning about community and entertainment offerings

With 1,200 to 1,500 employees working outside of their home countries at any given time, KPMG International, one of the world's largest accounting firms with a presence in 144 countries, attempts to deal with employee relocation adjustment issues by utilizing a "buddy" system. At work, the KPMG Global Code of Conduct, entitled "Performance with Integrity," sets out guidelines of ethical conduct that KPMG requires of all its employees worldwide. The code applies equally to partners and employees of all KPMG member firms regardless of their title or position.

To ease the social and cultural burden for new expatriates, the firm links the employee to a buddy for one-on-one support during the length of their assignment, which is typically 24 months. Timothy Dwyer, national director for international human resource advisory services at KPMG, points out that buddies—who usually do not have a direct working relationship with the new expatriate—function in a social role outside of work. They help the new employee and the family resolve the myriad of problems that can arise.

KPMG places a high value on the buddy support role, which is taken into account when performance evaluations are conducted each year. By creating a sense of shared identity within and outside of the organization, KPMG's international employees are more likely to stay on the job.[3]

Critical Thinking Questions

- The buddy system at KPMG is a value-added human resource service that is intangible and difficult to assess; nevertheless, it is important to identify and measure its benefits and costs. What do you think these are and how would you measure them?
- What are the top four or five job qualifications an employee should have to be considered for an overseas assignment?

Off-the-Job Training

Even with the advantages of on-the-job training, many firms recognize that it is often necessary to train employees away from the workplace. With off-the-job training, employees learn their duties away from the job. There are numerous popular methods of off-the-job training. Frequently, it takes place in a classroom, where cases, role-play exercises, films, videos, lectures, and computer demonstrations are utilized to develop workplace skills.

Web-based technology is being increasingly used along with more traditional off-the-job training methods. E-learning and e-training involve online computer presentation of information for learning new job tasks. Many companies with widely dispersed employees can deliver training materials electronically to save time and travel costs. For example, transportation companies can deliver technical and safety training through **programmed instruction**, a computer-assisted, self-paced, and highly structured training method that presents trainees with concepts and problems using a modular format. Software can make sure that employees receive, undergo, and complete, as well as sign off on, various training modules.

Computer-assisted training can also be done using a **simulation**, a scaled-down version of a manufacturing process or even a mock cockpit of a jet airplane. Air Canada uses a training simulator for pilots to practice hazardous flight manoeuvres or learn the controls of a new aircraft in a safe, controlled environment with no passengers. The simulator allows for more direct transfer of learning to the job.

programmed instruction
A form of computer-assisted off-the-job training.

simulation
A scaled down version or mock-up of equipment, process, or work environment.

concept check

Describe several types of on-the-job training.

What are the advantages of programmed instruction and simulation?

How is technology impacting off-the-job training?

Performance Planning and Evaluation

Along with employee orientation and training, new employees learn about performance expectations through performance planning and evaluation. Managers provide employees with expectations about the job. These are communicated as job objectives, schedules, deadlines, and product and/or service quality requirements. As an employee performs job tasks, the supervisor periodically evaluates the employee's efforts. A **performance appraisal** is a comparison of actual performance with expected performance to assess an employee's contributions to the organization and to make decisions about training, compensation, promotion, and other job changes. The performance planning and appraisal process is shown in Exhibit 10.7 and is described below:

performance appraisal
A comparison of actual performance with expected performance to assess an employee's contributions to the organization.

1. Performance standards are established.
2. The employee works to meet the standards and expectations.

EXHIBIT 10.7 > Performance Planning and Evaluation

Performance planning:
Setting standards
and expectations

Employee job task behaviour → Performance evaluation → Rewards and job changes

Performance feedback

CONCEPT *in Action* >>>

During a performance appraisal, a manager evaluates an employee's performance, comparing actual performance to expected performance goals. At General Electric, employees receive feedback from work teams, peers, and customers to develop perspective on their management style and skills. How does the performance appraisal help the employee and the organization?

3. The employee's supervisor evaluates the employee's work in terms of quality and quantity of output and various characteristics such as job knowledge, initiative, relationships with others, and attendance and punctuality.
4. Following the performance evaluation, reward (pay raise) and job change (promotion) decisions can be made.
5. Rewards are positive feedback and provide reinforcement, or encouragement, for the employee to work harder in the future.

concept check

What are the steps in the performance planning and appraisal process?

What purposes do performance appraisals serve?

Describe some sources of information for the performance appraisal..

Information for performance appraisals can be assembled using rating scales, supervisor logs of employee job incidents, and reports of sales and production statistics. Regardless of the source, performance information should be accurate and a record of the employee's job behaviour and efforts. Performance appraisals serve a number of purposes, but they are most often used to make decisions about pay raises, training needs, advancement opportunities, and employee terminations.

Employee Compensation and Benefits

LO 6

Compensation, which includes both pay and benefits, is closely connected to performance appraisal. Employees who perform better tend to get bigger pay raises. Several factors affect an employee's pay:

1. *Pay structure and internal influences.* Wages, salaries, and benefits usually reflect the importance of the job. The jobs that management considers more important are compensated at a higher rate; president, chief engineer, and chief financial

officer are high-paying jobs. Likewise, different jobs of equal importance to the firm are compensated at the same rate. For instance, if a drill-press operator and a lathe operator are considered of equal importance, they might both be paid $21 per hour.

2. *Pay level and external influences.* In deciding how much to pay workers, the firm must also be concerned with the salaries paid by competitors. If competitors are paying much higher wages, a firm might lose its best employees. Larger firms conduct salary surveys to see what other firms are paying. Wage and salary surveys conducted by Statistics Canada, for example, can also be useful.

An employer can decide to pay at, above, or below the going rate. Most firms try to offer competitive wages and salaries within a geographic area or an industry. If a company pays below-market wages, it might not be able to hire skilled people. The level, or competitiveness, of a firm's compensation is determined by the firm's financial condition (or profitability), efficiency, and employee productivity, as well as the going rates paid by competitors.

Types of Compensation or Pay

There are two basic types of compensation: direct and indirect. Direct pay is the wage or salary received by the employee; indirect pay consists of various employee benefits and services. Employees are usually paid directly on the basis of the amount of time they work, the amount they produce, or some combination of time and output. Hourly rates of pay or a monthly salary are considered base pay, or an amount of pay received by the employee regardless of output level.

The following are the most common types of compensation:

- *Hourly wages.* These will vary depending on the positions and job market. Each province and territory in Canada is responsible to set a "minimum hourly wage."
- *Salaries.* Managerial and professional employees are usually paid an annual salary on either a biweekly or a monthly basis.
- *Piecework and commission.* Some employees are paid according to how much they produce or sell. A car salesperson might be paid $500 for each car sold or a 3 percent commission on the car's sale price. Thus, a salesperson who sold four cars in one week at $500 per car would earn $2,000 in pay for that week. Alternatively, a 3 percent commission on four cars sold with total sales revenue of $70,000 would yield $2,100 in pay.

    Increasingly, business firms are paying employees using a base wage or salary and an incentive. The incentive feature is designed to increase individual employee, work group, and/or organizational performance. Incentive pay plans are commonly referred to as variable or contingent pay arrangements.
- *Accelerated commission schedule.* A salesperson could be paid a commission rate of 3 percent on the first $50,000 of sales per month, 4 percent on the next $30,000, and 5 percent on any sales beyond $80,000. For a salesperson that made $90,000 of sales in one month, the monthly pay would be as follows:

    3 percent $\times$ $50,000 = $1,500
    4 percent $\times$ $30,000 = $1,200
    5 percent $\times$ $10,000 = $ 500
    $90,000 $\rightarrow$ $3,200
- *Bonus.* A bonus is a payment for reaching a specific goal; it may be paid on a monthly, quarterly, or annual basis. A bank with several offices or branches might set monthly goals for opening new accounts, making loans, and customer service. Each employee of a branch that meets all goals would be paid a monthly bonus of $100. Although the bonuses are paid to the employees

Making Ethical Choices

individually, the employees must function as an effective, high-performing group to reach the monthly goals.

- *Profit sharing.* A firm that offers profit sharing pays employees a portion of the profits over a preset level. For example, profits beyond 10 percent of gross sales might be shared at a 50 percent rate with employees. The company retains the remaining profits. All employees might receive the same profit shares, or the shares might vary according to base pay.
- *Fringe benefits.* **Fringe benefits** are indirect compensation and include pensions, health insurance, vacations, and many others. Some fringe benefits are required by law (e.g., paid vacations and holidays, employment insurance [EI] and Canada or Quebec Pension Plan [CPP or QPP], the EI and CPP/QPP are paid at least in part by the employer).

Many employers also offer fringe benefits not required by law. Among these are paid time off (e.g., extra vacations, sick days), insurance (health care, disability, life, dental, vision, and accidental death and dismemberment), pensions and retirement savings accounts, and stock purchase options.

Some firms with numerous fringe benefits allow employees to mix and match benefit items or select items based on individual needs. This is a flexible, or cafeteria-style, benefit plan. A younger employee with a family might desire to purchase medical, disability, and life insurance, whereas an older employee might want to put more benefit dollars into a retirement savings plan. All employees are allocated the same number of benefit dollars but can spend these dollars on different items and in different amounts.

NORM BETTS / LANDOV

CONCEPT *in Action* >>>

Determining a CEO's fair salary isn't easy. CEOs are responsible for making decisions that can impact tens of thousands of employees and dramatically increase or decrease the value of a company. Indigo CEO Heather Reisman's compensation package would have to reflect her 25 years of extensive business experience. How do you think executive salaries should be determined?

fringe benefits
Indirect compensation, such as pensions, health insurance, and vacations.

Understanding Labour Relations in a Unionized Environment

LO 7

labour union
An organization that represents workers in dealing with management over issues involving wages, hours, and working conditions.

A **labour union** is an organization that represents workers in dealing with management over issues involving wages, hours, and working conditions. The labour relations process that produces a union–management relationship consists of three phases: union organizing, negotiating a labour agreement, and the day-to-day administering of the agreement. In Phase 1, a group of employees within a firm might form a union on their own, or an established union may target an employer and organize many of

collective bargaining
The process of negotiating labour agreements that provide for compensation and working arrangements mutually acceptable to the union and to management.

the firm's workers into a local labour union. The second phase constitutes **collective bargaining**, which is the process of negotiating labour agreements that provide for compensation and working arrangements mutually acceptable to the union and to management.

Finally, the third phase of the labour relations process involves the daily administering of the labour agreement primarily through the handling of worker grievances and other workforce management problems that require interaction between managers and labour union officials.

Modern Labour Movement

local union
A branch or unit of a national union that represents workers at a specific plant or in a specific geographic area.

A **local union** is a branch or unit of a **national union** that represents workers at a specific plant or over a specific geographic area. In conformance to national union rules, local unions determine the number of local union officers, procedures for electing officers, the schedule of local meetings, financial arrangements with the national organization, and the local's role in negotiating labour agreements.

national union
A union that consists of many local unions in a particular industry, skilled trade, or geographic area and thus represents workers throughout an entire country.

The largest national union is the Canadian Union of Public Employees (CUPE) with more than half a million members across Canada. CUPE represents workers in airlines, education, emergency services, health care, libraries, municipalities, public utilities, social services, transportation, and universities. Under the CUPE national union are the various local unions (e.g., CUPE local 774 in Abbotsford, British Columbia).

The three main functions of the local union are collective bargaining, worker relations and membership services, and community and political activities. Collective bargaining generally takes place every two or three years. Local union officers and shop stewards oversee worker-management relations on a day-to-day basis. A **shop steward** is an elected union official who represents union members to management when workers have issues. For most union members, his or her primary contact with the union is through union officials at the local level.

shop steward
An elected union official who represents union members to management when workers have issues.

Negotiating Union Contracts

A union contract is created through collective bargaining. Typically, both management and union negotiating teams are made up of a few persons. One person on each side is the chief spokesperson.

Bargaining begins with union and management negotiators setting a bargaining agenda, a list of contract issues that will be discussed. Much of the bargaining over the specific details takes place through face-to-face meetings and the exchange of written proposals. Demands, proposals, and counterproposals are exchanged during several rounds of bargaining. The resulting contract must then be approved by top management and by union members. The collective bargaining process is shown in Exhibit 10.8.

The union contract is a legally binding agreement that typically covers such issues as union security, management rights, wages and benefits, job security, and grievance procedures. Each of these is discussed in this section.

closed shop
A company where only union members can be hired.

Union Security   One of the key issues in a contract is union security. From the union's perspective, the most secure arrangement is the **closed shop**, a company where only union members can be hired. The union serves, in effect, as an employment agency for the firm. Today, the most common form of union security is the **union shop**. Non-union workers can be hired, but then they must join the union, normally within 30 or 60 days.

union shop
A company where non-union workers can be hired but must then join the union.

An **agency shop** does not require employees to join the union, but to keep working at the company, employees must pay the union a fee to cover its expenses in representing them. The union must fairly represent all workers, including those who do not become members.

agency shop
A company where employees are not required to join the union but must pay it a fee to cover its expenses in representing them.

EXHIBIT 10.8 > The Process of Negotiating Labour Agreements

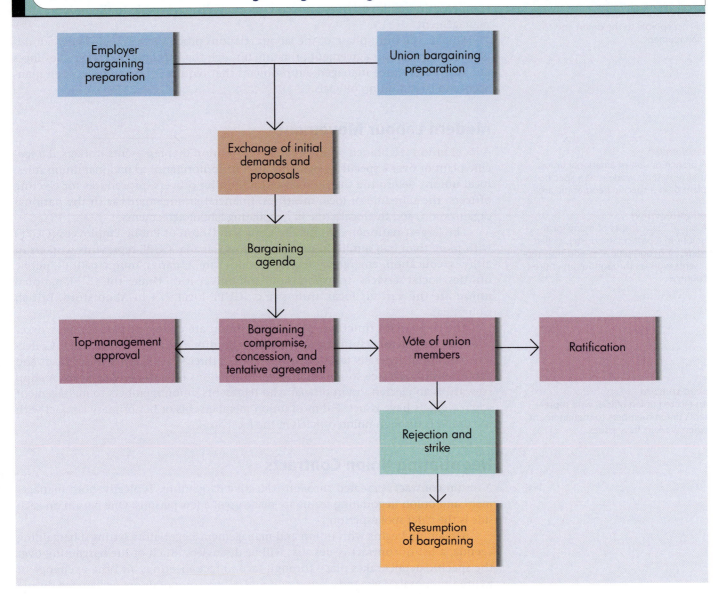

When employees can work at a unionized company without having to join the union, this arrangement is commonly known as an **open shop**. Workers don't have to join the union or pay dues or fees to the union.

Management Rights   When a company becomes unionized, management loses some of its decision-making abilities. But management still has certain rights that can be negotiated in collective bargaining.

One way to lessen a union's influence in the management of an organization is by having a *management rights clause* in the labour agreement. Most union contracts have one. A typical clause gives the employer all rights to manage the business except as specified in the contract. For instance, if the contract does not specify the criteria for promotions, with a management rights clause managers will have the right to use any criteria they wish. Another way to preserve management rights is to list areas that are not subject to collective bargaining. This list might secure management's right to schedule work hours, hire and fire workers, set production standards, determine the number of supervisors in each department, and promote, demote, and transfer workers.

Wages and Benefits   Much bargaining effort goes into wage increases and improvements in fringe benefits. Once agreed to, they remain in effect for the life of the contract. Some contracts provide for a **cost-of-living adjustment (COLA)**, under which wages increase automatically as the cost of living goes up.

Other contracts provide for *lump-sum wage adjustments*. The workers' base pay remains unchanged for the contract period (usually two or three years), but each worker receives a bonus (or lump sum) once or twice during the contract.

The union and the employer are usually both concerned about the firm's ability to pay higher wages. The firm's ability to pay depends greatly on its profitability. But even if profits have declined, average to above-average wage increases are still possible if labour productivity increases.

In addition to requests for wage increases, unions usually want better fringe benefits. In some industries, such as steel and auto manufacturing, fringe benefits are 40 percent of the total cost of compensation. Benefits might include higher wages for overtime work, holiday work, and less desirable shifts; insurance programs (life, health and hospitalization, dental care); payment for certain non-work time (rest periods, vacations, holidays, sick time); pensions; and income maintenance plans. A fairly common income maintenance plan is a *supplementary unemployment benefits fund* set up by the employer to help laid-off workers.

Job Security and Seniority   Cost-of-living adjustments, supplementary unemployment benefits, and certain other benefits give employees some financial security. But most financial security is directly related to job security—the assurance, to some degree, that workers will keep their jobs. Of course, job security depends primarily on the continued success and financial well-being of the company.

Seniority, the length of an employee's continuous service with a firm, is discussed in about 90 percent of all labour contracts. Seniority is a factor in job security; usually, unions want the workers with the most seniority to have the most job security.

Grievance and Arbitration   The union's main way of policing the contract is the grievance procedure. A **grievance** is a formal complaint, by an employee or by the union, that management has violated some part of the contract. Under a typical contract, the employee starts by presenting the grievance to the supervisor, either in person or in writing. The typical grievance procedure is illustrated in Exhibit 10.9.

If the problem isn't solved, the grievance is put in writing. The employee, one or more union officials, the supervisor, and perhaps the plant manager then discuss the grievance. If the matter still can't be resolved, another meeting takes place with higher level representatives of both parties present. If top management and the local union president can't resolve the grievance, it goes to arbitration.

Arbitration is the process of settling a labour-management dispute by having a third party—a single arbitrator or a panel—make a decision. The arbitrator is mutually chosen by labour and management and is expected to be impartial. The decision is final and binding on the union and the employer. The arbitrator reviews the grievance at a hearing and then makes the decision, which is presented in a document called the award.

Similar to arbitration is **mediation**, the process of settling issues in which the parties present their case to a neutral mediator. The mediator (the specialist) holds talks with union and management negotiators at separate meetings and at joint sessions. The mediator also suggests compromises. Mediators cannot issue binding decisions or impose a settlement on the disputing parties. Their only tools are communication and persuasion. Mediation almost always produces a settlement between the union and a firm, but sometimes the process takes months or even a year, and either or both sides can reject the mediator's assistance.

---

cost-of-living adjustment (COLA)
A provision in a labour contract that calls for wages to increase automatically as the cost of living rises (usually measured by the consumer price index).

grievance
A formal complaint, filed by an employee or by the union, charging that management has violated the contract.

arbitration
The process of settling a labour-management dispute by having a third party—a single arbitrator or a panel—make a decision, which is binding on both the union and the employer..

mediation
A method of attempting to settle labour issues in which a specialist (the mediator) tries to persuade management and the union to adjust or settle their dispute.

---

concept check

Discuss the difference between a local and national union.

Explain the collective bargaining process.

Explain each of the following: closed shop, union shop, agency shop, and open shop.

EXHIBIT 10.9 > Typical Grievance Procedure

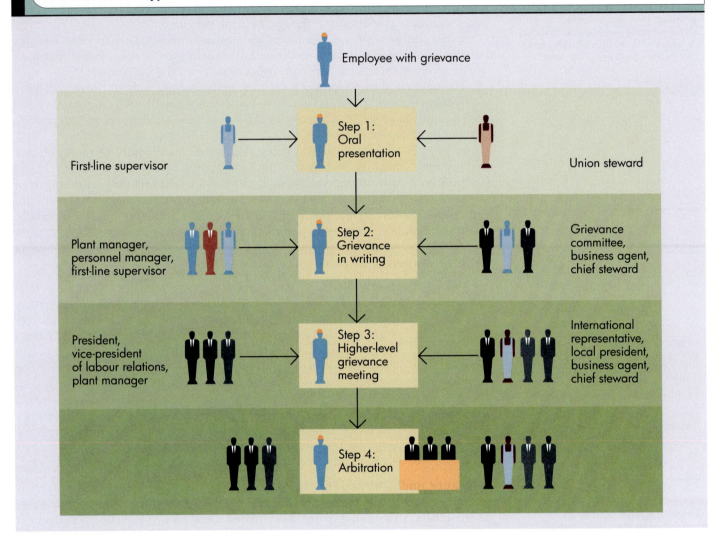

Tactics for Pressuring a Contract Settlement

Virtually all labour agreements specify peaceful resolution of conflicts, usually through arbitration. However, when a contract expires and a new agreement has not been reached, the union is free to strike or engage in other efforts to exert economic pressure on the employer. A strike occurs when employees refuse to work. Likewise, the employer can put pressure on the union through a lockout or hiring strike replacements if the union has called a strike. Some services which are seen to be critical do not have the option of a strike or lockout. Other strategies to force a contract settlement are listed in Exhibit 10.10.

> **concept check**
>
> Describe the grievance procedure.
>
> What is the distinction between arbitration and mediation?
>
> In what ways do arbitrators act like judges?

Laws Affecting Human Resource Management

Federal laws help ensure that job applicants and employees are treated fairly and not discriminated against. Hiring, training, and job placement must be unbiased. Promotion and compensation decisions must be based on performance. These laws help all Canadians who have talent, training, and the desire to get ahead.

EXHIBIT 10.10 > Strategies of Unions and Employers

Union Strategies		Employer Strategies	
Strike:	Employees refuse to work.	Lockout:	Employer refuses to let Employees enter plant to work.
Boycott:	Employees try to keep customers and others from doing business with employer.	Strike replacements:	Employer uses non-union employees to do jobs of striking union employees.
Picketing:	Employees march near entrance of firm to publicize their view of dispute and discourage customers.	Mutual-aid pact:	Employer receives money from other companies in industry to cover some of income lost because of strikes.
Corporate campaign:	Union disrupts shareholder meetings or buys company stock to have more influence over management.	Shift production:	Employer moves production to non-union plant or out of country.

CONCEPT *in Action* >>>

Strikes are powerful union tools, usually used as a last resort when labour and management cannot reach agreement on issues such as wages, pensions, vacation time, and other benefits. What other strategies are available to both unions and managements to force a contract?

CP PHOTO (BRENT REANEY)

HOT Links

Learn more about the Employment Equity Act by searching The Department of Justice Canada at (**www.justice.gc.ca**).

New legislation and the continual interpretation and reinterpretation of existing laws will continue to make the jobs of human resource managers challenging and complicated. The key laws that currently affect human resource management are shown in Exhibit 10.11.

Employers may not discriminate against persons with disability. They must make "reasonable accommodations," so that qualified employees can perform the job, unless doing so would cause "undue hardship" for the business. Altering

EXHIBIT 10.11 > Laws Impacting Human Resource Management

Law	Purpose	Applicability
Charter of Rights and Freedoms (contained in the Constitution Act of 1982)	Provides the right to live and seek employment anywhere in Canada	Takes precedence over all other laws
Human rights legislation	Provides equal opportunity for members of protected groups in areas such as accommodation, contracts, provision of goods and services, and employment	Comprised of federal, provincial, and territorial laws with a common objective
Canadian Human Rights Act (1977)	Prohibits discrimination on a number of grounds	Applies to federal government agencies, Crown corporations, and businesses under federal jurisdiction
Employment Equity Act (amended in 1996)	Attempts to remove employment barriers and promote equality for the members of four designated groups: women, visible minorities, Aboriginal people, and persons with disabilities	Every employer must implement the Act and make every reasonable accommodation to ensure that people in the designated groups are represented in their organization. The degree of representation in each occupational group should reflect the Canadian workforce and be consistent with their ability to meet reasonable occupational requirements
Occupational Health and Safety Act	Designed to protect the health and safety of workers by minimizing work-related accidents and illness	All provinces, territories, and the federal jurisdiction have occupational health and safety legislation
WHMIS (Workplace Hazardous Materials Information System)	Designed to protect workers by providing information about hazardous materials in the workplace	Canada-wide legally mandated system

work schedules, modifying equipment so a wheelchair-bound person can use it, and making buildings accessible by ramps and elevators are considered reasonable. Two companies often praised for their efforts to hire people with disabilities are McDonald's and IBM Canada.

Canada's overall employment equity record of the past decade has been mixed. The employment of women in professional occupations continues to grow, but minority representation among professionals has not significantly increased, even though professional jobs have been among the fastest-growing areas. Technical jobs have the most equitable utilization rates of minorities. Almost 400 federal and federally regulated organizations submit annual reports to Human Resources Development Canada (HRDC) under the Employment Equity Act. The organizations are then graded on an alphabetical scale.

concept check

What are the key laws affecting employment?

What is employment equity?.

Trends in Human Resource Management

Some of today's most important trends in human resource management are using employee diversity as a competitive advantage, improving efficiency through outsourcing and technology, and hiring employees who fit the organizational culture.

CONCEPT *in Action* >>>

For some occupations, danger is part of the job description. Tallies of work-related casualties routinely identify loggers, pilots, commercial fishermen, and steel workers as holding the most deadly jobs in industry. Job fatalities are often linked to the use of heavy or outdated equipment. However, many work-related deaths also happen in common highway accidents or as homicides. What laws and agencies are designated to improve occupational safety?

© NATALIE FOBES/CORBIS

competitive advantage
A set of unique features of an organization that are perceived by customers and potential customers as significant and superior to the competition.

outsource
The assignment of various functions, such as human resources, accounting, or legal work, to outside organizations.

Employee Diversity and Competitive Advantage

Canadian society and its workforce are becoming increasingly more diverse in terms of racial and ethnic status, age, educational background, work experience, and gender. A company with a demographic employee profile that looks like its customers may be in a position to gain a **competitive advantage**, which is a set of unique features of a company and its product or service that are perceived by the target market as superior to those of the competition. Competitive advantage is the factor that causes customers to patronize a firm and not the competition. Many things can be a source of competitive advantage: for WestJet Airlines it is route structure and high asset utilization; for the Four Seasons Hotels it is very high quality guest services; for Toyota it is manufacturing efficiency and product durability; and for Tim Hortons it is location, service, and outstanding coffee products. For these firms, a competitive advantage is also created by their HR practices.

Many firms are successful because of employee diversity which can produce more effective problem solving, a stronger reputation for hiring women and minorities, even greater employee diversity, quicker adaptation to change, and more robust product solutions because a diverse team can generate more options for improvement.[4]

In order for an organization to use employee diversity for competitive advantage, top management must be fully committed to hiring and developing women and minority individuals.

Outsourcing HR and Technology

The role of the HR professional has changed noticeably over the past 20 years. One significant change has been the use of technology in handling relatively routine HR tasks, such as payroll processing, initial screening of applicants, and benefits enrolments. Many businesses have purchased specialized software (SAP and Oracle/People-Soft) to perform the information processing aspects of many HR tasks. Other firms **outsource,** or contract out these tasks to HR service providers.

HR outsourcing is done when another firm can perform a task better and more efficiently, thus saving costs. Sometimes HR activities are outsourced because HR requirements are extraordinary and too overwhelming to execute in-house in a timely fashion. Frequently, HR activities are simply outsourced because a provider has greater expertise.

Organizational Culture and Hiring for Fit

Regardless of general business and economic conditions, many firms are expanding operations and hiring additional employees. For many growing firms, corporate culture can be a key aspect of developing employees into a competitive advantage for the firm. Corporate culture refers to the core values and beliefs that support the mission and business model of the firm and guide employee behaviour. Companies frequently hire for fit with their corporate cultures. This necessitates recruitment and selection of employees who exhibit the values of the firm. The companies might use carefully crafted applicant questionnaires to screen for values and behaviours that support corporate culture. In addition to cultural fit, firms are increasingly hiring for technical knowledge and skills fit to the job.

Great Ideas to Use Now

Planning Your Career

It's never too early to start thinking about your career in business. No, you don't have to decide today, but it's important to decide fairly soon to plan your life's work. A very practical reason for doing so is that it will save you a lot of time and money. We have seen too many students who aren't really sure what they want to do after graduation. The longer you wait to choose a profession, the more credit hours you might have to take in your new field, and the longer it will be before you start earning real money.

A second reason to choose a career field early is that you can get a part-time or summer job and "test-drive" the profession. If it's not for you, you will find out very quickly.

Your school career centre can give you plenty of information about various careers in business. We also describe many career opportunities at the end of each part of this text. Another source of career information is the Internet. Go to any search engine, such as Excite or Lycos, and enter "careers in business," or narrow your search to a specific area such as management or marketing.

Career planning will not end when you find your first professional job. It is a lifelong process that ends only with retirement. Your career planning will include conducting a periodic self-assessment of your strengths and weaknesses, gathering information about other jobs both within the firm and externally, learning about other industries, and setting career goals for yourself. You must always think about your future in business.

Human Resources Decision Making

During your professional career in business, you will likely have the opportunity to become a manager. As a manager, you will have to make many human resource decisions, including hiring, firing, promoting, giving a pay raise, sending an employee to a training program, disciplining a worker, approving a college tuition reimbursement request, and reassigning an employee to a different job. In short, you will be involved in virtually every human resource decision or activity affecting the employees you manage. Always treat people as you wish to be treated when making human resource decisions. Be fair, be honest, offer your experience and advice, and communicate frequently with your employees. If you follow this simple advice, you will be richly rewarded in your career.

Customer Satisfaction and Quality

Interviewing for a job can be a nerve-wracking experience. You show up on time in your interview suit expecting to meet someone equally prepared. But that is not always the case. One hears plenty of horror stories of personnel recruiters keeping interviewees waiting while they nonchalantly carry out some unimportant task, like watering their plants. Your meeting with a human resource representative is often your first exposure to the company you are applying to work for, and nothing is more demeaning than to be shown a lack of respect. Firms need to provide good customer service to applicants if they expect to hire the most qualified employees.

The following are further examples of poor customer service when dealing with job applicants:

- A firm reschedules your interview but doesn't let you know about the change
- A firm fails to acknowledge receiving your job application or résumé
- The interviewer eats his or her lunch during your job interview
- The interviewer interrupts the interview to answer cell phone calls that are clearly personal
- The firm fails to contact you for several weeks after your interview
- The interviewer is obviously not prepared to conduct the interview

Firms have several opportunities to create a positive impression of their organization during these key points in the employee selection process. These include a variety of communication channels, such as:

- in-person greetings at a job fair or at the interview itself,
- phone calls to a prospective employee from a human resource professional to set up the interview and any follow-up conversations between human resources and the applicant,

- e-mail correspondence to acknowledge receipt of an application and to thank applicants for submitting their job application,
- information packets given to the applicant, and
- a thank-you note from the employer following the second interview.

A firm that is recognized for treating prospective employees especially well is the Ritz-Carlton Hotel, a subsidiary of Marriott International. Ritz managers want to make a good impression, because an applicant could be a future Ritz-Carlton hotel guest. A department head or hotel executive greets each attendee personally at Ritz-Carlton job fairs. Every applicant receives a personal, formal thank-you note for coming to the job fair, and those who are considered for positions but later rejected receive another note. All job fair applicants complete a behavioural questionnaire and are briefly interviewed.

"The Ritz-Carlton knows how to take care of its employees and customers and the upshot is that it has amazing customer service," says David Saxby, president of Measure-X, a company that specializes in helping utilities improve their customer service and sales. "Ritz-Carlton officials know their efforts create a win-win-win situation. Employees feel good about themselves, guests are happy and the company stays in business."[5]

Critical Thinking Questions

- What are the benefits of an employer treating a job applicant like a customer? Are there costs associated with treating applicants poorly?
- Assume you are a hiring manager. What things can you do to ensure that applicants develop a favourable impression of your firm?

Summary of Learning Outcomes

1 | **Discuss the human resource management process, and how are human resource needs determined**

The human resource management process consists of a sequence of activities that begins with job analysis and HR planning; progresses to employee recruitment and selection; then focuses on employee training, performance appraisal, and compensation; and ends when the employee leaves the organization.

Creating a strategy for meeting human resource needs is called human resource planning, which begins with job analysis. Job analysis is the process of studying a job to determine its tasks and duties for setting pay, determining employee job performance, specifying hiring requirements, and designing training programs. Information from the job analysis is used to prepare a job description, which lists the tasks and responsibilities of the job. A job specification describes the skills, knowledge, and abilities a person needs to fill the job described in the job description. By examining the human resource demand forecast and the internal supply forecast, human resource professionals can determine if the company faces a personnel surplus or shortage.

2 Explain how firms recruit applicants.

When a job vacancy occurs, most firms begin by trying to fill the job from within. If a suitable internal candidate is not available, the firm begins an external search. Firms use local media to recruit non-technical, unskilled, and non-supervisory workers. To locate highly trained recruits, employers use college recruiters, executive search firms, job fairs, and company websites to promote job openings.

3 Summarize how firms select qualified applicants.

Typically, an applicant submits an application or résumé and then receives a short, structured interview. If an applicant makes it past the initial screening, he or she might be asked to take an aptitude, personality, or skills test. The next step is the selection interview, which is an in-depth discussion of the applicant's work experience, skills and abilities, education, and career interests.

4 List some of the types of training and development programs organizations offer their employees.

Training and development programs are designed to increase employees' knowledge, skills, and abilities to foster job performance improvements. Formal training (usually classroom in nature and off-the-job) takes place shortly after being hired. Development programs prepare employees to assume positions of increasing authority and responsibility. Job rotation, executive education programs, mentoring, and special-project assignments are examples of employee development programs.

5 Show how performance appraisals are used to evaluate employee performance.

A performance appraisal compares an employee's actual performance with the expected performance. Performance appraisals serve several purposes but are typically used to determine an employee's compensation, training needs, and advancement opportunities.

6 Analyze the various methods for compensating employees.

Direct pay is the hourly wage or monthly salary paid to an employee. In addition to the base wage or salary, direct pay may include bonuses and profit shares. Indirect pay consists of various benefits and services. Some benefits are required by law: unemployment compensation, worker's compensation, Canada or Quebec Pension Plan, and paid vacations and holidays. Others are voluntarily made available by employers to employees. These include pensions, health and other insurance products, employee wellness programs, and college tuition reimbursement.

7 Explain how labour-management relations are different in a unionized environment

Many organizations have unionized employees. A labour union is organized to represent workers in dealing with management over issues involving wages, hours, and working conditions. Contracts are negotiated that set out the responsibilities of management and the workers through collective bargaining.

8 Describe some of the key laws and federal agencies affecting human resource management and labour relations.

A number of federal, provincial, and territorial laws affect human resource management. These include the Charter of Rights and Freedoms (contained in the Constitution Act of 1982), the Canadian Human Rights Act (1977), the Employment Equity Act (amended in 1995), the Occupational Health and Safety Act, and the Workplace Hazardous Materials Information System.

9 List some of the trends and issues affecting human resource management and labour relations.

Today, more and more companies are actively recruiting minorities. A diverse workforce often leads to increased market share and profits. Organizations are becoming proactive in their management of diversity. Companies are creating initiatives to build effective multicultural organizations.

Outsourcing is becoming more popular as a means to increased cost savings and ease of obtaining expertise. Technology continues to improve the efficiency of human resource management. It also enables firms to outsource many functions done internally in the past. In addition to normal job requirements, selected workers must have the ability to adapt to a local culture and perhaps to learn a foreign language.

KEY TERMS

agency shop 305	layoff
apprenticeship 300	local union 305
arbitration 307	mediation 307
closed shop 305	mentoring 300
collective bargaining 305	mutual-aid pact
competitive advantage 311	national union 305
contigent workers 295	on-the-job training 300
corporate open house 296	open shop 306
cost-of-living adjustment (COLA) 307	orientation 299
fringe benefits 304	outsource 311
grievance 307	performance appraisal 301
human resource (HR) planning 293	programmed instruction 301
human resource management 292	recruitment 296
job analysis 294	selection 297
job description 294	selection interview 298
job fair 296	shop steward 305
job rotation 300	simulation 301
job specification 294	training and development 299
labour union 304	union shop 305

Experiential Exercises

1. Make telecommuting work for you. Maybe a part-time job requires too much driving time. Perhaps there are simply no jobs in the immediate area that suit you. Try telecommuting right now. Is telecommuting for you? Many people are more satisfied with their personal and family lives than before they started working at home. But telecommuting is not for every person or every job, and you'll need plenty of self-discipline to make it work for you. Ask yourself if you can perform your duties without close supervision. Think also about whether you would miss your coworkers. If you decide to give telecommuting a try, consider these suggestions to maintain your productivity:

- *Set ground rules with your family.* Spouses and small children have to understand that even though you're in the house, you are busy earning a living. It's fine to throw in a few loads of laundry or answer the door when the plumber comes. It's another thing to take the kids to the mall or let them play games on your office PC.
- *Clearly demarcate your work space by using a separate room with a door you can shut.* Let your family know that, emergencies excepted, the space is off-limits during working hours.
- *If you have small children, you might want to arrange for childcare during your working hours.*
- *Stay in touch with your coworkers and professional colleagues.* Go into the office from time to time for meetings to stay connected.

Above all, you can make telecommuting work for you by being productive. Doing your job well, whether on-site or telecommuting, will help assure you of a bright future.

2. The fringe benefit package of many employers includes numerous voluntarily provided items such as health care insurance, life insurance, a pension plan, tuition reimbursement, employee price discounts on products of the firm, and paid sick leave. At your age, what are the three or four most important benefits? Why? Twenty years from now, what do you think will be your three or four most important benefits? Why?

3. As a corporate recruiter, you must know how to screen prospective employees. The Integrity Center website, at (www.integctr.com), offers a brief tutorial on pre-employment screening, a glossary of key words and phrases, and related information. Prepare a short report that tells your assistant how to go about this process.

4. Go to the Monster Board at (http://resume.monster.ca) to learn how to prepare an electronic résumé that will get results. Develop a list of rules for creating effective electronic résumés, and revise your own résumé into electronic format.

5. Working as a contingent employee can help you explore your career options. Visit the Manpower website at (www.manpower.com), and search for several types of jobs that interest you. What are the advantages of being a temporary worker? What other services does Manpower offer job seekers?

6. Web-based training is becoming popular at many companies as a way of bringing a wider variety of courses to more people at lower costs. The Web-Based Training Information Center site, at (www.webbasedtraining.com), provides a good introduction. Learn about the basics of online training at its Primer page. Then link to the Resources section, try a demo, and explore other areas that interest you. Prepare a brief report on your findings, including the pros and cons of using the Web for training, to present to your class.

7. Your 250-employee company is considering outsourcing some of its HR functions because it wants to offer a wider range of services. You've been asked to prepare a report on whether it should proceed and if so, how. Visit BuyerZone.com, (www.buyerzone.com), click on HR Outsourcing and then HR Outsourcing Buyer's Guide, to learn more about why companies are going outside for this important function and the advantages and disadvantages of doing so. Summarize your finding and make a recommendation. Then use a search engine to locate two to three firms that offer HR outsourcing services. Compare them and recommend one, explaining the reasons for your choice.

Review Questions

1. Why is human resource management in today's organization instrumental in driving an organization toward its goals?

2. What is the human resource management process?

3. Why is human resource planning and forecasting so important?

4. What is recruitment? What are some recruitment methods?

5. What are the steps in employee selection?

6. Differentiate between training and development.

7. What are the steps in performance evaluation?

8. What is compensation? How is it determined?

9. Discuss the types of compensation.

10. What is a labour union?

11. How are labour agreements negotiated?

12. What are the management and union strategies for dealing with conflict?

13. What are the primary laws that affect human resource management?

14. Discuss the trends in HRM.

"People First" at FedEx

FedEx founder and CEO Frederick Smith wants employees to be an integral part of the decision-making process at FedEx. He believes that putting the people first leads to better service for the customer and this leads, ultimately, to higher profits for the company. The People-Service-Profit (P-S-P) focus ensures that employee satisfaction, empowerment, risk taking, and innovation are encouraged, leading to 100 percent customer satisfaction, 100 percent of the time, and resulting in corporate profits.

FedEx Canada employs more than 5,000 people in 56 locations, with more 1,300 drop-off locations, and three call centres dealing with more than 35,000 calls per day. To emphasize the "people first" approach, the president traded jobs with one of his couriers for a week, and had the experience televised. An unusual exercise such as this sent a clear message to customers and employees alike. "We are serious about putting people first."

To help employees with the P-S-P focus, the following processes are in place at FedEx:

- An annual employee satisfaction survey
- A promotion-from-within policy
- Employee recognition and reward programs
- Leadership evaluation
- Open communication including e-mail, print, broadcast and face-to-face
- Pay-for-performance remuneration
- An employee appeal procedure and guaranteed fair treatment policies.

The P-S-P philosophy, supported by the appropriate policies, leads to motivated employees who go beyond what might be delineated in the usual job description. Corporate legend reports a story of an employee who looked after a customer's cat after the cat was inadvertently wrapped into a package by the customer. Another story describes how a FedEx manager personally flew to Ottawa to hand-deliver lifesaving medication to a customer. These examples illustrate the service commitment FedEx has encouraged and obtained from their employees. Many companies profess that "people are our greatest asset," but FedEx has managed actually to live this philosophy through their "people first" focus.

Critical Thinking Questions
- To maintain the culture FedEx has developed, it is important to hire employees who "fit." How might FedEx do this?
- Look at the compensation and evaluation aspects of HR. Suggest strategies for FedEx in keeping with their P-S-P focus.

SOURCES: Brenda McWilams and Gary Burkett, "Empowered Employees," *Marketing*, 3 no. 22 (June 19, 2006), 40; FedEx Canada History, (www.fedex.com/ca) (accessed July 10, 2006); FedEx Philosophy, (www .fedex.com/ca) (accessed December 7, 2008).

PepsiCo: More than Just Personnel

How does a company with a massive international presence, doing business in multiple time zones and languages, manage its employees? PepsiCo does it with a Values Statement and Code of Conduct that spells out what the company stands for, the rules it lives by—and Strategic Human Resources Management. The Values Statement—which reflects the company's aspirations—and the Code of Conduct—which provides the operating principles to achieve those goals—apply to every PepsiCo (**www.pepsico.com**)

employee and to every business transaction the company makes worldwide. Chairman and chief executive officer Steven S. Reinemund believes the company's continued success comes from its employees' dedication to these principles.

At PepsiCo, Strategic Human Resources Management (SHRM) develops strategies that contribute to company expansion and innovation. It is fully integrated into the organization, "partnering" with every division of PepsiCo's business, and must produce hard line results.

One mode of SHRM divides the work into four "quadrants":

Administrative Experts manage basic human resource functions like paying employees, dealing with their benefits, ensuring they are treated fairly, and more.

Employee Champions represent the employees' perspective to management with a view to maximizing their contribution to the company.

Change Agents develop systems and processes to facilitate change within the organization.

Strategic Business Partners devise strategies for growth in the organization.

Let's look at SHRM in action. Darryl Claiborne, a human resources director for Frito-Lay, a PepsiCo snack division, sometimes heads out on field trips. "There's times that I actually jump on a route truck and spend a day with an employee. As we ride we talk about understanding the business and how to drive the numbers," he says.

In a conventional company, human resource personnel rarely leave their offices. But PepsiCo believes that it is important for HR managers to achieve a more complete integration into the organization's various departments, to everyone's benefit. For example, employee retention has improved as a result of this type of direct communication between managers and employees in the trenches.

When a sales rep asks Darryl about career advancement, Darryl suggests he first meet the obligations of his current job—improving sales figures and establishing a rapport with his customers—before taking advantage of the company's self-nomination procedure which allows employees to inform management they are interested in promotion. In some cases it could mean following an established progression of advancement before moving into management.

PepsiCo recognizes the value of a human resource function that goes beyond the basics to deliver strategies and measurable hard line results that contribute to the company's success.

It judges employee performance according to the person's contribution to company results and is committed to equal opportunity for all employees and job applicants. PepsiCo's focus on SHRM helps the company grow and innovate—keys to flourishing in today's competitive corporate environment.

Critical Thinking Questions

- What challenges do human resource organizations face in today's competitive business environment? How is PepsiCo meeting those challenges?
- Strategic Human Resources Management refers to an integrated personnel/ human resource function. Describe the components of the SHRM planning process and how each one contributes to PepsiCo's corporate development and growth.
- PepsiCo believes in an integrated human resource function, even sending senior human resource personnel out into the field. What important benefits have resulted from this unusual activity?

SOURCES: Adapted from the video case, "Human Resources Management—PepsiCo"; Society for Human Resource Management (SHRMOnline) (www.shrm.org); (October 15, 2005); Lin Grensing-Pophal, "First Day Impressions Set Stage for Retention," White Paper for The Society for Human Resources Management, CareerJournal.com, (www.careerjournal.com) (October 15, 2005); PepsiCo corporate Website, (www.pepsico.com) (October 15, 2005).

Is Trust in the Workplace *Really* Important?

According to the Great Place to Work Institute in San Francisco, which spent two and a half decades researching workplace culture, the answer is a resounding "YES." But does this finding hold true in Canada? "YES" again. The Great Place to Work Institute Canada conducted an analysis of almost 10,000 employee surveys in the fall of 2005. The Great Place to Work Model focuses on workplace trust as opposed to the usual attention-getters, such as compensation, benefits, and other perks. The Trust Index comprises 57 questions in the areas of credibility, respect, fairness, pride, and camaraderie. Accepted applicants for the Best Workplaces list are able to access the Trust Index as part of the employee survey section of the application process.

TD Bank Financial Group ranked high in the survey. With 74,000 employees, the merger of TD Bank and Canada Trust was the largest bank merger in Canadian history. Merging two different cultures could have been a huge problem, but obviously, management handled it well, with Ed Clark, of the acquired company, Canada Trust, becoming the new CEO. TD tends to focus on instilling pride in its employees as one aspect of its trust-based culture. Volunteerism is important in the company, and employees can access paid time off for volunteer activities.

Graham Lowe, one of the founding partners of the Great Place to Work Institute Canada, provides a number of principles to help managers move toward a "great" workplace. These include talking about employee trust openly, being aware of trust-building and breaking actions, focusing on a few trust-building changes and pursuing them, focusing on the *process* rather than the end result of these changes, and celebrating what already works well. By creating a high-trust culture, management can increase the company's competitive advantage, which benefits employees, management, shareholders, and customers.

Critical Thinking Questions

1. What sort of corporate culture would you, as an employee, prefer?

2. Focus on a potential employer, and investigate the culture through secondary research.

3. Look at (**www.greatplacetowork.ca**) and determine how this company would rank using the criteria discussed on the website.

SOURCES: Andrew Wahl "Best Workplaces," *Canadian Business*, April 10–23, 2006, 64–66; Andrew Wahl, "On the Money," *Canadian Business*, April 10–23, 2006, 68–69; and Peter Evans, "TD Bank Financial Group," *Canadian Business*, April 10–23, 2006, 77–79; (www/greatplacetowork.ca/best/list-ca.htm), accessed December 7, 2008.

CHAPTER 11

Making the Connection

Achieving World-Class Operations Management

This chapter, on the management of the operations area of a business, starts with a discussion of Harley-Davidson's operations. This example is very appropriate to the title of the chapter, as Harley definitely epitomizes world-class operations and offers many lessons for companies struggling to get there. For years Harley tried to sell freedom and adventure but with a poor-quality product sold at a high price because of outdated and inefficient facilities. Its *financial performance* was extremely poor, because it simply did not *meet customer needs*—poor *quality* at a high price did not provide the customer with anything of value. Once it stopped trying to produce quantity and focused instead on quality, Harley turned it all around. Today the company is a leader in quality management. But it required a view of the business as a whole—meeting the needs of the customer (*marketing*) through *committed employees* (*human resources*) and providing quality (*operations*) at the lowest cost to improve the bottom line (*finance*) while uniting all the *stakeholders* in the "Harley-Davidson family."

As explained in the chapter, sound operations management is vital to the financial success of the company because this area accounts for as much as three-quarters of the company's costs. It is a wonderful example of the integrative nature of business, as it must work very closely with the other functional areas to achieve maximum financial performance. Most obviously, operations must develop processes to provide for the demand created and forecasted by

marketing, but it must also work with marketing to develop and design products so that the operations processes used to provide them are the most efficient and effective and the distribution of those products—both an operations and a marketing issue—is done efficiently, cost-effectively, and in a manner that meets the customers' needs. Similarly, operations must work with human resources to have the right numbers of the best-qualified people available to produce products and service customers, as well as deciding whether to replace this human effort with robots or other computerized techniques. In fact, most of the decisions made in the operations area have wider functional implications. For example, the choice of location can affect transportation costs and thus the final cost of the product as well as the availability and cost of labour, whereas implementing a flexible manufacturing system is expensive but needs little labour to operate, and provides consistent quality products that meet individual customer specifications.

An excellent example in the chapter of the need for a successful business to integrate operations with the other functional areas is that of Designlore with its "Right the First Time" approach to designing products. Designlore recognizes the need to integrate innovative design that meets customer needs with traditional engineering and operations principles, in order to provide products that are designed in a way that keeps all members of the supply chain satisfied from engineering right through to the final

consumer Another area where we can see the integration of operations with the other facets of our business model is in the external environment. Many businesses today are faced with environmental challenges in an effort to meet their operational goals. For example, in the *social* environment, consumers are expecting customized products of greater quality delivered in a timely manner at a reasonable price. This requires using whatever *technology* is available to allow the company to stay ahead of the competition and improving relationships with suppliers and vendors (both important stakeholder groups), so that there is a smooth flow from provider to consumer. If consumers don't get what they want, they will simply go to the increasing number of competitors in the global *economic* environment who can often produce at a lower cost, and they will frequently do this at breakneck speed, using technology to shop over the Internet, switching their loyalties at the click of a mouse!

The technology that is available to the operations area of a business has improved tremendously. In this chapter, we outline many of these *innovations*. One of the most integrative examples of technology is manufacturing resource planning (MRPII). It uses a complex computerized system to integrate data from the different departments of the company, so that they are all working as one to meet customer needs. Enterprise resource planning (ERP) takes this a step further by going outside the business and integrating information about suppliers and customers into the system. These technologies and others help to manage the supply chain so that the entire sequence, from securing inputs into the process to delivering goods to the consumer, is done in a manner that meets the needs of the customer at the highest possible level.

Operations management is also an excellent example of the management process at work. You will read in the chapter about production *planning* and *control*, and the specific tools and techniques that are used to plan and control the production process. Quality control is a particularly important issue for management in meeting the customers' needs for a quality product. Part of the process is also deciding on the layout for the production or service facility, which involves *organizing* the company's resources in the most appropriate way to produce goods or provide services to the customer efficiently. The final management function is pivotal—*motivating*—as we know that workers must be committed to the task for it all to come together. Operations managers working directly with the workers that produce the goods or services for the customers have the ultimate responsibility to gain that commitment.

In this chapter, you'll learn about many trends in operations that allow companies to both enhance innovation to meet changing customer needs in a timely manner, and adapt to changes in technology. At the same time, they are improving quality, keeping costs down, and gaining employee commitment by involving teams of employees throughout the process. And isn't that what it's all about—meeting critical success factors by integrating the functional areas within the dynamic business environment?

CHAPTER 11

Achieving World-Class Operations Management

LEARNING OUTCOMES

1 Discuss why production and operations management is important in both manufacturing and service firms.

2 List the types of production processes used by manufacturers and service firms.

3 Describe how organizations decide where to put their production facilities and what choices must be made in designing the facility.

4 Explain why resource-planning tasks like inventory management and supplier relations are critical to production.

5 Discuss how operations managers schedule and control production.

6 Evaluate how quality management and lean-manufacturing techniques help firms improve production and operations management.

7 Identify the roles that technology and automation play in manufacturing and service industry operations management.

8 List some of the key trends affecting the way companies manage production and operations.

BUILDING ON SUCCESS AT HARLEY-DAVIDSON

© AP / WIDE WORLD PHOTOS

Harley-Davidsons aren't just motorcycles. They're an American legend, known for their unique style, sound, and power ever since the first one was assembled in a backyard workshop in 1903. "People want more than two wheels and a motor," explains former Harley-Davidson CEO Jeffrey Bleustein. "Harleys represent something very basic—a desire for freedom, adventure, and individualism."

Twenty years ago, Harley also represented everything that was wrong with American manufacturing. The company's production facilities were outdated and inefficient, keeping prices high. Quality was so poor that owners sometimes joked they needed two Harleys—one to ride and one for parts. As fed-up consumers turned to motorcycles made by Japanese and German manufacturers, Harley-Davidson's sales plummeted, and the company teetered on bankruptcy.

Today, however, Harley-Davidson (**www. harley-davidson.com**) is a company reborn. While 2007 was not as strong as 2006, with a decrease in revenue of 2.3%, Harley-Davidson Motorcycles still posted a revenue figure of $4.4 billion. The company's manufacturing facility in York, Pa. suffered a three week strike which impacted production at the Milwaukee plant as well.

The quest for excellence begins with product design. Every component in a Harley bike is put through a rigorous design process that examines its manufacturability according to quality standards. Special software estimates the cost of each design proposal, so that expenses can be carefully controlled. Vendors hoping to supply various components to Harley-Davidson automatically receive this same information electronically, integrating it into the product development cycle.

Lasers and robots automate many production tasks. Components ready for assembly are loaded onto specially designed carts that swivel 360 degrees and can be lowered or raised to suit different workers or tasks. The carts then move into workstations where groups of employees assemble them into motorcycle frames. No motorcycle leaves a Harley-Davidson plant without a final quality inspection. A team of test drivers revs up and rides each motorcycle, checking operating quality and listening for the classic Harley sound.

Employees play a critical role in Harley's production facilities. Working in teams, many employees are cross-trained to perform a variety of production tasks. Each work team is asked to look constantly for ways to build better motorcycles. The company has implemented many employee-generated ideas for improving equipment, factory layout, and production processes. They depend on their dealers and distributors as well, to create demand for their products and services.

Industry analysts say Harley-Davidson's rebirth and continued growth is intimately tied to its dedication to quality and efficiency in its operations and production processes. "Harley-Davidson succeeded because they aligned all stakeholders—from customers to shareholders to employees and suppliers," says consultant Stephen Shapiro. "They created the Harley-Davidson family, where everyone, including unions, are united in a common purpose."[1]

Critical Thinking Questions

As you read this chapter, consider the following questions as they relate to Harley-Davidson:

1. **How has focusing on quality in its operations and production supported Harley-Davidson's growth?**

2. **What external factors have led to this focus?**

3. **What future production decisions will Harley need to make if it is to continue to grow?**

Finding the most efficient and effective methods of producing the goods or services it sells to customers is an ongoing focus of nearly every type of business organization. Today more than ever, changing consumer expectations, technological advances, and increased competition are all forcing business organizations to rethink where, when, and how they will produce products or services.

Like Harley-Davidson, manufacturers have discovered that it is no longer enough simply to push products through the factory and onto the market. Consumers demand high quality at reasonable prices. They also expect manufacturers to deliver products in a timely manner. Firms that can't meet these expectations often face strong competition from businesses that can. To compete, many manufacturers are reinventing how they make their products by automating their factories, developing new production processes, using quality control techniques, and tightening their relationships with suppliers.

Service organizations are also facing challenges. Their customers are demanding better service, shorter waits, and more individualized attention. Just like manufacturers, service organizations are using new methods to deliver what customers need and want. Banks, for example, are using technology such as ATMs and the Internet to make their services more easily accessible to customers. Many universities and colleges now offer weekend and even online courses for students who find it more convenient. Tax services are filing tax returns via computer.

In this chapter, we examine how manufacturers and service firms manage and control the creation of products and services. We'll discuss production planning, including the choices firms must make concerning the type of production process they will use, the location where production will occur, the design of the facility, and the management of resources needed in production. Next, we'll explain routing and scheduling, two critical tasks for controlling production and operations efficiency. Many businesses are improving productivity by employing quality control methods and automation. We'll discuss these methods before summarizing some of the trends affecting production and operations management.

Production and Operations Management—An Overview

production
The creation of products and services by turning inputs, such as natural resources, raw materials, human resources, and capital, into outputs, which are products and services.

operations management
Management of the production process.

Production, the creation of products and services, is an essential function in every firm. Production turns inputs, such as natural resources, raw materials, human resources, and capital, into outputs, which are products and services. This process is shown in Exhibit 11.1. Managing this conversion process is the role of **operations management**.

In the 1980s, many Canadian industries, such as automotive and steel, lost customers to foreign competitors because their production systems could not provide the quality customers demanded. As a result, most Canadian companies, both large and small, now consider a focus on quality to be a central component of effective operations management.

The goal of customer satisfaction, closely linked to quality, is also an important part of effective production and operations. In the past, the manufacturing function in most companies was focused inward. Manufacturing had little contact with customers and didn't always understand their needs and desires. Today, however, stronger links between marketing and manufacturing have encouraged production managers to be more outwardly focused and to consider decisions in light

With oil reserves second only to Saudi Arabia, Canada's Alberta province is set to become a vast supplier of crude oil worldwide. Unlike the smooth petroleum that gushes from Arabian wells, however, most of Alberta's black gold has to be mined from oil-rich sands. The process is rigorous: 400-ton trucks transport excavated bitumen to crushers and mixers that separate the sands from the oil and the resulting slurry travels miles of pipeline to North American refineries. What are key inputs in the mining of oil sands?

BLOOMBERG VIA GETTY IMAGES

of their effect on customer satisfaction. Service companies have also found that making operating decisions with customer satisfaction in mind can be a competitive advantage.

Operations managers, the personnel charged with managing and supervising the conversion process, play a vital role in today's firm. They often control about three-fourths of a firm's assets, including inventories, wages, and benefits. They work closely with other major functions of the firm, such as marketing, finance, accounting, and human resources, to help ensure that the firm produces its goods

EXHIBIT 11.1 > Production Process for Products and Services

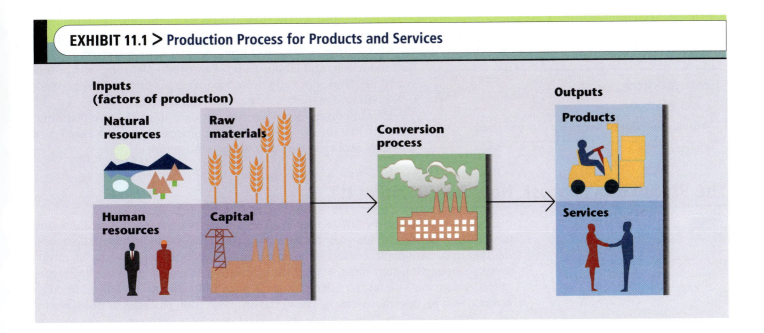

CONCEPT *in Action* >>>

From its storied creation in post-war Italy to its big-screen immortalization in movies like Roman Holiday and Quadrophenia, the Vespa scooter has a reputation for romance, rebellion, and style. Manufactured by Italy's Piaggio, the Vespa's svelte, stainless-steel chassis and aeronautic-inspired designs are seen everywhere in Europe and more and more in the United States. The Piaggio Group presently operates factories in Italy, Spain, India, and China. What important production-planning decisions does Piaggio need to make as it considers expanding into overseas markets?

production planning
The aspect of operations management in which the firm considers the competitive environment and its own strategic goals in an effort to find the best production methods.

> **concept check**
>
> Define production.
>
> What is production planning? Production control?

profitably and continually satisfies customers. They face the challenge of combining people and other resources to produce high quality goods on time and at a reasonable cost. Working with marketing, they help to decide which products to make or which services to offer. They become involved with the development and design of goods and determine what production processes will be most effective.

Production and operations management involves three main types of decisions that are made at three different stages:

1. **Production planning.** The first decisions facing operations managers come at the planning stage. At this stage, managers decide where, when, and how production will occur. They obtain resources and determine site locations.
2. **Production control.** At this stage, the decision-making process focuses on scheduling, controlling quality and costs, and the day-to-day operations of running a factory or service facility.
3. **Improving production and operations.** The final stage of operations management focuses on developing more efficient methods of producing the firm's goods or services.

These three types of decisions are ongoing and often occur simultaneously. In the following sections, we will take a closer look at the decisions and considerations firms face in each of these stages of production and operations management.

Gearing Up: Production Planning

An important part of operations management is **production planning**. During production planning, the firm considers the competitive environment and its own strategic goals in an effort to find the best production methods. Good production planning balances goals that might conflict, such as providing high quality service while keeping operating costs down, or keeping profits high while maintaining adequate inventories of finished products. Sometimes accomplishing all of these goals is quite difficult.

Production planning involves three phases. Long-term planning has a time frame of three to five years. It focuses on which goods to produce, how many to produce, and where they should be produced. Medium-term planning decisions cover about two years. They concern the layout of the factory or service facilities, where and how to obtain the resources needed for production, and labour issues. Short-term planning, with a one year time frame, converts these broader goals into specific production plans and materials management strategies.

Four important decisions must be made in production planning. They involve the type of production process that will be used, site selection, facility layout, and resource planning.

The Production Process: How Do We Make It?

production process
The way in which a good is made.

In production planning, the first decision involves which type of **production process**—the way in which a good is made—best fits with the company's goals and customer demands. Another important consideration is the type of good or service being produced, as different goods might require different production processes. In general, there are three types of production: mass production, mass customization, and customization. In addition to production type, operations managers also classify production processes in two ways: by how inputs are converted into outputs and by the timing of the process.

mass production
The ability to manufacture many identical goods at once.

One for All: Mass Production   **Mass production**, manufacturing many identical goods at once, was a product of the Industrial Revolution. Henry Ford's Model T automobile is a good example of mass production. Each car turned out by Ford's factory was identical, right down to its colour. If you wanted a car in any colour except black, you were out of luck. Canned goods, over-the-counter drugs, and household appliances are examples of goods that are still mass produced. The emphasis in mass production is on keeping manufacturing costs low by producing highly uniform products using repetitive and standardized processes. Mass production, therefore, relies heavily on standardization, mechanization, and specialization. As many products become more complicated to produce, however, mass production is becoming more complex. Automobile manufacturers, for example, must now incorporate more sophisticated electronics into their car designs. As a result, the number of assembly stations in most automobile manufacturing plants has increased.

mass customization
A manufacturing process in which goods are mass produced up to a point and then custom tailored to the needs or desires of individual customers.

Just for You: Customizing Goods   In **mass customization**, goods are produced using mass production techniques but only up to a point. At that point, the product or service is custom tailored to the needs or desires of individual customers. Many Canadian furniture manufacturers use mass customization to produce couches and chairs to customer specifications, usually within 30 days. The basic frames used to make the furniture are the same, but automated machinery pre-cuts the colour and type of leather or fabric ordered by each customer. These coverings are then added to the frame through mass production techniques. Dynasty Furniture Mfg. Ltd of Mississauga, Ontario uses mass customization for its sofas and other products.

customization
The production of goods or services one at a time according to the specific needs or wants of individual customers.

job shop
A manufacturing firm that produces goods in response to customer orders.

Customization is the opposite of mass production. In customization, the firm produces goods or services one at a time according to the specific needs or wants of individual customers. Unlike mass customization, each product or service produced is unique. For example, a print shop might handle a variety of projects, including newsletters, brochures, stationery, and reports. Each print job varies in quantity, type of printing process, binding, colour of ink, and type of paper. A manufacturing firm that produces goods in response to customer orders is called a **job shop**.

concept check

What is mass production?

Differentiate mass customization from customization.

Some types of service businesses also deliver customized services. Doctors, for instance, usually must consider the individual illnesses and circumstances of each patient before developing a customized treatment plan. Real estate agents also develop a customized service plan for each customer based on the type of house the person is selling or wants to buy. The differences between mass production, mass customization, and customization are summarized in Exhibit 11.2.

process manufacturing
A production process in which the basic input is *broken down* into one or more outputs (products).

assembly process
A production process in which the basic inputs are either *combined* to create the output or *transformed* into the output.

Converting Inputs to Outputs   Production involves converting *inputs* (raw materials, parts, human resources) into *outputs* (products or services). In a manufacturing company, the inputs, the production process, and the final outputs are usually obvious. Harley-Davidson, for instance, converts steel, rubber, paint, and other inputs into motorcycles. The production process in a service company involves a less obvious conversion. For example, a hospital converts the knowledge and skills of its medical personnel, along with equipment and supplies from a variety of sources, into health care services for patients. Exhibit 11.3 provides examples of the inputs and outputs used by several other types of businesses.

There are two basic processes for converting inputs into outputs. In **process manufacturing**, the basic input (raw materials, parts) is *broken down* into one or more outputs (products). For instance, bauxite (the input) is processed to extract aluminum (the output). The **assembly process** is just the opposite. The basic inputs, like parts, raw materials, or human resources, are either *combined* to create the output or *transformed* into the output. An airplane, for example, is created by assembling thousands of parts. Steel manufacturers use heat to transform iron and other materials into steel.

EXHIBIT 11.2 > Classification of Production Types

Mass Production

Highly uniform products or services. Many products made sequentially.

Examples: Breakfast cereals, soft drinks, and computer keyboards.

Mass Customization

Uniform standardized production to a point, then unique features added to each product.

Examples: Dell Computers, tract homes, and TaylorMade golf clubs.

Customization

Each product or service produced according to individual customer requirements.

Examples: Custom homes, legal services, and haircuts.

In services, customers may play a role in the transformation process. For example, a tax preparation service combines the knowledge of the tax preparer with the client's information about personal finances to complete tax returns.

continuous process
A production process that uses long production runs lasting days, weeks, or months without equipment shutdowns; generally used for high-volume, low-variety products with standardized parts.

Production Timing A second consideration in choosing a production process is timing. A **continuous process** uses long production runs that can last days, weeks, or months without equipment shutdowns. It is best for high-volume, low-variety products with standardized parts, such as nails, glass, and paper. Some services also use a continuous process. Your local electric company is one example. Per-unit costs are low, and production is easy to schedule.

CONCEPT *in Action* >>>

Mass customization has produced a thriving build-to-order society. This revolution in manufacturing is fueled, in part, by pop culture, where the compulsion to parade individuality is a hot commodity. Expressing oneself has never been easier. Consumers can design a new pair of sneakers with Vans Customs, build their own bags at Timbuk2, and customize a snowboard using the Burton Series 13 customization program—all while munching a pack of personalized M&M's candies. What developments have made mass customization a viable method of production?

COURTESY OF TIMBUK2

EXHIBIT 11.3 > Converting Inputs to Outputs

Type of Organization	Input	Output
Airline	Pilots, crew, flight attendants, reservations system, ticketing agents, customers, airplanes, fuel, maintenance crews, ground facilities	Movement of customers and freight
Grocery store	Merchandise, building, clerks, supervisors, store fixtures, shopping carts, customers	Groceries for customers
High school	Faculty, curriculum, buildings, classrooms, library, auditorium, gymnasium, students, staff, supplies	Graduates, public service
Manufacturer	Machinery, raw materials, plant, workers, managers	Finished products for consumers and other firms
Restaurant	Food, cooking equipment, serving personnel, chefs, dishwashers, host, patrons, furniture, fixtures	Meals for patrons

intermittent process
A production process that uses short production runs to make batches of different products; generally used for low-volume, high-variety products.

In an **intermittent process**, short production runs are used to make batches of different products. Machines are shut down to change them to make different products at different times. This process is best for low-volume, high-variety products, such as those produced by mass customization or customization. Job shops are examples of firms using an intermittent process.

Although some service companies use continuous processes, most rely on intermittent processes. For instance, a restaurant preparing gourmet meals, a physician performing physical examinations or surgical operations, and an advertising agency developing ad campaigns for business clients all customize their services to suit each customer. They use the intermittent process. Note that their "production runs" might be very short—one grilled salmon or one eye exam at a time.

concept check

Define process manufacturing and the assembly process.

What is the difference between continuous and intermittent processes?

Location, Location, Location: Where Do We Make It?

A big decision that managers must make early in production and operations planning is where to put the facility, be it a factory or a service office. The facility's location affects operating and shipping costs and, ultimately, the price of the product or service and the company's ability to compete. Mistakes made at this stage can be expensive, because moving a factory or service facility once production begins is difficult and costly. Firms must weigh a number of factors to make the right decision.

Availability of Production Inputs   As we discussed earlier, organizations need certain resources to produce products and services for sale. Access to these resources, or inputs, is a huge consideration in site selection. Executives must assess the availability of raw materials, parts, and equipment for each production site under consideration. The costs of shipping raw materials and finished goods can be as much as 25 percent of a manufacturer's total cost, so locating a factory where these and other costs are as low as possible can make a major contribution to a firm's success. Companies that use heavy or bulky raw materials, for example, might choose to be located near suppliers. Metal refiners want to be near ore deposits, oil refiners near oil fields, paper mills near forests, and food processors near farms.

The availability and cost of labour are also critical to both manufacturing and service businesses, and the unionization of local labour is another point to consider

Making Ethical Choices

SWEATING IT OUT AT NEW ERA CAP

As production manager for New Era Cap, the largest North American manufacturer of ball caps, you supervise operations at three factories. The oldest plant, in Derby, New York, has 600 workers and produces 120,000 caps a week, the lowest production rate of the three plants. The Derby factory also has the highest worker absentee rate of any plant, with as many as 13 percent of workers calling in sick on any given day.

In an attempt to bring the Derby plant up to the same level of efficiency as the other two, you've implemented several changes in the past few years. You've introduced new production schedules, made staff cuts, and tried to reduce absentee rates.

Unhappy with the changes you've made, Derby workers went on strike 10 months ago. After New Era executives refused to settle with the striking workers' demands for reduced hours and pay raises, their union, the Communications Workers of America (CWA), issued public statements accusing the Derby plant of "sweatshop" working conditions. At the CWA's urging, the United Students Against

Sweatshops (USAS) started a campaign to get colleges and universities to boycott New Era caps. Several universities have already joined the boycott.

You are convinced that the Derby plant is not a sweatshop. You've shifted most of Derby's production to New Era's other two factories with minimal problems. The union now says it will end the strike and call off the boycott if the company grants immediate pay raises and health benefit increases to all Derby workers. You feel this is blackmail.

ETHICAL DILEMMA: Should you recommend that New Era's president agree to the union's demands?

SOURCES: "New Era Union Plans Boycott," *Buffalo Business First*, July 20, 2001; "Cap Maker Shifts Production after Walkout," *Buffalo Business First*, July 16, 2001; "New Era Says 'Sweatshop' Label Is False," *Buffalo Business First*, June 4, 2002; "New Era Cap Makes New Offer to CWA Strikers," *Buffalo Business First*, February 26, 2002; all sources downloaded from (http://buffalo.bizjournals.com).

HOT Links

Learn more about the products Globe Motors manufactures at (**www.globe-motors.com**).

in many industries. Payroll costs can vary widely from one location to another due to differences in the cost of living, the number of jobs available, and the size, skills, and productivity of the local workforce.

Low labour costs were one reason why Globe Motors, a manufacturer of motors and power steering systems for automotive, aerospace, and defence applications, chose Portugal as the site for its production facility. In addition to low labour costs, Portugal offers manufacturers the lowest operating costs in the European Union.[2]

Marketing Factors   Businesses must also evaluate how their facility location will affect their ability to serve their customers. For some firms, it might not be necessary to be located near customers. Instead, the firm will need to assess the difficulty and costs of distributing its goods to customers from the chosen location.

Other firms might find that locating near customers can provide marketing advantages. When a factory or service centre is close to customers, the firm can often offer better service at a lower cost. Other firms might gain a competitive advantage by locating their facilities so that customers can easily buy their products or services. The location of competitors might also be a factor. Businesses with more than one facility might also need to consider how far to spread their locations to maximize market coverage. Globe Motors decided to build its new production facility in Europe because the continent is a major market for Globe's products. By building its motors closer to this large customer base, rather than exporting them to Europe after producing them elsewhere, Globe believes it will be able to improve customer service and response time.[3]

Manufacturing Environment   Another factor to consider is the manufacturing environment in a potential location. Some localities have a strong existing manufacturing base. When a large number of manufacturers, perhaps in a certain industry, are already located in an area, that area is likely to offer greater availability of resources, such as manufacturing workers, better accessibility to suppliers and transportation, and other factors that can increase a plant's operating efficiency.

Industry Week magazine conducts a regular survey of the manufacturing climate offered by areas around the world. Each area is rated on the productivity of its manufacturing sector, the percentage of the local workforce employed in manufacturing, the contribution of manufacturing to the area's overall economy, and several other factors. One such area that has been identified as a global "hot spot" is Turkey.[4]

HOT Links

What characteristics contribute to a city's manufacturing climate? Find out by reading more at Industry Week's website: (**www.industryweek.com**).

Local Incentives   Incentives offered by countries, states, or cities might also influence site selection. Tax breaks are a common incentive. A locality might reduce the amount of taxes the firm will pay on income, real estate, utilities, or payroll. Local governments also sometimes offer exemption from certain regulations or financial assistance to attract or keep production facilities in their area. For example, Portugal helped entice Globe Motors by offering $7.6 million USD in financial incentives, as well as tax breaks and assistance with employee-training programs.[5]

International Location Considerations   Like Globe Motors, many manufacturers have chosen to move much of their production to international locations in recent years. There are often sound financial reasons for considering this step. Labour costs are considerably lower in countries like Singapore, China, and Mexico. Foreign countries might also have fewer regulations governing how factories operate. A foreign location might place production closer to new markets. As we've seen, all of these considerations motivated Globe Motors to build a new production facility in Portugal.

Designing the Facility

After the site location decision has been made, the next focus in production planning is the facility's layout. Here, the goal is to determine the most efficient and effective design for the particular production process. A manufacturer might opt for a U-shaped production line, for example, rather than a long, straight one to allow products and workers to move more quickly from one area to another.

Service organizations must also consider layout, but they are more concerned with how it affects customer behaviour. It might be more convenient for a hospital to place its freight elevators in the centre of the building, for example, but doing so might block the flow of patients, visitors, and medical personnel between floors and departments.

There are three *main* types of facility layouts: process, product, and fixed-position layouts. All three are illustrated in Exhibit 11.4. Cellular manufacturing is another type of facility layout.

process layout
A facility arrangement in which work flows according to the production process. All workers performing similar tasks are grouped together, and products pass from one workstation to another.

Process Layout: All Welders Stand Here   The process layout arranges workflow around the production process. All workers performing similar tasks are grouped together. Products pass from one workstation to another (but not necessarily to every workstation). For example, all grinding would be done in one area, all assembling in another, and all inspection in yet another. The process layout is best for firms that produce small numbers of a wide variety of products, typically using general-purpose machines that can be changed rapidly to new operations for different product designs. For example, a manufacturer of custom machinery would use a process layout.

product (assembly line) layout
A facility arrangement in which workstations or departments are arranged in a line with products moving along the line.

Product Layout: Moving Down the Line   Products that require a continuous or repetitive production process use the product (or assembly line) layout. When large quantities of a product must be processed on an ongoing basis, the workstations or departments are arranged in a line with products moving along the line. Automobile and appliance manufacturers, as well as food-processing plants, usually use a product layout. Service companies may also use a product layout for routine processing operations. For example, overnight film processors use assembly line techniques.

fixed-position layout
A facility arrangement in which the product stays in one place and workers and machinery move to it as needed.

Fixed-Position Layout: Staying Put   Some products cannot be put on an assembly line or moved about in a plant. A fixed-position layout lets the product stay in one place while workers and machinery move to it as needed. Products that are impossible to move—ships, airplanes, and construction projects—are typically produced using a fixed-position layout. Limited space at a project site often means that parts of the product must be assembled at other sites, transported to the fixed site, and then assembled. Other examples of the fixed-position layout are on-site services like housecleaning services, pest control, and landscaping.

EXHIBIT 11.4 > Facility Layouts

Process layout arranges workflow around the production process. All workers performing similar tasks are grouped together.

Products that require a continuous or repetitive production process use the **product layout**.

A **fixed-position layout** lets the product stay in one place while workers and machinery move to it as needed.

cellular manufacturing
Production technique that uses small, self-contained production units, each performing all or most of the tasks necessary to complete a manufacturing order.

Cellular Manufacturing: A Start-to-Finish Focus   Cellular manufacturing combines some aspects of both product and fixed-position layout. Work cells are small, self-contained production units that include several machines and workers arranged in a compact, sequential order. Each work cell performs all or most of the tasks necessary to complete a manufacturing order. There are usually between 5 and 10 workers in a cell, and they are trained to perform all of the steps in the production process. The goal is to create a team environment where team members are involved in production from beginning to end. Clothing manufacturing can use cellular manufacturing by having small work cells completing all the work of each order.

Pulling It Together: Resource Planning

As part of the production-planning process, firms must ensure that the resources needed for production, such as raw materials, parts, and equipment, will be available at strategic moments in the production process. This can be a huge challenge. The components used to build just one Boeing airplane, for instance, number in the millions. Cost is also an important factor. In many industries, the cost of materials and supplies used in the production process amounts to as much as half of sales revenues. Resource planning is therefore a big part of any firm's production strategy.

Resource planners begin by specifying which raw materials, parts, and components will be required, and when, in order to produce finished goods. To determine the amount of each item needed, the expected quantity of finished goods to be produced must be forecast. A **bill of material** is then drawn up that lists the items and the number of each required to make the product. **Purchasing**, or *procurement*, is the process of buying production inputs from various sources.

bill of material
A list of the items and the number of each required to make a given product.

purchasing
The process of buying production inputs from various sources; also called *procurement*.

make-or-buy decision
The determination by a firm of whether to make its production materials or buy them from outside sources.

Make or Buy?   The firm must decide whether to make its production materials or buy them from outside sources. This is the **make-or-buy decision**. The quantity of items needed is one consideration. If a part is used in only one of many products, buying the part might be more cost-effective than making it. Buying standard items, such as screws, bolts, rivets, and nails, is usually cheaper and easier than producing them internally. Sometimes purchasing larger components from another manufacturing firm is cost-effective as well. Purchasing items from an outside source instead of making them internally is called **outsourcing**. Harley-Davidson, for example, purchases its tires, brake systems, and other motorcycle components from other businesses that make them to Harley's specifications. If a product has special design features that need to be kept secret to protect a competitive advantage, however, a firm might decide to produce all parts internally.

outsourcing
The purchase of items from an outside source rather than making them internally.

In deciding whether to make or buy, a firm must also consider whether outside sources can provide high-quality supplies in a reliable manner. Having to shut down production because vital parts weren't delivered on time can be a costly disaster. Just as bad are inferior parts or materials, which can damage a firm's reputation for producing high-quality goods. Therefore, firms that buy some or all of their production materials from outside sources should pay close attention to building strong relationships with quality suppliers.

HOT *Links*

How do companies decide whether to make or buy? Find out more at the Outsourcing Institute, a professional association where buyers and sellers network and connect:
(**www.outsourcing.com**).

Inventory Management: Not Just Parts   A firm's **inventory** is the supply of goods it holds for use in production or for sale to customers. Deciding how much inventory to keep on hand is one of the biggest challenges facing operations managers. With large inventories, the firm can meet most production and customer demands. Buying in large quantities can also allow a company to take advantage of quantity discounts. On the other hand, large inventories can tie up the firm's money, are expensive to store, and can become obsolete.

inventory
The supply of goods that a firm holds for use in production or for sale to customers.

Inventory management involves deciding how much of each type of inventory to keep on hand and the ordering, receiving, storing, and tracking of it. The goal of inventory management is to keep down the costs of ordering and holding inventories

inventory management
The determination of how much of each type of inventory a firm will keep on hand and the ordering, receiving, storing, and tracking of inventory.

while maintaining enough on hand for production and sales. Good inventory management enhances product quality, makes operations more efficient, and increases profits. Poor inventory management can result in dissatisfied customers, financial difficulties, and even bankruptcy.

One way to determine the best inventory levels is to look at three costs: the cost of holding inventory, the cost of reordering frequently, and the cost of not keeping enough inventories on hand. Managers must measure all three costs and try to minimize them.

To control inventory levels, managers often track the use of certain inventory items. Most companies keep a **perpetual inventory**, a continuously updated list of inventory levels, orders, sales, and receipts, for all major items. Today, companies often use computers to track inventory levels, calculate order quantities, and issue purchase orders at the right times.

Computerized Resource Planning   Many manufacturing companies have adopted computerized systems to control the flow of resources and inventory. **Materials requirement planning (MRP)** is one such system. MRP uses a master schedule to ensure that the materials, labour, and equipment needed for production are at the right places in the right amounts at the right times. The schedule is based on forecasts of demand for the company's products. It says exactly what will be manufactured during the next few weeks or months and when the work will take place. Sophisticated computer programs coordinate all the elements of MRP. The computer comes up with materials requirements by comparing production needs to the materials the company already has on hand. Orders are placed so that items will be on hand when they are needed for production. MRP helps ensure a smooth flow of finished products.

Manufacturing resource planning II (MRPII) was developed in the late 1980s to expand on MRP. It uses a complex computerized system to integrate data from many departments, including finance, marketing, accounting, engineering, and manufacturing. MRPII can generate a production plan for the firm as well as management reports, forecasts, and financial statements. The system lets managers make more accurate forecasts and assess the impact of production plans on profitability. If one department's plans change, the effects of these changes on other departments are transmitted throughout the company.

Whereas MRP and MRPII systems are focused internally, **enterprise resource planning (ERP)** systems go a step further and incorporate information about the

---

perpetual inventory
A continuously updated list of inventory levels, orders, sales, and receipts.

materials requirement planning (MRP)
A computerized system of controlling the flow of resources and inventory. A master schedule is used to ensure that the materials, labour, and equipment needed for production are at the right places in the right amounts at the right times.

manufacturing resource planning II (MRPII)
A complex computerized system that integrates data from many departments to allow managers to forecast and assess the impact of production plans on profitability more accurately.

enterprise resource planning (ERP)
A computerized resource-planning system that incorporates information about the firm's suppliers and customers with its internally generated data.

CONCEPT *in Action* >>>

Wal-Mart's retail dominance is built upon advanced logistics and inventory management. The company's vendor-managed inventory system puts the burden on suppliers to maintain stock until needed in stores and radio frequency identification tags (RFID) help automate the flow of goods. Wal-Mart's remarkable 2:1 sales-to-inventory ratio is expected to shrink further to a theoretical "zero inventory" state in which it won't pay for products until they're purchased by consumers. What costs are associated with keeping too much or too little inventory?

© DAVID MCNEW/GETTY IMAGES

CONCEPT *in Action* >>>

Manufacturing product labels for over 9,000 Estée Lauder cosmetics products would be impossible without enterprise resource planning (ERP). A daily data feed between ERP systems at Estée Lauder and label-supplier Topflight ensures that machines produce only the labels necessary for the next production run. The data-transfer link is flexible enough to accommodate dynamic design changes to colours and label copy while eliminating purchase orders, invoices, and price negotiations. What quality and cost benefits does ERP deliver to manufacturers and

supply chain
The entire sequence of securing inputs, producing goods, and delivering goods to customers.

supply chain management
The process of smoothing transitions along the supply chain, so that the firm can satisfy its customers with quality products and services; focuses on developing tighter bonds with suppliers.

firm's suppliers and customers into the flow of data. ERP unites all of a firm's major departments into a single software program. For instance, production can call up sales information and know immediately how many units must be produced to meet customer orders. By providing information about the availability of resources, including both human resources and materials needed for production, the system allows for better cost control and eliminates production delays. The system automatically notes any changes, such as the closure of a plant for maintenance and repairs on a certain date or a supplier's inability to meet a delivery date, so that all functions can adjust accordingly. Both large and small organizations use ERP to improve operations.

Keeping the Goods Flowing: Supply Chain Management

In the past, the relationship between purchasers and suppliers was often competitive and antagonistic. Businesses used many suppliers and switched among them frequently. During contract negotiations, each side would try to get better terms at the expense of the other. Communication between purchasers and suppliers was often limited to purchase orders and billing statements.

Today, however, many firms are moving toward a new concept in supplier relationships. The emphasis is increasingly on developing a strong **supply chain**. The supply chain can be thought of as the entire sequence of securing inputs, producing goods, and delivering goods to customers. If any links in this process are weak, chances are that customers—the end point of the supply chain—will end up dissatisfied.

Effective supply chain strategies reduce costs. For example, integration of the shipper and customer's supply chains allows companies to automate more processes and save time. Technology also improves supply chain efficiency by tracking goods through the various supply chain stages and also helping with logistics. With better information about production and inventory, companies can order and receive goods at the optimal point to keep inventory holding costs low.

Companies also need contingency plans for supply chain disruptions. Is there an alternative source of supply if a blizzard closes the airport so that cargo planes can't land or a drought causes crop failures? By thinking ahead, companies can avert major losses. The length and distance involved in a supply line is also a consideration. Importing parts from or outsourcing manufacturing to Asia creates a long supply chain for a manufacturer in Europe or Canada. Perhaps there are closer suppliers or manufacturers who can meet a company's needs at a lower overall cost. Companies should also re-evaluate outsourcing decisions periodically.

Strategies for Supply Chain Management

Ensuring a strong supply chain requires that firms implement supply chain management strategies. **Supply chain management** focuses on smoothing transitions along the supply chain, with the ultimate goal of satisfying customers with quality products and services. A critical element of effective supply chain management is to develop tighter bonds with suppliers. In many cases, this means reducing the number of suppliers used and asking those suppliers to offer more services or better prices in return for an ongoing relationship. Instead of being viewed as "outsiders" in the production process, many suppliers are now playing an important role in supporting the operations of their customers. They are expected to meet higher quality standards, offer suggestions that can help reduce production costs, and even contribute to the design of new products. The Expanding Around the Globe box shows the critical role of supply-chain management for global companies.

Talk to Us: Improving Supplier Communications   Effective supply chain management requires the development of strong communications with suppliers. Technology,

AP/WIDE WORLD PHOTOS

e-procurement
The process of purchasing supplies and materials using the Internet.

particularly the Internet, is providing new ways to do this. **E-procurement**, the process of purchasing supplies and materials online, is booming. Some manufacturing firms use the Internet to keep key suppliers informed about their requirements. Intel, for example, has set up a special website for its suppliers and potential suppliers. Would-be

Expanding Around The Globe

SOPHISTICATED SUPPLY-CHAIN STRATEGIES KEEP PRODUCTS ON THE MOVE

Headquartered in Tokyo but with offices around the world, shipping company MOL is taking integrating with its customers to new levels. It is joining its customers in a series of joint ventures to build and operate dedicated vessels for as long as 25 years. One such joint venture teamed MOL with a Chinese steel mill, to build and sail ships bringing Brazilian iron ore and coal across the Pacific Ocean for processing.

Sophisticated supply-chain systems that control every aspect of production and transportation are the key to making offshore manufacturing work. Supply-chain software that monitors operations and continually makes adjustments ensures that all processes are running at peak efficiency. By tightly mapping an entire sequence—from order to final delivery—and by automating it as much as possible, supply-chain management can deliver products from across the world while at the same time cutting costs. Companies that can carry a small inventory and get paid faster improve their cash flow and profitability.

Acer, a $7 billion Taiwanese computer and electronics maker, brings components from around the world and assembles them at factories in Taiwan and mainland China—into everything from PC notebooks to TVs. It then reverses the flow by shipping these products to international buyers. "In 2004, Acer sold 4 million portable systems. Without a solid supply-chain infrastructure behind us, we couldn't hope to do it," says Sumit Agnihotry, Acer's American director of notebook product marketing.

The synchronizing of trade is essential. If goods don't get into the stores in time, sales might be lost or the company might have to carry larger inventories to avoid sell-outs, which would cut into its profits. Companies need to continually monitor demand and react quickly by adjusting production. "This gets increasingly difficult when the supply chain stretches across thousands of miles and a dozen time zones," says David Bovet, managing director of Mercer Management Consulting, a Boston-based firm that advises on business tactics. "There are strategies that smart companies are using to bring costs down to earth. Getting the most of lower labour costs overseas requires an emphasis on transportation, and supply-chain skills are a required core competency," he says. His advice to global manufacturers: Cooperate with shippers and integrate supply chains into one cohesive system.

The acknowledged master of supply-chain dynamics is Dell, with its global logistics control room lined with big screens that monitor its shipping lanes at all times. Alongside Dell executives are representatives of its logistics suppliers for guidance and quick action if anything goes wrong.

Risk is the name of the game when it comes to international trade, and companies need to decide whether to play it safe with extra inventory or scramble if a disaster like a port strike occurs. Either way, they need to have contingency plans and be ready to react, and solid supply-chain strategies will ensure they are prepared for any eventuality.[6]

Critical Thinking Questions

- Why are solid supply-chain strategies so important?
- What problems is a company likely to experience without such strategies in place?

suppliers can visit the site to get information about doing business with Intel; once they are approved, they can access a secure area to make bids on Intel's current and future resource needs.

The Internet also streamlines purchasing by providing firms with quick access to a huge database of information about the products and services of hundreds of potential suppliers. Many large manufacturers now participate in *reverse auctions* online, whereby the manufacturer posts its specifications for the materials it requires. Potential suppliers then bid against each other to get the job. Reverse auctions can slash procurement costs.

However, there are risks with reverse auctions. For example, it can be difficult to establish and build ongoing relationships with specific suppliers using reverse auctions, because the job ultimately goes to the lowest bidder. Therefore, reverse auctions might not be an effective procurement process for critical production materials.[7]

electronic data interchange (EDI)
The electronic exchange of information between two trading partners.

Another communications tool is **electronic data interchange (EDI)**, in which two trading partners exchange information electronically. EDI can be conducted via a linked computer system or over the Internet. The advantages of exchanging information with suppliers electronically include speed, accuracy, and lowered communication costs.

> **concept check**
>
> What four important decisions must be made in production planning?
>
> What factors does a firm consider when making a site selection decision?
>
> How is technology being used in resource planning?

Dana Corporation, a manufacturer of auto and truck frames, has only one customer, New United Motor Manufacturing Inc. (NUMMI), a joint venture between Toyota and General Motors. In the past, NUMMI could give Dana only a six-week production forecast. A fax was sent to Dana each day updating NUMMI's needs. Dana and NUMMI then installed an EDI system that continually alerts Dana about NUMMI's purchasing requirements on an hourly basis. As a result, Dana has been able to cut its inventory, smooth its production scheduling, and meet NUMMI's needs more efficiently and rapidly.[8]

Production and Operations Control

Every company needs to have systems in place to see that production and operations are carried out as planned and to correct errors when they are not. The coordination of materials, equipment, and human resources to achieve production and operating efficiencies is called *production control*. Two of its key aspects are routing and scheduling.

Routing: Where to Next?

routing
The aspect of production control that involves setting out the workflow, the sequence of machines and operations through which the product or service progresses from start to finish.

Routing is the first step in production control. It sets out a workflow, that is, the sequence of machines and operations through which a product or service progresses from start to finish. Routing depends on the type of goods being produced and the facility layout. Good routing procedures increase productivity and cut unnecessary costs.

value-stream mapping
Routing technique that uses simple icons to visually represent the flow of materials and information from suppliers through the factory to customers.

One useful tool for routing is **value-stream mapping**, where production managers "map" the flow from suppliers through the factory to customers. Simple icons represent the materials and information needed at various points in the flow. Value-stream mapping can help identify where bottlenecks might occur in the production process and is a valuable tool for visualizing how to improve production routing.

Electronics manufacturer Rockwell Collins used value-stream mapping to automate more of its purchasing operations. The company evaluated 23 areas to identify where process changes would improve efficiency. Based on the study, managers decided to automate three steps: request for quote, quote receipt and total purchase cost, and automated purchase order. The company implemented a new system that automatically sends requests for quotes to appropriate suppliers and evaluates the responses to determine which best meets Rockwell Collins' requirements. Once in place, the new systems allowed purchasing professionals to focus on strategic rather than routine activities.[9]

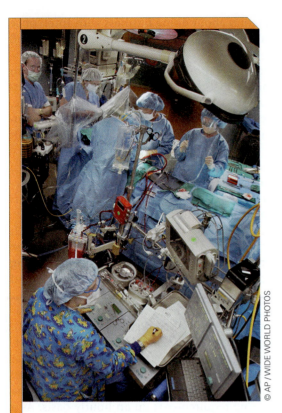
© AP / WIDE WORLD PHOTOS

CONCEPT *in Action* >>>

Routing and scheduling are just as important to service organizations as they are to manufacturing firms. Hospitals, for instance, must carefully schedule the equipment, personnel, and facilities needed to conduct patient surgeries and other treatments. What are some of the consequences if we do not properly plan the route and scheduling of services?

scheduling
The aspect of production control that involves specifying and controlling the time required for each step in the production process.

Gantt charts
Bar graphs plotted on a timeline that show the relationship between scheduled and actual production.

critical path method (CPM)
A scheduling tool that enables a manager to determine the critical path of activities for a project—the activities that will cause the entire project to fall behind schedule if they are not completed on time.

critical path
The longest path through the linked activities in a critical path method network.

Scheduling: When Do We Do It?

Closely related to routing is **scheduling**. Scheduling involves specifying and controlling the time required for each step in the production process. The operations manager prepares timetables showing the most efficient sequence of production and then tries to ensure that the necessary materials and labour are in the right place at the right time.

Scheduling is important to both manufacturing and service firms. The production manager in a factory schedules material deliveries, work shifts, and production processes. Trucking companies schedule drivers, clerks, truck maintenance, and repair with customer transportation needs. Scheduling at a polytechnic, college, or university entails deciding when to offer which courses, in which classrooms, with which instructors. A museum must schedule its special exhibits, ship the works to be displayed, market its services, and conduct educational programs and tours.

Scheduling can range from simple to complex. Giving numbers to customers waiting to be served in a bakery and making interview appointments with job applicants are examples of simple scheduling. Organizations that must produce large quantities of products or services, or service a diverse customer base, face more complex scheduling problems.

Three common scheduling tools used for complex situations are Gantt charts, the critical path method, and PERT.

Tracking Progress with Gantt Charts Named after their originator, Henry Gantt, **Gantt charts** are bar graphs plotted on a timeline that show the relationship between scheduled and actual production. Exhibit 11.5 is an example. On the left, the chart lists the activities required to complete the job or project. Both the scheduled time and the actual time required for each activity are shown, so the manager can easily judge progress.

Gantt charts are most helpful when only a few tasks are involved, when task times are relatively long (days or weeks rather than hours), and when job routes are short and simple. One of the biggest shortcomings of Gantt charts is that they are static. They also fail to show how tasks are related. These problems can be solved, however, by using two other scheduling techniques, the critical path method and PERT.

The Big Picture: Critical Path Method and PERT To control large projects, operations managers need to closely monitor resources, costs, quality, and budgets. They also must be able to see the "big picture"—the interrelationships of the many tasks necessary to complete the project. Finally, they must be able to revise scheduling and divert resources quickly if any tasks fall behind schedule. The critical path method (CPM) and the program evaluation and review technique (PERT) are related project management tools that were developed in the 1950s to help managers accomplish this.

In the **critical path method (CPM)**, the manager identifies all of the activities required to complete the project, the relationships between these activities, and the order in which they need to be completed. Then, he or she develops a diagram that uses arrows to show how the tasks are dependent on each other. The longest path through these linked activities is called the **critical path**. If the tasks on the critical path are not completed on time, the entire project will fall behind schedule.

To understand better how CPM works, look at Exhibit 11.6, which shows a CPM diagram for constructing a house. All of the tasks required to finish the house and an

EXHIBIT 11.5 > A Typical Gantt Chart

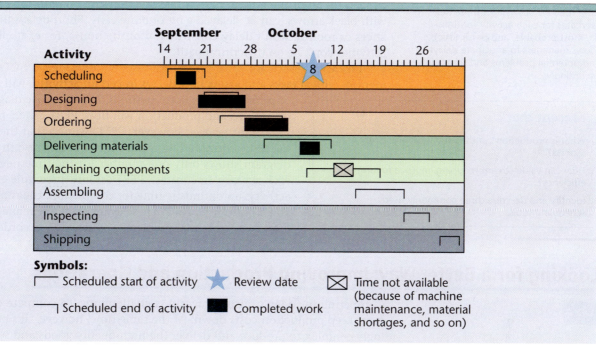

Symbols:

⌐ Scheduled start of activity   ★ Review date   ⊠ Time not available (because of machine maintenance, material shortages, and so on)

⌐ Scheduled end of activity   ■ Completed work

estimated time for each have been identified. The arrows indicate the links between the various steps and their required sequence. As you can see, most of the jobs to be done can't be started until the house's foundation and frame are completed. It will take five days to finish the foundation and an additional seven days to erect the house

EXHIBIT 11.6 > A CPM Network for Building a House

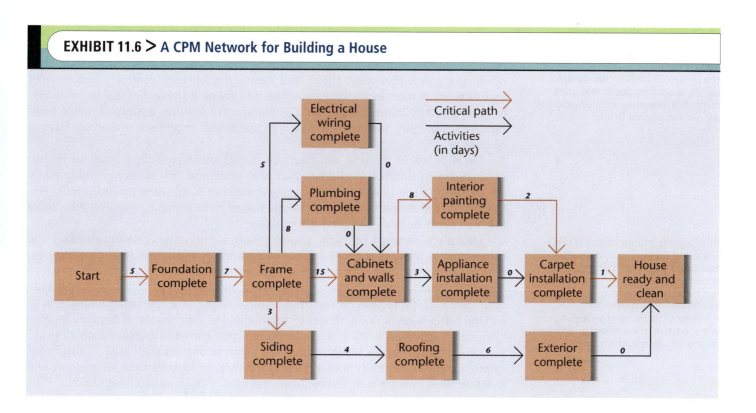

program evaluation and review technique (PERT)
A scheduling tool that is similar to the CPM method but assigns three time estimates for each activity (optimistic, most probable, and pessimistic); allows managers to anticipate delays and potential problems and schedule accordingly.

concept check

What is production control, and what are its key aspects?

How can value-stream mapping improve routing efficiency?

Identify and describe three commonly used scheduling tools.

frame. The activities linked by red arrows form the critical path for this project. It tells us that the fastest possible time the house can be built is 38 days, the total time needed for all of the critical path tasks. The non-critical path jobs, those connected with black arrows, can be delayed a bit or done early. Short delays in installing appliances or roofing won't delay construction of the house, for example, because these activities don't lie on the critical path.

Like CPM, **program evaluation and review technique (PERT)** helps managers identify critical tasks and assess how delays in certain activities will affect operations or production. In both methods, managers use diagrams to see how operations and production will flow. PERT differs from CPM in one important respect, however. CPM assumes that the amount of time needed to finish a task is known with certainty; therefore, the CPM diagram shows only one number for the time needed to complete each activity. In contrast, PERT assigns three time estimates for each activity: an optimistic time for completion, the most probable time, and a pessimistic time. These estimates allow managers to anticipate delays and potential problems and schedule accordingly.

Looking for a Better Way: Improving Production and Operations

Competing in today's business world is challenging. To compete effectively, firms must keep production costs down. At the same time, however, it's becoming increasingly complex to produce and deliver the high-quality goods and services customers demand. Methods to help meet these challenges include quality management techniques, lean manufacturing, and automation.

Putting Quality First

quality
Goods and services that meet customer expectations by providing reliable performance.

Successful businesses recognize that quality and productivity must go hand in hand. **Quality** goods and services meet customer expectations by providing reliable performance. Defective products waste materials and time, increasing costs. Worse, poor quality causes customer dissatisfaction, which usually means lost sales.

quality control
The process of creating standards for quality, producing goods that meet them, and measuring finished products and services against them.

A consumer measures quality by how well a good serves its purpose. From the company's point of view, quality is the degree to which a good conforms to a set of predetermined standards. **Quality control** involves creating those quality standards, producing goods that meet them, and measuring finished products and services against them. It takes more than just inspecting goods at the end of the assembly line to ensure quality control, however. Quality control requires a company-wide dedication to managing and working in a way that builds excellence into every facet of operations.

Dr. W. Edwards Deming, an American management consultant, was the first to say that quality control should be a company-wide goal. His ideas were adopted by the Japanese in the 1950s but were largely ignored in North America until the 1970s. Deming believed that quality control must start with top management, who must foster a culture dedicated to producing quality.

total quality management (TQM)
The use of quality principles in all aspects of a company's production and operations.

continuous improvement
A constant commitment to seeking better ways of doing things to achieve greater efficiency and improved quality.

Deming's concept of **Total Quality Management (TQM)** emphasizes the use of quality principles in all aspects of a company's production and operations. It recognizes that all employees involved with bringing a product or service to customers—marketing, purchasing, accounting, shipping, manufacturing—contribute to its quality. TQM focuses on **continuous improvement**, a constant commitment to seeking better ways of doing things to achieve greater efficiency and improve quality. Company-wide teams work together to prevent problems and systematically improve key processes instead of troubleshooting problems only as they arise. Continuous improvement continually measures performance using statistical techniques and looks for ways to apply new technologies and innovative production methods.

Sustainable Business, Sustainable World

One of the ways that a sustainable business can make the most impact is in its operations. One company that is making a real effort to be truly sustainable is the Hudson's Bay Company (Hbc). The Hudson's Bay Company, Canada's largest diversified general merchandise retailer, operates the Bay, Zellers, Home Outfitters, and Fields. It's commitment to sustainability can be seen very clearly in the statement on the front of its Corporate Social Responsibility Report: *"At Hbc, we understand that every one of us has a role to play in creating the kind of world we want to live in and pass on to our children. The possibilities are boundless when we act with a Global Mind."*

This global mindset is evident in Hbc's three core principles designed to reduce its environmental footprint: "#1. Continuous evaluation of our environmental policies and procedures; #2. Environmental improvement in our operations; and #3. Educating associates, customers and partners."

Hbc's Environmental Sustainability Team meets monthly and reports directly to Hbc senior management. It conducts annual audits of the company's operations to determine the amount of waste diverted from landfill, the amount of packaging and harmful PVCs in its private label products, energy consumption by store, and greenhouse gas (GHG) emissions. And most importantly, it continually looks for ways to improve its policies and practices.

Some of the new environmental improvements that Hbc introduced in its operations in 2007 include committing to zero waste, recycling in its stores, preserving water, opening green stores, increasing its number of biodiesel fuel trucks, and performing lighting retrofits. In fact Hbc's head office became the first office tower in Canada to be certified zero waste by Zero Waste International Alliance. This distinction for achieving a more than 95% diversion rate of waste away from landfills was also awarded to two other Hbc office buildings and seven of its retail locations. Now that's commitment. In 2007 Hbc also opened its greenest Zellers ever in Waterdown, Ontario. Some of the energy conservations measures include the use of two wind generators and solar panels to provide energy, a white roof to reflect heat, energy recovery ventilators, and heating/ventilating and air conditioning units that use non-ozone depleting refrigerant.

Hbc's efforts have won it several awards, including a 2007 Ontario Waste Minimization Award. This Facilities Platinum Award was presented to the Simpson Tower on Bay Street in Toronto in recognition of excellence and commitment to a sustainable environment. As well, the BOMA Go Green Plus Certificate of Achievement was awarded to the same building for environmental excellence in the management of the building.

How does your new knowledge of Hbc's commitment to environmental sustainability affect you and your decisions regarding where to shop? Should companies become more sustainable in their operations because it's the right thing to do for our planet or because it's better for the bottom line—leading to greater revenue generation by more conscious consumers, or both? Do you think that society is becoming sufficiently more conscious that environmental sustainability will pay off in terms of more customers, or does it simply pay off in more efficient operations? Is there an integrative effect?

SOURCE: www.hbc.com

Six Sigma
A quality control process that relies on defining what needs to be done to ensure quality, measuring and analyzing production results statistically, and finding ways of improving and controlling quality.

HOT Links

Learn more about Six Sigma at the Knowledge Management Group's website, (www.tkmg.org/services.html).

ISO 9000
A set of five technical standards of quality management created by the International Organization for Standardization to provide a uniform way of determining whether manufacturing plants and service organizations conform to sound quality procedures.

ISO 14000
A set of technical standards designed by the International Organization for Standardization to promote clean production processes to protect the environment.

Another quality control method is the **Six Sigma** quality program. Six Sigma is a company-wide process that focuses on measuring the number of defects that occur and systematically eliminating them to get as close to "zero defects" as possible. In fact, Six Sigma quality aims to have every process produce no more than 3.4 defects per million. Six Sigma focuses on designing products that not only have fewer defects but also satisfy customer needs. A key process of Six Sigma is called *DMAIC*. This stands for Define, Measure, Analyze, Improve, and Control. Employees at all levels define what needs to be done to ensure quality, then measure and analyze production results using statistics to see if the standards are met. They are also charged with finding ways of improving and controlling quality.

General Electric was one of the first companies to institute Six Sigma throughout the organization. All GE employees are trained in Six Sigma concepts, and many analysts believe this has given GE a competitive manufacturing advantage. Service firms have applied Six Sigma to their quality initiatives as well.

Worldwide Excellence: International Quality Standards   The International Organization for Standardization (ISO), located in Belgium, is an industry organization that has developed standards of quality that are used by businesses around the world. **ISO 9000**, introduced in the 1980s, is a set of five technical standards designed to offer a uniform way of determining whether manufacturing plants and service organizations conform to sound quality procedures. To register, a company must go through an audit of its manufacturing and customer service processes, covering everything from how it designs, produces, and installs its goods to how it inspects, packages, and markets them. More than 500,000 organizations worldwide have met ISO 9000 standards.

ISO 14000, launched after ISO 9000, is designed to promote clean production processes in response to environmental issues such as global warming and water pollution. To meet ISO 14000 standards, a company must commit to improving environmental management continually and reducing pollution resulting from its

CONCEPT *in Action* >>>

The Six Sigma quality program directly involves production employees in setting quality standards and in measuring and analyzing finished goods to ensure that quality has been achieved. Here, a worker in an electronics factory inspects a finished circuit board, looking for any defects. How can a service company (e.g., accountancy firm or dry cleaners) ensure quality?

lean manufacturing
Streamlining production by eliminating steps in the production process that do not add benefits customers are willing to pay for.

just-in-time (JIT)
A system in which materials arrive exactly when they are needed for production rather than being stored on-site.

HOT Links

Quality Management Products of Oakville, Ontario, helps its customers to improve their organization with a comprehensive line of quality software products and services. Visit their website at (www.qmproducts.com).

production processes. Some accredited ISO 14000 organizations include ASQR Canada, Intertek Testing Services NA Limited, and KPMG Performance Registrar Inc.

Lean Manufacturing Trims the Fat

Manufacturers are discovering that they can respond better to rapidly changing customer demands, while keeping inventory and production costs down, by adopting lean manufacturing techniques. **Lean manufacturing** streamlines production by eliminating steps in the production process that do not add benefits customers are willing to pay for. In other words, *non–value-added production processes* are cut, so that the company can concentrate its production and operations resources on items essential to satisfying customers. Toyota was a pioneer in developing these techniques, but today manufacturers in many industries subscribe to the lean-manufacturing philosophy.

Another Japanese concept, **just-in-time (JIT)**, goes hand in hand with lean manufacturing. JIT is based on the belief that materials should arrive exactly when they are needed for production rather than being stored on-site. Relying closely on computerized systems such as MRP, MRPII, and ERP, manufacturers determine what parts will be needed and when, and then order them from suppliers, so they arrive "just in time." Under the JIT system, inventory and products are "pulled" through the production process in response to customer demand. JIT requires close teamwork between vendors and purchasing and production personnel, because any delay in deliveries of supplies could bring JIT production to a halt.

Transforming the Factory Floor with Technology

LO 7

Technology is helping many firms improve their operating efficiency and ability to compete. Computer systems, in particular, are enabling manufacturers to automate factories in ways never before possible.

Among the technologies helping to automate manufacturing are computer-aided design and manufacturing systems, robotics, flexible manufacturing systems, and computer-integrated manufacturing.

HOT *Links*

Want to know more about how robots work? Find out at (**http://electronics. howstuffworks.com/robot.htm**).

Computer-Aided Design and Manufacturing Systems Computers have transformed the design and manufacturing processes in many industries. In **computer-aided design (CAD)**, computers are used to design and test new products and modify existing ones. Engineers use these systems to draw products and look at them from different angles. They can analyze the products, make changes, and test prototypes before making even one item. **Computer-aided manufacturing (CAM)** uses computers to develop and control the production process. The systems analyze the steps required to make the product. They then automatically send instructions to the machines that do the work. **CAD/CAM systems** combine the advantages of CAD and CAM by integrating design, testing, and manufacturing control into one linked computer system. The system helps design the product, control the flow of resources needed to produce the product, and operate the production process.

Cardianove Inc., a Montreal-based manufacturer of medical and surgical equipment, used CAD software to develop the world's smallest heart pump. The company says using computer-aided design shaved two years off the normal design time for cardiac devices. The company's CAD program ran complex three-dimensional simulations to confirm that the design would function properly inside the human body. Cardionove Inc. tested more than 100 virtual prototypes using the software before the top three designs were actually produced for real-life testing.[10]

Robotics *Robots* are computer-controlled machines that can perform tasks independently. **Robotics** is the technology involved in designing, constructing, and operating robots. The first robot, or "steel-collar worker," was used by General Motors in 1961. Today robots are used by many companies in many different industries.

Robots can be mobile or fixed in one place. Fixed robots have an arm that moves and does what the computer instructs. Some robots are quite simple, with limited movement for a few tasks such as cutting sheet metal and spot welding. Others are complex, with hands or grippers that can be programmed to perform a series of movements. Some robots are even equipped with sensing devices for sight and touch.

Robots usually operate with little or no human intervention. Replacing human effort with robots is most effective for tasks requiring accuracy, speed, or strength. Although manufacturers such as Harley-Davidson, as described at the beginning of this chapter, are most likely to use robots, some service firms are also finding them useful. Some hospitals, for example, use robots to sort and process blood samples, freeing medical personnel from a tedious, sometimes hazardous, repetitive task.

Adaptable Factories: Flexible Manufacturing Systems A **flexible manufacturing system (FMS)** automates a factory by blending computers, robots, machine tools, and materials-and-parts-handling machinery into an integrated system. These systems combine automated workstations with computer-controlled transportation devices. Automatic guided vehicles (AGVs) move materials between workstations and into and out of the system.

Flexible manufacturing systems are expensive. Once in place, however, a system requires little labour to operate and provides consistent product quality. The system can be changed easily and inexpensively. FMS equipment can be programmed to perform one job and then quickly be reprogrammed to perform another. These systems work well when small batches of a variety of products are required or when each product is made to individual customer specifications.

Quick Change with Computer-Integrated Manufacturing **Computer-integrated manufacturing (CIM)** combines computerized manufacturing processes (like robots and FMS) with other computerized systems that control design, inventory, production, and purchasing. With CIM, when a part is redesigned in the CAD system, the changes are quickly transmitted both to the machines producing the part and to all other departments that need to know about and plan for the change.

Technology and Automation at Your Service

concept check

Define total quality management, lean manufacturing, and just-in-time, and explain how each can help a firm improve its production and operations.

How are both manufacturing and non-manufacturing firms using technology and automation to improve operations?

Manufacturers are not the only businesses benefiting from technology. Non-manufacturing firms are also using automation to improve customer service and productivity. Banks now offer services to customers through automated teller machines (ATMs), via automated telephone systems, and over the Internet. Retail stores of all kinds use point-of-sale (POS) terminals that track inventories, identify items that need to be reordered, and tell which products are selling well. Wal-Mart, the leader in retailing automation, has its own satellite system connecting POS terminals directly to its distribution centres and headquarters.

Trends in Production and Operations Management

Some manufacturing employment has been eliminated as manufacturers attempt to cut operating costs. Many of these jobs have been moved overseas, where manufacturers have opened new production facilities or contracted out production to foreign firms with lower operating and labour costs. Continued growth in global competition, increasingly complex products, and more demanding consumers continue to force manufacturers to plan carefully how, when, and where they produce the goods they sell. New production techniques and manufacturing technologies are vital to keeping production costs as low as possible and productivity levels high. At the same time, many firms are re-evaluating the productivity of their production facilities and, in some cases, are deciding to close underperforming factories.

Non-manufacturing firms must carefully manage how they use and deploy their resources, while keeping up with the constant pace of technological change. Non-manufacturing firms must be ever vigilant in their search for new ways of streamlining service production and operation to keep their overall costs down.

Asset Management

In a tight economy, businesses must be careful about how their operating assets are used. From raw materials to inventories and manufacturing equipment, wasted, malfunctioning, or misused assets are costly. For example, one telephone company reported it had lost track of $5 billion worth of communications equipment. "I would say that every big company I have worked with has lost track of many major assets and a plethora of minor ones," said one executive. In fact, when chief financial officers of large companies were surveyed by *CFO Magazine*, 70 percent reported that asset management in their firms was "inefficient" or "erratic."[11]

Asset management software systems, many of which are Internet based, are beginning to help fix this problem. These programs automatically track materials, equipment, and inventory. They also automate inventory management, and maintenance and repairs scheduling.

ChevronTexaco has successfully implemented this type of system in its enormous production facility in Bakersfield, California. The facility is one of the largest outdoor factories in the world, stretching 160 kilometres from north to south, and containing a maze of storage tanks, filtering installations, and pipelines. In all, there are 230,000 separate pieces of equipment and machinery in hundreds of categories in the facility. To manage all of these assets, ChevronTexaco has installed an automated asset management system that schedules preventive maintenance for all equipment and tracks where surplus equipment and supplies are stored. ChevronTexaco estimates it is saving millions of dollars a year in the facility because of more effective asset management.[12]

Modular Production

Increasingly, manufacturers are relying on *modular production* to speed up and simplify production. Modular production involves breaking a complex product, service, or process into smaller pieces that can be created independently and then combined quickly to make a whole. Modular production not only cuts the cost of developing innovative products but also gives businesses a tool for meeting rapidly changing conditions. It also makes implementation of mass or pure customization strategies easier.

Johnson Controls Inc. (JCI), a manufacturer, works closely with its suppliers to build automotive interiors modularly. JCI uses 11 major components from 35 suppliers to build Jeep Liberty cockpits. The parts, designed to fit and function together, are then assembled in JCI's factory. "Our product development strategy is to build from the best capabilities and technologies in the world, but that doesn't mean they have to be owned and operated by us," says JCI vice-president Jeff Edwards.[13]

Designing Products for Production Efficiency

Today's operations managers recognize that production efficiency must begin *before* the first part reaches the factory floor. As a result, many manufacturers are investing in new methods of integrating product design and engineering with the manufacturing supply chain.

Designlore of Toronto, Ontario offers solutions and customized product design services to entrepreneurs and corporations. They specialize in taking product ideas to the finished product phase including: engineering, industrial and mechanical design, research and development, etc. The company prides itself on "Right the First Time" approach using innovative design with traditional engineering principles.

CONCEPT *in Action* >>>

Toyota focuses design and engineering on "crossover vehicles"—car model designs that appeal to different consumer segments yet are built using many of the same components and parts. This has allowed Toyota's factories to become flexible and modular. What other industries incorporate modular production?

© MICHAEL S. YAMASHITA/CORBIS

concept check

Explain modular production.

Why does production efficiency have to begin before the first part reaches the factory floor?

Another developing trend is the use of factory simulation tools for product design. These tools allow product designers to see the effects their designs will have on production equipment. For example, if a design calls for a specific size of drilled hole on a product, factory simulation tools will specify which particular drill bit and machine will be necessary for the task.

Great Ideas to Use Now

As we've seen throughout this chapter, every organization produces something. Cereal manufacturers turn grains into breakfast foods. Law firms turn the skills and knowledge of lawyers into legal services. Retailers provide a convenient way for consumers to purchase a variety of goods. Colleges and universities convert students into educated individuals. Therefore, no matter what type of organization you end up working for in the future, you will be involved, to one degree or another, with your employer's production and operations processes.

Some employees, such as plant managers and quality control managers, will have a direct role in the production process. However, employees of manufacturing firms are not the only ones involved with production. Software developers, bank tellers, medical personnel, magazine writers, and a host of other employees are also actively involved in turning inputs into outputs. If you manage people in these types of jobs, you'll need insight into the tools used to plan, schedule, and control production processes. Understanding production processes, resource management, and techniques for increasing productivity is vital to becoming a more valuable employee, one who sees how his or her job fits into "the big picture" of the firm's operating goals.

If you plan to start your own business, you'll also face many production and operations decisions. You can use the information from this chapter to help you find suppliers, design an operating facility (no matter how small), and put customer-satisfying processes in place. This information can also help you make decisions about whether to manufacture goods or rely on outside contractors to handle production.

Customer Satisfaction and Quality

Although we have talked a great deal in this chapter about methods for producing products faster and less expensively, it is important to remember that the most efficient factory in the world would be deemed a failure if the products it made broke soon after customers purchased them. Underlying every production and operations management decision is a very simple question: How will this affect our customers' satisfaction? To compete in today's marketplace, businesses must make sure they have the right answer.

The Honeywell Control Products plant realized it didn't have the right answer. The plant makes electromechanical snap-action switches that are used in machines such as icemakers and washing machines. In the face of foreign competition in the early 1990s, the plant had developed a successful strategy to improve productivity and reduce manufacturing costs. By 1998, however, it was

clear that customers weren't happy. Complaints and returns were constantly rising.

The problem? "We were driving the wrong behaviours," says Cynthia Knautz, manufacturing engineer at the plant. "All of our employee goals were set on output. Our production employees could build 36,000 bad switches in a day and still get rewarded." The plant set up new processes to help track and control quality and tied employee incentives to quality and customer satisfaction. As a result, customer reject rates have dropped dramatically, while production rates have actually increased.

SOURCE: Best Plant Winners 2002: Honeywell Control Products, *Industry Week Online*, 2002. Reprinted with permission of Penton Media. (http://www.industryweek.com/articles/iw_best_plants_profile_-_2002_9937.aspx).

Summary of Learning Outcomes

1 Discuss why production and operations management is important in both manufacturing and service firms.

In the 1980s, many manufacturers lost customers to foreign competitors because their production and operations management systems did not support the high-quality, reasonably priced products consumers demanded. Service organizations also rely on effective operations management to satisfy consumers. Operations managers, the personnel charged with managing and supervising the conversion of inputs into outputs, work closely with other functions in organizations to help ensure quality, customer satisfaction, and financial success.

2 List the types of production processes used by manufacturers and service firms.

Products are made using one of three types of production processes. In mass production, many identical goods are produced at once, keeping production costs low. Mass production, therefore, relies heavily on standardization, mechanization, and specialization. When mass customization is used, goods are produced using mass production techniques up to a point, after which the product or service is custom tailored to individual customers by adding special features. When a firm's production process is built around customization, the firm makes many products one at a time according to the very specific needs or wants of individual customers.

3 Describe how organizations decide where to put their production facilities and what choices must be made in designing the facility.

Site selection affects operating costs, the price of the product or service, and the company's ability to compete. In choosing a production site, firms must weigh the availability of resources—raw materials, human resources, and even capital—needed for production, as well as the ability to serve customers and take advantage of marketing opportunities. Other factors include the availability of local incentives and the manufacturing environment. Once a site is selected, the firm must choose an appropriate design for the facility. The three main production facility designs are process, product, and fixed-position layouts. Cellular manufacturing is another type of facility layout.

4 Explain why resource-planning tasks like inventory management and supplier relations are critical to production.

Production converts input resources, such as raw materials and labour, into outputs, finished products, and services. Firms must ensure that the resources needed for production will be available at strategic moments in the production process. If they are not, productivity, customer satisfaction, and quality might suffer. Carefully managing inventory can help cut production costs while maintaining enough supply for production and sales. Through good relationships with suppliers, firms can get better prices, reliable resources, and support services that can improve production efficiency.

5 Discuss how operations managers schedule and control production.

Routing is the first step in scheduling and controlling production. Routing involves analyzing the steps needed in production and setting out a workflow, the sequence of machines and operations through which a product or service progresses from start to finish. Good routing increases productivity and can eliminate unnecessary costs. Scheduling involves specifying and controlling the time and resources required for each step in the production process. Operations managers use three methods to schedule production: Gantt charts, the critical path method, and program evaluation and review techniques.

6 Evaluate how quality management and lean-manufacturing techniques help firms improve production and operations management.

Quality and productivity go hand in hand. Defective products waste materials and time, increasing costs. Poor quality also leads to dissatisfied customers. By implementing quality control methods, firms often reduce these problems and streamline production. Lean manufacturing also helps streamline production by eliminating unnecessary steps in the production process. When activities that don't add value for customers are eliminated, manufacturers can respond to changing market conditions with greater flexibility and ease.

7 **Identify the roles that technology and automation play in manufacturing and service industry operations management.**

Many firms are improving their operational efficiency by using technology to automate parts of production. Computer-aided design and manufacturing systems, for example, help design new products, control the flow of resources needed for production, and even operate much of the production process. By using robotics, human time and effort can be minimized. Factories are being automated by blending computers, robots, and machinery into flexible manufacturing systems that require less labour to operate. Service firms are automating operations too, using technology to cut labour costs and control quality.

8 **List some of the key trends affecting the way companies manage production and operations.**

The manufacturing sector has been faced with growing global competition, increased product complexity, and more demanding customers, so manufacturers must carefully plan how, when, and where they produce the goods they sell. New production techniques and manufacturing technologies can help keep costs as low as possible. Managing assets like inventory, raw materials, and production equipment is increasingly important. Asset management software systems automatically track materials and inventory to help reduce waste, misuse, and malfunctions. Modular production allows manufacturers to produce products using high-quality parts without investments in expensive technology. Production efficiency must begin before the factory floor. Many firms are using tools that integrate product design and engineering with the manufacturing supply chain to understand the cost and quality implications of producing new products.

Experiential Exercises

1. Track a project with a Gantt chart. Your instructor has just announced a huge assignment, due in three weeks. Where do you start? How can you best organize your time? A Gantt chart can help you plan and schedule more effectively. You'll be able to see exactly what you should be doing on a particular day.

   - First, break the assignment down into smaller tasks: pick a topic, conduct research at the library or on the Internet, organize your notes, develop an outline, and write, type, and proofread the paper.
   - Next, estimate how much time each task will take. Be realistic. If you've spent a week or more writing similar papers in the past, don't expect to finish this paper in a day.
   - At the top of a piece of paper, list all of the days until the assignment is due. Along the side of the paper, list all of the tasks you've identified in the order in which they need to be done.
   - Starting with the first task, block out the number of days you estimate each task will take. If you run out of days, you'll know you need to adjust how you've scheduled your time. If you know that you will not be able to work on some days, note them on the chart as well.
   - Hang the chart where you can see it.

2. Look for ways in which technology and automation are used at your school, in the local supermarket, and at your doctor's office. As a class, discuss how automation affects the service you receive from each of these organizations. Does one organization use any types of automation that might be effectively used by one of the others? Explain.

3. Pick a small business in your community. Make a list of the resources critical to the firm's production and operations. What would happen if the business suddenly couldn't acquire any of these resources? Discuss strategies that small businesses can use to manage their supply chain.

4. Today's Fashions is a manufacturer of women's dresses. The company's factory has 50 employees. Production begins when the fabric is cut according to specified patterns. After being cut, the pieces for each dress style are placed into bundles,

which then move through the factory from worker to worker. Each worker opens each bundle and does one assembly task, such as sewing on collars, hemming dresses, or adding decorative items such as appliqués. Then, the worker puts the bundle back together and passes it on to the next person in the production process. Finished dresses are pressed and packaged for shipment. Draw a diagram showing the production process layout in the Today's Fashions factory. What type of factory layout and process is Today's Fashions using? Discuss the pros and cons of this choice. Could Today's Fashions improve the production efficiency by using a different production process or factory layout? How? Draw a diagram to explain how this might look.

5. As discussed in this chapter, many firms have moved their manufacturing operations to overseas locations in the past decade. Although there can be sound financial benefits to this choice, moving production overseas can also raise new challenges for operations managers. Identify several of these challenges, and offer suggestions for how operations managers can use the concepts in this chapter to minimize or solve them.

6. Reliance Systems is a manufacturer of computer keyboards. The company plans to build a new factory and hopes to find a location with access to low-cost but skilled workers, national and international transportation, and favourable government incentives. As a team, use the Internet and your school library to research possible site locations, both domestic and international. Choose a location you feel would best meet the company's needs. Make a group presentation to the class explaining why you have chosen this location. Include information about the location's labour force, similar manufacturing facilities already located there, availability of resources and materials, possible local incentives, the political and economic environments, and any other factors you feel make this an attractive location. After all teams have presented their proposed locations, as a class rank all of the locations and decide the top two that Reliance should investigate further.

7. Find the supplier information websites of several firms by using the Google search engine, (**www.google.ca**), to conduct a search for "supplier information." Visit two or three of these sites. Compare the requirements the companies set for their suppliers. How do the requirements differ? How are they similar?

8. Find out about the manufacturing environment in Canada by using (**www .google.ca**) and searching for manufacturing in Canada. You will have many options for learning more about the manufacturing opportunities.

9. Using a search engine such as Excite (**www.excite.com**) or Info Seek (**www .infoseek.com**), search for information about technologies like robotics, CAD/ CAM systems, or ERP. Find at least three suppliers for one of these technologies. Visit their websites and discuss how their clients are using their products to automate production.

Key Terms

assembly process   327
bill of material   333
CAD/CAM systems   343
cellular manufacturing   333
computer-aided design (CAD)   343
computer-aided manufacturing
   (CAM)   343
computer-integrated manufacturing
   (CIM)   343
continuous improvement   340
continuous process   328

critical path   338
critical path method (CPM)   338
customization   327
electronic data interchange (EDI)   337
enterprise resource planning (ERP)   334
e-procurement   336
fixed-position layout   331
flexible manufacturing system
   (FMS)   343
Gantt charts   338
intermittent process   329

Review Questions

1. Define production and operations management.

2. What is production planning? What is the production process, and what options are available to manufacturers?

3. What are some of the considerations when determining the location of production facilities?

4. After management has decided on a location for the facilities, they need to design the facilities' layout. What are some options in the design?

5. What are the considerations when we are formulating our resource planning?

6. What are supply chain and supply chain management?

7. What is scheduling? What are the three (3) common scheduling tools available to management?

8. Discuss some ways of improving production and operations.

9. How can technology be used to improve operating efficiencies and the ability for companies to compete?

10. Discuss the importance of asset management.

11. What is modular production?

CREATIVE THINKING CASE >

Innovation Labs Spark Creativity

With sales of 12.5 million units in less than a year, no one is questioning why designers of the sleek Razr, Motorola's ultra-light, half-inch-thick cell phone, broke some internal rules in bringing the phone to market. Leaving their cubicles at the company's traditional research facility, engineers joined with designers and marketers at the company's innovation lab known as Moto City. Open space and waist-high cubicles—even for senior executives—fostered team spirit and a breaking down of barriers, which contributed to the project's success. Customary practices like running new product ideas past regional managers were bypassed. "We did not want to be distracted by the normal inputs we get," says Gary R. Weis, senior director of mechanical engineering. "It would not have allowed us to be as innovative."

Innovation labs are fast becoming a key element in the effort to revamp old-style research and development (R&D). In the past, scientists and engineers toiled away for years in pursuit of patents, and then handed their work over to product developers and marketers for eventual shipment to consumers. But today's sophisticated production and operations technology, as well as ferocious competition, can mean new innovations grow old quickly, so companies must work fast to get products to market. To keep pace with consumer demand, Motorola introduced new colours for the Razr, as well as follow-up phones like the Razr2, the candy-bar shaped Slvr and the rounded Pebl.

But the need for speed in innovation stretches beyond high-tech companies. Businesses as varied as Mattel, Boeing, Wrigley, Procter & Gamble, and even the Mayo Clinic also use such labs to shatter the bureaucratic barriers that existed among inventors, engineers, researchers, designers, marketers, and others. Now, teams of people from different disciplines gather to focus on a problem—brainstorming, tinkering, and toying with different approaches—and generate answers to test on customers. Successful products are then sped to the market.

Although innovation labs are typically created to generate new product ideas, they are also used to improve manufacturing processes. Large organizations have discovered that innovation labs can be a powerful tool for cutting through bureaucratic bloat. At Boeing Company, for instance, nearly 3,000 engineers and finance and program management staffers from scattered locations were moved last year to the factory that assembles 737 jetliners. To urge people to mingle, Boeing created common break areas where mechanics and engineers could talk shop over coffee or a snack, building informal relationships that improved both daily working processes and innovations.

But innovation labs are not panaceas. If ideas that emerge from these facilities are flawed, the products will undoubtedly be failures. And some older workers, especially baby boomers, may have a hard time giving up cherished perks such as private offices. Yet for companies in a creative rut, innovation labs can be places where something magical gets started.

Critical Thinking Questions

- How do innovation labs contribute to successful production and operations management?
- In what significant ways do they differ from a more traditional research and development approach?
- What market conditions lead companies to use innovation labs?

SOURCES: Joseph Weber, Stanley Holmes, and Christopher Palmieri, "'Mosh Pits of Creativity," Business Week, November 7, 2005, (www.businessweek.com); Rebecca Fannin, "Unlocking Innovation: CEOs Are Learning How to Better Tap University R & D," The Chief Executive, June 2005, (www.findarticles.com); Innovation Labs website, (www.innovationlabs.com) (May 22, 2006).

VIDEO CASE >

Big Blue Turns Small Businesses into Large Competitors

"It is like music, once it is in place and working," says Susan Jain, a marketing executive with IBM Global Services. She is talking about Enterprise Resource Planning, or ERP, complex software modules that do just about everything to help companies run more efficiently and competitively.

"The old systems couldn't relate one piece of information to another," she says. Separate databases meant information systems weren't integrated, so day-to-day operations were cumbersome and management reporting often inaccurate. With ERP, information is accessible immediately, greatly improving overall operating efficiency and speeding up and shortening internal reporting procedures, and even reducing the time it takes to bring new products to market.

ERP is a "relational database" that ties all aspects of information gathering and dissemination together in a tidy package. For example, ERP software modules can receive an order, check raw material stocks to make sure the order can be produced, order any additional materials that might be needed, place the order in the production schedule, and send it to shipping and invoicing. Its human resources module will even help hire and train the staff needed to produce and fulfill the order.

Companies no longer need to predict what products customers might want, or keep tons of product on warehouse shelves gathering dust. ERP literally allows companies to "build to order"—in fact, IBM has an automobile customer that does just that. It builds to order, one car at a time, eliminating the customary guessing games of what colours or styles might be popular at a given time.

Even small companies are investing in ERP systems to enable them to grow and compete, despite the substantial investment in time and dollars that is required. Jain is candid about the costs involved. The software costs about $1 million dollars, with an equal expenditure required for new hardware. Implementation, training, and education can cost two to three times that amount and take years in the case of very large companies.

IBM Global Financing supports all elements of an ERP acquisition with a broad array of financing offerings with flexible payment options. But after all that expense, return on investment is difficult to measure. With so many variables driving business success, good results could be due to other factors, such as changes in working styles or a general upswing in the current business environment. IBM's promotional material asks "Are You Ready for IBM?" It's a big decision for small companies to make.

Critical Thinking Questions

- As the production manager for a large manufacturing company, you recommend the acquisition of ERP software to your bosses. Be specific in describing how such a system would help your company be more competitive.
- What kind of information would you want such a system to integrate for your company?
- Explain how you would propose to track performance to justify the cost of installing such a system.

SOURCE: Adapted from material in the video "Are You Ready for IBM?" Information Management Systems at IBM, (www.ibm.com) (accessed April 8, 2003).

E-COMMERCE CASE >

Magna Moves Forward

In moving his company from a tool and die shop in Ontario to an automobile parts manufacturer and an auto-maker, Frank Stronach has practiced world-class operations management. Stronach began his rise to fame and fortune in 1957 with a business called Multimatic, employing only 10 people. In 1960, Multimatic produced sun visor brackets for General Motors Canada. Today, Magna international, Inc. (named in 1973) operates in 25 countries with over 70,000 employees and more than 300 facilities that focus on manufacturing, research and development, engineering and sales.

How has Stronach managed to remain successful in such a volatile industry as automobile manufacturing? Magna is on the cutting edge of the technological advances related to the industry. By engaging in the design, development and manufacture of systems, components and modules, as well as assembling vehicles, they have been able to control not only the research and development of many aspects of the final products, but also the design of the production process, if not the facility itself. Magna is able to control the inventory management, schedule production, monitor quality and effect lean manufacturing techniques. However, the industry profile is changing rapidly with GM declaring bankruptcy. Where does that leave auto parts manufacturers such as Magna? Apparently well positioned to move forward.

Magna is leading a consortium of partners in a bid to take over Opel, Germany's second largest automaker. The partnership is expected to include GM at 35%, Sherbank (Russian state-owned creditor of OAO GAZ, Russia's second largest automaker) at 35%, Magna at 20% and Opel employees at 10%. There are many advantages to this venture including access to the Russian market which is expected to become the largest in Europe, access to OAO GAZ excess factory capabilities, access to Opel's 10 vehicle assembly plants in Germany, Britain, Spain, Portugal, and Poland, and access to Opel's vast engineering expertise.

Magna is the only parts manufacturer to ever move into the realm of auto manufacturing. If the joint venture goes ahead as planned, the opportunities will be exciting, but, of course, the challenges of such a combination of players, all with their own agendas, will be just that … a challenge.

Critical Thinking Questions

1. What operations management challenges can you see in moving from one plant located in Austria to ten plants located in various countries?

2. With a 20% share in the joint venture, how much control over the production process would Magna actually have?

3. Check out (www.Magna.com) to see the status of the joint venture today.

SOURCES: Mike Ramsey, "Magna may build cars here for Europeans; Strong euro gives edge to N. A. assembly," The Windsor Star, June 7, 2007, accessed June 17, 2009; David Olive, "Car czar Stronach opening new opportunities; the road ahead for reviving Opel may be tough to navigate but Canadian auto-parts mogul is in the driver's seat," Toronto Star, June 14, 2009, accessed June 17, 2009 and (http://cobrands.hoovers.com) accessed June 17, 2009.

CHAPTER 12

Making the Connection

Understanding the Customer

In the next two chapters, we will continue to look at the functional areas of the company by examining the area of marketing. Marketers make decisions about what products to bring to market in conjunction with the overall strategic direction of the company, and then work with *operations* to design those products and allocate the resources needed to provide them—whether that be production facilities or alliances with other firms if it is a good that is being produced, or layouts and procedures to be followed if it is a service. And, of course, both marketing and operations need to work with *human resources* to make sure people with the needed skills are in place in all areas, as well as with *finance* to make sure the product is financially worthwhile for the company to pursue, and that funds will be available to pursue it. It is an integrated effort. This is evident from the example of Lexus in the chapter. The company "adopted a customer-driven approach with particular emphasis on service" by stressing "product *quality* with a standard of zero defects in manufacturing" and a service goal to "treat each customer as a guest in one's home." Marketing couldn't do this alone. It would have to work with operations to provide this level of product quality as well as human resources to provide this level of customer service. And it would also need an investment of funds to pull it all together.

But just think for a minute what would happen if there were no customer demand for the quality cars sold by Lexus? Just as the decisions that are made in the functional areas to bring a product to market are integrated, the decisions about which products to bring to market obviously have to be integrated with the outside environment—they must come ultimately from the customer. The customer is the central focal point of any successful business. Look at the critical success factors. As we've said many times, you can't *achieve financial success* if you aren't earning revenue, and you can't earn revenue if customers aren't buying your products. And they won't buy your products if they don't at least *meet and at best exceed* their expectations. That is what this chapter is all about—understanding your customers and creating a marketing strategy that satisfies their needs.

This requires that the company keep an eye on all areas of the external environment that may affect marketing decisions, as discussed in the chapter—but particularly on the *social* environment, including demographic changes—to understand the trends that affect customer needs, as well as to better understand the different factors that influence consumer decision making. As the chapter explains, it is important to do market research to understand the customer, and advances in *technology* have made that easier. Technology has also made it possible to create a unique marketing mix for each customer, discussed in the chapter as "one-to-one marketing," based on information kept on customers in the marketing database. The company also has to keep an eye on the *economic* environment to make sure it keeps ahead of the competition and that it takes into consideration the

effect of changing incomes and interest rates, etc., as well as the *political* environment to make sure it is meeting all the requirements in its package labelling, etc.

Many concepts in this chapter are important for understanding marketing and its integrative nature. For example, in this chapter you will read about the marketing concept—focusing on customer wants and needs, and integrating the organization's activities in the functional areas to satisfy the customer, but doing so with a responsibility toward the *stakeholders*—profitably for the owners, ethically for the customer, and fairly for the employee. The marketing concept is an important integrative concept as it is the thread that ties all the marketing activities, functional areas, and the business as a whole together to stay focused on the customer and make decisions responsibly so that success is achieved with all the stakeholders in mind and all critical success factors met.

You'll also learn about relationship marketing. This is critical to the long-term success of the company—meeting the critical success factors over time by establishing long-term relationships with customers. This can be done through loyalty programs as one example, but also requires *commitment* from your employees to be customer oriented. As discussed in the chapter, employee attitudes and actions are critical to building relationships. A good example of this is WestJet airlines. Just give them a call and chat with one of their reps, and then call another airline, and you'll see the difference in attitude toward the customer.

Target marketing is another important concept. Identifying a target market helps a company focus marketing efforts on those customers most likely to buy its products. The unique features of the product that appeal to the target group and are seen by the target group as superior to competitive offerings are the company's competitive advantage. If that competitive advantage is cost—operating at a lower cost than competitors and passing this saving on to the customer (as in Wal-Mart)—we see another integration of marketing with the other functional areas. This cost advantage is gained through using less expensive raw materials and/or controlling overhead costs (finance), and making plant operations more efficient and/or designing products that are easier to manufacture (operations), and so on. This is achieved by these areas through people committed to this goal, often with the help of technology.

And finally, the target market of consumers whose needs the company is focusing on is determined after segmenting the market. Though it seems like a purely marketing exercise—dividing up the market of consumers into different groups based on some common characteristics—it has some very definite integrative implications. Take Avon's foray into a new customer segment—teenagers and young women, as discussed in the opening vignette—with a new cosmetics line called "mark." The social environment would have influenced the move, with demographic variables and buying behaviour making the 15- to 24-year-old age group particularly appealing. This in turn caused changes in the functional areas to accommodate the new line, particularly the move to recruit teens as sales representatives, a very innovative move on the part of Avon. Marketing is without a doubt a very central integrative function within a successful business.

CHAPTER 12

Understanding the Customer

LEARNING OUTCOMES

1 Define marketing concept, and relationship marketing.

2 Show how managers create a marketing strategy.

3 Explain marketing mix.

4 Summarize how consumers and organizations make buying decisions.

5 List the five basic forms of market segmentation.

6 Identify how marketing research is used in marketing decision making.

7 List some of the trends in understanding the consumer.

AVON GOES FOR THE YOUNGER SET

© 2009 JUPITER IMAGES CORPORATION

Avon Products, Inc. (**www.avon.com**) is attempting to ring the doorbells of a new customer generation: teenagers and young women. The big direct seller of beauty products, eager to reach 16- to 24-year-old shoppers who mostly associate the Avon name with their mothers, launched a cosmetics line called "mark." The hip packaging was distinctly more upscale than other teen-focused brands, including Procter & Gamble's Cover Girl or mass market brands such as Bonne Bell. It was also trendier than Avon's traditional look, which is aimed squarely at 25- to 55-year-old women. However, the $65 million in revenue fell short of the $100 million projected for the first year of mark's introduction. The director of consumer marketing and creative services for the mark brand has focused on new products, new advertising, and new partnerships to attract the younger customers. The brand has become more recognizable through campaigns such as "Girls' empowerment." See the mark branding at (www.meetmark.com) or (www.markcanada.ca).[1]

Avon is recruiting teens as sales representatives, even as it pushes ahead on efforts to boost its main North American sales ranks. Although the company expects some door-to-door selling by its new recruits, it envisions youth sales mostly taking place among groups of friends at slumber parties and other informal gatherings. Avon hopes the opportunity to sell cosmetics to peers will prove more alluring than toiling behind the counter in fast-food restaurants.

About 2.2 million young women in Canada are in the 15- to 24-year-old age group,[2] and many of them spend money on beauty and beauty-related products. "It's not just lip gloss," says Deborah I. Fine, the former publisher of *Glamour* magazine tapped by Avon to lead the youth charge. "It's lip gloss with an earnings opportunity."

Avon executives say research shows that young women have a "neutral to positive" image of the company. But when mark made its debut, its own name was in lights. The name Avon appears, but only in tiny letters.[3]

Critical Thinking Questions

1. **Why do companies identify target customers for their products?**

2. **Why is it important to differentiate a product?**

3. **How does a company like Avon find out what customers and potential customers want in the way of cosmetics?**

SOURCE: Stephanie Thompson, "Avon struggles to make mark on young buyers," in *Advertising Age* (Midwest region edition). Chicago: February 28, 2005; Sally Beatty, "Avon Is Set to Call on Teens," *Wall Street Journal*, October 17. © 2002 by Dow Jones & Co. Inc.

marketing
The process of discovering the needs and wants of potential buyers and customers and then providing goods and services that meet or exceed their expectations.

products
In marketing, any good or service, along with its perceived attributes and benefits, that creates value for the customer.

exchange
The process in which two parties give something of value to each other to satisfy their respective needs.

HOT Links

What's new at Avon since it launched its mark line? Browse the company's website, at **(www.avoncompany.com)**, to find out how the teen products are doing.

*Marketing played an important role in Avon's successful launch of mark. Marketing is the process of getting the right goods or services to the right people at the right place, time, and price, using the right promotion techniques. This concept is referred to as the "right" principle. We can say that **marketing** is finding out the needs and wants of potential buyers and customers and then providing goods and services (i.e., **products**—discussed in more detail in Chapter 13) that meet or exceed their expectations. Marketing is about creating exchanges. An **exchange** takes place when two parties give something of value to each other to satisfy their respective needs. In a typical exchange, a consumer trades money for a good or service.*

To encourage exchanges, marketers follow the "right" principle. If your local Avon rep doesn't have the right lipstick for you when you want it, at the right price, you will not exchange money for a new lipstick from Avon. Think about the last exchange (purchase) you made: What if the price had been 30 percent higher? What if the store or other source had been less accessible? Would you have bought anything? The "right" principle tells us that marketers control many factors that determine marketing success. In this chapter, you will learn about the marketing concept and how organizations create a marketing strategy. You will learn how the marketing mix is used to create sales opportunities. Next, we examine how and why consumers and organizations make purchase decisions. Then, we will discuss the important concept of market segmentation, which helps marketing managers focus on the most likely purchasers of their wares. We conclude the chapter by examining how marketing research and decision support systems help guide marketing decision making.

The Marketing Concept

marketing concept
Identifying consumer needs, and then producing the goods or services that will satisfy them while making a profit for the organization.

If you study today's best organizations, you'll see that they have adopted the **marketing concept**, which involves identifying consumer needs and then producing the goods or services that will satisfy them while making a profit. The marketing concept is oriented toward pleasing consumers by offering value. Specifically, the marketing concept involves

- focusing on customer wants, so the organization can distinguish its product(s) from competitors' offerings;
- integrating all of the organization's activities, including production, to satisfy these wants; and
- achieving long-term goals for the organization by satisfying customer wants and needs legally and responsibly.

Today, companies of every size in all industries are applying the marketing concept. Enterprise Rent-A-Car found that its customers didn't want to have to drive to its offices. Therefore, Enterprise began delivering vehicles to customer homes or places of work. Disney found that some of its patrons really disliked waiting in lines. In response, Disney began offering FastPass at a premium price, which allows patrons to avoid standing in long lines waiting for attractions.

Firms have not always followed the marketing concept. Around the time of the Industrial Revolution in North America (1860–1910), firms had a **production orientation**, which meant that they worked to lower production costs without a strong desire to satisfy the needs of their customers. To do this, organizations concentrated on mass production, focusing internally on maximizing the efficiency of operations,

production orientation
An approach in which a firm works to lower production costs without a strong desire to satisfy the needs of customers.

increasing output, and ensuring uniform quality. They also asked such questions as: What can we do best? What can our engineers design? What is economical and easy to produce with our equipment?

There is nothing wrong with assessing a firm's capabilities. In fact, such assessments are necessary in planning. But the production orientation does not consider whether what the firm produces most efficiently also meets the needs of the marketplace. By implementing the marketing concept, an organization looks externally to the consumers in the marketplace and commits to customer value, customer satisfaction, and relationship marketing, as explained in this section.

Customer Value

Customer value is the ratio of benefits to the sacrifice necessary to obtain those benefits. The customer determines the value of both the benefits and the sacrifices. Creating customer value is a core business strategy of many successful firms. Customer value is rooted in the belief that price is not the only thing that matters. A business that focuses on the cost of production and price to the customer will be managed as though it were providing a commodity differentiated only by price. In contrast, businesses that provide customer value believe that many customers will pay a premium for superior customer service. Sir Colin Marshall, former chairman of the board of British Airways (BA), is explicit about his commitment to superior customer service, insisting that BA can succeed only by meeting all of its customer value-driven needs, not just price.[4]

The automobile industry also illustrates the importance of creating customer value. To penetrate the fiercely competitive luxury automobile market, Lexus adopted a customer-driven approach, with particular emphasis on service. Lexus stresses product quality with a standard of zero defects in manufacturing. The service quality goal is to treat each customer as one would treat a guest in one's home, to pursue the perfect person-to-person relationship, and to strive to improve continually. This strategy has enabled Lexus to establish a clear quality image and capture a significant share of the luxury car market.

Customer Satisfaction

Customer satisfaction is a theme that we have stressed throughout the text. **Customer satisfaction** is the customer's feeling that a product or service has met or exceeded expectations. Lexus consistently wins awards for its outstanding customer satisfaction. J. D. Power and Associates surveys car owners two years after they make their purchase. The Customer Satisfaction Survey is made up of four measures that each describes an element of overall ownership satisfaction at two years: vehicle quality/reliability, vehicle appeal, ownership costs, and service satisfaction from a dealer. Lexus continues to lead the industry. Lexus manager Stuart McCullough comments, "In close collaboration with our dealers we aim to provide the best customer service, not only in the car industry, but in any industry. The J. D. Power surveys are a testament to our success in making our customers happy."[5]

At Doubletree Hotels, guests are asked to fill out a CARE card several times during their stay to let staff know how they are doing. Managers check the cards daily to solve guests' problems before they check out. Guests can also use a CARE phone line to call in their complaints at the hotel. A CARE committee continually seeks ways to improve guest services. The goal is to offer a solution to a CARE call in 15 minutes. Embassy Suites goes one step further by offering a full refund to guests who are not satisfied with their stay.

customer value
The ratio of benefits to the sacrifice necessary to obtain those benefits, as determined by the customer; reflects the willingness of customers to buy a product.

customer satisfaction
The customer's feeling that a product has met or exceeded expectations.

© COURTESY OF GEICO

CONCEPT *in Action* >>>

Geico—the major auto insurer with the scaly mascot—famously boasts a 97 percent customer-satisfaction rating, based on an independent study conducted by Alan Newman Research, 2006. With this claim, communicated through the company's quirky and ubiquitous advertising, consumers get the message that Geico delivers quality insurance coverage at low prices. What factors do you think impact the customer-satisfaction ratings for an auto insurer like Geico?

Building Relationships

relationship marketing
A strategy that focuses on forging long-term partnerships with customers by offering value and providing customer satisfaction.

Relationship marketing is a strategy that focuses on forging long-term partnerships with customers. Companies build relationships with customers by offering value and providing customer satisfaction. Companies benefit from repeat sales and referrals that lead to increases in sales, market share, and profits. Costs fall because it is less expensive to serve existing customers than to attract new ones. Keeping an existing customer costs about one-fourth of what it costs to attract a new one, and the probability of retaining a customer is more than 60 percent, whereas the probability of landing a new customer is less than 30 percent.[6]

Customers also benefit from stable relationships with suppliers. Business buyers have found that partnerships with their suppliers are essential to producing high-quality products while cutting costs. Customers remain loyal to firms that provide them greater value and satisfaction than they expect from competing firms.

Customer relationship management (CRM)
The processes used by organizations to track and organize information about current and prospective customers.

Customer relationship management (CRM) are the processes an organization uses to track and organize information regarding current and prospective customers. This includes information about the customers or potential customers, past history with the organization, and future prospects. Usually this involves the implementation of CRM software that can automate the data collection and correlate the data to be used later to increase customer satisfaction and sales.

Loyalty programs, sometimes referred to as frequent-buyer clubs, are an excellent way to build long-term relationships. Most major airlines have frequent-flyer programs. After flying a certain number of miles, you become eligible for a free ticket. Now, cruise lines, hotels, car rental agencies, credit card companies, and even mortgage companies give away "airline miles" with purchases. Consumers patronize the airline and its partners, because they want the free tickets. Thus, the program helps to create a long-term relationship with the customer.

If an organization is to build relationships with customers, its employees' attitudes and actions must be customer oriented. Any person, department, or division that is not customer oriented weakens the positive image of the entire organization. An employee might be the only contact a potential customer has with the firm. In that

CONCEPT *in Action* >>>

As a "guest" on WestJet, you can expect friendly, casual, yet competent service from everyone you encounter, from captain to customer service representative. How does this create customer satisfaction and value to the customer?

PHOTO COURTESY OF WESTJET.

concept check

Explain the marketing concept.

Explain the difference between customer value and customer satisfaction.

What is meant by relationship marketing?

person's eyes, the employee is the firm. If greeted discourteously, the potential customer might well assume that the employee's attitude represents the whole firm.

Building long-term relationships with customers is an excellent way for small businesses to compete against the big chains. Sometimes small firms, with few employees, are in a better position to focus on a tiny segment of the market.

Creating a Marketing Strategy

LO 2

environmental scanning
The process by which a firm continually collects and evaluates information about its external environment.

There is no secret formula for creating goods and services that provide customer value and customer satisfaction. An organization that is committed to providing superior customer satisfaction puts customers at the very centre of its marketing strategy. Creating a customer-focused *marketing strategy* involves four main steps: understanding the external environment, defining the target market, creating a competitive advantage, and developing a marketing mix. In this section, we will examine the first three steps, and in the next section, we will discuss how a company develops a marketing mix.

Understanding the External Environment

Unless marketing managers understand the external environment, a firm cannot intelligently plan for the future. Thus, many organizations assemble a team of specialists to continually collect and evaluate environmental information, a process called **environmental scanning**. The goal in gathering the environmental data is to identify future market opportunities and threats.

Computer manufacturers understand the importance of environmental scanning to monitor rapidly changing consumer interests. Since the invention of the PC, techies have taken two things for granted: Processor speeds will grow exponentially, and PCs will become indistinguishable from televisions—that there will be, in industry lingo, convergence. The first prediction obviously has come true, and the second is beginning. Consumers may not like to watch movies on their PCs, but they love listening to music on them. They may not like to send e-mail from their couch, but they love having a PC—known as a digital video recorder—attached to the TV to automatically record all their favourite shows. And although they won't buy an old-fashioned TV from Dell or HP, when it comes to flat-screen TVs, they have no problem at all.

For PC makers, it's also good business. Prices and margins for computers keep falling; gross margins in consumer electronics are twice those in the PC world. And now that the music and movies consumers play on those systems are the same zeros and ones that are the foundation of PCs, there is little conversion cost.

In general, six categories of environmental data shape marketing decisions:

- *Social forces*, such as the values of potential customers and the changing roles of families
- *Demographic forces*, such as the ages, birth and death rates, and locations of various groups of people
- *Economic forces*, such as changing incomes, inflation, and recession
- *Technological forces*, such as advances in communications and data retrieval capabilities
- *Political and legal forces*, such as changes in laws and regulatory agency activities
- *Competitive forces* from domestic and foreign-based firms.

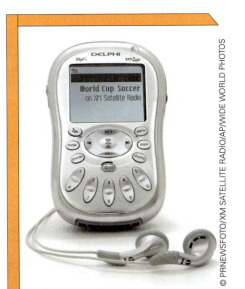

© PRNEWSFOTO/XM SATELLITE RADIO/AP/WIDE WORLD PHOTOS

CONCEPT *in Action* >>>

In the race to be Canada's premier satellite radio provider, two firms lead the pack. XM, the original pioneer of subscriber-based radio, offers listeners the best in entertainment including exclusive digital streams of major league sports and Oprah Winfrey. Rival company Sirius lures subscribers with a programming mix that includes NBA games and edgy adult banter from shock jock Howard Stern. What factors might constitute a competitive advantage for companies in the satellite radio business?

Defining the Target Market

Managers and employees focus on providing value for a well-defined target market. The **target market** is the specific group of consumers toward which a firm directs its marketing efforts. It is selected from the larger overall market. For instance, Carnival Cruise Lines says its main target market is "blue-collar entrepreneurs," people with an income of $25,000 to $50,000 a year who own auto supply shops, dry cleaners, and the like. Unlike other cruise lines, it does not seek affluent retirees. Laura's Shoppe Canada Limited has several different types of stores, each for a distinct target market: Laura's for average-size women, Laura Petites for petite women, Laura II for plus-size women, and Melanie Lyne for upscale women's apparel featuring designer labels.

Identifying a target market helps a company focus its marketing efforts on those who are most likely to buy its products or services. Concentrating on potential customers lets the firm use its resources efficiently. The target markets for Marriott International's lodging alternatives are shown in Exhibit 12.1. The latest in the Marriott family is SpringHill Suites. The SpringHill idea came from another Marriott chain, Fairfield Suites, an offshoot of Marriott's Fairfield Inns. The suites, opened in the late 1990's, were roomy but devoid of most frills: The closets didn't have doors, and the lobby floors were covered with linoleum. Some franchisees complained to Marriott that the suites were *under*priced: Fairfield Suites guests were saying they would pay a little more for a few more frills, so Marriott began planning an upgrade. To create each of the first 20 or so SpringHill locations, Marriott spent $200,000 renovating an existing Fairfield Suites unit, adding ergonomic chairs, ironing boards, and other amenities. Lobbies at SpringHill hotels are fancier than the rooms themselves: The lobbies have fireplaces, breakfast rooms, crown mouldings at the ceiling, and granite or ceramic tile floors.

Creating a Competitive Advantage

competitive advantage
A set of unique features of a company and its products that are perceived by the target market as significant and superior to those of the competition; also called *differential advantage*.

A competitive advantage, also called a differential advantage, is a set of unique features of a company and its products that are perceived by the target market as significant and superior to those of the competition. As Andrew Grove, CEO of Intel, says, "You have to understand what it is you are better at than anybody else and mercilessly focus your efforts on it." **Competitive advantage** is the factor or factors that cause customers to patronize a firm and not the competition. There are three types of competitive advantage: cost, product/service differential, and niche.

cost competitive advantage
A firm's ability to produce a product or service at a lower cost than all other competitors in an industry while maintaining satisfactory profit margins.

Cost competitive advantage   A firm that has a **cost competitive advantage** can produce a product (goods and/or services) at a lower cost than all its competitors

---

EXHIBIT 12.1 > The Target Markets for Marriott International

	Price Range	Target Market
Fairfield Inn	$45–65	Economizing business and leisure travellers
TownePlace Suites	$55–70	Moderate-tier travellers who stay three to four weeks
SpringHill Suites	$75–95	Business and leisure travellers looking for more space and amenities
Courtyard	$75–105	Travellers seeking quality and affordable accommodations designed for the road warrior
Residence Inn	$85–110	Travellers seeking a residential-style hotel
Marriott Hotels, Resorts, and Suites	$90–235	Grounded achievers who desire consistent quality
Renaissance Hotels and Resorts	$90–235	Discerning business and leisure travellers who seek creative attention to detail
Ritz-Carlton	$175–300	Senior executives and entrepreneurs looking for a unique, luxurious, personalized experience

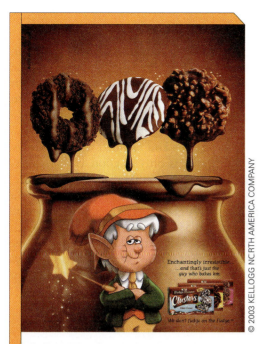

CONCEPT *in Action* >>>

A differential competitive advantage offers a unique value to consumers. The Keebler Company promises chocolate lovers that their Fudge Shoppe Clusters "don't fudge on the fudge." Considering some of the retail stores you are familiar with, what competitive advantages do they have?

differential competitive advantage
A firm's ability to provide a unique product or service with a set of features that the target market perceives as important and better than the competitor's.

niche competitive advantage
A firm's ability to target and effectively serve a single segment of the market within a limited geographic area.

while maintaining satisfactory profit margins. Firms become cost leaders by obtaining inexpensive raw materials, making plant operations more efficient, designing products for ease of manufacture, controlling overhead costs, and avoiding marginal customers.

Over time, the cost competitive advantage might fail. Typically, if one firm is using an innovative technology to reduce its costs, then others in the industry will adopt this technology and reduce their costs as well. For example, Bell Labs invented fibre optic cables, which reduced the cost of voice and data transmission by dramatically increasing the number of calls that could be transmitted simultaneously through a 5 cm cable. Within five years, however, fibre optic technology had spread through the industry, and Bell Labs lost its cost competitive advantage. Firms might also lose their cost competitive advantage if competing firms match their low costs by using the same lower cost suppliers. Therefore, a cost competitive advantage might not offer a long-term competitive advantage.

Differential Competitive Advantage   A product/service differential competitive advantage exists when a firm provides something unique that is valuable to buyers beyond simply offering a low price. Differential competitive advantages tend to be longer lasting than cost competitive advantages, because cost advantages are subject to continual erosion as competitors catch up.

The durability of a differential competitive advantage tends to make this strategy more attractive to many top managers. Common differential advantages are brand names (Lexus), a strong dealer network (Caterpillar Tractor for construction equipment), product reliability (Maytag washers), image (Holt Renfrew in retailing), and service (Federal Express). Brand names such as Coca-Cola, BMW, and Cartier stand for quality the world over. Through continual product and marketing innovations and attention to quality and value, managers at these organizations have created enduring competitive advantages. Arthur Doppelmayr, an Austrian manufacturer of aerial transport systems (Doppelmayr Lifts), believes his main differential advantage, besides innovative equipment design, is his service system which allows the company to come to the assistance of users anywhere in the world within 24 hours. Doppelmayr uses a worldwide system of warehouses and skilled personnel prepared to move immediately in emergency cases.

Niche Competitive Advantage   A company with a niche competitive advantage targets and effectively serves a single segment of the market within a limited geographic area. For small companies with limited resources that potentially face giant competitors, "niche-ing" might be the only viable option. A market segment that has good growth potential but is not crucial to the success of major competitors is a good candidate for a niche strategy. Once a potential segment has been identified, the firm needs to make certain it can defend against challengers through its superior ability to serve buyers in the segment. For example, STI Music Private Bank Group follows a niche strategy with its concentration on country music stars and entertainment industry professionals in Nashville. Its office is in the heart of Nashville's music district. STI has decided to expand its niche strategy to Miami, the "epicentre" of Latin music; and Atlanta. The latter is a long-time rhythm-and-blues capital and is now the centre of contemporary "urban" music. Both new markets have the kinds of music professionals—entertainers, record executives, producers, agents, and others—that have made STI so successful in Nashville.

concept check

What is environmental scanning?

What is a target market, and why should a company have one?

Explain the three types of competitive advantages, and provide examples of each.

Developing a Marketing Mix

marketing mix
The blend of product offering, pricing, promotional methods, and distribution system that brings a specific group of consumers superior value.

four Ps (4Ps)
Product, price, promotion, and place (distribution), which together make up the marketing mix.

product strategy
Taking the good or service and selecting a brand name, packaging, colours, a warranty, accessories, and a service program.

pricing strategy
Setting a price based on the demand and cost for a good or service.

distribution strategy
Creating the means by which products flow from the producer to the consumer.

Once a firm has defined its target market and identified its competitive advantage, it can create the **marketing mix**, that is, the blend of product offering, pricing, promotional methods, and distribution system that brings a specific group of consumers superior value. Distribution is sometimes referred to as place, so the marketing mix is based on the **four Ps (4Ps)**: product, price, promotion, and place. Every target market requires a unique marketing mix to satisfy the needs of the target consumers and meet the firm's goals. A strategy must be constructed for each of the 4Ps and blended with the strategies for the other elements. Thus, the marketing mix is only as good as its weakest part. An excellent product with a poor distribution system could be doomed to failure. A successful marketing mix requires careful tailoring. For instance, at first glance you might think that McDonald's and Wendy's have roughly the same marketing mix. After all, they are both in the fast-food business. But McDonald's targets parents with young children through Ronald McDonald, heavily promoted children's Happy Meals, and playgrounds. Wendy's is targeted to a more adult crowd. Wendy's has no playgrounds, but it does have carpeting in some locations (a more adult atmosphere) and has expanded its menu to include items for adult tastes.

Product Strategy

Marketing strategy typically starts with the product. You can't plan a distribution system or set a price if you don't know what you're going to market. Marketers use the term *product* to refer to both *goods*, such as tires, stereos, and clothing, and *services*, such as hotels, hair salons, and restaurants. Thus, the heart of the marketing mix is the good or service. Creating a **product strategy** involves choosing a brand name, packaging, colours, a warranty, accessories, and a service program.

Marketers view products in a much larger context than you might imagine. They include not only the item itself but also the brand name and the company image. The names Ralph Lauren and Gucci, for instance, create extra value for everything from cosmetics to bath towels. That is, products with those names sell at higher prices than identical products without the names. Another example, Holt Renfrew's company image is one of quality and superior service. We buy things not only for what they do but also for what they mean. Product strategies are discussed further in Chapter 13.

CONCEPT *in Action* >>>

With their computerized profile-matching capabilities, online dating services are a high-tech way to make a love connection. Today's date-seeking singles want more than automated personals, however. They want advice from experts. At Match.com, popular shrink Dr. Phil guides subscribers towards healthy relationships. At eHarmony.com, Dr. Neil Clark Warren helps the lovelorn find a soul mate. How do Internet dating services use various elements of the marketing mix to bolster the effectiveness of their product strategies?

Pricing Strategy

Pricing strategy is based on demand for the product and the cost of producing it. Some special considerations can also influence the price. Sometimes, for instance, a special introductory price is used to get people to try a new product. Some firms enter the market with low prices and keep them low, such as Carnival Cruise Lines and Suzuki cars. Others enter a market with very high prices and then lower them over time, such as producers of high-definition televisions and personal computers. You can learn more about pricing strategies in Chapter 13.

Distribution Strategy

Distribution strategy is creating the means (the channel) by which a product flows from the producer to the consumer. One aspect of distribution strategy is deciding how many stores and which specific wholesalers and retailers will handle the product in a geographic area. Cosmetics, for instance, are distributed in many different ways. Avon has a sales force of several hundred thousand representatives who call directly on consumers.

Clinique and Estée Lauder are distributed through selected department stores. Cover Girl and Del Laboratories use mostly chain drugstores and other mass merchandisers. Redken sells through beauticians. Revlon uses several of these distribution channels. Distribution is examined in detail in Chapter 13.

Promotion Strategy

promotion strategy
The unique combination of personal selling, advertising, publicity, and sales promotion to stimulate the target market to buy a product or service.

Many people feel that promotion is the most exciting part of the marketing mix. Promotion strategy covers personal selling, advertising, public relations, and sales promotion. Each element is coordinated with the others to create a promotional blend. An advertisement, for instance, helps a buyer get to know the company and paves the way for a sales call. A good promotion strategy can dramatically increase a firm's sales. Promotion is examined in Chapter 13.

Public relations plays a special role in promotion. It is used to create a good image of the company and its products. Bad publicity costs nothing to send out, but it can cost a firm a great deal in lost business. Good publicity, such as a television or magazine story about a firm's new product, can be the result of much time, money, and effort spent by a public relations department.

Sales promotion directly stimulates sales. It includes trade shows, catalogues, contests, games, premiums, coupons, and special offers. Tim Hortons discount coupons and "Roll up the rim to win" contests offering money and food prizes are examples of sales promotions.

Not-for-Profit Marketing

HOT Links

Considering a career in marketing? See various options in marketing (or any other field) at http://www.workopolis.ca.

Profit-oriented companies are not the only ones that analyze the marketing environment, find a competitive advantage, and create a marketing mix. The application of marketing principles and techniques is also vital to not-for-profit organizations. Marketing helps not-for-profit groups identify target markets and develop effective marketing mixes. In some cases, marketing has kept symphonies, museums, and other cultural groups from having to close their doors. In other organizations, marketing ideas and techniques have helped managers do their jobs better. In the private sector, the profit motive is both an objective for guiding decisions

CONCEPT in Action >>>

The Canadian Red Cross, a not-for-profit organization, uses social marketing to remind families to prepare their homes and families for emergencies and disasters. What are differences and similarities in marketing in for-profit and not-for-profit organizations?

CANADIAN PRESS

HOT Links

Visit the website for the Canadian Museum of Civilization at (**www.civilization.ca**).

social marketing
The application of marketing techniques to social issues and causes.

> ### concept check
>
> What is meant by the marketing mix?
>
> What are the components of the marketing mix?
>
> How can marketing techniques help not-for-profit organizations?
>
> Define social marketing.

and a criterion for evaluating results. Not-for-profit organizations do not seek to make a profit for redistribution to owners or shareholders. Rather, their focus is often on generating enough funds to cover expenses. For example, organized religions do not gauge their success by the amount of money left in offering plates. The Canadian Museum of Civilization does not base its performance evaluations on the dollar value of tokens put into the turnstile.

Not-for-profit marketing is also concerned with social marketing, that is, the application of marketing to social issues and causes. The goals of **social marketing** are to effect social change (for instance, by creating racial harmony), further social causes (for instance, by helping the homeless), and evaluate the relationship between marketing and society (for instance, by asking whether society should allow advertising on television shows for young children). Individual organizations also engage in social marketing. Mothers Against Drunk Driving (MADD) counsels against drunk driving, and the Canadian Wildlife Federation asks your help in protecting endangered animals and birds and their spaces.

Buyer Behaviour

buyer behaviour
The actions people take in buying and using goods and services.

© THINKSTOCK / GETTY IMAGES

CONCEPT *in Action* >>>

Many companies target consumers reaching retirement age and other baby boomers with advertisements promoting their products. Demographic segmentation is the most common form of market segmentation. What products are specifically targeted to the following groups: age 14–25, 25–50, and over 50?

An organization cannot reach its goals without understanding buyer behaviour. **Buyer behaviour** is the actions people take in buying and using goods and services. Marketers who understand buyer behaviour, such as how a price increase will affect a product's sales, can create a more effective marketing mix.

To understand buyer behaviour, marketers must understand how consumers make buying decisions. The consumer decision-making process has several steps, which are shown in Exhibit 12.2. The entire process is affected by cultural, social, individual, and psychological factors. The buying process starts with need recognition. This might be as simple as running out of coffee. Yes, I need to purchase more coffee. Or perhaps you recently got married and recognize that you need to start building equity instead of paying rent. Perhaps you are also considering starting a family. Therefore, you decide to buy your first home (Step 1 in Exhibit 12.2).

Next, you begin to gather information about financing, available homes, styles, locations, and so forth (Step 2). After you feel that you have gathered enough information, you begin to evaluate alternatives (Step 3). For example, you might eliminate all homes that cost more than $250,000 or are more than a 30-minute drive to your work. Then an offer is made and, if it is accepted, a purchase is made (Step 4). Finally, you assess the experience and your level of satisfaction with your new home (Step 5).

Influences on Consumer Decision-Making

Cultural, social, individual, and psychological factors have an impact on consumer decision-making from the time a person recognizes a need through post-purchase behaviour. We will examine each of these in more detail.

Culture   Purchase roles within the family are influenced by culture. **Culture** is the set of values, ideas, attitudes, and symbols created to shape human behaviour. Culture is environmentally oriented. The Sami of northern Europe (Kola Peninsula of Russia, Finland, Norway, and Sweden) have developed a culture for Arctic survival. Similarly, the indigenous people of the Brazilian jungle have created a culture suitable for jungle living.

Culture, by definition, is social in nature. It is human interaction that creates values and prescribes acceptable behaviour. Thus, culture gives

EXHIBIT 12.2 > Consumer Decision-Making Process

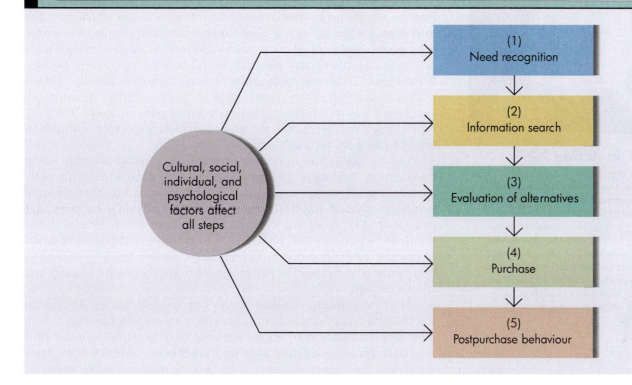

Cultural, social, individual, and psychological factors affect all steps

(1) Need recognition

(2) Information search

(3) Evaluation of alternatives

(4) Purchase

(5) Postpurchase behaviour

culture
The set of values, ideas, attitudes, and other symbols created to shape human behaviour.

order to society by creating common expectations. Sometimes these expectations are codified into law; for example, if you come to a red light, you stop the car. As long as a value or belief meets the needs of society, it will remain part of the culture; if it is no longer functional, the value or belief recedes. The value that very large families are "good" is no longer held by a majority of Canadians. As Canadians live more in an urban rather than a rural environment, children are no longer needed to perform farm chores.

Culture is not static. It adapts to changing societal needs and evolving environmental factors. The rapid growth of technology has accelerated the rate of cultural change. Inventions such as the elevator made possible modern high-rise cities. Television changed entertainment patterns and family communication flows, and heightened public awareness of political and other news events. The Internet has changed how we communicate and how most of us work.

Social Factors Most consumers are likely to seek out the opinions of others to reduce their search and evaluation effort or uncertainty, especially as the perceived risk of the decision increases. Consumers might also seek out others' opinions for guidance on new products or services, products with image-related attributes, or products where attribute information is lacking or uninformative. Specifically, consumers interact socially with reference groups, opinion leaders, and family members to obtain product information and decision approval. All the formal and informal groups that influence the buying behaviour of an individual are that person's **reference groups**. Consumers might use products or brands to identify with or become a member of a group. They learn from observing how members of their reference groups consume, and they use the same criteria to make their own consumer decisions. A reference

reference groups
Formal and informal groups that influence buyer behaviour.

CONCEPT *in Action* >>>

Since its launching in 2004, Facebook has the become the largest Internet social network with upwards of 50 million users. Originally created for Harvard university students, Facebook quickly spread to other colleges in the Boston area and then to the high schools. In September 2006, it became accessible to anyone with an e-mail address. "Friends" are quick to share their likes and dislikes as well as any aspect of their daily lives. How can online communities influence buyer behaviour?

opinion leaders
Those who influence others.

socialization process
The passing down of cultural norms and values to children.

personality
A way of organizing and grouping how an individual reacts to situations.

self-concept
How people perceive themselves.

group might be a fraternity or sorority, a group you work with, or a club to which you belong.

Reference groups frequently include individuals known as group leaders, or **opinion leaders**—those who influence others. Obviously, it is important for marketing managers to persuade such people to purchase their goods or services. Many products and services that are integral parts of Canadians' lives today got their initial boost from opinion leaders. For example, DVDs and sport utility vehicles were embraced by opinion leaders well ahead of the general public. Opinion leaders are often the first to try new products and services out of pure curiosity. They are typically self-indulgent, making them more likely to explore unproven but intriguing products and services.

The family is the most important social institution for many consumers, strongly influencing values, attitudes, and self-concept—and buying behaviour. For example, a family that strongly values good health will have a grocery list distinctly different from that of a family that views every dinner as a gourmet event. Moreover, the family is responsible for the **socialization process**, the passing down of cultural values and norms to children. Children learn by observing their parents' consumption patterns, and so they will tend to shop in a similar pattern.

Marketers should consider family purchase situations along with the distribution of consumer and decision maker roles among family members. Ordinary marketing views the individual as both decision maker and consumer. Family marketing adds several other possibilities: Sometimes more than one family member or all family members are involved in the decision; sometimes only children are involved in the decision; sometimes more than one consumer is involved; and sometimes the decision maker and the consumer are different people. For example, a parent will select a dentist for a child to visit.

Individual Influences on Consumer Buying Decisions   A person's buying decisions are also influenced by personal characteristics that are unique to each individual, such as gender, personality, and self-concept. Individual characteristics are generally stable over the course of one's life. For instance, most people do not change their gender, and the act of changing personality requires a complete reorientation of one's life.

Physiological differences between men and women result in different needs, such as health and beauty products. Just as important are the distinct cultural, social, and economic roles played by men and women and the effects that these have on their decision-making processes. Men and women also shop differently. Studies show that men and women share similar motivations in terms of where to shop—that is, seeking reasonable prices, merchandise quality, and a friendly, low-pressure environment—but they don't necessarily feel the same about shopping in general. Most women enjoy shopping; their male counterparts claim to dislike the experience and shop only out of necessity. Furthermore, men desire simple shopping experiences, stores with less variety, and convenience.

Each consumer has a unique personality. **Personality** is a broad concept that can be thought of as a way of organizing and grouping how an individual typically reacts to situations. Thus, personality combines psychological make-up and environmental forces. It includes people's underlying dispositions, especially their most dominant characteristics. Although personality is one of the least useful concepts in the study of consumer behaviour, some marketers believe that personality influences the types and brands of products purchased. For instance, the type of car, clothes, or jewellery a consumer buys can reflect one or more personality traits.

Self-concept, or self-perception, is how consumers perceive themselves. Self-concept includes attitudes, perceptions, beliefs, and self-evaluations. Although

ideal self-image
The way an individual would like to be.

real self-image
How an individual actually perceives him- or herself.

self-concept can change, the change is often gradual. Through self-concept, people define their identity, which, in turn, provides for consistent and coherent behaviour.

Self-concept combines the **ideal self-image** (the way an individual would like to be) and the **real self-image** (how an individual actually perceives him or herself). Generally, we try to raise our real self-image toward our ideal (or at least narrow the gap). Consumers seldom buy products that jeopardize their self-image. For example, someone who sees herself as a trendsetter wouldn't buy clothing that doesn't project a contemporary image.

Psychological Influences on Consumer Buying Decisions An individual's buying decisions are further influenced by psychological factors such as perception and beliefs and attitudes. These factors are what consumers use to interact with their world. They are the tools consumers use to recognize their feelings, gather and analyze information, formulate thoughts and opinions, and take action. Unlike the other three influences on consumer behaviour, psychological influences can be affected by a person's environment because they are applied on specific occasions. For example, you will perceive different stimuli and process these stimuli in different ways depending on whether you are sitting in class concentrating on the instructor, sitting outside of class talking to friends, or sitting in your dorm room watching television.

The world is full of stimuli. A stimulus is any unit of input affecting one or more of the five senses: sight, smell, taste, touch, and hearing. The process by which we select, organize, and interpret these stimuli into a meaningful and coherent picture is called **perception**. In essence, perception is how we see the world around us and how we recognize that we need some help in making a purchasing decision. People cannot perceive every stimulus in their environment. Therefore, they use **selective exposure** to decide which stimuli to notice and which to ignore. A typical consumer is exposed to more than 250 advertising messages a day but notices only between 11 and 20.

A **belief** is an organized pattern of knowledge that an individual holds as true about his or her world. A consumer might believe that Sony's camcorder makes the best home videos, tolerates hard use, and is reasonably priced. These beliefs might be based on knowledge, faith, or hearsay. Consumers tend to develop a set of beliefs about a product's attributes and then, through these beliefs, a *brand image*—a set of beliefs about a particular brand. In turn, the brand image shapes consumers' attitudes toward the product.

An **attitude** is a learned tendency to respond consistently toward a given object, idea, or concept, such as a brand. Attitudes rest on an individual's value system, which represents personal standards of good and bad, right and wrong, and so forth; therefore, attitudes tend to be more enduring and complex than beliefs. For an example of the nature of attitudes, consider the differing attitudes of consumers around the world toward the practice of purchasing on credit. North Americans have long been enthusiastic about charging goods and services and are willing to pay high interest rates for the privilege of postponing payment. To many European consumers, doing what amounts to taking out a loan—even a small one—to pay for anything seems absurd.

perception
The process by which we select, organize, and interpret stimuli into a meaningful and coherent picture.

selective exposure
The process of deciding which stimuli to notice and which to ignore.

belief
An organized pattern of knowledge that an individual holds as true about the world.

attitude
Learned tendency to respond consistently toward a given object, idea, or concept.

involvement
The amount of time and effort a buyer invests in the searches, evaluations, and decision processes of consumer behaviour.

Types of Consumer Buying Decisions

All consumer buying decisions generally fall along a continuum of three broad categories: routine response behaviour, limited decision-making, and extensive decision-making (see Exhibit 12.3). Goods and services in these three categories can best be described in terms of five factors: level of consumer involvement, length of time to make a decision, cost of the good or service, degree of information search, and the number of alternatives considered. The level of consumer involvement is perhaps the most significant determinant in classifying buying decisions. **Involvement** is the

EXHIBIT 12.3 > Continuum of Consumer Buying Decisions

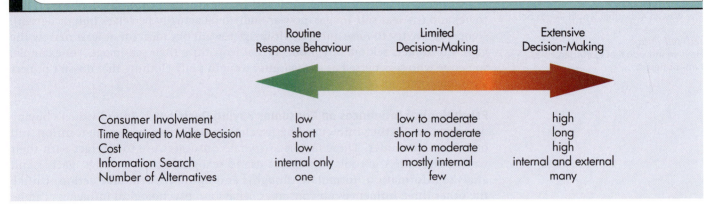

	Routine Response Behaviour	Limited Decision-Making	Extensive Decision-Making
Consumer Involvement	low	low to moderate	high
Time Required to Make Decision	short	short to moderate	long
Cost	low	low to moderate	high
Information Search	internal only	mostly internal	internal and external
Number of Alternatives	one	few	many

routine response behaviour
Purchase of low cost, frequently bought items with little search or decision making.

limited decision-making
Situation in which a consumer has previous product experience but is unfamiliar with the current brands available.

extensive decision-making
Purchasing an unfamiliar, expensive, infrequently bought item.

amount of time and effort a buyer invests in the search, evaluation, and decision processes of consumer behaviour.

Frequently purchased, low-cost goods and services are generally associated with **routine response behaviour**. These goods and services can also be called low-involvement products, because consumers spend little time on searching and decision-making before making the purchase. Usually, buyers are familiar with several different brands in the product category but stick with one brand. Consumers engaged in routine response behaviour normally don't experience need recognition until they are exposed to advertising or see the product displayed on a store shelf.

Limited decision-making typically occurs when a consumer has previous product experience but is unfamiliar with the current brands available. Limited decision-making is also associated with lower levels of involvement (although higher than routine decisions), because consumers do expend moderate effort in searching for information or in considering various alternatives. Suppose the children's usual brand of cereal, Kellogg's Corn Flakes, is unavailable in the grocery store. Completely out of cereal at home, the parent now must select another brand. Before making a final selection, he or she might pull from the shelf several brands similar to Kellogg's Corn Flakes, such as Cheerios, to compare their nutritional value and calories and to decide whether the children will like the new cereal.

Consumers practice **extensive decision-making** when buying an unfamiliar, expensive product or an infrequently bought item. This process is the most complex type of consumer buying decision and is associated with high involvement on the part of the consumer. This process resembles the model outlined in Exhibit 12.2. These consumers want to make the right decision, so they want to know as much as they can about the product category and available brands. Buyers use several criteria for evaluating their options and spend much time seeking information. Buying a home or a car, for example, requires extensive decision-making.

Business-to-Business Purchase Decision-Making Business buyer behaviour and business markets are different from consumer markets. Business markets include institutions such as hospitals and schools, manufacturers, wholesalers and retailers, and various branches of government. The key difference between a consumer product and a business product is the intended use. If you purchase a certain model of Dell computer for your home so you can surf the Internet, it is a consumer good. If a purchasing agent for MuchMusic buys exactly the same computer for a MuchMusic scriptwriter, it is a business good. Why? The reason is that MuchMusic is a business, so the computer will be used in a business environment.

Characteristics of the Business-to-Business Market   The main differences between consumer markets and business markets are as follows:

1. *Purchase volume.* Business customers buy in much larger quantities than consumers. Think how many truckloads of sugar M&M/Mars must purchase to make one day's output of M&Ms. Imagine the number of batteries Sears buys each day for resale to consumers. Think of the number of pens the federal government must use each day.

2. *Number of customers.* Business marketers usually have far fewer customers than consumer marketers. As a result, it is much easier to identify prospective buyers and monitor current needs. Think about how few customers for airplanes or industrial cranes there are compared to the more than 4 million consumer households in the Canada.

3. *Location of buyers.* Business customers tend to be much more geographically concentrated than consumers. For example, the automobile industry is concentrated in Ontario, and the oil industry is concentrated in Alberta. Suppliers to these industries often locate close to the industries to lower distribution costs and facilitate communication.

4. *Direct distribution.* Business sales tend to be made directly to the buyer, because such sales frequently involve large quantities or custom-made items like heavy machinery. Consumer goods are more likely to be sold through intermediaries, such as wholesalers and retailers.

> **concept check**
>
> Explain the consumer decision-making process.
>
> How do business markets differ from consumer markets?

Market Segmentation

 LO 5

market segmentation
The process of separating, identifying, and evaluating the layers of a market to identify a target market.

The study of buyer behaviour helps marketing managers better understand why people make purchases. To identify the target markets that might be most profitable for the firm, managers use **market segmentation**, which is the process of separating, identifying, and evaluating the layers of a market to identify a target market. For instance, a target market might be segmented into two groups: families with children and those without children. Families with young children are likely to buy hot cereals and pre-sweetened cereals. Families with no children are more likely to buy health-oriented cereals. You can be sure that cereal companies plan their marketing mixes with this difference in mind. A business market, on the other hand, might be segmented by large customers and small customers or by geographic area.

The five basic forms of consumer market segmentation are demographic, geographic, psychographic, benefit, and volume. Their characteristics are summarized in Exhibit 12.4 and are discussed in the following sections.

Demographic Segmentation

demographic segmentation
The differentiation of markets through the use of categories such as age, education, gender, income, and household size.

Demographic segmentation uses categories such as age, education, gender, income, and household size to differentiate among markets. This form of market segmentation is the most common. Statistics Canada provides a great deal of demographic data. For example, marketing researchers can use census data to find areas within cities that contain high concentrations of high-income consumers, singles, blue-collar workers, and so forth.

Many products are targeted to various age groups. Most music CDs, Pepsi, Coke, many movies, and thousands of other products are targeted toward teenagers and persons under 25 years old. In contrast, most cruises, medical products, fine jewellery, vacation homes, Buicks, and denture products are targeted toward people 50 years old

EXHIBIT 12.4 > **Forms of Consumer Market Segmentation**

Form	General Characteristics
Demographic segmentation	Age, education, gender, income, race, social class, household size
Geographic segmentation	Regional location (e.g., Maritimes and Newfoundland and Labrador, Central Canada, Western Canada, Northern Canada); population density (urban, suburban, rural); city or county size; climate
Psychographic segmentation	Lifestyle, personality, interests, values, attitudes
Benefit segmentation	Benefits provided by the good or service
Volume segmentation	Amount of use (light versus heavy)

and up. An example of how Frito Lay targets various age groups for three of its most popular products is shown is Exhibit 12.5.

Certain markets are segmented by gender. These include clothing, cosmetics, personal care items, magazines, jewellery, and footwear. Gillette, for example, is one of the world's best-known marketers of personal care products and has historically targeted men for the most part. Yet women's products have generated most of Gillette's growth since 1992. Gillette's shaving line for women has expanded into a $400 million global business, growing nearly 20 percent annually. Gillette has increased its advertising budget to help it reach a goal of more than $1 billion in revenues from women's shaving products worldwide.

Income is another popular way of segmenting markets. Income level influences consumers' wants and determines their buying power. Housing, clothing, automobiles, and alcoholic beverages are among the many markets segmented by income. Michelina's frozen dinners are targeted to lower income groups, whereas Stouffer's Lean Cuisine line is aimed at higher income consumers.

EXHIBIT 12.5 > **Age Segmentation for Fritos, Doritos, and Tostitos**

	Name Derivation	Year Introduced	Main Ingredients	Demographic	According to Frito-Lay
Frito	"Little fried bits" (Spanish)	1932	Corn, vegetable oil, salt	33- to 51-year-old males	"Hunger satisfaction"
Doritos	"Little bits of gold"	1964	Corn, vegetable oil, cheddar cheese, salt	Teens, mostly male	"Bold and daring snacking"
Tostitos	"Little toasted bits" (Spanish)	1981	White corn, vegetable oil, salt	Upscale consumers born between 1946 and 1964	"Casual interaction through friends and family . . . a social food that brings people together"

SOURCE: Frito-Lay.

Geographic Segmentation

geographic segmentation
The differentiation of markets by region of the country, city or county size, market density, or climate.

Geographic segmentation means segmenting markets by region of the country, city or county size, market density, or climate. *Market density* is the number of people or businesses within a certain area. Many companies segment their markets geographically to meet regional preferences and buying habits. Both Ford and Chevrolet, for instance, sell more pickup trucks and truck parts in the middle of the country than on either coast.

Psychographic Segmentation

psychographic segmentation
The differentiation of markets by personality or lifestyle.

Ethnic background, income, occupation, and other demographic variables help in developing strategies but often do not paint the entire picture of consumer needs. Demographics provide the skeleton, but psychographics add meat to the bones. **Psychographic segmentation** is market segmentation by personality or lifestyle. People with common activities, interests, and opinions are grouped together and given a "lifestyle name." For example, Harley-Davidson divides its customers into seven lifestyle segments, from "cocky misfits," who are most likely to be arrogant troublemakers, to "laid-back camper types" committed to cycling and nature, to "classy capitalists," who have wealth and privilege.

Benefit Segmentation

benefit segmentation
The differentiation of markets based on what a product will do rather than on customer characteristics.

Benefit segmentation is based on what a product will do rather than on consumer characteristics. For years Crest toothpaste was targeted toward consumers concerned with preventing cavities. Recently, Crest subdivided its market. It now offers regular Crest; Crest Tartar Control, for people who want to prevent cavities and tartar build-up; Crest for kids, with sparkles that taste like bubble gum; another Crest that prevents gum disease, and Crest Vivid White, for people wanting whiter teeth as well as a toothpaste that combines many of these in one tube. Sensodyne toothpaste is aimed at people with highly sensitive teeth.

> **concept check**
>
> Define market segmentation.
>
> List and discuss the five basic forms of market segmentation.

CONCEPT in Action >>>
L. L. Bean is a world-renowned outfitter serving people who love the outdoors. Psychographic segmentation is market segmentation by personality or lifestyle. How would you describe the psychographics of L.L. Bean's customers?

© 2009 JUPITERIMAGES CORPORATION

Volume Segmentation

volume segmentation
The differentiation of markets based on the amount of the product purchased.

The fifth main type of segmentation is **volume segmentation**, which is based on the amount of the product purchased. Just about every product has heavy, moderate, and light users, as well as non-users. Heavy users often account for a very large portion of a product's sales. Thus, a firm might want to target its marketing mix to the heavy user segment.

Using Marketing Research to Serve Existing Customers and Find New Customers

marketing research
The process of planning, collecting, and analyzing data relevant to a marketing decision.

HOT Links

A good place to learn more about marketing research is Quirks Marketing research review, **http://www.quirks.com**. In addition to articles, you can link to major marketing research firms.

How do successful companies learn what their customers value? Through marketing research, companies can be sure they are listening to the voice of the customer. Marketing research is the process of planning, collecting, and analyzing data relevant to a marketing decision. The results of this analysis are then communicated to management. The information collected through marketing research includes the preferences of customers, the perceived benefits of products, and consumer lifestyles. Research helps companies make better use of their marketing budgets. Marketing research has a range of uses from fine-tuning existing products to discovering whole new marketing concepts.

For example, everything at the Olive Garden restaurant chain, from the décor to the wine list, is based on marketing research. Each new menu item is put through a series of consumer taste tests before being added to the menu. Hallmark Cards uses marketing research to test messages, cover designs, and even the size of the cards. Hallmark's experts know which kinds of cards will sell best in which places. For instance, in geographic regions where engagement parties are popular, engagement cards sell best.

In this section, we examine the marketing research process, which consists of the following steps:

1. Define the marketing problem.
2. Choose a method of research.
3. Collect the data.
4. Analyze the research data.
5. Make recommendations to management.

Define the Marketing Problem

The most critical step in the marketing research process is defining the marketing problem. This involves writing either a problem statement or a list of research objectives. If the problem is not defined properly, the remainder of the research will be a waste of time and money. Two key questions can help in defining the marketing problem correctly:

1. Why is the information being sought? By discussing with managers what the information is going to be used for and what decisions might be made as a result, the researcher can get a clearer grasp of the problem.
2. Does the information already exist? If so, money and time can be saved, and a quick decision can be made.

Choose a Method of Research

After the problem is correctly defined, a research method is chosen. There are three basic research methods: survey, observation, and experiment.

survey research

A marketing research method in which data are gathered from respondents in person, by telephone, by mail, at a mall, or through the Internet to obtain facts, opinions, and attitudes.

observation research

A marketing research method in which the investigator monitors respondents' actions without interacting directly with the respondents; for example, by using cash registers with scanners.

experiment

A marketing research method in which the investigator changes one or more variables—price, packaging, design, shelf space, advertising theme, or advertising expenditures—while observing the effects of these changes on another variable (usually sales).

primary data

Information collected directly from the original source to solve a problem.

secondary data

Information that has already been collected for a project other than the current one but that can be used to solve the current problem.

HOT Links

Find out what information Statistics Canada collects at **http://www.statcan.ca**.

With **survey research**, data are gathered from respondents in person, at a mall, or through the Internet, by telephone, or mail to obtain facts, opinions, and attitudes. A questionnaire is used to provide an orderly and structured approach to data gathering. Face-to-face interviews might take place at the respondent's home, in a shopping mall, or at a place of business.

Observation research is research that monitors respondents' actions without direct interaction. In the fastest-growing form of observation research, researchers use cash registers with scanners that read tags with bar codes to identify the item being purchased. Technological advances are rapidly expanding the future of observation research. For example, ACNielsen has been using black boxes for years on television sets to obtain information on a family's viewing habits silently. But what if the set is on but no one is in the room? To overcome that problem, researchers will soon rely on infrared passive "people meters," which will identify the faces of family members watching the television program. Thus, the meter can duly record when the set is on and no one is watching.

In the third research method, **experiment**, the investigator changes one or more variables—price, package, design, shelf space, advertising theme, or advertising expenditures—while observing the effects of those changes on another variable (usually sales). The objective of experiments is to measure causality. For example, an experiment might reveal the impact that a change in package design has on sales.

Collect the Data

Two types of data are used in marketing research: **primary data**, which are collected directly from the original source to solve a problem; and **secondary data**, information that has already been collected for a project other than the current one but that can be used to help solve it. Secondary data can come from a number of sources, among them government agencies, trade associations, research bureaus, universities, the Internet, commercial publications, and internal company records. Company records include sales invoices, accounting records, data from previous research studies, and historical sales data.

Primary data are usually gathered through some form of survey research. As described earlier, survey research often relies on interviews. See Exhibit 12.6 for the different types of surveys. Today, conducting surveys over the Internet is the fastest-growing form of survey research.

Analyze the Data

After the data have been collected, the next step in the research process is data analysis. The purpose of this analysis is to interpret and draw conclusions from the mass of collected data. Many software statistical programs, such as SAS and SPSS, are available to make this task easier for the researcher.

Make Recommendations to Management

After completing the data analysis, the researcher must prepare the report and communicate the conclusions and recommendations to management. This is a key step in the process, because marketing researchers who want their conclusions acted on must convince the manager that the results are credible and justified by the data collected. Today, presentation software like PowerPoint and Astound provides easy-to-use tools for creating reports and presentations that are more interesting, compelling, and effective than was possible just a few years ago.

concept check

Define marketing research.

Explain the marketing research process.

What are the three basic marketing research methods?

EXHIBIT 12.6 > Common Types of Survey Research

Internet surveys	Conducted on the Internet, often using respondents from huge Internet panels (persons agreeing to participate in a series of surveys).
Executive surveys	Interviews of professionals (e.g., engineers, architects, doctors, executives) or decision makers that are conducted at their place of business.
Mall-intercept surveys	Interviews with consumers that are conducted in a shopping mall or other high-traffic location. Interviews may be done in a public area of the mall, or respondents might be taken to a private test area.
Central location telephone surveys	Interviews are conducted from a telephone facility set up for that purpose. These facilities typically have equipment that permits supervisors to monitor the interviewing unobtrusively while it is taking place. Many of these facilities do national sampling from a single location. An increasing number have computer-assisted interviewing capabilities. At these locations, the interviewer sits in front of a computer terminal attached to a mainframe or personal computer. The questionnaire is programmed into the computer, and the interviewer uses the keyboard to enter responses directly.
Self-administered questionnaires	Self-administered questionnaires are most frequently employed at high-traffic locations, such as shopping malls, or in captive audience situations, such as classrooms and airplanes. Respondents are given general information on how to fill out the questionnaire and are expected to fill it out on their own. Kiosk-based point-of-service touch screens provide a way of capturing information from individuals in stores, health clinics, and other shopping or service environments. Sometimes software-driven questionnaires on diskettes are sent to individuals who have personal computers.
Ad hoc (one-shot) mail surveys	Questionnaires are mailed to a sample of consumers or industrial users, without prior contact by the researcher. Instructions are included, and respondents are asked to fill out the questionnaire and return it via mail. Sometimes a gift or monetary incentive is provided.
Mail panels	Questionnaires are mailed to a sample of individuals who have been pre-contacted. The panel concept has been explained to them, and they have agreed to participate for some period of time in exchange for gratuities. Mail panels typically generate much higher response rates than do ad hoc mail surveys.

Trends in Marketing

To discover exactly what customers value most, organizations are using innovative techniques for collecting customer information. Some of the more sophisticated marketing research techniques that are growing in popularity are the use of the Internet, scanner-based research, capitalizing on loyalty cards, and one-to-one marketing.

Internet Marketing Research

Current methods of conducting some types of research soon may seem as quaint as a steam-engine train. New techniques and strategies for conducting traditional marketing research are appearing online in increasing numbers every day. The growth of Internet marketing research is being fuelled because the Internet:

- Provides more rapid access to business intelligence and thus allows for better and faster decision making.
- Improves a firm's ability to respond quickly to customer needs and market shifts.
- Facilitates conducting follow-up studies and longitudinal research.
- Slashes labour- and time-intensive research activities (and associated costs), including mailing, telephone solicitation, data entry, data tabulation, and reporting.

CHALLENGES OF CONDUCTING GLOBAL MARKETING RESEARCH

Global companies, like Research In Motion (RIM), Procter & Gamble, McDonald's, and 3M, want global marketing research to help them make good strategic marketing decisions around the world. Yet, doing marketing research in some countries is not easy.

For example, using the same questionnaire asking "How did you like the taste of the new Pizza Hut crust?" might be followed with a scale that goes (1) excellent through (7) poor. Canadians might rank the new crust at 3.3 and Asians at 1.7. Thus, the conclusion is that the Asians prefer the new crust more than the Canadians. The answer would be wrong! Asians don't like to offend others and therefore rate the new crust higher. In fact, they both liked the new crust the same!

There are many other problems in conducting global research. Cultural habits in some countries virtually prohibit communication with a stranger, particularly for women. For example, a researcher simply may not be able to speak on the phone with a housewife in an Islamic country to find out what she thinks of a particular brand. Second, in many societies, such matters as preferences for hygienic products are too personal to be shared with an outsider. In many Latin American countries, a woman may feel ashamed to talk with a researcher about her choice of a brand of sanitary pad, hair shampoo, or perfume. Third, respondents in many cases may be unwilling to share their true feelings with interviewers because they suspect the interviewers may be agents of the government (for example, seeing information for imposition of additional taxes). Fourth, middle-class people, in developing countries in particular, are reluctant to accept their status and may make false claims to reflect the lifestyle of wealthier people. For example, in a study on the consumption of tea in India, more than 70 percent of the respondents from middle-income families claimed they used one of the several national brands of tea. This finding could not be substantiated because more than 60 percent of the tea sold nationally in India is unbranded, generic tea sold unpackaged. Fifth, many respondents, willing to cooperate, may be illiterate, so that even oral communication may be difficult.[7]

Critical Thinking Questions
- What cultural factors (values, attitudes, ideas, and symbols) may influence the market research conducted in a third-world country?
- How can market researchers improve the accuracy and quality of market research conducted in a foreign country?

Internet surveys have several specific advantages:

- Rapid development, real-time reporting. Internet surveys can be broadcast to thousands of potential respondents simultaneously. The results can be tabulated and posted for corporate clients to view as the returns arrive. Thus, Internet survey results can be in a client's hands in significantly less time than traditional survey results.
- Dramatically reduced costs. The Internet can cut costs by 25 to 40 percent while providing results in half the time it takes to do a traditional telephone survey. Data-collection costs account for a large proportion of any traditional market research budget. Telephone surveys are labour-intensive efforts incurring training, telecommunications, and management costs. Using the Internet eliminates these costs completely.
- Personalization. Internet surveys can be highly personalized for greater relevance to each respondent's own situation, thus speeding the response process. Respondents enjoy answering only pertinent questions, being able to pause and resume the survey as their schedule allows, and having the ability to see previous responses and correct inconsistencies.
- Higher response rates. Busy respondents are growing increasingly intolerant of "snail mail" or telephone-based surveys. Internet surveys take half the time to complete than phone interviews do, can be accomplished at the respondent's convenience (after work hours), and are much more stimulating and engaging. Graphics, interactivity, links to incentive sites, and real-time summary reports make Internet surveys more enjoyable. This results in much higher response rates.
- Ability to contact the hard-to-reach. Busy professionals—doctors, engineers, and top management in Global 2000 firms—are the most difficult to reach through traditional survey methods. Many of these groups are well represented online. Internet surveys provide convenient anytime/anywhere access that makes it easy for busy professionals to participate.[8]

Conducting Internet marketing research is possible only in countries that have a high Internet penetration rate such as in Western Europe. When marketing researchers "go global" they face many challenges, as discussed in the Expanding Around the Globe box.

Scanner-Based Research

scanner-based research
System for gathering information from a single group of respondents by continuously monitoring the advertising, promotion, and pricing they are exposed to and the things that they buy.

Scanner-based research is a system for gathering information from a single group of respondents by continuously monitoring the advertising, promotion, and pricing they are exposed to and the things they buy. The variables measured are advertising campaigns, coupons, displays, and product prices. The result is a huge database of marketing efforts and consumer behaviour. Scanner-based research is bringing ever closer the Holy Grail of marketing research: an accurate, objective picture of the direct causal relationship between different kinds of marketing efforts and actual sales.

The two major scanner-based suppliers are Information Resources, Inc. (IRI), and the ACNielsen Company. Each has about half the market. However, IRI is the founder of scanner-based research.

IRI's first product was called *BehaviorScan*. A household panel (a group of 3,000 long-term participants in the research project) were recruited and maintained in each BehaviorScan town. Panel members shop with an ID card, which is presented at the checkout in scanner-equipped grocery stores and drugstores, allowing IRI to track each household's purchases electronically, item by item, over time. It uses microcomputers to measure TV viewing in each panel household and can send special commercials to panel member television sets. With such a measure of household purchasing, it is possible to manipulate marketing variables, such as TV advertising or consumer promotions, or to introduce a new product and analyze real changes in consumer buying behaviour.

IRI's most successful product is *InfoScan*—a scanner-based sales-tracking service for the consumer packaged-goods industry. Retail sales, detailed consumer purchasing information (including measurement of store loyalty and total grocery basket expenditures), and promotional activity by manufacturers and retailers are monitored and evaluated for all bar-coded products. Data are collected weekly from more than 31,000 supermarkets, drugstores, and mass merchandisers.

Making Ethical Choices

HITTING THE LONG SHOT

As a marketing manager at a beverage company, you are always looking for new products to offer—especially in the under-18 market where you are weak. A hot new drink has been a hit with kids in Japan—sales were up to 75,000 bottles a month—and it is making its way to Europe. Kidsbeer is a cola-like soft drink that is packaged to look like beer. The same colour as lager beer, the drink is formulated to pour with a beer-like foam. It includes guarana, a South American plant extract used in energy drinks. Tomomasu, the Japanese bottler, markets it with the slogan "Even kids cannot stand life unless they have a drink."

The impending arrival of such a drink has raised the ire of consumer groups outside Japan. They are alarmed that any company would glamorize drinking. Already beer drinking is showing up in movies that target kids and teens—for example, DodgeBall and HellBoy. Says Amon Rappaport of the Marin Institute, an alcohol industry watchdog group, "The last thing we need is another product that introduces kids to drinking when the alcohol industry already spends billions doing that."

Nonetheless, you are intrigued and begin to investigate. Besides, several companies still sell candy cigarettes to kids (although some countries have banned them).

Using a Web search tool, locate articles about this topic and then write responses to the following questions. Be sure to support your arguments and cite your sources.

ETHICAL DILEMMA: Kidsbeer would boost your company's revenues, because kids love to mimic their parents' behaviour. Do you recommend it to top management?

SOURCES: "Beer-Flavored Soda Headed for Europe," UPI NewsTrack, September 19, 2005; "Here's Looking at You, Kid," Food Management, October 2005, p. 104; Andrew Adam Newman, "If the Children Can Drink Uncola, What about Unbeer?" New York Times, September 19, 2005, p. C8(L); Andrew Adam Newman, "Youngsters Enjoy Beer Ads, Arousing Industry's Critics," New York Times, February 13, 2006, p. C15(L); "Drink That Looks Like Beer Getting Popular with Kids, Kyodo News International, August 5, 2005.

Loyalty Cards

loyalty cards
Cards issued by a manufacturer, service organization, or retailer that give discounts to loyal and frequent shoppers.

Just swipe the card at the checkout register and get a discount on tomatoes, toothpaste, or other specials. You save money, and the store builds a record that lets it know how to serve its best customers. **Loyalty cards** are cards issued by a service organization, retailer, or manufacturer that give discounts to loyal and frequent shoppers. Most companies require the shopper to fill out a demographic profile questionnaire before the card is issued.

Loyalty cards have been around for a few years now, and supermarket and drugstore chains are beginning to reap the benefits. With a huge amount of data being collected on shoppers, from the types of pop they buy to whether they like to shop late at night, merchants are getting smarter at tracking consumer trends. And they're changing their merchandise, store layout, and advertising accordingly to keep their most loyal customers spending.

Retailers estimate that 20 percent of their shoppers account for 80 percent of store sales, so finding out what their best customers want is essential. By simply scanning purchases, stores track what's selling, but when that information is tied to loyalty cards, merchants obtain richer information on who is buying what. This is the prized asset of supermarkets' future.[9]

One-To-One Marketing

one-to-one marketing
Creating a unique marketing mix for every customer.

marketing database
Computerized file of customers' and potential customers' profiles and purchase patterns.

One-to-one marketing is creating a unique marketing mix for every consumer. The key to creating one-to-one marketing is a good marketing database. The information contained in a marketing database helps managers know and understand customers, and potential customers, on an individual basis. A **marketing database** is a computerized file of customers' and potential customers' profiles and purchase patterns.

In the 1960s, network television enabled advertisers to "get the same message to everyone simultaneously." Database marketing can get a customized, individual message to everyone simultaneously through direct mail. This is why database marketing is sometimes called *micromarketing*. Database marketing can create a computerized form of the old-fashioned relationship that people used to have with the corner grocer, butcher, or baker. "A database is sort of a collective memory," says Richard G. Barlow, president of Frequency Marketing, Inc., a consulting firm. "It deals with you in the same personalized way as a mom-and-pop grocery store, where they knew customers by name and stocked what they wanted."

The size of some databases is impressive: at the Ford Motor Company it contains about 50 million names; Kraft General Foods, 30 million; and Citicorp, 30 million. American Express can pull from its database all cardholders who made purchases at golf pro shops in the past six months, who attended symphony concerts, or who travelled to Europe more than once in the past year, as well as the very few people who did all three.

Companies are using their marketing databases to implement one-to-one marketing. For example, Novartis Seeds, Inc., an agriculture business, produces individually customized, full-colour brochures for 7,000 farmers. Each piece features products selected by Novartis dealers specifically for the farmer based on information collected about the farm operation and the types of crops grown. Instead of the 30-page catalogue Novartis traditionally sent, these customers get a one-page brochure with only the five or six products they need, plus other complementary products dealers feel they should consider.

concept check

Describe how scanner-based research helps measure the effectiveness of marketing.

Explain how loyalty cards are of benefit to manufacturers and retailers.

Describe one-to-one marketing and the role of marketing databases.

Great Ideas to Use Now

As a consumer, you participate in shaping consumer products by the choices you make and the products and services you buy. You can become a better consumer by actively participating in marketing surveys and learning more about the products you buy.

Participate in Marketing Research Surveys

All of us get tired of telephone solicitations where people try to sell us everything from new carpet to chimney cleaning. Recognize that marketing research surveys are different. A true marketing research survey will *never* involve a sales pitch, nor will the research firm sell your name to a database marketer. The purpose of marketing research is to build better goods and services for you and me. Help out the researchers and ultimately help yourself. The Canadian Marketing Association (CMA) is the largest marketing association in Canada. CMA members include major financial institutions, publishers, retailers, charitable organizations, agencies, relationship marketers and those involved in e-business and Internet marketing. A key objective of CMA is to increase consumer confidence in the marketing industry.

Understanding Cognitive Dissonance

cognitive dissonance
The condition of having beliefs or knowledge that are internally inconsistent or that disagree with one's behaviour.

When making a major purchase, particularly when the item is expensive and choices are similar, consumers typically experience **cognitive dissonance**; that is, they have beliefs or knowledge that are internally inconsistent or that disagree with their behaviour. In other words, instead of feeling happy with their new purchase, they experience doubts, feel uneasy, and wonder if they have done the right thing. Understand that this feeling of uneasiness is perfectly normal and goes away over time. Perhaps the best way to avoid cognitive dissonance is to insist on a strong warranty or money-back guarantee. A second approach is to read everything you can find about your purchase. Go to the Internet, and use the search engines to find articles relevant to your purchase. Find Internet chat rooms about your product, and join in the discussion. And, before you buy, check out the *Consumer Reports* ratings on your product at **http://www.consumerreports.org**. For electronic products, also go to **http://www.CNET.com** and **http://www.ZDNET.com**.

HOT Links

Visit the Canadian Marketing Association at **http://www.the-cma.org** to learn more about how they take a leadership role in responding to consumer concerns and to learn more about their "Code of Ethics and Standards of Practice."

Customer Satisfaction and Quality

We have stressed the importance of product/service quality throughout the text. But how does a company know if it is offering high quality and satisfaction to its customers? The answer is marketing research. Marketing research provides the feedback to managers through customer satisfaction surveys about how well the company is doing.

Conducting a survey is a rather easy task; however, making changes based on the research can be a different story. It all begins with the commitment of top management. If top management makes customer satisfaction a top priority, then the chance of creating satisfied customers increases greatly. For example, Jean Gourdon, General Manager of the Montreal Novotel hotel, consistently earns the highest customer satisfaction ratings in the entire Accor system (more than 3,800 Novotel, Sofitel, Red Roof Inns, Ibis, and Motel 6 hotels). Jean Gourdon is devoted to satisfying customers, and he accomplishes this by making employees number one. Gourdon says,

"I tell my customers that it is staff first, customers second, profit third. I tell them that the management of this hotel does not spend time with customers. I have six department heads who concentrate on the staff. That means being attentive to family life as well, since I believe the organization has a role [to play] in life, not just work."

As a result, it is the employees' responsibility to not only clean rooms or change menus but also to take care of problems and represent the hotel to guests. "These people are the ambassadors of the hotel," Gourdon says. "They are extremely motivated, not just because they don't have supervision, but because they are empowered. It gives their job another dimension and also leverage in the industry." According to Gourdon, customers say it works. "They tell me that when they are here they are treated like kings," he says.[10]

SOURCE: "GM's Winning Vision: Staff First, Profit Follows," *Hotels* (March, 2003), p. 14. Reprinted with permission.

Summary of Learning Outcomes

1 **Define the marketing concept, and relationship marketing.**

Marketing includes those business activities that are designed to satisfy consumer needs and wants through the exchange process. Marketing managers use the "right" principle—getting the right goods or services to the right people at the right place, time, and price, using the right promotional techniques. Today, many firms have adopted the marketing concept. The marketing concept involves identifying consumer needs and wants and then producing goods or services that will satisfy them while making a profit. Relationship marketing entails forging long-term relationships with customers, which can lead to repeat sales, reduced costs, and stable relationships.

2 **Show how managers create a marketing strategy.**

A firm creates a marketing strategy by understanding the external environment, defining the target market, determining a competitive advantage, and developing a marketing mix. Environmental scanning enables companies to understand the external environment. The target market is the specific group of consumers toward which a firm directs its marketing efforts. A competitive advantage is a set of unique features of a company and its products that are perceived by the target market as significant and superior to those of the competition.

3 **Explain the marketing mix.**

To carry out the marketing strategy, firms create a marketing mix—a blend of products, distribution systems, prices, and promotion. Marketing managers use this mix to satisfy target consumers. The mix can be applied to non-business as well as business situations.

4 **Summarize how consumers and organizations make buying decisions.**

Buyer behaviour is what people and businesses do in buying and using goods and services. The consumer decision-making process consists of the following steps: recognizing a need, seeking information, evaluating alternatives, purchasing the product, judging the purchase outcome, and engaging in post-purchase behaviour. A number of factors influence the process. Cultural, social, individual, and psychological factors have an impact on consumer decision-making. The main differences between consumer and business markets are purchase volume, number of customers, location of buyers, direct distribution, and rational purchase decisions.

5 **List the five basic forms of market segmentation.**

Success in marketing depends on understanding the target market. One technique used to identify a target market is market segmentation. The five basic forms of segmentation are demographic (population statistics), geographic (location), psychographic (personality or lifestyle), benefit (product features), and volume (amount purchased).

6 **Identify how marketing research is used in marketing decision-making.**

Much can be learned about consumers through marketing research, which involves collecting, recording, and analyzing data important in marketing goods and services, and communicating the results to management. Marketing researchers can use primary data, which are gathered through door-to-door, mall-intercept, telephone, the Internet, and mail interviews. The Internet is becoming a quick, cheap, and efficient way of gathering primary data. Secondary data are available from a variety of sources including government, trade, and commercial associations. Secondary data save time and money, but they might not meet researchers' needs. A huge amount of secondary data is available on the Internet. Both primary and secondary data give researchers a better idea of how the market will respond to the product. Thus, they reduce the risk of producing something the market doesn't want.

7 **List some of the trends in understanding the consumer.**

New techniques and strategies for conducting traditional marketing research are appearing online in increasing numbers every day, including Internet marketing research. The growth of Internet marketing research is being fuelled because the

Internet and its acceptance in business today. BehaviorScan uses scanners and television meters to measure the impact of marketing on sales of specific products. BehaviorScan panels can also measure the impact of coupons, free samples, store displays, new packaging, and pricing. A second trend is retailers capitalizing on shopper loyalty cards. These enable managers to track customer shopping patterns. A third trend is the growing use of one-to-one marketing by using databases to target the needs of customers and non-customers more accurately.

Experiential Exercises

1. Can the marketing concept be applied effectively by a sole proprietorship, or is it more appropriate for larger businesses with more managers? Explain.

2. Before starting your own business, you should develop a marketing strategy to guide your efforts. Choose one of the business ideas listed, and develop a marketing strategy for the business. Include the type of market research (both primary and secondary) you will perform and how you will define your target market.

   a. Crafts store to capitalize on the renewed interest in knitting and other crafts

   b. Online corporate-training company

   c. Ethnic restaurant near your campus

   d. Another business opportunity that interests you

3. "Market segmentation is the most important concept in marketing." Why do you think some marketing professionals make this statement? Give an example of each form of segmentation.

4. Pick a specific product that you use frequently, such as a cosmetic or toiletry item, a snack food, article of clothing, book, computer program, or music CD. What is the target market for this product, and does the company's marketing strategy reflect this? Now consider the broader category of your product. How can this product be changed and/or the marketing strategy adjusted to appeal to other market segments?

5. Can marketing research be carried out in the same manner all over the world? Why or why not?

6. Visit the SRI Consulting site, **http://www.sric-bi.com**, and click on the VALS Survey link. First read about the VALS survey and how marketers can use it. Describe its value. Then take the survey to find out which psychographic segment you're in. Do you agree or disagree with the results? Why or why not?

7. How good was the marketing strategy you developed in Question 2? Using advice from the marketing section of *Entrepreneur* (**http://www.entrepreneur.com**) or other resources, revisit your marketing strategy for the business you selected and revise the plan accordingly. (*Entrepreneur*'s article "Write a Simple Marketing Plan" is a good place to start.) What did you overlook? (If you didn't do this exercise, pick one of the businesses and draft a marketing strategy using online resources to guide you.)

8. As the number of people online continues to grow, more of the Web surfers are also buying products online. What do researchers say about the characteristics of the online market? What market segments are appearing? Visit several sites to research this topic, and then prepare a report on the demographics of online markets and other key considerations for marketers. NUA Internet Surveys is a good place to start: **http://www.gdsourcing.ca/**. You'll find summaries of the latest research studies and can search for others by category. From there, you can link to the sites of market research companies. (Many research company sites require registration

or subscriptions; however, you can check press releases for summaries of research findings.) Also search for "Internet marketing" or "online marketing" using search engines and business publication sites such as *Business Week*, *Entrepreneur*, and *Inc.*

Key Terms

attitude   369
belief   369
benefit segmentation   373
buyer behaviour   366
cognitive dissonance   380
competitive advantage   362
cost competitive advantage   362
culture   367
customer satisfaction   359
customer value   359
customer relationship management
   (CRM)   360
demographic segmentation   371
differential competitive advantage   363
distribution strategy   364
environmental scanning   361
exchange   358
experiment   375
extensive decision-making   370
four Ps (4Ps)   364
geographic segmentation   373
ideal self-image   369
involvement   369
limited decision-making   370
loyalty cards   379
market segmentation   371
marketing   358
marketing concept   358
marketing database   379

marketing mix   364
marketing research   374
niche competitive advantage   363
observation research   375
one-to-one marketing   379
opinion leader   368
perception   369
personality   368
pricing strategy   364
primary data   375
product   358
product strategy   364
production orientation   358
promotion strategy   365
psychographic segmentation   373
real self-image   369
reference groups   367
relationship marketing   360
routine response behaviour   370
scanner-based research   378
secondary data   375
selective exposure   369
self-concept   368
social marketing   366
socialization process   368
survey research   375
target market   362
volume segmentation   374

Review Questions

1. What is marketing? What is an exchange in marketing?

2. What does the marketing concept involve?

3. What is the difference between customer value and customer satisfaction? How are these related to building relationships?

4. Why is it important for marketers to understand the external environment? What are the six general categories of the environment that marketers must evaluate?

5. What is a target market?

6. What are the various competitive advantages that a company can create?

7. What are the four variables in the marketing mix?

8. What influences consumers in their decision-making?

9. What are the characteristics of the business-to-business market?

10. What is market segmentation? What are the five basic forms of consumer market segmentation?

11. What is market research, and what are the steps in the market research process?

Teen Power: A Force to be Reckoned With

Cell phones, surfing gear, X-treme sports, video games—these are just some of the lucrative markets where companies focus major marketing dollars on some very important consumers—teenagers. Understanding youth trends and dynamics in the constantly changing teen market remains an ongoing challenge for companies needing to know how best to spend those dollars.

That's where Teen Research Unlimited (TRU) comes in. Started by youthful entrepreneur Peter Zollo in 1982, TRU was the first company to specialize in teen-focused market research. It keeps companies in touch with teen thinking, making it possible for them to forecast trends and remain a step ahead of the competition. Based in Northbrook, Illinois, TRU has worked closely with many of the world's leading youth brands and advertising agencies, playing a key role in groundbreaking advertising and marketing campaigns, and the development of successful products and services. TRU has worked with over half a million teenagers nationwide to assemble data for use in advertising campaigns, product development, store designs, and other strategic business activities. Last year TRU conducted more than 1,000 focus groups and personal in-depth interviews in addition to several major quantitative studies. TRU also applies its expertise to teen advocacy on important social issues and high-risk youth behaviours such as anti-tobacco and drug use, sexual assault, life safety, education, crisis management, and skin cancer.

So how does TRU gather its data and help its clients create effective marketing strategies? When a burgeoning fashion retailer needed ethnographic research to learn more about their target consumer, they asked TRU to help them. TRU spent months scouring malls, sitting down with shoppers, and carrying out a comprehensive national quantitative analysis to gain a well-rounded view of the client and its competitors. At project completion, TRU was able to provide its client with a strategically sound, actionable plan that built on previous strengths, addressed areas requiring improvement, and set a benchmark for future measurements.

In another study a leading manufacturer of backpacks and luggage hired TRU to explore "personal carrying device" trends. To meet the client's research objective, TRU devised a series of in-home interviews focused on which bags people own, when they use them, and what they use them for. These interviews, as well as "intercepts" on snowy train platforms and the sunny West Coast beaches, were videotaped to reveal an "on-the-street" take on emerging trends.

The only full-service marketing-research firm dedicated solely to understanding teens, TRU's initial vision remains in place today: to develop an unparalleled expertise in the teenage market, and to offer clients virtually unlimited methods for researching teens. And with more businesses than ever focused on marketing to teenage consumers—Abercrombie & Fitch, PepsiCo, Nintendo, and Nokia are just some of TRU's prestigious clients—companies count on TRU's research to remain in touch with what teenagers want.

Critical Thinking Questions

*   What makes TRU's research so important?
*   In what way is the company unique?
*   How does TRU help its customers understand their target market and create effective marketing strategies?

SOURCES: Adapted from the video "Teenage Research Unlimited," http://www.swlearning.com; Parija Bhatnagar, "More Cheese for the 'Mall Rats,'" CNN/Money, February 4, 2005; Ruth Laferla, "Teenagers Shop for Art of the Deal," New York Times, September 22, 2005; Mary Ellen Podmolik, "Teen Stores Leading the Herd," Chicago Tribune, January 14, 2006, p. 1; TRU corporate website (www .teenresearch.com), April 26, 2006.

Building Customer Relationships—One Kid at a Time

If giving consumers what they want is an excellent way to ensure loyalty and build long-term customer relationships, Fisher-Price has the right idea. Inviting its customers to participate in product design and development studies is an integral part of its marketing research programs. It is also one way Fisher-Price makes sure that products will achieve high levels of customer acceptance and success when they finally do reach the marketplace.

Founded in 1930, Fisher-Price is the most widely recognized brand of infant and preschool toys in the industry, and a trusted name in early childhood development. The company has earned a reputation for designing and producing high-quality toys that provide both developmental benefits and fun for children from birth to age 5.

Shelly Glick Gryfe, Director of Marketing Research at Fisher-Price, is proud of its Play Lab and Mom Talks, which are conducted in-house. Drawing from a list of several thousand volunteers, Gryfe and her team invite mothers with children who meet a specific demographic requirement to spend the day at their facility. In the Play Lab children do arts and crafts, read stories, and are encouraged to interact with a selection of toys. Some of the toys are still in development, whereas others, including those from competing companies, are already on the market.

These sessions are designed to provide the marketing research team with "directional information." Their designers, who observe the children from behind a one-way mirror, are looking for feedback on how they can make Fisher-Price products even better. It was this level of detailed observation that was responsible for the large feet on the company's preschool-age action figures called Rescue Heroes. The designers noted how frustrated the children became when a competitor's action figures kept toppling over.

Mothers are also an important part of the process. After viewing models, videos, and photo boards, and observing children's interactions with the toys, they are consulted on such topics as ranking products in order of desirability and giving opinions on age appropriateness and product pricing. Gryfe says parents participate because they "want to have good toys coming out for their children."

There is no doubt that kids and moms know what they like. Mothers loved the "good guy" theme of the Rescue Heroes line when it was first introduced in 1998 and declared it a winner. CBS television agreed, creating a Rescue Heroes TV series for young viewers, which has helped boost ongoing demand for the products. At Fisher-Price, giving the customer a voice means everyone wins.

Critical Thinking Questions

- How does Fisher-Price's marketing research strategy help build customer loyalty?
- What other "spin-off" benefits does it produce for the company? For the consumer?
- Is there a downside to having customers involved in the product development process? Explain.

SOURCES: Adapted from the video "Fisher-Price: The Pre-School Boy;" and information on Fisher-Price brands from the Mattel corporate Web site, http://www.mattel.com (accessed April 22, 2003).

Sunworks Organic Farm: For Profit or Health?

In the case of Sunworks Farm, the original idea was to produce organic products to help Sheila, one of the owners, battle fibromyalgia, which had been plaguing her for four years. A naturopath had suggested that Sheila use organic food, and within six weeks, she recovered, marking the beginning of great things for the family. The Hamilton farm has been certified organic since 1997. They started with 80 chickens, and they now raise over 25,000 chickens during the outdoor season. Sunworks Farm provides 600 dozen eggs every week, and they always sell out early in the weekend. The farm also produces whole chickens, roasts, sausages, bison, pork, yogurt, and other products, all organic.

The Hamiltons have a strong family orientation as well, with Sheila's sister raising pigs and lambs, which the Hamiltons then market. Sheila's daughters and their families also work in the business. The Sunworks philosophy is heavily influenced by their ethics. As Ron Hamilton says, "When our customers buy our food, they buy our ethics package." This package includes a concern for the health of the earth as well as people and animals. Only a very small percentage of their products are not sold directly to the consumer primarily through year-round farmers' markets.

By offering a choice to consumers, the Hamiltons are living their values (The animals are raised outdoors when weather permits and graze naturally, supplemented only by organic feed). There are no chemicals, medications, or other toxins applied to their land or fed to their animals. In addition, products such as sausage, wieners, and bacon contain no fillers, nitrates, sulphites, or MSG. The philosophy, as stated on their website (**www.sunworksfarm.com**), is as follows:

We believe that:

1. It is our privilege to be stewards of the land and that we should leave it in a better state than when we got it. We do our best to work with nature and not against it.

2. Our children should be raised in a healthy mental and physical environment.

3. Animals should be treated kindly, humanely, ethically and have access to fresh air, clean water, green grass, and sunshine.

4. A healthy environment and gentle handling grows healthy animals, which reduces disease and the need for medication.

5. We want to grow good healthy food for our customers. We guarantee that you will not taste better meat than our pasture-raised products.

Under this philosophy, based on the ancient Haida saying "We do not inherit the land from our ancestors, we borrow it from our children," Sunworks Farms has continued to prosper, with many customers reaping the benefits of the superior product produced with care and concern for the animals and the earth.

Critical Thinking Questions

1. As a consumer, you might have noticed that organic products are generally more expensive than traditionally mass-produced products. Why are these products more expensive? Are you willing to pay the extra cost? Why or why not?

2. Suggest a marketing strategy for a company such as Sunworks Farm.

SOURCES: Pamela Irving, "Farming for the Love of It: Organic Food," Edmonton Journal, March 22, 2006; and Sunworks Farms Web site, http://www.sunworksfarm.com (accessed September 30th, 2008).

CHAPTER 13

Making the Connection

Creating Marketing Strategies

In this chapter we will continue to look at the functional area of marketing but more specifically at the 4P's of the marketing mix—product, price, place, and promotion. One of the keys to success in marketing is to provide something of unique value to the customer in order to achieve the critical success factor of *meeting their needs*. The second is to market it in such a way that you convince the customer of its benefit. They must believe that it will satisfy their needs or they won't buy it. This is where the 4Ps come in. Not only does marketing have to work with the other functional areas in an integrative fashion, as we discussed last chapter, but the marketing functions themselves must work together in an integrative way to convince the customer of the unique benefit of the product. For example, if a company wants to promote a product that is of better quality than the competition—such as Tivoli Florist in our opening vignette—and therefore designs it to have the features as well as the look of higher quality, promotes it in ways that appeal to high-end customers, distributes it in high-end stores, but prices it below the competition, consumers will be confused as to its quality. All four elements must give a consistent message—they must form an integrative whole—or the customer will be confused rather than convinced.

This is quite evident when you consider, as the chapter explains, that consumers make purchase decisions after considering both the tangible and intangible attributes of the product, including price. They consider the total value

package—what they get at the price they have to pay. Another very integrative product concept is that of the product life cycle. It sounds like just a product concept, but the implications of what stage in the life cycle a product is at goes far beyond the product itself and into how it is priced, promoted and distributed.

Integration is also evident in looking at product design alone. The chapter discusses how consumers buy packages of benefits, such as: Burger King sells burgers and fries, but along with that quick food preparation and cleanliness. In other words, the product design must take into consideration *human resource* and *operations* issues as well.

When new products are developed, there are also obvious connections to the other parts of our business model. New product goals are usually financially stated, for example, so that the company only pursues products that help it *achieve financial performance*, and ideas are rejected if they don't meet financial goals. The firm must also determine if it has the operational facilities to produce the product, plus access to the necessary technology, human, and financial resources. New product ideas need to be checked against long-range strategies. Remember that planning takes place at different levels, but all levels are always connected so that they move in the same direction.

Pricing has obvious connections to *finance* of course, just as it affects the total value package for the consumer. The company must set a price that will earn a fair return

for the company, but provide value to the consumer as well. This connection with finance is no more obvious than in the discussion of breakeven. If the costs from operations, human resources and marketing cannot be covered from the revenue generated by the product, then financially it is not feasible and can't be done within the current cost structure, regardless of its marketing appeal.

Place or distribution is one of the 4Ps that is, by its very nature, the most integrative since any discussion of place must combine two functional areas—operations and marketing. Distribution is typically the responsibility of operations, but is critical to marketing's ability to meet the needs of the customer—getting products to customers when and where they want them. The importance placed on managing the supply chain in today's businesses, that is, the route the product takes from provider to consumer, makes these two areas inseparable.

Promotion appears to most students to be the purest form of marketing, but it is also affected by other areas of the business. For example, one of the elements of a promotional mix is personal selling. This has definite human resource implications. The sales force must be managed to communicate the intended message. And how much is spent on personal selling as opposed to other forms of promotion depends to a great extent on the financial situation of the company. As the chapter suggests, "Money, or the lack of it, is one of the biggest influences on the promotional mix." But the factors in the external environment also affect promotion—the government (*political*) sets guidelines on what can and cannot be done in advertising, the competition has to be monitored carefully to be aware of what message they are projecting vs. your company's message, *social* trends will influence your advertising design and, of course, the *technology* is always changing and expanding the limits of what can be done. For example, the Internet is discussed in the chapter as a potential vehicle for building a brand presence, in fact more quickly than traditional methods, and it is also a powerful tool for tailoring the message to meet the needs of specific consumers. Just go visit (amazon.com).

The clearest example of integration in promotion is the need for integrated marketing communications. Just as all of the 4Ps must project the same message, so must all elements of the promotional mix. If this is not done, the company risks confusing the consumer, and they will simply buy a different product. The area where there is the least control is in personal selling. You are not designing an ad with a consistent message; your salespeople are your message. Therefore, the message may not be the same every time—again you have human resource issues that must be handled very carefully to ensure consistency.

CHAPTER 13

Creating Marketing Strategies

LEARNING OUTCOMES

1. Describe what is meant by a product.
2. Explain the stages of the product life cycle.
3. Discuss the role of pricing and the strategies used for pricing products.
4. Explain distribution and distribution channels.
5. Illustrate how supply chain management can increase efficiency and customer satisfaction.
6. Briefly list the goals of promotional strategy.
7. Discuss the elements of the promotional mix, and integrated marketing communications.
8. Identify the factors that affect the promotional mix.
9. List some of the trends in marketing.

SHIRLEY A. ROSE

For approximately 20 years, Michael Corbeil has been operating his own retail florist business. Tivoli Florist offers distinctive arrangements designed to suit the tastes and requirements of a wide range of clients. Now a successful business owner with two locations, Michael struggled to make the business what it is today. Michael says that he did not realize how long it would take to develop a client base to make the business economically viable. A strong basic knowledge of marketing served him well.

Michael's *product* is several levels up from your run-of-the-mill flower shop. He has 70-80 different types of flowers, none of which are carnations or baby's breath. Fresh flowers arrive daily from such places as Africa, Ecuador, Thailand, Holland, and other European countries. Arrangements are custom designed and range from corporate requirements to weddings, funerals, and other personal occasions. The flowers are fairly-traded and eco-friendly. Other products offered include rare and unusual plants, garden accents, and giftware.

The *price* of Tivoli's flowers reflects the higher quality of the product. In the industry, 3.5 times is the standard markup for an arrangement but some of Tivoli's arrangements are marked up 4 times due to the extra time required to custom design the arrangement. Some of the vases used are very expensive and can be marked up to reflect that, but others are pricey without the same customer appeal, therefore it is sometimes difficult to even get a 1 time markup. At particular times of the year, such as Christmas, Valentine's Day, Easter, and Mother's Day, the markup may be greater, but because of higher shipping costs, the net profit on the arrangement does not increase.

Promotion is done primarily through word-of-mouth. The quality and exclusiveness of the design appeals to the quality-conscious consumer and the reputation of Tivoli Florist spreads throughout the Ottawa area. Michael also uses the telephone directory but finds the cost quite high relative to the results. Tivoli has an attractive website (**www.tivoliflorist.com**) with an interesting array of colourful photographs as well as useful information to inform the inquiring consumer. Another promotional tool used by Michael is the donation of flowers for charitable events that are sponsored by Tivoli's clientele as well as support for and from artistic endeavours.

For now, the *distribution* is from the two existing locations, one a large shop dedicated to Tivoli products, the other a smaller shop as part of another business, Paper Papier, in the Ottawa ByWard Market area. The secondary location is a card and paper store which provides the flowers as a complementary product when customers come in looking for "just the right card" for whatever the occasion. Usually flowers can complete the message the customer wishes to send. Tivoli also offers local and worldwide delivery service.

Obviously in tough economic times, flower sales will suffer since they are covered by one's disposable income. Corporate clients also tend to cut back on non-essentials. But Michael is optimistic, and given his loyal client base and superior product, will probably continue to help brighten the day of his Ottawa customers.

Critical Thinking Questions

1. **In tough economic times, what would you suggest someone like Michael Corbeil might do to maintain the viability of his business?**

2. **What component(s) of the marketing mix should he change? Why? How?**

3. **Check out Michael's website (www.tivoliflorist. com). What suggestions would you make to help encourage more business via the Web?**

The creation of a marketing mix combines the four Ps into a concise plan that will meet or exceed the target market's expectations. Organizations prepare for long-term success by creating and packaging products that add value, and pricing them to meet the organization's financial objectives. The businesses must use the distribution system that enhances the value of the product and determine what methods they will use to move products to locations where consumers wish to buy them. At the same time, the organizations build demand for their products through their promotional strategies. This chapter will discuss the product, price, promotion, and place of goods and services.

What Is a Product?

product
In marketing, any good or service, along with its perceived attributes and benefits, that creates value for the customer.

In marketing, a **product** is any good or service, along with its perceived attributes and benefits, that creates value for the customer. Attributes can be tangible or intangible. Among the tangible attributes are packaging and warranties, as illustrated in Exhibit 13.1. Intangible attributes are symbolic, such as brand image. People make decisions about which products to buy after considering both tangible and intangible attributes of a product. For example, when you buy a pair of jeans, you consider price, brand, store image, and style before you buy.

Products are often a blend of goods and services, as shown in Exhibit 13.2. For example, a Honda Civic (a good) would have less value without Honda's maintenance agreement (a service). Although Tim Hortons sells such goods as sandwiches and coffee, customers expect quality service as well, including quick food preparation and cleanliness. When developing a product, an organization must consider how the combination of goods and services will provide value to the customer.

Classifying Consumer Products

Because most things sold are a blend of goods and services, the term *product* can be used to refer to both. After all, consumers are really buying packages of benefits that deliver

EXHIBIT 13.1 > Tangible and Intangible Attributes of a Product Create Value for the Buyer

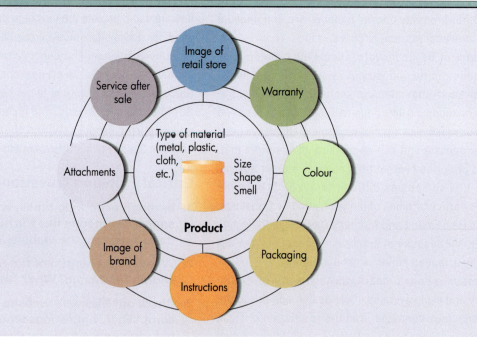

EXHIBIT 13.2 > Products Are Typically a Blend of Goods and Services

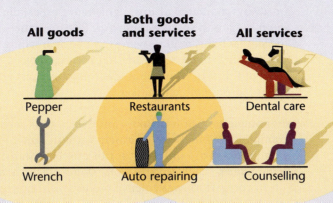

value. The person who buys a plane ride on Air Canada is looking for a quick way to get from one city to another (the benefit). Providing this benefit requires goods (a plane) and services (ticketing, maintenance, piloting).

Marketers must know how consumers view the types of product their companies sell, so that they can design the marketing mix to appeal to the selected target market. To help them define target markets, marketers have devised product categories. Products that are bought by the end user are called *consumer products* (e.g., razors, sandwiches, cars, stereos, magazines, and houses). Consumer products that get used up, such as Lay's potato chips, are called *consumer non-durables*. Those that last for a long time, such as Kenmore washing machines and Apple computers, are *consumer durables*.

Another way to classify consumer products is by the amount of effort consumers are willing to make to acquire them. The four major categories of consumer products are unsought products, convenience products, shopping products, and specialty products, as summarized in Exhibit 13.3.

EXHIBIT 13.3 > Classification of Consumer Products by the Effort Expended to Buy Them

Consumer Product	Examples	Degree of Effort Expended by Consumer
Unsought products	Life insurance Burial plots New products	No effort
Convenience products	Soft drinks Bread Milk Coffee	Very little or minimum effort
Shopping products	Automobiles Homes Vacations	Considerable effort
Specialty products	Expensive jewellery Gourmet dinners Limited-production automobiles	Maximum effort

unsought products
Products that either are unknown to the potential buyer or are known but not actively sought by the buyer.

convenience products
Relatively inexpensive items that require little shopping effort and are purchased routinely without planning.

shopping products
Items that are bought after considerable planning, including brand-to-brand and store-to-store comparisons of price, suitability, and style.

specialty products
Items for which consumers search long and hard, and for which they refuse to accept substitutes.

capital products
Large, expensive items with a long life span that are purchased by businesses for use in making other products or providing a service.

expense items
Items purchased by businesses that are smaller and less expensive than capital products and usually have a life span of less than one year.

CONCEPT in Action >>>

After seeing the Scooba floor-washing robot in action, consumers may never want to touch a mop again. The self-propelled circular bot navigates around hard surfaces, washing and scrubbing floors so they shine like new. A follow-up to the popular Roomba vacuum, Scooba sweeps loose debris, sprays cleaning solution, scrubs surfaces with a brush, and sucks up dirty water—all on its own. How do marketers classify products like the Scooba floor-cleaning robot?

Unsought products are products unknown to the potential buyer or known products that the buyer does not actively seek. New products fall into this category until advertising and distribution increase consumer awareness of them. Some goods are always marketed as unsought items, especially products we do not like to think about or care to spend money on. Life insurance, cemetery plots, medical services, and similar items require aggressive personal selling and highly persuasive advertising. Salespeople actively seek leads to potential buyers. Because consumers usually do not seek out this type of product, the company must go directly to them through a salesperson, direct mail, telemarketing, or direct-response advertising.

Convenience products are relatively inexpensive items that require little shopping effort. Soft drinks, candy bars, milk, bread, and small hardware items are examples. We buy them routinely without much planning. This does not mean that such products are unimportant or obscure. Many, in fact, are well known by their brand names—such as Pepsi-Cola, Domino's Pizza, and UPS shipping.

In contrast to convenience products, **shopping products** are bought only after a brand-to-brand and store-to-store comparison of price, suitability, and style. Examples are furniture, automobiles, a vacation in Europe, and some items of clothing. Convenience products are bought with little planning, but shopping products might be chosen months or even years before their actual purchase.

Specialty products are products for which consumers search long and hard, and for which they refuse to accept substitutes. Expensive jewellery, designer clothing, state-of-the-art stereo equipment, limited-production automobiles, and gourmet dinners fall into this category. Because consumers are willing to spend much time and effort to find specialty products, distribution is often limited to one or two sellers in a given region, such as Holt Renfrew, Gucci, or the Porsche dealer.

Classifying Business Products

Products bought by businesses or institutions for use in making other products or in providing services are called *business* or *industrial products*. They are classified as either capital products or expense items. **Capital products** are usually large, expensive items with a long life span. Examples are buildings, large machines, and airplanes. **Expense items** are typically smaller, less expensive items that usually have a life span of less than a year. Examples are printer cartridges and paper. Industrial products are sometimes further classified in the following categories:

- *Installations.* These are large, expensive capital items that determine the nature, scope, and efficiency of a company. Capital products like the Ford assembly plant represent a big commitment against future earnings and profitability. Buying an installation requires longer negotiations, more planning, and the judgments of more people than buying any other type of product.
- *Accessories.* Accessories do not have the same long-run impact on the firm as installations, and they are less expensive and more standardized, but they are still capital products. Xerox copy machines, IBM personal computers (PCs), and smaller machines such as Black & Decker table drills and saws are typical accessories. Marketers of accessories often rely on well-known brand names and extensive advertising as well as personal selling.
- *Component parts and materials.* These are expense items that are built into the end product. Some component parts are custom-made, such as a drive shaft for an automobile, a case for a computer, or a special pigment for painting harbour buoys; others are standardized for sale to many industrial users. Intel processors for computers and cement for the construction trade are examples of standardized component parts and materials.
- *Raw materials.* Raw materials are expense items that have undergone little or no processing and are used to create a final product. Examples include lumber, copper, and zinc.

- *Supplies.* Supplies do not become part of the final product. They are bought routinely and in fairly large quantities. Supply items run the gamut from pencils and paper to paint and machine oil. They have little impact on the firm's long-run profits. Bic pens, Unisource copier paper, and Pennzoil machine oil are typical supply items.
- *Services.* These are expense items used to plan or support company operations; for example janitorial cleaning and management consulting.

The Product Life Cycle

product life cycle
The pattern of sales and profits over time for a product or product category; consists of an introductory stage, growth stage, maturity, and decline (and death).

Product managers create marketing mixes for their products as they move through the life cycle. The **product life cycle** is a pattern of sales and profits over time for a product (Sunlight dishwashing liquid) or a product category (liquid detergents). As the product moves through the stages of the life cycle, the firm must keep revising the marketing mix to stay competitive and meet the needs of target customers.

Stages of the Life Cycle

As illustrated in Exhibit 13.4, the product life cycle consists of the following stages.

1. *Introduction.* When a product enters the life cycle, it faces many obstacles. Although competition might be light, the *introductory stage* usually features frequent product modifications, limited distribution, and heavy promotion. The failure rate is high. Production and marketing costs are also high, and sales volume is low. Hence, profits are usually small or negative.
2. *Growth stage.* If a product survives the introductory stage, it advances to the *growth stage* of the life cycle. In this stage, sales grow at an increasing rate, profits are healthy, and many competitors enter the market. Large companies might start to acquire small pioneering firms that have reached this stage. Emphasis switches from primary demand promotion to aggressive brand advertising and communicating the differences between brands. For example, the goal changes from convincing people to buy compact DVD players to convincing them to buy Sony versus Panasonic or Sharp.

   Distribution becomes a major key to success during the growth stage, as well as in later stages. Manufacturers scramble to acquire dealers and distributors and to build long-term relationships. Without adequate distribution, it is impossible to establish a strong market position.

   Toward the end of the growth phase, prices normally begin falling and profits peak. Price reductions result from increased competition and from cost reductions from producing larger quantities of items (economies of scale). As well, most firms have recovered their development costs by now, and their priority is in increasing or retaining market share and enhancing profits.
3. *Maturity.* After the growth stage, sales continue to mount—but at a decreasing rate. This is the *maturity stage.* Most products that have been on the market for a long time are in this stage. Thus, most marketing strategies are designed for mature products. One such strategy is to bring out several variations of a basic product (line extension). Kool-Aid, for instance, was originally offered in six flavours. Today there are many flavours, as well as sweetened and unsweetened varieties.
4. *Decline (and death).* When sales and profits fall, the product has reached the decline stage. The rate of decline is governed by two factors: the rate of change in consumer tastes and the rate at which new products enter the market. An example of a product that is at the death stage in Canada is the VCR player. The demand for VCRs is virtually nil (except those that have tapes that have not been converted to DVD).

EXHIBIT 13.4 > Sales and Profits During the Product Life Cycle

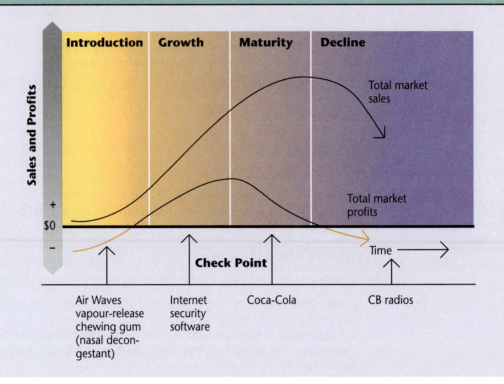

The Product Life Cycle as a Management Tool

The product life cycle can be used in planning. Marketers who understand the cycle concept are better able to forecast future sales and plan new marketing strategies. Exhibit 13.5 is a brief summary of strategic needs at various stages of the product life cycle. Marketers must be sure that a product has moved from one stage to the next before changing the company's marketing strategy. A temporary sales decline should not be interpreted as a sign that the product is dying. Pulling back marketing support can become a self-fulfilling prophecy that brings about the early death of a healthy product.

EXHIBIT 13.5 > Strategies for Success at Each Stage of the Product Life Cycle

Category	Introduction	Growth	Maturity	Decline
Marketing objectives	Encourage trial, establish distribution	Get triers to repurchase, attract new users	Seek new users or uses	Reduce marketing expenses, keep loyal users
Product	Establish competitive advantage	Maintain product quality	Modify product	Maintain product
Distribution	Establish distribution network	Solidify distribution relationships	Provide additional incentives to ensure support	Eliminate trade allowances
Promotional	Build brand awareness	Provide information	Reposition product	Eliminate most advertising and sales promotions
Pricing	Set introductory price (skimming or penetration pricing)	Maintain prices	Reduce prices to meet competition	Maintain prices

Pricing Products Right

LO 3

An important part of the product development process is setting the right price. Price is the perceived value that is exchanged for something else. Value in our society is most commonly expressed in dollars and cents. Thus, price is typically the amount of money exchanged for a good or service. Note that perceived value refers to the time of the transaction. After you've used a product you've bought, you may decide that its actual value was less than its perceived value at the time you bought it. The price you pay for a product is based on the expected satisfaction you will receive and not necessarily the actual satisfaction you will receive.

Although price is usually a dollar amount, it can be anything with perceived value. When goods and services are exchanged for each other, the trade is called barter. If you exchange this book for a math book at the end of the term, you have engaged in barter.

Pricing Objectives

Price is important in determining how much a firm earns. The prices charged customers times the number of units sold equals the gross revenue for the firm. Revenue is what pays for every activity of the company (production, finance, sales, distribution, and so forth). What's left over (if anything) is profit. Managers strive to charge a price that will allow the firm to earn a fair return on its investment.

The chosen price must be neither too high nor too low. And the price must equal the perceived value to target consumers. If consumers think the price is too high, sales opportunities will be lost. Lost sales mean lost revenue. If the price is too low, consumers may view the product as a great value, but the company may not meet its profit goals. Three common pricing objectives are maximizing profits, achieving a target return on the investment, and offering good value at a fair price.

Maximizing Profits

profit maximization
A pricing objective that entails getting the largest possible profit from a product by producing it for as long as the revenue from selling the product exceeds the cost of producing it.

Profit maximization means producing a product for as long as the revenue from selling it exceeds the cost of producing it. In other words, the goal is to get the largest possible profit from the product. For example, suppose Carl Morgan, a builder of houses, sells each house for $300,000. His revenue and cost projections are shown in Exhibit 13.6. Notice in column 3 that the cost of building each house drops for the second through the fifth house. The lower cost per house results from two things: First, by having several houses under construction at the same time, Morgan can afford to hire a full-time crew. The crew is more economical than the independent contractors to whom he would otherwise subcontract each task. Second, Morgan can order materials in greater quantities than usual and thus get quantity discounts on his orders.

Morgan decides that he could sell 15 houses a year at the $300,000 price. But he knows he cannot maximize profits at more than seven houses a year. Inefficiencies begin to creep in at the sixth house. (Notice in column 3 that the sixth house costs more to build than any of the first five houses.) Morgan can't supervise more than seven construction jobs at once, and his full-time crew can't handle even those seven. Thus, Morgan has to subcontract some of the work on the sixth and seventh houses. To build more than seven houses, he would need a second full-time crew.

The exhibit also shows why Morgan should construct seven houses a year. Even though the profit per house is falling for the sixth and seventh houses (column 4), the total profit is still rising (column 5). But at the eighth house, Morgan would go beyond profit maximization. That is, the eighth unit would cost more than its selling price. He would lose $15,000 on the house, and total profit would fall to $154,000 from $169,000 after the seventh house.

EXHIBIT 13.6 > Revenue, Cost, and Profit Projections for Morgan's Houses

(1) Unit of Output (House)	(2) Selling Price (Revenue)	(3) Cost of Building House	(4) Profit on House	(5) Total Profit
1st	$ 300,000	$ 276,000	$ 24,000	$ 24,000
2nd	300,000	275,000	25,000	49,000
3rd	300,000	273,000	27,000	76,000
4th	300,000	270,000	30,000	106,000
5th	300,000	270,000	30,000	136,000
6th	300,000	277,000	23,000	159,000
7th	300,000	290,000	10,000	169,000
8th	300,000	315,000	(15,000)	154,000

Achieving a Target Return on Investment

target return on investment
A pricing objective where the price of a product is set so as to give the company the desired profitability in terms of return on its money.

Another pricing objective used by many companies is **target return on investment,** whereby a price is set to give the company the desired profitability in terms of return on its money. Among the companies that use target return on investment as their main pricing objective are 3M, Procter & Gamble, General Electric, and DuPont.

To get an idea of how target return works, imagine that you are a marketing manager for a cereal company. You estimate that developing, launching, and marketing a new hot cereal will cost $2 million. If the net profit for the first year is $200,000, the return on investment will be $200,000 ÷ $2,000,000, or 10 percent. Let's say that top management sets a 15 percent target return on investment. As a net profit of $200,000 will yield only a 10 percent return, one of two things will happen: Either the cereal won't be produced, or the price and marketing mix will be changed to yield the 15 percent target return.

CONCEPT *in Action* >>>

Some automobile makers have announced Employee-Discount-for-Everyone prices that boosted car sales. But when the bargain blowout ended, so did sales, leaving automakers with an inventory hangover and the need to re-examine their pricing strategies. Some manufacturers switched to value pricing, slashing prices across the board while abandoning incentives like employee discounts and zero-percent financing. Why might some car buyers prefer value pricing to traditional price haggling?

ALAMY

Value Pricing

value pricing
A pricing strategy in which the target market is offered a high-quality product at a fair price and with good service.

Value pricing has become a popular pricing strategy. **Value pricing** means offering the target market a high-quality product at a fair price and with good service. It is the notion of offering the customer a good value. Value pricing doesn't mean high quality that's available only at high prices, nor does it mean bare-bones service or low-quality products. Value pricing can be used to sell a variety of products, from a $30,000 Jeep Wrangler to a $1.99 package of dinner napkins.

A value marketer does the following:

- *Offers products that perform.* This is the price of entry because consumers have lost patience with shoddy merchandise.
- *Gives consumers more than they expect.* Soon after Toyota launched Lexus, the company had to order a recall. The weekend before the recall, dealers phoned every Lexus owner that was affected and arranged to pick up their cars and provide replacement vehicles.
- *Gives meaningful guarantees.* Hyundai offers a five year, 100,000 kilometre power train protection. Michelin recently introduced a tire warranted to last 140,000 kilometres.
- *Gives the buyer facts.* Today's sophisticated consumer wants informative advertising and knowledgeable salespeople.
- *Builds long-term relationships.* The Aeroplan program, Hyatt's Passport Club, and Moen's 800-number hotline all help build good customer relations.

> **concept check**
>
> Explain the concept of price.
>
> What is meant by target return on investment, and how does it differ from profit maximization?
>
> What is value pricing?

How Managers Set Prices

After establishing a pricing objective, managers must set a specific price for the product. Two techniques that are often used to set a price are markup pricing and breakeven analysis.

Markup Pricing

markup pricing
A method of pricing in which a certain percentage (the markup) is added to the product's cost to arrive at the price.

One of the most common forms of pricing is **markup pricing.** In this method, a certain dollar amount is added to a product's cost to arrive at the retail price. (The retail price is thus *cost plus markup*.) The cost is the expense of manufacturing the product or acquiring it for resale. The markup is the amount added to the cost to cover expenses and leave a profit. For the purpose of discussion, there can be two types of markup pricing: one on cost and one on selling price.

For example, if Banana Boat suntan cream costs Shoppers Drug Mart $8 and sells for $11:

based on cost or markup-on-cost,

$$\text{markup amount} = \frac{\text{markup percentage}}{\text{item cost}} \text{ or } \frac{3}{8} = 37.5\%$$

based on selling price or markup-on-selling-price,

$$\text{markup amount} = \frac{\text{markup percentage}}{\text{selling price}} \text{ or } \frac{3}{11} = 27.3\%$$

Several elements influence markups. Among them are tradition, the competition, store image, and stock turnover. Traditionally, department stores used a 40 percent markup. But today, competition and economic conditions have forced retailers to respond to consumer demand and meet competitors' prices. A department store that tried to sell household appliances at a 40 percent markup would lose customers to discounters such as Wal-Mart. However, a retailer trying to develop a prestige image will use markups that are much higher than those used by a retailer trying to develop an image as a discounter.

CONCEPT *in Action* >>>

In recent years, gas prices have soared and fallen. Top producers have defended their pricing methods, citing global demand and political instability as causes of pain at the pump. What are some reasons gas prices rise and fall?

AP/WIDE WORLD PHOTOS

Breakeven Analysis

breakeven point
The price at which a product's costs are covered, so additional sales result in profit.

fixed costs
Costs that do not vary with different levels of output; for example, rent.

variable costs
Costs that change with different levels of output; for example, wages and cost of raw materials.

fixed-cost contribution
The selling price per unit (revenue) minus the variable costs per unit.

total revenue
The selling price per unit times the number of units sold.

total cost
The sum of the fixed costs and the variable costs.

total profit
Total revenue minus total cost.

HOT Links

Companies are turning to Web-based, smart-pricing software to improve margins on products. Find out how one company's software works at Oracle's website, (**www.oracle.com**).

Manufacturers, wholesalers (companies that buy from manufacturers and sell to retailers and institutions), and retailers (firms that sell to end users) need to know how much of a product must be sold at a certain price to cover all costs. The point at which the costs are covered and additional sales result in profit is the **breakeven point**.

To find the breakeven point, the firm measures the various costs associated with the product:

- **Fixed costs** do not vary with different levels of output. The rent on a manufacturing facility is a fixed cost. It must be paid whether production is one unit or a million.
- **Variable costs** change with different levels of output. Wages and expenses of raw materials are considered variable costs.
- The **fixed-cost contribution** is the selling price per unit (revenue) minus the variable costs per unit.
- **Total revenue** is the selling price per unit times the number of units sold.
- **Total cost** is the total of the fixed costs and the variable costs.
- **Total profit** is total revenue minus total cost.

Knowing these amounts, the firm can calculate the breakeven point:

Breakeven point in units = Total fixed cost ÷ Fixed cost contribution

Let's see how this works: Gray Corporation, a manufacturer of aftershave lotion, has variable costs of $3 per bottle and fixed costs of $50,000. Gray's management believes the company can sell up to 100,000 bottles of aftershave at $5 a bottle without having to lower its price. Gray's fixed-cost contribution is $2 ($5 selling price per bottle minus $3 variable costs per bottle). Therefore, $2 per bottle is the amount that can be used to cover the company's fixed costs of $50,000.

To determine its breakeven point, Gray applies the previous equation:

$$\text{Breakeven point in bottles} = \frac{\$50{,}000 \text{ fixed cost}}{\$2 \text{ fixed-cost contribution}}$$

$$= 25{,}000 \text{ bottles}$$

Gray Corporation will, therefore, break even when it sells 25,000 bottles of aftershave lotion. After that point, at which the fixed costs are met, the $2 per bottle becomes profit. If Gray's forecasts are correct and it can sell 100,000 bottles at $5 a bottle, its total profit will be $150,000 ($2 per bottle × 75,000 bottles).

By using the equation, Gray Corp. can quickly find out how much it needs to sell to break even. It can then calculate how much profit it will earn if it sells more units. A firm that is operating close to the breakeven point might change the profit picture in two ways. Reducing costs will lower the breakeven point and expand profits. Increasing sales will not change the breakeven point, but it will provide more profits.

Product Pricing Strategies

Managers use various pricing strategies when determining the price of a product, as we explain in this section. Price skimming and penetration pricing are strategies used in pricing new products; other strategies, such as leader pricing and bundling, might be used for established products as well.

Price Skimming

price skimming
The strategy of introducing a product with a high initial price and lowering the price over time as the product moves through its life cycle.

The practice of introducing a new product on the market with a high price and then lowering the price over time is called **price skimming**. As the product moves through its life cycle, the price usually is lowered because competitors are entering the market. As the price falls, more and more consumers can buy the product.

Price skimming has four important advantages. First, a high initial price can be a way to find out what buyers are willing to pay. Second, if consumers find the introductory price too high, it can be lowered. Third, a high introductory price can create an image of quality and prestige. Fourth, when the price is lowered later, consumers might think they are getting a bargain. The disadvantage is that high prices attract competition.

Price skimming can be used to price virtually any new product, such as high-definition televisions, PCs, and colour computer printers. For example, the Republic of Tea has launched new Imperial Republic White Tea, which it says is among the rarest of teas. Because it is minimally processed, white tea is said to retain the highest level of antioxidants and has less caffeine than black and green teas. The company says the tea is picked only a few days each year, right before the leaves open, yielding a small harvest. The product retails for $14 per tin of 50 bags. Products don't have to be expensive to use a skimming strategy.

Penetration Pricing

penetration pricing
The strategy of selling new products at low prices in the hope of achieving a large sales volume.

A company that doesn't use price skimming will probably use **penetration pricing**. With this strategy, the company offers new products at low prices in the hope of achieving a large sales volume. Procter & Gamble did this with SpinBrush. Penetration pricing requires more extensive planning than skimming does, because the company must gear up for mass production and marketing. If the company significantly overestimates demand, its losses are considerable.

Penetration pricing has two advantages. First, the low initial price might induce consumers to switch brands or companies. Using penetration pricing on its jug wines, Gallo has lured customers away from Taylor California Cellars and Inglenook. Second, penetration pricing might discourage competitors from entering the market. Their costs would tend to be higher, so they would need to sell more at the same price to break even.

© AP/WIDE WORLD PHOTOS

Leader Pricing

leader pricing
The strategy of pricing products below the normal markup or even below cost to attract customers to a store where they would not otherwise shop.

loss leader
A product priced below cost as part of a leader pricing strategy.

Pricing products below the normal markup or even below cost to attract customers to a store where they wouldn't otherwise shop is **leader pricing.** A product priced below cost is referred to as a **loss leader.** The customers go to the retailer and will often purchase many other products that are competitively priced, not just the loss leader. Retailers hope that this type of pricing will increase their overall sales volume and thus their profit.

Items that are leader priced are usually well known and priced low enough to appeal to many customers. They also are items that consumers will buy at a lower price, even if they have to switch brands. Supermarkets often feature coffee and bacon in their leader pricing. Department stores and specialty stores also rely heavily on leader pricing.

Bundling

bundling
The strategy of grouping two or more related products together and pricing them as a single product.

Bundling means grouping two or more related products together and pricing them as a single product. Weston Hotels' special weekend rates often include the room, breakfast, and one night's dinner. Department stores might offer a washer and dryer together for a price lower than if the units were bought separately. Rogers Communications and Shaw Cable bundle services such as telephone, Internet, and television into one package. This is not only convenient for the customer but, as the next paragraph highlights, allows the companies to sell more products.

The idea behind bundling is to reach a segment of the market that the products sold separately would not reach as effectively. Some buyers are more than willing to buy one product but have much less use for the second. Bundling the second product to the first at a slightly reduced price thus creates some sales that otherwise would not be made. Aussie 3 Minute Miracle Shampoo is typically bundled with its conditioner, because many people use shampoo more than conditioner, so they don't need a new bottle of conditioner.

Odd-Even Pricing

odd-even (psychological) pricing
The strategy of setting a price at an odd number to connote a bargain and at an even number to suggest quality.

Psychology often plays a big role in how consumers view prices and what prices they will pay. **Odd-even pricing** (or **psychological pricing**) is the strategy of setting a price at an odd number to connote a bargain and at an even number to imply quality. For years, many retailers have priced their products in odd numbers—for example, $99.95 or $49.95—to make consumers feel that they are paying a lower price for the product.

Some retailers favour odd-numbered prices because they believe that $9.99 sounds much less imposing to customers than $10.00. Other retailers believe that an odd-numbered price signals to consumers that the price is at the lowest level possible, thereby encouraging them to buy more units. Neither theory has ever been proved conclusively, although one study found that consumers perceive odd-priced products as being on sale. Even-numbered pricing is sometimes used to denote quality. Examples include a fine perfume at $100 a bottle, a good watch at $500, or a Holt Renfrew coat at $3,000.

prestige pricing
The strategy of increasing the price of a product so that consumers will perceive it as being of higher quality, status, or value.

Prestige Pricing

The strategy of raising the price of a product so consumers will perceive it as being of higher quality, status, or value is called **prestige pricing.** This type of pricing is common where high prices indicate high status. In the specialty shops on Rodeo Drive in Beverly Hills, which cater to the super-rich of Hollywood, shirts that would sell for $40 elsewhere sell for at least $150. If the price were lower, customers would perceive them as being of low quality.

concept check

What is the difference between penetration pricing and price skimming?

Explain the concept of price bundling.

Describe odd-even pricing and prestige pricing.

The Nature and Functions of Distribution

 LO 4

distribution (logistics)
Efficiently managing the acquisition of raw materials to the factory and the movement of products from the producer to industrial users and consumers.

manufacturer
A producer; an organization that converts raw materials to finished products.

Distribution (or logistics) is efficiently managing the acquisition of raw materials to the factory and the movement of products from the producer or **manufacturer** to industrial users and consumers. Logistics activities are usually the responsibility of the marketing department and are part of the large series of activities included in the supply chain. As discussed in Chapter 11, a supply chain is the system through which an organization acquires raw material, produces products, and delivers the products and services to its customers. Exhibit 13.7 illustrates a supply chain. Supply chain management helps increase the efficiency of logistics service by minimizing inventory and moving goods efficiently from producers to the ultimate users.

EXHIBIT 13.7 > Supply Chain

Suppliers of raw materials

CD factory

Finished product

Wholesaler or distribution center

Retailers, wholesalers distribution centres

Customers

On their way from producers to end users and consumers, goods and services pass through a series of marketing entities known as a distribution channel. We will look first at the entities that make up a **distribution channel** and then will examine the functions that channels serve.

Marketing Intermediaries in the Distribution Channel

A distribution channel is made up of **marketing intermediaries**, or organizations that assist in moving goods and services from producers to end users and consumers. Marketing intermediaries are in the middle of the distribution process between the producer and the end user. The following marketing intermediaries most often appear in the distribution channel:

- *Agents and brokers*. Agents are sales representatives of manufacturers and wholesalers, and brokers are entities that bring buyers and sellers together. Both agents and brokers are usually hired on commission basis by either a buyer or a seller. Agents and brokers are go-betweens whose job is to make deals. They do not own or take possession of goods.
- *Industrial distributors*. Industrial distributors are independent wholesalers that buy related product lines from many manufacturers and sell them to industrial users. They often have a sales force to call on purchasing agents, make deliveries, extend credit, and provide information. Industrial distributors are used in such industries as aircraft manufacturing, mining, and petroleum.
- *Wholesalers*. Wholesalers are firms that sell finished goods to retailers, manufacturers, and institutions (such as schools and hospitals). Historically, their function has been to buy from manufacturers and sell to retailers.
- *Retailers*. Retailers are firms that sell goods to consumers and to industrial users for their own consumption.

At the end of the distribution channel are final consumers, like you and me, and industrial users. Industrial users are firms that buy products for internal use or for producing other products or services. They include manufacturers, utilities, airlines, railroads, and service institutions, such as hotels, hospitals, and schools.

Exhibit 13.8 shows various ways marketing intermediaries can be linked. For instance, a manufacturer may sell to a wholesaler that sells to a retailer that in turn sells to a customer. In any of these distribution systems, goods and services are physically transferred from one organization to the next. As each takes possession of the products, it may take legal ownership of them. As the exhibit indicates, distribution channels can handle either consumer products or industrial products.

Alternative Channel Arrangements

Rarely does a producer use just one type of channel to move its product. It usually employs several different or alternative channels, which include multiple channels, non-traditional channels, and strategic channel alliances.[1]

Multiple Channels   When a producer selects two or more channels to distribute the same product to target markets, this arrangement is called **dual distribution (or multiple distribution)**. For example, Avon, a direct supplier of health and beauty products for women, offers consumers four alternatives for purchasing products. They can contact a representative in person (the original business model), purchase on the Web, order direct from the company, or pick up products at an Avon Salon & Spa. With Avon, identical products are being distributed to existing markets using more than one channel of distribution.

Dual channels don't always work out as planned. Tupperware finally stopped a 15-year slide in sales with new booths at shopping malls and a push onto the Internet. New buzz led to more Tupperware parties where salespeople set up shop in

---

distribution channel
The series of marketing entities through which goods and services pass on their way from producers to end users.

marketing intermediaries
Organizations that assist in moving goods and services from producers to end users.

agents
Sales representatives of manufacturers and wholesalers.

brokers
Go-betweens that bring buyers and sellers together.

industrial distributors
Independent wholesalers that buy related product lines from many manufacturers and sell them to industrial users.

wholesalers
Firms that sell finished goods to retailers, manufacturers, and institutions.

retailers
Firms that sell goods to consumers and to industrial users for their own consumption.

dual distribution (or multiple distribution)
Two or more channels that distribute the same product to target markets.

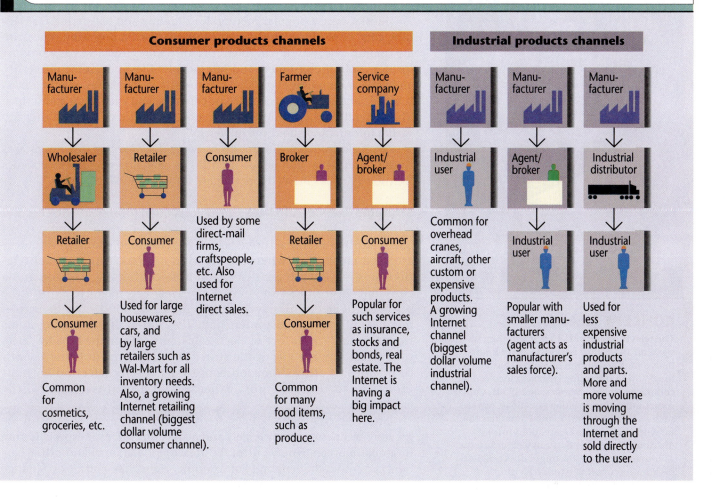

people's living rooms to show off plastic food storage containers and such. Then the company decided to place Tupperware in some stores with salespeople in the aisles to demonstrate the merchandise. It looked like the answer to a chronic problem: how to sell face-to-face in an era when shoppers don't have time for a door-to-door sales pitch. Tupperware also figured the move would give it a stream of potential party hosts and sales-force recruits.

But moving into stores turned out to be one of the worst disasters ever at Tupperware. It was so easy to find the company's products that interest in its parties plummeted. Fewer parties meant fewer chances to land other parties and new salespeople—which Tupperware needs to offset turnover that often hits 100 percent a year.[2]

Non-traditional Channels   Often non-traditional channel arrangements help differentiate a firm's product from the competition. For example, manufacturers may decide to use non-traditional channels such as the Internet, mail-order channels, or infomercials to sell products instead of going through traditional retailer channels. Although non-traditional channels may limit a brand's coverage, they can give a producer serving a niche market a way to gain market access and customer attention without having to establish channel intermediaries. Non-traditional channels can also provide another avenue of sales for larger firms. For example, a London publisher sells short stories through vending machines in the London

Underground. Instead of the traditional book format, the stories are printed like folded maps making them an easy-to-read alternative for commuters.

Kiosks, long a popular method for ordering and registering for wedding gifts, dispersing cash through ATMs, and facilitating airline check-in, are finding new uses. Ethan Allen furniture stores use kiosks as a product locator tool for consumers and salespeople. Kiosks on some university and college campuses allow students to register for classes, see their class schedule and grades, check account balances, and even print transcripts. The general public, when it has access to the kiosks, can use them to gather information about the university.

With electronic media rapidly evolving, downloading first-run movies to cell phones may not be too far off! The changing world of electronics technology opens many doors for new, non-traditional channels.

Strategic Channel Alliances   Producers often form **strategic channel alliances** which enable the producers to deliver products and services using another manufacturer's already-established channel. Alliances are used most often when the creation of marketing channel relationships may be too expensive and time-consuming. Amazon and a consumer electronics store have a multiyear agreement to expand the selection of electronics available on Amazon.com. Under the agreement, Amazon.com customers have the option of purchasing items from Amazon's inventory of electronic items or from the broader selection offered by the electronic store. The arrangement benefits both companies: it allows Amazon.com to deepen its selection without increasing its own inventory expense, and it increases sales for the electronics store.

Strategic channel alliances are proving to be more successful for growing businesses than mergers and acquisitions. This is especially true in global markets where cultural differences, distance, and other barriers can prove challenging. For example, Heinz has a strategic alliance with Kagome, one of Japan's largest food companies. The companies are

© TERRI MILLER/E-VISUAL COMMUNICATIONS INC.

CONCEPT *in Action* >>>

The television networks are scrambling to stave off the end of television as we know it, as a new generation of viewers has taken to watching streaming Internet video on computers, mobile phones, and iPods. Consumer migration to video download services such as YouTube, In2TV, and iTunes has the networks rushing to create multi-format distribution systems that can deliver Internet TV programming. How might direct digital distribution upset network television's traditional distribution channel?

CONCEPT *in Action* >>>

Cabela's started as a two-person, direct-mail operation in the early 1960s. Today, the outdoor outfitter is the world's largest direct marketer and specialty retailer of hunting, fishing, and related merchandise. In addition to operating its famed catalogue business, Cabela's now sells goods to customers through the Internet and at retail superstores. Cabela's showrooms bring the outdoors inside—the stores' museum-quality displays of wildlife, fishing ponds, and mountain replicas are veritable tourist attractions. What logistical challenges arise from using multiple distribution channels?

© AP/WIDE WORLD PHOTOS

CONCEPT *in Action* >>>

An efficient distribution system allows Home Depot to offer customers a vast assortment of building materials, appliances, and tools economically. What do you think the distribution channels for Home Depot are?

strategic channel alliances
One manufacturer using another manufacturer's previously established channel to distribute its goods.

working together to find ways to reduce operating costs while expanding both brands' market presence globally.

The Functions of Distribution Channels

Why do distribution channels exist? Why can't every firm sell its products directly to the end user or consumer? Why are go-betweens needed? Channels serve a number of functions.

Channels Reduce the Number of Transactions   Channels make distribution simpler by reducing the number of transactions required to get a product from the manufacturer to the consumer. Assume for the moment that only four students are in your class. Also assume that your professor requires five textbooks, each from a different publisher. If there were no bookstore, 20 transactions would be necessary for all students in the class to buy the books, as shown in Exhibit 13.9. If the bookstore serves as a go-between, the number of transactions is reduced to nine. Each publisher sells to one bookstore rather than to four students. Each student buys from one bookstore instead of from five publishers.

Dealing with channel intermediaries frees producers from many of the details of distribution activity. Producers are traditionally not as efficient or as enthusiastic about selling products directly to end users as channel members are. First, producers may wish to focus on production. They may feel that they cannot both produce and distribute in a competitive way. On the other hand, manufacturers are eager to deal directly with larger retailers, such as Sport Chek. Sport Chek offers huge sales opportunities to producers.

Channels Ease the Flow of Goods   Channels make distribution easier in several ways. The first is by sorting, which consists of the following:

- *Sorting out*. Breaking many different items into separate stocks that are similar. Eggs, for instance, are sorted by grade and size.
- *Accumulating*. Bringing similar stocks together into a larger quantity. Twelve large Grade A eggs could be placed in some cartons and 12 medium Grade B eggs in other cartons.
- *Allocating*. Breaking similar products into smaller and smaller lots. (Allocating at the wholesale level is called **breaking bulk**.) For instance, a tank-car load of milk could be broken down into gallon jugs. The process of allocating generally is done when the goods are dispersed by region and as ownership of the goods changes.

breaking bulk
The process of breaking large shipments of similar products into smaller, more usable lots.

EXHIBIT 13.9 > How Distribution Channels Reduce the Number of Transactions

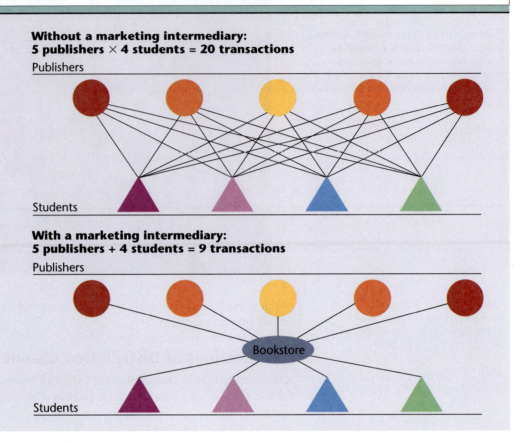

Without a marketing intermediary:
5 publishers $\times$ 4 students = 20 transactions
Publishers

Students

With a marketing intermediary:
5 publishers + 4 students = 9 transactions
Publishers

Bookstore

Students

Without the sorting, accumulating, and allocating processes, modern society would not exist. We would have home-based industries providing custom or semicustom products to local markets. In short, we would return to a much lower level of consumption.

A second way channels ease the flow of goods is by locating buyers for merchandise. A wholesaler must find the right retailers to sell a profitable volume of merchandise. A sporting-goods wholesaler, for instance, must find the retailers who are most likely to reach sporting-goods consumers. Retailers have to understand the buying habits of consumers and put stores where consumers want and expect to find the merchandise. Every member of a distribution channel must locate buyers for the products it is trying to sell.

Channel members also store merchandise so that goods are available when consumers want to buy them. The high cost of retail space often means that many goods are stored by the wholesaler or the manufacturer.

Channels Perform Needed Functions   The functions performed by channel intermediaries help increase the efficiency of the channel. Yet consumers sometimes feel that the go-betweens create higher prices. They doubt that these intermediaries perform useful functions. Actually, however, if channel intermediaries did not perform important and necessary functions at a reasonable cost, they would cease to exist. If firms could earn a higher profit without using certain channel members, they would not use them.

Channel intermediaries perform three general functions: transactional, logistical, and facilitating. We have already discussed logistics. Transactional functions involve contacting and communicating with prospective buyers to make them aware of goods and services that are available. Sellers attempt to explain why their offerings provide more features, benefits, and value than the competition. The third function is facili-

EXHIBIT 13.10 > Marketing Channel Functions Performed by Intermediaries

Type of Function	Description
Transaction Functions	**Contacting and promoting:** Contacting potential customers, promoting products, and soliciting orders **Negotiating:** Determining how many goods or services to buy and sell, type of transportation to use, when to deliver, and method and timing of payment **Risk taking:** Assuming the risk of owning inventory
Logistical Functions	**Physically distributing:** Transporting and sorting goods **Storing:** Maintaining inventories and protecting goods **Sorting out:** Breaking down a heterogeneous supply into separate homogeneous stocks **Accumulation:** Combining similar stocks into a larger homogeneous supply **Allocation:** Breaking a homogeneous supply into smaller and smaller lots ("breaking bulk") **Assortment:** Combining products into collections or assortments that buyers want available at one place
Facilitating Functions	**Researching:** Gathering information about other channel members and consumers **Financing:** Extending credit and other financial services to facilitate the flow of goods through the channel to the final consumer

tating, which includes financing and market research. Research answers questions such as who is buying the products, where do they like to buy the items, and what are the characteristics of the users. The three basic functions that channel intermediaries perform are summarized in Exhibit 13.10.

A useful rule to remember is that, although channel intermediaries can be eliminated, their functions cannot. The manufacturer must either perform the functions of the intermediaries itself or find new ways of getting them carried out. Publishers can bypass bookstores, for instance, but the function performed by the bookstores then has to be performed by the publishers or by someone else.

concept check

List and define the marketing intermediaries that make up a distribution channel.

Provide an example of a strategic channel alliance.

How do channels reduce the number of transactions?

Expanding Around The Globe

EASY DOES IT ALL

It's just after midnight on the French Riviera, and while the rich and famous sip champagne in Cannes at the annual film festival, something unsightly and orange cruises into the harbour and plops down its anchor among the majestic yachts. An enormous "EasyCruise.com" logo runs down the length of the ship, with all the subtlety of a flashing neon sign. This is the maiden voyage of a new concept in budget cruising, the 14th venture of low-cost superbrand EasyGroup.

The Easy empire was built on experiments in low-cost living like EasyCruise, and life on the inside is a study in value trumping aesthetics. The company is the brainchild of 38-year-old Greek shipping heir Stelios Haji-Ioannou, who popped up on the international radar screen in 1995 when he founded budget airline EasyJet at the tender age of 28. Now, he is merrily slapping the Easy brand on an almost unlimited array of discount products and services, many of which seem to have little in common. There are Easy movie rentals and an Easy shaving cream. There are Easy Internet cafes, Easy pizzas, and an Easy hotel. There's even an Easy wristwatch. "In an industry where consumers are being ripped off, if I can find a way to give them real value, I'm going to do it," he says.

It's an audacious—some would say delusional—notion. But then, nobody thought Stelios had much of a chance with his low-cost debut, the airline. The airline is now fourth only to Lufthansa, Air France, and KLM in the number of passengers carried within Europe. And although

it's true that 11 of the other 14 Easy companies have yet to turn an annual profit, they're still young—half have existed for less than a year.

Competitors, however, often feel threatened by Easy's incursions. Stelios starts price wars almost everywhere he goes, and that has earned him plenty of detractors across many industries. "His assumption that he can take any idea and just slap his brand on it is somewhat arrogant," says Paolo Pescatore, a wireless analyst with research firm IDC. Easy's mobile-phone venture, launched in March, illustrates the typical pattern. It sells SIM cards that can be put into existing handsets and then charges for service. Its debut prices were as much as 40 percent below prevailing norms, and rival Carphone Warehouse countered with deep discounts of its own. Orange, a heavyweight in the United Kingdom, sued Easy—for using orange, the same colour that Orange uses in its ads.[3]

Critical Thinking Questions
- With 15 Easy brands on the market, in many different industries, do you think that Stelios has diversified too much? Is he destroying the mystique of the brand?
- Stelios says North America will be "Easy pickings" for the Easy Group. Do you agree? Why or why not?

SOURCE: "Easy Does It All," *Business 2.0*, August 2005, pg. 69–74. Copyright © Time Inc. All rights reserved. Reproduced by permission.

The Intensity of Market Coverage

exclusive distribution
A distribution system in which a manufacturer selects only one or two dealers in an area to market its products.

selective distribution
A distribution system in which a manufacturer selects a limited number of dealers in an area (but more than one or two) to market its products.

intensive distribution
A distribution system in which a manufacturer tries to sell its products wherever there are potential customers.

All types of distribution systems must be concerned with market coverage. How many dealers will be used to distribute the product in a particular area? The three degrees of coverage are exclusive, selective, and intensive. The type of product determines the intensity of the market coverage.

When a manufacturer selects one or two dealers in an area to market its products, it is using **exclusive distribution**. Only items that are in strong demand can be distributed exclusively because consumers must be willing to travel some distance to buy them. If Dentyne chewing gum were sold in only one drugstore per city, Dentyne would soon be out of business. However, Bang and Olufsen stereo components, Jaguar automobiles, and top name designer clothing are distributed exclusively with great success.

A manufacturer that chooses a limited number of dealers in an area (but more than one or two) is using **selective distribution**. Since the number of retailers handling the product is limited, consumers must be willing to seek it out. Timberland boots, a high-quality line of footwear, are distributed selectively. So are Sony televisions, Maytag washers, Waterford crystal, and Tommy Hilfiger clothing. When choosing dealers, manufacturers look for certain qualities. Sony may seek retailers that can offer high-quality customer service. Tommy Hilfiger may look for retailers with high-traffic locations in regional shopping malls. All manufacturers try to exclude retailers that are a poor credit risk or that have a weak or negative image.

A manufacturer that wants to sell its products everywhere there are potential customers is using **intensive distribution**. Such consumer goods as bread, tape, and light bulbs are often distributed intensively. Usually, these products cost little and are bought frequently, which means that complex distribution channels are necessary. Coca-Cola is sold in just about every type of retail business, from gas stations to grocery stores.

> **concept check**
>
> Name the three degrees of market coverage.
>
> Describe the types of products that are distributed using intensive distribution.

Supply Chain Management: Increasing Efficiency and Customer Satisfaction

Distribution is an important part of the marketing mix. Retailers don't sell products they can't deliver, and salespeople don't (or shouldn't) promise deliveries they can't make. Late deliveries and broken promises may mean loss of a customer. Accurate order filling and billing, timely delivery, and arrival in good condition are important to the success of the product.

The goal of supply chain management is to create a satisfied customer by coordinating all of the activities of the supply chain members into a seamless process. Therefore, an important element of supply chain management is that it is completely customer driven. In the mass-production era, manufacturers produced standardized products that were "pushed" down through the supply channel to the consumer. In today's marketplace by contrast, products are being driven by customers who expect to receive product configurations and services matched to their unique needs. For example, Dell only builds computers according to its customers' precise specifications, such as the amount of RAM memory; type of monitor, modem, or CD drive; and amount of hard-disk space. The process begins by Dell purchasing partly built laptops from contract manufacturers. The final assembly is done in Dell factories in Ireland, Malaysia, or China where microprocessors, software, and other key components are added. Those finished products are then shipped to Dell-operated distribution centres in Canada where they are packaged with other items and shipped to the customer.

Through the channel partnership, suppliers, manufacturers, wholesalers, and retailers along the entire supply chain work together toward the common goal of creating customer value. Supply chain management allows companies to respond with the unique product configuration and mix of services demanded by the customer. Today, supply chain management plays a dual role: first, as a communicator of customer demand that extends from the point of sale all the way back to the supplier, and second, as a physical flow process that engineers the timely and cost-effective movement of goods through the entire supply pipeline.

Accordingly, supply chain managers are responsible for making channel strategy decisions, coordinating the sourcing and procurement of raw materials, scheduling production, processing orders, managing inventory, transporting and storing supplies and finished goods, and coordinating customer service activities. Supply chain managers are also responsible for the management of information that flows through the supply chain. Coordinating the relationships between the company and its external partners, such as vendors, carriers and third-party companies, is also a critical function of supply chain management. Because supply chain managers play such a major role in both cost control and customer satisfaction, they are more valuable than ever.

Managing the Logistical Components of the Supply Chain

Logistics, discussed earlier, is a term borrowed from the military that describes the process of strategically managing the efficient flow and storage of raw materials, in-process inventory, and finished goods from the point of origin to the point of consumption. The supply chain team manages the logistical flow. Key decisions in managing the logistical flow are: finding and procuring raw materials and supplies, production scheduling, choosing a warehouse location and type, inventory control, setting up a materials-handling system, and making transportation decisions.

Sourcing and Procurement

One of the most important links in the supply chain is between the manufacturer and the supplier. Purchasing professionals are on the front lines of supply chain management. Purchasing departments plan purchasing strategies, develop specifications, select suppliers, and negotiate price and service levels.

The goal of most sourcing and procurement activities is to reduce the costs of raw materials and supplies and to have the items available when they are needed, for production or for the office, but not before (see just-in-time manufacturing in Chapter 11).

Retailers like 1-800-Flowers.com and FTD use local florists as the backbone of their distribution networks; flowers travel from the farm to a distributor and then to a wholesaler before finally reaching the flower shop. By the time they reach consumers, flowers can be 8 to 12 days old. ProFlowers.com found this procurement system too inefficient and costly. The company developed a network-based system that transforms each domestic flower farm into a self-contained distribution facility. Growers handle everything from receiving real-time flower orders to adding personalized message cards.[4]

Production Scheduling

In traditional mass-market manufacturing, production begins when forecasts call for additional products to be made or inventory control systems signal low inventory levels. The firm then makes a product and transports the finished goods to its own warehouses or those of intermediaries, where the goods wait to be ordered by retailers or customers. Production scheduling based on pushing a product down to the consumer obviously has its disadvantages, the most notable being that companies risk making products that may become obsolete or that consumers don't want in the first place.

In a customer "pull" manufacturing environment, which is growing in popularity, production of goods or services is not scheduled until an order is placed by the customer specifying the desired configuration. This process, known as mass customization, or build-to-order, uniquely tailors mass-market goods and services to the needs of the individuals who buy them. Mass customization was explained in Chapter 11. Companies as diverse as BMW, Dell Computer, Levi Strauss, Mattel, and many Web-based businesses are adopting mass customization to maintain or obtain a competitive edge.

Choosing a Warehouse Location and Type

Deciding where to put a warehouse is mostly a matter of deciding which markets will be served and where production facilities will be located. A storage warehouse is used to hold goods for a long time. For instance, Jantzen makes bathing suits at an even rate throughout the year to provide steady employment and hold down costs. It then stores them in a warehouse until the selling season.

distribution centres
Warehouses that specialize in rapid movement of goods to retail stores by making and breaking bulk.

Distribution centres are a special form of warehouse. They specialize in changing shipment sizes rather than storing goods. Such centres make bulk (put shipments together) or break bulk. They strive for rapid inventory turnover. When shipments arrive, the merchandise is quickly sorted into orders for various retail stores. As soon as the order is complete, it is delivered. Distribution centres are the wave of the future, replacing traditional warehouses. Companies simply can't afford to have a lot of money tied up in idle inventory.

Inventory Control

inventory control system
A system that maintains an adequate assortment of items to meet users' or customers' needs.

Closely interrelated with the procurement, manufacturing, and ordering processes is the inventory control system—a method that develops and maintains an adequate assortment of materials or products to meet manufacturers' or customers' demands.

Inventory decisions, for both raw materials and finished goods, have a big impact on supply chain costs and the level of service provided. If too many products are kept in inventory, costs increase—as do risks of obsolescence, theft, and damage. If too few products are kept on hand, then the company risks product shortages, angry customers, and ultimately lost sales.

Many of the chain retailers have used supply-chain technology to control inventories and dramatically raise profitability. In a matter of seconds, any store manager can tap into the chain's proprietary computer system and pull up real-time data on what products are selling best at that location or across the country.

Setting Up a Materials-Handling System

A materials-handling system moves and handles inventory. The goal of such a system is to move items as quickly as possible while handling them as little as possible. For example, Rival Material Handling Systems Inc. of Ontario specializes in the manufacture and supply of ergonomic industrial and commercial materials-handling products. By using customized materials-handling, companies operate more efficiently at lower costs.

Making Transportation Decisions

Transportation typically accounts for between 5 and 10 percent of the price of goods. Physical-distribution managers must decide which mode of transportation to use to move products from producer to buyer. This decision is, of course, related to all other physical-distribution decisions. The five major modes of transportation are railroads, motor carriers, pipelines, water transportation, and airways. Distribution managers generally choose a mode of transportation on the basis of several criteria:

- *Cost.* The total amount a specific carrier charges to move the product from the point of origin to the destination.
- *Transit time.* The total time a carrier has possession of goods, including the time required for pickup and delivery, handling, and movement between the point of origin and the destination.
- *Reliability.* The consistency with which the carrier delivers goods on time and in acceptable condition.
- *Capability.* The carrier's ability to provide the appropriate equipment and conditions for moving specific kinds of goods, such as those that must be transported in a controlled environment (for example, under refrigeration).

EXHIBIT 13.11 > Criteria for Ranking Modes of Transportation

	Highest				Lowest
Relative cost	Air	Truck	Rail	Pipe	Water
Transit time	Water	Rail	Pipe	Truck	Air
Reliability	Pipe	Truck	Rail	Air	Water
Capability	Water	Rail	Truck	Air	Pipe
Accessibility	Truck	Rail	Air	Water	Pipe
Traceability	Air	Truck	Rail	Water	Pipe

concept check

What is the goal of supply chain management?

Describe the key decisions in managing the logistical flow.

What factors are considered when selecting a mode of transportation?

- *Accessibility.* The carrier's ability to move goods over a specific route or network.
- *Traceability.* The relative ease with which a shipment can be located and transferred.

Using these six criteria, a shipper selects the mode of transportation that will best meet its needs. Exhibit 13.11 shows how the basic modes of transportation rank in terms of these criteria.

Promotional Goals

LO 6

promotion
The attempt by marketers to inform, persuade, or remind consumers and industrial users to engage in the exchange process.

Very few goods or services can survive in the marketplace without good **promotion**. Marketers promote their products to build demand. Promotion is an attempt by marketers to inform, persuade, or remind customers and industrial users in order to influence their opinion or elicit a response. Once the product has been created, promotion is often used to convince target customers that it has a differential advantage over the competition. A differential competitive advantage, as explained in Chapter 12, is a set of unique features that the target market perceives as important, and better than the competition's features; the advantage ideally results in purchase of the brand.

Most firms use some form of promotion, a word whose Latin root means "to move forward." Hence, actions that move a company toward its goals are promotional

CONCEPT *in Action* >>>

Reliable and inexpensive water transportation is one of the five major modes of transportation that distribution managers can choose from to move products from the producer to the buyer. What are the other four modes of transportation?

S-OLEG/SHUTTERSTOCK

in nature. Because company goals vary widely, so do promotional strategies. The goal is to stimulate action. In a profit-oriented firm, the desired action is for the consumer to buy the promoted item. McCain's, for instance, wants people to buy more frozen French fries. Not-for-profit organizations seek a variety of actions with their promotions. They tell us not to litter, to buckle up, and to attend the ballet.

Promotional goals include creating awareness, getting people to try products, providing information, retaining loyal customers, increasing the use of products, and identifying potential customers. Any promotional campaign may seek to achieve one or more of these goals:

1. *Creating awareness.* All too often, firms go out of business because people don't know they exist or what they do. Small restaurants often have this problem. Simply putting up a sign and opening the door is rarely enough. Promotion through ads on local radio or television, coupons in local papers, flyers, and so forth can create awareness of a new business or product.

2. *Getting consumers to try products.* Promotion is almost always used to get people to try a new product or to get non-users to try an existing product. Sometimes free samples are given away.

3. *Providing information.* Informative promotion is more common in the early stages of the product life cycle. An informative promotion may explain what ingredients (like fibre) will do for your health, tell you why the product is better (high-definition television versus regular television), inform you of a new low price, or explain where the item may be bought. People typically will not buy a product or support a not-for-profit organization until they know what it will do and how it may benefit them. Thus, an informative ad may stimulate interest in a product. Consumer watchdogs and social critics applaud the informative function of promotion because it helps consumers make more intelligent purchase decisions.

4. *Keeping loyal customers.* Promotion is also used to keep people from switching brands. Slogans such as Campbell's Soups are "M'm! M'm! Good!" and "Intel Inside" remind consumers about the brand. Marketers also remind users that the brand is better than the competition. For years, Pepsi has claimed it has the taste that consumers prefer. Such advertising reminds customers about the quality of the product. Firms can also help keep customers loyal by telling them when a product or service is improved.

5. *Increasing the amount and frequency of use.* Promotion is often used to get people to use more of a product and to use it more often. The most popular promotion to increase the use of a product may be loyalty programs such as, frequent-flyer or -user programs. For example, most larger grocery stores have loyalty cards that reward customers with discounts or redeemable points.

6. *Identifying target customers.* Promotion helps find customers. One way to do this is to list a website. For instance, *Canadian Business* magazine and *Business Week* include web addresses for more information on computer systems, corporate jets, colour copiers and other types of business equipment to help target those who are truly interested.

The Promotional Mix and Integrated Marketing Communications

promotional mix
The combination of advertising, personal selling, sales promotion, and public relations used to promote a product.

The combination of advertising, personal selling, sales promotion, and public relations used to promote a product is called the **promotional mix**. Each firm creates a unique mix for each product. But the goal is always to deliver the firm's message efficiently and effectively to the target audience. These are the elements of the promotional mix:

advertising
Any paid form of non-personal presentation by an identified sponsor.

personal selling
A face-to-face sales presentation to a prospective customer.

sales promotion
Marketing events or sales efforts—not including advertising, personal selling, and public relations—that stimulate buying.

public relations
Any communication or activity designed to win goodwill or prestige for a company or person.

integrated marketing communications (IMC)
The careful coordination of all promotional activities—media advertising, sales promotion, personal selling, and public relations, as well as direct marketing, packaging, and other forms of promotion—to produce a consistent, unified message that is customer focused.

- **Advertising**. Any paid form of non-personal promotion by an identified sponsor.
- **Personal selling**. A face-to-face presentation to a prospective buyer.
- **Sales promotion**. Marketing activities (other than personal selling, advertising, and public relations) that stimulate consumer buying, including coupons and samples, displays, shows and exhibitions, demonstrations, and other types of selling efforts.
- **Public relations**. The linking of organizational goals with key aspects of the public interest and the development of programs designed to earn public understanding and acceptance.

Ideally, marketing communications from each promotional-mix element (personal selling, advertising, sales promotion, and public relations) should be integrated. That is, the message reaching the consumer should be the same regardless of whether it comes from an advertisement, a salesperson in the field, a magazine article, or a coupon in a newspaper insert.

This unintegrated, disjointed approach to promotion has propelled many companies to adopt the concept of **integrated marketing communications (IMC)**. IMC involves carefully coordinating all promotional activities—media advertising, sales promotion, personal selling, and public relations, as well as direct marketing, packaging, and other forms of promotion—to produce a consistent, unified message that is customer focused. Following the concept of IMC, marketing managers carefully work out the roles the various promotional elements will play in the marketing mix. Timing of promotional activities is coordinated, and the results of each campaign are carefully monitored to improve future use of the promotional mix tools. Typically, a marketing communications director is appointed who has overall responsibility for integrating the company's marketing communications.

Pepsi relied on IMC to launch Pepsi One. The $100 million program relied on personal selling in the distribution channels, a public-relations campaign with press releases to announce the product, and heavy doses of advertising and sales promotion. The company toured the country's shopping malls setting up Pepsi One "lounges"—

CONCEPT *in Action* >>>
Whether making a cameo appearance or starring in a major role, brands are top talent in the entertainment world. Coca-Cola sits at the judges' table on American Idol; Under Armour is the performance apparel of choice for the virtual characters in top-selling computer games like Tom Clancy's Ghost Recon 2; and Reese's Pieces are forever immortalized in E.T: The Extra-Terrestrial. Does product placement blur the lines between advertising and content and should viewers be concerned?

F. MICELOTTA/AMERICAN IDOL 2009/GETTY IMAGES FOR FOX

inflatable couches with plastic carpeting—for random taste tests. It also produced 11,000 end-cap displays for supermarket aisles and created stand-up displays for 12-packs to spark impulse purchases. It secured Oscar-winning actor Cuba Gooding Jr. as spokesperson for the ad campaign. The ads made their debut during the World Series. The tagline for the ad campaign was "Only One has it all."

Factors that Affect the Promotional Mix

Promotional mixes vary a great deal from product to product and from one industry to the next. Advertising and personal selling are usually a firm's main promotional tools. They are supported by sales promotion. Public relations help develop a positive image for the organization and its products. The specific promotional mix depends on the nature of the product, market characteristics, available funds, and whether a push or a pull strategy is used.

The Nature of the Product

Selling toothpaste differs greatly from selling overhead industrial cranes. Personal selling is most important in marketing industrial products and least important in marketing consumer nondurables (consumer products that get used up). Broadcast advertising is used heavily in promoting consumer products, especially food and other nondurables. Print media and the Internet are used for all types of consumer products. Industrial products may be advertised through special trade magazines. Sales promotion, branding, and packaging are roughly twice as important (in terms of percentage of the promotional budget) for consumer products as for industrial products.

Market Characteristics

When potential customers are widely scattered, buyers are highly informed, and many of the buyers are brand loyal, the promotional mix should include more advertising and sales promotion and less personal selling. But sometimes personal selling is required even when buyers are well informed and geographically dispersed, as is the case with super computers and airplanes. Industrial installations and component parts may be sold to knowledgeable people with much education and work experience. Yet a salesperson must still explain the product and work out the details of the purchase agreement.

Salespeople are also required when the physical stocking of merchandise—called detailing—is the norm. Soft drinks and potato chips, for instance, are generally stocked by the person who makes the delivery, rather than by store personnel. This practice is becoming more common for convenience products as sellers try to get the best display space for their wares.

detailing
The physical stocking of merchandise at a retailer by the salesperson who delivers the merchandise.

Available Funds

Money, or the lack of it, is one of the biggest influences on the promotional mix. A small manufacturer with a tight budget and a unique product may rely heavily on free publicity. The media often run stories about new products.

If the product warrants a sales force, a firm with little money may turn to manufacturers' agents. They work on commission, with no salary, advances, or expense accounts. The Duncan Co., which makes parking meters, is just one of the many that rely on manufacturers' agents.

Push and Pull Strategies

Manufacturers may use aggressive personal selling and trade advertising to convince a wholesaler or a retailer to carry and sell their merchandise. This approach is known as a **push strategy**. The wholesaler, in turn, must often push the merchandise forward by persuading the retailer to handle the goods. A push strategy relies on extensive personal selling to channel members, or trade advertising, and price incentives to wholesalers and retailers. The retailer then uses advertising, displays, and other promotional forms to convince the consumer to buy the "pushed" products. This approach also applies to services. For example, the Jamaican Tourism Board targets promotions to travel agencies, which are members of its distribution channel.

At the other extreme is a **pull strategy**, which stimulates consumer demand in order to obtain product distribution. Rather than trying to sell to wholesalers, a manufacturer using a pull strategy focuses its promotional efforts on end consumers. As they begin demanding the product, the retailer orders the merchandise from the wholesaler. The wholesaler, confronted with rising demand, then places an order from the manufacturer. Thus, stimulating consumer demand pulls the product down through the channel of distribution. Heavy sampling, introductory consumer advertising, cents-off campaigns, buzz marketing, and couponing may all be used as part of a pull strategy. For example, using a pull strategy, the Jamaican Tourism Board may entice travelers to come to its island by offering discounts on hotels or airfare. The push and pull promotional strategies are illustrated in Exhibit 13.12.

Rarely does a company use a pull or a push strategy exclusively. Instead, the mix will emphasize one of these strategies. For example, pharmaceutical company Sanofi Aventis uses a push strategy by using personal selling and sampling of Allegra D, the allergy drug, to physicians and pharmacies. The company also uses print ads in consumer magazines, network TV, newspaper ads, and a Website aimed at final consumers to pull the product through the channel.

concept check

Explain how the nature of the product, market characteristics, and available funds can affect the promotional mix.

Distinguish between push and pull strategies.

EXHIBIT 13.12 > Push and Pull Promotional Strategies

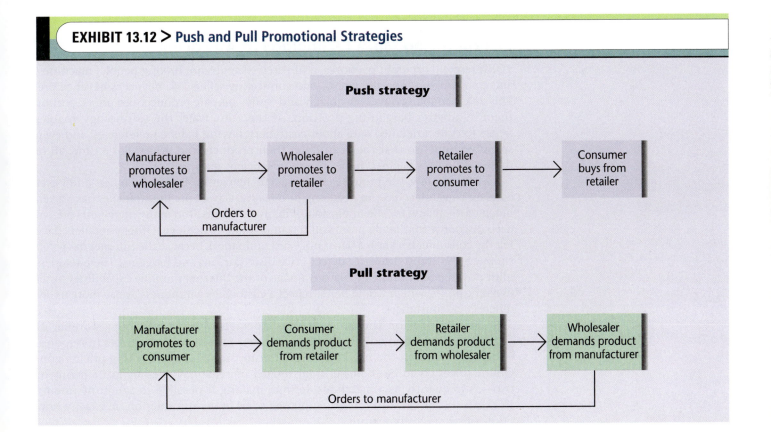

Making Ethical Choices

After working really hard to distinguish yourself, you've finally been promoted to a senior account executive at a major advertising agency and placed in charge of the agency's newest account, a nationally known cereal company. Their product is one you know contains excessive amounts of sugar as well as artificial colorings, and lacks any nutritional value whatsoever. In fact, you have never allowed your own children to eat it.

Your boss has indicated that the cereal company would like to use the slogan, "It's good for you," in their new television and print advertising campaign. You know that a $2 billion lawsuit has been filed against the Kellogg and Viacom corporations for marketing junk food to young children. The suit cited "alluring product packaging, toy giveaways, contests, collectibles, kid-oriented Websites, magazine ads, and branded toys and clothes." In addition, two consumer groups have brought suit against children's television network, Nickelodeon, for "unfair and deceptive junk-food marketing."

Your new role at the agency will be tested with this campaign. Doing a good job on it will cement your position and put you in line for a promotion to vice president. But as a responsible parent you have strong feelings about misleading advertising targeted at susceptible children.

Using a Web search tool, locate articles about this topic and then write responses to the following questions. Be sure to support your arguments and cite your sources.

ETHICAL DILEMMA: Do you follow your principles and ask to be transferred to another account? Or do you help promote a cereal you know may be harmful to children in order to secure your career?

SOURCES: Stephanie Thompson, "Standing Still, Kellogg Gets Hit with a Lawsuit," Advertising Age, January 23, 2006; Stephanie Thompson, "Kellogg Co. Might as Well Have Painted a Bull's-eye on Itself," Advertising Age, January 23, 2006; and Abbey Klaassen, "Viacom Gets Nicked," Advertising Age, January 23, 2006 (all from (http://galenet.thomsonlearning.com).

Trends in Marketing

LO 9

As customer expectations increase and competition becomes fiercer, perceptive marketers will find innovative strategies to satisfy demanding consumers and establish unique products in the market at the right prices. By using new distribution strategies and harnessing new technology to hone their marketing message and reach more customers, companies can boost profits and gain a competitive edge. Some of the significant trends in marketing include: incorporating more technology at all levels, increased use of yield management systems, category management, and outsourcing logistics functions.

Incorporating More Technology at All Levels

The Internet, corporate networks, and wireless setups are linking people, machines, and companies around the globe—and connecting sellers and buyers as never before. This link is enabling buyers to quickly and easily compare products and prices, putting them in a better bargaining position. At the same time, the technology enables sellers to collect detailed data about customers' buying habits, preferences, and even spending limits so that they can tailor their products and prices. For a time, all of these developments raised hopes of a more efficient marketplace.

Unfortunately, the promise of pricing efficiencies for Internet retailers and lower costs for consumers has run headlong into reality. Flawed pricing strategies have taken much of the blame for the implosion of many dot-coms. Too many merchants offered deep discounts that made profits all but impossible to achieve. Other e-retailers have felt the consumer backlash against price discrimination, because the Internet has given shoppers the ability to better detect price discrepancies and bargains. The e-retailers must now figure out how to take advantage of the Internet's unique capabilities to set dynamic prices, which would better reflect a customer's willingness to pay more under different circumstances.

Setting prices on the Internet was expected to offer retailers a number of advantages. To begin with, it would be far easier to raise or lower prices in response to demand, without the need for a clerk to run through a store with a pricing gun. Online prices could be changed in far smaller increments—even by just a penny or two—as frequently as a merchant desired, making it possible to fine-tune pricing strategies. But the real payoff was supposed to be better information on exactly how price-conscious customers are.

The idea was to charge exactly what the market will bear. But putting this into practice online has turned out to be exceptionally difficult, in part because the Internet has also empowered consumers to compare prices to find out if other merchants are offering a better deal or if other consumers are getting a bigger break. And the Internet has also made it easier for consumers to complain.

Online retail sales have been increasing and one reason is the economics of shopping. Think time spent, cost of travel, finding a parking spot, locating your intended store, and then driving home. Now think a mouse click. Countless small businesses have taken the plunge to serve the growing demand of the online shoppers.

The increasing sophistication of search technology and comparison-shopping sites have allowed online businesses cheaply and effectively to market their products to millions of potential customers. Often, these innovations are bringing less-well-known brands and merchants to consumers' attention.

Online merchants can offer a far broader array of merchandise than specialty brick-and-mortar retailers, because they don't have to keep the products on store shelves.

All forms of promotion are applying more and more technology to enhance effectiveness. For example, blogs provide marketers with a real-time dialogue with customers and an avenue to promote their products or services. A blog is an online journal with regularly updated content. This content is pushed to subscribers by RSS (really simple syndication) or e-mail and allows for response and discussion from site visitors. RSS enables users to automatically gather updates from various websites, especially news sites and blogs, and display headlines and a brief summary of those updates in a single location.

As we can see, all areas of marketing are increasing the use of technology to provide better customer service and satisfaction.

Yield Management Systems Help Companies Maximize Their Revenues

When competitive pressures are high, a company must know when it can raise prices to maximize its revenues. More and more companies are turning to **yield management systems (YMS)** to help adjust prices. First developed in the airline industry, yield management systems use complex mathematical software to profitably fill unused capacity. The software employs techniques such as discounting early purchases, limiting early sales at these discounted prices, and overbooking capacity. YMS now are appearing in other services such as lodging, other transportation forms, rental firms, and even hospitals. A key factor in easy group's success (see the expanding around the globe box) is its use of YMS.

Yield management systems are spreading beyond service industries as their popularity increases. The lessons of airlines and hotels aren't entirely applicable to other industries however, because plane seats and hotel beds are perishable—if they go empty, the revenue opportunity is lost forever. So it makes sense to slash prices to move toward capacity if it's possible to do so without reducing the prices that other customers pay. Cars and steel aren't so perishable. Still, the capacity to make these goods is perishable. An underused factory or mill is a lost revenue opportunity. So it makes sense to cut prices to use up capacity if it's possible to do so while getting other customers to pay full price.

Category Management

Category management is when retailers ask one supplier in a category to determine how the retailer should best stock its shelves. Category management is becoming standard practice at nearly every Canadian grocery store, convenience store, mass merchant, and drugstore chain.

A retailer can increase profits by managing itself not as a collection of products, but product categories. People don't shop for soft drinks the way that they shop for meat.

With soft drinks, it may be more effective to group brands (Pepsi, Coke, store brand) together; in another category, freshness is most important. Sophisticated computer programs and marketing research help decide which products and how much should be carried. Manufacturers that supply most of the category management are called captains. Category captains include: soft drinks—Coca-Cola; shaving—Gillette; pet food—Nestlé Purina; and detergent—Procter & Gamble.

The best retailers are far from passive when it comes to accepting category captains' recommendations. Walmart runs the captain's plan by a "validator," which is a second supplier. So Dole, for example, runs a check on what Del Monte proposes.

Outsourcing Logistics Functions

External partners are becoming increasingly important in the efficient deployment of supply chain management. Outsourcing, or contract logistics, is a rapidly growing segment of the distribution industry in which a manufacturer or supplier turns over the entire function of buying and managing transportation or another function of the supply chain, such as warehousing, to an independent third party. Many manufacturers are turning to outside partners for their logistics expertise in an effort to focus on the core competencies that they do best. Partners create and manage entire solutions for getting products where they need to be, when they need to be there. Logistics partners offer staff, an infrastructure, and services that reach consumers virtually anywhere in the world. Because a logistics provider is focused, clients receive service in a timely, efficient manner, thereby increasing customers' level of satisfaction and boosting their perception of added value to a company's offerings.

Third-party contract logistics enable companies to cut inventories, locate stock at fewer plants and distribution centers, and still provide the same service level or even better. The companies then can refocus investment on their core business.

> ### concept check
>
> What are some ways that technology has been incorporated in marketing?
>
> How are yield management systems and category management used in marketing?
>
> Why are more retailers outsourcing their logistics functions?

Great Ideas to Use Now

Chances are that someday you will be a buyer or seller on eBay. The auction site has more than 100 million registered members from around the world with more than 18,000 categories of items on the auction block. Yet, finding what you want or getting the best deal can be tough. Following are a few helpful tips.

A Buyer's Guide

Browsing/Searching

- Before diving in, get a solid sense of what the items you're interested in are worth. Use the "completed items" advanced search to see the prices that similar items actually sold for, or check eBay's library for the category-specific "inside scoop," which generally features a useful page titled "Factors Influencing Value."
- Search in both related and general categories, as sellers often classify their wares differently. For example, if you're looking for a CD by Elvis Costello, check classic rock, pop, and punk in addition to alternative rock.
- Be descriptive when searching. Specify dates, colours, brands, sizes, and model numbers. Try variations—if a model number has a hyphen, search both with and without it.
- Conduct searches often, as items are constantly added and removed. Save yourself from having to monitor the site on a daily basis by using the "favourite searches" service, which will notify you by e-mail when items matching your search criteria are put up for sale.
- Think eBay for retail too. Many companies, such as Dell and Handspring, off-load surplus inventory at deep discounts, so check here before you try standard retail outlets.

Bidding

- Don't bid if you don't intend to buy, as bids are binding contracts. Bids can be retracted only under exceptional circumstances (e.g., the seller changes the product description after you've placed your bid).
- Don't bid in the first days of an auction. Doing so merely reveals your interest and increases the likelihood of other bidders joining the fray, causing the price to rise quickly. Instead, wait until the auction is near its close (10 to 30 seconds before, depending on the speed of your Internet connection), and then bid the maximum amount you are willing to pay, regardless of any previous bids—a strategy known as sniping. To do this, open a second browser window and fill in all the relevant information, stopping just short of submitting your bid. Watch the auction wind down in the first window, and when the time is right, place your bid in the second. Don't fret—you can always use a professional sniper service to handle this for you automatically.
- Factor in shipping costs, which typically fall on the buyer. If the item is bulky or the seller lives overseas, your "bargain" might end up costing more than you bargained for.
- Try adding a penny or two to your bid. Since many bids are placed in round-number increments, this little extra something can mean the difference between winning by a nose and coming up short.

A Seller's Guide

Listing   Online auctions bring out the competitive nature in bidders, especially as the clock runs out. Bidding wars are a seller's dream; to make sure your auction gets significant play, follow these steps:

- Include specifics, such as manufacturer or product name, in both the title and description.
- Be honest in describing imperfections. This gives buyers comfort that you're being honest and could head off conflicts later.
- Set a low initial bid amount to attract more bidders. The mere *possibility* of getting a great deal on that rare Tony Gwynn rookie card encourages competition and increases the likelihood of rival bidders' driving up the price. This can also save you money, as eBay's listing fees are based on the minimum bid you set.
- Include a picture, as most buyers are reluctant to make a big purchase sight unseen. But don't overdo it: Including too many photos, or big ones with large file sizes, slows download times and tends to frustrate buyers with dial-up connections.
- Set a "buy it now" price, which allows buyers to subvert the bidding process and nab an item outright for a predetermined amount.
- Don't set a "reserve" price, which requires bidders to meet or exceed a certain minimum. As bidders can't see this minimum price, many avoid such auctions altogether out of fear that they'll be wasting their time.
- Accept multiple forms of payment, which increases the likelihood that interested buyers will place bids.
- Pay attention to when your auction is scheduled to end. eBay auctions run 3, 5, 7, or 10 days; to get the most traffic, make sure that yours includes a full weekend and ends at a time when people will be around to bid up the price.

Closing the Deal

- Congratulate the winner by e-mail. Include the auction number, a description of the item, the amount of the winning bid, and estimated shipping charges.
- Send the item as soon as the buyer's payment clears, and alert the buyer by e-mail (be sure to include the tracking number).
- Include links to your other auctions in all e-mail correspondence with buyers; if they are satisfied with their experience, they might want to check out what else you have.[5]

Customer Satisfaction and Quality

Distribution is all about getting the right product to the right person, at the right place, at the right time. Even if only one of these things does not occur, then the firm will have a dissatisfied customer. Sophisticated supply chain management programs, using the latest software, have dramatically reduced distribution errors in addition to lowering costs for the firm.

Oracle, the giant software company, has switched from an overly aggressive sales force to making customer service its top priority. "It's more than just the sale," said Paul Ciandrini, former Oracle senior vice president who headed up the company's commercial sales in the western region of North America. "I can make the sale and be a hero, but I can't go back in and expand that sale if it's of no value to the customer."[6]

Even the smallest details have been reconsidered. Oracle used to offer slick presentations on its products and the features that distinguished them from those of SAP AG of Germany. Now, it uses demonstrations that map its customers' specific technology environment, so it can put itself in its customers' shoes by focusing on problems as they see them.

Summary of Learning Outcomes

1 Describe what is meant by a product.

A product is any good or service, along with its perceived attributes and benefits, that creates customer value. Tangible attributes include the good itself, packaging, and warranties. Intangible attributes are symbolic, such as a brand's image. Products are categorized as either consumer products or industrial products. Consumer products are goods and services that are bought and used by the end users. They can be classified as unsought products, convenience products, shopping products, or specialty products, depending on how much effort consumers are willing to exert to get them. Industrial products are those bought by organizations for use in making other products or in rendering services and include capital products and expense items.

2 Explain the stages of the product life cycle.

After a product reaches the marketplace, it enters the product life cycle. This cycle typically has four stages: introduction, growth, maturity, and decline (and possibly death). Profits usually are small in the introductory phase, reach a peak at the end of the growth phase, and then decline. Marketing strategies for each stage are listed in Exhibit 13.5.

3 Discuss the role of pricing and the strategies used for pricing products.

Price indicates value, helps position a product in the marketplace, and is the means for earning a fair return on investment. If a price is too high, the product won't sell well, and the firm will lose money. If the price is too low, the firm might lose money, even if the product sells well. Prices are set according to pricing objectives. Among the most common objectives are profit maximization, target return on investment, and value pricing.

A cost based method for determining price is markup pricing. A certain percentage is added to the product's cost to arrive at the retail price. The markup is the amount added to the cost to cover expenses and earn a profit. Breakeven analysis determines the level of sales that must be reached before total cost equals total revenue. Breakeven analysis provides a quick look at how many units the firm must sell before it starts earning a profit. The technique also reveals how much profit can be earned with higher sales volumes.

The two main strategies for pricing a new product are price skimming and penetration pricing. Price skimming involves charging a high introductory price and then, usually, lowering the price as the product moves through its life cycle. Penetration pricing involves selling a new product at a low price in the hope of achieving a large sales volume.

Pricing tactics are used to fine-tune the base prices of products. Sellers that use leader pricing set the prices of some of their products below the normal markup or even below cost to attract customers who might otherwise not shop at those stores. Bundling is grouping two or more products together and pricing them as one. Psychology often plays a role in how consumers view products and in determining what they will pay. Setting a price at an odd number tends to create a perception that the item is cheaper than the actual price. Prices in even numbers denote quality or status. Raising the price so an item will be perceived as having high quality and status is called prestige pricing.

4 Explain distribution and distribution channels.

Physical distribution is efficiently managing the acquisition of raw materials to the factory and the movement of products from the producer or manufacturer to industrial users and consumers. Physical distribution activities are usually the responsibility of the marketing department and are part of the large series of activities included in the supply chain. Distribution channels are the series of marketing entities through which goods and services pass on their way from producers to end users. Distribution systems focus on the physical transfer of goods and services and on their legal ownership at each stage of the distribution process. Channels (a) reduce the number of transactions, (b) ease the flow of goods, and (c) increase channel efficiency.

5 Illustrate how supply chain management can increase efficiency and customer satisfaction.

The goal of supply chain management is to coordinate all of the activities of the supply chain members into a seamless process, thereby increasing customer satisfaction. The logistical components of the supply chain include sourcing and procurement, production scheduling, choosing a warehouse location and type, setting up a materials-handling system, and making transportation decisions.

6 Briefly list the goals of promotional strategy.

Promotion aims to stimulate demand for a company's goods or services. Promotional strategy is designed to inform, persuade, or remind target audiences about those products. The goals of promotion are to create awareness, get people to try products, provide information, keep loyal customers, increase use of a product, and identify potential customers.

7 Discuss the elements of the promotional mix, and integrated marketing communications.

The unique combination of advertising, personal selling, sales promotion, and public relations used to promote a product is the promotional mix. Advertising is any paid form of non-personal promotion by an identified sponsor. Personal selling consists of a face-to-face presentation in a conversation with a prospective purchaser. Sales promotion consists of marketing activities—other than personal selling, advertising, and public relations—that stimulate consumers to buy. These activities include coupons and samples, displays, shows and exhibitions, demonstrations, and other selling efforts. Public relations is the marketing function that links the policies of the organization with the public interest and develops programs designed to earn public understanding and acceptance. Integrated marketing communications (IMC) is being used by more and more organizations. It is the careful coordination of all of the elements of the promotional mix to produce a consistent, unified message that is customer focused.

8 Identify the factors that affect the promotional mix.

The factors that affect the promotional mix are the nature of the product, market characteristics, available funds, and whether a push or a pull strategy is emphasized. Personal selling is used more with industrial products, and advertising is used more heavily for consumer products. With widely scattered, well-informed buyers and with brand-loyal customers, a firm will blend more advertising and sales promotion and less personal selling into its promotional mix. A manufacturer with a limited budget might rely heavily on publicity and manufacturers' agents to promote the product.

9 List some of the trends in marketing.

Four trends that we are seeing in marketing include: incorporating more technology at all levels, increased use of yield management systems, category management, and outsourcing logistics functions.

Technology is becoming more prevalent in all aspects of business including marketing. Technology is incorporated from the development of strategies and goals to the final stage – the customer. Companies can use yield management systems (yms) to help them adjust prices to maximize revenue and retailers can use category management to manage the inventory of a category of products for them. Outsourcing, or contract logistics, is a rapidly growing segment of the distribution industry in which a manufacturer or supplier turns over the entire function of buying and managing transportation or another function of the supply chain, such as warehousing, to an independent third party.

Key Terms

advertising 415	odd-even (psychological) pricing 402
agents 404	penetration pricing 401
breakeven point 400	personal selling 415
breaking bulk 407	prestige pricing 403
brokers 404	price skimming 401
bundling 402	product 392
capital products 394	product life cycle 395
category management 419	profit maximization 397
convenience products 394	promotion 413
detailing 416	promotional mix 414
distribution (logistics) 403	public relations 415
distribution centres 412	pull strategy 417
distribution channel 404	push strategy 417
dual distribution (multiple distribution) 404	retailers 404
	sales promotions 415
exclusive distribution 410	selective distribution 410
expense items 394	shopping products 394
fixed costs 400	specialty products 394
fixed-cost contribution 400	strategic channel alliances 407
industrial distributors 404	target return on investment 398
integrated marketing communications (IMC) 415	total cost 400
	total profit 400
intensive distribution 410	total revenue 400
inventory control system 412	unsought products 394
leader pricing 402	value pricing 399
loss leader 402	variable costs 400
manufacturer 403	wholesalers 404
marketing intermediaries 404	yield management systems (YMS) 419
markup pricing 399	

Experiential Exercises

1. Under what circumstances would a jeans maker market the product as a convenience product? A shopping product? A specialty product?

2. Go to the library and look through magazines and newspapers to find examples of price skimming, penetration pricing, and value pricing. Make copies and show them to the class.

3. Write down the names of two brands to which you are loyal. Indicate the reasons for your loyalty.

4. Visit an online retailer such as Amazon.ca (**www.amazon.ca**), PCConnection. com (**www.pcconnection.com**), or Drugstore.com (**www.drugstore.com**). At the site, try to identify examples of leader pricing, bundling, odd-even pricing, and other pricing strategies. Do online retailers have different pricing considerations from "real-world" retailers? Explain.

5. Do a search on Yahoo (**www.yahoo.ca**) for online auctions for a product you are interested in buying. Visit several auctions to get an idea of how the product is priced. How do these prices compare with the price you might find in a local store? What pricing advantages or disadvantages do companies face in selling their products through online auctions? How do online auctions affect the pricing strategies of other companies? Why?

6. Do some comparison shopping. A beauty of the Internet is the ability to comparison shop like never before. Tour and Internet travel companies offer many last-minute specials where travellers can save on their trips. To compare brands, features, and prices of products, go to one of these sites: (**www.airtransat.com**), (**www.aircanadavacations.com**), (**www.expedia.com**), (**www.itravel2000.com**), and any others that you have researched.

7. Kick the tires before you buy. At some point you are going to buy a car. The Web can simplify the process, help you make an intelligent decision, and save you money. Start at (**www.edmunds.com**). The online version of the respected car buying guide is crammed with information about new and used cars. The site offers thousands of car reviews and current loan rates.

8. Trace the distribution channel for some familiar product. Compose an e-mail explaining why the channel has evolved as it has and how it is likely to change in the future.

9. Go to a successful, independent specialty store in your area that has been in business for quite a while. Interview the manager and try to determine how the store successfully competes with the national chains.

10. Visit a local manufacturer. Interview managers to determine how its supply chain functions. Make a report to the class.

11. One of the biggest challenges for retailers is integrating their various channels to provide a seamless experience for customers, regardless of the channel. Pick two of the following companies, explore their Websites, and compare the channel integration strategies: Staples (**www.staples.com**), Gap (**www.gap.com**), or Borders (**www.borders.com**). In addition to looking at the websites from a channel perspective, you might want to look at the company information and news sites.

12. Protect your privacy online. Here are some pointers to protect yourself against spam.

   • Use free Web-based e-mail services like Microsoft's Hotmail.com to create a second e-mail address to give out when shopping at an e-commerce site. This will prevent your corporate or primary account from being deluged with targeted spam.
   • Use websites like (**www.spychecker.com**) to check if you have unwittingly downloaded spyware—nettlesome programs that are secretly installed when you download many free programs. Visitors to Spychecker are prompted to enter the names of programs, and the site tells them whether the software contains spyware.
   • Activate your Web browser's security functions to block out cookies or alert you when a site is trying to install one on your computer. In Internet Explorer, you would go to Tools, and then click on the Internet Options command. That brings up a series of tabs, including one for Security. Moving the sliding bar to its highest setting will disable all cookies. This, however, might make it difficult to visit many popular Websites, as the sites tend to require the ability to install cookies on your machine.
   • Use e-mail re-mailers like the one at (**www.gilc.org/speech/anonymous/ remailer.html**) to bounce your message through a series of computers that forward it on, in theory making it untraceable. Sending anonymous e-mail through these re-mailers also reduces the odds of its being read by hackers, who try to monitor data traffic to and from companies and sites like Hotmail.

- Use privacy software to shield the content and addresses of the Websites you visit from employers and other prying eyes. One of the best such programs is available at (**www.anonymizer.com**).

13. Think of a product that you use regularly. Find several examples of how the manufacturer markets this product, such as ads in different media, sales promotions, and publicity. Assess each example for effectiveness in meeting one or more of the six promotional goals described in the chapter. Then analyze them for effectiveness in reaching you as a target consumer. Consider such factors as the media used, the style of the ad, and ad content. Present your findings to the class.

14. Choose a current advertising campaign for a beverage product. Describe how the campaign uses different media to promote the product. Which medium is used the most, and why? What other promotional strategies does the company use for the product? Evaluate the effectiveness of the campaign. Present your results to the class.

15. The Zenith Media site at (**www.zenithmedia.com**) is a good place to find links to Internet resources on advertising. At the site, click on "Leading Corporate and Brand Sites." Pick three of the company sites listed and review them, using the concepts in this chapter.

16. Does a career in marketing appeal to you? Start your journey at Careers in Marketing, (**www.careers-in-marketing.com**), and explore the five areas listed there: Advertising & Public Relations, Market Research, Non-Profit, Product Management, and Retailing. Which one appeals to you most, and why? Briefly describe the type of work you would be doing, the career path, and how you will prepare to enter this field (courses, part-time jobs, etc.).

Review Questions

1. What is a product? How do products create value for the buyer?

2. What are the four (4) classifications of consumer products?

3. How are business products classified?

4. Discuss the strategies for success at each stage of the product life cycle.

5. What is the role of pricing in marketing?

6. How are product prices determined?

7. What are the various pricing strategies available to managers?

8. What is physical distribution?

9. Define *marketing intermediaries*. What are four common marketing intermediaries?

10. What is the distribution channel? What are the functions of distribution channels?

11. What are some alternative channel arrangements?

12. What are the three (3) degrees of market coverage for consumer products?

13. What is the goal of supply chain management? What are the logistical components of the supply chain?

14. What are some of the key decision in managing the logistical flow of products?

15. Explain some of the criteria that managers must consider when deciding the mode of transportation.

16. What are the goals of promotion?

17. What is the promotional mix, and what options are available in this mix?

18. Explain integrated marketing communications (IMC).

19. List the factors that affect the promotional mix.

20. What are some of the trends in marketing?

Advertisers Score with the World Cup

What sporting event is televised in 213 countries and watched by more passionate fans than any other? If you guessed the Olympics, you'd be wrong. It's the world cup football (soccer) matches, which last a month and are held every four years. An estimated 1.5 billion people watched the 2006 world cup opener, and web surfers registered over 2 billion page views at (www.fifaworldcup.com). Online venues such as chat rooms, blogs, and discussion boards added another media channel for fans to get more of the action.

Soccer's worldwide popularity makes it a prime advertising buy for many global companies, who want to get their message out to these large audiences. More than 240 million players on 1.4 million teams around the world play the game, supporting its claim to be the world's favourite sport. As the FIFA world cup website explains, "the FIFA world cup™ reaches an audience of a size and diversity that is unrivalled by any other single-sports body. Add to this a passion for the game found in all corners of the world, and you have a sporting, social, and marketing phenomenon." As a result, companies vie to become official partners with global marketing rights as well as custom opportunities. The 2006 FIFA world cup™ official partners were Adidas, Avaya, Budweiser, Coca-Cola, Continental, Deutsche Telekom, Emirates, Fujifilm, Gillette, Hyundai, MasterCard, McDonald's, Philips, Toshiba, and Yahoo!.

The world cup's global nature presents major challenges as well as opportunities for its advertisers. Unlike the Grey Cup, which focuses on Canada, the world cup requires even greater levels of creativity to produce ads that make a strong connection with soccer fans from very diverse cultures. Ads may have to appeal to viewers in countries as different as Ireland, Mexico, Malaysia, and Bangladesh.

Companies accomplish this task in various ways. They can select the countries that see their ads. Some have one ad for all countries, whereas others customize ads. MasterCard overcame the language barrier by showing soccer fans from many countries cheering. The only words appear at the end with the company logo: "football fever. Priceless." Anheuser-Busch, which spent more for its 2006 world cup ads than it did for its Olympics or super bowl ads, also opted for a visual rather than verbal ad: people in the stands at a sporting event do the "wave," holding cards that show beer flowing from a Budweiser bottle into a glass, which then empties. "If you get too complicated, you lose people with different cultures and perspectives," says Tony Ponturo, vice president of global sports marketing for the brewer. Gillette starts with the same ad but uses digital techniques so that each ad features the team colors for the country where the spot is showing.

Critical Thinking Questions

- What are some of the challenges global marketers encounter when developing advertising and promotion campaigns? How does the type of product affect the promotional strategies?
- You work for an ad agency that has a world cup sponsor as a client. What approach would you recommend for your agency as it develops a campaign—universal, customized for each geographical region, or something else, and why?
- What types of companies could benefit from placing ads on the fifa website, and how can they use the Internet effectively to promote their products?

SOURCES: Adapted from "Marketing & TV," Fédération Internationale de Football Association, (www.fifa.com), May 3, 2006; Aaron O. Patrick, "World Cup's advertisers hope one size fits all," Wall Street Journal, March 28, 2006, p. B7; "The Wave, " TV commercials, budweiser.com, (www.budweiser.com), May 3, 2006; "World cup advertising analysis," Analyst Wire, March 3, 2006, (http://galenet. thomsonlearning.com); "3 billion eyes to view World Cup opener, (www.worldcupblog.org/world-cup-2006/3-billion-eyes-to-view-world-cup-opener.html), accessed February 26, 2009.

The Toronto Blue Jays Hit a Home Run with Pricing

Can doubling the number of ticket categories bring more fans out to the ball game? For the Toronto Blue Jays, an improved pricing strategy and additional promotional strategies helped the team raise its profile in its hometown.

Prior to the 1999 baseball season, the Toronto Blue Jays (**www.bluejays.ca**) had just five ticket-pricing categories. After thorough study of their ticket prices, the Blue Jays established a new pricing structure with 10 levels to provide fans different product value. From single-ticket $7 seats to season tickets costing more than $13,000 ($165 per game) for the "In the Action" seats, fans can pick the ticket program that suits them best. In-between seats range from $24 to $49, depending on location. In addition to individual seats and season passes, Blue Jays fans can buy Flex-Packs with 5, 20, or 40 tickets to the games they choose. These packages sell at a discount from the single-ticket price. Group ticket sales, an important component of the Blue Jays product mix, are targeted toward the seats priced at about $40 and under.

As part of the Toronto team's effort to provide a high-quality product at a fair price, the Blue Jays added several regularly occurring special promotions during many home games. For example, every Tuesday home game is a TIM-BR Mart Tuesday. The building supplies chain collaborates with the Blue Jays in a three-part promotion. When a Toronto player hits the official TIM-BR Mart target, a fan chosen at random wins a cottage supplied and built by TIM-BR Mart. Another fan chosen at random gets to watch the game from a custom-built wood deck in the Toronto Rogers Centre. This fan is also provided food and beverage service. A third lucky fan wins a custom-built deck for his or her home by TIM-BR Mart.

Saturday home games have special promotions for children. On Junior Jays Saturdays, sponsored by *The Toronto Star,* children 14 and under are admitted at discounted prices. The gates open early, so fans can watch batting practice, and kids can participate in many activities and contests, win prizes, and get player autographs. Children can enter a drawing to throw out the ceremonial first pitch at the next Junior Jays Saturday game; nine youngsters get to take the field along with the Blue Jays starting lineup, and a child is selected to announce the Blue Jays batters for one inning. Children can also run the bases following the game. Each child 14 and under also receives Blue Jays souvenir giveaways.

The Blue Jays' marketing staff continue to add special promotions to please their fans. For example, they asked fans what they enjoy the most about attending a Blue Jays game and combined many of these elements to create Premium Games. Tickets for these games cost a few dollars more but include a pre-game party, early admission to watch batting practice, autograph signing, giveaway items, and post-game entertainment. Staples Business Depot "Deal of the Game," the FedEx Home Run Club, and Schneider's Juicy Jumbo Toss are among the team's recent promotions.

This well-planned package of special promotions, along with different ticket prices for seats providing different amenities, has increased the Toronto Blue Jays' popularity. As a result, attendance at games is up and the fan base is growing.

Critical Thinking Questions

- How would you describe the Toronto Blue Jays' baseball franchise as a product?
- What decision criteria do you think the Blue Jays used in establishing their new ticket price structure? Do you agree with this pricing strategy?

SOURCE: Toronto Blue Jays web site, (http://toronto.bluejays.mlb.com).

Success Blooms At 1-800-FLOWERS

Do you need to send flowers for a relative's birthday in Germany, to celebrate your daughter's first big business presentation in the United Kingdom, or to congratulate your neighbours across the street on the birth of their new baby? One call to 1-800- FLOWERS does it all—floral arrangements individually created by the nation's top floral artists, hand-delivered the same day at the peak of freshness and perfection—whether your loved ones are in Australia, the Philippines, Mexico, Italy, Japan, Hawaii, Alaska, or Puerto Rico.

So how do they do it? After opening his first retail store in 1976, Jim McCann, chief executive officer of 1-800-FLOWERS, built a chain of 14 flower shops in the New York metropolitan area before acquiring the 1-800-FLOWERS telephone number in 1986 and continuing to grow his business under that name. His understanding of his customer base and market helped him create a reliable brand his customers could trust.

He knew that when selling such a perishable product, efficient access and distribution is critical to success. The company's sophisticated fulfillment system includes its BloomNet; an international network of florists. BloomNet partners are selected based on their commitment to quality and service and strictly monitored by 1-800-FLOWERS—part of its focus on customer service.

McCann extended his business into other channels, going online in 1992 and opening a website in 1995. He maintains strategic marketing relationships with a number of online services, including America Online, Microsoft Network (MSN), and Yahoo! The company's third-party vendor-direct program allows for easy and efficient delivery of gourmet foods, candies, and gift baskets, among other items. Its collection of brands includes home décor and garden merchandise sold under Plow & Hearth; premium popcorn and other food gifts sold under The Popcorn Factory; chocolates from Fannie May, Godiva, and others; and baked cookies and desserts from Cheryl & Co.

Headquartered on long island, New York, 1-800-FLOWERS, (**www.1800flowers.com**) is today one of the most recognized brands in flower and gift retailing. Available online 24 hours a day, seven days a week, customers can also visit a company-operated or franchised store. The website also allows customers to send free virtual flowers—building their own virtual bouquet complete with flowers, accents, a beautiful vase, and even a personalized message.

1-800-FLOWERS maintains a comprehensive quality assurance program that incorporates ongoing blind test orders, telephone surveys with customers and recipients, in-store and mail surveys, and customer service reports. With customers assured of a 100 percent satisfaction and freshness guarantee on all products and services, the company's fortunes should continue to blossom.

Critical Thinking Questions

1. Describe the unique challenges faced by companies that sell highly perishable products.

2. How does 1-800-FLOWERS meet and address those challenges?

3. What other types of distribution or product access should the company consider?

SOURCES: Adapted from the video "1-800 FLOWERS," (www.swlearning.com); Tim Beyers, "budding growth at 1-800-flowers?" The Motley Fool, (www.fool.com), August 11, 2005; Tony Goins, "1-800-flowers to buy Cheryl & Co.," Business First of Columbus, March 11, 2005; Rich Smith, "1-800-flowers buys Fannie May," The Motley Fool, April 10, 2006, (www.fool.com); 1-800-flowers corporate website, (http://1800flowers.com); April 29, 2006.

CHAPTER 14

Making the Connection

Using Financial Information and Accounting

In the previous four chapters, we examined the functional areas of human resources, operations, and marketing, and saw that they must work together in a very integrative way to achieve the goals of the company. It is obvious that these three areas affect the ability of the company to *gain employee commitment, increase the* level of product *quality* and *innovativeness,* and thus *meet customer needs,* and that they therefore affect the ability of the company to *achieve financial performance.* In this chapter we will begin to look more specifically at the last functional area of *finance,* starting with how a firm develops and uses financial information through the function of accounting.

It's clear from the beginning of this chapter that, regardless of your position in an organization, you need to understand accounting. It is the "financial language of businesses," and all decisions that are made in an organization eventually have financial consequences and therefore show up in the accounting information. For example, on the income statement, you might find advertising expenses and sales revenue from *marketing,* production and operating costs from *operations,* payroll and training costs from *human resources,* and, of course, the interest costs on debt financing to pay for it all. On the statement of financial position, you can also see the impact of each area on the numbers. For example, in the accounts payable section, there might be payments outstanding for employee wages, for marketing expenses, and for operating expenses, as well as for interest

on debt financing or dividends payable to shareholders. In the current assets sections, you might find marketable securities (money invested in financial products to earn a return for a short period—a financing decision), accounts receivable from customers for invoices they have not yet paid (a marketing decision), and inventories of goods on hand (an operating decision).

All areas of the company, and employees at all levels, must therefore understand the financial implications of the decisions they make. They must see the integration of their decisions with each area and eventually on the "bottom line." Internal accounting reports help functional areas make these decisions; for example, marketing sales reports can be used to assess how well different marketing strategies are working, and production cost reports help in efforts to control operating costs.

On the other hand, external accounting reports, such as statement of financial position and income statements, which are contained in annual reports to shareholders, are used by many outside *stakeholder* groups. Potential employees use them to assess the stability of a company, and therefore job security and job prospects, before taking job offers, and potential investors use them to assess investment opportunities, just as current shareholders use them to assess the investments they have already made. These stakeholder relationships cannot be dealt with casually, particularly in light of scandals that have called into question

the integrity of the accounting profession. The impact that these scandals, such as those involving WorldCom and Enron, have had on the financial markets (*economic* environment) demonstrate quite clearly the far-reaching integrative impact of financial information and the importance of operating with the highest ethical standards. In fact, this demand for greater ethical conduct (*social* environment) has resulted in many new regulations (*political* environment) governing what firms can and cannot do in reporting accounting information.

The other aspect of the external environment that affects this functional area is *technology*. The advances in technology today have sped up the pace with which accounting information can be gathered and disseminated throughout an organization, thus giving all areas an opportunity to examine the impact of their decisions in an integrative way and focus more on the analysis of the information to make better decisions. In the remaining chapters, we'll continue with the finance area and look at these decisions in more detail.

CHAPTER 14

Using Financial Information and Accounting

LEARNING OUTCOMES

1 Explain the importance of financial reports and accounting information to the targeted users.

2 Show an understanding of the accounting profession.

3 Identify the six steps in the accounting cycle.

4 Understand how a statement of financial position describes the financial condition of an organization.

5 Explain the purpose of the income statement.

6 Describe the importance of the statement of cash flows.

7 Explain how ratio analysis is used to identify a firm's financial strengths and weaknesses.

8 List some of the major trends that are impacting the accounting industry.

ACCOUNTING IN EVERYDAY LIFE

SHIRLEY A. ROSE

When first introduced to accounting, many students are unsure of what they are getting into. "But," says longtime accounting instructor, Rafik Kurji, "they are already using accounting principles in their everyday lives." Rafik's explains: the individual gets their paycheque (income) and pays the rent (expense), then they make a mortgage payment (reducing a longterm liability), they make a car payment (reducing another liability by paying down the car loan, the car being an asset), a friend pays back the $100.00 he owes (increasing the cash balance and reducing the accounts receivables), etc. At a very basic level, these activities represent accounting. Once on a career path, accounting is important to anyone wishing to move up in the organization.

A marketing manager has to have a sound understanding of accounting principles in order to plan. Many questions need to be answered. What is the revenue stream comprised of? How can it be increased? Can the quantity sold be increased or the cost to produce the goods and services be reduced? Can the other expenses be reduced? Which are fixed expenses and which are variable? What are the assets and what condition are they in? Without this sort of information and knowledge, how can a marketer make recommendations that are in the best interests of the company as a whole? Without careful planning, the company may end up practicing crisis management on a regular basis. The projections on which the plans are based must be constantly compared with the accounting actuals and variances identified and explained. If marketers, HR professionals, purchasers or general managers wish to be active participants in the strategic planning for their companies, they must understand accounting.

With the increase in globalization, it has become necessary to standardize accounting around the world. Rafik feels that, without this standardization, we are often comparing apples and oranges. The International Financial Accounting Standards (IFAS) will help accomplish this standardization and enable accountants around the world to more readily understand statements prepared by their counterparts in other countries.

Accountants are always in demand, whether the economy is in a growth or a recessionary period. If the company is not doing well, management still needs to know how just how badly they are doing in order to deal with the situation. As managers sit around the strategic planning table, their knowledge of accounting will serve them well as they contribute valuable information from their own functional areas, enabling the team to make well-informed decisions.

Critical Thinking Questions

As you read this chapter, consider the following questions:

1. **Why is accounting so important to the decision-making activities of managers?**

2. **Can a business be incredibly busy, with high sales volumes, and still not have a good bottom line? If so, explain how this could happen?**

3. **Do you agree that all business students, including marketing, HR and MIS should have a good understanding of accounting? Explain your answer.**

Financial information is central to every organization. To operate effectively, businesses must have a way to track income, expenses, assets, and liabilities in an organized manner. Financial information is also essential for decision making. Managers prepare financial reports using accounting, a set of procedures and guidelines for companies to follow when preparing financial reports. Unless you understand basic accounting concepts, you will not be able to "speak" the standard financial language of business.

All of us—whether we are self-employed, work for a local small business or a multinational Fortune 100 firm, or are not currently in the workforce—benefit from knowing the basics of accounting and financial statements. We can use this information to educate ourselves about companies before interviewing for a job or buying a company's shares or bonds. Employees at all levels of an organization use accounting information to monitor operations. They must also decide which financial information is important for their company or business unit, what those numbers mean, and how to use them to make decisions.

We start this chapter by discussing why accounting is important for businesses and for users of financial information. We then provide a brief overview of the accounting profession and recent problems in the industry, and the new regulatory environment. Following that, we present an overview of accounting procedures, followed by a description of the three main financial statements: the statement of financial position, the income statement, and the statement of cash flows. Using these statements, we then demonstrate how ratio analysis of financial statements can provide valuable information about a company's financial condition. Finally, we will explore current trends affecting the accounting profession.

Accounting: More than Numbers

Accounting is the process of collecting, recording, classifying, summarizing, reporting, and analyzing financial activities. It results in reports that describe the financial condition of an organization. All types of organizations—businesses, hospitals, schools,

CONCEPT *in Action* >>>

Financial accounting information, such as asset values, sales, and inventory, helps managers in all types of organizations make business decisions that enhance organizational effectiveness and efficiency. What are some of the consequences of not understanding accounting in business?

© BONNIE KAMIN / PHOTOEDIT

EXHIBIT 14.1 > The Accounting System

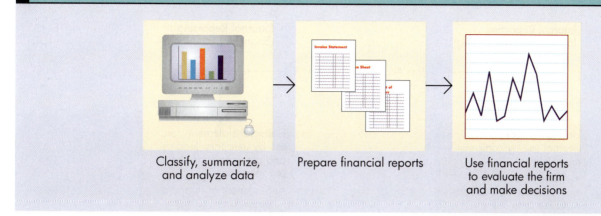

Classify, summarize, and analyze data → Prepare financial reports → Use financial reports to evaluate the firm and make decisions

accounting
The process of collecting, recording, classifying, summarizing, reporting, and analyzing financial activities.

managerial accounting
Accounting that provides financial information that managers inside the organization can use to evaluate and make decisions about current and future operations.

financial accounting
Accounting that focuses on preparing external financial reports that are used by outsiders such as creditors, lenders, suppliers, investors, and government agencies to assess the financial strength of a business.

generally accepted accounting principles (GAAP)
The financial accounting rules, standards, and usual practices followed by accountants in Canada when preparing financial statements, until January 2011.

International Financial Reporting Standards (IFRS)
A set of globally accepted accounting standards adopted in Canada on January 1st, 2011.

HOT Links

Check out what is new at the International Accounting Standards Committee: (**www.iasb.org).**

government agencies, and civic groups—use accounting procedures. Accounting provides a framework for looking at past performance, current financial health, and possible future performance. It also provides a framework for comparing the financial positions and financial performances of different firms. Understanding how to prepare and interpret financial reports will enable you to evaluate two computer companies and choose the one that is more likely to be a good investment.

As Exhibit 14.1 shows, the accounting system converts the details of financial transactions (sales, payments, purchases, and so on) into a form that people can use to evaluate the firm and make decisions. Data become information, which, in turn, becomes reports. These reports describe a firm's financial position at one point in time and its financial performance during a specified period. Financial reports include *financial statements,* such as the statement of financial position and income statements, and special reports, such as sales and expense breakdowns by product line.

Who Uses Financial Reports?

The accounting system generates two types of financial reports, as shown in Exhibit 14.2: internal and external. Internal reports are used within the organization. As the term implies, **managerial accounting** provides financial information that managers inside the organization can use to evaluate and make decisions about current and future operations. For instance, the sales reports prepared by managerial accountants show how well marketing strategies are working. Production cost reports help departments track and control costs. Managers might prepare very detailed financial reports for their own use and provide summary reports to top management.

Financial accounting focuses on preparing external financial reports that are used by outsiders, that is, people who have an interest in the business but are not part of management. Although these reports also provide useful information for managers, they are primarily used by shareholders (the owners of the company), lenders, suppliers, investors, and government agencies to assess the financial strength of a business.

At the time this book was published, accountants in Canada were following the Canadian **generally accepted accounting principles (GAAP)** to ensure accuracy and consistency in the way financial information is reported. On January 1st, 2011, Canada will adopt the **International Financial Reporting Standards (IFRS)** for publicly accountable organizations. These organizations must use the IFRS for fiscal periods beginning on or after the January 1st, 2011 date. As well, since financial statements include comparative figures, these companies must present their 2010 financial information using IFRS. The

EXHIBIT 14.2 > Reports Provided by the Accounting System

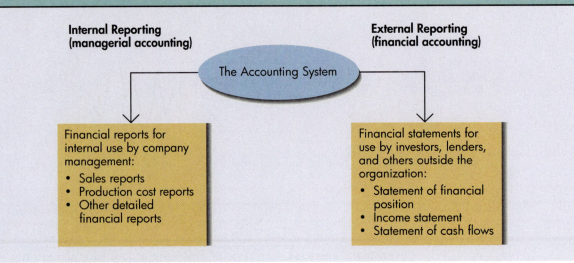

Internal Reporting
(managerial accounting)

External Reporting
(financial accounting)

The Accounting System

Financial reports for
internal use by company
management:
- Sales reports
- Production cost reports
- Other detailed
  financial reports

Financial statements for
use by investors, lenders,
and others outside the
organization:
- Statement of financial
  position
- Income statement
- Statement of cash flows

annual report
A yearly document that describes a firm's
financial status and usually discusses the
firm's activities during the past year and
its prospects for the future.

adoption of the IFRS was designed to provide consistency in financial reporting internationally and replace the GAAP of over 100 countries.[1] The Expanding Around the Globe box discusses the challenges in changing from GAAP to IFRS.

Financial statements are the chief element of the **annual report**, a yearly document that describes a firm's financial status. Annual reports usually discuss the firm's activities during the past year and its prospects for the future. Three primary financial statements included in the annual report discussed and illustrated later in this chapter are

- the statement of financial position,
- the income statement, and
- the statement of cash flows.

concept check

Explain who uses financial information.

Differentiate between financial accounting and managerial accounting.

Expanding Around The Globe

MOVING TOWARD ONE WORLD OF NUMBERS

Imagine being treasurer of a major multinational company with significant operations in ten other countries. Because the accounting rules in those countries don't conform to IFRS, your staff has to prepare nine sets of financial reports that comply with the host country's rules—and also translate the figures to IFRS for consolidation into the parent company's statements. It's a massive undertaking.

The Canadian Accounting Standards Board (AcSB) and the international accounting standards board (IASB) are working together to develop international accounting standards that will remove disparities between national and international standards, improve the quality of financial information worldwide, and simplify comparisons of financial statements across borders for both corporations and investors.

The AcSB and the IASB desire to create uniform global accounting standards. Presently, there are approximately 100 countries that use IFRS with more signing on each year. As they worked toward convergence, the board members decided to develop a new set of common standards, rather than try to reconcile the two standards.

These new standards must be better than existing ones, not simply eliminate differences. Merging GAAP and IFRS into a consistent set of international accounting standards has proven to be very difficult because of different approaches used in the two sets.

However, the convergence project is moving ahead more quickly than the sponsoring groups anticipated. Raising capital outside a corporation's home country overseas will be easier for companies because they will not have to restate their financial reports to conform to either GAAP or IFRS. Because the goal is to develop improved accounting standards, the boards take the big picture view in seeking solutions.[2]

Critical Thinking Questions
- Is it important to have a single set of international accounting standards for at least publicly owned companies? Defend your answer.
- What are some of the major changes from Canadian GAAP to IFRS? (Hint: Use your search engine to find out the answer!)

The Accounting Profession

When you think of accountants, do you picture someone who works alone in a back room, hunched over a desk, scrutinizing pages and pages of numbers? Although today's accountants still must love working with numbers, they now work closely with their clients not only to prepare financial reports but also to help them develop good financial practices. Computers have taken the tedium out of the number-crunching and data-gathering parts of the job and now offer powerful analytical tools as well. Therefore, accountants must keep up with information technology trends. The accounting profession has grown due to the increased complexity, size, and number of businesses and the frequent changes in the tax laws. There are approximately 200,000 accountants in Canada working in the private sector, public sector, or as self-employed accountants.[3]

HOT *Links*

To find out more about the accounting profession, visit the Canadian Institute of Chartered Accountants site at (www.cica.ca), the CMA Canada site at (www.cma-canada.org), or the Certified General Accountants site at (www.cga-canada.org).

The Accounting Designations

In Canada, there are three accounting associations that grant professional designations. They are the Canadian Institute of Chartered Accountants (CICA), the Society of Management Accountants of Canada (CMA Canada), and the Certified General Accountants Association of Canada (CGA-Canada). Each of the professional accounting associations provides specialized services and has certain educational and work experience requirements for the accountant to be granted the professional designation.

CONCEPT *in Action* >>>

The financial information contained in the CIBC Annual Accountability Report is prepared using generally accepted accounting principles. Lenders, suppliers, investors, and government agencies refer to the annual report to assess the financial strength of a business. What decisions can be made by reviewing a company's annual report?

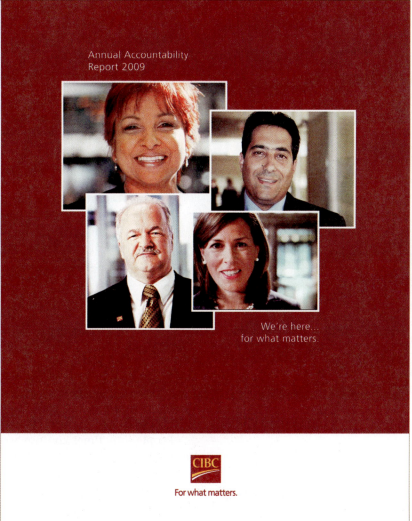

COURTESY CIBC

chartered accountant (CA)
An accountant who has completed an approved bachelor's degree program, completed an educational program, and passed a comprehensive examination.

A **chartered accountant (CA)** typically provides tax, audit, and management services. CAs focus on the external reporting and provide an opinion as to whether the financial statements accurately reflect the company's financial health (this can also be provided by a CGA—discussed below). Most CAs first work for public accounting firms and later become private accountants or financial managers.

CAs generally work in four key areas: public practice, industry, government, or education. In public practice they provide accounting and business advice to clients such as small business taxation, auditing, information technology, personal finance planning, business valuation, receivership, insolvency, and forensic investigation. In industry, CAs develop financial and administrative policies, analyze information, and provide strategic leadership.

certified management accountant (CMA)
An accountant who works primarily in industry and focuses on internal management accounting.

A **certified management accountant (CMA)** works primarily in industry and focuses on internal management accounting. CMAs combine their accounting expertise and business know-how with professional management skills to provide strategic financial management, strategic planning, sales and marketing, information technology, human resources, finance, and operations. According to CMA Canada, "*Working in organizations of all sizes and types, CMAs provide an integrating perspective to business decision making, applying best management practices in strategic planning, finance, operations, sales and marketing, information technology, and human resources to identify new market opportunities, ensure corporate accountability, and help organizations maintain a long-term competitive advantage.*"[4]

certified general accountant (CGA)
An accountant who focuses primarily on external financial reporting.

Certified general accountant (CGA) roles have far expanded from the primary focus on external financial reporting. CGAs also provide tax and financial advice to individuals and businesses. Many own their own accounting businesses, whereas others are employed in industry and government. According to CGA Canada, "*CGAs work throughout the world in industry, commerce, finance, government, public practice and other areas where accounting and financial management is required. CGA clients range from major corporations and industries to entrepreneurs. Their expertise is valued in the public sector, government and the corporate world.*"[5]

The requirements to become a CA, CMA, or CGA are quite extensive. Each requires a degree plus additional professional studies that cover the full spectrum of financial and business management. Candidates must also complete a period of articling (that results in real-world skills and development of practical problem-solving abilities) and, finally, pass comprehensive exams that demonstrate their knowledge of the profession.

Accountants add value to organizations as CEO/president, treasurer/VP finance, controller, or systems developer. All areas of government require accounting expertise to guide the financial planning and to maintain fiscal control. Additionally, many of Canada's top educators are accountants.

concept check

What are the three accounting designations in Canada?

Basic Accounting Procedures

Using generally accepted accounting principles, accountants record and report financial data in similar ways for all firms. They report their findings in financial statements that summarize a company's business transactions over a specified time period. As mentioned earlier, the three major financial statements are the statement of financial position, income statement, and statement of cash flows.

People sometimes confuse accounting with bookkeeping. Accounting is a much broader concept. *Bookkeeping,* the system used to record a firm's financial transactions, is a routine, clerical process. Accountants take bookkeepers' transactions, classify and summarize the financial information, and then prepare and analyze financial reports. Accountants also develop and manage financial systems and help plan the firm's financial strategy.

The Accounting Equation

assets
Things of value owned by a firm.

liabilities
What a firm owes to its creditors; also called *debts*.

owners' equity
The total amount of investment in the firm minus any liabilities; also called *net worth*.

The accounting procedures used today are based on the three main accounting elements of assets, liabilities, and owners' equity. **Assets** are things of value owned by a firm. They might be *tangible,* such as cash, equipment, and buildings, or *intangible,* such as a patent or trademarked name. **Liabilities**—also called *debts*—are what a firm owes to its creditors. **Owners' equity** is the total amount of investment in the firm minus any liabilities. Another term for owners' equity is *net worth.*

The relationship among these three elements is expressed in the accounting equation:

$$\text{Assets} = \text{Liabilities} + \text{Owners' equity}$$
$$\text{(own)} \qquad \text{(owe)} \qquad \text{(net worth)}$$

The accounting equation must always be in balance (that is, the total of the elements on one side of the equals sign must equal the total on the other side).

Suppose you start a bookstore and put $10,000 in cash into the business. At that point, the business has assets of $10,000 and no liabilities. This would be the accounting equation:

$$\text{Assets} \quad = \text{Liabilities} + \text{Owners' equity}$$
$$\$10,000 = \$0 \qquad\qquad + \$10,000$$

The liabilities are zero, and owner's equity (the amount of your investment in the business) is $10,000. The equation balances.

To keep the accounting equation in balance, every transaction must be recorded as at least two entries. As each transaction is recorded, there is an equal and opposite event so that the accounts or records are changed. This method is called **double-entry bookkeeping**.

double-entry bookkeeping
A method of accounting in which each transaction is recorded as at least two entries, so that the accounts or records are changed.

Suppose that, after starting your bookstore with $10,000 cash, you borrow an additional $10,000 from the bank. The accounting equation will change as follows:

Assets	= Liabilities	+ Owners' equity	
$10,000	= $0	+ $10,000	Initial equation
$10,000	= $10,000	+ $0	Borrowing transaction
$20,000	= $10,000	+ $10,000	Equation after borrowing

Now you have $20,000 in assets—your $10,000 in cash and the $10,000 loan proceeds from the bank. The bank loan is also recorded as a liability of $10,000, because it's a debt that you must repay. Making two entries keeps the equation in balance.

The Accounting Cycle

The *accounting cycle* refers to the process of generating financial statements, beginning with a business transaction and ending with the preparation of the report. Exhibit 14.3 shows the six steps in the accounting cycle. The first step in the cycle is to analyze the data collected from many sources. All transactions that have a financial impact on the firm—sales, payments to employees and suppliers, interest and tax payments, purchases of inventory, and the like—must be documented. The accountant must review the documents to make sure they're complete.

Next, each transaction is recorded in a *journal,* a listing of financial transactions in chronological order. Then the journal entries are recorded in *ledgers,* which show increases and decreases in specific asset, liability, and owners' equity accounts. The ledger totals for each account are summarized in a *trial balance,* which is used to confirm the accuracy of the figures. These values are used to prepare financial statements and management reports. Finally, individuals analyze these reports and make decisions based on the information in them.

EXHIBIT 14.3 > The Accounting Cycle

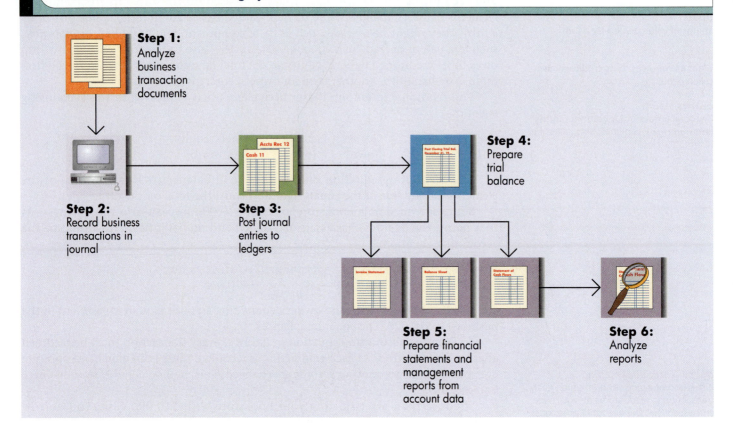

Step 1: Analyze business transaction documents

Step 2: Record business transactions in journal

Step 3: Post journal entries to ledgers

Step 4: Prepare trial balance

Step 5: Prepare financial statements and management reports from account data

Step 6: Analyze reports

Computers in Accounting

Computerized accounting programs do many different things. Most accounting packages offer six basic modules that handle general ledger, sales order, accounts receivable, purchase order, accounts payable, and inventory control functions. Tax programs use accounting data to prepare tax returns and tax plans. Computerized point-of-sale terminals used by many retail firms automatically record sales and do some of the bookkeeping.

Accounting and financial applications typically represent one of the largest portions of a company's software budget. Accounting software ranges from off-the-shelf programs for small businesses to full-scale customized enterprise resource planning systems for major corporations. Besides the accounting packages mentioned above, many large accounting firms have customized accounting software developed for them and their clients.

concept check

Explain the accounting equation.

Describe the six-step accounting cycle.

What role do computers play in accounting?

The Statement of Financial Position

LO 4

statement of financial position (balance sheet)
A financial statement that summarizes a firm's financial position at a specific point in time.

The **statement of financial position (balance sheet),** one of three financial statements generated from the accounting system, summarizes a firm's financial position at a specific point in time. It reports the resources of a company (assets), the company's obligations (liabilities), and the difference between what is owned (assets) and what is owed (liabilities), which is known as owners' equity.

liquidity
The speed with which an asset can be converted to cash.

The assets are listed in order of their **liquidity**, the speed with which they can be converted to cash. The most liquid assets come first, and the least liquid are last. Because cash is the most liquid asset, it is listed first. Buildings, on the other hand, have to be sold to be converted to cash, so they are listed after cash. Liabilities are arranged similarly: liabilities due in the short term are listed before those due in the long term.

The statement of financial position at December 31, 2011, for Delicious Desserts, an imaginary manufacturer, is illustrated in Exhibit 14.4. The basic accounting equation is reflected in the three totals highlighted on the statement of financial position: assets of $148,900 equal the sum of liabilities and owners' equity ($70,150 + $78,750). The three main categories of accounts on the statement of financial position are explained below.

EXHIBIT 14.4 > Statement of Financial Position for Delicious Desserts

Delicious Desserts, Inc.
Statement of Financial Position as of December 31, 2011

Assets

Current assets:			
Cash		$15,000	
Marketable securities		4,500	
Accounts receivable	$45,000		
Less: Allowance for doubtful accounts	1,300	43,700	
Notes receivable		5,000	
Inventory		15,000	
Total current assets			$ 83,200
Fixed assets:			
Bakery equipment	$56,000		
Less: Accumulated depreciation	16,000	$40,000	
Furniture and fixtures	$18,450		
Less: Accumulated depreciation	4,250	14,200	
Total fixed assets			54,200
Intangible assets:			
Trademark		$ 4,500	
Goodwill		7,000	
Total intangible assets			11,500
Total assets			**$148,900**

Liabilities and Owners' Equity

Current liabilities:			
Accounts payable	$30,650		
Notes payable	15,000		
Accrued expenses	4,500		
Income taxes payable	5,000		
Current portion of long-term debt	5,000		
Total current liabilities		$60,150	
Long-term liabilities:			
Bank loan for bakery equipment	$10,000		
Total long-term liabilities		10,000	
Total liabilities			**$ 70,150**
Owners' equity:			
Common shares (10,000 shares outstanding)		$30,000	
Retained earnings		48,750	
Total owners' equity			**78,750**
Total liabilities and owners' equity			**$148,900**

Assets

Assets can be divided into three broad categories: current assets, fixed assets, and intangible assets. **Current assets** are assets that can or will be converted to cash within the next 12 months. They are important because they provide the funds used to pay the firm's current bills. They also represent the amount of money the firm can raise quickly. Current assets include

- *cash*—funds on hand or in a bank;
- *marketable securities (trading securities)*—temporary investments of excess cash that can readily be converted to cash;
- *accounts receivable*—amounts owed to the firm by customers who bought goods or services on credit;
- *notes receivable*—amounts owed to the firm by customers or others to whom it lent money; and
- *inventory*—stock of goods being held for production or for sale to customers.

Fixed assets are long-term assets used by the firm for more than a year. They tend to be used in production and include land, buildings, machinery, equipment, furniture, and fixtures. Except for land, fixed assets wear out and become outdated over time. Thus, they decrease in value every year. This declining value is accounted for through amortization. **Amortization (also called depreciation)** is the allocation of the asset's original cost to the years in which it is expected to produce revenues. A portion of the cost of a depreciable asset—a building or piece of equipment, for instance—is charged to each of the years in which it is expected to provide benefits. This practice helps match the asset's cost against the revenues it provides. As it is impossible to know exactly how long an asset will last, estimates are used. They are based on past experience with similar items or on Canada Revenue Agency's guidelines. Notice that, through 2011, Delicious Desserts has taken a total of $16,000 in amortization on its bakery equipment.

Intangible assets are long-term assets with no physical existence. Common examples are patents, copyrights, trademarks, and goodwill. *Patents* and *copyrights* shield the firm from direct competition, so their benefits are more protective than productive. For instance, no one can use more than a small amount of copyrighted material without permission from the copyright holder. *Trademarks* are registered names that can be sold or licensed to others. One of Delicious Desserts' intangible assets is a trademark valued at $4,500. Delicious Desserts' other intangible asset is goodwill of $7,000. *Goodwill* occurs when a company pays more for an acquired firm than the value of its tangible assets.

Liabilities

Liabilities are the amounts a firm owes to creditors. Those liabilities coming due sooner—current liabilities—are listed first on the statement of financial position, followed by long-term liabilities.

Current liabilities are those due within a year of the date of the statement of financial position. These short-term claims can strain the firm's current assets because they must be paid in the near future. Current liabilities include the following:

- *Accounts payable.* This is the amount that the firm owes for credit purchases due within a year. This account is the liability counterpart of accounts receivable.
- *Notes payable.* These are short-term loans from banks, suppliers, or others that must be repaid within a year. For example, Delicious Desserts has a six-month, $15,000 loan from its bank that is a note payable.
- *Accrued expenses.* These represent expenses, typically for wages and taxes, that have accumulated and must be paid at a specified future date within the year, although no bill has been received by the firm.

---

current assets
Assets that can or will be converted to cash within the next twelve months.

fixed assets
Long-term assets used by a firm for more than a year, such as land, buildings, and machinery.

amortization (depreciation)
The allocation of an asset's original cost to the years in which it is expected to produce revenues.

intangible assets
Long-term assets with no physical existence, such as patents, copyrights, trademarks, and goodwill.

current liabilities
Short-term claims that are due within a year of the date of the statement of financial position.

CONCEPT *in Action* >>>

On its statement of financial position, a bakery would list its bakery equipment, furniture, and fixtures as fixed assets. The amount it owes its vendors for supplies would appear as a current liability—accounts payable—and its bank loan would be under long-term liabilities. On the income statement, you'll find a summary of revenues and expenses for a particular time period. What information can a potential investor find out from the statement of financial position?

IZAOKAS SAPIRO/SHUTTERSTOCK

- *Income taxes payable.* These are taxes owed for the current operating period but not yet paid. Taxes are often shown separately when they are a large amount.
- *Current portion of long-term debt.* This represents any repayment on long-term debt due within the year. Delicious Desserts is scheduled to repay $5,000 on its equipment loan in the coming year.

Long-term liabilities come due more than one year after the date of the statement of financial position. They include bank loans (such as Delicious Desserts' $10,000 loan for production equipment), mortgages on buildings, and the company's bonds sold to others.

long-term liabilities
Claims that come due more than one year after the date of the statement of financial position.

retained earnings
The amounts left over from profitable operations since the firm's beginning; equal to total profits minus all dividends paid to shareholders.

Owners' Equity

Owners' equity is the owners' total investment in the business after all liabilities have been paid. For sole proprietorships and partnerships, amounts put in by the owners are recorded as capital. In a corporation, the owners provide capital by buying the firm's common shares. For Delicious Desserts, the total common shares investment is $30,000. **Retained earnings** are the amounts left over from profitable operations since the firm's beginning. They are total profits minus all dividends (distributions of profits) paid to shareholders. Delicious Desserts has $48,750 in retained earnings.

> **concept check**
>
> *What is a statement of financial position?*
>
> *What are the three main categories of accounts on the statement of financial position, and how do they relate to the accounting equation?*
>
> *How do retained earnings relate to owners' equity?*

The Income Statement

LO 5

income statement
A financial statement that summarizes a firm's revenues and expenses, and shows its total profit or loss over a period of time.

The statement of financial position shows the firm's financial position at a certain point in time. The **income statement** summarizes the firm's revenues and expenses and shows its total profit or loss over a period of time. Most companies prepare monthly income statements for management and quarterly and annual statements for use by investors, creditors, and other outsiders. The primary elements of the income statement are revenues, expenses, and net income (or net loss). The income statement for Delicious Desserts for the year ended December 31, 2011, is shown in Exhibit 14.5.

NEL   **CHAPTER 14 Using Financial Information and Accounting   443**

EXHIBIT 14.5 > Income Statement for Delicious Desserts

Delicious Desserts, Inc.
Income Statement for the Year Ending December 31, 2011

Revenues		
Gross sales	$275,000	
Less: Sales discounts	2,500	
Less: Returns and allowances	2,000	
Net sales		$270,500
Cost of Goods Sold		
Beginning inventory, January 1	$ 18,000	
Cost of goods manufactured	109,500	
Total cost of goods available for sale	$127,500	
Less: Ending inventory December 31	15,000	
Cost of goods sold		112,500
Gross profit		**$158,000**
Operating Expenses		
Selling expenses		
Sales salaries	$31,000	
Advertising	16,000	
Other selling expenses	18,000	
Total selling expenses	$ 65,000	
General and administrative expenses		
Professional and office salaries	$20,500	
Utilities	5,000	
Office supplies	1,500	
Interest	3,600	
Insurance	2,500	
Rent	17,000	
Total general and administrative expenses	50,100	
Total operating expenses		115,100
Net profit before taxes		**$ 42,900**
Less: Income taxes		10,725
Net profit		**$ 32,175**

Revenues

revenues
The dollar amount of a firm's sales plus any other income it received from sources such as interest, dividends, and rents.

Revenues are the dollar amount of sales plus any other income received from sources such as interest, dividends, and rents. The revenues of Delicious Desserts arise from sales of its products. Revenues are determined starting with **gross sales,** the total dollar amount of a company's sales. Delicious Desserts had two deductions from gross sales. *Sales discounts* are price reductions given to customers who pay their bills early. For example, Delicious Desserts gives sales discounts to restaurants that buy in bulk and pay at delivery. *Returns and allowances* is the dollar amount of merchandise returned by customers because they didn't like a product or because it was damaged or defective. **Net sales** is the amount left after deducting sales discounts and returns and allowances from gross sales. Delicious Desserts gross sales were reduced by $4,500, leaving net sales of $270,500.

gross sales
The total dollar amount of a company's sales.

net sales
The amount left after deducting sales discounts and returns and allowances from gross sales.

Expenses

expenses
The costs of generating revenues.

cost of goods sold (COGS)
The total expense of buying or producing a firm's goods or services.

Expenses are the costs of generating revenues. Two types are recorded on the income statement: cost of goods sold and operating expenses.

The **cost of goods sold (COGS)** is the total expense of buying or producing the firm's goods or services. For manufacturers, cost of goods sold includes all costs directly related to production: purchases of raw materials and parts, labour, and factory overhead (utilities, factory maintenance, and machinery repair). For wholesalers and retailers, it is the cost of goods bought for resale. For all sellers, cost of goods sold includes all the expenses of preparing the goods for sale, such as shipping and packaging.

The value of COGS can be calculated using:

Beginning Inventories
+   Inventory Purchases
=   Inventories Available for Sale
−   Ending Inventories
=   COGS

Delicious Desserts cost of goods sold is based on the value of inventory on hand at the beginning of the accounting period, $18,000 (from the statement of financial position of the last accounting period). During the year, the company spent $109,500 to produce its manufactured goods. This figure includes the cost of raw materials, labour costs for production workers, and the cost of operating the production area. Adding the cost of goods manufactured to the value of beginning inventory, we get the total cost of goods available for sale, $127,500. To determine the cost of goods sold for the year, we subtract the cost of inventory at the end of the period:

$$\$18,000 + \$109,500 - \$15,000 = \$112,500$$

The amount a company earns after paying to produce or buy its products but before deducting operating expenses is the **gross profit.** It is the difference between net sales and cost of goods sold. As service firms do not produce goods, their gross profit equals net sales. Gross profit is a critical number for a company, because it is the source of funds to cover all the firm's other expenses.

The other major expense category is **operating expenses.** These are the expenses of running the business that are not related directly to producing or buying its products. The two main types of operating expenses are selling expenses and general and administrative expenses. *Selling expenses* are those related to marketing and distributing the company's products. They include salaries and commissions paid to salespeople and the costs of advertising, sales supplies, delivery, and other items that can be linked to sales activity, such as insurance, telephone and other utilities, and postage. *General and administrative expenses* are the business expenses that cannot be linked to either cost of goods sold or sales. Examples of general and administrative expenses are salaries of top managers and office support staff; utilities; office supplies; interest expense; fees for accounting, consulting, and legal services; insurance; and rent. Delicious Desserts operating expenses totalled $115,100.

Net Profit or Loss

The final figure—or bottom line—on an income statement is the **net profit** (or **net income**) or **net loss.** It is calculated by subtracting all expenses from revenues. If revenues are more than expenses, the result is a net profit. If expenses exceed revenues, a net loss results and is usually shown in brackets.

Several steps are involved in finding net profit or loss. (These are shown in the right-hand column of Exhibit 14.5.) First, the cost of goods sold is deducted from net sales to get the gross profit. Then, total operating expenses are subtracted from gross profit to get the net profit before taxes. Finally, income taxes are deducted to get the net profit. As shown in Exhibit 14.5, Delicious Desserts earned a net profit of $32,175 in 2011.

It is very important to recognize that profit does not represent cash. The income statement is a summary of the firm's operating results during some time period. It does not present the firm's actual cash flows during the period. Those are summarized in the statement of cash flows, which is discussed briefly in the next section.

gross profit
The amount a company earns after paying to produce or buy its products but before deducting operating expenses.

operating expenses
The expenses of running a business that are not directly related to producing or buying its products.

net profit (net income)
The amount obtained by subtracting all of a firm's expenses from its revenues, when the revenues are more than the expenses.

net loss
The amount obtained by subtracting all of a firm's expenses from its revenues, when the expenses are more than the revenues.

concept check

What is an income statement? How does it differ from the statement of financial position?

Describe the key parts of the income statement. Distinguish between gross sales and net sales.

How is net profit or loss calculated?

The Statement of Cash Flows

 LO 6

HOT Links

Choose any public Canadian company. Search its website for their financial statements, and review the statement of financial position and income statement.

Net profit or loss is one measure of a company's financial performance. However, creditors and investors are also keenly interested in how much cash a business generates and how it is used. The **statement of cash flows,** a summary of the money flowing into and out of a firm, is the financial statement used to assess the sources and uses of cash during a certain period, typically one year. All publicly traded firms must include a statement of cash flows in their financial reports to shareholders. The statement of cash flows tracks the firm's cash receipts and cash payments. It gives financial managers and analysts a way of identifying cash flow problems and of assessing the firm's financial viability.

Using income statement and statement of financial position data, the statement of cash flows divides the firm's cash flows into three groups:

- *cash flow from operating activities*—those related to the production of the firm's goods or services;
- *cash flow from investment activities*—those related to the purchase and sale of assets; and
- *cash flow from financing activities*—those related to debt and equity financing.

Delicious Desserts' statement of cash flows for 2011 is presented in Exhibit 14.6. It shows that the company's cash and marketable securities have increased over the last year. Furthermore, during the year, the company generated enough cash flow to increase inventory and fixed assets and to reduce accounts payable, accruals, notes payable, and long-term debt.

Analyzing Financial Statements

 LO 7

Individually, the statement of financial position, income statement, and statement of cash flows provide insight into the firm's operations, profitability, and overall financial condition. By studying the relationships among the financial statements,

---

EXHIBIT 14.6 > Statement of Cash Flows for Delicious Desserts

Delicious Desserts, INC.
Statement of Cash Flows for 2011

Cash Flow from Operating Activities		
Net profit after taxes	$ 27,175	
Amortization	1,500	
Decrease in accounts receivable	3,140	
Increase in inventory	(4,500)	
Decrease in accounts payable	(2,065)	
Decrease in accruals	(1,035)	
Cash provided by operating activities		$ 24,215
Cash Flow from Investment Activities		
Increase in gross fixed assets	($ 5,000)	
Cash used in investment activities		($ 5,000)
Cash Flow from Financing Activities		
Decrease in notes payable	($ 3,000)	
Decrease in long-term debt	(1,000)	
Cash used by financing activities		($ 4,000)
Net increase in cash and marketable securities		**$ 15,215**

---

ratio analysis
The calculation and interpretation of financial ratios using data taken from the firm's financial statements to assess its condition and performance.

however, one can gain even more insight into a firm's financial condition and performance.

Ratio analysis involves calculating and interpreting financial ratios using data taken from the firm's financial statements to assess its condition and performance. A financial ratio states the relationship between financial data on a percentage of three to five years. A firm's ratios can also be compared to industry averages or to basis. For instance, current assets might be viewed relative to current liabilities or sales relative to assets. The ratios can then be compared over time, typically to those of another company in the same industry. Period-to-period and industry ratios provide a meaningful basis for comparison, so that we can answer questions such as, "Is this particular ratio good or bad?"

It's important to remember that ratio analysis is based on historical data and might not indicate future financial performance. Ratio analysis merely highlights potential problems; it does not prove that they exist. However, ratios can help managers monitor the firm's performance from period to period, to understand operations better and identify trouble spots.

Ratios are also important to a firm's present and prospective creditors (lenders), who want to see if the firm can repay what it borrows and assess the firm's financial health. Often loan agreements require firms to maintain minimum levels of specific ratios. Both present and prospective shareholders use ratio analysis to look at the company's historical performance and trends over time.

Ratios can be classified by what they measure: liquidity, profitability, activity, and debt. Using Delicious Desserts' 2011 statement of financial position and income statement (Exhibits 14.4 and 14.5), we can calculate and interpret the key ratios in each group. In Exhibit 14.7, we have summarized the calculations of these ratios for Delicious Desserts. We will now discuss how to calculate the ratios and, more important, how to interpret the ratio value.

Liquidity Ratios

liquidity ratios
Ratios that measure a firm's ability to pay its short-term debts as they come due.

Liquidity ratios measure the firm's ability to pay its short-term debts as they come due. These ratios are of special interest to the firm's creditors. The three main measures of liquidity are the current ratio, the acid-test (quick) ratio, and net working capital.

CONCEPT *in Action* >>>

How is Best Buy doing this quarter compared to historical results? With ratio analysis, managers can track performance. For example, the net profit margin shows how much profit is left after all expenses. Why would a company want to compare their financial ratios with the industry averages?

© AP/WIDE WORLD PHOTOS

EXHIBIT 14.7 > Ratio Analysis for Delicious Desserts at Year-End 2011

Ratio	Formula	Calculation	Result
Liquidity Ratios			
Current ratio 1.42	$\dfrac{\text{Total current assets}}{\text{Total current liabilities}}$	$\dfrac{\$83,200}{\$60,150}$	1.4
Acid-test (quick) ratio	$\dfrac{\text{Total current assets} - \text{inventory}}{\text{Total current liabilities}}$	$\dfrac{\$83,200 - \$15,000}{\$60,150}$	1.1
Net working capital	Total current assets − Total current liabilities	$\$83,200 - \$60,150$	$23,050
Profitability Ratios			
Net profit margin	$\dfrac{\text{Net profit}}{\text{Net sales}}$	$\dfrac{\$13,175}{\$270,500}$	11.9%
Return on equity	$\dfrac{\text{Net profit}}{\text{Total owners' equity}}$	$\dfrac{\$32,175}{\$78,750}$	40.9%
Earnings per share	$\dfrac{\text{Net profit}}{\text{Number of shares of common shares outstanding}}$	$\dfrac{\$32,175}{10,000}$	$3.22
Activity Ratio			
Inventory turnover	$\dfrac{\text{Cost of goods sold}}{\text{Average inventory}}$		
	$\dfrac{\text{Cost of goods sold}}{(\text{Beginning inventory} + \text{Ending inventory})/2}$	$\dfrac{\$112,500}{(\$18,000 + \$15,000)/2}$	
		$\dfrac{\$112,500}{\$16,500}$	6.8 times
Debt Ratio			
Debt-to-equity ratio	$\dfrac{\text{Total liabilities}}{\text{Owners' equity}}$	$\dfrac{\$70,150}{\$78,750}$	89.1%

current ratio
The ratio of total current assets to total current liabilities; used to measure a firm's liquidity.

acid-test (quick) ratio
The ratio of total current assets excluding inventory to total current liabilities; used to measure a firm's liquidity.

The **current ratio** is the ratio of total current assets to total current liabilities. Traditionally, a current ratio of 2 ($2 of current assets for every $1 of current liabilities) has been considered good. Whether it is sufficient depends on the industry in which the firm operates. Public utilities, which have a very steady cash flow, operate quite well with a current ratio well below 2. A current ratio of 2 might not be adequate for manufacturers and merchandisers that carry high inventories and have lots of receivables. The current ratio for Delicious Desserts for 2011, as shown in Exhibit 14.7, is 1.4. This means little without a basis for comparison. If the analyst found that the industry average was 2.4, Delicious Desserts would appear to have low liquidity.

The **acid-test (quick) ratio** is like the current ratio except that it excludes inventory, which is the least liquid current asset. The acid-test ratio is used to measure the firm's ability to pay its current liabilities without selling inventory. The name *acid-test* implies that this ratio is a crucial test of the firm's liquidity. An acid-test ratio of at least 1 is preferred, but again, what is an acceptable value varies by industry. The acid-test ratio is a good measure of liquidity when inventory cannot easily be converted to cash (for instance, if it consists of very specialized goods with a limited market). If inventory is liquid, the current ratio is better. Delicious Desserts' acid-test ratio for 2011 is 1.1. Because Delicious Desserts does not carry large inventories, the values of its acid test and current ratios are fairly close. For manufacturing companies, however,

net working capital
The amount obtained by subtracting total current liabilities from total current assets; used to measure a firm's liquidity.

profitability ratios
Ratios that measure how well a firm is using its resources to generate profit and how efficiently it is being managed.

net profit margin
The ratio of net profit to net sales, also called *return on sales*. It measures the percentage of each sales dollar remaining after all expenses, including taxes, have been deducted.

return on equity (ROE)
The ratio of net profit to total owners' equity; measures the return that owners receive on their investment in the firm.

earnings per share (EPS)
The ratio of net profit to the number of common shares outstanding; measures the number of dollars earned by each share.

activity ratios
Ratios that measure how well a firm uses its assets.

inventory turnover ratio
The ratio of cost of goods sold to average inventory; measures the speed with which inventory moves through a firm and is turned into sales.

debt ratios
Ratios that measure the degree and effect of a firm's use of borrowed funds (debt) to finance its operations.

inventory typically makes up a large portion of current assets, so the acid-test ratio will be lower than the current ratio.

Net working capital, though not really a ratio, is often used to measure a firm's overall liquidity. It is calculated by subtracting total current liabilities from total current assets. Delicious Desserts' net working capital for 2011 is $23,050. Comparisons of net working capital over time often help in assessing a firm's liquidity.

Profitability Ratios

To measure profitability, a firm's profits can be related to its sales, equity, or shares value. Profitability ratios measure how well the firm is using its resources to generate profit and how efficiently it is being managed. The main profitability ratios are net profit margin, return on equity, and earnings per share.

The ratio of net profit to net sales is the net profit margin, also called *return on sales*. It measures the percentage of each sales dollar remaining after all expenses, including taxes, have been deducted. Higher net profit margins are better than lower ones. The net profit margin is often used to measure the firm's earning power. "Good" net profit margins differ quite a bit from industry to industry. A grocery store usually has a very low net profit margin, perhaps below 1 percent, whereas a jewellery store's net profit margin would probably exceed 10 percent. Delicious Desserts' net profit margin for 2011 is 11.9 percent. In other words, Delicious Desserts is earning 11.9 cents on each dollar of sales.

The ratio of net profit to total owners' equity is called return on equity (ROE). It measures the return that owners receive on their investment in the firm, a major reason for investing in a company's shares. Delicious Desserts has a 40.9 percent ROE for 2011. On the surface, a 40.9 percent ROE seems quite good, but the level of risk in the business and the ROE of other firms in the same industry must also be considered. The higher the risk, the greater the ROE investors look for. A firm's ROE can also be compared to past values to see how the company is performing over time.

Earnings per share (EPS) is the ratio of net profit to the number of shares of common shares outstanding. It measures the number of dollars earned by each share. EPS values are closely watched by investors and are considered an important sign of success. EPS also indicates a firm's ability to pay dividends. Note that EPS is the dollar amount earned by each share, not the actual amount given to shareholders in the form of dividends. Some earnings may be put back into the firm. Delicious Desserts' EPS for 2011 is $3.22.

Activity Ratios

Activity ratios measure how well a firm uses its assets. They reflect the speed with which resources are converted to cash or sales. A frequently used activity ratio is inventory turnover.

The inventory turnover ratio measures the speed with which inventory moves through the firm and is turned into sales. It is calculated by dividing cost of goods sold by the average inventory. (Average inventory is estimated by adding the beginning and ending inventories for the year and dividing by 2.) Based on its 2011 financial data, Delicious Desserts' inventory, on average, is turned into sales 6.8 times each year, or about once every 54 days (365 days ÷ 6.8). The acceptable turnover ratio depends on the line of business. A grocery store would have a high turnover ratio, maybe 20 times a year, whereas the turnover for a heavy equipment manufacturer might be only 3 times a year.

Debt Ratios

Debt ratios measure the degree and effect of the firm's use of borrowed funds (debt) to finance its operations. These ratios are especially important to

Making Ethical Choices

SUPERMARKETS SHELVE REVENUES AND CAN AUDITORS

As the assistant controller of a major supermarket company, you work closely with the company's independent auditor. Overall, you have been pleased with your auditor's performance and believe that the firm has shown high standards of integrity.

During this year's review of your firm's financial reports and its internal controls, the auditor raised a question about the timing of incentive payments received from vendors and when they would be recognized as revenue. The issue of such incentive payments from vendors is a big one in the grocery industry. Several of your competitors recorded vendor payments received of $2 to $3 billion in 2011—more than those companies' operating profits. You are aware that your chain uses these payment receipts to manipulate earnings, choosing the supplier that offers the largest up-front incentive payments for shelf space to boost quarterly earnings by a sizable amount. Although this is legal, it is a practice that has come under closer scrutiny in the wake of investigations of other accounting irregularities.

You are called into a meeting with the CFO and the controller to discuss what to do about the warning from the audit firm that it might have a "reportable condition" relating to this situation. The CFO wants to fire the audit firm and hire another one. The controller asks for your opinion.

ETHICAL DILEMMA: Should you go along with the CFO and recommend firing the audit firm?

SOURCES: David Henry, "Accounting Games in the Grocer's Aisle," *Business Week*, April 14, 2003, 64; and Stephen Taub, "D&T Warned A&P Dismissed," *CFO.com*, September 19, 2002, (www.cfo.com).

---

debt-to-equity ratio
The ratio of total liabilities to owners' equity; measures the relationship between the amount of debt financing and the amount of equity financing (owner's funds).

> ### concept check
>
> How can ratio analysis be used to interpret financial statements?
>
> Name the main liquidity and profitability ratios, and explain what they indicate.
>
> What kinds of information do activity ratios give? Why are debt ratios of concern to lenders and investors?

lenders and investors. They want to make sure the firm has a healthy mix of debt and equity. If the firm relies too much on debt, it might have trouble meeting interest payments and repaying loans. The most important debt ratio is the debt-to-equity ratio.

The **debt-to-equity ratio** measures the relationship between the amount of debt financing (borrowing) and the amount of equity financing (owners' funds). It is calculated by dividing total liabilities by owners' equity. In general, the lower the ratio, the better, but it is important to assess the debt-to-equity ratio against both past values and industry averages. Delicious Desserts' ratio for 2011 is 89.1 percent. The ratio indicates that the company has 89 cents of debt for every dollar the owners have provided. A ratio above 100 percent means the firm has more debt than equity. In such a case, the lenders are providing more financing than the owners.

Trends in Accounting

LO 8

HOT Links

Learn more accounting terms at Small Business: Canada, (http://sbinfocanada.about.com/od/accounting) or (http://sbinfocanada.about.com/cs/businessinfo/a/biztermsall.htm).

The role of accountants has been changing and expanding. Although accountants still perform the important task of assuring that a company's financial reporting conforms to IFRS, they have become a valuable part of the financial team and consult with clients on information technology and other areas as well.

The increasing complexity of today's business environment creates additional challenges for the accounting profession. As we move to a more knowledge-based economy, this creates a problem with being able to value and account for the knowledge assets. By far the most significant accounting change in Canada is the move to IFRS.

Accountants Expand Their Role

Moving beyond their traditional task of validating a company's financial information, accountants now take an active role in advising their clients on systems and procedures, accounting software, and changes in accounting regulations. They also delve into operating information to discover what's behind the numbers. By examining the risks and weaknesses in a company, they can help managers develop financial controls and procedures to prevent future trouble spots. For example, auditors in a manufacturing company might spend a significant amount of time on inventory, a likely problem area.

Accounting firms have greatly expanded the consulting services they provide clients. As a result, accountants have become more involved in the operations of their clients. This raises the question of potential conflicts of interest. Can auditors serve both the public and the client? Auditors' main purpose is to certify financial statements. Will they maintain sufficient objectivity to raise questions while auditing a client that provides them with significant consulting revenues? Can auditors review systems and methods that they recommended? According to one expert, "If the financial markets don't believe in a firm's audit, the firm has nothing."

Valuing Knowledge Assets

As the world's economy becomes knowledge-based rather than industrial-based, more of a company's value might come from internally generated, intangible intellectual assets. Intellectual capital is an important resource to any organization, but are we serious about actually attaching a dollar value to it? Dr. Nick Bontis, a researcher and practitioner in knowledge management, intellectual capital, and organizational learning at McMaster University in Hamilton, Ontario, discovered that the main reason cited by his research subjects for leaving their employment was that they felt they were underutilized. With voluntary turnover in Canadian organizations reaching 15 percent, we are watching these knowledge assets walk out the door.[6]

Whether and how to value intangibles are controversial issues. Some people believe that because intangibles are uncertain and risky, they do not belong on the statement of financial position. Costs related to intangibles might bear no relationship to their actual value. On the other hand, placing a value on intangibles allows companies to know whether they are earning adequate returns on R&D, whether patents are worth renewing, and whether they should invest more to build brands. Clearly, there are no quick and easy solutions to this issue, which will continue to be studied in the coming years.

Canada Moves to International Financial Reporting Standards (IFRS)

The most significant trend in accounting presently is the move to IFRS. As we have seen, international trade and investment is important to the Canadian economy and our standard of living. As more and more Canadian companies are operating globally, the various accounting methods used internationally has created duplicate work and more expenses. By moving to IFRS, international companies can use one accounting method. This creates many advantages.

Some of the advantages include: lower costs associated with preparation of financial information, consistency in reports internationally, ease of financial comparisons with other companies, etc. Some notable changes to IFRS include: revenue is called income, the balance sheet is called the Statement of Financial Position and the cash flow statement is called the Statement of Cash Flows.

concept check

What new roles are accountants playing? Do you see any potential problems from these new roles?

What are knowledge assets, and why have they become so important?

How will Canada's moving to IFRS benefit our companies?

Great Ideas to Use Now

By now it should be very clear that basic accounting knowledge is a valuable skill to have, whether you start your own company or work for someone else. Analyzing a company's financial statements before you take a job there can tell you quite a bit

Customer Satisfaction and Quality

The recent upheaval in corporate financial reporting makes customer satisfaction and quality very relevant to financial statement preparation and the accounting profession. As noted earlier, auditing firms often gave good reports to companies later charged with accounting irregularities.

The customers for financial reports are not just the corporate clients who hire the auditors. The investing public—both institutions who buy large blocks of shares and individuals—rely heavily on the quality and reliability of reported financial information to make investment decisions. They are demanding that auditors and corporations demonstrate their compliance with higher standards.

Companies are now giving new respect to the external auditing process. "If you want an audit that will detect management fraud, you must be willing to pay more for it and pay far greater attention to the process and what will be included and analyzed," says Robert G. Eccles, PricewaterhouseCoopers senior fellow and coauthor of *Building Public Trust: The Future of Corporate Reporting.* "The audit committee must be the customer for the audit, and this will require more time on the part of the audit committee."

Better quality control will result from new corporate governance standards and financial disclosure practices. Management at Airgas Inc., an industrial gases distributor, now spends more time on these issues. It was already in compliance with the latest legislative and regulatory reforms. Recently, the company implemented a more formal approach to financial quality control. The audit committee will hold a special meeting every year to review current business issues. "This focus is closely tied to our growth strategy," says Roger Millay, Airgas senior vice-president and CFO. "Good governance, and the perception and understanding of good governance, are important to our growth strategy. The market's confidence in our governance is essential to attracting capital."

SOURCE: Outlook 2003: More Changes, Greater Challenges, (www.businessfinance-mag.com), December 2002. Reprinted with permission from Penton Media.

about its financial health. Once you are on the job, you need to understand how to read financial statements and how to develop financial information for business operations. It's almost impossible to operate effectively in a business environment otherwise. In a small company, you will wear many hats, and having accounting skills may help you get the job. In addition, accounting will help you manage your personal finances.

If you own your own firm, you can't rely on someone else to take charge of your accounting system. You must decide what financial information you need to manage your company better and to track its progress. If you can't understand the reports your accountant prepares, you will have no idea whether they are accurate.

Summary of Learning Outcomes

1 Explain the importance of financial reports and accounting information to the targeted users?

Accounting involves collecting, recording, classifying, summarizing, reporting, and analyzing a firm's financial activities according to a standard set of procedures. The financial reports resulting from the accounting process give managers, employees, investors, customers, suppliers, creditors, and government agencies a way of analyzing a company's past, current, and future performance. Financial accounting is concerned with the preparation of financial reports using generally accepted accounting principles. Managerial accounting provides financial information that management can use to make decisions about the firm's operations.

2 Show an understanding of the accounting profession.

Although today's accountants still must love working with numbers, they now work closely with their clients not only to prepare financial reports but also to help them develop good financial practices. Computers have taken the tedium out of the number-crunching and data-gathering parts of the job and now offer powerful analytical tools as well. Therefore, accountants must keep up with information technology trends.

In Canada there are three accounting associations that grant professional designations. They are the Canadian Institute of Chartered Accountants (CICA), the Society of Management Accountants of Canada (CMA Canada), and the Certified

General Accountants Association of Canada (CGA-Canada). Each of the professional accounting associations provides specialized services and has certain educational and work experience requirements for the accountant to be granted the professional designation.

3 **Identify the six steps in the accounting cycle.**

The accounting cycle refers to the process of generating financial statements. It begins with analyzing business transactions, recording them in journals, and posting them to ledgers. Ledger totals are then summarized in a trial balance that confirms the accuracy of the figures. Next, the accountant prepares the financial statements and reports. The final step involves analyzing these reports and making decisions.

4 **Understand how a statement of financial position describes the financial condition of an organization.**

The statement of financial position represents the financial condition of a firm at one moment in time, in terms of assets, liabilities, and owners' equity. The key categories of assets are current assets, fixed assets, and intangible assets. Liabilities are divided into current and long-term liabilities. Owners' equity, the amount of the owners' investment in the firm after all liabilities have been paid, is the third major category.

5 **Explain the purpose of the income statement.**

The income statement is a summary of the firm's operations over a stated period of time. The main parts of the statement are revenues (gross and net sales), cost of goods sold, operating expenses (selling and general and administrative expenses), taxes, and net profit or loss.

6 **Describe the importance of the statement of cash flows.**

The statement of cash flows summarizes the firm's sources and uses of cash during a financial-reporting period. It breaks the firm's cash flows into those from operating, investment, and financing activities. It shows the net change during the period in the firm's cash and marketable securities.

7 **Explain how ratio analysis is used to identify a firm's financial strengths and weaknesses.**

Ratio analysis is a way to use financial statements to gain insight into a firm's operations, profitability, and overall financial condition. The four main types of ratios are liquidity ratios, profitability ratios, activity ratios, and debt ratios. Comparing a firm's ratios over several years and comparing them to ratios of other firms in the same industry or to industry averages can indicate trends and highlight financial strengths and weaknesses.

8 **List some of the major trends that are impacting the accounting industry.**

The accounting industry is responding to the rise in information technology in several ways. The role of accountants has expanded beyond the traditional audit and tax functions and now includes management consulting in areas such as computer systems, human resources, and electronic commerce. A major issue facing the industry is how to treat key intangible assets—knowledge assets such as patents, brands, and research and development—and whether they should be valued and included on a company's statement of financial position. The most significant trend is Canada's move to the IFRS. This allows Canadian companies operating internationally to potentially benefit from decreased costs of financial reporting, consistency in financial reporting, ease of financial comparisons, etc.

Key Terms

accounting   434
acid-test (quick) ratio   448
activity ratios   449
amortization (depreciation)   442
annual report   436

assets   439
certified general accountant (CGA)   438
certified management accountant (CMA)   438
chartered accountant (CA)   438

Experiential Exercises

1. Learn to read financial statements. To become more familiar with annual reports and key financial statements, head for IBM's "Guide to Understanding Financials" at (**www.ibm.com/investor/financialguide**). The material offers a good overview of financial reporting and shows you what to look for when you read these documents.

2. **Prepare personal financial statements.** One of the best ways to learn about financial statements is to prepare them. Put together your personal statement of financial position and income statement, using Exhibits 14.4 and 14.5 as samples. You will have to adjust the account categories to fit your needs. Here are some suggestions:

    *   Current assets–cash on hand, balances in savings and chequing accounts.
    *   Investments–shares and bonds, retirement funds.
    *   Fixed assets–real estate, personal property (cars, furniture, jewellery, etc.).
    *   Current liabilities–credit card balances, loan payments due in one year.
    *   Long-term liabilities–auto loan balance, mortgage on real estate, other loan balances that will not come due until after one year.
    *   Income–employment income, investment income (interest, dividends).
    *   Expenses–housing, utilities, food, transportation, medical, clothing, insurance, loan payments, taxes, personal care, recreation and entertainment, and miscellaneous expenses.

    After you complete your personal financial statements, use them to see how well you are managing your finances. Consider the following questions:

    *   Should you be concerned about your debt ratio?
    *   Would a potential creditor conclude that it is safe or risky to lend you money?
    *   If you were a company, would people want to invest in you? Why or why not? What could you do to improve your financial condition?

3. Your firm has been hired to help several small businesses with their year-end financial statements.

a. Based on the following account balances, prepare the Marbella Design Enterprises statement of financial position as of December 31, 2011:

Cash	$30,250
Accounts payable	28,500
Fixtures and furnishings	85,000
Notes payable	15,000
Retained earnings	64,450
Accounts receivable	24,050
Inventory	15,600
Equipment	42,750
Accumulated amortization on fixtures and furnishings	12,500
Common shares (50,000 shares outstanding)	50,000
Long-term debt	25,000
Accumulated amortization on equipment	7,800
Marketable securities	13,000
Income taxes payable	7,500

b. The following are the account balances for the revenues and expenses of the Windsor Gift Shop for the year ending December 31, 2011. Prepare the income statement for the shop.

Rent	$15,000
Salaries	23,500
Cost of goods sold	98,000
Utilities	8,000
Supplies	3,500
Sales	195,000
Advertising	3,600
Interest	3,000
Taxes	12,120

4. During the year ended December 31, 2011, Lawrence Industries sold $2 million worth of merchandise on credit. A total of $1.4 million was collected during the year. The cost of this merchandise was $1.3 million. Of this amount, $1 million has been paid, and $300,000 is not yet due. Operating expenses and income taxes totalling $500,000 were paid in cash during the year. Assume that all accounts had a zero balance at the beginning of the year (January 1, 2011). Write a brief report for the company controller that includes calculation of the firm's (a) net profit and (b) cash flow during the year. Explain why there is a difference between net profit and cash flow.

5. A friend has been offered a sales representative position at Draper Publications, Inc., a small publisher of computer-related books, but wants to know more about the company. Because of your expertise in financial analysis, you offer to help analyze Draper's financial health. Draper has provided the following selected financial information:

Account balances on December 31, 2011:	
Inventory	$ 72,000
Net sales	450,000
Current assets	150,000
Cost of goods sold	290,000
Total liabilities	180,000
Net profit	35,400
Total assets	385,000
Current liabilities	75,000
Other information	
Number of common shares outstanding	25,000
Inventory at January 1, 2011	48,000

Calculate the following ratios for 2011: acid-test (quick) ratio, inventory turnover ratio, net profit margin, return on equity (ROE), debt-to-equity ratio, and earnings per share (EPS). Summarize your assessment of the company's financial performance, based on these ratios, in a report for your friend. What other information would you like to have to complete your evaluation?

6. Two years ago, Rebecca Mardon started a computer consulting business, Mardon Consulting Associates. Until now, she has been the only employee, but business has grown enough to support an administrative assistant and another consultant this year. Before she adds staff, however, she wants to hire an accountant and computerize her financial record keeping. Divide the class into small groups, assigning one person to be Rebecca and the others to represent members of a medium-sized accounting firm. Rebecca should think about the type of financial information systems her firm requires and develop a list of questions for the firm. The accountants will prepare a presentation, making recommendations to her as well as explaining why their firm should win the account.

7. Do annual reports confuse you? Many websites can take the mystery out of this important document. See IBM's "Guide to Understanding Financials" at (**www.prars.com/ibm/ibmframe.html**). Moneychimp's "How to Read an Annual Report" features an interactive diagram that provides a big picture view of what the report's financial information tells you: (**www.moneychimp.com/articles/financials/fundamentals.htm**). Which site was more helpful to you, and why?

8. Can you judge an annual report by its cover? What are the most important elements of a top annual report? Go to Sid Cato's Official Annual Reportwebsite, (**www.sidcato.com**), to find his 15 standards for annual reports and read about the reports that receive his honours. Then, get a copy of an annual report and evaluate it using Cato's 135-point scale. How well does it compare to his top picks?

Review Questions

1. What is accounting? What is the difference between managerial and financial accounting?

2. What is IFRS? What is its function?

3. Discuss the accounting profession in terms of public versus private accountants, CAs, CMAs, and CGAs.

4. What is the accounting equation?

5. Explain the various categories of a statement of financial position.

6. What is the purpose of the income statement? What does it include?

7. What is the purpose of a statement of cash flows?

8. What is ratio analysis?

9. Name and provide the formulas of the liquidity ratios mentioned in the chapter.

10. What do profitability ratios tell us? Which ratios are mentioned in the chapter?

11. What are activity ratios and which ones are mentioned in the chapter?

12. What do debt ratios measure? What does the debt-to-equity ratio measure?

13. What trends are happening in the accounting field?

Accounting: Who Are We Responsible To?

Arthur Andersen started the accounting firm that bore his name in 1913. From the start, he embraced the highest business ethics, refusing to manipulate unsatisfactory financial results at a client's request. Andersen's motto, "Think straight, talk straight," was the foundation of the company's culture of honesty and integrity. The company was known for its disciplined and strict attention to accounting standards.

By the 1990s, the Andersen culture had strayed far from its founder's philosophy. Andersen was "a place where the mad scramble for fees had trumped good judgment," says Barbara Ley Toffler, author of *Final Accounting: Ambition, Greed and the Fall of Arthur Andersen*. These fees came not only from auditing but increasingly from the rapidly growing consulting practices of Andersen and its industry colleagues. Business units competed with each other and were rewarded for bringing in revenues, not for evaluating a deal's risks.

The growth of consulting revenues was in itself a problem. Andersen often provided business services to the same companies it audited, earning as much from consulting as auditing. This conflict of interest placed pressure on the auditors to go along with aggressive accounting practices in order to preserve the consulting relationships and earnings.

Andersen's culture also placed a loyalty to the firm before loyalty to clients or shareholders. Partners who raised questions were penalized. This attitude went straight down the line, as Toffler discovered when leading a meeting of young Andersen employees. She asked how they would respond if a supervisor told them to do something they considered wrong. Only one person spoke up: "If he insisted I do it, yes, I would." Toffler then asked if he would tell anyone about it: "No. It could hurt my career."

Turning a blind eye to accounting irregularities at clients was a common practice. Says Toffler, who—ironically—ran Andersen's business ethics consulting practice from 1995 to 1999, "High-level members of that organization knew much of what was going on." As Enron's wrongdoings became public, the firm's top management became Enron's partner in duplicity instead of demonstrating the industry leadership its founder would have expected.

In June 2002, Andersen was convicted of obstruction of justice in the Enron case for shredding documents. Later that summer, the doors shut at the accounting firm that once set the standards to which other firms aspired.

Critical Thinking Questions

- Toffler says that Andersen executives expected that aggressive accounting would have an impact when the economy tanked but issued few warning memos and did nothing to change the culture of greed. With the benefit of hindsight, what steps could Andersen's leadership have taken to preserve the firm as the accounting scandals unfolded?
- Andersen's Enron audit team was aware of monkey business as early as 1987, when management covered up the oil-trading scandal mentioned in the chapter opener. It also caved in to pressure to sign off on questionable deals and participated in document destruction that led to its obstruction-of-justice conviction. Suggest procedures that auditors and corporations should adopt and enforce to prevent these abuses.
- Discuss why providing consulting services to audit clients in such areas as business strategy, financial strategy, human resources, and information technology systems planning, design, and implementation can create a conflict of interest.

SOURCES: Greg Farrell, "Former Andersen Exec Tells of Stressful Internal Culture," *USA Today*, March 3, 2003; William J. Holstein, "Lessons of a Fallen Rival for Accounting's Big 4," *The New York Times*, February 23, 2003; and Rob Walker, "Inside a Culture of Greed," *Newsday*, March 6, 2003.

Doug Hall Fixes Tofino

Tofino is a remote community on the west coast of Vancouver Island. Many of the small businesses there depend on the tourism industry, which is, to a large degree, seasonal. Doug Hall is a successful business consultant who has been hired to advise three of Tofino's entrepreneurs on how to be more profitable. The operations include a fish/ice-cream market, Mike's Market; a whale-watching/museum company, and a cleaning business, Dust Bunnies. Each enterprise is able to cover its expenses and make a bit of money, but the profits are small, and there is virtually no growth. The owners report working long hours at their respective endeavours and are interested in what a high-profile American consultant might suggest.

The fish market owner has several other businesses and lacks focus. The whale-watching entrepreneur has tried to differentiate by offering whale bones for the tourists to admire as part of his museum. The owner of the cleaning service, although successful, is simply tired of cleaning toilets.

An analysis of each statement of financial position might show a reasonable current ratio and acid-test ratio but nothing particularly strong. The ROE ratios might not look very good for the fish market and the whale-watching, as each of these probably has significant owner's equity. To help these businesses increase their cash flow, Doug Hall suggests strategies such as diversification for the whale-watching business, greater focus and branding for the fish/ice-cream market, and the addition of a totally new operation for the owner of the cleaning business.

In an area that depends heavily on tourism, it is more difficult to have money coming in regularly, and the stress of having to make enough money in the summer to last the entire year is enormous. The whale-watching does occur year-round, but summer is the busiest time. Dust Bunnies primarily cleans vacation rentals, and Mike's Market, although serving the locals, depends on the tourists as well.

Doug Hall makes excellent recommendations to the owners, and the results are interesting.

Critical Thinking Questions

- If these three entrepreneurs were to implement Doug's suggestions, how would they finance the changes?
- Why would having significant owner's equity negatively affect the ROE for the market and the whale-watching businesses?
- Which of the three companies profiled in the video found a strategy to allow year-round income? Check (**www.tofinotime.com/main**) and look at Bodi Bikes. Also look at (**www.tofinowhalecentre.com**).

SOURCE: CBC, *Venture*, "Doug Hall Fixes Tofino Part 1, 2, and 3," February 20, 2005.

Accounting for the Dollars Spent on the Gun Registry

Whether you disagree philosophically with the Canadian gun registry or not, most Canadian taxpayers would certainly disagree with the amount of tax dollars spent on it.

Criticisms of the gun registry have been voiced for years, and with a cost of approximately $2 billion, have we spent our tax dollars wisely? The annual cost of the registry is $2.9 million a year with daily usage of 9400 inquiries per day by police officials, a cost of $308.51 per inquiry. How can we assign a dollar value to a human life? Does the use of the Registry reduce the incidence of murder by firearms?

The rate of spousal murder by firearms has dropped considerably and the RCMP report these are the most common weapons used in domestic disputes. A Swiss study suggests that the gun registry may, in fact, be saving Canada money by lowering the costs associated with firearms injuries. Their estimated savings, based on costing studies, is a savings of $1.4 billion a year. Others argue that it is impossible to establish a direct causal link to the gun control and do not agree that the decreases in deaths and injuries can be attributed to the gun registry.

The Conservatives are still attempting to abolish the gun registry and have put forward a third bid to do so. They are aware of the importance of the rural vote and recognize that most rural constituents do not support the gun registry. Since 2006, the government has granted amnesties, fee rebates, and has overall not collected a possible $56.5 million while spending $35.9 million to run the registry.

Critical Thinking Questions

1. From an accounting perspective, can you justify the money spent on the gun registry to date? In this chapter, we discussed valuing knowledge assets and other intangibles. How would you attach a dollar value to a human life? If this could be done, could you then make an argument for the money spent on the gun registry?

2. Check online to determine if the Conservatives have, in fact, abolished the registry. What research can you find on valuing intangible assets? What further research has been done on the effectiveness of the Registry or gun control in general?

SOURCES: Tonda MacCharles, "Conservatives make Third Attempt to Kill Gun Registry," TheStar.com, April 1, 2009; Nathanial Gronewold, "Swiss study says Canada's gun registry may help cut costs from violence," Canadian Press, June 27, 2006; and Frances Russell, " Canadian Police want to keep gun registry going, Winnipeg Free Press, Apr. 1, 2009.

CHAPTER 15

Making the Connection

Understanding Money, Financial Institutions, and the Securities Markets

In this chapter, we will look at the finance area by examining where the money to run a successful business comes from. It would be wonderful if all the capital needed to operate and grow a business came from income alone. However, to move past a company's current level of income and to grow it to new heights, implementing its chosen *strategy* to achieve its *vision*, it typically must bring fresh capital in from outside. In the chapter, we introduce the role of money and financial institutions as well as the securities markets, which provide the fuel for companies—an arena for raising capital.

Among the major *stakeholders* in any business are the owners. As discussed in previous chapters, companies must consider the impact on stakeholders of any decisions they make. Certainly the choice of how a business is financed has a tremendous impact on the owners. Particularly in the publicly traded corporation, it is critical that financial managers consider this seriously, as there is a very integrative relationship between this major stakeholder and the firm's financing. Much of the firm's financial resources will come from investments from its owners—the shareholders—through the purchase of shares or stocks in the company. However, how those financial resources are managed will, in turn, affect the value of the company and the owners' stake in it, and therefore whether they would consider the company worth continuing to invest in. This affects the company's ability to raise additional money through the sale of more shares.

If the financial manager does not focus on the first of the critical success factors—*achieving financial performance*—then the shareholders will be less inclined to invest further and perhaps even sell their shares, which could, if there is enough selling activity, drive down the price of the shares on the stock market, making the shares even less appealing to most investors. The ability to raise additional funds through the sale of shares will then be hindered. However, to achieve financial performance, we know that it is essential to achieve the other success factors as well—*meeting customer needs, providing quality, encouraging innovation*, and *gaining employee commitment*—because they are all related. So all the functional area managers—*marketing, operations*, and *human resources*, as well as *finance*, are responsible for making sure the company is successful for its stakeholders. They all have an impact on financial performance.

Companies, of course, have other options for raising capital. In the securities markets, one of the major options besides selling equity investments—a piece of ownership through shares—is to sell bonds. Selling bonds is essentially borrowing money and so is debt rather than equity financing. The balancing act that the company plays between the amount of debt it uses to finance the company and the amount of equity also has an impact on the financial performance of the firm and, again, on its ability to raise more capital.

Whatever amount of debt it chooses to use versus equity, or the amount of bonds it sells as opposed to shares,

the external environment will have an enormous impact, just as we've seen with all other aspects of the business. The external environment forms the context in which the company operates and thus affects its decisions and its success. For example, the *political* environment lays the foundation for how the company can raise capital—regulations exist surrounding the criteria that a company must meet to be able to sell its shares to the public—as well as the composition of the Board of Directors, the highest level of *management* in the firm, whose main job is to protect the interests of the shareholders. The *economic* environment certainly has an impact, both from a competitive standpoint, as firms compete not only for customers but for investors as well, and from a purely economic one, as the economy affects what investments are the most attractive to investors (influencing what type of financing is likely to be the more marketable—selling shares or bonds) and the cost of debt financing to the company through interest rates. The *social* environment

also impacts a company's financing. This is evident in the popularity of ethical funds—mutual funds that invest in companies that have a strong social conscience. And finally, the impact of the *technological* environment was very obvious and extreme a few years back, when technological companies were the darlings of the stock market, before the "bubble burst" and they just as dramatically fell in value. But the impact of technology is also felt in how the market operates. Each year, more and more advances are made to automate the securities exchanges. Gone are the days of traders shouting across trading floors.

For investors, though, the markets are still exciting and offer an opportunity for ordinary people like you and me to become part owners in a company and share in its success. This is all made possible by companies' entering the market to raise capital to operate their businesses and, in turn, increasing value for the owners, their primary stakeholders.

CHAPTER 15

Understanding Money, Financial Institutions, and the Securities Markets

LEARNING OUTCOMES

1 Understand the characteristics of money and its functions.

2 Describe the basic functions of the Bank of Canada, and how it manages the Canadian money supply.

3 Identify the key financial institutions, and the role they play in the process of financial intermediation.

4 Outline how the Canada Deposit Insurance Corporation protects depositors' funds.

5 Summarize the role of Canadian banks in the international marketplace.

6 Distinguish between common shares and preferred shares.

7 Understand the investment advantages and disadvantages of bonds.

8 List other types of securities available to investors.

9 Describe the function of the securities markets.

10 List some of the trends that are reshaping the financial industry.

THE CHANGING ROLE OF BANKING

SHIRLEY A. ROSE

Ron Munaweera is the former senior vice-president and chief financial officer of Bank West, a subsidiary of the Western Financial Group, Inc. Ron's career has spanned more than 30 years in the banking and insurance industries, in positions ranging from teller at the BC Teachers' Credit Union, through Coronado Mortgage Corporation, Seaboard Life and People's Trust, to VP and CFO.

As Ron has moved forward in his career, he has seen many changes in the Canadian banking industry. In the 1970s, when Ron began his banking career, there were numerous financial institutions but only the six major banks. Today there are 21 domestic banks, 25 Canadian banks that are subsidiaries of foreign banks, and 23 foreign bank branches in Canada.[1] Institutions such as Canadian Tire Bank and Manulife Bank of Canada are both domestic banks. Over the years, there have been trust company mergers as well as bank acquisitions of trust companies (e.g., TD Canada Trust, part of the TD Financial Group). These institutions manage approximately $1.8 trillion in assets.

In addition to the expansion occurring in the industry, there have been many changes in the focus of banking. Ron has identified three very important trends that have definitely changed the flavour of banking over the years. First, the regulation of the industry with respect to proper governance is stronger. Second, there is an emphasis on anti-terrorist financing and anti-money laundering financing. The banks must know their clients and also know where the clients are getting their money. Third, there is movement toward strengthening the international banking system to ensure consistent and proper measurement of risk. Banks face many types of risk in addition to the obvious interest rate fluctuations. These include other banking risks such as credit risks, liquidity risks, market risks and foreign exchange risks. Non-banking risks include factors such as IT risks, HR risks, reputational risks and regulatory/statutory risks. The Bank for International Settlements (BIS), which is a group of bankers from the developed countries, has developed a framework for international standards known as Basel II.

In an attempt to focus more intently on issues of risk, the Office of the Superintendent of Financial Institutions Canada (OSFI–(www.osfi-bsif.gc.ca)) is requiring banks to submit a report analyzing their risks. This report (ICAAP–Internal Capital Adequacy Assessment Process) requires the banks to analyze not only the risks listed above, but also examine the magnitude and probability of losses, calculate the impact losses would have on capital, devise plans to divert or raise capital and quantify all risks.

As well, any financial institution traded on an American exchange must comply with the Canadian equivalent of Sarbanes-Oxley, known in the Canadian industry as SOX North.

These trends toward greater regulation have tremendously increased the compliance effort required, leading to time-consuming and complex decision making. But Ron finds it a very exciting time to be in the industry—a role far removed from the "old-time" bank manager of the '70s, '80s, and '90s.[2]

Critical Thinking Questions

1. **Given the trends toward increased regulation in the industry, is banking a reasonable career goal for a business student?**

2. **Research the Basel II accord. What can you see as possible problems if economic powers such as China do not join BIS?**

Advanced technology, globalization of markets, and the relaxation of regulatory restrictions are accelerating the pace of change in the financial services industry. These changes are giving businesses and consumers new options for conducting their financial transactions. The competitive landscape for financial institutions is also changing, creating new ways for these firms to increase their market share and boost profits.

Because financial institutions connect people with money, we begin this chapter with a discussion of money, its characteristics and functions, and the components of the Canadian money supply. Next we explain the role of the Bank of Canada (Canada's central bank—first introduced in Chapter 1) in managing the money supply. Then we describe different types of financial institutions and their services, and the organizations that insure customer deposits. We continue with a discussion of international banking and the securities markets. Finally, we look at trends in the banking industry.

Show Me the Money

money
Anything that is acceptable as payment for goods and services.

Money is anything that is acceptable as payment for goods and services. It affects our lives in many ways. We earn it, spend it, save it, invest it—and often wish we had more of it. Business and government use money in similar ways. Both require money to finance their operations. By controlling the amount of money in circulation, the Bank of Canada can promote economic and financial well-being in Canada. For this reason, money has been called the lubricant for the machinery of our economic system. Our banking system was developed to ease the handling of money.

Characteristics of Money

For money to be a suitable means of exchange, it should have these key characteristics.

- *Scarcity.* Money should be scarce enough to have some value but not so scarce as to be unavailable. Pebbles, which meet some of the other criteria, would not work well as money, because they are widely available. Too much money in circulation increases prices. Central banks control the scarcity of money by limiting the quantity of money produced.
- *Durability.* Any item used as money must be durable. A perishable item such as a banana becomes useless as money when it spoils. Even early societies used durable forms of money, such as metal coins and paper money that lasted for a long time.
- *Portability.* Money must be easily moved around. Large or bulky items, such as boulders or heavy gold bars, cannot be transported easily from place to place.
- *Divisibility.* Money must be capable of being divided into smaller parts. Divisible forms of money help make possible transactions of all sizes and amounts.

HOT Links

How durable is Canadian printed money? To discover the life expectancy of Canadian bills, visit (**www.bankofcanada.ca/en/banknotes/facts.html**).

Functions of Money

Using a variety of goods as money would be confusing. Thus, societies develop a uniform money system to measure the value of goods and services. For money to be acceptable, it must function as a medium of exchange, as a standard of value, and as a store of value.

As a *medium of exchange*, money makes transactions easier. Having a common form of payment in each country is much less complicated than having a barter system—where goods and services are exchanged for other goods and services. Money allows the exchange of products to be a simple process.

Money also serves as a *standard of value*. With a form of money whose value is accepted by all, goods and services can be priced in standard units. This makes it easy to measure the value of products and allows transactions to be recorded in consistent terms.

As a *store of value*, money is used to hold wealth. It retains its value over time. Someone who owns money can keep it for future use rather than exchange it today for other types of assets.

The Canadian Money Supply

The Canadian money supply has three parts: currency, demand deposits, and **time deposits**. The amount of money in circulation in Canada can be measured in various ways. The most common measurements are called the monetary aggregates and include these:

M1 is the narrowest measure. M1 includes all **currency** (bank notes and coins) plus **demand deposits** (personal chequing accounts) and other current accounts at banks. Other forms of currency include traveller's cheques, cashier's cheques, and money orders.

M2 is a broader measure that includes not only M1 but also personal savings accounts, other chequing accounts, **term deposits**, and non-personal deposits that require notice before the money can be withdrawn.

Because banks are not the only providers of deposit facilities, we can use an even broader measurement of money, *M2+ (also known as M3)*. This includes not only M1 and M2 but also all deposits at non-bank deposit institutions, such as money-market mutual funds and life insurance companies. Exhibit 15.1 shows these three measurements of the Canadian money supply.

Credit cards, sometimes referred to as "plastic money," are used as a substitute for cash and cheques. Credit cards are simply a form of borrowing. When RBC issues a credit card to a small business owner, it gives a short-term loan to the business by directly paying the seller for the business's purchases. The business pays RBC when it receives its monthly statement. Credit cards do not replace money; they simply defer payment.

currency
Bank notes and coins used as a medium of exchange.

demand deposits
Money kept in chequing accounts that can be withdrawn by depositors on demand

time deposits
Money invested for a specific period of time.

term deposits
Deposits at a bank or other financial institution that pay interest but cannot be withdrawn on demand.

concept check

What is money, and what are its characteristics?

What are the main functions of money?

What are the components of the Canadian money supply?

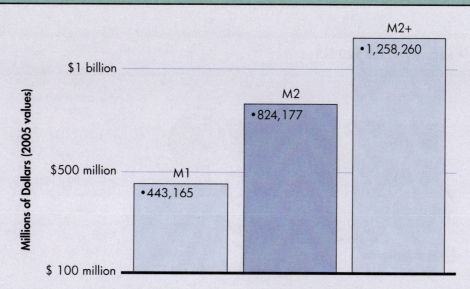

EXHIBIT 15.1 > Three Measures of the Money Stock for the Canadian Economy

SOURCE: Statistics Canada, "Exchange Rates, Interest Rates, Money Supply and Stock Prices," (www40.statcan.ca/101/cst01/econ07-eng.htm) (Accessed April 6th, 2009). Statistics Canada, CANSIM, tables 176-0025, 176-0043, 176-0047 and 176-0064; Bank of Canada, Bank of Canada Review, Ottawa.

The Bank of Canada

LO 2

Before the 20th century, there was very little government regulation of the Canadian financial system. In 1934 the Bank of Canada (also discussed in Chapter 1) was founded as a privately owned corporation. In 1938 it became a Crown corporation belonging to the federal government, with all shares held by the federal minister of finance.

The Bank of Canada is the sole issuer of bank notes in Canada and is responsible for facilitating the management of Canada's financial system. As an independent institution, the Bank of Canada has the power to create money, which is separate from the government's power to spend the money.

The Bank of Canada promotes the economic and financial welfare of Canada by

- conducting monetary policy in a way that fosters confidence in the value of money,
- supplying quality bank notes that are readily accepted and secure against counterfeiting (see Exhibit 15.2),
- promoting the safety and efficiency of Canada's financial system,
- providing efficient and effective funds-management services, and
- communicating their objectives openly and effectively and standing accountable for their actions.[3]

Carrying Out Monetary Policy

The most important function of the Bank of Canada is carrying out monetary policy. It uses its power to change the money supply to control inflation and interest rates, increase employment, and influence economic activity. Two tools used by the Bank of Canada in managing the money supply are open market operations and the overnight rate. Exhibit 15.3 summarizes the short-term effects of these tools on the economy.

In **open market operations,** the Canadian government issues securities to obtain the extra money needed to run the government (if taxes and other revenues aren't enough). In effect, these securities are long-term loans made by businesses and individuals to the government. When the Bank of Canada buys securities, it puts money into the economy. Banks have more money to lend so they reduce interest rates, and lower rates generally stimulate economic activity. The opposite occurs when the Bank of Canada sells government securities.

Although the **bank rate** still exists, the Bank of Canada is now putting more emphasis on the **target for the overnight rate.** The bank rate is the interest rate that

---

HOT Links

To learn more about how the Bank of Canada works, visit (www.bankofcanada.ca).

open market operations
The purchase or sale of Canadian government securities by the Bank of Canada to stimulate or slow down the economy.

bank rate
The interest rate that the Bank of Canada charges on one-day loans to financial institutions.

target for the overnight rate
The signal to the major participants in the money market as to what the Bank of Canada is aiming for when participants borrow and lend one-day funds to each other.

EXHIBIT 15.2 > Security of the $20 Bill

All security features for this note:

- Holographic Stripe
- Watermark Portrait
- Windowed Security Thread
- See-through Number
- Raised Print (Intaglio)
- Fine-line Printing
- Fluorescence
- Serial Number
- Colours

SOURCE: Bank of Canada, Medium-Term Plan 2007–2009, Moving Forward: Building the Future Together, http://www.bankofcanada.ca/en/pdf/mtp_2007-09e.pdf. Reprinted by permission.

EXHIBIT 15.3 > The Bank of Canada's Monetary Tools and Their Effects

Tool	Effect on Action	Effect on Money Supply	Effect on Interest Rates	Economic Activity
Open market operations	Buy government securities	Increases	Lowers	Stimulates
	Sell government securities	Decreases	Raises	Slows Down
Overnight rate	Raise overnight rate	Decreases	Raises	Slows Down
	Lower overnight rate	Increases	Lowers	Stimulates

the Bank of Canada charges member banks that borrow from the Bank of Canada. On the other hand, the target for the overnight rate is a signal from the Bank of Canada to the major participants in the money market as to what rate the Bank of Canada is aiming for in the market for overnight funds.[4] The target for the overnight rate is more relevant to the Canadian monetary policy. It is the average interest rate that the Bank of Canada wants to see in the overnight market (one-day loans). Under the current system, the Bank of Canada will always change the target for the overnight rate and the bank rate at the same time and in the same amount.

> **concept check**
>
> What are the key functions of the Bank of Canada?
>
> What tools does the Bank of Canada use in managing the money supply, and how does each affect economic activity?

The Canadian Financial System

The well-developed financial system in Canada supports our high standard of living. The system allows those who wish to borrow money to do so with relative ease. It also gives savers a variety of ways of earning interest on their savings. For example, a computer company that wants to build a new headquarters in New Brunswick might be financed partly with the savings of families in British Columbia. The British Columbians deposit their money in a local financial institution. That institution looks for a profitable and safe way to use the money and decides to make a real estate loan to the computer company. The transfer of funds from savers to investors enables businesses to expand and the economy to grow.

Households are important participants in the Canadian financial system. Although many households borrow money to finance purchases, they supply funds to the financial system through their purchases and savings. Overall, businesses and governments are users of funds. They borrow more money than they save.

Sometimes those who have funds deal directly with those who want them. A wealthy realtor, for example, might lend money to a client to buy a house. But most often, financial institutions act as intermediaries—or go-betweens—between the suppliers of and demanders for funds. The institutions accept savers' deposits and invest them in financial products (such as loans) that are expected to produce a return. This process, called **financial intermediation**, is shown in Exhibit 15.4. Households are shown as suppliers of funds, and businesses and governments are shown as demanders, but a household, business, or government can be either a supplier or a demander, depending on the circumstances.

Financial institutions are the heart of the financial system, as they are convenient vehicles for financial intermediation. They can be divided into two broad groups: depository institutions (those that accept deposits) and non-depository institutions (those that do not accept deposits).

financial intermediation
The process in which financial institutions act as intermediaries between the suppliers and demanders of funds.

EXHIBIT 15.4 > The Financial Intermediation Process

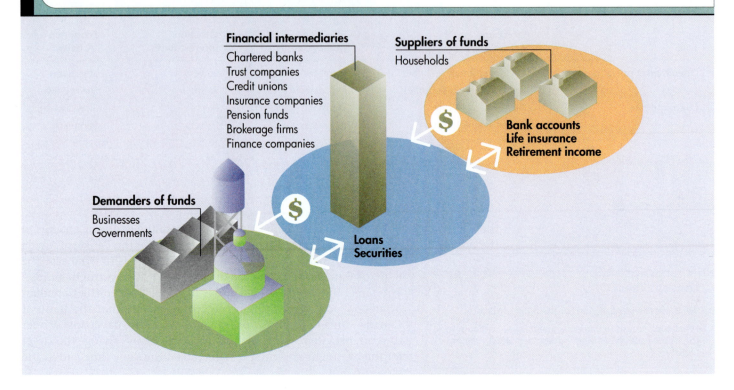

Depository Financial Institutions

Not all depository financial institutions are alike. Most people call the place where they save their money a "bank." Some of those places are, indeed, banks, but other depository institutions include trust companies and credit unions.

Chartered Banks   A **chartered bank** is a profit-oriented financial institution that accepts deposits, makes business and consumer loans, invests in government and corporate securities, and provides other financial services. There are 21 domestic banks, 25 Canadian banks that are subsidiaries of foreign banks, and 23 foreign bank branches operating in Canada. These banks operate through approximately 8,000 branches and manage more than $1.7 trillion in assets. Collectively, the chartered banks account for more than 70 percent of the total assets of the Canadian financial services sector.[5]

Customers' deposits are a chartered bank's main source of funds; the main use of those funds is loans. The differences between the interest earned on loans and the interest paid on deposits, plus fees earned from other financial services, pay the bank's costs and provide a profit. Chartered banks are corporations owned and operated by individuals or other corporations. In Canada, banks are regulated through the Bank Act.

Trust Companies   A **trust company** is the only financial institution allowed to administer trusts, such as those set up to manage estates. Like banks, they operate through a network of branches and may operate either under provincial or federal legislation. When the Canadian government radically changed the financial regulations in the 1990s, this allowed banks to purchase trust companies (e.g., Toronto Dominion Bank purchased Canada Trust to become TD Canada Trust).[6]

Credit Unions and Caisses Populaires   Credit unions, or caisses populaires, are not-for-profit, member-owned financial cooperatives that operate for the benefit of

---

chartered banks
Profit-oriented financial institutions that accept deposits, make business and consumer loans, invest in government and corporate securities, and provide other financial services.

HOT *Links*

Did you know that there is money unclaimed by depositors in Canada? Check out **(ucbswww.bank-banque-canada.ca)** to determine if you have deposits that you have forgotten about.

trust company
A financial institution that conducts the same activities as a bank but can also administer estates, trusts, pension plans, and agency contracts.

HOT *Links*

Check out the services offered by TD Canada Trust at **(www.tdcanadatrust.com)**.

credit unions and caisses populaires
Not-for-profit, member-owned financial cooperatives.

CONCEPT *in Action* >>>

One of the most popular services offered by depository institutions is the automated teller machine. ATMs on college campuses make it easy for students to deposit and withdraw money. How has technology changed the way we bank in Canada today?

© THINKSTOCK/GETTY IMAGES

the members. They are subject to provincial regulation, are usually small and locally owned, and members typically have something in common—their employer, union, professional group, or church, for example.

Chartered banks, trust companies, and credit unions offer a wide range of financial services for businesses and consumers. Typical services offered by depository institutions are listed in Exhibit 15.5. These services play an important role in helping to fuel the Canadian economy and foster individual financial security.

EXHIBIT 15.5 > Services Offered by Depository Institutions

Service	Description
Savings accounts	Pay interest on deposits
Chequing accounts	Allow depositors to withdraw any amount of funds at any time up to the amount on deposit
Money market deposit accounts	Savings accounts on which the interest rate is set at market rates
Certificates of deposit (CDs)	Pay a higher interest rate than regular savings accounts, provided that the deposit remains for a specified period
Consumer loans	Loans to individuals to finance the purchase of a home, car, or other expensive items
Business loans	Loans to businesses and other organizations to finance their operations
Money transfer	Transfer of funds to other banks
Electronic funds transfer	Use of telephone lines and computers to conduct financial transactions
Automated teller machines (ATMs)	Allow bank customers to make deposits and withdrawals from their accounts 24 hours a day
Debit cards	Allow customers to transfer money from their bank account directly to a merchant's account to pay for purchases
Smart cards	Cards that store monetary value and can be used to buy goods and services instead of using cash, cheques, and credit and debit cards
Online and telephone banking	Allows customers to conduct financial transactions via the Internet or through a dial-in line that operates with a bank's software

Non-Depository Financial Institutions

Some financial institutions provide a few banking services but do not accept deposits. These non-depository financial institutions include insurance companies, pension funds, brokerage firms, and finance companies. They serve both individuals and businesses.

Insurance Companies   Insurance companies are major suppliers of funds. Policyholders make payments (called *premiums*) to buy financial protection from the insurance company. Insurance companies invest the premiums in shares, bonds, real estate, business loans, and real estate loans for large projects.

Pension Funds   Corporations, unions, and governments set aside large pools of money for later use in paying retirement benefits to their employees or members. These **pension funds** are managed by the employers or unions themselves or by outside managers, such as life insurance firms, chartered banks, and private investment firms. Pension plan members receive a specified monthly payment when they reach a given age. After setting aside enough money to pay near-term benefits, pension funds invest the rest in business loans, shares, bonds, or real estate. They often invest large sums in the shares of the employer.

pension funds
Large pools of money set aside by corporations, unions, and governments for later use in paying retirement benefits to their employees or members.

concept check

What is the financial intermediation process?

What are the types of depository institutions, and what services do they offer?

What are the main types of non-depository institutions?

Brokerage Firms   A *brokerage firm* buys and sells securities (shares and bonds) for its clients and gives them related advice. Many brokerage firms offer some banking services. They might offer clients a combined chequing and savings account with a high interest rate and also make loans, backed by securities, to them.

HOT Links

To find out if your institution is a member of the CDIC or to see any new announcements, visit (www.cdic.ca).

Finance Companies   A *finance company* makes short-term loans for which the borrower puts up tangible assets (such as an automobile, inventory, machinery, or property) as security. Finance companies often make loans to individuals or businesses that cannot get credit elsewhere. To compensate for the extra risk, finance companies usually charge higher interest rates than banks do. *Consumer finance companies* make loans to individuals.

Insuring Bank Deposits

Canada Deposit Insurance Corporation (CDIC)
The Canada Deposit Insurance Corporation is a federal Crown Corporation created in 1967 to provide deposit insurance and contribute to the stability of Canada's financial system.

The **Canada Deposit Insurance Corporation (CDIC)** is a federal Crown corporation created in 1967 to provide deposit insurance and to contribute to the stability of Canada's financial system. The CDIC insures eligible deposits at member institutions and reimburses depositors for the amount of their insured deposits when a member institution fails. Since 2005, the amount insured at a single member institution is $100,000 and depositors are automatically insured for their deposits (to the maximum) if their deposits are with a member institution and in Canadian currency.

CDIC is governed by the Canada Deposit Insurance Corporation Act and is accountable to Canada's Parliament through the Minister of Finance. Since its creation, 43 member institutions have failed, at a cost of about $4.7 billion.[7]

concept check

What is the CDIC, and what are its responsibilities?

How does this encourage confidence in the Canadian economy?

International Banking

The financial marketplace spans the globe, with money routinely flowing across international borders. Multinational corporations need many special banking services, such as foreign currency exchange. Many Canadian banks have started expanding into trans-border and overseas markets by opening offices in the United States, Europe,

Expanding Around The Globe

BREACHING BANKING BARRIERS IN CHINA

If Citigroup's bid to purchase a majority stake in Guangdong Development Bank—with its nationwide network of over 500 branches and booming credit-card business—had been successful, it would have captured the largest ownership stake held by a foreign investor in a Chinese bank and thereby gained full management control. It could have ended regulatory limits on foreign ownership of Chinese financial institutions, overcoming the current regulatory limits of 20 percent ownership for a single foreign investor in a Chinese bank and less than 25 percent for all foreign shareholders.

But the Chinese government refused to put aside the ownership rule, killing Citigroup's bid to be the first foreign firm to surpass the ownership limit in a mainland lender. The government's denial indicates an increasing resistance to state-asset sales in the country. "There's real concern about losing control of the banking system and fears that the local banks have no way to compete with the more sophisticated foreign banks," said Stephan Rothlin, secretary general of the Centre for International Business Ethics in Beijing.

So Citigroup abandoned its larger stake bid in an effort to keep its bid for a smaller stake in the bank alive. China forbids foreign companies from purchasing more than 19.9 percent of a bank. Citigroup wanted 40 percent of Guangdong development as part of an investment consortium that sought an overall 85 percent stake.

The question of control is vital in China, where banks are striving to introduce modern risk-management systems after decades of uncontrolled lending. "China should pass a law to prevent 'malicious' mergers and acquisitions by overseas companies seeking monopolies," Li Deshu, the former head of the National Statistics Bureau and a ministerial-level official, said during the National People's Congress in March 2006. Other critics say that foreign companies are profiteering after paying too little for their stakes. "Pricing China's big four banks only on their net assets fails to factor in the value of their brand and customers," said Shi Jianping, dean of the School of Finance at Central University of Finance & Economics.

Banking forecasters say it is doubtful that authorities will permit any of the "big four" state-owned Chinese banks to come under overseas rule any time soon. Any relaxation of the limits is more liable to concern smaller provincial and city banks, which would benefit from foreign investment and expertise.[8]

Critical Thinking Questions
- Why is China so reluctant to allow foreign companies a major ownership stake in their banks?
- Why are Chinese banks attractive to foreign investors? Explain.

Latin America, and the Far East. They provide better customer service than local banks in many countries and have access to more sources of funding.

Competing against foreign banks can be difficult. Foreign banks are subject to fewer regulations, making it easier for them to undercut Canadian banks on the pricing of loans and services to multinational corporations and governments. Some governments protect their banks against foreign competition. In China, for example, the government prohibits foreign banks from acquiring more than 19.9 percent of any of its domestic financial institutions as explained in the "Expanding Around the Globe" box.

Canadian banks play an important role in global business by providing loans to foreign governments and businesses. They also offer trade-related services. For example, Scotiabank's global cash management services help firms manage their cash flows to improve their payment efficiency and reduce their exposure to operational risks. The bank's advanced information systems enable corporate customers to access their accounts electronically throughout the world. Other Canadian banks are taking advantage of their technological expertise and information systems to sell more financial services throughout the world.

International banking can be profitable, but it's also a high-risk business. The global financial crisis beginning in 2008 resulted in many Canadian financial institutions writing down assets especially as a result of the "sub-prime mortgage" failure in the United States.

HOT Links

Scotiabank is Canada's most international bank, with more than 12.5 million customers in approximately 50 countries around the world. Check out their website at (www.scotiabank.com).

concept check

What is the role of Canadian banks in international banking?

What challenges do Canadian banks face in foreign markets?

Investor's Choice: Shares and Bonds

LO 6

securities
Investment certificates issued by corporations or governments that represent either equity or debt.

A central concern of most businesses is raising capital to finance operations and expansion. Many corporations use securities as a source of long-term financing. **Securities** are investment certificates that represent either equity (ownership in the issuing organization) or debt (a loan to the issuer). Corporations and governments sell securities to investors, who, in turn, take on a certain amount of risk with the hope of receiving a profit from their investment.

Sharing the Wealth—and the Risks

Equity securities, commonly called *shares,* represent ownership in a corporation. A share is issued for each unit of ownership, and the shareholder (owner) gets a share certificate to prove ownership. If you own a share in TD Canada Trust, for example, you are a partial owner of TD Canada Trust. Your ownership interest isn't very big, because TD Canada Trust has over 800 million shares outstanding,[9] but your ownership gives you certain rights and potential rewards. The two types of equity securities are common shares and preferred shares. Each has advantages and disadvantages for investors.

Common Shares *Common shares* are the most widespread form of ownership. Holders of common shares receive the right to vote on many important corporate decisions, such as who should sit on the company's board of directors and whether the firm should merge with another company. In most cases, common shareholders get one vote for each share they own. Common shares also give investors the opportunity to share in the company's success, through either dividends or share price increases.

Dividends are the part of corporate profits that the firm distributes to shareholders. Dividends for common shares can be paid either in cash or in additional shares (called *stock dividends*). Common share dividends are usually declared either annually or quarterly (four times a year) by a corporation's board of directors. However, these dividends are paid only after all other obligations of the firm—payments to suppliers, employees, bondholders, and other creditors, plus taxes and preferred share dividends—have been met. Some firms, especially rapidly growing companies and those in high-technology industries, choose not to pay any dividends on their common shares. Instead, they reinvest their profits in more buildings, equipment, and new products in hope of earning greater profits in the future. These reinvested profits are called *retained earnings.*

One advantage of common shares ownership is its liquidity: Many common shares are actively traded in securities markets and can be bought and sold quickly. An investor can benefit by selling common shares when the price increases, or *appreciates,* above the original purchase price.

Although the returns from common share dividends and price appreciation can be quite attractive, common shareholders have no guarantee that they will get any return on their investment. Share prices are subject to many risks related to the economy, the industry, and the company. Like any commodity, the price of a specific company's shares are affected by supply and demand. The supply of shares is limited by the number of shares a company has issued, whereas demand is created by the number of investors who want to buy the shares from those who already own them. Factors that can increase demand for shares—and their price—include strong financial reports, new-product market opportunities, and positive industry trends. However, demand can fall—and a share's price drop—when negative events occur.

The threat of a lawsuit or increased government regulation of a firm's industry can send share prices downward. Market conditions can also affect a company's share price. Factors like these can hold down a common share's dividends and its price, making it hard to predict the share's return. For example, Merck & Co., a major pharmaceutical firm, recalled Vioxx after it was revealed that the popular painkiller could increase the risk of heart attacks and strokes. Its shares price fell 38 percent from September to December 2004 and never fully regained lost ground. The result of the lawsuits from the danger of Vioxx resulted in the courts awarding injured parties compensation.[10] Factors like these can hold down a common share's dividends and its price, making it hard to predict the share's return.

Preferred Shares *Preferred shares* are a second form of corporate ownership. Unlike common shareholders, preferred shareholders do not receive voting rights. However, preferred shares provide several advantages to investors that common shares do not, specifically in the payment of dividends and the distribution of assets if the firm is liquidated.

The dividend for preferred shares is usually set at the time the shares are issued, giving preferred shareholders a clearer picture of the dividend proceeds they can expect from their investment. This dividend can be expressed either in dollar terms or as a percentage of the share's par (stated) value. As with common shares, the company's board of directors might decide not to pay dividends if the company encounters financial hardships. However, most preferred shares are *cumulative preferred shares*, which means that preferred shareholders must receive all unpaid dividends before any dividends can be paid to common shareholders. Suppose, for example, that a company with a $5 annual preferred dividend misses its quarterly payment of $1.25 ($5.00 ÷ 4). The following quarter, the firm must pay preferred shareholders $2.50—$1.25 in unpaid preferred dividends from the previous quarter plus the $1.25 preferred dividend for the current quarter—before it can pay any dividends to common shareholders. Similarly, if the company goes bankrupt, preferred shareholders are paid off before common shareholders.

Investors like preferred shares because of the fixed dividend income. Although companies are not legally obligated to pay preferred dividends, most have an excellent record of doing so. However, the fixed dividend can also be a disadvantage, because it limits the cash paid to investors. Thus, preferred shares have less potential for price appreciation than common shares.

Cashing in with Bonds

LO 7

Bonds are long-term debt obligations (liabilities) of corporations and governments. A bond certificate is issued as proof of the obligation. The issuer of a bond must pay the buyer a fixed amount of money—called **interest**, stated as the *coupon rate*—on a regular schedule, typically every six months. The issuer must also pay the bondholder the amount borrowed—called the **principal**, or *par value*—at the bond's maturity date (due date). Bonds are usually issued in units of $1,000—for instance, $1,000, $5,000, or $10,000. The two sources of return on bond investments are interest income and gains from the sale of the bonds.

Unlike common and preferred shareholders, who are owners, bondholders are creditors (lenders) of the issuer. In the event of liquidation, the bondholders' claim on the assets of the issuer comes before that of any shareholders.

Bonds do not have to be held to maturity. They can be bought and sold in the securities markets. However, the price of a bond changes over its life as market interest rates fluctuate. When the market interest rate drops below the fixed interest rate on a bond, it becomes more valuable, and the price rises. If interest rates rise, the bond's price will fall.

Corporate Bonds *Corporate bonds*, as the name implies, are issued by corporations. They usually have a par value of $1,000. They may be secured or unsecured, include special provisions for early retirement, or be convertible to common shares.

High-yield, or **junk, bonds** are high-risk, high-return bonds that became popular during the 1980s, when they were widely used to finance mergers and take-overs. Today, they are used by companies whose credit characteristics would not otherwise allow them access to the debt markets. Because of their high risk, these bonds generally earn 3 percent or more above the returns on high-quality corporate bonds.

Corporate bonds can be either secured or unsecured. **Secured bonds** have specific assets pledged as collateral, which the bondholder has a right to take if

interest
A fixed amount of money paid by the issuer of a bond to the bondholder on a regular schedule, typically every six months; stated as the *coupon rate*.

principal
The amount borrowed by the issuer of a bond; also called *par value*.

high-yield (junk) bonds
High-risk, high-return bonds.

secured bonds
Corporate bonds for which specific assets have been pledged as collateral.

CHAPTER 15 **Understanding Money, Financial Institutions, and the Securities Markets**

mortgage bonds
Corporate bonds that are secured by property, such as land, equipment, or buildings.

debentures
Unsecured bonds that are backed only by the reputation of the issuer and its promise to pay the principal and interest when due.

convertible bonds
Corporate bonds that are issued with an option that allows the bondholder to convert them into common shares.

bond ratings
Letter grades assigned to bond issues to indicate their quality, or level of risk; assigned by rating agencies such as Moody's and Standard & Poor's (S&P).

the bond issuer defaults. **Mortgage bonds** are secured by property, such as land, equipment, or buildings. **Debentures** are unsecured bonds. They are backed only by the reputation of the issuer and its promise to pay the principal and interest when due. In general, debentures have a lower risk of default than secured bonds and therefore have lower interest rates. Of course, a debenture issued by a financially shaky firm probably has greater default risk than a mortgage bond issued by a sound one.

Corporate bonds may be issued with an option for the bondholder to convert them into common shares. **Convertible bonds** generally allow the bondholder to exchange each bond for a specified number of shares. For instance, a $1,000 par value convertible bond might be convertible into 40 shares—no matter what happens to the market price of the common shares. Because convertible bonds could be converted to shares when the price is very high, these bonds usually have a lower interest rate than non-convertible bonds.

Government Securities   Both the federal government and provincial governments also issue bonds to finance programs. When the government of Canada borrows money on a short-term basis, it issues Treasury bills (T-bills); whereas bonds are meant to be held for a longer period.

Bond Ratings   Bonds vary in quality, depending on the financial strength of the issuer. Because the claims of bondholders come before those of shareholders, bonds are generally considered less risky than shares. However, some bonds are, in fact, quite risky. Companies can *default*—fail to make scheduled interest or principal payments—on their bonds.

Investors can use **bond ratings**, letter grades assigned to bond issues to indicate their quality or level of risk. Ratings for corporate bonds are easy to find. The two largest and best-known rating agencies are Moody's and Standard & Poor's (S&P), whose publications are in most libraries and in stock brokerages. Exhibit 15.6 lists the letter grades assigned by Moody's and S&P. A bond's rating can change with events.

> **concept check**
>
> What are the advantages and disadvantages of common shares for investors and corporations?
>
> What is a preferred share, and how is it different from a common share?
>
> Describe the common features of all bonds and the advantages and disadvantages of bonds for investors.

EXHIBIT 15.6 > Moody's and Standard & Poor's Bond Ratings

Moody's Ratings	S & P Ratings	Description
Aaa	AAA	**Prime-quality investment bonds:** Highest rating assigned; indicates extremely strong capacity to pay.
Aa A	AA A	**High-grade investment bonds:** Also considered very safe bonds, although not quite as safe as Aaa/AAA issues; Aa/AA bonds are safer (have less risk of default) than single As.
Baa	BBB	**Medium-grade investment bonds:** Lowest of investment-grade issues; seen as lacking protection against adverse economic conditions.
Ba B	BB B	**Junk bonds:** Provide little protection against default; viewed as highly speculative.
Caa Ca C	CCC CC C D	**Poor-quality bonds:** Either in default or very close to it.

Playing the Market with Other Types of Securities

LO 8

In addition to equity and debt, investors have several other types of securities available to them. The most popular are mutual funds, futures contracts, and options. Mutual funds appeal to a wide range of investors. Futures contracts and options are more complex investments for experienced investors.

Mutual Funds

Suppose that you have $1,000 to invest but don't know which shares or bonds to buy, when to buy them, or when to sell them. By investing in a mutual fund, you can buy shares in a large, professionally managed *portfolio*, or group, of shares and bonds. A **mutual fund** is a financial service company that pools its investors' funds to buy a selection of securities—marketable securities, shares, bonds, or a combination of securities—that meet its stated investment goals.

Each mutual fund focuses on one of a wide variety of possible investment goals, such as growth or income. Many large financial service companies sell a wide variety of mutual funds, each with a different investment goal. Investors can pick and choose funds that match their particular interests. Some specialized funds invest in a particular type of company or asset: in one industry, such as transportation or technology; in a geographical region, such as Asia; or in an asset, such as precious metals. Mutual funds appeal to investors for three main reasons:

- They are a good way to hold a diversified and, thus, less risky, portfolio. Investors with only $500 or $1,000 to invest cannot diversify much on their own. Buying shares in a mutual fund lets them own part of a portfolio that might contain 100 or more securities.
- Mutual funds are professionally managed.
- Mutual funds might offer higher returns than individual investors could achieve on their own.

Exchange-Traded Funds

A relatively new type of investment, the **exchange-traded fund (ETF)**, also called Index Participation Unit (IPU) has become very popular with investors. The world's

mutual fund
A financial service company that pools its investors' funds to buy a selection of securities that meet its stated investment goals.

exchange-traded fund (ETF)
A basket of marketable securities in a category, such as industry sector, investment objective, or geographical area, or that track an index. ETFs are similar to mutual funds but trade like shares.

first ETFs originated in the Toronto Stock Exchange in 1990. ETFs are considered to be a special type of mutual fund that holds a broad basket of marketable securities with a common theme, giving investors instant diversification. ETFs trade on stock exchanges so their price changes throughout the day, whereas mutual fund net asset values (NAVs) are calculated once a day, at the end of trading.

Futures Contracts

futures contracts
Legally binding obligations to buy or sell specified quantities of commodities or financial instruments at an agreed-on price at a future date.

Futures contracts are legally binding obligations to buy or sell specified quantities of commodities (agricultural or mining products) or financial instruments (securities or currencies) at an agreed-on price at a future date. An investor can buy commodity futures contracts in cattle, pork bellies (large slabs of bacon), eggs, coffee, flour, gasoline, fuel oil, lumber, wheat, gold, and silver. Financial futures include Treasury securities and foreign currencies, such as the British pound or Japanese yen.

Futures contracts do not pay interest or dividends. The return depends solely on favourable price changes. These are very risky investments, because the prices can vary a great deal.

options
Contracts that entitle holders to buy or sell specified quantities of common shares or other financial instruments at a set price during a specified time.

Options

Options are contracts that entitle holders to buy or sell specified quantities of common shares or other financial instruments at a set price during a specified time. As with futures contracts, investors must correctly guess future price movements in the underlying financial instrument to earn a positive return. Unlike futures contracts, options do not legally obligate the holder to buy or sell and the price paid for an option is the maximum amount that can be lost. However, options have very short maturities, so it is easy to lose a lot of money quickly with them.

Securities Markets

Shares, bonds, and other securities are traded in securities markets. These markets streamline the purchase and sales activities of investors by allowing transactions to be made quickly and at a fair price. They make the transfer of funds from lenders to borrowers much easier. Securities markets are busy places. On an average day, individual and institutional investors trade billions of shares in more than 10,000 companies through securities markets. They also trade bonds, mutual funds, futures contracts, and options. *Individual investors* invest their own money to achieve their personal financial goals. **Institutional investors** are investment professionals who are paid to manage other people's money. Most of these professional money managers work for financial institutions, such as banks, mutual funds, insurance companies, and pension funds. Institutional investors control very large sums of money, often buying shares in 10,000-share blocks. They aim to meet the investment goals of their clients. Institutional investors are a major force in the securities markets, accounting for about half of the dollar volume of equities traded.

institutional investors
Investment professionals who are paid to manage other people's money.

HOT Links

You have probably heard of buying on margin. Find out how this works at (**www.investopedia.com/university/margin/margin1.asp**).

Businesses and governments also take part in the securities markets. Corporations issue bonds and shares to raise funds to finance their operations. They are also among the institutional investors that purchase corporate and government securities.

investment bankers
Firms that act as intermediaries, buying securities from corporations and governments and reselling them to the public.

The Role of Investment Bankers and Stockbrokers

Two types of investment specialists play key roles in the functioning of the securities markets. **Investment bankers** help companies raise long-term financing. These firms act as intermediaries, buying securities from corporations and governments and reselling them to the public. This process, called **underwriting**, is the main activity of

underwriting
The process of buying securities from corporations and governments and reselling them to the public, with the aim of reselling at a higher price; the main activity of investment bankers.

CONCEPT in Action >>>

Linking investors and public companies, stockbrokers serve a vital role in the securities marketplace. Today, most customer buy-sell orders are transacted electronically. What are the benefits of using a stockbroker?

stockbroker
A person who is licensed to buy and sell securities on behalf of clients.

HOT Links

Check online investment information at the following: (www.questrade.com), (www.bmoinvestorline.com), and (www.tradefreedom.com).

the investment banker, which acquires the security for an agreed-on price and hopes to be able to resell it at a higher price to make a profit. Investment bankers advise clients on the pricing and structure of new securities offerings, as well as on mergers, acquisitions, and other types of financing. Most Canadian banks now offer investment banking services.

A **stockbroker** is a person who is licensed to buy and sell securities on behalf of clients. Also called *account executives*, these investment professionals work for brokerage firms and execute the orders customers place for shares, bonds, mutual funds, and other securities.

Stockbrokers are the link between public companies and the investors interested in buying their shares. Before investing in securities, investors must select a stock brokerage firm, select a stockbroker at that firm, and open an account. Investors are wise to seek a broker who understands their investment goals and can help them pursue their objectives.

Brokerage firms are paid commissions for executing clients' transactions. Although brokers can charge whatever they want, most firms have fixed commission schedules for small transactions. These commissions usually depend on the value of the transaction and the number of shares involved.

Online Investing

Improvements in Internet technology have made it possible for investors to research, analyze, and trade securities online. Although traditional brokerage firms still dominate the investment industry, many investors use online brokerage firms for their securities transactions. Online brokerages are popular with "do-it-yourself" investors who choose their own shares and don't want to pay a full-service broker for these services. Lower transaction costs are a major benefit. Fees at online brokerages range from approximately $4 to $20 depending on the number of trades a client makes and the size of the client's account. Presently many traditional brokerage firms now have added online trading options to their list of services.

CONCEPT in Action >>>

Online brokerages like E*Trade and RBC Direct Investing have given rise to a new market player: the self-directed investor. These "do-it-yourselfers" take their financial futures into their own hands, buying and selling shares over the Internet for a fraction of the cost associated with traditional brokerage firms. Online investors pay commission fees as low as $4 while accessing streaming quotes and charts, financial news, and risk analyzers—all on their computer screens. What are the pros and cons of online investing?

Types of Markets

primary market
The securities market where new securities are sold to the public, usually with the help of investment bankers.

Securities markets can be divided into primary and secondary markets. The **primary market** is where *new* securities are sold to the public, usually with the help of investment bankers. In the primary market, the issuer of the security gets the proceeds from the transaction. A security is sold in the primary market just once—when it is first issued by the corporation or government.

Later transactions take place in the **secondary market,** where *old* (already issued) securities are bought and sold, or traded, among investors. The issuers generally are not involved in these transactions. The vast majority of securities transactions take place in secondary markets, which include the organized stock exchanges, the over-the-counter securities market, and the commodities exchanges. You'll see announcements of both primary and secondary shares and bond offerings in *The Globe and Mail* and other newspapers.

secondary market
The securities market where old (already issued) securities are bought and sold, or traded, among investors.

> **concept check**
>
> How do securities markets help businesses and investors? How does an investment banker work with companies to issue securities?
>
> How is online investing changing the securities industry?
>
> Distinguish between primary and secondary securities markets.

Buying and Selling at Securities Exchanges

When we think of stock markets, we are typically referring to secondary markets, which handle most of the securities trading activity. The two key types of securities markets are **broker markets**, more commonly referred to as "organized stock exchanges" and dealer markets. **Organized stock exchanges** are organizations on whose premises securities are resold. They operate using an auction-style trading system. All other securities are traded in the dealer markets.

broker markets or organized stock exchanges
Organizations on whose premises securities are resold using an auction-style trading system.

Trading in an organized stock exchange is done by exchange members, who act as agents for individual and institutional investors. To make transactions in an organized stock exchange, an individual or firm must be a member and own a "seat" on that exchange. Owners of the limited number of seats must meet certain financial requirements and agree to observe a broad set of rules when trading securities.

The Primary Canadian Stock Exchanges

The cornerstone of the Canadian financial system is the TSX Group. The TSX Group owns and operates the two national stock exchanges, the Toronto Stock Exchange

CONCEPT *in Action* >>>

Once a customer order is transmitted to the trading floor, getting the most competitive price for the customer is the job of the brokerage's floor broker. Floor brokers must act quickly and aggressively to outbid other brokers. How does the traditional Toronto Stock Exchange differ from fully automated electronic trading?

© AP/WIDE WORLD PHOTOS

and the TSX Venture Exchange. The Toronto Stock Exchange serves the senior equity market (a broad range of established businesses from across Canada, the United States, and other countries), and the public venture equity market is served by the TSX Venture Exchange (which provides emerging companies with access to capital).

Other Exchanges Important to Canadian Businesses

Of all the foreign exchanges, the New York Stock Exchange (NYSE) is the most important to Canadian business. Canadian companies that are listed on the NYSE have access to a greater pool of potential investors because of the sheer number of people who live and invest in the United States. Only companies that meet certain minimum requirements are eligible to be listed on the NYSE.

Global Trading and Foreign Exchanges

Improved communications and the elimination of many legal barriers are helping the securities markets go global. The number of securities listed on exchanges in more than one country is growing.

Stock exchanges also exist in foreign countries. The London and Tokyo Stock Exchanges rank behind the NYSE and NASDAQ (described below). Other important foreign stock exchanges include those in Buenos Aires, Zurich, Sydney, Paris, Frankfurt, Hong Kong, and Taiwan.

Dealer Markets

Unlike broker markets, **dealer markets** do not operate on centralized trading floors but instead use sophisticated telecommunications networks that link dealers throughout the world. Buyers and sellers do not trade securities directly, as they do in broker markets. They work through securities dealers called market makers, who make markets in one or more securities and offer to buy or sell securities at stated prices. A security transaction in the dealer market has two parts: the selling investor sells his or her securities to one dealer, and the buyer purchases the securities from another dealer (or in some cases, the same dealer).

NASDAQ   The largest dealer market is the **National Association of Securities Dealers Automated Quotation system**, commonly referred to as NASDAQ. The first electronic-based stock market, the NASDAQ is a sophisticated telecommunications network that links dealers throughout the world. Founded in 1971 with origins in the over-the-counter market (discussed below). Today NASDAQ is a separate securities exchange that is no longer part of the over-the-counter market.

The Over-the-Counter Market   The **over-the-counter (OTC) markets** refer to those other than the organized exchanges described above. As mentioned previously, NASDAQ, until January 2006 was part of the OTC. Today the OTC consists of dealers who make trades over the telephone and computer. It is also called the "unlisted market," or the "street market."

Market Conditions: Bull Market or Bear Market?

Two terms that often appear in the financial press are "bull market" and "bear market." Securities prices rise in **bull markets**. These markets are normally associated with investor optimism, economic recovery, and government action to encourage economic growth. In contrast, prices go down in **bear markets**. Investor pessimism, economic slowdown, and government restraint are all possible causes. As a rule, investors earn better returns in bull markets; they earn low, and sometimes negative, returns in bear markets.

HOT *Links*

To learn more about the Toronto Stock Exchange, the TSX Venture Exchange, how companies get listed on the exchanges, and the most current share price quotes, visit **(www.tsx.com)**.

HOT *Links*

The Montreal Exchange trades primarily in the options, futures, and derivative markets. To find out more about these, visit **(www.m-x.ca)**.

dealer markets
Securities markets where buy and sell orders are executed through dealers, or "market makers" linked by telecommunications networks.

National Association of Securities Dealers Automated Quotation (NASDAQ) system
The first electronic-based stock market and the fastest-growing part of the stock market.

over-the-counter (OTC) market
A sophisticated telecommunications network that links dealers and enables them to trade securities.

bull markets
Markets in which securities prices are rising.

bear markets
Markets in which securities prices are falling.

Bull and bear market conditions are hard to predict, as seen in the economic crisis beginning in 2008. Usually, they can't be identified until after they begin. Over the past 50 years, the stock market has generally been bullish, reflecting general economic growth and prosperity. Bull markets tend to last longer than bear markets.

Trends in the Financial Industry

LO 10

Once a highly regulated industry offering limited services, the banking industry continues to change. Trends influencing the direction of banking are online banking, consolidation, and the integration of banking with brokerage and insurance services.

Changing the Way We Bank

The federal government has strict controls regulating the financial industry in Canada. These strict regulations caused Canada to be less affected by the financial crisis of 2008 than many other countries. But today, the regulations are less restrictive regarding financial business operations than they were in the later part of the 20th century.

Today, our financial systems are using Internet technology to expand their services. "Online banking may be the critical service that enables banks to maintain their role as the dominant provider of financial services," says Paul Johnson, an analyst with International Data.[11]

One service that has given banks tremendous profit potential is online bill statements and payments. The service has benefited many businesses, such as utility firms, because it will eliminate the time-consuming and costly process of printing bills, mailing them to customers, and waiting for the cheques to arrive and clear.[12]

In 1992, the federal government reduced the various barriers and created a new framework for competition. These far-reaching changes include the ability of banks to offer a wider range of services to their customers. The deregulation of the financial industry saw financial services being consolidated, and now banks offer many of the services that were traditionally offered by industry-specific institutions. For example, insurance, brokerage services, and so on were not offered by the banks prior to the deregulation.

HOT Links

To learn more about Canadian banks online, visit (www.canadabanks.net).

Making Ethical Choices

TRIALS AND MANIPULATIONS

You have just joined a prestigious investment banking firm as a junior securities analyst covering the pharmaceutical industry. Eager to make a good impression on your boss, you diligently monitor the companies your group follows and search for unique ways to get the scoop on new drugs currently under development. Rumour has it that a biotechnology firm has come out with a new drug for insomnia with the potential to be a blockbuster. You've heard that other analysts, posing as doctors or patients, have called the managers of clinical trials to get inside information or have paid doctors involved in the trials to disclose confidential data. They then use what they learn in their share reports, making recommendations that can significantly impact the price of the share.

Why not go a step further, you wonder, and participate in the trial for the insomnia drug yourself? After all, you've had many sleepless nights and believe you'd qualify for the study. Not only would you help the cause of science, but you'd also get the chance to talk to doctors about the other patients in the study to find out more about the results of the trial so far.

With your boss's approval, you apply for the trial. When you arrive for your first appointment, you are asked to sign a confidentiality agreement to not disclose any treatment information based on your experiences or anything you learn about other patients.

ETHICAL DILEMMA: Should you honour the confidentiality agreement or share your findings with your boss to use in writing the share report?

SOURCES: Getta Anand and Randall Smith, "Biotech Analysts Strive to Peek Inside Clinical Tests of Drugs," *Wall Street Journal*, August 8, 2002; and Penni Crabtree, "Firm Fined for 'Creative' Research on Neurocrine," *San Diego Union-Tribune*, October 29, 2002.

After reading this chapter, you might be wondering if investing in shares or bonds is right for you. Like millions of others, you've probably read headlines about the markets' rise and fall. How can you minimize the risks while reaping the benefits of securities investments? The basic information presented in this chapter is a good starting point. It's also important to understand some of the key strategies used by successful investors.

The Time Is Now

As the TSX Composite tumbled starting in 2008, many investors panicked. They rushed to sell off their shares—often at a loss—because they believed doing otherwise would spell financial ruin.

These investors fell prey to some common mistakes of novice investors. For one thing, they got caught up in the mystique of the S&P/TSX Composite. Although it is the most publicized market indicator in Canada, it only represents the activity of approximately 220 of the roughly 1600 companies listed on the TSX.[13] A milestone on the TSX composite is just another number. It doesn't tell investors where their individual investments are going or how long the market will stay at a particular level.

The stock market has always been cyclical in nature. Share prices rise and fall depending on many factors. A bull market is almost invariably followed by a bear market. Although every investor dreams of buying a share at its low point and selling it at its peak, predicting the market's ups and downs is impossible.

Successful investors think of the stock market as a long-term investment. They know that it's important to let their investments grow over time, and they avoid falling into the trap of thinking that they should sell their shares whenever there's a market downturn. They also recognize that the best time to buy shares is when the market is at a low point.

Financial advisers suggest investing small amounts over time. Start early and invest regularly, whether the market is up or down. Don't immediately panic if the market takes a nosedive. The highs and lows will average out over time, and you'll find yourself with long-term gains.

Another reason many investors lost money in recent years is that they failed to diversify their investment portfolios. Many poured money into technology shares while ignoring the shares of businesses in other industries. When the technology boom ended, these investors were hit the hardest. Building a portfolio of individual shares in different industries can help cushion losses. Investing in mutual funds can also help spread your risk over a broad group of securities. Also, consider investing in

Customer Satisfaction and Quality

Some would say that the first obligation of a public corporation is to make money for its shareholders. Of course, companies have many stakeholders—employees, customers, and the communities where they operate—but building shareholder value has been front and centre of the concerns facing most corporate executives for the past 20 years.

As the stock markets boom, corporations face tremendous pressure from shareholders to keep pace. Many CEOs made strategic decisions that were focused mainly on pushing the share price. Unfortunately, as investors at some companies eventually discovered, some corporate executives responded to the pressure by making unscrupulous choices.

Shareholder value will always be a central concern of publicly traded companies, but now many chief executives have discovered that providing shareholder value means more than just inflated share prices. It also means serving investors with financial results built on honesty and realistic expectations. It means keeping an eye on the basic principle of business: Make your customers happy first.

Procter & Gamble's chief executive A. G. Lafley sums it up best when asked how P&G shares soared nearly 60 percent in the first part of the 21st century. "Over the last half of the 1990s, we were a little bit too shareholder focused, too growth-at-any-cost focused," he says. "I tried to get people to flip that around. If we create brands that make a difference to our customers and focus on the fundamentals, ultimately shareholder growth will take care of itself."

SOURCES: Joseph Nocera, "Value Judgments," *Money*, December 2001, (www.business2.com); and Nicholas Stein, "America's Most Admired Companies," *Fortune*, March 3, 2003, 81, modified March 30th, 2009.

a mix of shares and bonds. Bonds tend to rise in value as share prices drop, and vice versa, further lessening the risk of losing it all when one investment vehicle declines.

Most important, do your homework. Don't make investment decisions based only on what you find on a website or in a single magazine. It's easy to be taken in by someone hyping a share. To avoid investment scams, do your own research. Investigate the company's standing with the TSX, and look at its historic performance over a number of years. Remember, if it sounds too good to be true, it probably is!

Summary of Learning Outcomes

1 **Understand the characteristics of money and its functions.**

Money is anything accepted as payment for goods and services. For money to be a suitable means of exchange, it should be scarce, durable, portable, and divisible. Money functions as a medium of exchange, a standard of value, and a store of value. The Canadian money supply consists of currency (coins and paper money), demand deposits (chequing accounts), and time deposits (interest-bearing deposits that cannot be withdrawn on demand).

2 **Describe the basic functions of the Bank of Canada, and how it manages the Canadian money supply.**

The Bank of Canada promotes the economic and financial welfare of Canada by

- conducting monetary policy in a way that fosters confidence in the value of money,
- supplying quality bank notes that are readily accepted and secure against counterfeiting,
- promoting the safety and efficiency of Canada's financial system,
- providing efficient and effective funds management services, and
- communicating their objectives openly and effectively, and standing accountable for their actions.

The Bank of Canada uses the Monetary Policy to manage the money supply.

3 **Identify the key financial institutions, and the role they play in the process of financial intermediation.**

Financial institutions can be divided into two main groups: depository institutions and non-depository institutions. Depository institutions include chartered banks, trust companies, and credit unions and caisses populaires. Non-depository institutions include insurance companies, pension funds, brokerage firms, and finance companies. Financial institutions ease the transfer of funds between suppliers and demanders.

4 **Outline how the Canada Deposit Insurance Corporation protects depositors' funds.**

The CDIC is a Crown corporation that insures eligible deposits at member institutions and reimburses depositors for the amount of their insured deposits when a member institution fails.

5 **Summarize the role of Canadian banks in the international marketplace.**

Canadian banks provide loans and trade-related services to foreign governments and businesses. They also offer specialized services such as cash management and foreign currency exchange.

6 **Distinguish between common shares and preferred shares.**

Common and preferred shares represent ownership—equity—in a corporation. Common shareholders have voting rights, but their claim on profits and assets ranks behind that of holders of other securities. Preferred shareholders receive a stated dividend; it must be paid before any dividends are distributed to common shareholders.

Common shares are more risky than preferred shares. They offer the potential for increased value through growth in the share price and income through dividend payments. However, neither price increases nor dividends are guaranteed. Preferred shares are usually bought for their dividend income rather than potential price appreciation.

7 **Understand the investment advantages and disadvantages of bonds.**

Bonds are a form of debt and may be secured or unsecured. Bondholders are creditors of the issuing organization, and their claims on income and assets rank ahead of those of preferred and common shareholders. The corporation or government entity that issues the bonds must pay interest periodically and repay the principal at maturity. Bonds provide a steady source of income and the potential for price appreciation if interest rates fall below the coupon rate. However, investors also bear the risk that rising interest rates might erode the bond's price.

8 **List other types of securities available to investors.**

Mutual funds are financial service companies that pool the funds of many investors to buy a diversified portfolio of securities. Investors choose mutual funds because they offer a convenient way of diversifying and are professionally managed. Futures contracts are legally binding obligations to buy or sell specified quantities of commodities or financial instruments at an agreed-on price at a future date. They are very risky investments, because the price of the commodity or financial instrument can change drastically. Options are contracts that entitle the holder to buy or sell specified quantities of common shares or other financial instruments at a set price during a specified time. They, too, are high-risk investments.

9 **Describe the function of the securities markets.**

Securities markets allow shares, bonds, and other securities to be bought and sold quickly and at a fair price. New issues are sold in the primary market. After that, securities are traded in the secondary market. Investment bankers specialize in issuing and selling new security issues. Stockbrokers are licensed professionals who buy and sell securities on behalf of their clients.

Securities are resold on organized share exchanges, such as the Toronto Stock Exchange and regional share exchanges, and in the over-the-counter market, a telecommunications network linking dealers throughout North America. The most actively traded securities are listed on the NASDAQ system, so dealers and brokers can perform trades quickly and efficiently.

10 **List some of the trends that are reshaping the financial industry.**

By using Internet technology, banks are delivering more services online. Mergers and acquisitions in the financial industry continue to consolidate the industry, helping financial institutions to improve their operating efficiency, reduce costs, and extend their geographic reach. Recent passage of bank reform legislation that allows banks to market securities and insurance products will help banks compete with non-depository institutions and with banks in other countries.

Key Terms

Bank of Canada   466
bank rate   466
bear markets   479
bond ratings   474
broker markets   478
bull markets   479
caisses populaires   468
Canada Deposit Insurance
    Corporation (CDIC)   470
chartered banks   468
convertible bonds   474
credit unions   468

currency   465
dealer markets   479
debentures   474
demand deposits   465
exchange-traded fund (ETF)   475
financial intermediation   467
futures contracts   476
high-yield (junk) bonds   473
institutional investors   476
interest   473
investment bankers   476
money   464

Experiential Exercises

1. Is it really free? How much is your chequing account really costing you? Maybe more than you think. Even "free" chequing accounts aren't always a good deal when you add up extra costs such as ATM fees, lost interest, bounced-cheque charges, and other hidden expenses. Take a closer look at your current chequing account, and then comparison shop to see if you could be getting a better deal elsewhere. Here's how.

   - Ask yourself how you really use your chequing account. What's the average balance you keep in your account? How many cheques do you write in a typical month? What time of day do you do most of your banking, and where do you prefer to do it?

   - Zero in on the real cost of your current chequing account. Once you know how you use your chequing account, you can get a clearer idea of its true cost—beyond just the monthly account fee. Do you write more cheques per month than allowed by your "free" account? What is the cost of each cheque? How many times do you use the ATM instead of a branch? How much does it cost each time? Do you pay extra for overdraft protection? What does your bank charge for bounced cheques? Add in any bonuses you receive with your chequing account as well. For example, does your bank waive your credit card's annual fee for keeping your chequing account with them?

   - Comparison shop. Check the websites of the major banks and credit unions in your area. Could you pay lower fees elsewhere? Could you earn interest on your chequing account at a credit union? Would you be better off paying a monthly fee with unlimited cheque-writing privileges? Crunch the numbers to find the best deal.

2. Compare brokerages. Visit the sites of two online brokerages, such as E*Trade (**www.etrade.ca**) or BMO (**www.bmoinvestorline.com**), or any others you know. Compare them for ease of use, quality of information, and other criteria you select. Summarize your findings. Which firm would you prefer to use, and why?

3. Track share prices. Pick a portfolio of five companies in at least three different industries. Choose companies you know, read the financial press to find good candidates, or follow the shares on the TSX. Set up a table to track the share prices. Record the end-of-month prices for the past six months, and track the daily price movements for at least two weeks (longer is even better!). Visit the websites of these companies to view their investor relations information. Finally, monitor economic and market trends and other events that affect market conditions. Share the performance of the portfolio with your classmates. Explain your basis for selecting each share, and analyze its price changes.

4. Research the trends in the initial public offering (IPO) marketplace from 2000 to present. Then select two IPO success stories and two failures. Prepare a report for the class on their performance. What lessons about the securities markets can you learn from their stories?

5. What role do a CEO's actions/strategies have in influencing a company's share performance? Prepare a class presentation that answers this question using both positive and negative examples from at least three companies covered in recent business news. In your presentation, discuss what your recommendations for each CEO would be.

6. At the Vanguard Group's site, (**www.vanguard.com**), go to the page for "Personal Investors," then to the "Planning & Education" section. Read about investor education and mutual funds. After learning about the fundamentals of mutual funds, prepare a presentation for the class based on the materials.

7. You've been asked to address your investment club on socially responsible investing and how companies qualify as socially responsible. Research this topic at the websites of the Social Investment Forum, (**www.socialinvest.org**). Prepare a detailed outline of the key points you would include in the speech. How can your personal financial decisions have a positive impact on communities and the environment? Do you support socially responsible investing?

Review Questions

1. What are the characteristics of money?
2. What are the functions of money?
3. Differentiate between M1, M2, and M2+ (M3).
4. What are the roles of the Bank of Canada?
5. What are chartered banks, and what are their roles?
6. What are some of the non-depository financial institutions?
7. What agency protects depositors, and to what limit?
8. Discuss the differences between common and preferred shares.
9. Discuss the use of bonds as a form of liability.
10. What are some other types of securities (other than common shares, preferred shares, and bonds)?
11. What are the security markets? What are the two key securities markets?
12. What is the role of investment bankers and stockbrokers?
13. What are the current trends in financial institutions?

CREATIVE THINKING CASE >

ING DIRECT—A Different Way to Bank

ING DIRECT began here in Canada in 1997. As they have no branches, our first introduction to the company was a television commercial announcing, " We are new here." We are all familiar with Frederik's face on television reminding us to "Save your money." ING DIRECT's business is conducted through the Internet, phone system, and ATM's. To open an account you simply mail them a cheque, payable to yourself, drawn on your existing account at another bank. And start saving your money. They have no service fees, higher interest rates on savings and lower interest rates on loans. Since 1999, ING DIRECT Funds Limited, a wholly owned subsidiary, has been selling mutual funds in all provinces except Quebec. Do they make any money with this approach that is so contradictory to that of the big five banks? Actually they do. They first became profitable in 2001 and are still profitable today. ING DIRECT Canada has over 1.6 million clients, employs over 900 people and has over $23 billion in assets. In addition, they have paid out over $3.6 billion in interest to clients while collecting nothing in fees and service charges. ING DIRECT's goal is not to have clients waiting on hold when they phone, but when this cannot be avoided, the clients are entertained by Frederik, the spokesperson we are all familiar with.

In addition to radically different operating procedures, ING DIRECT also hopes to create a different feel to banking with their unusual ads, bright orange colour schemes and off-beat activities. For example, they wanted to show Canadians that it felt good to save as they encouraged people to adopt the savings habit by engaging in 'random acts of saving.' They offered free coffee, snacks, and rides on public transit in locations all across the country. ING DIRECT does not even use the word 'bank' in their name but yet they are an amazingly successful bank that 'believes in service, not service charges.'

Critical Thinking Questions

- Do you think that most banking customers would choose higher interest rates and simplified loans over extra banking services? Why or why not?
- Compare the structure of ING DIRECT and the traditional bank, such as one of the 'big five.' How are they alike? How are they different?
- How might ING Direct's current strategy affect its future growth?

SOURCE: Adapted from http//www.ingdirect.ca/en/aboutus/index.html, accessed April 2, 2009. Reprinted by permission of ING Direct.

VIDEO CASE >

Card Tricks

Can't wait for your new credit card to arrive in the mail? A little trip to Mexico on spring break? Or how about Fort Lauderdale?

Stop right there! Have you read the agreement? Most of us never do. Credit card agreements are written by lawyers, for lawyers. The lender is in charge of this relationship. You are simply borrowing from them. Interest is charged on the entire balance if you do not pay it in full. Hard to do on your 20 hours a week at Starbucks.

Credit card companies will often start you out at perhaps 1.5 percent interest for six months. What happens at the end of six months? Unfortunately the interest rate is not tied to the prime rate in any way. The lender can change your rate at its discretion and without any warning. You might also be charged an extra fee for using your card in another country, in addition to the currency conversion fee rolled into your exchange rate. There are approximately 68 low interest options on the market. If you do make your minimum monthly payment on time, the credit card company might increase your spending limit. But is this really a problem?

It most definitely is. There are more than *68 million* Visas and MasterCards in circulation in Canada with more than 27% of these carrying balances. Over 550 institutions in Canada issue credit cards and over 660,000 outlets in Canada accept them. Interest rates on Visa and MasterCard can vary widely, but some department store cards are at an interest rate of almost 30 percent!

So what do we do to avoid trouble? The first and best course of action is to pay off the balance each month. However that is not always possible. Other options include the use of a personal line of credit, which has a lower interest rate, or at the very least, finding a credit card that has a lower rate. Check out (www.fcac.gc.ca), an interactive site of the Financial Consumer Agency of Canada, for a credit card comparison table. You might be surprised by what you see.

Critical Thinking Questions

- Assume you charge your spring break trip on your Visa. If the trip costs $1,500 and your interest rate is 17.9 percent, how much would you actually pay if you make regular payments of $125 per month for one year? Do you still owe a balance? How much?
- Using the PEST model, what environmental factors can impact your ability to handle your debt?

SOURCE: (www.cba.ca/contents/files/background/bkg_20090123_creditcards_en_pdf) accessed April 2nd, 2009; SOURCE: CBC, *Marketplace*, "Card Tricks," February 27, 2005.

Canadian Banks' International Presence

Canadian banks want to evolve and expand, but how they do this has been the subject of much debate and controversy. One obvious strategy would be horizontal integration, through merger or acquisition, involving banks, credit unions, or insurance companies. The Canadian Bankers Association supports allowing this strategy, as do the major banks and some of the large insurance companies, whereas Sun Life and Great-West Life want a ban on such mergers. Given the limited opportunities for growth in Canada, the big banks are looking at foreign markets. Prime Minister Stephen Harper has urged Canadian banks to expand abroad. Canada's major banks have remained profitable despite bank failures in the United States in the recession that began in 2008. Dividends have remained stable and are expected to continue that way assuming the economic downturn does not last beyond 2011.

The Bank of Montreal purchased the Harris Bank of Chicago in 1984 and has been building up its U.S. presence ever since. The Royal Bank is visible in the southern United States. The Bank of Nova Scotia/Scotiabank has been visible in Latin America and the Caribbean for decades, and in 2005, it acquired two banks in Peru. Toronto-Dominion is the majority shareholder of TD Banknorth, and more acquisitions are planned in the U.S. northeast.

However, all ventures into the United States have not been pretty. The drop in the technology sector of North America contributed to a net loss for TD in 2002, and CIBC's long-standing relationship with Enron cost the bank $80 million in settlement payments to the U.S. Securities and Exchange Commission and $2.4 billion in settlement of a class action suit by Enron investors. BMO engaged in an unfortunate deal with AIG which could have resulted in a drop in dividends if they had not received a US$1.1billion payout from the U.S. government after the AIG bailout. Fortunately for the Canadian banks, they have strong retail banking operations in Canada and have relied on this stable income source to buoy their bottom line when things have soured south of the border.

It seems we have a classic catch-22 situation. The Canadian banks argue that they need to expand outside of Canada, but if they are to be able to gain greater access to foreign markets, then Canada must allow foreign access to the domestic market. Harper has reiterated that he does not intend to promote greater protectionism. If this is allowed, competition will increase, supporting the Canadian banks' argument for domestic consolidation. The Bloc, Liberals, and Conservatives are generally on the same side of the debate, with the NDP teetering on the edge. Positions range from advocating on behalf of the banks, to allowing domestic mergers, to blocking any mergers until protection is assured for bank employees and consumers. Major reforms suggested are in the areas of transparency, accountability, community reinvestment, credit card interest rates, as well as consumer and employee protection. However, a very important point is the fact that the Canadian public is not supportive of bank mergers, with small and large businesses both finding the idea less than appealing. If bank reforms are instituted, requiring more transparency and accountability, we might just see more Canadian mergers in the financial sector.

Critical Thinking Questions

1. What are the arguments for and against the merger of banks in Canada?

2. Look once again at the PEST model, and identify which environmental factors could impact, either positively or negatively, Canadian banks operating domestically and internationally.

SOURCES: Murray Cole, "The Bank Merger Debate in the Harper Era," *Canadian Dimension*, 40, no.3 (May/June 2006); and Matthias Rieker, "TD Banknorth on Naming of President," *American Banker*, 171, no. 123 (June 28, 2006), (http://financialpost.com/news-sectors/story.html?id=1447994), accessed April 2, 2009.

CHAPTER 16

Making the Connection

Managing the Firm's Finances

In this chapter, we will continue to look at the finance area of business. The primary role of the financial manager is to maximize the value of the firm for the owners, achieving the main critical success factor of *financial performance*. This, we know, cannot be done without the other four success factors, reiterating the need for managers in all departments to work closely with one another, and the finance area in particular.

As we saw in Chapter 15, the relationship between finance and the major *stakeholders*, particularly the owners, is a difficult but important one. Financial managers make many important decisions regarding the acquisition, disposition, and management of financial resources to maximize the value of the firm for its owners. They must decide what projects to invest the firm's money into, and how to finance those projects, whether through issuing debt—borrowing the money—or selling more shares—equity financing. Each has its own advantages and disadvantages, or rewards and risks in 'finance speak.' If the firm chooses to use equity financing, one of the major decisions that will affect this stakeholder group is how much of the company's profit will be distributed to the shareholders in the form of a dividend. The shareholders expect a return, so if a regular dividend is not paid, then they expect the return in the form of an increased share price. This can happen only if the investing community sees potential in the value of the shares. If neither of these happens, the price of the shares will fall as

shareholders sell their shares. The company must therefore consider the stakeholder response to the decisions it makes, as they will affect its ability to maximize the value of the firm for the owners.

As we also saw in Chapter 15, all decisions have financial consequences, but financial decisions have consequences in other areas as well. For example, policies for granting credit affect *marketing's* ability to generate sales. Just imagine if BMW did not offer financing packages on its vehicles. Furthermore, money spent on research and development or new production facilities has an impact on what *operations* is capable of doing, just as the company's policies on payroll costs have an impact on attracting and keeping key employees (*human resources*). To make money, the firm must first spend money, but it must also control that money to continue to be profitable and stay viable. A fine balance must be achieved between taking the risks and reaping the rewards—one that the finance manager must consider and that affects all areas of the company.

Cash flow provides an example of this need for integration and balance. To aid marketing in selling the firm's products, the supply chain must be set up to make sure that inventory is available for customers and that credit is generally extended. However, that means that finance must balance the time that it takes to sell the inventory and then collect the accounts receivable from customers with the payments on that inventory and other expenses. If it does not

do this, the company will not have enough cash coming in to pay its bills and will go bankrupt! Another example is with inventory. The operations area needs raw materials on hand to avoid delays in production, and marketing needs enough finished goods on hand to *satisfy customers*, but finance must balance these needs with the cost of carrying inventory, and therefore tries to keep inventory levels at a minimum. In Chapter 11, we discussed techniques for dealing with inventory and saw that technology provides many new options.

Technology is just one of the many environmental factors that must be taken into account in making financial decisions. For example, as market demand changes (*social* environment), funds need to be shifted between projects. As discussed in this chapter, the social environment has also had a significant impact on changing the role of the typical CFO in an organization—from being "just numbers people" to helping to develop and implement the firm's overall *strategy* and "re-establish public trust" in the wake of recent financial scandals. As interest and exchange rates fluctuate (*economic* environment), some projects and methods

of financing projects either will need to be abandoned or will become more possible. General economic conditions in domestic and world markets, like the recent global meltdown created by the sub-prime mortgage crisis, might cause firms to speed up or slow down the rate of investment in different projects, and government policies in the home and foreign countries (*political* environment) might make investment in certain projects more attractive than others. Finally, as *technology* advances and costs drop, some projects become more accessible.

In the internal business environment, when budgets are set, the finance area must work with the other functional areas to develop *plans* for financing the company that help it meet its strategic goals. Each area has a role to play in helping the organization achieve its strategic goals, and the resources they will need must be considered by the finance area. Finance uses various forecasts, as discussed in the chapter, to develop financial plans for the business to ensure that its goals are met in a way that balances risks and rewards, maximizing the value of the firm for its owners.

CHAPTER 16

Managing the Firm's Finances

LEARNING OUTCOMES

1   Explain the roles finance and the financial manager play in the firm's overall strategy.

2   Describe how a firm develops its financial plans, including forecasts and budgets.

3   List the types of short- and long-term expenditures a firm makes.

4   Summarize the main sources and costs of unsecured and secured short-term financing.

5   Identify and compare the two primary sources of long-term financing.

6   Understand the major types, features, and costs of long-term debt.

7   Discuss how firms issue equity, and the costs to the company.

8   Understand risk, how it can be managed and what makes a risk insurable.

9   Describe the types of insurance coverage that businesses should consider.

10   List some of the trends that are affecting the practice of financial management.

WHY WE NEED AN UNDERSTANDING OF FINANCE

SHIRLEY A. ROSE

Victoria Calvert has operated a consulting practice specializing in venture launch and expansion since 1984. Having guided clients through both recessions and periods of rapid expansion has required her to develop financing strategies to both downsize and expand client operations.

Calvert indicated that there would be significant opportunities for acquisition and expansion despite slower economic conditions in the 2010 to 2012 period. She said "A report published by the Canadian Federation of Business implied that almost 500,000 ventures would be for sale in the 2010 to 2015 period as owners retire. That ownership transfer will require a great deal of financial creativity. As banks may still be reluctant to lend to new owners, a patchwork financial strategy could be employed. Buyers could ask for a long term loan from the current owner, as well as issuing shares to friends and family (love money). In a crunch, the new owner can use their credit card, as many entrepreneurs do, to finance short-term assets such as inventory."

Calvert reflected that many clients have had to deal with short-term cash shortages. She suggested that managers of small- and medium-sized organizations tend to focus on marketing issues rather than managing their cash flow. They have costs (such as rent) that may increase dramatically; ensuring that their sales or profit margins have increased in a similar manner is essential. While she does not recommend cutting advertising and promotion during tight economic times, she does have her clients critically evaluate each of their products or service lines to ensure they are contributing to profits. Cut the dogs; get rid of products that are not turning over or that have thin margins. She does, however, caution clients to keep up to date on some important expenses, indicating, "Don't forget to pay for your insurance; a lawsuit or fire damage will put you out of business if you are not covered."

Clients are advised to match the type of financing to the operation needed by their business. She suggests that short-term financing, such as operating lines or short-term loans, be used to fund inventory or accounts receivable. Alternatively, long-term assets such as equipment or buildings, should be funded with long-term financing—long-term loans, the issuing of shares, or a mortgage. She laughs as she remembers one client who used six different credit cards for short term cash requirements, and got a call from the bank to cancel his account. He had been busy, and focused only on staff and customers, forgetting to manage the money. "We took some time, assessed the profitability of his activities, sold some materials and equipment, and restructured his funding to give him some cash to pay bills. He introduced a better software package and manages the finances now. He even has enough equity to consider a second location."

Calvert recommends clients track their expenses and prepare trend analyses; if margins start slipping they can address the problem quickly. She also provides them with standard costs for their industry by referring them to (www.sme.ic.gc.ca). She suggests, "If they know what is common for their industry, they can aim to contain their expenses to the industry norm—it provides a goalpost for them."

When asked if she had any parting words of advice for new managers she quipped, "Sure. It is not what you earn, it is what you keep that is important."

Critical Thinking Questions

1. Why is a basic knowledge of finance important to *any* manager?

2. What can happen if you tend to ignore the implications of financial issues in your day-to-day operations? In your strategic planning?

3. What financial strategies might you suggest to a small business looking to expand, given the current economic climate?

In today's fast-paced global economy, managing a firm's finances is more complex than ever. A thorough command of traditional finance activities—financial planning, investing money, and raising funds—is only part of the job. Financial managers are more than number crunchers. As part of the top-management team, chief financial officers (CFOs) need a broad understanding of their firm's business and industry, as well as leadership ability and creativity. They must never lose sight of the primary goal of the financial manager: to maximize the value of the firm to its owners.

All firms, whether start-up companies with three employees or major multinational corporations with billions of dollars in annual revenue, need to manage their finances efficiently and effectively. Otherwise, the firm will not have the resources it needs to pay its bills and run its daily operations or to make investments in future growth.

Financial management—spending and raising a firm's money—is both a science and an art. The science part is analyzing numbers and flows of cash through the firm. The art is answering questions like these: Is the firm using its financial resources in the best way? Aside from costs, why choose a particular form of financing? How risky is each option?

Whether you are a marketing manager, purchasing agent, or systems analyst, knowledge of finance will help you to do your job better. You'll be able to understand your company's financial statements, its financial condition, and management's investment and financing decisions. Financial information also provides feedback on how well you are doing and identifies problems. On a more practical note, you may be asked to prepare a budget for your department or unit. Employees who understand the financial decision-making process will be able to prepare proposals that address financial concerns. As a result, they will be more likely to get the resources they require to accomplish the firm's goals.

If you own a business, you must pay close attention to financial management. Without financial plans you may find yourself running out of cash. It's easy to get so caught up in growing sales that you neglect your billing and collection methods. In fact, managing accounts receivable is often one of the more challenging aspects of running a young company.

This chapter focuses on the financial management of a firm. We'll start with an overview of the role of finance and of the financial manager in the firm's overall business strategy. Next we consider the basics of financial planning: forecasts and budgets. Discussions of short- and long-term uses of funds and sources of short- and long-term financing follow. The importance of understanding and managing risk and insurance is examined, and finally, we'll look at key trends affecting financial management.

The Role of Finance and the Financial Manager

financial management
The art and science of managing a firm's money so that it can meet its goals.

HOT Links

What challenges do today's financial managers face? To find out, browse through recent issues of *CFO* magazine at (**www.cfo.com**).

cash flows
The inflows and outflows of cash for a firm.

Any company—whether it's a two-lawyer law partnership or an integrated oil company, such as Suncor Energy—needs money to operate. To make money, it must first spend money—on inventory and supplies, equipment and facilities, and employee wages and salaries. Therefore, finance is critical to the success of all companies. It might not be as visible as marketing or production, but management of a firm's finances is just as much a key to the firm's success.

Financial management—the art and science of managing a firm's money so that it can meet its goals—is not just the responsibility of the finance department. All business decisions have financial consequences. Managers in all departments must work closely with financial personnel. If you are a sales representative, for example, the company's credit and collection policies will affect your ability to make sales.

Revenues from sales of the firm's products should be the chief source of funding, but money from sales doesn't always come in when it's needed to pay the bills. Financial managers must track how money is flowing into and out of the firm (see Exhibit 16.1). They work with the firm's other department managers to determine how available funds will be used and how much money is needed. Then they choose the best sources to obtain the required funding.

For example, a financial manager will track day-to-day operational data such as cash collections and disbursements to ensure that the company has enough cash to meet its obligations. Over a longer time horizon, the manager will thoroughly study whether and when the company should open a new manufacturing facility. The manager will also suggest the most appropriate way to finance the project, raise the funds, and then monitor the project's implementation and operation.

Financial management is closely related to accounting. In most firms, both areas are the responsibility of the vice-president of finance or the CFO (many of whom have an accounting designation). But the accountant's main function is to collect and present financial data. Financial managers use financial statements and other information prepared by accountants to make financial decisions. Financial managers focus on **cash flows**, the inflows and outflows of cash. They plan and monitor the firm's cash flows to ensure that cash is available when needed.

CONCEPT *in Action* >>>

Because all business decisions have financial consequences, managers in all departments must work closely with financial personnel. A company's credit and collection policies, for example, might impact a sales representative's ability to close a sale. Who is responsible for making key financial decisions for businesses?

© ROYALTY-FREE/CORBIS

EXHIBIT 16.1 > How Cash Flows Through a Business

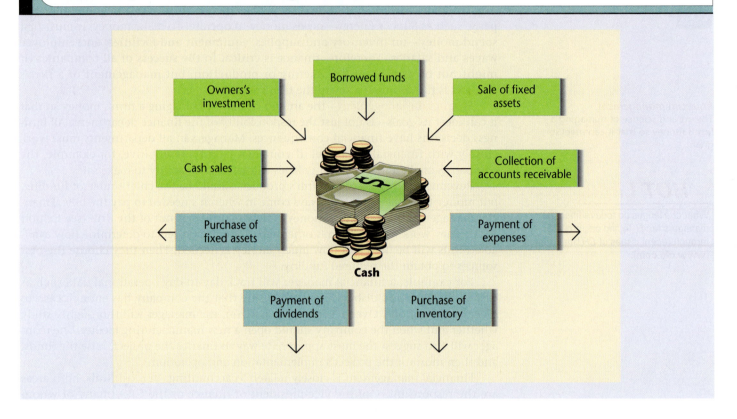

Owners's investment

Borrowed funds

Sale of fixed assets

Cash sales

Collection of accounts receivable

Purchase of fixed assets

Payment of expenses

Payment of dividends

Purchase of inventory

Cash

The Financial Manager's Responsibilities and Activities

Financial managers have a complex and challenging job. They analyze financial data prepared by accountants, monitor the firm's financial status, and prepare and implement financial plans. One day they might be developing a better way to automate cash collections; the next they might be analyzing a proposed acquisition. The key activities of the financial manager are

- *financial planning*—preparing the financial plan, which projects revenues, expenditures, and financing needs over a given period;
- *investment (spending money)*—investing the firm's funds in projects and securities that provide high returns in relation to their risks; and
- *financing (raising money)*—obtaining funding for the firm's operations and investments and seeking the best balance between debt (borrowed funds) and equity (funds raised through the sale of ownership in the business).

The Goal of the Financial Manager

How can financial managers make wise planning, investment, and financing decisions? The main goal of the financial manager is *to maximize the value of the firm to its owners*. The value of a publicly owned corporation is measured by the share price of its shares. A private company's value is the price at which it could be sold.

To maximize the firm's value, the financial manager has to consider both short- and long-term consequences of the firm's actions. Maximizing profits is one approach, but it should not be the only one. Such an approach favours making short-term gains over achieving long-term goals. What if a firm in a

HOT Links

When you come across a finance term you don't understand, visit (www.fiscalagents.com/newsletter/gloss/Glossary/a.shtml).

highly technical and competitive industry did no research and development? In the short run, profits would be high because research and development are very expensive, but in the long run, the firm might lose its ability to compete because of its lack of new products.

This is true regardless of a company's size or point in its life cycle. David Deeds was cofounder of a company that developed an innovative computer-aided design hardware and software package for architects and engineers. He and his partners made some decisions early in the company's life to pursue opportunities such as consulting projects that generated revenue quickly. The company saw its profits grow, adding staff and offices to handle the increased business, but this side-tracked the founders from their initial vision: designing revolutionary new products to address client needs. "We managed ourselves into a niche where we could survive and make a little money but never offer anything unique or grow significantly," says Deeds. Although they built a reasonably successful small business, the desire for the quick buck overrode the long-term goal of building a $100 million company.[1]

Financial managers constantly strive for a balance between the opportunity for profit and the potential for loss. In finance, the opportunity for profit is termed **return**; the potential for loss, or the chance that an investment will not achieve the expected level of return, is **risk**. A basic principle in finance is that the higher the risk, the greater the return that is required. This widely accepted concept is called the **risk–return trade-off**. Financial managers consider many risk and return factors when making investment and financing decisions. Among them are changing patterns of market demand, interest rates, general economic conditions, market conditions, and social issues (such as environmental effects and equal employment opportunity policies).

return
The opportunity for profit.

risk
The potential for loss or the chance that an investment will not achieve the expected level of return.

risk–return trade-off
A basic principle in finance that holds that the higher the risk, the greater the return that is required.

Financial Planning: Looking Ahead

As we learned in Chapter 7, companies use several types of plans to determine how to achieve organizational objectives. A company's *financial plan* is part of the overall company plan and guides the firm toward its business goals and the maximization of its value. The financial plan enables the firm to estimate the amount and timing of its investment and financing needs.

To prepare a financial plan, the financial manager must first consider existing and proposed products, the resources available to produce them, and the financing needed to support production and sales. Forecasts and budgets are essential to the firm's financial planning. They should be part of an integrated planning process that links them to strategic plans and performance measurement.

Forecasting the Future

The financial-planning process starts with financial forecasts, or projections of future developments within the firm. The estimated demand for the firm's products (the sales forecast) and other financial and operating data are key inputs. At Ford Motor Company, economic analysts estimate expected production and sales for each line of cars and trucks. Then, financial analysts prepare detailed short- and long-term financial forecasts based on these assumptions.

Short-term forecasts, or *operating plans*, project revenues, costs of goods, and operating expenses over a one-year period. Using short-term forecasts, financial managers at Ford estimate the next year's expenses for inventory, labour, advertising, and other operating activities. These estimates form the basis for cash

short-term forecasts
Projections of revenues, costs of goods, and operating expenses over a one-year period.

long-term forecasts
Projections of a firm's activities and the funding for those activities over a period that is longer than a year, typically 2 to 10 years.

budgets (described next), which forecast cash inflows and outflows over the same period.

Long-term forecasts, or strategic plans, cover a period that is longer than a year, typically 2 to 10 years, and take a broader view of the firm's financial activities. With these forecasts, management can assess the financial effects of various business strategies: What would be the financial results of investing in new facilities and equipment? Of developing new products? Of eliminating a line of business? Of acquiring other firms? Long-term forecasts also show where the funding for these activities is expected to come from.

Lenders typically ask potential borrowers for forecasts that cover the period during which the loan will be outstanding. The forecasts are used to evaluate the risk of the loan and to see that adequate cash flow will be available to pay off the debt. Then they structure loan terms and covenants (requirements that the company comply with certain operating and financial measures during the loan period) based on those statements.

Budgets

budgets
Formal written forecasts of revenues and expenses that set spending limits based on operational forecasts; include cash budgets, capital budgets, and operating budgets.

Businesses prepare budgets to plan and control their future financial activities. **Budgets** are formal written forecasts of revenues and expenses that set spending limits based on operational forecasts. All budgets begin with forecasts. Budgets provide a way to control expenses and compare the actual performance to the forecast. By monitoring actual revenues and expenses and comparing them to budgets on a regular basis, companies gain critical information about operations. When variances to the budget occur, managers can analyze them to determine if they need to take steps to correct them. Suppose the owner of a small printing company sees that May sales are down and expenses are over budget because a major press broke down and the company was unable to fulfill many orders on time. This situation would require asking such questions as: How old is the press, has it broken down before, should the company continue to repair it or is it time to replace it, can the company afford a new press, and how would it finance the new press? A back-up plan to prevent lost orders would be another possible outcome of this budget review.

Firms use several types of budgets, most of which cover a one-year period:

cash budgets
Budgets that forecast a firm's cash inflows and outflows and help the firm plan for cash surpluses and shortages.

- **Cash budgets** forecast the firm's cash inflows and outflows, and help the firm plan for cash surpluses and shortages. Because having enough cash is so critical to their financial health, many firms prepare annual cash budgets subdivided into months or weeks. Then they project the amount of cash needed in each shorter time period.

capital budgets
Budgets that forecast a firm's outlays for fixed assets (plant and equipment), typically covering a period of several years.

- **Capital budgets** forecast outlays for fixed assets (plant and equipment). They usually cover a period of several years and ensure that the firm will have enough funds to buy the equipment and buildings it needs.

operating budgets
Budgets that combine sales forecasts with estimates of production costs and operating expenses to forecast profits.

- **Operating budgets** combine sales forecasts with estimates of production costs and operating expenses to forecast profits. They are based on individual budgets for sales, production, purchases of materials, factory overhead, and operating expenses. Operating budgets then are used to plan operations: dollars of sales, units of production, amounts of raw materials, dollars of wages, and so forth.

Budgets are routinely used to monitor and control the performance of a division, a department, or an individual manager. When actual outcomes differ from budget expectations, management must take action.

concept check

What is a financial plan? Name two types of financial-planning documents.

Distinguish between short- and long-term forecasts. How are both used by financial managers?

Briefly describe three types of budgets.

CONCEPT *in Action* >>>

Budgets of all types help companies plan and control their future financial activities. What types of fixed assets would a fast-growing, outdoor video-billboard company include in its capital budget?

How Organizations Use Funds

LO 3

To grow and prosper, a firm must keep investing money in its operations. The financial manager decides how best to use the firm's money. Short-term expenses support the firm's day-to-day activities. For instance, an athletic-apparel maker regularly spends money to buy raw materials such as leather and fabric, and to pay employee salaries. Long-term expenses are typically for fixed assets. For the athletic-apparel maker, these would include outlays to build a new factory, buy automated manufacturing equipment, or acquire a small manufacturer of sports apparel.

Short-Term Expenses

Short-term expenses, often called *operating expenses,* are outlays used to support current selling and production activities. They typically result in current assets, which include cash and any other assets (accounts receivable and inventory) that can be converted to cash within a year. The financial manager's goal is to manage current assets so the firm has enough cash to pay its bills and to support its accounts receivable and inventory.

cash management
The process of making sure that a firm has enough cash on hand to pay bills as they are due, and to meet unexpected expenses.

Cash Management: Assuring Liquidity   Cash is the lifeblood of business. Without it, a firm could not operate. An important duty of the financial manager is **cash management,** or making sure that enough cash is on hand to pay bills as they are due and to meet unexpected expenses.

Businesses use budgets to estimate the cash requirements for a specific period. Many companies keep a minimum cash balance to cover unexpected expenses or changes in projected cash flows. The financial manager arranges loans to cover any shortfalls. If the size and timing of cash inflows closely match the size and timing of cash outflows, the company needs to keep only a small amount of cash on hand. A company whose sales and receipts are fairly predictable and regular throughout the year needs less cash than a company with a seasonal pattern of sales and receipts. A toy company, for instance, whose sales are concentrated in the fall, spends a great deal of cash during the spring and summer to build inventory. It has excess cash during the winter and early spring, when it collects on sales from its peak selling season.

Because cash held in current accounts earns little, if any, interest, the financial manager tries to keep cash balances low and to invest the surplus cash. Surpluses are invested temporarily in marketable securities, short-term investments that are easily converted into cash. The financial manager looks for low-risk investments that offer high returns. Three of the most popular marketable securities are Treasury bills, certificates of deposit, and **commercial papers**. (Commercial paper is unsecured short-term debt—an IOU—issued by a financially strong corporation.)

Companies with overseas operations face even greater cash management challenges, as the Expanding Around the Globe box explains. Developing the systems for international cash management may sound simple in theory, but in practice it's extremely complex. In addition to dealing with multiple foreign currencies, treasurers must understand and follow banking practices and regulatory and tax requirements in each country. Regulations may impede their ability to move funds freely across borders. Also, issuing a standard set of procedures for every office may not work because local business practices differ from country to country. Moreover, local managers may resist the shift to a centralized structure because they don't want to give up control of cash generated by their units. Corporate financial managers must be sensitive to and aware of local customs and adapt the centralization strategy accordingly.

In addition to seeking the right balance between cash and **marketable securities**, the financial manager tries to shorten the time between the purchase of inventory or services (cash outflows) and the collection of cash from sales (cash inflows). The three key strategies are to collect money owed to the firm (accounts receivable) as quickly as possible, to pay money owed to others (accounts payable) as late as possible without damaging the firm's credit reputation, and to turn inventory quickly to minimize the funds tied up in it.

commercial paper
Unsecured short-term debt—an IOU—issued by a financially strong corporation.

marketable securities
Short-term investments that are easily converted into cash.

Expanding Around the Globe

FOLLOW THE MONEY

If you think it's hard to balance your chequing account, imagine trying to deal with $4 billion or more in 1,400 accounts in 46 different currencies for 233 legal entities, at 145 banks worldwide! That's the job facing Jim Colby, assistant treasurer of Honeywell International Inc., and his counterparts at other multinational companies who grapple with complex treasury operations like this on a daily basis. With so much at stake, international cash management becomes a priority for financial managers.

Many companies are joining Honeywell in the quest for more efficient global cash management systems. Corporate treasurers want to identify and pool cash from overseas operations so that these cash balances can be put to work. In addition, recent regulatory changes have brought huge amounts of cash back to North America from overseas operations—and too much cash can be as much of a problem as too little. "Cash is a wonderful thing to have, but when it's yielding 3.5 percent pre-tax, then it's also a burden. That is not a viable return on a large asset," says David O'Brien, assistant treasurer of EDS Corp.

At Honeywell, Colby and his team turned to a Web-based technology solution to improve its global cash pooling system. Prior to 2002, Honeywell couldn't track its cash, most of which was outside North America and earning little or no interest. The company launched a centralized Web portal in 2002, and Honeywell's business units began reporting their cash holdings. By 2005, Honeywell upgraded to an automated treasury platform.

Once Honeywell knew where its cash holdings were, it could manage this cash more efficiently and profitably. Treasury managers developed budgets and goals for interest income that were tied to cash balance forecasts, exchange rates in each country, and other factors. Next, they pooled cash from individual bank accounts and invested it in marketable securities. The interest income goals established performance benchmarks and were factored into incentive compensation. The results were significant. Today, most of Honeywell's cash is now actively managed and the interest income is about twice what it was in 2002. The company can also quickly identify which cash reserves are available to make an acquisition or fund a large capital project.[2]

Critical Thinking Questions

- Why is managing cash such an important part of a financial manager's job? Why is having too much cash a problem?
- What were the benefits from Honeywell's new cash management procedures worldwide? For a multinational company? Are there any disadvantages?

Adapted from Richard Gamble, "Got Cash? Who Doesn't?" Treasury & Risk Management, December 2005/January 2006, http://www.treasuryandrisk.com; Richard Gamble, Susan Kelly, and John Labate, "The 2005 Alexander Hamilton Award Winners: Cash Management; Bronze Award Winner: Honeywell International," Treasury & Risk Management, November 2005, all from http://www.treasuryandrisk.com; and Karen M. Kroll, "Treasury Today: To Centralize or Not?" Business Finance, April 2006, http://businessfinancemag.com.

accounts receivable
Sales for which a firm has not yet been paid.

Managing Accounts Receivable   Accounts receivable represent sales for which the firm has not yet been paid. Because the product has been sold but cash has not yet been received, an account receivable amounts to a use of funds. For the average manufacturing firm, accounts receivable represent about 15 to 20 percent of total assets.

The financial manager's goal is to collect money owed to the firm as quickly as possible while offering customers credit terms attractive enough to increase sales. Accounts receivable management involves setting *credit policies,* guidelines on offering credit, and *credit terms,* specific repayment conditions, including how long customers have to pay their bills and whether a cash discount is given for quicker payment. Another aspect of accounts receivable management is deciding on *collection policies,* the procedures for collecting overdue accounts.

Setting up credit and collection policies is a balancing act for financial managers. On the one hand, easier credit policies or generous credit terms (a longer repayment period or larger cash discount) result in increased sales. On the other hand, the firm has to finance more accounts receivable, and the risk of uncollectible accounts receivable rises. Businesses consider the impact on sales, timing of cash flow, experience with bad debt, customer profiles, and industry standards when developing their credit and collection policies.

Companies that want to speed up collections actively manage their accounts receivable rather than passively letting customers pay when they want to. Companies that take this approach can usually collect from anyone.

Technology plays a big role in helping companies improve their credit and collections performance. When the tech sector fell on hard times, Cisco saw its global Days Sales Outstanding (DSO) climb to a high of 47 days. The company then developed Web-based reporting tools that improved overall cash management. Managers received frequently updated accounts receivable and cash collection reports, along with real-time collection and credit reports. The new system also flagged potential problems with customers. Within nine months of implementation, Cisco exceeded its goal of reducing DSO to 30 days, slashing that number to 24 days.[3]

Inventory   One use of funds is to buy inventory needed by the firm. In a typical manufacturing firm, inventory is nearly 20 percent of total assets. The cost of inventory includes not only its purchase price but also ordering, handling, storage, interest, and insurance costs.

Production, marketing, and finance managers usually have differing views about inventory. Production managers want lots of raw materials on hand to avoid production delays. Marketing managers want lots of finished goods on hand so that customer orders can be filled quickly, but financial managers want the least inventory possible without harming production efficiency or sales. Financial managers must work closely with production and marketing to balance these conflicting goals. Techniques for reducing the investment in inventory—inventory management, the just-in-time system, and materials requirement planning—were described in Chapter 11.

Long-Term Expenditures

capital expenditures
Investments in long-lived assets such as land, buildings, machinery, and equipment, that are expected to provide benefits extending beyond one year.

A firm also uses funds for its investments in long-lived assets—such items as land, buildings, machinery, equipment, and information systems. These are called capital expenditures. Unlike operating expenses, which produce benefits within a year, the benefits from capital expenditures extend beyond one year. For instance, a printer's purchase of a new printing press with a usable life of seven years is a capital expenditure. It appears as a fixed asset on the firm's balance sheet. Paper, ink, and other supplies, however, are expenses. Mergers and acquisitions, discussed in Chapter 5, are also considered capital expenditures.

Firms make capital expenditures for many reasons. The most common are to expand and to replace or renew fixed assets. Another reason is to develop new products. Most manufacturing firms have a big investment in long-term assets. Boeing Company, for instance, puts millions of dollars a year into airplane-manufacturing facilities.

capital budgeting
The process of analyzing long-term projects and selecting those that offer the best returns while maximizing the firm's value.

Because capital expenditures tend to be costly and have a major effect on the firm's future, the financial manager must analyze long-term projects and select those that offer the best returns, while maximizing the firm's value. This process is called **capital budgeting**. Decisions involving new products or the acquisition of another business are especially important. Managers look at project costs and forecast the future benefits the project will bring—for example, from increased productivity, staff reductions, and other cost savings—to calculate the firm's estimated return on the investment.

For instance, consider the period during which Air Canada or WestJet Airlines is planning for new aircraft. Before going ahead, the company must consider not only its present aircraft and load factors (i.e., how many seats are typically full during any of its routes) but also the actual acquisition costs, maintenance costs, how to finance the aircraft (i.e., debt capital or equity capital), the amount that the aircraft will actually be flying (and therefore making revenue), and the anticipated payback period (i.e., how long will it take for the revenue that the aircraft generates to pay off its costs).

> **concept check**
>
> Distinguish between short- and long-term expenses.
>
> What is the financial manager's goal in cash management? List the three key cash management strategies.
>
> Describe the firm's main motives in making capital expenditures.

Obtaining Short-Term Financing

How do firms raise the funding they need? They borrow money (debt), sell ownership shares (equity), and retain earnings (profits). The financial manager must assess all of these sources and choose the one most likely to help maximize the firm's value.

Like expenses, borrowed funds can be divided into short- and long-term loans. A short-term loan comes due within a year; a long-term loan has a maturity greater than one year. Short-term financing is shown as a current liability on the balance sheet and is used to finance current assets and support operations. Short-term loans can be unsecured or secured.

Unsecured Short-Term Loans

unsecured loans
Loans for which the borrower does not have to pledge specific assets as security.

Unsecured loans are made on the basis of the firm's creditworthiness and the lender's previous experience with the firm. An unsecured borrower does not have to pledge specific assets as security. The three main types of *unsecured short-term loans* are trade credit, bank loans, and commercial paper.

trade credit
The extension of credit by the seller to the buyer between the time the buyer receives the goods or services and when it pays for them.

accounts payable
Purchase for which a buyer has not yet paid the seller.

Trade Credit: Accounts Payable   When Magna International Inc. (Magna) sells auto parts to its customers; the customers do not have to pay cash on delivery. Instead, Magna regularly bills its customers for the purchases, and they pay at a later date. This is an example of **trade credit**: The seller extends credit to the buyer between the time the buyer receives the goods or services and when it pays for them. Trade credit is a major source of short-term business financing. The buyer enters the credit on its books as an **account payable**. In effect, the credit is a short-term loan from the seller to the buyer of the goods and services. Until the customers pay Magna, Magna has an account receivable from its customers and the customers have an account payable to Magna.

Bank Loans   Unsecured bank loans are another source of short-term business financing. Companies often use these loans to finance seasonal (cyclical) businesses. For instance, a swimwear manufacturer has strong sales in the spring and summer and lower sales during the fall and winter. It needs short-term bank financing to increase inventories before its strongest selling season and to finance accounts receivable during late winter and early spring, as shown in Exhibit 16.2. The company repays these bank loans when it sells the inventory and collects the receivables.

EXHIBIT 16.2 > Swimwear Manufacturer's Seasonal Cash Flows

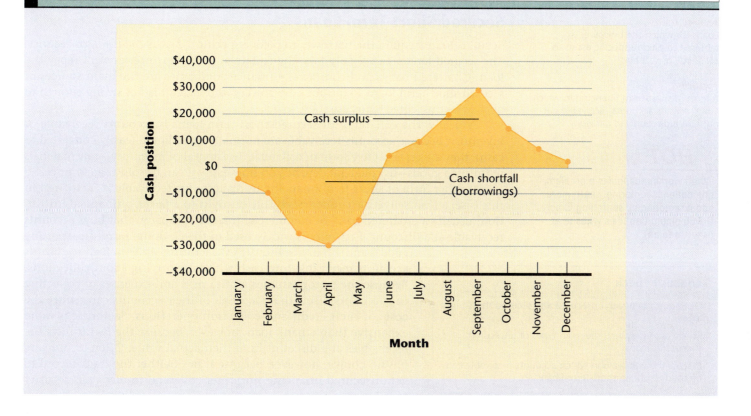

line of credit
An agreement between a bank and a business that specifies the maximum amount of short-term borrowing the bank will make available to the business or an individual.

revolving credit agreement (or revolving line of credit)
A line of credit that allows the borrower to have access to funds again once it has been repaid.

Unsecured bank loans include lines of credit and revolving credit agreements (although in Canada most are secured). A **line of credit** is an agreement between a bank and a business or an individual. It specifies the maximum amount of short-term borrowing the bank will make available to the firm or the individual. This allows the borrower to obtain a number of loans without reapplying each time, as long as they do not exceed the prearranged amount.

Most lines of credit are a **revolving credit agreement (or revolving line of credit)**. A revolving credit agreement allows the borrower to continue to have access to funds as long as the maximum has not been exceeded. Therefore, the business or individual can pay off the line of credit and have access to the available funds again. Most credit cards offer revolving lines of credit.

Firms often obtain annual lines of credit based on their expected seasonal needs. Then they can quickly borrow without having to reapply to the bank each time funds are needed. Suppose the swimwear manufacturer projected a cash shortfall of $80,000 for the period from February to June. The financial manager might get a $100,000 line of credit from the bank. (The extra $20,000 would be there to cover any unexpected outlays.) The firm could borrow funds as needed—$10,000 in February, $25,000 in March, $30,000 in April. Then it could gradually repay the loan as it collects cash during the summer months.

Commercial Paper   As noted earlier, *commercial paper* is an unsecured short-term debt—an IOU—issued by a financially strong corporation. Thus, it is a short-term investment for firms with temporary cash surpluses, and it is a financing option for major corporations. Corporations issue commercial paper in multiples of $100,000 for periods ranging from 3 to 270 days. Many big companies use commercial paper instead of short-term bank loans because the interest rate on commercial paper is usually 1 to 3 percent below bank rates.

Secured Short-Term Loans

secured loans
Loans for which the borrower is required to pledge specific assets as *collateral,* or security.

factoring
A form of short-term financing in which a firm sells its accounts receivable outright, at a discount, to a *factor*.

Secured loans require the borrower to pledge specific assets as *collateral,* or security. The secured lender can legally take the collateral if the borrower doesn't repay the loan. Chartered banks and commercial finance companies are the main sources of secured short-term loans to business. Borrowers whose credit is not strong enough to qualify for unsecured loans use these loans.

Typically, the collateral for secured short-term loans is accounts receivable or inventory. Because accounts receivable are normally quite liquid (easily converted to cash), they are an attractive form of collateral. The appeal of inventory—raw materials or finished goods—as collateral depends on how easily it can be sold at a fair price.

Another form of short-term financing using accounts receivable is **factoring**. In this case, a firm sells its accounts receivable outright to a *factor*, a financial institution (usually a chartered bank or commercial finance company) that buys accounts receivable at a discount. Factoring is widely used in the clothing, furniture, sporting goods, and appliance industries. Factoring allows a firm to turn its accounts receivable into cash without worrying about collections. Because the factor assumes all the risks and expenses of collecting the accounts, firms that factor all of their accounts can reduce the costs of their credit and collection operations. Factoring is more expensive than a bank loan, however, because the factor buys the receivables at a discount from their actual value. Often a company has no choice, however, because it has neither the track record to get unsecured financing nor other collateral to pledge as security for a loan.

HOT Links

When working capital is a problem, one option is factoring. Learn more about factoring by searching Export Development Canada's website at (www.edc.ca).

concept check

Distinguish between unsecured and secured short-term loans.

Briefly describe the three main types of unsecured short-term loans.

Discuss the two ways in which accounts receivable can be used to obtain short-term financing.

CONCEPT *in Action* >>>

For businesses with steady orders but a lack of cash to make payroll or other immediate payments, factoring is a popular way to obtain financing. In factoring, a firm sells its invoices to a third-party funding source for cash. The factor purchasing the invoices then collects on the due payments over time. Trucking companies with voluminous accounts are good candidates for factoring. Why might firms choose factoring instead of loans?

© ROBERT MCGOUEY/ALAMY

Raising Long-Term Financing

A basic principle of finance is to match the term of the financing to the period over which benefits are expected to be received from the associated outlay. Short-term items should be financed with short-term funds, and long-term items should be financed with long-term funds. Long-term financing sources include both debt (borrowing) and equity (ownership). Equity financing comes either from selling new ownership interests or from retaining earnings.

Debt Versus Equity Financing

Say that Bombardier plans to spend $2 billion over the next four years to build and equip new factories to make regional jets. The company's top management will assess the pros and cons of both debt and equity and then consider several possible sources of the desired form of long-term financing.

The major advantage of debt financing is the deductibility of interest expense for income tax purposes, which lowers its overall cost. In addition, there is no loss of ownership. The major drawback is **financial risk**: the chance that the firm will be unable to make scheduled interest and principal payments. The lender can force a borrower that fails to make scheduled debt payments into bankruptcy. Most loan agreements have restrictions to ensure that the borrower operates efficiently.

Equity, on the other hand, is a form of permanent financing that places few restrictions on the firm. The firm is not required to pay dividends or repay the investment. However, equity financing gives common shareholders voting rights that provide them with a voice in management. Equity is more costly than debt. Unlike the interest on debt, dividends to owners are not tax-deductible expenses.

Exhibit 16.3 summarizes the major differences between debt and equity financing.

Financial managers try to select the mix of long-term debt and equity that results in the best balance between cost and risk. If a company's debt load gets too high, in the view of investors and securities analysts, the costs of borrowing will rise. Company policies about the mix of debt and equity vary. Some companies have high debt

financial risk
The chance that a firm will be unable to make scheduled interest and principal payments on its debt.

---

concept check

Discuss the major differences between debt and equity financing.

What is financial risk?

EXHIBIT 16.3 > Major Differences Between Debt and Equity Financing

	Debt Financing	Equity Financing
Voice in management	Creditors typically have none, unless borrower defaults on payments. Creditors may be able to place restraints on management in event of default.	Common shareholders have voting rights.
Claim on income and assets	Debt holders rank ahead of equity holders. Payment of interest and principal is a contractual obligation of the firm.	Equity owners have a residual claim on income (dividends are paid only after interest and any scheduled principal payments are paid) and assets. The firm has no obligation to pay dividends.
Maturity	Debt has a stated maturity and requires repayment of principal by a specified maturity date.	The company is not required to repay equity, which has no maturity date.
Tax treatment	Interest is a tax-deductible expense.	Dividends are not tax-deductible and are paid from after-tax income.

compared to equity. Debt as a percentage of equity is 163 percent at International Paper, a capital-intensive manufacturer. Others keep debt to a minimum. The long-term debt-to-equity ratio for Nike is about 12 percent; Starbucks, 4 percent; Microsoft, 3 percent; and Apple Computer, 0 percent.

Long-Term Debt Financing

term loan
A business loan with an initial maturity of more than one year; can be unsecured or secured.

Long-term debt is used to finance long-term (capital) expenditures. The initial maturities of long-term debt typically range between 5 and 20 years. Three important forms of long-term debt are term loans, bonds, and mortgage loans.

A **term loan** is a business loan with an initial maturity of more than one year. Term loans generally have 5- to 12-year maturities and can be unsecured or secured. They are available from chartered banks, insurance companies, pension funds, commercial finance companies, and manufacturers' financing subsidiaries. A contract between the borrower and the lender spells out the amount and maturity of the loan, the interest rate, payment dates, the purpose of the loan, and other provisions, such as operating and financial restrictions on the borrower to control the risk of default. Term loans may be repaid on a quarterly, semiannual, or annual schedule. The payments include both interest and principal, so the loan balance declines over time. Borrowers try to arrange a repayment schedule that matches the forecast cash flow from the project being financed.

bonds
Long-term debt obligations (liabilities) issued by corporations and governments.

Bonds are long-term debt obligations (liabilities) issued by corporations and governments. Like term loans, corporate bonds are issued with formal contracts that set forth the obligations of the issuing corporation and the rights of the bondholders. Most bonds are issued in multiples of $1,000 (par value) with initial maturities of 10 to 30 years. The stated interest rate, or *coupon rate*, is the percentage of the bond's par value that the issuer will pay each year as interest.

mortgage loan
A long-term loan made against real estate as collateral.

A **mortgage loan** is a long-term loan made against real estate as collateral. The lender takes a mortgage on the property, which lets the lender seize the property, sell it, and use the proceeds to pay off the loan if the borrower fails to make the scheduled payments. Long-term mortgage loans are often used to finance office buildings, factories, and warehouses. Life insurance companies are an important source of these loans. They make billions of dollars' worth of mortgage loans to businesses each year.

> **concept check**
>
> What is a long-term loan used for?
>
> What is a term loan? A bond? A mortgage loan?

Equity Financing

Equity is the owners' investment in the business. In corporations, the preferred and common shareholders are the owners. A firm obtains equity financing by selling new ownership shares (external financing), by retaining earnings (internal financing), or, for small and growing, typically high-tech companies, through venture capital (external financing).

common shares
A security that represents an ownership interest in a corporation.

Selling New Issues of Common Shares **Common shares** are securities that represent an ownership interest in a corporation. In March 2006, Tim Hortons offered 29 million shares of common shares at the initial price of $27 and began trading on the Toronto Stock Exchange and the New York Stock Exchange.

The Tim Hortons offering is an example of a company *going public*—its first sale of shares to the public. Usually, a high-growth company has an *initial public offering* (IPO), because it needs to raise funds to finance continuing growth. An IPO often enables existing shareholders, usually employees, family, and friends who bought the shares privately, to earn big profits on their investment. (Companies that are already public can also issue and sell additional common shares to raise equity funds.)

HOT Links

What are some of the IPOs available today? Check out the premium investor resource centre at (http://ipo.investcom.com).

But going public has some drawbacks. For one thing, there is no guarantee an IPO will sell. It is also expensive. Big fees must be paid to investment bankers, brokers, lawyers, accountants, and printers. And once the company is public, it is watched closely by regulators, shareholders, and securities analysts. The firm must reveal information such as operating and financial data, product details, financing plans, and operating strategies. Providing this information is often costly.

Going public can be successful when a company is well established and market conditions are right. Strong equity markets in the late 1990s and into 2000 prompted many companies, especially very young Internet-related companies, to go public. Frequently companies that were only a year or two old rushed to go public to take advantage of market conditions. Their prices popped up to what many believed were unrealistic levels. When the recession started in 2008 and capital markets dried up, far fewer companies were willing to brave the IPO waters. Instead, they turned to other financing sources to tide them over until the market for new issues picked up.

Dividends and Retained Earnings **Dividends** are payments to shareholders from a corporation's profits. A company does not have to pay dividends to shareholders, but if investors buy the shares expecting to get dividends and the firm does not pay them, the investors might sell their shares. If too many sell, the value of the shares decreases. Dividends can be paid in cash or in shares. **Share dividends** are payments in the form of more shares. Share dividends may replace or supplement cash dividends. After a share dividend has been paid, more shares have a claim on the same company, so the value of each share often declines.

At their quarterly meetings, the company's board of directors (with the advice of its financial managers) decides how much of the profits to distribute as dividends and how much to reinvest. A business's basic approach to paying dividends can greatly affect its share price. A stable history of dividend payments indicates good financial health. If a firm that has been making regular dividend payments cuts or skips a dividend, investors start thinking it has serious financial problems. The increased uncertainty often results in lower share prices. Thus, most firms set dividends at a level they can keep paying. They start with a relatively low dividend payout ratio, so that they can maintain a steady or slightly increasing dividend over time.

Retained earnings, profits that have been reinvested in the firm, have a big advantage over other sources of equity capital: They do not incur underwriting costs. Financial managers strive to balance dividends and retained earnings to maximize the value of the firm. Often the balance reflects the nature of the firm and its industry. Well-established and stable firms and those that expect only modest growth, such as public utilities, financial services companies, and large industrial corporations, typically pay out much of their earnings in dividends.

Most high-growth companies, like those in technology-related fields, finance much of their growth through retained earnings and pay little or no dividends to shareholders.

Preferred Shares Another form of equity is **preferred shares**. Unlike common shares, preferred shares usually have a dividend amount that is set at the time the shares are issued. These dividends must be paid before the company can pay any dividends to common shareholders. Furthermore, if the firm goes bankrupt and sells its assets, preferred shareholders get their money back before common shareholders do. Preferred shares are described in greater detail in Chapter 15.

Like debt, preferred shares increase the firm's financial risk because it obligates the firm to make a fixed payment, but preferred shares are more flexible. The firm can miss a dividend payment without suffering the serious results of failing to pay back a debt.

dividends
Payments to shareholders from a corporation's profits.

share or stock dividends
Payments to shareholders in the form of more shares; can replace or supplement cash dividends.

retained earnings
Profits that have been reinvested in a firm.

preferred shares
Equity securities for which the dividend amount is set at the time the shares are issued.

Making Ethical Choices

THE FRIENDS AND FAMILY IPO PLAN

As a financial analyst at an up-and-coming high-technology firm, you are involved in your most exciting project to date: helping to prepare pro forma financial statements (pro forma is a projection or estimate of what will happen in the future based on what is happening now) for the prospectus for the firm's initial public offering.

During your visits to various departments, you hear rumours about promises of IPO shares for favoured customers and suppliers. Researching if this is legal, you learn your company can give up to 5 percent of its offering to anyone it chooses. Because this price is not offered to the general public, inviting these "friends and family" to buy shares at the IPO price presents an attractive opportunity. At the height of the bull market, IPO share prices were jumping an average of 65 percent on the first day. Even though times are more normal now, the growth prospects make these shares a good buy. "Companies are continuing to be approached for shares by analysts and others who wield influence," says David Helfrich, a venture capitalist.

However, some legal experts believe that allocating IPO share to customers and vendors borders on bribery and creates conflicts of interest. Those receiving shares could feel pressured to send business to your firm. Yet such practices are common; other businesses in your industry use shares to gain a competitive advantage (perhaps as a way of saying "thank you" or of obtaining obligations from people who they want to help them in the future).

If your company is giving out only small allocations of shares, such as 100 to 200 shares, and the offering price is $18 to $20, the profit from flipping the shares on the first days is negligible and the potential for conflicts of interest reduced. If the invitation is for larger amounts, at what point does it become a problem?

ETHICAL DILEMMA: Should you bring this situation to your superiors' attention and urge them to develop a corporate policy that covers offers to sell shares at special prices?

SOURCES: Linda Himelstein, "CEOs to Eliot Spitzer: 'Give It Back? No Way!' " *Business Week*, June 9, 2003, 113; and Linda Himelstein and Ben Elgin, "High Tech's Kickback Culture," *Business Week*, February 10, 2003, 74–77.

HOT Links

Which companies are getting funding from venture capital firms? For this and other information, visit vFinance. com at (**www.vfinance.com**).

HOT Links

Find out about the Canada's Venture Capital & Private Equity Association at (**www.cvca.ca**).

concept check

Define each of the following:
- Common shares
- Dividends
- Share or stock dividends
- Retained earnings
- Preferred shares
- Venture capital

Preferred shares are more expensive than debt financing, however, because preferred dividends are not tax-deductible. Furthermore, because the claims of preferred shareholders on income and assets are second to those of debt holders, preferred shareholders require higher returns to compensate for the greater risk.

Venture Capital   As we learned in Chapter 6, *venture capital* is another source of equity capital. It is most often used by small and growing firms that aren't big enough to sell securities to the public. This type of financing is especially popular among high-tech companies that need large sums of money.

Venture capitalists invest in new businesses in return for part of the ownership, sometimes as much as 60 percent. They look for new businesses with high growth potential, and they expect a high investment return within 5 to 10 years. By getting in on the ground floor, venture capitalists buy shares at a very low price. They earn profits by selling the shares at a much higher price when the company goes public. Venture capitalists generally get a voice in management through a seat on the board of directors.

Getting venture capital is difficult, even though there are many private venture capital firms in this country. Most venture capitalists finance only about 1 to 5 percent of the companies that apply. Venture capital investors, many of whom experienced losses from their investments in failed dot-coms, are less willing nowadays to take risks on very early-stage companies with unproven technology. They are looking for companies with high growth potential that are already on a demonstrated track to profitability.

As a result, other sources of venture capital, including private foundations, governments, and wealthy individuals (called *angel investors*), are helping start-up firms find equity capital. These private investors are motivated by the potential for earning a high return on their investment. Accountants, lawyers, business associates, financial consultants, bankers, and others can help the small firm find an angel.

Managing Risk And Insurance

 LO 8

Every day, businesses and individuals are exposed to many different kinds of risk. Investors who buy shares or speculate in commodities can earn a profit, but they also take the risk of losing all or part of their money. Illness is another type of risk, involving financial loss from not only the cost of medical care but also the loss of income.

Businesses, too, are exposed to many types of risk. Market risks, such as lower demand for a product or worsening economic conditions, can hurt a firm. Other risks involve customers—they could be injured on a company's premises or by a company's product. Like homes and cars owned by individuals, business property can be damaged or lost through fire, floods, and theft. Businesses must also protect themselves against losses from theft by dishonest employees. The loss of a key employee is another risk, especially for small firms.

It is impossible to avoid all risks, but individuals and businesses can minimize risks or buy protection—called insurance—against them. Although some risks are uninsurable, many others are insurable. Let's now look at basic risk concepts and the types of insurance available to cover them.

Risk Management

risk management
The process of identifying and evaluating risks and selecting and managing techniques to adapt to risk exposures.

Every business faces risks like the ones previously listed. **Risk management** involves analyzing the firm's operations, evaluating the potential risks, and figuring out how to minimize losses in a cost-efficient manner. In today's complex business environment, the concern for public and employee welfare and the potential for lawsuits have both increased. Risk management thus plays a vital role in the overall management of a business.

peril
A hazard or a source of danger.

speculative risk
The chance of either loss or gain, without insurance against the possible loss.

Types of Risk Individuals and firms need to protect themselves against the economic effects of certain types of risk. In an insurance sense, risk (sometimes called *pure risk*) is the chance of financial loss due to a **peril** (a hazard or a source of danger). Insurable risks include fire, theft, auto accident, injury or illness, a lawsuit, or death. **Speculative risk** is the chance of either loss or gain. Someone who buys shares in the hope of later selling it at a profit is taking a speculative risk and cannot be insured against it.

HOT *Links*

Learn about how Reuters Risk Management Services, at (http://risk.reuters.com), helps companies with global operations identify, measure, and manage financial risk.

Strategies to Manage Risk Risk is part of life. Nevertheless, people have four major ways of dealing with it.

- *Risk avoidance.* This means staying away from situations that can lead to loss. A person can avoid the risk of a serious injury by choosing not to go skydiving. A daycare centre could avoid risk by not transporting children to and from the facility or taking them on field trips. Manufacturers who wish to avoid risks could produce only goods that have a proven track record, but these risk-avoidance strategies could stifle growth in the long run. Thus, risk avoidance is not good for all risks.
- *Risk Retention (Self-insurance).* This is the willingness to bear a risk without insurance, also called *risk assumption*. This offers a more practical way of handling many types of risks. Many large firms with warehouses or stores spread out over Canada might choose not to insure them. They assume that even if disaster strikes one location, the others won't be harmed. The losses will probably be less than the insurance premiums for all of the locations. Many companies retain losses, because it is cheaper to assume some risks than to insure against them. Some choose to pay small claims and insure only for catastrophic losses. Others "go naked," paying for all claims from current company funds. This is clearly the most risky strategy. A big claim could cripple the firm or lead to bankruptcy.

CONCEPT *in Action* **>>>**

Companies must constantly manage risk which is often not foreseen. What ways can businesses manage unforeseen risks?

---

insurance
The promise of compensation for certain financial losses.

• *Risk Control (Risk reduction).* This is done by adopting techniques to prevent financial losses. For example, companies adopt safety measures to reduce accidents. Construction workers are required to wear hard hats and safety glasses. Airlines keep their aircraft in good condition and require thorough training programs for pilots and flight attendants. Hotels install smoke alarms, sprinkler systems, and firewalls to protect guests and minimize fire damage.

• *Risk transfer.* This means paying someone else to bear some or all of the risk of financial loss for certain risks that can't be avoided, assumed, or controlled to acceptable levels. One way to transfer risk is through **insurance**. Individuals and organizations can pay a fee (a *premium*) and get the promise of compensation for certain financial losses. The companies that take on the risks are called *insurance companies.*

concept check

What is risk management?

What are the types of risk?

What are some strategies for managing risk?

Insurance Concepts

insurance policy
A written agreement that defines what the insurance covers and the risks that the insurance company will bear for the insured party.

underwriting
A review process of all insurance applications and the selection of those who meet the standards.

Companies purchase insurance to cover insurable risks. An **insurance policy** is the written agreement that defines what the insurance covers and the risks that the insurance company will bear for the insured party. It also outlines the policy's benefits (the maximum amount that it will pay in the event of a loss) and the premium (the cost to the insured for coverage). Any demand for payment of losses covered by the policy is a *claim.*

Before issuing a policy, an insurance company reviews the applications of those who want a policy and selects those that meet its standards. This **underwriting** process also determines the level of coverage and the premiums. Each company sets its own underwriting standards based on its experience. For instance, a life insurance company might decide not to accept an applicant who has had a heart attack within the previous five years (or to charge a 50 to 75 percent higher premium). A property insurer might refuse to issue a policy on homes near brush-filled canyons, which present above-average fire hazards.

insurable interest
An insurance applicant's chance of loss if a particular peril occurs.

To get insurance, the applicant must have an **insurable interest**: the chance of suffering a loss if a particular peril occurs. In most cases, a person cannot insure the life of a friend, because the friend's death would not be considered a financial loss. But business partners can get life insurance on each other's lives, because the death of one of them would have a financial impact on their firm.

insurable risk
A risk that an insurance company will cover. It must meet certain criteria.

Insurable Risks Insurance companies are professional risk takers, but they won't provide coverage against all types of risk. Some risks are insurable; some are not. For instance, changes in political or economic conditions are not insurable. An **insurable risk** is one that an insurance company will cover. For a risk to be insurable, it must meet these criteria:

- *The loss must not be under the control of the insured.* The loss must be accidental—that is, unexpected and occurring by chance. Insurance companies do not cover losses purposely caused by the insured party. No insurance company will pay for the loss of a clothing store that the insured set on fire, nor will most companies pay life insurance benefits for a suicide.
- *There must be many similar exposures to that peril.* Insurance companies study the rates of deaths, auto accidents, fires, floods, and many other perils. They know about how many of these perils will occur each year. The **law of large numbers** lets them predict the likelihood that the peril will occur and then calculate premiums.

law of large numbers
Insurance companies' predictions of the likelihood that a peril will occur; used to calculate premiums.

Suppose that an insurance company has 150 policies in a city. The company knows from past experience that these policyholders are likely to have a total of 12 car accidents a year and that the average payment for a claim in this city has been $1,000. The total claims for one year's car accidents in the city would be $12,000 (12 accidents × $1,000). Thus, the company would charge each policyholder a premium of at least $80 ($12,000 ÷ 150). Profits and administrative expenses would serve to increase the premium from this base rate.

- *Losses must be financially measurable.* The dollar amount of potential losses must be known, so that the insurance company can figure the premiums. Life insurance is for a fixed amount specified at the time the policy is bought. Otherwise, the company and the beneficiary (the one who gets the funds) would have to agree on the value of the deceased's life at the time of death. Premiums have to be calculated before then, however.
- *The peril must not be likely to affect all the insured parties at the same time.* Insurance companies must spread out their risks by insuring many people and businesses in many locations. This strategy helps minimize the chance that a single calamity will wipe out the insurance company.
- *The potential loss must be significant.* Insurance companies cannot afford to insure trivial things for small amounts. Many policies have **deductibles**, amounts that the insured must pay before insurance benefits begin.
- *The company must have the right to set standards for insurance coverage.* Insurance companies can refuse to cover people with health problems such as AIDS, cancer, or heart trouble, a poor driving record, or a dangerous job or hobby. They can also charge higher premiums because of the higher risks they are covering.

deductibles
The amounts that the insured must pay before insurance benefits begin.

Premium Costs Insurance policies must be economical—relatively low in cost compared to the benefits—so that people will want to buy them. Yet the premiums must also cover the risks that the insurance company faces. Insurance companies collect statistics on many perils. Then specially trained mathematicians called *actuaries* use the law of large numbers to develop actuarial tables, which show how likely each peril is. Actuarial tables are the basis for calculating premiums. For example, actuaries use a mortality table showing average life expectancy and the expected number of deaths per 1,000 people at given ages to set life insurance premiums.

Almost every homeowner buys insurance to cover the perils of fire, theft, vandalism, and other home-related risks. With such a large pool of policyholders, homeowners' policies are usually inexpensive. Annual premiums are about 0.5 percent (or less) of the value of the home. This low cost encourages people to buy policies and thereby helps spread the insurance companies' risk over many homes throughout the country.

When setting premiums, insurers also look at the risk characteristics of certain groups to assess the probability of loss for those groups. For instance, smokers tend to die younger than non-smokers do and thus pay higher life insurance premiums. Female drivers under the age of 25 have a lower rate of accidents than male drivers, so their car insurance premiums are lower.

Insurance Providers   Insurers can be either public or private. Public insurance coverage is offered by specialized government agencies (e.g., provincial health care plans and employment insurance). Private insurance coverage is provided by privately organized (non-government) companies.

Public Insurance   Government-sponsored insurance can be regulated by either the provinces or the federal government. These are some of the main programs:

- *Employment Insurance (EI).* The employment insurance program pays laid-off workers weekly benefits while they seek new jobs. Persons who terminate their employment voluntarily or are fired for cause are generally not eligible for **employment insurance**. These programs also provide job counselling, education opportunities, and placement services. The size of the weekly benefit depends on the workers' previous income. Employment insurance is funded by the employees and through contributions by the employers.
- *Workers' compensation.* The provinces and territories have laws requiring employers in many industries to fund **workers' compensation** insurance to cover the expenses of job-related injuries and diseases, including medical costs, rehabilitation, and job retraining if necessary. It also provides disability income benefits (salary and wage payments) for workers who can't perform their jobs. Employers can buy workers' compensation policies or self-insure. A company's premium is based on the amount of its payroll and the types of risks present in the workplace. For instance, a construction company would pay a higher premium for workers' compensation insurance than would a jewellery store.
- *Canada Pension Plan (CPP).* The **Canada Pension Plan** provides retirement, disability, survivor benefits, and death benefits. CPP is funded by equal contributions from workers and employers. Canadians that have paid into the plan can collect as early as age 60. The province of Quebec administers its own pension plan.
- *Provincial health care.* Health care is provided to all Canadians through their respective **provincial health care** programs. In some provinces the premiums are not collected separately but are included in other taxes, and in others there are direct payments to the provincial health care insurance program.

Private Insurance Companies   Private insurance companies sell property and liability insurance, health insurance, and life insurance. Generally they can be either not-for-profit (e.g., Blue Cross) or shareholder insurance companies (e.g., Manulife Financial).

For example, all eligible residents in every province and territory can obtain Blue Cross coverage through their provincial/territorial independent member plan. Blue Cross provides products such as health care, dental care, life insurance, and disability income.

Just like other publicly owned corporations, *shareholder insurance companies* are profit-oriented companies owned by shareholders. The shareholders do not have to be policyholders, and the policyholders do not have to be shareholders. Their profits come from insurance premiums in excess of claim payments and operating expenses and from investments in securities and real estate.

---

employment insurance
Payment of benefits to laid-off workers while they seek new jobs.

workers' compensation
Payments to cover the expenses of job-related injuries and diseases, including medical costs, rehabilitation, and job retraining if necessary.

Canada Pension Plan
Insurance that provides retirement, disability, death, and health benefits.

provincial health care
Health insurance programs provided by the provinces.

Types of Insurance

Most companies offer group health and life insurance plans for their employees as a fringe benefit. Employers typically pay some of the health insurance premiums, and employees pay the rest. The cost is usually considerably less than for individual policies, although it pays to check before signing up. For example, companies might pay for the entire cost of life insurance equal to one or two times the employee's annual salary, with an option to purchase more under the group plan, but the premiums might be more expensive than buying an individual policy.

Businesses often insure the lives of key employees, such as top executives, salespeople, inventors, and researchers, whose death could seriously limit the income or value of a firm. To protect themselves, businesses buy **key person life insurance**, a life insurance policy that names the company as beneficiary. In the case of a partnership, which is dissolved when a partner dies, key person insurance is often bought for each partner, with the other partner named as the beneficiary, so that the surviving partner can buy the partnership interest from the estate of the deceased and continue operating.

Property and Liability Insurance

Property and liability insurance is important for businesses that wish to protect against losses of property and lawsuits arising from harm to other people. *Property insurance* covers financial losses from damage to or destruction of the insured's assets as a result of specified perils, whereas *liability insurance* covers financial losses from injuries to others and damage to or destruction of others' property when the insured is considered to be the cause. It also covers the insured's legal defence fees up to the maximum amount stated in the policy. Automobile liability insurance is an example. It would pay for a fence damaged when the insured person lost control of his or her car. Commercial and product liability insurance also fall into this category.

Commercial liability insurance covers a variety of damage claims, including harm to the environment from pollution. In the case of *product liability,* if a defective furnace exploded and damaged a home, the manufacturer would be liable for the damages. If the manufacturer were insured, the insurance company would cover the losses or pay to dispute the claim in court.

Property and liability insurance is a broad category. Businesses buy many types of property and liability insurance. These protect against loss of property due to fire, theft, accidents, or employee dishonesty, and financial losses arising from liability cases. Landlords and owners of business property buy *building insurance,* a type of property coverage, for protection against both property damage and liability losses. For instance, if a person broke an arm slipping on a wet floor in a hardware store, the business's insurance policy would cover any claim.

Special Types of Business Liability Insurance

Businesses also purchase several other types of insurance policies, depending on their particular needs.

- *Business interruption insurance.* This optional coverage is often offered with fire insurance. It protects business owners from losses occurring when the business must be closed temporarily after property damage. **Business interruption insurance** might cover costs such as rental of temporary facilities, wage and salary payments to employees, payments for leased equipment, fixed payments (for instance, rent and loans), and profits that would have been earned during the period. *Contingent business interruption insurance* covers losses to the insured in the event of property damage to a major supplier or customer.
- *Theft insurance.* Businesses also want to protect their property against financial losses due to crime. **Theft insurance** is the broadest coverage and protects businesses against losses from an act of stealing. Businesses can also buy more limited types of theft insurance.

---

key person life insurance
A term insurance policy that names the company as beneficiary.

business interruption insurance
Covers costs such as rental of temporary facilities, wage and salary payments to employees, payments for leased equipment, fixed payments, and profits that would have been earned during that period.

theft insurance
A broad insurance coverage that protects businesses against losses from an act of stealing.

- *Fidelity and surety bonds*. What if a firm has a dishonest employee? This situation is covered by a *fidelity bond*, an agreement that insures a company against theft committed by an employee who handles company money. If a restaurant manager is bonded for $50,000 and steals $60,000, the restaurant will recover all but $10,000 of the loss. Banks, loan companies, and retail businesses that employ cashiers typically buy fidelity bonds.

  A *surety bond,* also called a *performance bond,* is an agreement to reimburse a firm for non-performance of acts specified in a contract. This form of insurance is most common in the construction industry. Contractors buy surety bonds to cover themselves in case the project they are working on is not completed by the specified date or does not meet specified standards. In practice, the insurance company often pays another contractor to finish the job or to redo shoddy work when the bonded contractor fails to perform.

- *Title insurance.* A title policy protects the buyer of real estate against losses caused by a defect in the title—that is, a claim against the property that prevents the transfer of ownership from seller to purchaser. It eliminates the need to search legal records to be sure that the seller was actually the owner of (had clear title to) the property.

- *Professional liability insurance*. This form of insurance covers financial losses (legal fees and court-awarded damages up to specific limits) resulting from alleged malpractice by professionals in fields like medicine, law, architecture, and dentistry. *Directors and officers insurance* is a type of **professional liability insurance** designed to protect top corporate management, who have also been the target of malpractice lawsuits. It pays for legal fees and court-awarded damages up to specific limits.

professional liability insurance
Insurance designed to protect top corporate management, who have been the target of malpractice lawsuits.

> **concept check**
>
> What is an insurance policy? Underwriting? Insurable interest?
>
> What are premiums and deductibles?
>
> What types of insurance policies are available? What is the purpose of each?

Trends in Financial Management

Finance has moved from a relatively isolated, inward-looking function to a unit that is heavily involved in shaping and implementing a company's overall strategic objectives. Many of the key trends shaping the practice of financial management echo those in other disciplines. For example, technology is improving the efficiency with which financial managers run their operations. The "Customer Satisfaction and Quality" box, on page 515, describes how Dell Computer uses technology to improve its cash forecasts. The continued expansion of the financial manager's role in risk management is a natural outgrowth of the new regulations in the United States, as Canadian companies that trade on the United States exchanges must adhere not only to Canadian law but also American standards (e.g., the Sarbanes-Oxley Act).

The CFO's Role Continues to Expand

During the 1990s, CFOs expanded their jobs beyond the ordinary finance responsibilities. No longer just numbers people, they joined top management in developing and implementing the firm's strategic direction. Negotiating billion-dollar mergers and finding creative financing vehicles were all part of the day's work. They were the company's face to the Bay Street analysts, who watched to see if the company would meet each quarter's earnings estimates.

CFOs are more highly visible and active in company management than ever before. They serve as both business partner to the chief executive and a fiduciary to the board. "Today, in what I'll call the post-Enron, post-WorldCom era, there's been a restored emphasis on the fiduciary and control aspects," says Robert Lumpkins, vice chairman and CFO of Cargill Inc., a privately owned international agricultural and industrial products company. "Finance today is well-balanced between what

I'll call the value-adding and the value-preservation aspects." In global organizations such as Cargill, with 142,000 employees in 61 countries, finance managers must also be sensitive to cultural differences and different approaches to solving problems.[4]

Finance professionals need to have a broad view of company operations to communicate effectively with business unit managers, board members, creditors, and investors. Douglas Oberheim, a group president at Caterpillar, credits his years as CFO with providing him the broad perspective to see the company from the shareholder's viewpoint and the understanding of the importance of cross-functional activities. In addition to such traditional duties as arranging mergers and acquisitions, raising and allocating capital, and managing treasury operations, CFOs are also key players in matters pertaining to information technology, human resources, and the supply chain. Interpersonal skills are essential because they must motivate employees and encourage a positive environment that promotes accountability and ethical behaviour down through the organization. Finance managers must learn to be team players who can work with employees in other functional areas. At times finance and business unit executives have differing positions, and it takes careful negotiation to resolve issues. For example, business units may want to maintain larger cash balances than finance recommends. Educating unit managers about the cost of idle cash and establishing appropriate incentives can change corporate culture.[5]

Weighing the Risks

The job of managing a company's risk, which became even more difficult after the September 11, 2001 terrorist attacks, continues to be challenging for financial executives. Adding to the complexity are the volatile economy and financial markets at home and abroad. No longer does risk management focus narrowly on buying insurance to protect against loss of physical assets and interruption of business. Instead, more companies now consider **enterprise risk management (ERM)** a priority. ERM goes beyond just identifying, monitoring, and lowering risk to include a strategic approach to defining and managing all elements of a company's risk.

enterprise risk management (ERM)
A company-wide, strategic approach to identifying, monitoring, and managing all elements of a company's risk.

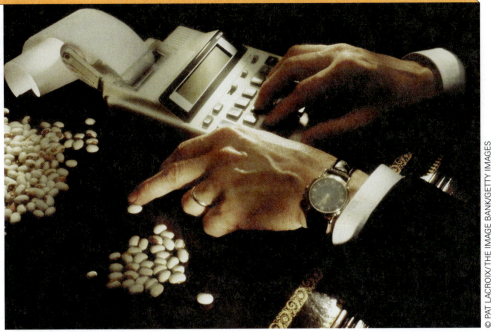

CONCEPT *in Action* >>>

The CFO-as-busy-bean counter image has undergone an extreme makeover, as today's financial chiefs increasingly perform highly visible decision-making roles alongside CEOs. Intense pressure for financial reporting compliance along with expectations of beating the numbers each quarter are major factors behind both the rising prominence and turnover of financial officers. And as responsibility increases, so does pay. Have CFOs become chief executive material?

© PAT LACROIX/THE IMAGE BANK/GETTY IMAGES

© AP/WIDE WORLD PHOTOS

CONCEPT *in Action* >>>

Many companies have created a new position, chief risk officer, to study risk potential and coordinate risk management procedures throughout the company. How can a company anticipate catastrophic events and minimize the devastating impact on business?

concept check

How has the role of CFO changed since the passage of the Sarbanes-Oxley Act?

Why are improved risk management procedures important to shareholders?

As the risk management function expands beyond its traditional role, companies recognize that ERM can make significant contributions to financial performance and shareholder returns. Because a failure in a company's risk control procedures can lead to substantial financial losses, corporate CFOs and treasurers are taking a proactive, leadership role in ERM. This requires them to get more involved with operations and form partnerships with business unit executives. "Effective risk management requires the ability to walk in the shoes of operations," says David Kelsey, senior vice president and CFO of Sealed Air Corp., a packaging products manufacturer. "Risk management can't be perceived as getting in the way of what business wants to do. Risk management needs to manage exposures, but not by creating more work or increasing costs."[6]

Companies face a wide range of risks, including:

- credit risk—exposure to loss as a result of default on a financial transaction, or a reduction in a security's market value due to decline in the credit quality of the debt issuer;
- market risk—risk resulting from adverse movements in the level or volatility of market prices of securities, commodities, and currencies; and
- operational risk—the risk of unexpected losses arising from deficiencies in a firm's management information, support, and control systems and procedures.

Jennifer Ceran, treasurer of eBay Inc., was an early adopter of ERM. Ceran recognized the need for the finance area to go beyond the traditional risk tasks assigned to the treasury operation, such as insurance, and take a broader view of all the risks affecting the company. Evaluating all types of risk and their impact on each other is critical to reducing overall risk for any company. As Rossini Zumwalt, assistant treasurer and director of finance at software firm Symantec explains,

"We identified the risks we already knew about, but what were we leaving out? It's not just the risk you know. It's the risks you don't know. We forgot the 'E' in ERM. I think that's why companies are challenged. It's important to attach the 'E,' to go beyond traditional risks."[7]

Companies are also using risk management in response to new corporate governance guidelines. Better risk management procedures are important to shareholders in the post-Enron era. They want to know that companies have taken steps to minimize risks that would affect the company's values.

Great Ideas to Use Now

Whether you are a marketing manager, purchasing agent, or systems analyst, knowledge of finance will help you to do your job better. You'll be able to understand your company's financial statements, its financial condition, and management's investment and financing decisions. Financial information also provides feedback on how well you are doing and identifies problems. On a more practical note, you might be asked to prepare a budget for your department or unit. Employees who understand the financial decision-making process will be able to prepare proposals that address financial concerns. As a result, they will be more likely to be given the resources they require to accomplish the firm's goals.

If you own a business, you must pay close attention to financial management. Without financial plans, you might find yourself running out of cash. It's easy to get so caught up in growing sales that you neglect your billing and collection methods. In fact, managing accounts receivable is often one of the more challenging aspects of running a young company. But you can't rely on revenue increases to solve your cash flow problems. Good receivables practices start with credit policies. Be choosy when it comes to offering trade credit, and check customers' credit references and payment history thoroughly. Set the initial credit limit fairly low until the customer establishes a prompt payment history. Here are some other ways to improve collections.

- Bill frequently, not just at the end of the month, so that money flows in throughout the month. Send bills when milestones are reached, such as making a presentation or completing a phase of a project.
- Clearly state payment terms, and make sure that the language on the invoice matches the contract.
- Establish regular and frequent follow-up procedures. Some companies call to notify the customer that the bill has been sent and to make sure the customer is satisfied. Weekly calls are in order for late payments.
- Try to get a firm date by which you will be paid, and be prepared to say what you will do if you aren't paid on time—for example, stopping work on a project or not shipping the next part of the order.
- Keep detailed notes of all conversations relating to a collection: your contact, date of the call, what was promised, and what you replied. You can then e-mail this as confirmation of your understanding and as another reminder.
- Monitor results of outstanding receivables collection.
- Don't fill new orders from customers who are continually delinquent.[8]

Customer Satisfaction and Quality

Because an organization's finance department affects every other area of the firm, it must adhere to the highest quality standards. "Our decision-making needs to be near-perfect, if not perfect," says Ruth Ann M. Gillis, former CFO of Exelon, an electric utility company.

Reliable and consistent financial reports and analyses are critical for managers throughout the firm and also to investors, creditors, suppliers, and customers. Because CEOs and CFOs must now certify the company's financial reports under the Sarbanes-Oxley Act (although this is American legislation, Canadian companies listed on U.S. exchanges must also adhere to the act), they are demanding that their managers adhere to strict quality control procedures and guidelines. To minimize risks of errors, companies are establishing formal rules and procedures for corporate finance. Some CFOs, including Home Depot's Carol Tomé and Consolidated Edison's Joan Freilich, ask key finance managers to sign personal statements that the financial statements they submit are correct.

Financial managers are continually looking for ways to improve the quality of their forecasts and budgets. Unhappy with the level of accuracy in its cash forecasts, Dell Computer developed the Enzo Liquidity Forecasting Tool. It chose the name in honour of race car designer Enzo Ferrari, to underscore the speed of Dell's cash forecasts. Complex cash flow forecasts now take one person an afternoon to prepare instead of three people working for two days. Accuracy is extremely high: The variance is less than $30 million on an accounts payable balance of $5 billion, a 99.4 percent accuracy level. Better cash forecasts were one reason Dell was able to raise its investment income above $1.5 million annually. In addition, Enzo's sophisticated analytical powers give financial managers a broader view of the cash picture. "Any question you can have about a scenario, you can answer," says Nathan Brunner, senior finance consultant at Dell.

SOURCES: Joseph Weber, "CFOs on the Hot Seat," *Business Week*, March 17, 2003, 67–70; and "Stand Back! Enzo Has Arrived," in Jay Sherman and Susan Kelly, "Uphill Racer—The 2002 Alexander Hamilton Award Winners," *Treasury & Risk Management*, October 2002, (www.treasuryandrisk.com).

Summary of Learning Outcomes

1 **Explain the roles finance and the financial manager play in the firm's overall strategy.**

Finance is the art and science involved in managing the firm's money. The financial manager must decide how much money is needed and when, how best to use the available funds, and how to get the required financing. The financial manager's responsibilities include financial planning, investing (spending money), and financing (raising money). Maximizing the value of the firm is the main goal of the financial manager, whose decisions often have long-term effects.

2 **Describe how a firm develops its financial plans, including forecasts and budgets.**

Financial planning enables the firm to estimate the amount and timing of the financial resources it needs to meet its business goals. The planning process begins with forecasts based on the demand for the firm's products. Short-term forecasts project expected revenues and expenses for one year. They are the basis for cash budgets, which show the flow of cash into and out of the firm and are used to plan day-to-day operations. Long-term forecasts project revenues and expenses over more than a year, typically 2 to 10 years. These strategic plans allow top management to analyze the impact of different options on the firm's profits.

3 **List the types of short- and long-term expenditures a firm makes.**

A firm invests in short-term expenses—supplies, inventory, and wages—to support current production, marketing, and sales activities. The financial manager manages the firm's investment in current assets, so that the company has enough cash to pay its bills and support accounts receivable and inventory. Long-term expenditures (capital expenditures) are made for fixed assets such as land, buildings, machinery, and equipment. Because of the large outlays required for capital expenditures, financial managers carefully analyze proposed projects to determine which offer the best returns.

4 **Summarize the main sources and costs of unsecured and secured short-term financing.**

Short-term financing comes due within one year. The main sources of unsecured short-term financing are trade credit, bank loans, and commercial paper. Secured loans require a pledge of certain assets, such as accounts receivable or inventory, as security for the loan. Factoring, or selling accounts receivable outright at a discount, is another form of short-term financing.

5 **Identify and compare the two primary sources of long-term financing.**

Financial managers must choose the best mix of debt and equity for their firm. The main advantage of debt financing is the tax-deductibility of interest, but debt involves financial risk, because it requires the payment of interest and principal on specified dates. Equity—common and preferred shares—is considered a permanent form of financing on which the firm might or might not pay dividends. Dividends are not tax-deductible.

6 **Understand the major types, features, and costs of long-term debt.**

The main types of long-term debt are term loans, bonds, and mortgage loans. Term loans can be secured or unsecured and generally have 5- to 12-year maturities. Bonds usually have initial maturities of 10 to 30 years. Mortgage loans are secured by real estate. Long-term debt usually costs more than short-term financing because of the greater uncertainty that the borrower will be able to make the scheduled loan payments.

7 **Discuss how firms issue equity and the costs to the company.**

The chief sources of equity financing are common shares, retained earnings, and preferred shares. The cost of selling shares includes issuing costs and potential dividend payments. Retained earnings are profits reinvested in the firm. For the issuing firm, preferred shares are more expensive than debt, because its dividends are not tax-deductible and its claims are secondary to those of debt holders, but less expensive than common shares. Venture capital is often a source of equity financing for small and growing, typically high-tech companies.

8 Understand risk, how it can be managed, and what makes a risk insurable.	Risk is the potential for loss or the chance that an investment will not achieve the expected level of return. Risk can be managed by identifying and evaluating the potential risks and selecting and managing techniques to adapt to risk exposures. To get insurance, the applicant must have an insurable interest: the chance of suffering a loss if a particular peril occurs. An insurable risk is one that an insurance company will cover. To qualify, the following conditions must be met: The loss must not be under the control of the insured; there must be many similar exposures to that peril; losses must be financially measurable; the peril must not be likely to affect all the insured parties at the same time; the potential loss must be significant; and the company must have the right to set standards for insurance coverage.
9 Describe the types of insurance coverage that businesses should consider.	The main types of insurance that businesses should consider include property and liability, commercial liability, business interruption, theft, fidelity and surety bonds, title insurance, and professional liability insurance.
10 List some of the trends that are affecting the practice of financial management.	The role of the CFO has changed, with CFOs taking the central role in overseeing corporate compliance with the various regulations and re-establishing public trust. They must balance the roles of corporate cop and strategic planner. The continued expansion of the financial manager's role in risk management is a natural outgrowth as companies face a wide range of risks, including credit, market, and operational risk. More companies are adopting risk management to identify and evaluate risks and select techniques to control and reduce risk.

Key Terms

accounts payable   500
accounts receivable   499
bonds   504
budgets   496
business interruption insurance   511
Canada Pension Plan   510
capital budgeting   500
capital budgets   496
capital expenditures   499
cash budgets   496
cash flows   493
cash management   497
commercial paper   498
common shares   504
deductibles   509
dividends   505
employment insurance   510
enterprise risk management (ERM)   513
factoring   502
financial management   493
financial risk   503
insurable interest   509
insurable risk   509
insurance   508
insurance policy   508
key person life insurance   511

law of large numbers   509
line of credit   501
long-term forecasts   496
marketable securities   498
mortgage loan   504
operating budgets   496
peril   507
preferred shares   505
professional liability insurance   512
provincial health care   510
retained earnings   505
return   495
revolving credit agreement† (revolving line of credit)   501
risk   495
risk management   507
risk-return trade-off   495
secured loans   502
share or stock dividends   505
short-term forecasts   495
speculative risk   507
term loan   504
theft insurance   511
trade credit   500
underwriting   508
unsecured loans   500
workers' compensation   510

Experiential Exercises

1. Prepare a personal budget. A personal budget is one of the most valuable tools for personal financial planning. It will help you evaluate your current financial situation, spending patterns, and goals. Use the following steps to create your budget.

   Using credit card receipts, cheque records, and other documents, record your income and expenses for the past 30 days. Based on this information, develop a personal budget for the next month. Record your budget in the "Planned" column of the worksheet in Exhibit 16.4. Include scholarships or grants as other income sources.

   Track your actual income and expenses for one month. Write down everything you spend on a daily basis, or you will forget little things (like snacks) that add up over the course of a month. Record your actual totals in the "Actual" column of the worksheet.

   At the end of the budget period, compare your budget to your actual results. Record any differences between the "Planned" and "Actual" values in the "Variance" column of the worksheet. How close were you to your budget estimates? In what categories did you overspend? Where did you underspend? Did creating the budget have any impact on how you allocated your money to different categories and how you spent your money?

   Optional: Use the results of your first month's budget to project next month's income and expenses. Repeat the monitoring process.

2. The head of your school's finance department has asked you to address a group of incoming business students about the importance of finance to their overall business education. Develop an outline with the key points you would cover in your speech.

3. As a financial manager at Nature's Food Company, you are preparing forecasts and budgets for a new line of high-nutrition desserts. Why should the finance department prepare these plans for the product development group? What factors would you consider in developing your projections and assessing their impact on the firm's profits?

4. You are the cash manager for a chain of sporting goods stores facing a cash crunch. To date, the chain has always paid accounts payable within the credit period. The CFO wants to consider extending payments beyond the due date. Write a memo that discusses the pros, cons, and ethics of stretching accounts payable as well as other cash-saving options to investigate.

5. You are the chief financial officer of Discovery Labs, a privately held, five-year-old biotechnology company that needs to raise $3 million to fund the development of a new drug. Prepare a report for the board of directors that discusses the types of long-term financing available to the firm, their pros and cons, and the key factors to consider in choosing a financing strategy.

6. GetSmart (www.getsmart.com) is an information service that offers advice on personal loans. Try the questionnaires in each area, using different answers, to see what is necessary to qualify for that financing option.

7. If factoring accounts receivable is still a mystery to you, visit the 21st Financial Solutions site, (www.21stfinancialsolutions.com). Follow the links on the home page to answer these questions: What are factoring's advantages? What are the additional benefits, and what types of companies can use factoring to their advantage? Then summarize the factoring process.

8. Visit your bank's website to learn about the bank's products and services for corporate customers. Describe briefly each type of loan it offers. Then do the same for another financial institution.

9. Visit the Treasury Board of Canada Secretariat website at (www.tbs-sct.gc.ca/tbs-sct/index-eng.asp) to learn more about risk management.

EXHIBIT 16.4 > Monthly Budget Worksheet

Name: _____

Month of _____

	Planned	Actual	Variance
Income			
Wages (take-home pay)	_____	_____	_____
Support from relatives	_____	_____	_____
Loans	_____	_____	_____
Withdrawals from savings	_____	_____	_____
Other _____	_____	_____	_____
Other _____	_____	_____	_____
(1) Total Available Income	_____	_____	_____
Expenses			
Fixed Expenses			
Housing	_____	_____	_____
Automobile payment	_____	_____	_____
Insurance	_____	_____	_____
Loan repayment	_____	_____	_____
Savings for goals	_____	_____	_____
Tuition and fees	_____	_____	_____
Other _____	_____	_____	_____
Subtotal, Fixed Expenses	_____	_____	_____
Flexible Expenses			
Food	_____	_____	_____
Clothing	_____	_____	_____
Personal care	_____	_____	_____
Entertainment and recreation	_____	_____	_____
Transportation	_____	_____	_____
Telephone	_____	_____	_____
Utilities (electricity, gas, water)	_____	_____	_____
Cable TV	_____	_____	_____
Medical and dental	_____	_____	_____
Books, magazines, educational supplies	_____	_____	_____
Gifts	_____	_____	_____
Other _____	_____	_____	_____
Other _____	_____	_____	_____
Subtotal, Flexible Expenses	_____	_____	_____
(2) Total Expenses	_____	_____	_____
Cash Surplus (Deficit) [(1)–(2)]	_____	_____	_____

Review Questions

1. What is financial management?

2. List the responsibilities of the financial manager.

3. What is the goal of the financial manager? What are risk, return, and the risk-return trade-off?

4. What is the purpose of the three types of budgets mentioned in this chapter?

5. What is cash management, and why is it important in business?

6. How can technology be used to help companies improve their credit and collection performance?

7. What are the sources of short-term financing?

8. How do companies obtain long-term financing?

9. Describe the major differences between debt and equity financing.

10. What are dividends and retained earnings?

11. What is the difference between common shares and preferred shares?

12. What is risk management? What are some strategies to manage risk?

13. What are the various types of insurance available to businesses?

CREATIVE THINKING CASE >

Investors Hang Up on Vonage

Founded in 2002, Vonage quickly became a major player in Voice over Internet Protocol (VoIP) phone service. Using Internet connections instead of traditional phone lines, it offered customers an attractive flat rate of about $25 a month for calls to the United States, Canada, and many European countries. By its May IPO, Vonage had 1.7 million customers and more than half the U.S. market for Internet phone service. Vonage claimed to be the fastest growing phone company in the United States. Revenues in 2005 were almost triple 2004 levels.

Management thought the time was right to go public and raise funds for expansion. Investors were again interested in IPOs after several years of low demand. So on May 24, 2006, it sold 31.25 million shares and raised $531 million. It also offered its individual customers—usually closed out of high-profile IPOs—the chance to buy 100 shares at the IPO price, an unusual move. So why was the Vonage IPO the worst in two years?

Timing is everything, and Vonage's timing was off. The market fell sharply on inflation concerns. The shares opened on the New York Stock Exchange at $17, fell to $14.85 by the end of the first day, and were trading below $7 by September 2006.

The offer to individual investors worked against Vonage, sending a message to some analysts that institutions were not interested in buying the stock and that Vonage needed help from its customers. Chad Brand of Peridot Capital Management considered this a "huge red flag. . . . If that's not a sign that nobody else wanted their stock, I don't know what is," he posted on his website.

Several factors negatively affected the Vonage offering. Increased competition creates pricing pressure. Rivals range from small VoIP players similar to Vonage to Internet powerhouses including Google, Yahoo, and MSN. Cable companies such as Time Warner, that offer phone service bundled with television and broadband services, and Verizon and other traditional providers are lowering prices as well. Vonage's sales are already falling, while costs-per-subscriber are rising. The company's marketing costs are very high, and the per-line cost of providing service is also rising at the same time as customer complaints about service quality are mounting.

Regulatory uncertainty adds another layer of complexity. Telecommunications providers are campaigning to charge for carrying other company's calls. This would add to Vonage's costs. As Vonage grows, it will be required to collect sales tax and other fees, pushing customer bills well above the $25 flat rate they were expecting to pay and removing pricing advantages.

These are just a few of the issues that stand in the way of Vonage's profitability. In fact, Vonage's IPO prospectus says that it will focus on growth rather than profitability and went so far as to say that it might never become profitable. As a public company, Vonage will be under greater pressure to execute its business plan and also face close scrutiny from its investors. Only time will tell if investors hang up when Vonage calls.

Critical Thinking Questions

- What issues should executives of a company such as Vonage consider before deciding to go public? In your opinion, was the company ready for an IPO, and why?
- How else could Vonage have raised funds to continue to grow? Compare the risks of raising private equity to going public.
- Use a search engine and a site such as Yahoo Finance to learn about Vonage's current situation. Prepare a brief summary, including its current financial situation. Is it still a public company, and how has its stock fared?

SOURCES: David A. Gaffen, "Tale of Two IPOs," Wall Street Journal Online, May 24, 2006, (www.wsj.com); Olga Kharif, "Vonage's Iffy IPO," Business Week Online, February 9, 2006, (www.businessweek.com); Timothy J. Mullaney, "Vonage's Lackluster IPO," Business Week Online, May 24, 2006, (www.businessweek.com); Shawn Young and Li Yuan, "Vonage Faces User Complaints as IPO Looms," Wall Street Journal, May 18, 2006, p. B1; Shawn Young and Lynn Cowan, "Vonage Lacks Voltage in Its IPO, with Weakest Debut in 2 Years," Wall Street Journal, May 25, 2006, p. C4; Shawn Young and Randall Smith, "How Vonage's High Profile IPO Stumbled on the Stock Market," Wall Street Journal, June 3, 2006, p. A1.

VIDEO CASE >

Debt Nation

Many Canadians are finding themselves in deep financial trouble, even though they make a reasonable income. The primary contributing factor seems to be credit card debt. Many items purchased with major credit cards are intangible, which means that you have nothing to show for it when the bill comes in. For example, trips, restaurant meals, shows, and gas are often purchased with credit cards. And the credit card companies are pushing hard.

In 2003, there were approximately 23.9 million *retailer-issued* credit cards in circulation in Canada. These are the ones at 28.8 percent interest (e.g., HBC/Zellers). Students often start out in debt simply from educational expenses, with the average amount being $22,700 for four-year programs. Add that to a credit card (or two, or three,) and financial trouble can follow.

Family 1, Wayne and Theresa, are not that unusual, and many Canadians behave in a similar manner—the ostrich approach: If I can't see it, it's not a problem. Family 2, Joanne and Travis, admit that Joanne is a shopaholic. Some people get a genuine high from shopping, similar to that of drugs and alcohol. For Family 3, Hanna Laura might have to forgo her trip to England to curb her debt. How did this happen to ordinary Canadians? In 2001, Canadians received 208.3 million credit card solicitations. If you pay your monthly amount regularly, what happens? The credit card company probably raises your limit! This is a very slippery slope. With an increase in credit card debt of 90 percent between 1997 and 2001, as well as an estimated household debt owed by Canadians in 2003 of $731 billion compared to saving of $9.39 billion, it is obvious we need to step back and look at what we are doing.

Critical Thinking Questions

- If a large number of Canadians suddenly stopped using their credit cards (and did not have the cash to make intended purchases) what effect would this have on the Canadian economy?
- Are the credit card companies acting responsibly by encouraging Canadians to accept more cards? How might they build their business in a more ethical matter?

SOURCES: CBC, *Marketplace*, "Debt Nation Part 1," January 15, 2006.

CBC, *Marketplace*, "Debt Nation Part 2," January 22, 2006.

Investing Your Money: Is the Target of Your Investment Managing Risk Adequately?

An important aspect of managing a firm's finances (the chapter title) involves understanding and managing risk. Do we have enough assets to cover our liabilities? Currently some Canadian corporate pension plans do *not* have enough assets to cover the value of the current pension plan obligations. In fact, these plans are underfunded. For example, Air Canada had a pension plan deficit of $3.2 billion on January 1st, 2009.

Investors in pension plans are sometimes unaware of this problem, as it is not readily apparent from the financial statements. An item such as pension plan underfunding would have to be discovered by examining the off-balance sheet obligations of the company.

What are the implications of an underfunded plan for the investor? A cash infusion might be required in a few cases; however, there is an impact on the share value. Keeping in mind that the asset value of the fund is an estimate, as is the value of future obligations, is this really a serious problem? It depends. Interest rates are relatively low right now—as this book is being printed—and when they rise, the current value of future obligations will decrease. Furthermore, the assets supporting the plan should appreciate in value, causing the underfunding gap to disappear. Again, given that the numbers reflect management estimates, of greater concern might be the trust in the firm's management.

Al Rosen, a commentator for *Canadian Business Online,* feels that attention needs to be given to the lack of accounting principles that might prevent the pension plan underfunding issue. In his opinion, the inadequacy of a system that does not look out for the interests of investors is the problem, with the pension issues being only a symptom.

SOURCE: (www.theglobeandmail.com/servlet/story/LAC.20090326.Race26/TPStory/Business), accessed March 29, 2009.

Critical Thinking Questions

1. Do you agree or disagree with Al Rosen's point of view? Why?

2. Choose a Canadian company at random, and see if you can tell from the financial statements whether the pension plan is adequately funded. Does the result of the exercise change your answer to question 1?

SOURCES: Al Rosen, "Time Bombs," *Canadian Business,* 79 no. 10 (Summer 2006), 23; Al Rosen, "The Pension Fun Never Stops," *Canadian Business,* 76 no. 13 (July 7–21, 2003), 23; April 29, 2003; and Boston Beer Company corporate website, www.bostonbeer.com, accessed May 1, 2003.

APPENDIX

Making the Connection

Corporate Governance, the Legal Environment, and Taxation

In this appendix we're back to our PEST model. Corporate governance, the legal environment, and taxes fit most directly in the *political* environment, as the government at all levels regulates business activity. It lays out the laws for business to follow and taxes businesses in many different ways.

However, these laws are not shaped by the political environment alone. The political environment responds to the changing needs of the social, economic, and technological environments, changing laws and creating new ones as appropriate. You'll read in this appendix, for example, about laws relating to the natural environment, as the *social* environment becomes increasingly aware and protective of the natural environment, particularly as climate change accelerates; laws relating to employment equity, as the workforce becomes more diverse; laws relating to competition (the *economic* environment) to protect consumers from businesses engaging in anticompetitive behaviour; and laws relating to privacy issues and the Internet (the *technological* environment). An interesting integrative example is in the economic trend toward deregulation—removing regulations governing competition in certain industries, as opposed to creating new regulations. This practice has led to one of the major trends discussed in Chapter 6—the increase in the number of new small and entrepreneurial businesses in the economy as opportunities have opened up in deregulated industries. For these reasons, business needs to see the whole of the external environment in an integrative and proactive way to stay within the boundaries created by the legal system.

There are many examples in this appendix of how the legal system affects decisions made by business and therefore, ultimately, the success of the business. For example, in the area of *operations*, the law of negligence requires that "businesses comply with industry standards in the manufacture" of products or "liability to consumers may result." This makes it extremely critical to monitor product *quality* (one of our critical success factors) to prevent strict liability resulting from defective products or packaging. In the area of *human resources*, the Employment Standards Act covers minimum wage, hours of work, and other workplace regulations. In the area of *marketing*, the Trademarks Act applies to all businesses and affects the ability of the company to

create a unique brand in the customer's mind. Patent law also affects the ability to create a competitive advantage and *meet customer needs* by protecting *innovations* from competitive threats (more critical success factors). And finally, there is the tax system, which, of course, affects the *financial* area of business and cannot be ignored. If not managed correctly, the amount of taxes that a business is required to pay can severely affect its ability to *achieve financial performance*.

Associations, industry, and governments are working closely together to protect the *stakeholders of business*. Clearly, as with the changes in the other areas of the external environment, the legal and tax environment of a business is a certain yet virtually uncontrollable factor that must be monitored and managed in an integrative way, for the business to achieve success in all areas.

APPENDIX

Corporate Governance, the Legal Environment, and Taxation

LEARNING OUTCOMES

1 Explain corporate governance, and why it is important.

2 Review how the legal system governs business transactions and settles business disputes.

3 Discuss the required elements of a valid contract.

4 Explain some of the Canadian laws that protect businesses and consumers.

5 Discuss the Employment Standards Acts.

6 List the most common taxes paid by businesses.

A Basic Understanding of Canadian Business Law and the Tax System Adds Certainty

According to Sandra Malach, LLB, LLM, the law has an effect on how business is conducted in Canada, because it sets standards, defines business risks, and defines business relationships. As an instructor of business law, securities, and corporate tax, as well as being a contributing author on legal issues in small-business publications, Sandra believes that a business law course for management students is invaluable, because it provides a background to areas that are not, in the strictest sense, day-to-day management issues but affect managers and the way they conduct their operations, both internally and externally. "Managers need to be aware of the laws that affect their day-to-day operations," she says. "And more importantly, recognize legal issues and contact the appropriate professional to resolve the issue."

"Many businesspeople see the law as solely establishing rules regarding permissible and illegal business activities. But the law goes beyond dictating what can and what cannot be done. By understanding the basics of the laws as they affect business, it can add certainty to business activity, particularly with regard to activities that affect third parties. For example, the law of contract allows businesses to know when they have formed an enforceable contract allowing them to seek compensation if the contracting party does not fulfill its obligations." Sandra continues, "The law of negligence has established that businesses must comply with industry standards in the manufacture and inspection of their products or liability to consumers may result. Regulations establish standards for the import of certain products and the conduct of certain kinds of business."

"The Employment Standards Act is one of the most important areas for any employer. Each of the provinces has its own act that covers topics such as minimum wage, allowable deductions, hours of work, and so on. Without the knowledge of the act (or in some cases its existence) business owners may be violating laws that they are not aware of, which could amount to considerable costs if violations occur."

PHOTO BY LINDA CRAIG

Another vital area to have at least some knowledge of is the tax system and the obligations of a corporation and its directors. "Often when businesses are having financial difficulties, they will not remit their payroll deduction amounts and the directors are often surprised to find out that they are personally responsible," she says.

In a final thought, Sandra states, "As a result, it is important for businesspeople to become familiar with the law, as it affects their business, so that they can minimize their risk exposure through proper conduct of the operational aspects of their business."[1]

Critical Thinking Questions

As you read this appendix, consider Sandra Malach's thoughts on why it is important for employees, business owners, and corporations to have at least a basic understanding of Canadian business law and the tax system. Consider the following:

1. **Why are there laws that relate to external business practices?**

2. **How do contracts help the parties to the contract?**

3. **What laws apply to the business when it has employees?**

4. **How are consumers protected by the laws?**

5. **Why is the tax system important to Canada and its society?**

Corporate Governance

corporate governance
The way in which an organization is governed, directed, and administered.

Corporate governance refers to the way in which an organization is governed, directed, and administered.[2] As discussed in Chapter 5, the board of governors is responsible for the organization's being managed in the best interest of the corporation. Recent experiences in Canada, the United States, and around the world have highlighted the outcome of poor corporate governance on the organization's performance and survival. Increasingly, stakeholders are looking at the corporate governance and control systems of businesses to ensure that they are being managed with the interests of the stakeholders in mind. Although the debate has focused primarily on the financial position and reporting of companies, other concerns are being discussed (honesty in other information, respect for the environment, etc.).

Since the early 1990s, the debate on corporate governance has been flourishing, and regulators in Canada have been setting guidelines to address this issue. This has been in response to worldwide incidents that have raised questions about boards of directors' performance and alleged management incompetence. Most notable have been the WorldCom and Enron scandals (where financial statements proved to be inaccurate), but Canada has not escaped its own examples (e.g., Bre-X and YBM).[3] As well, companies are expected to be socially responsible in their investing. According to Brian A. Schofield and Blair W. Feltmate in Sustainable Development Investing,

> Stakeholders now require that companies be committed to minimizing environmental disruptions and to contribute to the economic and social advancement of the communities in which they operate, known as sustainable development.[4]

In July 2002, the Canadian Institute of Chartered Accountants, the Canadian Securities Administrators, and the Office of the Superintendent of Financial Institutions announced the creation of the Canadian Public Accountability Board (CPAB). Its mission is to "contribute to public confidence in the integrity of financial reporting of public companies by promoting high-quality, independent auditing."[5]

So what has brought about the need to create the CPAB? There have been many successful attempts by associations to regulate their industries. The provincial legal associations, medical associations, faculty associations, accounting associations, and others have developed strict guidelines that control the responsibilities and actions of their members, but this does not guarantee that every member will follow the guidelines. Typically, when there are serious violations, government bodies react and enact regulations (in the form of laws) to protect society, or, in some cases, governments have been proactive in anticipation of violations.

HOT Links

For more news and updated events, search the Office of the Superintendent of Financial Institutions' Web site at (www.osfi-bsif.gc.ca).

The Legal System

Our legal system affects everyone who lives and does business in Canada. The smooth functioning of society depends on the law, which protects the rights of people and businesses. The purpose of law is to keep the system stable while allowing orderly change. The law defines which actions are allowed or banned and regulates some practices. It also helps settle disputes. The legal system both shapes and is shaped by political, economic, and social systems. All three levels of government—federal, provincial, and municipal—regulate various business activities as set out in the laws of Canada and the provinces.

laws
The rules of conduct in a society, created and enforced by a controlling authority, usually the government.

In any society, **laws** are the rules of conduct created and enforced by a controlling authority, usually the government. They develop over time in response to the changing needs of people, property, and business. The legal system in Canada is thus the result of a long and continuing process. In each generation, new social problems occur, and new laws are created to solve them. For instance, the Combines Investigation Act and its successor, the Competition Act, were enacted to protect consumers in areas such as misleading advertising and abusive marketing practices. These acts also contain provisions that can be grouped under three categories: conspiracies, monopolies, and mergers.

Environmental law is an area over which the federal and provincial governments have concurrent jurisdiction. Increased awareness of pollution and a social movement toward the protection of our environment has made this area an important public issue. The appropriate federal and provincial Environmental Protection Acts apply to all the elements of the environment: air, land, and water.

Another area of law that is important to businesses is the Employment Equity Act. Passed in the late 1980s, the act initially applied to all employers with 100 or more employees. Employment rights go beyond requiring employers to treat potential and existing employees equally, regardless of their personal characteristics. The employers, at a minimum, were encouraged to make their workforce reflect various underrepresented peoples (i.e., their organizations should reflect society as much as possible). Because of the increase of businesses geared toward social responsibility, not only did employers with 100 or more employees try to follow the Employment Equity standards, smaller organizations did so as well.

The Employment Equity Act was amended in 1996 to include that every employer (not only those with 100 or more employees) shall implement employment equity. The amendment also states that all employers shall make reasonable accommodations to persons of one of the four designated groups (i.e., women, persons with disabilities, Aboriginal people, and visible minorities) to achieve a degree of representation that is consistent with their representation in the Canadian workforce. The Act allows employers to consider the potential employee's availability to meet reasonable occupational requirements.

Today new areas of law are developing to deal with the Internet. The increasing use of the Internet, as discussed in Chapter 4, requires that industry and the governments respond to various applicable issues, such as privacy.

Public and Private Law

public law
The law relating to the relationship between the individual or business and the government (or its agencies).

private law
The law relating to the relationship between individuals, businesses, or individuals and businesses.

Public law is the law relating to the relationship between the individual or business and the government (or its agencies). The Criminal Code and the Income Tax Act are two examples at the federal level. Liquor laws are an example of public law at the provincial level.

Private law is the law relating to the relationship between individuals, businesses, or individuals and businesses. Statutes that protect one person from the harm of another are private laws.

CONCEPT *in Action* >>>
Statute laws at the federal level are the end result of the legislative process in Ottawa. What are some of the laws that affect the day-to-day operations of business?

© PHOTODISC COLLECTION/GETTY IMAGES

The Main Sources of Law

common law
The body of unwritten law that has evolved out of judicial (court) decisions rather than being enacted by a legislature; also called *case law*.

Common law is the body of unwritten law that has evolved out of judicial (court) decisions rather than being enacted by legislatures. It is also called case law. It developed in England and applies to most of the English-speaking world. Common law is based on community customs that were recognized and enforced by the courts. Therefore, it is based on previous decisions. The reliance on previous decisions creates certainty and predictability.

civil code
A body of written law that sets out the private rights of the citizens.

Civil code is a body of written law that sets out the private rights of the citizens. In Quebec much of what would be found in the common law of other provinces has been codified and is known as the Civil Code.

statute law (or statutory law)
Written law enacted by a legislature (municipal, provincial, or federal).

Statute law (or statutory law) is written law enacted by legislatures at all levels, from municipal and provincial governments to the federal government. Statutes are the end result of the legislative process. Statutory laws are expected to represent the people's wishes. The particular advantage of statute law over common law is the relative ease with which the statutes can be changed.

administrative law
The rules, regulations, and orders passed by boards, commissions, and agencies of government (municipal, provincial, and federal).

Related to statutory law is **administrative law**, or the rules, regulations, and orders passed by boards, commissions, and agencies of municipal, provincial, and federal governments. The scope and influence of administrative law has expanded as the number of these government bodies has grown. Examples of the activities of regulatory agencies include the sale of securities by public companies, employment standards, and broadcasting.

Business Law

business law
The body of law that governs commercial dealings.

Business law is the body of law that governs commercial dealings. These laws provide a certainty within which businesses can operate, serving as guidelines for business decisions. Every businessperson should be familiar with the laws governing his or her field. Some laws, such as the Trademarks Act, apply to all businesses. Other types of business laws might apply to a specific industry, such as the Canadian Radio-television and Telecommunications Commission Act, which regulates and supervises all aspects of the Canadian broadcasting system and regulates telecommunications carriers and service providers that fall under federal jurisdiction.

The Court System

Canada has a highly developed court system. There are four levels of courts in Canada. The trials of most business disputes are heard in the Provincial/Territorial Superior Courts. These courts also hear appeals from Provincial Court judgments and judgments from the Provincial Administrative Tribunals. Appeals of these decisions are made to the Provincial Court of Appeal and subsequently to the Supreme Court of Canada. The Federal Court, Trial Division, and the Court of Appeals hear appeals of federally regulated Administrative Tribunals. The highest court in Canada is the Supreme Court of Canada and it is the final court of appeal from all other Canadian courts. Also, there are specialized Federal Courts, including the Tax Court of Canada, where individuals and companies have an opportunity to settle matters relating to federal tax and revenue legislation. See Exhibit A.1 for an outline of Canada's court system.[6]

Nonjudicial Methods of Settling Disputes

arbitration
A method of settling disputes in which the parties agree to present their case to an impartial third party and are required to accept the arbitrator's decision.

Settling disputes by going to court is both expensive and time-consuming. Even if the case is settled prior to the trial, a sizable legal expense can be incurred in preparing for trial. Therefore, many companies now use private arbitration and mediation firms as alternatives to litigation. Private firms offer these services, which are a high-growth area within the legal profession.

mediation
The intervention of a third party with a view to persuading the parties to adjust or settle their dispute.

With **arbitration,** the parties agree to present their case to an impartial third party and are required to accept the arbitrator's decision. **Mediation** is similar, but the

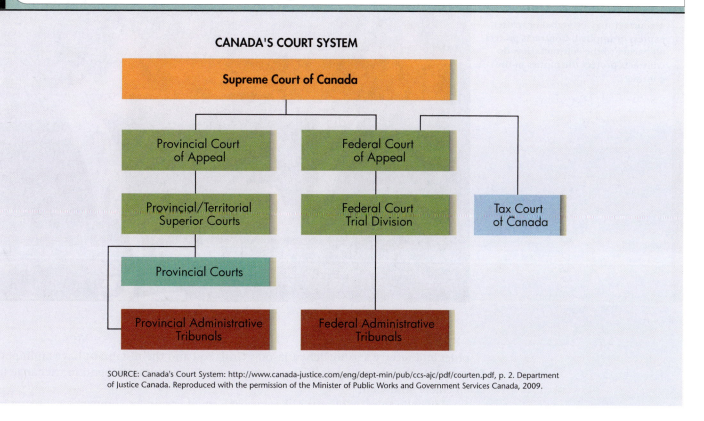

CANADA'S COURT SYSTEM

Supreme Court of Canada

Provincial Court of Appeal — Federal Court of Appeal

Provincial/Territorial Superior Courts — Federal Court Trial Division — Tax Court of Canada

Provincial Courts

Provincial Administrative Tribunals — Federal Administrative Tribunals

SOURCE: Canada's Court System: http://www.canada-justice.com/eng/dept-min/pub/ccs-ajc/pdf/courten.pdf, p. 2. Department of Justice Canada. Reproduced with the permission of the Minister of Public Works and Government Services Canada, 2009.

HOT Links

Whether we are purchasing a computer or a vehicle, it is important to fill out a bill of sale. To see what a legal bill of sale should contain to ensure that both the purchaser and the buyer are protected in case of later disagreements, go to: (http://www.lawdepot.com).

contract
An agreement that sets forth the relationship between parties regarding the performance of a specified action; creates a legal obligation and is enforceable in a court of law.

express contract
A contract in which the terms are specified in either written or spoken words.

implied contract
A contract that depends on the acts and conduct of the parties to show agreement; the terms are not specified in writing or orally.

mediator intervenes with the view of persuading the parties to adjust or settle their dispute. The mediator might or might not offer a resolution, but even if the mediator does offer a solution, neither party is bound by the mediator's decision. The mediator may suggest alternative solutions and primarily tries to help the parties negotiate a settlement. Mediation is more flexible than arbitration and allows for compromise. If the parties cannot reach a settlement, they can then go to court, an option not available in most arbitration cases.

In addition to saving time and money, corporations like the confidentiality of testimony and settlement terms in these proceedings. Arbitration and mediation also allow businesses to avoid the risks associated with going to trial. Generally speaking, once court action is initiated, the information is then public.

Contract Law

A **contract** is an agreement that sets forth the relationship between parties regarding the performance of a specified action. The contract creates a legal obligation and is enforceable in a court of law. Contracts are an important part of business law. Contract law is also incorporated into other fields of business law, such as property and agency law, which we'll discuss later. Some of the business transactions that involve contracts are buying materials and property, selling goods, leasing equipment, and hiring consultants.

A contract can be an **express contract,** which specifies the terms of the agreement in either written or spoken words, or an **implied contract,** which depends on the acts and conduct of the parties to show agreement. An example of an express contract is the written contract an employee might sign that outlines the obligations of the employee and the employer. On the other hand, an implied contract exists when you

CONCEPT *in Action* >>>

A contract may be verbal or written, express or implied. Contracts protect all parties to the contract. How do contracts protect the parties of the contract?

order and receive a sandwich at Jason's Grill. You and the restaurant have an implied contract that you will pay the price shown on the restaurant's menu in exchange for an edible sandwich.

Michelle Sales, a 22-year-old owner of a small cosmetics company, is looking for a supplier to provide her store with inventory. She found a supplier she had confidence in, and after some negotiating, she and the supplier agree on a price of $11,000. The supplier writes up a contract, which they both sign. Has Michelle legally bought the inventory for $11,000? The answer is yes, because the transaction meets all the requirements for a valid contract.

Contract Requirements[7]

Businesses deal with contracts all the time, so it's important to know the requirements of a valid contract. For a contract to be legally enforceable, all of the following elements must be present.

- *Mutual agreement.* This is evidenced by the offer of one party being accepted by another party. Each party to the contract must have entered into it freely, without duress, and without improper inducements. Using physical or economic harm to force the signing of the contract—threatening injury or refusing to place another large order, for instance—invalidates a contract. Likewise, fraud—misrepresenting the essential facts of a transaction—makes a contract unenforceable. Telling a prospective used-car buyer that the brakes are new when, in fact, they have not been replaced can make the contract of sale invalid.
- *Capacity of the parties.* This refers to the legal ability of a party to enter into contracts. Under the law, minors (those who have not attained the age of majority according to the law of their province or territory), people who are mentally incompetent, and those whose judgment has been obviously impaired by drugs or alcohol cannot enter into validly enforceable contracts.
- *Legal consideration.* This is the exchange of something of legal value or benefit between the parties. Consideration can be in the form of money, goods, or giving

© ALISTAR BERG/PHOTODISC/GETTY IMAGES

up a legal right. Suppose that an electronics manufacturer agrees to rent an industrial building for a year at a monthly rent of $1,500. Its consideration is the rent payment of $1,500, and the building owner's consideration is permission to occupy the space. But if you offer to type a term paper for a friend for free and your offer is accepted, there is no contract. Your friend has not given up anything, so you are not legally bound to honour the deal.

- *Lawful object (legal purpose).* This means absence of illegality. The purpose of the contract must be legal for it to be valid. A contract cannot require performance of an illegal act. A contract to smuggle a banned substance into Canada for a specified amount of money would not be legally enforceable.
- *Legal form.* A contract can be in oral or written form, as required. Many can be oral (although a written contract provides an accurate record to the parties of their obligations). For instance, an oral contract exists when Bridge Corp. orders office supplies by phone from Ace Stationery Store and Ace delivers the requested goods. Written contracts include leases, sales contracts, and property deeds. Some types of contracts must be in writing to be legally binding.

As you can see, Michelle's inventory purchase meets all the requirements for a valid contract. Both parties have freely agreed to the terms of the contract. Michelle is not a minor and presumably does not fit any of the other categories of incapacity. Both parties are giving consideration, Michelle by paying the money and the supplier by delivering the inventory. The purchase of the inventory is a legal activity, and the written contract is in the correct form, because the cost of the inventory is over the legal amount that requires a written contract (this varies by province).

Breach of Contract

breach of contract
The failure by one party to a contract to fulfill the terms of the agreement without a legal excuse.

A **breach of contract** occurs when one party to a contract fails (without legal excuse) to fulfill the terms of the agreement. The other party then has the right to seek a remedy in the courts. There are three legal remedies for breach of contract.

- *Payment of damages*—money awarded to the party who was harmed by the breach of contract, to cover losses incurred because the contract wasn't fulfilled. Suppose that Ajax Roofing contracts with Fred Wellman to fix the large hole in the roof of his factory within three days, but the roofing crew doesn't show up as promised. When a thunderstorm four days later causes $45,000 in damage to Wellman's machinery, Wellman can sue for damages to cover the costs of the water damage, because Ajax breached the contract.
- *Specific performance of the contract*—a court order that requires the breaching party to perform the duties under the terms of the contract. Specific performance is a common method of settling a breach of contract. Wellman might ask the court to direct Ajax to fix the roof at the price and conditions in the contract.
- *Restitution*—cancelling the contract and returning both parties to the situation that existed before the contract. If one party fails to perform under the contract, neither party has any further obligation to the other. Because Ajax failed to fix Wellman's roof under the terms of the contract, Wellman does not owe Ajax any money. Ajax must return the 50 percent deposit it received when Wellman signed the contract.

Protecting Businesses and Consumers

The legal environment is meant to not only protect the citizens in everyday life, but also to provide protection to owners and consumers alike. Below is a brief discussion of some of these protections.

Patents, Copyrights, and Trademarks

Canadian law protects authors, inventors, and creators of other intellectual property by giving them the rights to their creative works. Patents, copyrights, and registration of trademarks are legal protection for key business assets.

A **patent** gives an inventor the exclusive right to manufacture, use, and sell an invention for 20 years. The Patent Act grants patents for ideas that meet its requirements of being new, unique, and useful. The physical process, machine, or formula is what is patented. Patent rights—pharmaceutical companies' rights to produce drugs they discover, for example—are considered intangible personal property (i.e., they do not have physical form but are of value).

The government also grants copyrights. A **copyright** is an exclusive right, shown by the symbol © (but does not necessarily need to be shown), given to a writer, artist, composer, or playwright to use, produce, and sell her or his creation. This protection is automatic. Works protected by copyright include printed materials (books, magazine articles, lectures), works of art, photographs, and movies. Under current copyright law, the copyright is issued for the life of the creator plus 50 years after the creator's death. Patents and copyrights, which are considered intellectual property, are the subject of many lawsuits today.

A **trademark** is a design, name, or other distinctive mark that a manufacturer uses to identify its goods in the marketplace. Apple Computer's multicoloured apple logo (symbol) is an example of a trademark.

Trademarks are valuable because they create uniqueness in the minds of customers. At the same time, companies don't want a trademark to become so well known that it is used to describe all similar types of products. For instance, Coke is often used to refer to any cola soft drink, not just those produced by the Coca-Cola Company. Companies spend millions of dollars each year to keep their trademarks from becoming generic words, terms used to identify a product class rather than the specific product. Coca-Cola employs many investigators and files 70 to 80 lawsuits each year to prevent its trademarks from becoming generic words.

Once a trademark becomes generic (which a court decides), it is public property and can be used by any person or company. Names that were once trademarked but are now generic include aspirin, thermos, linoleum, and zipper.

Bankruptcy and Insolvency Act

It might be possible to save a business, even though it is insolvent, by using the provisions under the Bankruptcy and Insolvency Act. **Bankruptcy** is the legal act by which individuals or businesses that cannot meet their financial obligations are relieved of some, if not all, of their debt. Working through a Trustee in Bankruptcy, the company (or individual) files a Proposal ("offer") to the company's creditors asking them to accept less than the actual monies owed so that the company can survive.

Deregulation of Industries

Since the 1980s, the Canadian governments (federal and provincial/territorial) have actively promoted deregulation, the removal of rules and regulations governing business competition. **Deregulation** has drastically changed some once-regulated industries (especially the transportation, telecommunications, and financial services industries) and created many new competitors. The result has been entries into and exits from some industries.

Tort Law

A **tort** is a civil, or private, act that harms other people or their property. The harm might involve physical injury, emotional distress, invasion of privacy, or defamation (injuring a person's character by publication of false statements). The injured party

---

patent
A form of protection (limited monopoly) established by the government to inventors; gives an inventor the exclusive right to manufacture, use, and sell an invention for 20 years.

copyright
A form of protection established by the government for creators of works of art, music, literature, or other intellectual property; gives the creator the exclusive right to use, produce, and sell the creation during the lifetime of the creator and the creator's estate for 50 years thereafter.

trademark
The legally exclusive design, name, or other distinctive mark that a manufacturer uses to identify its goods in the marketplace.

HOT Links

For more information about patents, copyrights, and trademarks, go to CanadaOne's website and search for information at (**www.canadaone.com**).

bankruptcy
The legal procedure by which individuals or businesses that cannot meet their financial obligations are relieved of some, it not all, of their debt.

HOT Links

For more information on corporate bankruptcy, see the website that helps people and businesses get a fresh financial start at (**www.BankruptcyCanada.com**).

deregulation
The removal of rules and regulations governing business competition.

tort
A civil, or private, act that harms other people or their property.

may sue the wrongdoer to recover damages for the harm or loss. A tort is not the result of a breach of contract, which would be settled under contract law. Torts are part of common law. Examples of tort cases are medical malpractice, slander (an untrue oral statement that damages a person's reputation), libel (an untrue written statement that damages a person's reputation), product liability (discussed in the next section), professional negligence, and fraud.

A tort is generally not a crime, although some acts can be both torts and crimes. (Assault and battery, for instance, is a criminal act that would be prosecuted by the government and is also a tort because of the injury to the person.) Torts are private wrongs and are settled in courts. Crimes are violations of public law punishable by the government in the criminal courts. The purpose of criminal law is to punish the person who committed the crime. The purpose of tort law is to provide remedies to the injured party.

For a tort to exist and damages to be recovered, the harm must be done through either negligence or deliberate intent. Negligence occurs when reasonable care is not taken for the safety of others. For instance, a woman attending a baseball game was struck on the head by a foul ball that came through a hole in the screen behind home plate. The court could rule that a sports team charging admission has an obligation to provide structures free from defects and seating that protects spectators from danger. Therefore, the baseball organization could be found negligent. Negligence does not apply when an injury is caused by an unavoidable accident, an event that was not intended and could not have been prevented even if the person used reasonable care. This area of tort law is quite controversial, because the definition of negligence leaves much room for interpretation.

Consumer Protection

consumerism
A movement that seeks to increase the rights and powers of buyers vis-à-vis sellers.

Consumerism reflects the struggle for power between buyers and sellers. Specifically, it is a movement seeking to increase the rights and powers of buyers vis-à-vis sellers, often resulting in consumer protection laws. Sellers' rights and powers include the right

- to introduce into the marketplace any product, in any size and style, that is not hazardous to personal health or safety, or, if it is hazardous, to introduce it with the proper warnings and controls;
- to price the product at any level they wish, provided they do not discriminate among similar classes of buyers;
- to spend any amount of money they wish to promote the product, so long as the promotion does not constitute unfair competition;
- to formulate any message they wish about the product, provided that it is not misleading or dishonest in content or execution; and
- to introduce any buying incentives they wish.

    Meanwhile, buyers have the rights and powers

- to refuse to buy any product that is offered to them,
- to expect products to be safe,
- to expect a product to be essentially as the seller represents it, and
- to receive adequate information about the product.

Warranties

Express warranties are specific statements of fact or promises about a product by the seller. This form of warranty is considered part of the sales transaction that influences the buyer. Express warranties appear in the form of statements that can be interpreted as fact. The statement "This machine will process 1,000 gallons of paint per hour" is an express warranty, as is the printed warranty that comes with a computer or a telephone answering machine.

Implied warranties are neither written nor oral. These guarantees are imposed on sales transactions by statute or court decision. They promise that the product will perform up to expected standards. For instance, a man bought a used car from a dealer, and the next day the transmission fell out as he was driving on the highway. The dealer fixed the car, but a week later the brakes failed. The man sued the car dealer. The court ruled in favour of the car owner, because any car without a working transmission or brakes is not fit for the ordinary purpose of driving. Similarly, if a customer asks to buy a copier to handle 5,000 copies per month, she relies on the salesperson to sell her a copier that meets those needs. The salesperson implicitly warrants that the copier purchased is appropriate for that volume.

Product-liability Law

product liability
The responsibility of manufacturers and sellers for defects in the products they make and sell.

Product liability refers to manufacturers' and sellers' responsibility for defects in the products they make and sell. It has become a specialized area of law combining aspects of contracts, warranties, torts, and statutory law.

strict liability
A concept in products liability laws under which a manufacturer or seller is liable for any personal injury or property damage caused by defective products or packaging that does not meet industry standards.

An important concept in product-liability law is **strict liability**. A manufacturer or seller is liable for any personal injury or property damage caused by defective products or packaging that does not meet industry standards.

Competition Act

The Competition Act was enacted to protect consumers and provide provisions that can be grouped under three categories: conspiracies, monopolies, and mergers. Each of these three categories is briefly discussed below.

Many measures have been taken to try to keep the marketplace free from influences that would restrict competition. The Competition Act sets out the basic prohibition against cartels, (the expression that is often used is *antitrust law*), among other issues. A **cartel** is an agreement between enterprises to lessen competition. If it can be proven that enterprises entered into an agreement or arrangement (a conspiracy) to lessen competition, they can be charged with a criminal offence.

cartel
An agreement between enterprises to lessen competition.

Some of the more common methods of reducing or eliminating competition are

- *parallel pricing*—competing firms adopt similar pricing strategies;
- *setting quotas*—imposing limits of production;
- *market sharing*—dividing the market based on a geographical basis; and
- *product specialization*—whereby each firm agrees to specialize its products.

According to the free market economy (as discussed in Chapter 1), the essential characteristic of an efficient market is competition. If customers have a choice of products to purchase (i.e., competition), prices will be generally lower, and quality will be better, or both. A **monopoly** is a situation when there is no competition and the benefits of a free market are lost.

monopoly
A situation where there is no competition and the benefits of a free market are lost.

For various reasons (e.g., small population, large geographical area) some monopolies are allowed to exist in Canada. Some examples have been utilities and telecommunications services, but these have been governed by regulatory agencies (e.g., utility boards) that protected the consumers' rights. These *natural monopolies* have been disappearing in the past decade as government regulations have promoted more competition in reaction to the stronger move to increased competition.

The third area where the Competition Act protects the consumer is mergers and acquisitions. As discussed in Chapter 6, mergers and acquisitions are often an important means of seeking efficiencies in business. The Competition Act allows the government to stop any mergers and acquisitions that might lessen competition.

Employment Standards Acts

One issue that many businesses face is the ability to recruit good employees. Furthermore, each province has an Employment Standards Act (or an equivalent, such as an Employment Standards Code) that outlines the minimum terms of employment in such areas as minimum wages, payment of earnings, hours of work, overtime, general (statutory) holidays, vacations, maternity and parental leaves, termination, layoff and recall, and the employment of children.

Without the knowledge of these minimum standards, employers can potentially be violating the standards and can incur considerable costs if action is taken against them. Particularly at risk are the smaller organizations that do not have a human resource department with professional human resource personnel.

Taxation of Business

Taxes are sometimes seen as the price we pay to live in this country. Taxes are assessed by all levels of government on both business and individuals, and they are used to pay for the services provided by government.

Income Taxes

income taxes
Taxes that are based on the income received by businesses and individuals.

Income taxes are based on the income received by businesses and individuals. Most personal income taxes are progressive, meaning that rates increase as income increases (one exception is the flat tax for individuals in Alberta). The tax rates for the federal government apply to all Canadians (with few exceptions) equally, but the provinces are free to set their own rates. Income taxes for businesses are flat (i.e., same rate regardless of income).

As we discussed in Chapter 5, the net income for sole proprietorships and partnerships are included in the personal income of the owners. For corporations, taxes are the responsibility of the corporation.

Other Types of Taxes

property taxes
Taxes that are imposed on real and personal property based on the *assessed value* of the property.

Besides income taxes, individuals and businesses pay a number of other taxes. The four main types are property taxes, payroll taxes (only as a remittance), sales taxes, and excise taxes.

Property taxes are assessed on real property, based on its assessed value. Most jurisdictions tax land and buildings. Property taxes may be based on fair market value (what a buyer would pay), a percentage of fair market value, or replacement value (what it would cost today to rebuild or buy something like the original). The value on which the taxes are based is the *assessed value.*

Any individual that is employed is required to pay federal and provincial taxes on the money that he or she earns (after the personal exemption is deducted), called income taxes. These taxes must be paid on wages, salaries, and commissions. The employer deducts the income taxes from the employee's pay and remits them to the federal government, where they are called **payroll taxes.**

payroll taxes
Income taxes that are collected by the employer and remitted to the federal government, usually in the form of a deduction from the employee's pay.

sales taxes
Taxes that are levied on goods and services when they are sold; calculated as a percentage of the price.

Sales taxes are levied on goods when they are sold and are a percentage of the sales price. These taxes are imposed by the federal government (the goods and services tax, or GST) and most provincial governments in the form of a provincial sales tax (PST). (One exception is that there is no provincial sales tax in Alberta.) Some provinces now have a harmonized sales tax (HST), which is a combination of the GST and the PST. The PSTs vary in amount and in what is considered taxable. Sales taxes increase the cost of goods to the consumer. Businesses are responsible for collecting sales taxes and remitting them to the government.

excise taxes
Taxes that are imposed on specific items such as gasoline, alcoholic beverages, and tobacco.

Excise taxes are placed on specific items, such as gasoline, alcoholic beverages, and tobacco. They can be assessed by federal and provincial governments. In many cases, these taxes help pay for services related to the item taxed. For instance, gasoline excise taxes are often used to build and repair highways. Other excise taxes—like those on alcoholic beverages and tobacco—are used to control practices that can cause harm.

Summary

This appendix has been about businesses governing themselves in a legal manner to respond to their stakeholders. Corporate governance is increasingly becoming important, and it is necessary for businesses to be aware of their ethical and legal responsibilities.

Our environment is always changing, and businesses must be proactive in responding to the changes, or governments are forced to act. Associations can encourage strict adherence to the ethical standards that they set out, but these have little power to stop someone from acting unethically, or even illegally, often until it is too late.

Organizations, associations, industry, and government are increasingly working together to protect the stakeholders to ensure that business is governed in an ethical and legal manner.

Summary of Learning Outcomes

1 Explain corporate governance, and why is it important.

Corporate governance is the way in which an organization is governed, directed, and administered. Increasingly, organizations must be seen as acting in the interests of its various stakeholders, or its survival could be in jeopardy. If a corporation is acting in a perceived unethical manner, it could lose sales, have regulations imposed on it, have difficulty attracting employees, and so on.

2 Review how the legal system governs business transactions and settles business disputes.

Laws are the rules governing a society's conduct that are created and enforced by a controlling authority. The Canadian court system governs the legal system and includes both federal and provincial courts, each organized into three levels. The courts settle disputes by applying and interpreting laws. Most cases start in trial courts. Decisions can be appealed to appellate courts. The Supreme Court of Canada is the nation's highest court and the court of final appeal. To avoid the high costs of going to court, many firms now use private arbitration or mediation as alternatives to litigation.

3 Discuss the required elements of a valid contract.

A contract is an agreement between two or more parties that meets five requirements: mutual agreement, capacity of the parties, legal consideration, lawful object (legal purpose), and legal form. If one party breaches the contract terms, the remedies are damages, specific performance, or restitution.

4 Explain some of the Canadian laws that protect businesses and consumers.

A patent is a form of protection (limited monopoly) established by the government to protect inventors. It gives an inventor the exclusive right to manufacture, use, and sell an invention for 20 years. A copyright is established by the government to protect creators of works of art, music, literature, or other intellectual property. It gives the creator the exclusive right to use, produce, and sell the creation during his or her lifetime and for 50 years thereafter. A trademark is a design, name, or other distinctive mark that a manufacturer uses to identify its goods in the marketplace.

Patents, copyrights, and trademarks help businesses protect their rights for the exclusive use of their inventions, creations (e.g., music), names, and designs. Tort law settles disputes involving civil acts that harm people or their property. Torts include physical injury, mental anguish, and defamation. Product-liability law governs the responsibility of manufacturers and sellers for product defects. Bankruptcy law gives business or individuals who cannot meet their financial obligations a way of being relieved of their debts. Some laws are designed to keep the marketplace free from influences that would restrict competition, such as price fixing and deceptive advertising. Laws protecting consumer rights are another important area of government control.

5 **Discuss the Employment Standards Acts.**

Each province has an Employment Standards Act (or an equivalent act) that outlines the minimum terms of employment in such areas as minimum wages, payment of earnings, hours of work, overtime, statutory holidays, vacations, maternity and parental leaves, termination, layoff and recall, and the employment of children.

6 **List the most common taxes paid by businesses.**

Income taxes are based on the income received by businesses and individuals. They are paid to both the federal and provincial governments, who are responsible for setting their own rates. In addition to income taxes, individuals and businesses also pay property taxes (assessed on real property), payroll taxes (employers are responsible for collecting the income taxes from their employees and remitting them to the federal government), sales taxes (e.g., GST and HST, which are levied on goods and services), and excise taxes (levied on specific products such as gasoline, alcoholic beverages, and tobacco).

Key Terms

administrative law   530
arbitration   530
bankruptcy   534
breach of contract   533
business law   530
cartel   536
civil code   530
common law   530
consumerism   535
contract   531
copyright   534
corporate governance   528
deregulation   534
excise taxes   537
express contract   531
implied contract   531

income taxes   537
laws   528
mediation   530
monopoly   536
patent   534
payroll taxes   537
private law   529
product liability   536
property taxes   537
public law   529
sales taxes   537
statute law (statutory law)   530
strict liability   536
tort   534
trademark   534

GLOSSARY

A

absolute advantage The situation when a country can produce and sell a product at a lower cost than any other country or when it is the only country that can provide the product.

accounting The process of collecting, recording, classifying, summarizing, reporting, and analyzing financial activities.

accounts payable Purchase for which a buyer has not yet paid the seller.

accounts receivable Sales for which a firm has not yet been paid.

acid-test (quick) ratio The ratio of total current assets excluding inventory to total current liabilities; used to measure a firm's liquidity.

acquisition The purchase of a corporation by another corporation or by an investor group; the identity of the acquired company can be lost.

activity ratios Ratios that measure how well a firm uses its assets.

administrative law The rules, regulations, and orders passed by boards, commissions, and agencies of government (municipal, provincial, and federal).

advertising Any paid form of non-personal presentation by an identified sponsor.

agency shop A company where employees are not required to join the union but must pay it a fee to cover its expenses in representing them.

agents Sales representatives of manufacturers and wholesalers.

amortization (depreciation) The allocation of an asset's original cost to the years in which it is expected to produce revenues.

angel investors Individual investors or groups of experienced investors who provide funding for start-up businesses.

annual report A yearly document that describes a firm's financial status and usually discusses the firm's activities during the past year and its prospects for the future.

application service providers (ASPs) A service company that buys and maintains software on its servers and distributes it through high-speed networks to subscribers for a set period and price.

apprenticeship A form of on-the-job training that combines specific job instruction with classroom instruction.

arbitration A method of settling disputes in which the parties agree to present their case to an impartial third party and are required to accept the arbitrator's decision.

assembly process A transformation process in which the basic inputs are either combined to create the output or transformed into the output.

assets Possessions of value owned by a firm.

Association of Southeast Asian Nations (ASEAN) Organization initially established in 1967 to promote economic growth, social progress, and cultural development in the region; currently has 10 members.

attitude Learned tendency to respond consistently toward a given object, idea, or concept.

authority Legitimate power, granted by the organization and acknowledged by employees, that allows an individual to request action and expect compliance.

autocratic leaders Directive leaders who prefer to make decisions and solve problems on their own with little input from subordinates.

B

baby boomers People born between the late 1940s (after World War II) and the mid-1960s.

balance of payments A summary of a country's international financial transactions showing the difference between the country's total payments to and its total receipts from other countries.

balance of trade The differences between the value of a country's exports and the value of its imports during a certain time.

balance sheet See statement of financial position.

Bank of Canada Canada's central bank whose objective is to "promote the economic and financial well-being of Canada."

bank rate The interest rate that the Bank of Canada charges on one-day loans to financial institutions.

bankruptcy The legal procedure by which individuals or businesses that cannot meet their financial obligations are relieved of some, if not all, of their debt.

barriers to entry Factors, such as technological or legal conditions, that prevent new firms from competing equally with a monopoly.

batch processing A method of updating a database in which data are collected over some time period and then processed together.

bear markets Markets in which securities prices are falling.

belief An organized pattern of knowledge that an individual holds as true about the world.

benefit segmentation The differentiation of markets based on what a product will do rather than on customer characteristics.

bill of material A list of the items and the number of each required to make a given product.

board of directors A group of people elected by the shareholders to handle the overall management of a corporation, such as setting corporate goals and policies, hiring corporate officers, and overseeing the firm's operations and finances.

bond ratings Letter grades assigned to bond issues to indicate their quality, or level of risk; assigned by rating agencies such as Moody's and Standard & Poor's (S&P).

bonds Securities that represent long-term debt obligations (liabilities) issued by corporations and governments.

breach of contract The failure by one party to a contract to fulfill the terms of the agreement without a legal excuse.

breakeven point The price at which a product's costs are covered, so additional sales result in profit.

breaking bulk The process of breaking large shipments of similar products into smaller, more usable lots.

broker markets (organized stock exchanges) Organizations on whose premises securities are resold using an auction-style trading system.

brokers Go-betweens that bring buyers and sellers together.

budgets Formal written forecasts of revenues and expenses that set spending limits based on operational forecasts; include cash budgets, capital budgets, and operating budgets.

bull markets Markets in which securities prices are rising.

bundling The strategy of grouping two or more related products together and pricing them as a single product.

business An organization that strives for a profit by providing goods and services desired by its customers.

business cycles Upward and downward changes in the level of economic activity.

Business Development Bank of Canada (BDC) Bank that provides small and medium-sized businesses with flexible financing, affordable consulting services, and venture capital.

business interruption insurance Covers such costs as rental of temporary facilities, wage and salary payments to employees, payments for leased equipment, fixed payments, and profits that would have been earned during that period.

business law The body of law that governs commercial dealings.

business plan A formal written statement that describes in detail the idea for a new business and how it will be carried out; includes a general description of the company, the qualifications of the owner(s), a description of the product or service, an analysis of the market, and a financial plan.

business-to-business (B2B) e-commerce Electronic commerce that involves transactions between companies.

business-to-consumer (B2C) e-commerce Electronic commerce that involves transactions between businesses and the end user of the goods or services; also called *e-tailing*.

business-to-enterprise (B2E) Electronic collecting, storing, updating, and using of information within the business.

buyer behaviour The actions people take in buying and using goods and services.

C

CAD/CAM systems Linked computer systems that combine the advantages of *computer-aided design* and *computer-aided manufacturing*. The system helps design the product, control the flow of resources, and operate the production process.

caisses populaires Credit unions operating in Quebec and other areas of Canada with francophone populations.

Canada Deposit Insurance Corporation (CDIC) A federal Crown Corporation created in 1967 to provide deposit insurance and contribute to the stability of Canada's financial system.

Canadian Charter of Rights and Freedoms Legislation that guarantees the rights and freedoms of Canadians.

Canada Pension Plan Insurance that provides retirement, disability, death, and health benefits.

capital Tools, machinery, equipment, and buildings used to produce goods and services and get them to the consumer. Sometimes refers to the money that buys machinery, factories, and other production and distribution facilities.

capital budgeting The process of analyzing long-term projects and selecting those that offer the best returns while maximizing the firm's value.

capital budgets Budgets that forecast a firm's outlays for fixed assets (plant and equipment), typically for a period of several years.

capital expenditures Investments in long-lived assets, such as land, buildings, machinery, and equipment, that are expected to provide benefits over a period longer than one year.

capital products Large, expensive items with a long life span that are purchased by businesses for use in making other products or providing a service.

cartel An agreement between enterprises to lessen competition.

cash budgets Budgets that forecast a firm's cash inflows and outflows and help the firm plan for cash surpluses and shortages.

cash flows The inflow and outflow of cash for a firm.

cash management The process of making sure that a firm has enough cash on hand to pay bills as they come due and to meet unexpected expenses.

category management Suppliers manage the inventory of a category of products for a retailer.

cellular manufacturing Production technique that uses small, self-contained production units, each performing all or most of the tasks necessary to complete a manufacturing order.

centralization The degree to which formal authority is concentrated in one area or level of an organization.

certified general accountant (CGA) An accountant who focuses primarily on external financial reporting.

certified management accountant (CMA) An accountant who works primarily in industry and focuses on internal management accounting.

chain of command The line of authority that extends from one level of an organization's hierarchy to the next, from top to bottom, and makes clear who reports to whom.

chartered accountant (CA) An accountant who has completed an approved bachelor's degree program, completed an educational program, and passed a comprehensive examination. Only a CA can issue an auditor's opinion on a firm's financial statements.

chartered banks Profit-oriented financial institutions that accept deposits, make business and consumer loans, invest in government and corporate securities, and provide other financial services.

chief information officer (CIO) An executive with responsibility for managing all information resources in an organization.

circular flow The movement of inputs and outputs among households, businesses, and governments; a way of showing how the sectors of the economy interact.

civil code A body of written law that sets out the private rights of the citizens.

code of ethics A set of guidelines prepared by a firm to provide its employees with the knowledge of what the firm expects in terms of their responsibilities and behaviour toward fellow employees, customers, and suppliers.

coercive power Power that is derived from an individual's ability to threaten negative outcomes.

cognitive dissonance The condition of having beliefs or knowledge that are internally inconsistent or that disagree with one's behaviour.

collective bargaining The process of negotiating labour agreements that provide for compensation and working arrangements mutually acceptable to the union and to management.

command economy An economic system characterized by government ownership of virtually all resources and economic decision-making by central government planning; also known as a *planned economy*.

commercial paper Unsecured short-term debt (an IOU) issued by a financially strong corporation.

committee structure An organizational structure in which authority and responsibility are held by a group rather than an individual.

common law The body of unwritten law that has evolved out of judicial (court) decisions rather than being enacted by a legislature; also called *case law*.

common shares Securities that represent one form of ownership interest in a corporation.

competitive advantage A set of unique features of a company and its products that are perceived by the target market as significant and superior to those of the competition; also called *differential advantage*.

component lifestyle A lifestyle made up of a complex set of interests and choices.

computer network A group of two or more computer systems linked together by communications channels to share data and information.

computer virus A computer program that copies itself into other software and can spread to other computer systems.

computer-aided design (CAD) The use of computers to design and test new products and modify existing ones.

computer-aided manufacturing (CAM) The use of computers to develop and control the production process.

computer-integrated manufacturing (CIM) The combination of computerized manufacturing processes (such as robots and flexible manufacturing systems) with other computerized systems that control design, inventory, production, and purchasing.

conceptual skills A manager's ability to view the organization as a whole, understand how the various parts are interdependent, and assess how the organization relates to its external environment.

conglomerate merger A merger of companies in unrelated businesses; done to reduce risk.

consensual leaders Leaders who encourage discussion about issues and then require that all parties involved agree to the final decision.

consultative leaders Leaders who confer with subordinates before making a decision but who retain the final decision-making authority.

consumer price index (CPI) A measure of retail price movements that compares a representative "shopping basket" of goods and services.

consumerism A movement that seeks to increase the rights and powers of buyers vis-à-vis sellers.

consumer-to-business (C2B) e-commerce Electronic commerce that involves transactions between consumers and businesses initiated by the consumer.

consumer-to-consumer (C2C) e-commerce Electronic commerce that involves transactions between consumers.

contingency plans Plans that identify alternative courses of action for very unusual or crisis situations; typically stipulate the chain of command, standard operating procedures, and communication channels the organization will use during an emergency.

contingent workers Persons who prefer temporary employment, either part- or full-time.

continuous improvement A constant commitment to seeking better ways of doing things to achieve greater efficiency and improve quality.

continuous process A production process that uses long production runs lasting days, weeks, or months without equipment shutdowns; generally used for high-volume, low-variety products with standardized parts.

contract An agreement that sets for the relationship between parties regarding the performance of a specified action; creates a legal obligation and is enforceable in a court of law.

contract manufacturing The practice in which a foreign firm manufacturers private-label goods under a domestic firm's brand name.

contractionary policy The use of monetary policy by the Bank of Canada to tighten the money supply by selling government securities or raising interest rates.

controlling The process of assessing the organization's progress toward accomplishing its goals; includes monitoring the implementation of a plan and correcting deviations from the plan.

convenience products Relatively inexpensive items that require little shopping effort and are purchased routinely without planning.

conventional ethics The second stage in the ethical development of individuals in which people move from an egocentric viewpoint to consider the expectations of an organization or society; also known as social ethics.

convertible bonds Corporate bonds that are issued with an option that allows the bondholder to convert them into common shares.

cooperatives Legal entities typically formed by people with similar interests, such as customers or suppliers, to reduce costs and gain economic power. A cooperative has limited liability, an unlimited life span, an elected board of directors, and an administrative staff; all profits are distributed to the member-owners in proportion to their contributions.

copyright A form of protection established by the government for creators of works of art, music, literature, or other intellectual property; gives the creator the exclusive right to use, produce, and sell the creation during the lifetime of the creator and the creator's estate for 50 years thereafter.

corporate culture The set of attitudes, values, and standards of behaviour that distinguishes one organization from another.

corporate governance The way in which an organization is being governed, directed, and administered.

corporate open house Persons are invited to an open house on the premises of the corporation. Qualified applicants are encouraged to complete an application before leaving.

corporate philanthropy The practice of charitable giving by corporations; includes contributing cash, donating equipment and products, and supporting the volunteer efforts of company employees.

corporation A legal entity with an existence and life separate from its owners who, therefore, are not personally liable for the entity's debts. A corporation has many of the same legal rights and responsibilities as that of a person: it can own property, enter into contracts, sue and be sued, and engage in business operations.

cost competitive advantage A firm's ability to produce a product or service at a lower cost than all other competitors in an industry while maintaining satisfactory profit margins.

cost of goods sold (COGS) The total expense of buying or producing a firm's goods or services.

cost-of-living adjustment (COLA) A provision in a labour contract that calls for wages to increase automatically as the cost of living rises (usually measured by the consumer price index).

cost-push inflation Inflation that occurs when increases in production costs push up the prices of final goods and services.

costs Expenses incurred in creating and selling goods and services.

countertrade A form of international trade in which part or all of the payment for goods or services is in the form of other goods and services.

credit unions Not-for-profit, member-owned financial cooperatives.

critical path In a critical path method network, the longest path through the linked activities.

critical path method (CPM) A scheduling tool that enables a manager to determine the critical path of activities for a project—the activities that will cause the entire project to fall behind schedule if they are not completed on time.

cross-functional teams Teams of employees who are from about the same level in the organizational hierarchy but from different functional areas; for example, task forces, organizational committees, and project teams.

crowding out The situation that occurs when government spending replaces spending by the private sector.

Crown corporations Companies that only the provincial and federal government can set up.

culture The set of values, ideas, attitudes, and other symbols created to shape human behaviour.

currency Bank notes and coins used as a medium of exchange.

current assets Assets that can or will be converted to cash within the next 12 months (within the next fiscal year).

current liabilities Short-term claims that are due within a year of the date of the balance sheet.

current ratio The ratio of total current assets to total current liabilities; used to measure a firm's liquidity.

custom regulations Regulations on products that are different from generally accepted international standards.

customer departmentalization Departmentalization that is based on the primary type of customer served by the organizational unit.

customer relationship management (CRM) The processes used by organizations to track and organize information about current and prospective customers.

customer satisfaction The customer's feeling that a product has met or exceeded expectations.

customer value (in economics) The customer's perception of the ratio of benefits (functionality, performance, durability, design, ease of use, and serviceability) to the sacrifice (of money, time, and effort) necessary to obtain those benefits.

customer value (in marketing) The ratio of benefits to the sacrifice necessary to obtain those benefits, as determined by the customer; reflects the willingness of customers to buy a product.

customization The production of goods or services one at a time according to the specific needs or wants of individual customers.

cyclical unemployment Unemployment that occurs when a downturn in the business cycle reduces the demand for labour throughout the economy.

D

database An electronic filing system that collects and organizes data and information.

data mart Special subset of a data warehouse that deals with a single area of data and is organized for quick analysis.

data warehouse An information technology that combines many databases across a whole company into one central database that supports management decision making.

dealer markets Securities markets where buy and sell orders are executed through dealers, or "market makers" linked by telecommunications networks.

debentures Unsecured bonds that are backed only by the reputation of the issuer and its promise to pay the principal and interest when due.

debt A form of business financing consisting of borrowed funds that must be repaid with interest over a stated time period.

debt ratios Ratios that measure the degree and effect of a firm's use of borrowed funds (debt) to finance its operations.

debt-to-equity ratio The ratio of total liabilities to owners' equity; measures the relationship between the amount of debt financing and the amount of equity financing.

decentralization The process of pushing decision-making authority down the organizational hierarchy.

decision support system (DSS) An interactive, flexible, computerized information system that allows managers to make decisions quickly and accurately; used to conduct sales analyses, forecast sales, evaluate advertising, analyze product lines, and keep tabs on market trends and competitors' actions.

decisional roles A manager's activities as an entrepreneur, resource allocator, conflict resolver, or negotiator.

deductibles The amounts that the insured must pay before insurance benefits begin.

delegation of authority The assignment of some degree of authority and responsibility to persons lower in the chain of command.

demand The quantity of a good or service that people are willing to buy at various prices.

demand curve A graph showing the quantity of a good or service that people are willing to buy at various prices.

demand deposits Money kept in chequing accounts that can be withdrawn by depositors on demand.

demand-pull inflation Inflation that occurs when the demand for goods and services is greater than the supply.

democratic leaders Leaders who solicit input from all members of the group and then allow the members to make the final decision through a vote.

demographic segmentation The differentiation of markets through the use of categories such as age, education, gender, income, and household size.

demography The study of people's vital statistics, such as their age, race and ethnicity, and location.

departmentalization The process of grouping jobs together so that similar or associated tasks and activities can be coordinated.

depreciation (amortization) The allocation of an asset's original cost to the years in which it is expected to produce revenues; also referred to as *amortization*.

deregulation The removal of rules and regulations governing business competition.

detailing The physical stocking of merchandise at a retailer by the salesperson who delivers the merchandise.

devaluation A lowering of the value of a nation's currency relative to other currencies.

differential competitive advantage A firm's ability to provide a unique product or service that offers something of value to buyers besides simply a lower price.

distribution (logistics) Efficiently managing the acquisition of raw materials to the factory and the movement of products from the producer to industrial users and consumers.

distribution centres Warehouses that specialize in changing shipment sizes rather than in storing goods.

distribution channel The series of marketing entities through which goods and services pass on their way from producers to end users.

distribution strategy The part of the marketing mix that involves deciding how many stores and which specific wholesalers and retailers will handle the product in a geographic area.

diversity Employee differences in age, race and ethnicity, gender, educational background, and work experience.

dividends Payments to shareholders from a corporation's profits.

division of labour The process of dividing work into separate jobs and assigning tasks to workers.

double-entry bookkeeping A method of accounting in which each transaction is recorded as two entries so that two accounts or records are changed.

dual distribution (or multiple distribution) Two or more channels that distribute the same product to target markets.

dumping The practice of charging a lower price for a product in foreign markets than in the firm's home market.

E

earnings per share (EPS) The ratio of net profit to the number of common shares outstanding; measures the number of dollars earned by each share.

economic growth An increase in a nation's output of goods and services.

economic system The combination of policies, laws, and choices made by a nation's government to establish the systems that determine what goods and services are produced and how they are allocated.

economics The study of how a society uses scarce resources to produce and distribute goods and services.

effectiveness The ability to produce the desired result or good (doing the right thing).

efficiency Using the least amount of resources to accomplish the organization's goals (doing things right).

electronic business (e-business) The entire process that involves the full value chain (the entire value-adding process, from the raw materials to the eventual end user, including the disposing of the packaging after use) and how all units of a business operate.

electronic commerce (e-commerce) The actual transaction of selling a product or service via the Internet.

electronic data interchange (EDI) The electronic exchange of information between two trading partners.

embargo A total ban on imports or exports of a product.

employment insurance Payment of benefits to laid-off workers while they seek new jobs.

empowerment The process of giving employees increased autonomy and discretion to make decisions, as well as control over the resources needed to implement those decisions.

enterprise portal A customizable internal website that provides proprietary corporate information to a defined user group, such as employees, supply chain partners, or customers.

enterprise resource planning (ERP) A computerized resource planning system that includes information about the firm's suppliers and customers as well as data generated internally.

enterprise risk management (ERM) A company-wide, strategic approach to identifying, monitoring, and managing all elements of a company's risk.

entrepreneurs People with vision, drive, and creativity who are willing to take the risk of starting and managing a new business to make a profit or greatly changing the scope and direction of an existing firm.

environmental scanning The process in which a firm continually collects and evaluates information about its external environment.

e-procurement The process of purchasing supplies and materials online using the Internet.

equilibrium The point on the supply and demand curve at which quantity demanded equals quantity supplied.

equity A form of business financing consisting of funds raised through the sale of stock in a business.

equity theory A theory of motivation that holds that worker satisfaction is influenced by employees' perceptions about how fairly they are treated compared with their coworkers.

ethics A set of moral standards for judging whether something is right or wrong.

European Union (EU) An organization of 15 European nations (as of early 2004) that works to foster political and economic integration in Europe; formerly called the European Community.

exchange The process in which two parties give something of value to each other to satisfy their respective needs.

exchange controls Laws that require a company earning foreign exchange (foreign currency) from its exports to sell the foreign exchange to a control agency, such as a central bank.

exchange-traded fund (ETF) A basket of marketable securities in a category, such as industry sector, investment objective, or geographical area, or that track an index. ETFs are similar to mutual funds but trade like shares.

excise taxes Taxes that are imposed on specific items such as gasoline, alcoholic beverages, and tobacco.

exclusive distribution A distribution system in which a manufacturer selects only one or two dealers in an area to market its products.

executive information system (EIS) A management support system that is customized for an individual executive; provides specific information for strategic decisions.

expansionary policy The use of monetary policy by the Bank of Canada to increase the growth of the money supply.

expectancy theory A theory of motivation that holds that the probability of an individual acting in a particular way depends on the strength of that individual's belief that the act will have a particular outcome and on whether the individual values that outcome.

expense items Items, purchased by businesses, that are smaller and less expensive than capital products and usually have a life span of less than one year.

expenses The costs of generating revenues.

experiment A marketing research method in which the investigator changes one or more variables—price, packaging, design, shelf space, advertising theme, or advertising expenditures—while observing the effects of these changes on another variable (usually sales).

expert power Power that is derived from an individual's extensive knowledge in one or more areas.

expert system A management support system that gives managers advice similar to what they would get from a consultant; it uses artificial intelligence to enable computers to reason and learn to solve problems in much the same way humans do.

exporting The practice of selling domestically produced goods to buyers in another country.

exports Goods and services produced in one country and sold in other countries.

express contract A contract in which the terms are specified in either written or spoken words.

extensive decision making Purchasing an unfamiliar, expensive, infrequently bought item.

F

factoring A form of short-term financing in which a firm sells its accounts receivable outright at a discount to a *factor*.

factors of production The resources that are necessary to produce goods and services: labour, capital, entrepreneurs, physical resources, and information.

federal budget deficit The condition that occurs when the federal government spends more for programs than it collects in taxes.

financial accounting Accounting that focuses on preparing external financial reports that are used by outsider stakeholders such as creditors, suppliers, investors, and government agents to assess the financial strength of a business.

financial intermediation The process in which financial institutions act as intermediaries between the suppliers and demanders of funds.

financial management The art and science of managing a firm's money so that it can meet its goals.

financial risk The chance that a firm will be unable to make scheduled interest and principal payments on its debt.

fiscal policy The government's use of taxation and spending to affect the economy.

fixed assets Long-term assets used by a firm for more than a year, such as land, buildings, and machinery; also referred to as *capital assets* or *property, plant, and equipment (PPE)*.

fixed costs Costs that do not vary with different levels of output; for example, rent.

fixed-cost contribution The selling price per unit (revenue) minus the variable costs per unit.

fixed-position layout A facility arrangement in which the product stays in one place and workers and machinery move to it as needed.

flexible manufacturing system (FMS) A system that combines automated workstations with computer-controlled transportation devices—automatic guided vehicles (AGVs)—that move materials between workstations and into and out of the system.

floating exchange rates A system in which prices of currencies move up and down based upon the demand for and supply of the various currencies.

foreign direct investment Active ownership of a foreign company or of manufacturing or marketing facilities in a foreign country.

formal organization The order and design of relationships within a firm; consists of two or more people working together with a common objective and clarity of purpose.

four Ps (4Ps) Product, price, promotion, and place (distribution), which together make up the marketing mix.

franchise agreement A contract setting out the terms of a franchising arrangement, including the rules for running the franchise, the services provided by the franchisor, and the financial terms. Under the contract, the franchisee is allowed to use the franchisor's business name, trademark, and logo.

franchisee In a franchising arrangement, the individual or company that sells the goods or services of the franchisor in a certain geographic area.

franchising A form of business organization based on a business arrangement between a franchisor, which supplies the product concept, and the franchisee, who sells the goods or services of the franchisor in a certain geographic area.

franchisor In a franchising arrangement, the company that supplies the product concept to the franchisee.

free-rein (laissez-faire) leadership A leadership style in which the leader turns over all authority and control to subordinates.

free trade The policy of permitting the people of a country to buy and sell where they please without restrictions.

free trade zone An area where the nations allow free, or almost free, trade among each other while imposing tariffs on goods of nations outside the zone.

frictional unemployment Short-term unemployment that is not related to the business cycle.

friendly takeover A takeover that is supported by the management and board of directors of the targeted company.

fringe benefits Indirect compensation such as pensions, health insurance, and vacations.

full employment Situation when the economy is producing to its maximum sustainable capacity, using labour, technology, land, capital, and other factors of production to their fullest potential.

functional departmentalization Departmentalization that is based on the primary functions performed within an organizational unit.

futures contracts Legally binding obligations to buy or sell specified quantities of commodities or financial instruments at an agreed-on price at a future date.

G

Gantt charts Bar graphs plotted on a time line that show the relationship between scheduled and actual production.

general partners Partners who have unlimited liability for all of the firm's business obligations and who control its operations.

general partnership A partnership in which all partners share in the management and profits. Each partner can act on behalf of the firm and has unlimited liability for all its business obligations.

generally accepted accounting principles (GAAP) The financial accounting standards followed by accountants in Canada in preparing financial statements.

Generation X Those born between the mid-1960s and the late 1970s.

Generation Y Those born from the early 1980s to the mid 1990s.

geographic departmentalization Departmentalization based on the geographic segmentation of the organizational units.

geographic segmentation The differentiation of markets by region of the country, city or county size, market density, or climate.

global management skills A manager's ability to operate in diverse cultural environments.

global vision The ability to recognize and react to international business opportunities, be aware of threats from foreign competition, and use international distribution networks effectively to obtain materials and move finished products to customers.

goal-setting theory A theory of motivation based on the premise that an individual's intention to work toward a goal is a primary source of motivation.

goods Tangible items manufactured by businesses.

grievance A formal complaint, filed by an employee or by the union, charging that management has violated the contract.

gross domestic product (GDP) The total market value of all final goods and services produced within a nation's borders each year.

gross national product (GNP) The total market value of all final goods and services produced by a country regardless of where the factors of production are located.

gross profit The amount a company earns after paying to produce or buy its products but before deducting operating expenses.

gross sales The total dollar amount of a company's sales.

group cohesiveness The degree to which group members want to stay in the group and tend to resist outside influences.

H

Hawthorne effect The phenomenon that employees perform better when they feel singled out for attention or feel that management is concerned about their welfare.

high-yield (junk) bonds High-risk, high-return bonds.

horizontal merger A merger of companies at the same stage in the same industry; done to reduce costs, expand product offerings, or reduce competition.

hostile takeover A takeover that goes against the wishes of the target company's management and board of directors.

human relations skills A manager's interpersonal skills that are used to accomplish goals through the use of human resources.

human resource (HR) planning Creating a strategy for meeting future human resource needs.

human resource management (HRM) The process of hiring, developing, motivating, and evaluating employees to achieve organizational goals.

hygiene factors Extrinsic elements of the work environment that do not serve as a source of employee satisfaction or motivation.

I

ideal self-image The way an individual would like to be.

implied contract A contract that depends on the acts and conduct of the parties to show agreement; the terms are not specified in writing or orally.

import quota A limit on the quantity of a certain good that can be imported; also known as a *quantitative restraint*.

imports Goods and services that are bought from other countries.

income statement A financial statement that summarizes a firm's revenues and expenses and shows its total profit or loss over a period of time; also referred to as a *profit and loss statement* or *statement of earnings*.

income taxes Taxes that are based on the income received by businesses and individuals.

industrial distributors Independent wholesalers that buy related product lines from many manufacturers and sell them to industrial users.

inflation The situation in which the average of all prices of goods and services is rising.

informal organization The network of connections and channels of communication based on the informal relationships of individuals inside an organization.

information system (IS) The hardware, software, people, data, and so on, that provide information about all aspects of a firm's operations.

information technology (IT) The equipment and techniques used to manage and process information.

informational roles A manager's activities as an information gatherer, an information disseminator, or a spokesperson for the company.

infrastructure The basic institutions and public facilities upon which an economy's development depends.

initial public offer (IPO) A company's first issuance of shares to the public.

institutional investors Investment professionals who are paid to manage other people's money.

insurable interest An insurance applicant's chance of loss if a particular peril occurs.

insurable risk A risk that an insurance company will cover. It must meet certain criteria.

insurance The promise of compensation for certain financial losses.

insurance policy A written agreement that defines what the insurance covers and the risks that the insurance company will bear for the insured party.

intangible assets Long-term assets with no physical existence, such as patents, copyrights, trademarks, and goodwill.

integrated marketing communications (IMC) The careful coordination of all promotional activities—media advertising, sales promotion, personal selling, and public relations, as well as direct marketing, packaging, and other forms of promotion—to produce a consistent, unified message that is customer focused.

intensive distribution A distribution system in which a manufacturer tries to sell its products wherever there are potential customers.

interest A fixed amount of money paid by the issuer of a bond to the bondholder on a regular schedule, typically every six months; stated as the *coupon rate*.

intermittent process A production process that uses short production runs to make batches of different products; generally used for low-volume, high-variety products.

International Financial Reporting Standards (IFRS) A set of globally accepted accounting standards to be adopted in Canada on January 1st, 2011.

International Monetary Fund (IMF) An international organization, founded in 1945, that promotes trade, makes short-term loans to member nations, and acts as a lender of last resort for troubled nations.

interpersonal roles A manager's activities as a figurehead, company leader, or liaison.

intranet An internal corporate-wide area network that uses Internet technology to link employees in many locations and with different types of computers.

intrapreneurs Entrepreneurs who apply their creativity, vision, and risk taking within a large corporation, rather than starting a company of their own.

inventory The supply of goods that a firm holds for use in production or for sale to customers.

inventory control system A system that maintains an adequate assortment of items to meet a user or customer's needs.

inventory management The determination of how much of each type of inventory a firm will keep on hand and the ordering, receiving, storing, and tracking of inventory.

inventory turnover ratio The ratio of cost of goods sold to average inventory; measures the speed with which inventory moves through a firm and is turned into sales.

investment bankers Firms that act as underwriters, buying securities from corporations and governments and reselling them to the public.

involvement The amount of time and effort a buyer invests in the searches, evaluations, and decision processes of consumer behaviour.

ISO 14000 A set of five technical standards of quality management created by the International Organization for Standardization to provide a uniform way of determining whether manufacturing plants and service organizations conform to sound quality procedures.

ISO 9000 A set of technical standards designed by the International Organization for Standardization to promote clean production processes to protect the environment.

J

job analysis A study of the tasks required to do a particular job well.

job description The tasks and responsibilities of a job.

job enlargement The horizontal expansion of a job by increasing the number and variety of tasks that a person performs.

job enrichment The vertical expansion of a job by increasing the employee's autonomy, responsibility, and decision-making authority.

job fair An event, typically one day, held at a convention centre to bring together thousands of job seekers and hundreds of firms searching for employees.

job rotation Reassignment of workers to several different jobs over time so that they can learn the basics of each job; also called *cross-training*.

job sharing A scheduling option that allows two individuals to split the tasks, responsibilities, and work hours of one 40-hour-per-week job.

job shop A manufacturing firm that produces goods in response to customer orders.

job specification A list of the skills, knowledge, and abilities a person must have to fill a job.

joint venture An agreement in which a domestic firm buys part of a foreign firm to create a new entity.

justice What is considered fair according to the prevailing standards of society; in the 21st century, an equitable distribution of the burdens and rewards that society has to offer.

just-in-time (JIT) A system in which materials arrive exactly when they are needed for production, rather than being stored on site.

K

key person life insurance A term insurance policy that names the company as beneficiary.

knowledge The understanding or awareness of information about a subject.

knowledge management (KM) A worker who develops or uses knowledge, contributing to and benefiting from information used in performing various tasks, including planning, acquiring, searching, analyzing, organizing, storing, programming, producing, distributing, marketing, or selling functions.

knowledge worker A worker who develops or uses knowledge, contributing to and benefiting from information used in performing various tasks, including planning, acquiring, searching, analyzing, organizing, storing, programming, producing, distributing, marketing, or selling functions.

L

labour Economic contributions of people.

labour union An organization that represents workers in dealing with management over issues involving wages, hours, and working conditions.

law of large numbers Insurance companies' predictions of the likelihood that a peril will occur, used to calculate premiums.

laws The rules of conduct in a society, created and enforced by a controlling authority, usually the government.

leader pricing The strategy of pricing products below the normal markup or even below cost to attract customers to a store where they would not otherwise shop.

leadership The process of guiding and motivating others toward the achievement of organizational goals.

leadership style The relatively consistent way that individuals in leadership positions attempt to influence the behaviour of others.

lean manufacturing Streamlining production by eliminating steps in the production process that do not add benefits that customers are willing to pay for.

legitimate power Power that is derived from an individual's position in an organization.

leveraged buyout (LBO) A corporate takeover financed by large amounts of borrowed money; can be done by outside investors or by a company's own management.

liabilities What a firm owes to its creditors; also called *debts*.

licensing The legal process whereby a firm agrees to allow another firm to use a manufacturing process, trademark, patent, trade secret, or other proprietary knowledge in exchange for the payment of a royalty.

limited decision-making Situation in which a consumer has previous product experience but is unfamiliar with the current brands available.

limited liability partnership (LLP) In a limited liability partnership, each individual partner is protected from responsibility for the acts of other partners, and each party's liability is limited to harm resulting from that party's own actions.

limited partners Partners whose liability for the firm's business obligations is limited to the amount of their investment. They help to finance the business and/or promote the business, but do not participate in the firm's day-to-day operations.

limited partnership A partnership with one or more general partners who have unlimited liability, and one or more limited partners whose liability is limited to the amount of their investments.

line of credit An agreement between a bank and a business that specifies the maximum amount of unsecured short-term borrowing the bank will allow the firm over a given period, typically one year.

line organization An organizational structure with direct, clear lines of authority and communication flowing from the top managers downward.

line positions All positions in the organization directly concerned with producing goods and services and which are directly connected from top to bottom.

line-and-staff organization An organizational structure that includes both line and staff positions.

liquidity The speed with which an asset can be converted to cash.

liquidity ratios Ratios that measure a firm's ability to pay its short-term debts as they come due.

local area network (LAN) A network that connects computers at one site, enabling the computer users to exchange data and share the use of hardware and software from a variety of computer manufacturers.

local union A branch or unit of a national union that represents workers at a specific plant or in a specific geographic area.

logistics management The management of the physical distribution process.

long-term forecasts Projections of a firm's activities and the funding for those activities over a period that is longer than a year; from a financial point typically covers 2 to 10 years.

long-term liabilities Claims that come due more than one year after the date of the balance sheet.

loss leader A product priced below cost as part of a leader pricing strategy.

loyalty cards Cards issued by a manufacturer, service organization, or retailer that give discounts to loyal and frequent shoppers.

M

Maastricht Treaty A 1993 treaty concluded by the members of the European Community (now the European Union) that outlines plans for tightening bonds among the members and creating a single market; officially called the Treaty on European Union.

macroeconomics The sub-area of economics that focuses on the economy as a whole by looking at aggregate data for large groups of people, companies, or products.

make-or-buy decision The determination by a firm of whether to make its own production materials or buy them from outside sources.

management The process of guiding the development, maintenance, and allocation of resources to attain organizational goals.

management information system (MIS) The methods and equipment that provide information about all aspects of a firm's operations

management support system (MSS) A dynamic information system that helps managers make decisions by allowing them to analyze data, identify business trends, make forecasts, and model business strategies.

managerial accounting Accounting that provides financial information that managers inside the organization can use to evaluate and make decisions about current and future operations.

managerial hierarchy The levels of management within an organization; typically includes top, middle, and supervisory management.

manufacturer A producer; an organization that converts raw materials to finished products.

manufacturing resource planning II (MRPII) A complex computerized system that integrates data from many departments to control the flow of resources and inventory.

market economy An economic system based on competition in the marketplace and private ownership of the factors of production (resources); also known as the *private enterprise system* or *capitalism*.

market segmentation The process of separating, identifying, and evaluating the layers of a market to design a marketing mix.

market structure The number of suppliers in a market.

marketable securities Short-term investments that are easily converted into cash.

marketing The process of discovering the needs and wants of potential buyers and customers and then providing goods and services that meet or exceed their expectations.

marketing concept Identifying consumer needs and then producing the goods or services that will satisfy them while making a profit for the organization.

marketing database Computerized file of customers' and potential customers' profiles and purchase patterns.

marketing intermediaries Organizations that assist in moving goods and services from producers to end users.

marketing mix The blend of product offering, pricing, promotional methods, and distribution system that brings a specific group of consumers superior value.

marketing research The process of planning, collecting, and analyzing data relevant to a marketing decision.

markup pricing A method of pricing in which a certain percentage (the markup) is added to the product's cost to arrive at the price.

Maslow's hierarchy of needs A theory of motivation developed by Abraham Maslow; holds that humans have five levels of needs and act to satisfy their unmet needs. At the base of the hierarchy are fundamental physiological needs, followed in order by safety, social, esteem, and self-actualization needs.

mass customization A manufacturing process in which modules are mass-produced and then assembled to meet the needs or desires of individual customers.

mass production The ability to manufacture many identical goods or provide many identical services at once.

materials requirement planning (MRP) A computerized system of controlling the flow or resources and inventory. A master schedule is used to ensure that the materials, labour, and equipment needed for production are at the right places in the right amounts at the right times.

matrix structure (project management) An organizational structure that combines functional and product departmentalization by bringing together people from different functional areas of the organization to work on a special project.

mechanistic organization An organizational structure that is characterized by a relatively high degree of job specialization, rigid departmentalization, many layers of management, narrow spans of control, centralized decision-making, and a long chain of command.

mediation The intervention of a third party with a view to persuading the parties to adjust or settle their dispute.

mentoring A form of on-the-job training in which a senior manager or other experienced employee provides job- and career-related information to a protégé.

Mercosur A trade agreement among Argentina, Brazil, Paraguay, and Uruguay that eliminates most tariffs among the member nations.

merger The combination of two or more firms to form a new company, which often takes on a new corporate identity.

microeconomics The sub area of economics that focuses on individual parts of the economy such as households or firms.

middle management Managers who design and carry out tactical plans in specific areas of the company.

mission An organization's purpose and reason for existing; its long-term goals.

mission statement The formalized statement of an organization's purpose and reason for existing.

mixed economies Economies that combine several economic systems; for example, an economy where the government owns certain industries but others are owned by the private sector.

monetary policy The measures taken by the Bank of Canada to regulate the amount of money in circulation to influence the economy.

money Anything that is acceptable as payment for goods and services.

monopolistic competition A market structure in which many firms offer products that are close substitutes and in which entry is relatively easy.

monopoly A situation in which there is no competition and the benefits of a free market are lost.

mortgage bonds Corporate bonds that are secured by property, such as land, equipment, or buildings.

mortgage loan A long-term loan made against real estate as collateral.

motivating factors Intrinsic job elements that lead to worker satisfaction.

multiculturalism The condition when all major ethnic groups in an area, such as a city, county, or province, are about equally represented.

multinational corporations Corporations that move resources, goods, services, and skills across national boundaries without regard to the country in which their headquarters are located.

mutual fund A financial service company that pools its investors' funds to buy a selection of securities that meet its stated investment goals.

mutual-aid pact An agreement by companies in an industry to create a fund that can be used to help cover fixed costs of any member company whose workers go on strike.

N

National Association of Securities Dealers Automated Quotation (NASDAQ) system The first electronic-based stock market and the fastest-growing part of the stock market.

national debt The accumulated total of all of the federal government's annual budget deficits.

national union A union that consists of many local unions in a particular industry, skilled trade, or geographic area and thus represents workers throughout an entire country.

nationalism A sense of national consciousness that boosts the culture and interests of one country over those of all other countries.

natural resources Commodities that are useful inputs in their natural state.

net loss The amount obtained by subtracting all of a firm's expenses from its revenues, when the expenses are more than the revenues.

net profit (net income or net earnings) The amount obtained by subtracting all of a firm's expenses from its revenues, when the revenues are more than the expenses.

net profit margin The ratio of net profit to net sales; also called *return on sales*. It measures the percentage of each sales dollar remaining after all expenses, including taxes, have been deducted.

net sales The amount left after deducting sales discounts and returns and allowances from gross sales.

net working capital The amount obtained by subtracting total current liabilities from total current assets; used to measure a firm's liquidity.

niche competitive advantage A firm's ability to target and effectively serve a single segment of the market within a limited geographic area.

non-programmed decisions Responses to infrequent, unforeseen, or very unusual problems and opportunities where the manager does not have a precedent to follow in decision-making.

North American Free Trade Agreement (NAFTA) An agreement, launched in 1994, creating a free-trade zone including Canada, the United States, and Mexico.

not-for-profit organization An organization that exists to achieve some goal other than the usual business goal of profit.

O

observation research A marketing research method in which the investigator monitors respondents' actions without interacting directly with the respondents; for example, by using cash registers with scanners.

odd-even (psychological) pricing The strategy of setting a price at an odd number to connote a bargain and at an even number to suggest quality.

office automation system An information system that uses information technology tools such as word processing systems, e-mail systems, cellular phones, pagers, and fax machines to improve communications throughout an organization.

oligopoly A market structure in which a few firms produce most or all of the output and in which large capital requirements or other factors limit the number of firms.

one-person corporation A corporation with only one person as the shareholder; common in professional practices (e.g., medical doctors, accountants, or lawyers).

one-to-one marketing Creating a unique marketing mix for every customer.

on-line (real-time) processing A method of updating a database in which data are processed as they become available.

on-the-job training Training in which the employee learns the job by doing it with guidance from a supervisor or experienced coworker.

open market operations The purchase or sale of Canadian government securities by the Bank of Canada to stimulate or slow down the economy.

open shop A company where employees do not have to join the union or pay dues or fees to the union; established under right-to-work laws.

operating budgets Budgets that combine sales forecasts with estimates of production costs and operating expenses to forecast profits.

operating expenses The expenses of running a business that are not directly related to producing or buying its products.

operational planning The process of creating specific standards, methods, policies, and procedures that are used in specific functional areas of the organization; helps guide and control the implementation of tactical plans.

operations management The design and management of the transformation process.

opinion leaders Leaders who influence others.

options Contracts that entitle holders to buy or sell specified quantities of common shares or other financial instruments at a set price during a specified time.

orientation Training that prepares a new employee to perform on the job; includes information about job assignments, work rules, equipment, and performance expectations, as well as about company policies, salary and benefits, and parking.

organic organization An organizational structure that is characterized by a relatively low degree of job specialization, loose departmentalization, few levels of management, wide spans of control, decentralized decision-making, and a short chain of command.

organization chart A visual representation of the structured relationships among tasks and the people given the authority to do those tasks.

organized stock exchanges Organizations on whose premises securities are resold using an auction-style trading system.

organizing The process of coordinating and allocating a firm's resources to carry out its plans.

outsource The assignment of various functions, such as human resources, accounting, or legal work, to outside organizations. Also refers to the purchase of items from an outside source rather than making them internally.

over-the-counter (OTC) market A sophisticated telecomunications network that links dealers and enables them to trade securities.

owners' equity The total amount of investment in the firm minus any liabilities; also called *net worth*.

P

participative leaders Leaders that share decision making with group members and encourages discussion of issues and alternatives; includes democratic, consensual, and consultative styles.

partnership An association of two or more persons who agree to operate a business together for profit.

patent A form of protection (limited monopoly) established by the government to inventors; gives an inventor the exclusive right to manufacture, use, and sell an invention for 20 years.

payroll taxes Income taxes that are collected by the employer and remitted to the federal government, usually in the form of a deduction from the employee's pay.

penetration pricing The strategy of selling new products at low prices in the hope of achieving a large sales volume.

pension funds Large pools of money set aside by corporations, unions, and governments for later use in paying retirement benefits to their employees or members.

perception The process by which we select, organize, and interpret stimuli into a meaningful and coherent picture.

perfect (pure) competition A market structure in which a large number of small firms sell similar products, buyers and sellers have good information, and businesses can be easily opened or closed.

performance appraisal A comparison of actual performance with expected performance to assess an employee's contributions to the organization.

peril A hazard or a source of danger.

perpetual inventory A continuously updated list of inventory levels, orders, sales, and receipts.

personal selling A face-to-face sales presentation to a prospective customer.

personality A way of organizing and grouping how an individual reacts to situations.

physical distribution (logistics) The movement of products from the producer to industrial users and consumers.

planning The process of deciding what needs to be done to achieve organizational objectives, identifying when and how it will be done, and determining by whom it should be done.

postconventional ethics The third stage in the ethical development of individuals in which people adhere to the ethical standards of a mature adult and are less concerned about how others view their behaviour than about how they will judge themselves in the long run; also known as *principled ethics*.

power The ability to influence others to behave in a particular way.

preconventional ethics A stage in the ethical development of individuals in which people behave in a childlike manner and make ethical decisions in a calculating, self-centred way, based on the possibility of immediate punishment or reward; also known as *self-centred ethics*.

preferential tariff A tariff that is lower for some nations than for others.

preferred shares Equities for which the dividend amount is set at the time the stock is issued.

prestige pricing The strategy of increasing the price of a product so that consumers will perceive it as being of higher quality, status, or value.

price skimming The strategy of introducing a product with a high initial price and lowering the price over time as the product moves through its life cycle.

pricing strategy The part of the marketing mix that involves establishing a price for the product based on the demand for the product and the cost of producing it.

primary data Information collected directly from the original source to solve a problem.

primary market The securities market where *new* securities are sold to the public.

principal The amount borrowed by the issuer of a bond; also called *par value*.

principle of comparative advantage The concept that each country should specialize in the products that it can produce most readily and cheaply and trade those products for those that other countries can produce more readily and cheaply.

private corporation A corporation that does not trade publicly and, therefore, is not listed on a stock exchange.

private law The law relating to the relationship between individuals, businesses, or individuals and businesses.

problem-solving teams Teams of employees from the same department or area of expertise and from the same level of the organizational hierarchy who meet regularly to share information and discuss ways to improve processes and procedures in specific functional areas.

process The way a good is made or a service provided.

process departmentalization Departmentalization that is based on the production process used by the organizational unit.

process layout A facility arrangement in which work flows according to the production process. All workers performing similar tasks are grouped together, and products pass from one workstation to another.

process manufacturing A transformation process in which the basic input is broken down into one or more outputs (products).

producer price index (PPI) An index of the prices paid by producers and wholesalers for various commodities such as raw materials, partially finished goods, and finished products.

product In marketing, any good or service, along with its perceived attributes and benefits, that creates value for the customer.

product (assembly line) layout A facility arrangement in which workstations or departments are arranged in a line with products moving along the line.

product departmentalization Departmentalization that is based on the goods or services produced or sold by the organizational unit.

product liability The responsibility of manufacturers and sellers for defects in the products they make and sell.

product life cycle The pattern of sales and profits over time for a product or product category; consists of an introductory state, growth stage, maturity, and decline (and death).

product strategy The part of the marketing mix that involves choosing a brand name, packaging, colours, a warranty, accessories, and a service program for the product.

production The creation of products and services by turning inputs, such as natural resources, raw materials, human resources, and capital, into outputs, which are products and services.

production orientation An approach in which a firm works to lower production costs without a strong desire to satisfy the needs of customers.

production planning The aspect of operations management in which the firm considers the competitive environment and its own strategic goals in an effort to find the best production methods.

production process The way in which a good is made.

professional liability insurance Insurance designed to protect top corporate management, who have been the target of malpractice lawsuits.

profit The money left over after all expenses are paid.

profit maximization A pricing objective that entails getting the largest possible profit from a product by producing the product as long as the revenue from selling it exceeds the cost of producing it.

profitability ratios Ratios that measure how well a firm is using its resources to generate profit and how efficiently it is being managed.

program evaluation and review technique (PERT) A scheduling tool that is similar to the CPM method but assigns three time estimates for each activity (optimistic, most probable, and pessimistic); allows managers to anticipate delays and potential problems and schedule accordingly.

programmed decisions Decisions made in response to frequently occurring routine situations.

programmed instruction A form of computer-assisted off-the-job training.

promotion (in marketing) The attempt by marketers to inform, persuade, or remind consumers and industrial users to engage in the exchange process.

promotion strategy The part of the marketing mix that involves personal selling, advertising, public relations, and sales promotion of the product.

promotional mix The combination of advertising, personal selling, sales promotion, and public relations used to promote a product.

property taxes Taxes that are imposed on real and personal property based on the assessed value of the property.

protectionism The policy of protecting home industries from outside competition by establishing artificial barriers such as tariffs and quotas.

protective tariffs Tariffs that are imposed to make imports less attractive to buyers than domestic products are.

provincial health care Health insurance programs provided by the provinces.

psychographic segmentation The differentiation of markets by personality or lifestyle.

public corporation Corporation that has the right to issue shares to the public.

public law The law relating to the relationship between the individual or business and the government (or its agencies).

public relations Any communication or activity designed to win goodwill or prestige for a company or person.

pull strategy A promotional strategy in which a manufacturer focuses on stimulating consumer demand for its product rather than on trying to persuade wholesalers or retailers to carry the product.

purchasing The process of buying production inputs from various sources; also called *procurement*.

purchasing power The value of what money can buy.

pure monopoly A market structure in which a single firm accounts for all industry sales and in which there are barriers to entry.

push strategy A promotional strategy in which a manufacturer uses aggressive personal selling and trade advertising to convince a wholesaler or retailer to carry and sell its merchandise.

Q

quality Goods and services that meet customer expectations by providing reliable performance.

quality control The process of creating standards for quality and then measuring finished products and services against them.

quality of life The general level of human happiness based on such things as life expectancy, educational standards, health, sanitation, and leisure time.

R

ratio analysis The calculation and interpretation of financial ratios taken from the firm's financial statements to assess its condition and performance.

real self-image How an individual actually perceives him- or herself.

recession A decline in GDP that lasts for at least two consecutive quarters.

recruitment The attempt to find and attract qualified applicants in the external labour market.

re-engineering The complete redesign of business structures and processes to improve operations.

reference groups Formal and informal groups that influence buyer behaviour.

referent power Power that is derived from an individual's personal charisma and the respect and/or admiration the individual inspires.

relationship management The practice of building, maintaining, and enhancing interactions with customers and other parties to develop long-term satisfaction through mutually beneficial partnerships.

relationship marketing A strategy that focuses on forging long-term partnerships with customers by offering value and providing customer satisfaction.

retailers Firms that sell goods to consumers and to industrial users for their own consumption.

retained earnings (in accounting) Profits that have been reinvested in a firm.

retained earnings (in financial management) The amounts left over from profitable operations since the firm's beginning; equal to total profits minus all dividends paid to shareholders.

return The opportunity for profit.

return on equity (ROE) The ratio of net profit to total owners' equity; measures the return that owners receive on their investment in the firm.

revenues The money a company earns from providing services or selling goods to customers.

revolving credit agreement (revolving line of credit) A guaranteed line of credit whereby a bank agrees that a certain amount of funds will be available for a business to borrow over a given period.

reward power Power that is derived from an individual's control over rewards.

risk (financial) The potential for loss or the chance that an investment will not achieve the expected level of return.

risk (general) The potential for losing time and money or otherwise not being able to accomplish an organization's goals.

risk management The process of identifying and evaluating risks and selecting and managing techniques to adapt to risk exposures.

risk-return trade-off A basic principle in finance that holds that the higher the risk, the greater the return that is required.

robotics The technology involved in designing, constructing, and operating computer-controlled machines that can perform tasks independently.

routine response behaviour Purchase of low-cost, frequently bought items with little search or decision making.

routing The aspect of production control that involves setting out the workflow—the sequence of machines and operations through which the product or service progresses from start to finish.

S

sales promotions Marketing events or sales efforts—not including advertising, personal selling, and public relations—that stimulate buying.

sales taxes Taxes that are levied on goods and services when they are sold; calculated as a percentage of the price.

scanner-based research System for gathering information from a single group of respondents by continuously monitoring the advertising, promotion, and pricing they are exposed to and the things that they buy.

scheduling The aspect of production control that involves specifying and controlling the time required for each step in the production process.

scientific management A system of management developed by Frederick W. Taylor and based on four principles: developing a scientific approach for each element of a job, scientifically selecting and training workers, encouraging cooperation between workers and managers, and dividing work and responsibility between management and workers according to who can better perform a particular task.

seasonal unemployment Unemployment that occurs during specific seasons in certain industries.

secondary data Information that has already been collected for a project other than the current one but that can be used to solve the current problem.

secondary market The securities market where (already issued) old securities are traded among investors; includes the organized stock exchanges, the over-the-counter market, and the commodities exchanges.

secured bonds Corporate bonds for which specific assets have been pledged as collateral.

secured loans Loans for which the borrower is required to pledge specific assets as collateral, or security.

securities Investment certificates issued by corporations or governments that represent either equity or debt.

selection The process of determining which persons in the applicant pool possess the qualifications necessary to be successful on the job.

selection interview An in-depth discussion of an applicant's work experiences, skills and abilities, education, and career interests.

selective distribution A distribution system in which a manufacturer selects a limited number of dealers in an area (but more than one or two) to market its products.

selective exposure The process of deciding which stimuli to notice and which to ignore.

self-concept How people perceive themselves.

self-managed work teams Highly autonomous teams of employees who manage themselves without any formal supervision and take responsibility for setting goals, planning and scheduling work activities, selecting team members, and evaluating team performance.

servers Computers that store data and "serve" information to other computers, called clients, on request.

services Intangible offerings of businesses that can't be held, touched, or stored.

share or stock dividends Payments to shareholders in the form of more shares; can replace or supplement cash dividends.

shareholders The owners of a corporation, who hold shares of stock that provide certain rights; also known as *stockholders*.

shop steward An elected union official who represents union members to management when workers have issues.

shopping products Items that are bought after considerable planning, including brand-to-brand and store-to-store comparisons of price, suitability, and style.

short-term forecasts Projections of revenues, costs of goods, and operating expenses over a one-year period.

simulation A scaled down version or mock-up of equipment, process, or work environment.

Six Sigma A quality control process that relies on defining what needs to be done to ensure quality, measuring and analyzing production results statistically, and finding ways of improving and controlling quality.

small business A business that is independently owned, is owned by an individual or a small group of investors, is based locally, and is not a dominant company in its industry.

social investing The practice of limiting investments to securities of companies that behave in accordance with the investor's beliefs about ethical and social responsibility.

social marketing The application of marketing techniques to social issues and causes.

social responsibility The concern of businesses for the welfare of society as a whole; consists of obligations beyond those required by law or contracts.

socialism An economic system in which the basic industries are owned either by the government itself or by the private sector under strong government control.

socialization process The passing down of cultural norms and values to children.

software The general term for various programs used to operate computers; a set of instructions that directs a computer's activities.

sole proprietorship A business that is established, owned, operated, and often financed by one person.

span of control The number of employees a manager directly supervises; also called span of management.

specialization The degree to which tasks are subdivided into smaller jobs.

specialty products Items for which consumers search long and hard and for which they refuse to accept substitutes.

speculative risk The chance of either loss or gain, without insurance against the possible loss.

staff positions Positions in an organization held by individuals who provide the administrative and support services that line employees need to achieve the firm's goals.

stakeholders Individuals or groups (including organizations) to whom the business has a responsibility; including the investors or shareholders (those with a financial interest), employees, customers, suppliers (business partners), governments, local communities, the environment, and society as a whole.

standard of living A country's output of goods and services that people can buy with the money they have.

statement of cash flows A financial statement that provides a summary of the money flowing into and out of a firm.

statement of financial position A financial statement that summarizes a firm's financial position at a specific point in time.

statute law (or statutory law) Written law enacted by a legislature (municipal, provincial, or federal).

stock dividends See share dividends.

stockbroker A person who is licensed to buy and sell securities on behalf of clients.

strategic alliance A cooperative agreement between business firms; sometimes called a *strategic partnership*.

strategic channel alliances One manufacturer using another manufacturer's previously established channel to distribute its goods.

strategic giving The practice of tying philanthropy closely to the corporate mission or goals and targeting donations to regions where a company operates.

strategic planning The process of creating long-range (one to five years), broad goals for the organization and determining what resources will be needed to accomplish those goals.

strict liability A concept in products-liability laws under which a manufacturer or seller is liable for any personal injury or property damage caused by defective products or packaging that do not meet industry standards.

structural unemployment Unemployment that is caused by a mismatch between available jobs and the skills of available workers in an industry or region; not related to the business cycle.

supervisory management Managers who design and carry out operational plans for the ongoing daily activities of the firm.

supply The quantity of a good or service that businesses will make available at various prices.

survey research A marketing research method in which data are gathered from respondents in person, by telephone, by mail, at a mall, or through the Internet to obtain facts, opinions, and attitudes.

supply chain The entire sequence of securing inputs, producing goods, and delivering goods to customers.

supply chain management The process of using information along the supply chain so that the firm can satisfy its customers with quality products and services; includes working closely with suppliers.

supply curve A graph showing the quantity of a good or service that a business will make available at various prices.

T

tactical planning The process of beginning to implement a strategic plan by addressing issues of coordination and allocating resources to different parts of the organization; has a shorter time frame (less than one year) and more specific objectives than strategic planning.

target for the overnight rate The signal to the major participants in the money market as to what the Bank of Canada is aiming for when participants borrow and lend one-day funds to each other.

target market The specific group of consumers toward which a firm directs its marketing efforts.

target return on investment A pricing objective where the price of a product is set so as to give the company the desired probability in terms of return on its money.

tariff A tax imposed on imported goods.

technical skills A manager's specialized areas of knowledge and expertise, as well as the ability to apply that knowledge.

telecommuting An arrangement in which employees work at home and are linked to the office by phone, fax, and computer or other communication devices.

term deposits Deposits at a bank or other financial institution that pay interest but cannot be withdrawn on demand.

term loan A business loan with a maturity of more than one year; can be unsecured or secured.

theft insurance A broad insurance coverage that protects business against losses for an act of stealing.

Theory X A management style, formulated by Douglas McGregor, which is based on a pessimistic view of human nature and assumes that the average person dislikes work, will avoid it if possible, prefers to be directed, avoids responsibility, and wants security above all.

Theory Y A management style, formulated by Douglas McGregor, that is based on a relatively optimistic view of human nature; assumes that the average person wants to work, accepts responsibility, is willing to help solve problems, and can be self-directed and self-controlled.

Theory Z A theory developed by William Ouchi that combines U.S. and Japanese business practices by emphasizing long-term employment, slow career development, moderate specialization, group decision-making, individual responsibility, relatively informal control over the employee, and concern for workers.

time deposits Interest-bearing deposits that cannot be withdrawn on demand.

top management The highest level of managers; includes CEOs, presidents, and vice-presidents, who develop strategic plans and address long-range issues.

tort A civil, or private, act that harms other people or their property.

total cost The sum of the fixed costs and the variable costs.

total profit Total revenue minus total cost.

total quality management (TQM) The use of quality principles in all aspects of a company's production and operations.

total revenue The selling price per unit times the number of units sold.

trade credit The extension of credit by the seller to the buyer between the time the buyer receives the goods or services and when it pays for them.

trade deficit An unfavourable balance of trade that occurs when a country imports more than it exports.

trade surplus A favourable balance of trade that occurs when a country exports more than it imports.

trademark The legally exclusive design, name, or other distinctive mark that a manufacturer uses to identify its goods in the marketplace.

training and development Activities that provide learning situations in which an employee acquires additional knowledge or skills to increase job performance.

transaction processing system (TPS) An information system that handles the daily business operations of a firm. The system receives and organizes raw data from internal and external sources for storage in a database.

trust company A financial institution that conduct the same activities as a bank but can also administer estates, trusts, pension plans, and agency contracts.

U

underwriting The process of buying securities from corporations and governments and reselling them to the public; the main activity of investment bankers.

unemployment rate The percentage of the total labour force that is not working but is actively looking for work.

union shop A company where non-union workers can be hired but must then join the union.

unsecured loans Short-term loans for which the borrower does not have to pledge specific assets as security.

unsought products Products that either are unknown to the potential buyer or are known but the buyer does not actively seek them.

Uruguay Round A 1994 agreement by 117 nations to lower trade barriers worldwide.

utilitarianism A philosophy that focuses on the consequences of an action to determine whether it is right or wrong; holds that an action that affects the majority adversely is morally wrong.

V

value pricing A pricing strategy in which the target market is offered a high-quality product at a fair price and with good service.

value-stream mapping Routing technique that uses simple icons to visually represent the flow of materials and information from suppliers through the factory and to customers.

variable costs Costs that change with different levels of output; for example, wages and cost of raw materials.

venture capital Financing obtained from investment firms that specialize in financing small, high-growth companies and receive an ownership interest and a voice in management in return for their money.

vertical merger A merger of companies at different states in the same industry; done to gain control over supplies of resources or to gain access to different markets.

virtual corporation A network of independent companies linked by information technology to share skills, costs, and access to one another's markets; allows the companies to come together quickly to exploit rapidly changing opportunities.

virtual private networks (VPNs) Private corporate networks connected over a public network, such as the Internet. VPNs include strong security measures to allow only authorized users to access the network.

volume segmentation The differentiation of markets based on the amount of the product purchased.

W

warranty A guarantee of the quality of a good or service.

whistle blower An employee, former employee, or any other member of an organization that reports misconduct by others in the organization that have the power to take corrective action.

wholesalers Firms that sell finished goods to retailers, manufacturers, and institutions.

wide area network (WAN) A network that connects computers at different sites via telecommunications media such as phone lines, satellites, and microwaves.

work groups Groups of employees who share resources and coordinate efforts so as to help members perform their individual duties and responsibilities better. The performance of the group can be evaluated by adding up the contributions of the individual group members.

work teams Groups of employees who not only coordinate their efforts, but also collaborate by pooling their knowledge, skills, abilities, and resources in a collective effort to attain a common goal, causing the performance of the team to be greater than the sum of the members' individual efforts.

workers' compensation Payments to cover the expenses of job-related injuries and diseases, including medical costs, rehabilitation, and job retraining if necessary.

World Bank An international bank that offers low-interest loans, as well as advice and information, to developing nations.

World Trade Organization (WTO) An organization established by the Uruguay Round in 1994 to oversee international trade, reduce trade barriers, and resolve disputes among member nations.

Y

yield management system (YMS) Mathematical software that helps companies adjust prices to maximize revenue

ENDNOTES

Prologue

1. Marlene Caroselli, *Interpersonal Skills*, (Thomson South-Western, a part of The Thomson Corporation, 2003), The section "Getting Ahead in Business and Life" is also adapted from the above text.
2. The Persuasion self-test was created by the authors and from the following sources: *Persuade Others to Follow Your Way of Thinking*, (www.winstonbrill.com/ bril001/html/ article_index/articles/251-300/ article271_body.html); *Six Unique Ways to Persuade Others*, (www.micaworld.com/pdfs/Six%20 Unique%20%20Ways%20%20 Persuade%20Others.pdf); *Strategies of Influence and Persuasion*, Kenrick Cleveland, (www.maxpersuasion.com); (www.gowerpub.com/pdf/ imppeopleconstch1.pdf); *Power Persuasion—How to Persuade People*, (www.1000ventures.com/business_ guide/crosscutings/persuading_ people.html); and *How to Persuade and Influence People*, Wolf J. Rinke, Ph.D., CSP, #554 Innovative Leader Volume 11, Number 6, June 2002, (www.winstonbrill.com/bril001/ html/article_index/articles/551-600/ article554_body.html).
3. The Office Politics scale was developed by the authors and from the following sources: *Don't Sabotage Your Success!—Make Office Politics Work*, Karen Ginsburg Wood, (www.atlasbooks.com/ markplc/00492.htm); *Play the Office Politics Game*, Cynthia A. Broderick, (www.bankrate.com/brm/ news/advice/19990914a.asp); *The Fairness of Office Politics . . . Integrity and Political Motivation!* Edward B. Toupin, (www.hotlib.com/articles/ show.php?t=The_Fairness_of_ Office_Politics_...Integrity_and_ Political_Motivation!); *Fly Under the Radar to Absorb Delicate Office Politics*, Peter Vogt, MonsterTRAK Career Coach, (http://content. monstertrak.monster.com/resources/ archive/onthejob/politics); *The New Office Politics: We've Seen the Enemy at Work, and Sometimes It's Us,* Audrey Edwards, *Essence*, March 2005, (www.findarticles. com/p/articles/mi_ml264/is_11_35/ ai_n11830673); *Assessment—Office Politics*, First Edition, (www.course. com/downloads/courseilt/ e-assessments/0619254394.pdf); and *Play Office Politics and Keep Your Soul*, (www.createyourvision.com/ playofficepolitics.htm).
4. The section on planning is adapted from: *Investing in Your Future* (Thomson South-Western, a part of The Thomson Corporation, 2007), pp. 1–10.
5. The material on **Don't Let Go** is adapted from Abby Marks-Beale, *Success Skills: Strategies for Study and Lifelong Learning* (Thomson South-Western, a part of The Thomson Corporation, 2007).
6. The Time Management scale was created by the authors and: *Time Management Quiz*, (www.nus.edu.sg/ osa/guidance/quiz/timemgmtquiz. html); *Manage Your Time in Ten Steps*, (www.familyeducation.com/ article/0,1120,1-263,00.html); *TimeManagement Quiz, (*http://tools. monster.com/quizzes/pareto); *Stress Management, Better Health Channel,* (www.betterhealth.vic.gov.au/bhcv2/ bhcsite.nsf/pages/quiz_manage_ stress?) *Stress Management Quiz,* (www.betterhealth.vic.gov.au/bhcv2/ bhcsite.nsf/pages/quiz_manage_ stress?); *Time Management*, (http:// uwadmnweb.uwyo.edu/RanchRecr/ handbook/time_management.htm); and *Time Management: Importance of Good Practice*, (www.accel-team.com/ techniques/time_management.html).
7. The Ability to Manage Money scale was created by your authors and: *Quiz—Can You Manage Money?*, (http://collegeanduniversity.net/ collegeinfo/index.cfm?catid=20&p ageid=2339&affid=75); *Boston.com/ Business/YourMoney;* (www.boston. com/business/personalfinance/ articles/2005/04/03can_you_manage_ your_ own_month?mode=PF); *Psychology of Money Management*, (www. uwec.edu/counsel/pubs/Money.htm); *Managing Your Money*, (www.nelliemae. com/managingmoney); *The Importance of Managing Money*, (www.mtstcil.org/ skills/budget-12.html); and *How Do You Rate as a Money Manager?*, (http://cahe. nmsu.edu/pubs/_g/G-219.pdf).
8. The self-quiz on How to Study was prepared by the authors using: *EDinformatics–Education for the Information Age*, (www.edinformatics. com/education/howtostudy.htm); *The Manila Times*, March 20, 2004, (www. manilatimes.net/national/2004/ mar/20/yehey/life/20040320lif2. html); *Ten Traps of Studying— Improving Your Studying Skills—CAPS— UNC—Chapel Hill*, (http://caps.unc. edu/TenTraps.html); and *Language Study Skills*, (www.usingenglish.com/ study-skills.html).
9. Julie Griffin Levitt. *Your Career: How to Make It Happen*, 5th edition (Thomson South-Western, a part of The Thomson Corporation, 2006), pp. 2–4.
10. The Assertiveness test was prepared by the authors using: *Test Your Assertive Level*, (www.hodu.com/ assertiveness-skills.shtml); *Assertive Action Plan*, (www.headinjury.com/ assertplan.html); *Assertiveness*, (www. coping.org/relations/assert.htm); *Perception of Assertiveness as a Function of Tag Questions*, (www.ycp.edu/besc/ Journal2002/paper%201.htm); and *Assertion Training*, (http://front.csulb. edu/tstevens/assertion_training.htm).
11. Levitt, p. 36.
12. Barbara Ling, (www.riseway.com).
13. CBS, "Web Largely Untapped by Job Seekers," (http://MarketWatch.com) (accessed January 24, 2003).
14. Levitt, Your Career, 100.
15. Levitt, Your Career, 189–205.
16. Levitt, Your Career, 205.

Chapter 1

1. Lester Thurow, "Changing the Nature of Capitalism", in *Rethinking the Future,* ed. Rowan Gibson (London: Nicholas Brealey, 1997), 228.
2. Peter Burrows, "Notebooks without Wide Margins", *Business Week*, September 5, 2005, (www. businessweek.com), Jason Dean and Pui-Wing Tam, "The Laptop Trail", *Wall Street Journal*, June 9, 2005, pp. B1, B8; and H-P website, (www.hp.com).

3. Lertzman D. and H. Vredenburg, 2005: "Indigenous Peoples, Resource Extraction and Sustainable Development", *Journal of Business Ethics*, 56/3: 239-254.
4. See: (www.footprintnetwork.org/en/index.php/GFN/page/world_footprint/).
5. See: (http://ucatlas.ucsc.edu/income.php).
6. Pui-Wing Tam and Ann Zimmerman, "Wal-Mart's H-P Elves", *Wall Street Journal*, December 15, 2005, pp. B1, B4.
7. Phred Dvorak and Evan Ramstad, "TV Marriage: Behind Sony-Samsung Rivalry, an Unlikely Alliance Develops", *Wall Street Journal*, January 3, 2006, pp. A1, A6.
8. James McGregor, Advantage, China," *Washington Post*, July 31, 2005; Page B1.
9. Don Clark, "In Setting Up Its New Plants, Chip Maker Clones Older Ones Down to the Paint on the Wall", *Wall Street Journal*, October 28, 2002. ©2002 by Dow Jones & Co. Inc. Reproduced with permission of Dow Jones & Co. Inc., in the format Textbook via Copyright Clearance Center; (www.intel.com).

Chapter 2

1. Domino's Pizza, *"Domino's Around the World"*, (www.dominosbiz.com/Biz-Public-EN/Site+Content/Secondary/International/), accessed March 20th, 2009.
2. Statistics Canada, *"Imports, exports and trade balance of goods on a balance-of-payments basis, by country or country grouping"*, (www40.statcan.ca/cbin/fl/cstprintflag.cgi), accessed March 13, 2009.
3. "Armchairs, TVs and Expresso—Is It McDonald's?" *Wall Street Journal*, August 30, 2002. © 2002 by Dow Jones & Co. Inc. Reproduced with permission of Dow Jones & Co. Inc., in the format Textbook via Copyright Clearance Center.
4. Government of Canada, Department of Foreign Affairs and International Trade, "Trade Negotiations and Agreements—Why Trade Matters," (www.dfait.maeci.gc.ca/tna-nac/text-e.asp) (accessed June 4, 2002).
5. Foreign Affairs and International Trade Canada, *"Trade Matters"*, (www.international.gc.ca/trade-agreements-accords-commerciaux/matters-important/index.aspx?lang=en), accessed March 13, 2009; Statistics Canada, *"Imports, exports and trade balance of goods on a balance-of-payments*

basis, by country or country grouping", (www40.statcan.ca/cbin/fl/cstprintflag.cgi), accessed March 13, 2009.
6. Government of Canada, "Team Canada—What Is Team Canada," (www.tcm-mec.gc.ca/what-e.asp) (accessed June 4, 2002).
7. "Team Canada—What Is Team Canada."
8. Government of Canada, Department of Foreign Affairs and International Trade, "Trade Negotiations and Agreements—Why Trade Matters," (www.dfait.maeci.gc.ca/tna-nac/text-e.asp) (accessed June 4, 2002).
9. Statistics Canada, *"Merchandise trade of Canada (monthly)"*, (www40.statcan.gc.ca/l01/cst01/trad45a-eng.htm?sdi=merchandise%20trade), accessed March 13, 2009.
10. Statistics Canada, *"Imports, exports and trade balance of goods on a balance-of-payments basis, by country or country grouping"*.
11. "Anti-Trade/Pro-Poverty," Fortune, January 10, 2000, 40.
12. "Globalization: What Americans Are Worried About," *Business Week*, April 24, 2000, 44.
13. Government of Canada, Department of Foreign Affairs and International Trade, "About EPD, Export and Import Controls Bureau," (www.dfait-maeci.gc.ca/~eicb/eicbintro-e.htm) (accessed June 4, 2002).
14. European Commission's Trade SIA Mercosur, *"Final–Overview"*, (http://sia-trade.org/mercosur/phase2/Mercosur_final_overview_SIAv5.pdf), Novermber 2008, accessed March 20th, 2009.
15. Association Of Southeast Asian Nations, "Overview", (www.aseansec.org/64.htm), accessed March 13th, 2009.
16. Neil King, "A Whole New World," *Wall Street Journal* (September 17, 2004), pp. R1–R2.
17. "Survey: Coming Out," *The Economist* (London), 378, no. 8470 (2005): 4.
18. "India's Coming Eclipse of China," Far *Eastern Economic Review*, 169, no. 2 (2006): 12-18.
19. Hal Lancaster, "Global Managers Need Boundless Sensitivity, Rugged Constitutions," *Wall Street Journal*, October 13, 1998.

Chapter 3

1. "100-Calorie Snack Packs: Fad or Diet Tool?" *San Diego Union-Tribune*, October 12, 2005, pp. E1, E3.
2. Statistics Canada, "Women in Canada: Work Chapter Updates", (www.statcan.gc,ca/

pub/89f0133x/89f0133x20006000-eng.htm), (accessed, February 9, 2009).
3. Roger Schilling, "Reaching Those Female Fans," *American Coin-Op*, September 2005, pp. 31–37.
4. "Generation Y Defined," *On-Point Marketing and Promotions*, (www.onpoint-marketing.com/generation-y.htm), (May 23, 2006); and "Q&As from Howe and Strauss, authors of Millennials Rising," *MillennialsRising.com*, (www.millenialsrising.com), (May 23, 2006).
5. Desiree J. Hanford, "Long-Term Success of E-Tailers Will Hinge on 'Echo Boomers'," *Wall Street Journal*, July 27, 2005, p. B3A; and Jilian Mincer, "Generation Y Is New Territory For Financial-Service Marketers," *Wall Street Journal*, September 26, 2005, p. B3A.
6. Caron Alarab, "Generation Y Spending Trends: Gotta Have It," *Detroit Free Press*, August 25, 2005, (www.freep.com/money/tech/youngcomps25e_20050825.htm).
7. Jilian Mincer, "Generation Y Is New Territory For Financial-Service Marketers," *Wall Street Journal*, September 26, 2005, p. B.5; Robin Sidel, "Hip Check: American Express Tries to Find Its Place with a Younger Crowd," *Wall Street Journal*, September 22, 2005, pp. A1, A8.
8. Katherine Yung, "Generation Xers Hit Middle Age," *Houston Chronicle*, July 10, 2005, p. 3.
9. Jeanette Borzo, "Follow the Money: More Businesses Are Starting to Cater to an Affluent—and Discriminating —'Mature Market'," *Wall Street Journal*, September 26, 2005. p. R9 and Anne D'Innocenzio, "Revlon Targets Older Women to Boost Sales," *Associated Press*, April 10, 2006, (http://news.yahoo.com).
10. Greene, "When We're All 64," p. R1; Johnson, "Half of Boomers Hit the 50 Mark," p. 18; and Kevin Kelly, "Aging Buyers Dictate Trends," *Ward's Auto World*, June 2005.
11. Section based on Andrea Coombes, "The Case for Older Workers: Value," *San Diego Union-Tribune*, January 29, 2006, p. H7; Peter Coy, "Old. Smart. Productive." *Business Week*, June 27, 2005, (www.businessweek.com); Ellen M. Heffes, "Dramatic Workforce Trends Require Planning Now," *Financial Executive*, July/August 2005, pp. 18–21; - Patricia Kitchen, "The 4 Generation Workplace, It's Not What It Used to Be," *Newsday*, - August 14, 2005, p. A52; and Jennifer J. Salopek, "The New Brain Drain," *T+D*, June 2005, pp. 23–24.

12. Canadian Policy Research Network, "Diversity: Canada's Strength," Release date: April 19, 2007, (www.cprn.com/doc.cfm?doc=1652&l=en) (accessed March 2, 2009).

13. Canadian Heritage, Government of Canada, "What is Multiculturalism," (www.pch.gc.ca/progs/multi/what_e.cfm) (accessed July 11, 2006).

14. Canadian Policy Research Network, "Population Projections for 2017," (www.cprn.com/en/diversity-2017.cfm) (accessed April 10, 2006).

15. Statistics Canada, "Births and Birth Rate, by Province and Territory," (www40.statcan.ca/101/cst01/demo04a-eng.htm) (accessed March 2, 2009).

16. Marianne Moody Jennings, *Case Studies in Business Ethics*, 2nd ed. (St. Paul, MN: West Publishing Company, 1996 pp xx-xxiii).

17. Milton Borden, "The Three R's of Ethics," *Management Review*, (1998), 59–61.

18. Sarah Ellison and Eric Bellman, "Clean Water, No Profit," *Wall Street Journal* (February 3, 2005), pp. B1, B2.

19. Canadian Tire Corporation, "Canadian Tire & The Community," (www2.canadiantire.ca/CTenglish/enreop_wrd.html) (accessed May 23, 2002).

20. Manulife Financial, "Corporate Giving," (www.manulife.com/corporate/Corporate2.nsf/Public/corporategiving.html) (accessed April 11, 2006).

21. *Business Ethics Online*, (www.business-ethics.com).

22. Adapted from "In the Bag," *Fast Company*, March 2005, (www.fastcompany.com); Andrew Tilin, "Bagging the Right Customers," *Business 2.0*, May 2005, pp. 56–57; Timbuk2 corporate website, (www.timbuk2.com) (November 13, 2005); David Worrell, "Go for the Gold" *Entrepreneur*, July 2005, (www.entrepreneur.com); and "It's All in the Bag for Timbuk2," *San Francisco Chronicle*, (May 1, 2006).

Chapter 4

1. CGI, "*About Us*", (http://cgi.com/web/en/cgi_canada/contact_us.htm), accessed June 22, 2009.

2. Jerry McElhatton, "Data BPO Can End Restless Nights for CIOs," *Bank Technology News*, February 2006, p.31.

3. "Electronic Trading Hubs," (www.com-met2005.org.uk) April 4, 2006; David Luckham, "The Global Information Society and the Need for New Technology," (http://.informit.com), April 4, 2006; "Trading Hubs," (www.investni.com) April 4, 2006; "Trading Hubs in Asia," *Oikono*, December 6, 2005, (www.oikono.com).

4. "St. Agnes Hospital Improves Patient Care and Management, Reduces Costs with Pervasive Meru Wireless LAN Deployment," *Meru Networks*, press release, February 13, 2006, (www.merunetworks.com/news/press_releases/021306.shtml).

5. Rita Zeidner, "Building a Better Intranet," *HR Magazine*, November 1, 2005, p. 99.

6. James Brown, "Hotel Group Installs Global Staff Intranet," *Computing*, October 20, 2005, (www.computing.co.uk).

7. "Executive Guides. Wireless," *Darwin Executive Guides* http://guide.darwinmag.com/technology/communications/wireless/index.html (accessed January 31, 2003); and "Wi-Fi," Webopedia, (www.webopedia.com).

8. "Bluetooth® Wireless Technology Becoming Standard in Cars," *Bluetooth SIG*, February 13, 2006, (www.bluetooth.com).

9. Find VPN.com, "(VPN) Virtual Private Network FAQs," (http://findvpn.com/articles/faq.php) (accessed January 31, 2003); and About.com: Computer Networking, "VPN Tutorial," (http://compnetworking.about.com/library/weekly/aa010701a.htm) (accessed January 24, 2003).

10. Mae Kowalke, "Bell Canada Intros VoIP managed Services for Cisco and Nortel Enterprise Customers", *TMCnet.com*, November 17, 2008, (http://voipservices.tmcnet.com) (accessed February 2, 2009).

11. Kathleen Melymuka, "Far from the Mother Ship," *Computerworld*, December 9, 2002, (www.computerworld.com).

12. Section based on "Executive Guides: Knowledge Management," *Darwin Executive Guides*, (http://guide.darwinmag.com/technology/enterprise/knowledge/index.html) (April 3, 2006).

13. "Cybercrime Cost about $400 Billion," Computer Crime Research Center, July 6, 2005, (www.crime-research.org).

14. "The Difference Between a Virus, Worm and Trojan Horse?" *Webopedia*, (www.webopedia.com) (April 1, 2006).

15. "Spam Costs World Businesses $50 Billion," *InternetWeek*, February 23, 2005; and "Spam Rates Rebound," *InternetWeek*, March 7, 2006, both from (http://galenet.thomsonlearning.com).

16. Scott Berinato, "The Global State of Information Security 2005," *CIO*, September 15, 2005, (www.cio.com).

17. "Security Policies 101," *Intranet Journal*, January 6, 2003, (www.intranetjournal.com).

18. Tom Standage, "The Weakest Link" (Survey of Digital Security, Special Section), *Economist*, October 26, 2002, 11–16.

19. Lucas Mearian, "IT Managers See Portable Storage Device Security Risk," *Computerworld*, March 17, 2006, (www.computerworld.com).

20. Tech Trends 2002, Volume 2 (City: Deloitte & Touche LLP, Technology, Media and Telecommunications Group), (www.deloitte.com).

21. Matthew Boyle, "Tech in Action The Latest Hit: CSI in Your Hard Drive," *Fortune,* November 14, 2005, p. 39.

22. Matthew Boyle, "Tech In Action—The Latest Hit: CSI in Your Hard Drive."; "Guidance Software Introduces the World's Most Complete and Advanced eDiscovery Solution," Press Release, Guidance Software Corporate Web site, January 30, 2006, (www.guidancesoftware.com).

23. Doug Bartholomew, "IT On Tap?" *Industry Week*, June 1, 2005, p. 64.

24. Office of the Privacy Commissioner of Canada, "Top 10 Ways Your Privacy is Threatened," (www.privcom.gc.ca/resource/dpd/top10_e.asp), (accessed February 2, 2009).

Chapter 5

1. Christopher Halpin, personal communication, April 10, 2009.

2. Anne Stuart, "Where Do Great Ideas Come From?" *Inc.*, October 2002, 43, 45.

3. Mike Hofman, "The Bad Boy," *Inc.*, September 2002, 78–80.

4. (http://www.digitrustgroup.com), accessed March 12, 2009.

5. Government of Canada Co-operatives Secretariat, "*About Co-ops in Canada*", modified August 22, 2008, accessed March 9, 2009.

6. Canadian Co-operative Association. "About Co-operatives," (http://www.coopscanada.coop/aboutcoop/) (accessed November 1, 2005).

7. Hydrocarbons Technology, "Syncrude 21 Expansion Project, Alberta, Canada," (http://www.hydrocarbons-technology.com/projects/syncrude/), (accessed March 16, 2009).

8. McDonald's Canada, "FAQs", (http://www.mcdonalds.ca/en/aboutus/faq.aspx), Copyright © 2008, (accessed March 9, 2009).

9. Carlye Adler, "How China Eats a Sandwich," *Fortune*, March 21, 2005, p. F210-B; Julie Bennett, "Chinese Market Offers Franchise Challenges," *Startup Journal–The Wall Street Journal Online*, (http://www.startupjournal.com); Subway corporate website, (http://www.subway.com) (accessed March 25, 2006).

10. Home Instead Senior Care, *"About Us-Helping You Care for the Seniors in Your Life"*, (http://www.homeinstead.com/aboutus/default.aspx), accessed March 9, 2009.

11. "Sarah Adult Day Services," *Franchise Zone*, (http://www.entrepreneur.com/franzone/) (accessed May 31, 2006).

12. Stephanie Clifford, "What You Need To Know Now," *Inc. Magazine*, September 2005, p. 27.

13. Devlin Smith, "One Big Happy Family," January 2003, (http://www.entrepreneur.com).

14. Caliber Collision Centers website, (http://www.calibercollision.com); and Justin Martin, David Birch, "Slump? What Slump?" *Fortune Small Business*, December 2002/January 2003, (http://www.ask.elibrary.com); Robert McGarvey, "When It Comes to Customer Service Actions Speak Louder than Words," *Entrepreneur Magazine*, January 1997, (http://www.entrepreneur.com).

15. Jane Applegate, "Novelty Pillow Catches Manufacturer's Eye," February 2002, (http://www.entrepreneur.com); Carolyn Morton, e-mail correspondence, January 17 and 24, 2003; and Peeramid website, (http://www.peeramid.com).

16. Hilary Potkewitz, "Geek Support: Techies Make House Calls Like Old-Time Docs," *Los Angeles Business Journal*, June 13, 2005, (http://www.findarticles.com); "Stand Alone Geek Squads Target Small Business," *DSN Retailing Today*, February 7, 2005, (http://www.findarticles.com); corporate websites for Geek Squad, (http://www.geeksquad.com), and Best Buy, (http:www.bestbuy.com), (April 27, 2006).

Chapter 6

1. Personal interview with Gino Panucci, August 2008.

2. "Key Small Business Statistics, July 2008", Industry Canada's website, (www.ic.gc.ca/epic/site/sbrp-rppe.nsf/en/h_rd01252e.html), accessed November 24th, 2008.

3. "About OGIO International," OGIO International website, (www.ogio.com), accessed November 24th, 2008.

4. "Famous Canadian Entrepreneurs", Westmount Collegiate Institute website, (www.westmount.ci.yrdsb.edu.on.ca/entrepreneurs.html), accessed on November 24th, 2008.

5. April Y. Pennington, "Entrepreneurial Snapshot: Katrina Markoff," *Entrepreneur*, November 2002, (www.entrepreneur.com).

6. David Shook, "Jeff Bezos: Finally Relaxing?" *Business Week Online*, October 1, 2002, (www.businessweek.com).

7. "About Us", The Jim Pattison Group website, (www.jimpattison.com/corporate/about-us.htm), accessed on November 24th, 2008.

8. Gregory Katz, "Her Daily Bread," *American Way Magazine*, July 15, 2005, p. 34; Poilane website (www.poilane.com) (October 27, 2005).

9. "Are You Building an Inc. 500 Company?" *Inc. 500*, October 15, 2002, (www.inc.com/inc500).

10. "Key Small Business Statistics, July 2008", Industry Canada's website, (www.ic.gc.ca/epic/site/sbrp-rppe.nsf/en/h_rd01252e.html), accessed on November 24th, 2008.

11. "Key Small Business Statistics, July 2008", Industry Canada's website, (www.ic.gc.ca/epic/site/sbrp-rppe.nsf/en/h_rd01252e.html), accessed on November 24th, 2008.

12. David Noonan, "Be Your Own Master," *Newsweek*, September 23, 2002, 61.

13. Keith McFarland, "What Makes Them Tick," *Inc. 500*, October 19, 2005, http://www.inc.com.

14. Kimberly McCall, "Then There Were Two: Should You Hire a Staff?" *Startup Journal.com*, November 4, 2002, (www.inc.com).

15. Andreea Dulipovici, "Small Business—Big Picture", Canadian Federation of Independent Business, (www.cfib.ca) (accessed February 9, 2006).

16. Dun & Bradstreet, "D&B 21st Annual Small Business Survey Summary Report," (www.dnb.com).

17. Jeff Cornwall, "We Will Not Go Quietly," *The Entrepreneurial Mind*, June 22, 2004, (www.belmont.edu) (October 27, 2005).

18. Stacy Zhao, "Web-Based Companies Significant Part of U.S. Small Business," *Inc.com*, June 7, 2005, (www.inc.com).

19. Jeff Bailey, "Growing Up," *Wall Street Journal*, March 27, 2002, R6; Case, "Trading Places," 74–82; Brenda L. Moore, "Changing Classes," *Wall Street Journal*, March 27, 2002, R8; and "Be Your Own Master."

20. Geoff Williams, "Looks like Rain," *Entrepreneur*, September 2002, (www.entrepreneur.com).

21. "Got ID?" *Entrepreneur*, November 2002, (www.entrepreneur.com) (accessed July, 2006).

22. Martha Irvine, "More 20-Somethings Are Blazing Own Paths in Business," *San Diego Union-Tribune*, November 22, 2004, p. C6.

Chapter 7

1. "Now for the Hard Part," *Fortune*, November 18, 2002, 95–106.

2. David Bank, "Autodesk Stages Revival," *Wall Street Journal*, August 19, 2005, p. B3.

3. Jeffrey Garten, "Jack Welch: A Role Model for Today's CEO," *Business Week*, September 10, 2001, 32.

4. Max Messmer, "Surviving and Thriving as a New Manager," *National Public Accountant*, June 2000, 22–24.

5. Waterstone Human Capital, "Canada's 10 Most Admired Corporate Cultures™ 2007," http://canadasmostadmired.com, (accessed September 29, 2008).

6. Robert Ramsey, "What Will You Do if the Worst Case Scenario Really Happens?" *Supervision*, June, 2002, 6–7.

7. Tom McDonald, "A World of Challenges," *Successful Meetings*, July 2002, 25.

8. Cora Daniels, "The Last Taboo: It's Not Sex. It's Not Drinking. It's Stress—And It's Soaring," *Fortune*, October 28, 2002, 136–140 and David Noonan, Jill Sieder, and Kevin Peraino, "Stop Stressing Me," *Newsweek*, January 29, 2001, 54–56.

9. Fara Warner, "Keeping the Crisis in Chrysler," *Fast Company*, September 2005, pp. 69–73.

Chapter 8

1. "Building the Right Team," *Maclean's*, October 28, 2002, 31.

2. "Re-Inventing H-P the Hurd Way," *Information Age*, September 10, 2005.

3. Hiroshi Ikematsu, "Sony's Restructuring No Easy Task," *The Yomiuri Shimbun*, September 23, 2005; Cliff Edwards with Tom Lowry, Moon Ihlwan, and Kenji Hall, "The Lessons for Sony at Samsung," *Business Week*, October 10, 2005, p. 37.

4. See R. Z. Gooding and J. A. Wagner III, "A Meta-Analytic Review of the Relationship—between Size and Performance: The Productivity and Efficiency of Organizations and Their Subunits," *Administrative Science Quarterly*, December 1985, pp. 462–481.

5. Peter Burrows, "HP Says Goodbye to Drama; Five months in, CEO Mark

Hurd's no-nonsense approach is being felt in a big way—and the Street has taken notice," *Business Week Online*, September 1, 2005.

6. Novartis, "Welcome to Citizenship@ Novartis", (www.corporatecitizenship. novartis.com), downloaded December 11th, 2008.

7. Traci Purdum, "Teaming, Take 2: Once a Buzzword, Teaming Today Is One of the Fundamentals of Manufacturing," *Industry Week*, May 2005, p. 41.

8. Joseph B. White, "LaSorda's Chrysler Challenge," *The Wall Street Journal*, August 15, 2005, p. B5.

9. Alan Deutschman, "The Fabric of Creativity: Pound for Pound, W. L. Gore Just Might Be the Most Innovative Company in America. Here's Why," *Fast Company*, December 2004, pp. 54–60.

10. Diane Brady, "Reaping the Wind: GE's Energy Initiative Is a Case Study in Innovation without Borders," *Business Week*, October 11, 2004, p. 201; Patricia Sellers, "Blowing in the Wind: To Build a Better Wind Turbine, General Electric Built a Global Team of Researchers in Germany, China, India, and the U.S.," *Fortune*, July 25, 2005, p. 130.

11. "New Study Shows That Workers Believe the Office Grapevine More Than They Do Management," *M2 Presswire*, September 14, 2005.

12. *Ibid.*

Chapter 9

1. UPS website, (www.ups.com); Keith Hammonds, "Handle with Care," *Fast Company*, August, 2002, 102–107.

2. Kim Clark, "No Pink Slips at the Plant," *U.S. News & World Report*, February 2002, 40.

3. Kayte Vanscoy, "The Hiring Crisis," *Smart Business for the New Economy*, July 2000, 84–94.

4. From Alder, *International Dimensions*, 174–181.

5. "Strategies for Developing an Effective Employee Absenteeism Policy," *HR Focus*, September 11, 2001, 5.

6. Jeffrey Marshall, "Employee Retention Linked to Better Customer Service," Financial Executive, March/April 2001, 11–12.

7. Gary Wallace, "Satisfied Employees Help Attract and Retain Members," *Credit Union Magazine*, September 2002, 32.

Chapter 10

1. "Gore-Text," *Fast Company*, January 1999, 160.

2. Melanie Peacock, personal interview, conducted March 31, 2006.

3. Michael A. Tucker, "E-Learning Evolves," *HR Magazine*, vol. 50 (October, 2005), pp.75–78.

4. Taylor Cox and Stacy Blake, "Managing Cultural Diversity: Implications for Organizational Competitiveness," *Academy of Management Executive*, Vol. 5 (1991), pp. 45–56.

5. Gene J. Koprowski, "Rude Awakening", *HR Magazine*, vol. 49 (September 2004), pp. 50–55.

Chapter 11

1. Mark Haines and David Farber, "Harley-Davidson—CEO Interview," *CNBC/Dow Jones Business*, Video, October 11, 2002; Tim Stevens, "Technologies of the Year—DFM Concurrent Costing Version 2.0," *Industry Week*, December 12, 2002, (www.industryweek.com); John Teresko, "Technology Leader of the Year—Fueled by Innovation," *Industry Week*, December 1, 2002, (www.industryweek.com); and John Teresko, "Driven by Cost," *Industry Week*, September 1, 2002, (www. industryweek.com); Harley-Davidson, *"Harley-Davidson update guidance as a result of strike"*, Harley-Davidson press release, February 27, 2007, (www. harley-davidson.com/wcm/Content/Pages/HD_News/c).

2. Jill Jusko, "Locations—Globe Motors Turns to Portugal," *Industry Week*, November 1, 2002, (www. industryweek.com).

3. Jill Jusko, "Locations."

4. Adrienne Selko, "GLOBAL HOT SPOTS 2008: Revealing Global Manufacturing's Best Kept Secrets," *Industry Week*, June 2008, Vol. 257, Iss. 6; pg.46, 4 pages.

5. John S. McClenahen, "The World's Best," *Industry Week*, April 16, 2001, (www.industryweek.com).

6. Brian Nadel, "Chain and Command," *Fortune,* July 25, 2005; Dell company website (www.dell.com) (May 20, 2006); MOL company website (www.mol.) (May 20, 2006); Acer company website (www.global.acer. com) (May 20, 2006).

7. Michael A. Verespej, "E-Procurement Explosion," *Industry Week*, March 1, 2002, (www.industryweek.com).

8. John S. McClenahen, "The World's Best," *Industry Week*, April 16, 2001, (www.industryweek.com).

9. Maria Varmazis, "Automation Frees Time for Strategic Activities," *Purchasing*, September 2005, p. 40.

10. Doug Bartholomew, "Faster CAD Design Called a Lifesaver," *Industry Week*, June 4, 2001, (www. industryweek.com).

11. Gene Bylinsky, "Elite Factories: They're Setting Lofty Standards in Quality Control, Preventive Maintenance, and Automation," *Fortune*, September 2, 2002, 172B.

12. Gene Bylinsky, "Elite Factories."

13. Tim Stevens, "Factories of the Future—Integrated Product Development," *Industry Week*, June 1, 2002, (www.industryweek.com).

Chapter 12

1. Stephanie Thompson, "Avon struggles to make mark on young buyers", in *Advertising Age* (Midwest region edition). Chicago: February, 28, 2005.

2. Statistics Canada, "Population Characteristics," http://www.statcan. ca (accessed November 20, 2008).

3. Sally Beatty, "Avon Is Set to Call on Teens," *Wall Street Journal*, October 17. © 2002 by Dow Jones & Co. Inc. Reproduced with permission of Dow Jones & Co. Inc., in the format Textbook via Copyright Clearance Center. Sally Beatty, "Avon Is Set to Call on Teens," *Wall Street Journal*, October 17. © 2002 by Dow Jones & Co. Inc. Reproduced with permission of Dow Jones & Co. Inc., in the format Textbook via Copyright Clearance Center.

4. Prokesch, S. E. (1995). "Competing on customer service: An interview with British Airways' Sir Colin Marshall." Harvard Business Review 73: 101-112.

5. "Caring for the Customer Pays Off for Lexus Again," *Essex Chronicle Series*, May 10, 2002.

6. American Marketing Association Web site, http://www.marketingpower.com (accessed August 28, 2003).

7. Carl McDaniel and Roger Gates, *Marketing Research Essentials*, 5th ed. (Hoboken, NJ: John Wiley & Sons, 2006), p. 131–133.

8. "How Cool Is That," *Smart Money*, June 2005, p. 13.

9. Ann D'Innocenzio, "Stores Putting Data from Loyalty Cards to Work," *Fort Worth Star Telegram*, March 25, 2003.

10. "GM's Winning Vision: Staff First, Profit Follows," *Hotels*, March 2003, 14.

Chapter 13

1. This section partially adapted from: Charles Lamb, Joe Hair, and Carl McDaniel, *Marketing 8th ed.*, (Mason, Ohio: Thomson Publishing, 2006), p. 402–403.

2. "A Deal with Target Put Lid on Revival at Tupperware," *Wall Street Journal*, February 18, 2004, p. A1, A9; and "Tupperware Announces Second Quarter EPS," news release, (www.tupperware.com) (July 26, 2005).
3. "Easy Does It All," *Business 2.0*, August 2005, p. 69–74. Copyright © Time Inc. All rights reserved. Reproduced by permission.
4. "A More Profitable Harvest," *Business 2.0*, May 2005, p. 66–67.
5. "Making the Most of eBay," *Business 2.0* (June 2002), 129–130. © 2002-Time Inc. All rights reserved; *"The Company"*, ebay.ca, (http://pages.ebay.ca/aboutebay/thecompany/companyoverview.html), accessed February 26, 2009.
6. "Oracle Puts Priority on Customer Service, *Wall Street Journal*, January 21, 2003.

Chapter 14

1. Chartered Accountants of Canada, *"Filling the GAP to IFRS: Teaching Supplements for Canada's Accounting Academics"*, ISBN 978-1-55385-370-1
2. Glenn Cheney, "FASB, IASB Agree to Push on with Convergence Effort," *Accounting Today* April 3, 2006, (http://ask.elibrary.com); "FASB and IASB Reaffirm Commitment to Enhance Consistency, Comparability and Efficiency in Global Capital Markets" *Financial Accounting Standards Board,* February 27, 2006, (www. fasb.org/news); "FASB Issues Accounting Standard That Improves the Reporting of Accounting Changes as Part of Convergence Effort with IASB," *Financial Accounting Standards Board,* June 1, 2005, (www.fasb.org/news); Tim Reason, "The Narrowing GAAP," *CFO*, December 1, 2005, (www.cfo.com).
3. The Certified General Accounts Association of Canada, *"Statement delivered to the Standing Committee on Industry, Science and Technology—Review of Canada's Service Sector"*, February 7, 2008.
4. CMA Canada, "What is a CMA" and "About CMA," (www.cma-canada.org) (accessed March 31, 2009).
5. CMA Canada, *"Overview"*, (www.cga-canada.org/en-ca/aboutcgacanada/pages/_ca_about_overview.aspx), accessed March 31st, 2009.
6. Anne Papmehl, "Accounting for Knowledge: Measuring Our Intellectual Assets Helps Us Manage Them Effectively," *CMA Management*, March 2004, (www.allbusiness.com) (accessed April 1, 2006).

Chapter 15

1. Office of the Superintendent of Financial Institutions Canada, *"Federally Regulated Financial Institutions"*, (www.osfi.gc.ca/WWWapps/lists/eng.asp?s=1&g=1&i=2), accessed April 6, 2009.
2. The author's personal interview with Ron Munaweera, March 28, 2009.
3. The Bank of Canada, *"Medium-Term Plan 2007–2009, Moving Forward: Building The Future Together"*, (www.bankofcanada.ca/en/about/do.html), accessed March 30, 2009.
4. The Bank of Canada, *"Monetary Policy–key interest rate: target for the overnight rate"*, (www.bankofcanada.ca/en/monetary/target.html), accessed March 30, 2009.
5. Statistics Canada, "Chartered Banks," (http://142.206.72.67/03/03e/03e_001a_e.htm), accessed March 8, 2005.
6. Statistics Canada, "Trust Companies," (http://142.206.72.67/03/03e/03e_001b_e.htm), accessed March 8, 2005.
7. Canadian Deposit Insurance Corporation, *"History of Member Institution Failures"*, (www.cdic.ca/1/7/0/7/index1.shtml), accessed March 30, 2009.
8. "Overview of Economic Benefits to the United States from the Activities of International Banks," Institute of International Bankers website, (www.iib.org), accessed June 3, 2006.
9. TD Canada Trust, *"Consolidated Financial Statements–2008"*, (www.td.com/ar2008/index.jsp), accessed March 30, 2009.
10. Mike Adams, The Health Ranger, Naturalnews Editor, *"Merck Loses Vioxx Lawsuit: Jury Awards $253.4 Million to Widow"*, (www.naturalnews.Com/011064.html), accessed March 30, 2009.
11. "Online Banking Booming, Says IDC," (www.electronicbanker.com), accessed June 2, 1999.
12. Reuters, "Top Banks Plan Online Billing Network," *The Sheboy-Gan Press*, June 24, 1999, C5.
13. Toronto Stock Exchange, *"An Exchange of Opportunity"*, (www.tsx.com/en/pdf/Factsheet0607-e.pdf), accessed March 31, 2009.

Chapter 16

1. David Deeds, "Extra! Extra!" *Inc.*, September 2002, 110–112.
2. Adapted from Richard Gamble,"Got Cash? Who Doesn't?" *Treasury & Risk Management*, December 2005/January 2006, (www.treasuryandrisk.com); Richard Gamble, Susan Kelly, and John Labate, "The 2005 Alexander Hamilton Award Winners: Cash Management; Bronze Award Winner: Honeywell International," *Treasury & Risk Management*, November 2005, all from (www.treasuryandrisk.com); and Karen M. Kroll, "Treasury Today: To Centralize or Not?" *Business Finance*, April 2006, (http://businessfinancemag.com).
3. Jay Sherman and Susan Kelly, "Uphill Racer—The 2002 Alexander Hamilton Award Winners," *Treasury & Risk Management*, October 2002, (www.treasuryandrisk.com).
4. John Cummings, "Guiding the Global Enterprise," *Business Finance*, June 2005, (www.businessfinancemag.com).
5. Laurie Brannen, "A Bird's Eye View of Finance," *Business Finance*, May 2005; and Laurie Brannen "Finance at the Forefront," *BusinessFinance*, April 2006, both from (www.businessfinancemag.com); and Richard Gamble, "Straddling the Great Divide," *Treasury & Risk Management*, September 2005, (www.treasuryandrisk.com).
6. Joanne Sammer, "What CFOs Want From Risk Management," *Business Finance*, April 2006, (www.businessfinancemag.com).
7. Ann Lubart, "Saving a Seat at the Table," *Treasury & Risk Management,* March 2005, (www.treasuryandrisk.com).
8. Ilan Mochari, How to Collect from Anyone (Even Enron)", Inc., September 1, 2002, pp. 67–68.

Appendix

1. Personal interview with Sandra Malach, April 13, 2003.
2. Mohammed B Hemraj, "Preventing Corporate Failure: The Cadbury Committee's Governance Report," *Journal of Financial Crime*, October 2002.
3. Colin P. MacDonald, "Where Were the Directors?" *Business Credit*, January 2003.
4. Adapted in part from Brian A. Schofield and Blair W. Feltmate, "Sustainable Development Investing," *Employee Benefits Journal*, March 2003.
5. Government of Canada, Canadian Public Accountability Board (CPAB), Office of the Superintendent of Financial Institutions website, (www.osfi-bsif.gc.ca/eng/issues/cpab_e.asp) (accessed July 10, 2003).
6. Canada, Department of Justice, "Canada's Court System," (www.canada.justice.gc.ca/en/dept/pub/trib/page3.html).
7. Adapted from the notes of Robert Malach, LLB, LLM.

COMPANY INDEX

Foot Locker, 174
Ford Motor Company, 3, 8, 16, 88, 240, 373, 379, 495
Forzani Group, 96
Four Seasons Hotels, 311
Frequency Marketing, Inc., 379
Frito Lay, 372
Fruit-of-the-Loom, 59
FTD, 411
Fuji Xerox, 63
Funko, Inc., 178, 179

G

Gallo, 33, 401
Gartner Inc., 127
Gateway Computers, 19, 402
Geekcorps, 104
Geeks on Call, 157
Geeks on the Way, 136
Geek Squad, 136, 168–69, 271
Geico, 359
General Electric (GE), 210, 213, 248, 302, 341, 398
General Motors, 8, 337, 343, 352, 353
Gillette, 211, 372, 420, 427
Globe Motors, 330, 331
Golden Lane Honey, 187
Google Inc., 171, 520
Gotcha, 173, 174
Gray Corporation, 400–401
Greenpeace, 3
Guangdong Development Bank, 471
Gucci, 364, 394
Guidance Software, 129

H

Hallmark Cards, 374
Halsall Associates, 230, 237
Harley-Davidson, 320, 323, 327, 333, 343, 373
Harris Bank of Chicago, 487
HBO, 70
Heinz, 406
Hermell Products, 167
Hershey Foods, 35
Hewlett-Packard (H-P), 19, 33, 63, 130, 208, 213, 241, 245, 402
Hitachi, 269
H.J. Heinz, 35
Holt Renfrew, 363, 364, 394, 403
Home Depot, 82, 83, 407, 515
Home Instead Senior Care, 160
Honda, 3, 63, 115, 224, 392
Honeywell Control Products, 346
Honeywell International Inc., 498
HSBC, 276

I

i2T, 152
IBM, 60, 96, 130, 176, 208, 310, 352
IBM Global Financing, 352
IBM Global Services, 351–52

IKEA, 234
Imax, 65, 175
Imperial Oil Resources, 154
Indigo, 304
Information Resources, Inc. (IRI), 378
ING Direct, 485–86
Inglenook, 401
Intel, 38–39, 89, 176, 189, 214, 362
Interactive Travel Services Association (ITSA), 40
Intercontinental Hotels Group (IHG), 115
iRobot Corporation, 176
Irving Oil, 197

J

Jaguar, 410
J.D. Power and Associates, 359
The Jim Pattison Group, 176
Johnson Controls Inc. (JCI), 345

K

Kagome, 406
Keebler Company, 363
Kellogg's, 370
Kentucky Fried Chicken (KFC), 156, 158
Kodak, 32
KPMG International, 300
Kraft General Foods, 379

L

L. L. Bean, 373
Labatt Brewing Company, 59
Laura's Shoppe Canada Limited, 362
Levi Strauss, 59, 97, 411
Lexus, 35, 354, 359, 363
Lockheed Martin, 30
Lonely Planet, 258
L'Oreal, 82
LT Designs, 187
Lucent Technologies, 93
Lululemon Athletic, Inc., 177
Lycos, 104

M

Mad Science Group, 167–68
Magna International Inc., 63, 240, 352–53, 500
Manna Catering Services, 143–44
Manulife Bank of Canada, 463
Manulife Financial, 95, 510
Maple Leaf Foods, 94
Mark's Work Wearhouse (MWW), 34, 94, 107, 109
Marriott, 98, 313
Marriott International, 362
Mars, 35
MasterCard, 111, 189, 427
Mattel, 351, 411
Max Call Centre, 283–84
Maytag, 35, 363, 410
McCain Foods, 34, 414

McDonald's, 46, 47, 97, 98, 155, 156, 158, 310, 364, 377, 427
Measure-X, 313
Mercedes-Benz, 35, 39–40
Merck & Co., 472
Michael H. Seid & Associates, 157
Microsoft, 129, 504
Microsoft Network (MSN), 429, 520
Mitsubishi Motors, 61
MOL, 336
Molly Maid, 161
Monster Worldwide, 285
Moody's, 474
Morton and York, 167
Motorola, 115, 350–51
Mountain Equipment Co-op, 154, 155
Mr. Handyman, 161
MTV, 69–70
MTV Networks International (MTVNI), 69, 70
MuchMusic, 370–71

N

Nabisco, 79
National Museum of Science and Technology, 152
Navistar International Corporation, 230, 233
NEC, 19
Nerds on Site, 136
Nestlé, 18–19, 64, 420
New Era Cap, 330
New United Motor Manufacturing Inc. (NUMMI), 337
Nexen, Inc., 154
Nike, 30, 33, 102, 213, 214, 504
Nintendo, 384
Nokia, 115, 384
Nortel Networks Corporation, 117
North Face, 28
Northwest Airlines, 40
Novartis Seeds, Inc., 137, 245, 379
Novotel, 380

O

OGIO International, 171, 174
Olive Garden, 374
1-800-FLOWERS, 411, 429
180s, 195–96
Ontario Co-operative Association (OnCoop), 154
Opel, 353
Oracle, 130, 259, 422
Orange, 409
Orangina, 61
Orbitz, 40–41
Otis Elevator, 63

P

Parmalat Canada, 240
PepsiCo, 288–89, 291, 317–18, 384, 414, 415–16

SUBJECT INDEX

United States (U.S.), 48, 50, 51, 56
unity of command, 238
unsecured loans
   definition/overview, 500
   short-term, 500–502
unsecured short-term loans
   bank loans, 500–501
   commercial paper, 501–2
   trade credit/accounts payable, 500
unsought products, 393, 394
Uruguay Round, 54–55
utilitarianism, 84–85

V

value. *See also* Customer value
   critical success factor of quality
     products at reasonable price and
     providing, 5, 6, 43
   currencies changing, 50–51
   pricing, 398, 399
value-stream mapping, 337
variable costs, 400
venture capital, 184, 506

vertical merger, 159
virtual corporation, 231, 251
virtual private networks (VPNs),
   115–16
virtual teams, 247, 252
vision, 42
   global, 46
   top management, 5, 7
volume segmentation, 372, 374

W

want, 263
warranties, 535–36
Welch, Jack, 210
whistle blower
   definition, 95
   protection for, 95
wholesalers, 404
wide area network (WAN), 113
wireless LANs (WLANs), 113
wireless technologies, 115
women
   entrepreneurs, 170–71, 189

   in workforce, 75, 79–80
workers' compensation, 510
workforce. *See also* Employee
   creating competitive, 32, 34
   critical success factors and committed,
     6, 9, 43, 106
   distributed, 129
   knowledge of, 13
   women in, 75, 79–80
work groups, 246–47
work-life benefits, 278
workplace trust, 319
work-scheduling options, 275–76
work teams, 246
   definition, 247
   types, 247–49
World Bank, 52, 55
World Trade Organization (WTO), 52,
   54–55

Y

yield management system (YMS), 419